DAVID DICKSON is Professor in Modern History at Trinity College, Dublin and has published ~~extensively on the social, economic~~ and cultural history of ~~...~~ Irish Academy in 2006.

DUBLIN

THE MAKING OF A CAPITAL CITY

DAVID DICKSON

P

PROFILE BOOKS

This paperback edition published in 2015

First published in Great Britain in 2014 by
Profile Books Ltd
3 Holford Yard
Bevin Way
London WC1X 9HD
www.profilebooks.com

1 3 5 7 9 10 8 6 4 2

Typeset in Garamond by MacGuru Ltd
info@macguru.org.uk

Printed and bound in Great Britain by
CPI Group (UK) Ltd, Croydon CR0 4YY

A CIP catalogue record for this book is available from the British Library.

ISBN 978 1 86197 586 7
eISBN 978 1 84765 056 6

Mixed Sources
Product group from well-managed forests and other controlled sources
www.fsc.org   Cert no. TT-COC-002227
© 1996 Forest Stewardship Council
FSC

For Charlie and Tom

CONTENTS

PREFACE

'No city exists in the present tense,' wrote James Stephens, Dublin journalist and poet in 1923, 'it is the only surviving mass-statement of our ancestors, and it changes inversely to its inhabitants. It is old when they are young, and when they grow old it has become amazingly and shiningly young again.'[1] More recent cultural commentators like Henri Lefebvre might take a less sanguine view: 'the city historically constructed is no longer lived and is no longer understood ...' For most of us, the past is indeed lost, the evidence indecipherable.[2] The city of Dublin in the Celtic Tiger years (*c*.1995–*c*.2007) was a city of youthful excess, manic and present-centred. Yet it was framed by a soft historical narrative, which became integral to the commercial branding of its identity. Dublin's history was packaged and commodified as never before. Amiable tour guides enlarged on 'the rare ould times', more artful purveyors of cultural tourism invoked the world of Joyce's Leopold Bloom, and the city government celebrated the city's history and championed its physical and literary 'heritage'.

But what constitutes the city? Is Dublin merely the territory ruled from the Civic Offices? That would exclude many districts that have been entirely urban since the mid-nineteenth century, and many more that have been urbanised in the twentieth. Does Dublin mean the *whole* urbanised area, stretching nowadays from Malahide in north County Dublin to Bray in County Wicklow and westwards to Leixlip in County Kildare? This million-strong 'city' is politically quite fragmented and at present straddles six county councils. And there is an even bigger Dublin in the form of the metropolitan city-region – the commuting zone – be it to work, to school, or to recreation.

The problems of identifying Old Dublin are rather different. They are not so much where was Dublin, but what was Dublin. The city has attracted many labels, Viking, Norman, English, Protestant, Georgian, nationalist and republican, but such labels have nearly always oversimplified. Incontrovertibly, Dublin has been the biggest urban place in a deeply contested island since towns first appeared west of the Irish Sea. For seven centuries it was the epicentre of English power and for much of that time it was the principal channel of anglicisation. But the city has also provided shelter and opportunity for radical challenges to that power. It was therefore at different times a colonial fortress and a contested space. There have been many other contested cities in the European and Mediterranean world, some of which have suffered much harsher histories than Dublin (be it Prague or Königsberg/Kaliningrad, Smyrna/Izmir or Algiers). And unlike many cities of Britain and western Europe, Dublin almost escaped the devastating effects of industrial warfare in the twentieth century. But in the longer run there have been much sharper discontinuities and reverses in Dublin's history than in almost any other European capital city – and these have left their mark. Yet, like all great cities, Dublin has been a cultural hybrid and that hybridity has shaped its creative history, even though cultural differences have at times been a source of bitter tension, even of bloody conflict.

Dublin has also had the reputation of being a city divided to an extreme degree by class and material wealth, an arena for Neapolitan excess and unspeakable poverty. Again, the story is more complex. The city has been centre of social and economic innovation within Ireland, but at times of change it was also an economic battlefield, suffering as a result of its metropolitan status and the strength of vested interests working within it. A century ago it had the largest brewery in the world, with quite exceptional welfare arrangements for its employees, at the same time that the housing of the city's labouring classes was an international scandal and excessive alcohol consumption was a near-universal problem.

The ambiguities and paradoxes were never so evident as in the epoch-changing years between 1916 and 1922. The Easter Rising that convulsed a war-weary city in April 1916 was a bolt from the blue. The insurrection initially lacked popular support. Yet within a year public opinion had shifted and substantial segments of Dublin's citizenry supported the aggressive pursuit of separatism. Less than three years later, Sinn Féin, the champions of separatism, were able to hold a national convention (the first Dáil) in an annex to the Lord Mayor's house. The ensuing guerrilla campaign that took place across much of the country and the British resistance to that campaign were both – albeit in varying degrees – run from the city, even though most of the action took place far outside the Dublin region. Much of the political drama in 1921 surrounding the Anglo-Irish Truce and Treaty was also acted out primarily within the city of Dublin.

Then in January 1922 came the handover of Dublin Castle, the symbol of English ascendancy in Ireland since the twelfth century. Between the twelfth and the twentieth centuries Dublin's fortunes had flowed and ebbed with English ascendancy. Could the city now reinvent itself in 1922 as an Irish-Ireland capital for the first time? Five months after the formal handover of power came civil war. In the first act of a short but vicious conflict, the Public Record Office of Ireland, beside the Dublin quays, was destroyed, following the bombardment of the Four Courts complex. Seven centuries in the making, the central archives of English governance of Ireland were lost in a couple of hours.

The year 1922 also witnessed the appearance of a unique literary text. Seven years in the making, James Joyce's 'little story of a day', set in pre-war Dublin but echoing Homer's *Odyssey*, was published in Paris. Its initial local reception was furtive and disapproving and its global impact slow in coming, but long before the end of twentieth century *Ulysses* had been accepted as one of the canonical texts of modernism. That moment in Dublin's imagined history thus became utterly familiar to every student of modern English literature and Dublin itself became a distinctive corner of the global cultural landscape. It was quite an irony that the year when Joyce universalised the city was also the time when the potential to explore its deeper history was catastrophically diminished by the PRO fire.

There were, however, two projects at that time which opened up the history of Dublin. The first was the publication of *Calendar of the ancient records of Dublin*; this had begun in 1889, and the nineteenth and final volume appeared in 1944. Edited by Sir John Gilbert and his widow, the *Calendar* provided a critical edition of the assembly rolls that recorded the formal decisions of the city's governing body, running from 1447 down to the reconfiguration of city government in 1840. These parchments, together with other key municipal archives, were unaffected by the

PRO fire, but their full-scale publication was a rare acknowledgement by the then nationalist local government of the city's deep and complex history. Gilbert had written an innovative history of the city in the 1850s and remained a passionate champion of archives, their protection and publication; he had been a key advocate for the professional protection of the city's records and for the establishment of an Irish Public Record Office. The other *fin de régime* project was entirely unofficial. The Irish Georgian Society, formed in 1908, was led by a group of amateur enthusiasts, mainly unionist in their politics, whose declared mission was to document and publish the architectural and decorative history of Dublin in its 'classical' age, the long eighteenth century. By 1922 five volumes had appeared and they included detailed photographic and archival evidence of many buildings and archives that were destroyed during the Easter Rising of 1916 or in 1922 during the Civil War. The initiative was at that point quietly abandoned.

The scholarly study of the history of Dublin made little progress in the wake of these events, and indeed, in most respects, the old capital made an awkward transition into the new Ireland. Its particular historical story did not fit easily into the dominant national narrative, and its civic development was in no way a priority for the new state. Neither the national cultural institutions located within the city nor the principal agency of local government, Dublin Corporation, had the resources or the vision to champion the problematic heritage of the city. An amateur-run city museum was opened in 1944 and remained a quietly unassuming place, and the National Museum's treatment of Dublin history was (at least until the 1990s) restricted to a celebration of the Easter Rising. For decades it was left to the amateurs of the Old Dublin Society, founded in 1934, to illuminate and popularise the city's past and on occasion to lobby for its protection. In retrospect we can see that the publication of Maurice Craig's *Dublin: A social and architectural history* in 1952 marks the beginning of rigorous scholarship on the city's history. A strikingly elegant and subtle reading of two hundred years of Dublin's physical history, it wore its scholarship lightly but made its arguments cogently. Craig saw the Restoration city, patronised by the Duke of Ormond, as an apprenticeship for the 'Georgian' capital, which reached its fullest flowering in the late eighteenth century when it was the social and political playground of the Protestant ruling class, a city which then lost much of its *raison d'être* after Anglo-Irish parliamentary union in 1801.

Craig's survey has deservedly remained in print, but in the last thirty years books on Dublin history have appeared in unprecedented quantity, some of them original, others light in tone and designed for the general reader. Then came the huge public controversy rumbling through the 1970s over whether or not to protect the Viking-age archaeological treasure trove discovered between Wood Quay and Christ Church Cathedral: this created a public fascination in the tiny medieval city, which has been sustained ever since, thanks in part to an ongoing programme of archaeological research and its publication in the *Medieval Dublin* volumes. Work on the post-medieval period, archaeological, architectural and documentary, has been more uneven but voluminous nonetheless.

The intention here is to draw on the modern proliferation of research projects and academic publications, many of which have been stimulated by the recent growth in public and civic interest in the city's past, and to present a synthesis of our understanding of the evolution of the city. Parts of that canvas have been worked on by historians much more energetically than others. But it is sobering to reflect that there has been more research, reflection and publication on the city's past carried out since the city's millennium year of 1988 than over the whole of the previous millennium. This, therefore, is a report of work (of many people's work) in progress, and my enormous debt to that small army who have been writing on Dublin and Dubliners will, I hope, be apparent throughout the volume.

As a contemporary of James Joyce observed in 1902, 'Dublin is a big village and a dirty village where gossip reigns supreme'. Almost a century later, a perceptive outsider reckoned its defining characteristic was 'the gregarious intimacy, rare in a town of this size, the vivacious gossip, the cultural *fizz*, the wit and repartee at every social level ...'[3] Joyce in *Dubliners* and *Ulysses* captured the conversation of the city, and many illustrious writers have tried to do the same with varying success ever since. Historical documents rarely – and material artefacts never – capture the power of the spoken word. There is now a rich audio and visual record of modern Dublin talk, but this is both too recent and too abundant for the historian to absorb. So a written history has to be based on documents, historical images and the physical evidence of architecture, archaeology and material culture, and the aim here is to try to understand the past rather than to recreate it. But in the process some actors from the past crowd others into the shadows, for the powerful, the rich and the adult male world dominate all forms of historical record before the twentieth century, and this is inevitably reflected in any general historical analysis. As extenuation, one can argue that if the object here is to understand the evolution of the city, the focus has to remain disproportionately on those who actually wielded influence. The silent voices, unheard even in the twentieth century – the prisoners, the institutionalised patients, the casually abused – are silent in the historical record because they had very little influence over their personal fate or their city's shape. It is only extraordinary events, natural disasters, explosions and major crimes that generate the incidental detail about such Dubliners who are otherwise hidden from the historical record. Where possible, such revealing cameos have been exploited.

The focus, then, is on the documented history of the city after it emerged from its medieval chrysalis. The Prologue looks back at the life-cycle of the walled town in the medieval era, first as a Norse micro-kingdom, then as a royal borough of the English Crown. Politically, Dublin was important from the ninth century, but its economic impact on Ireland and beyond was modest and quite contained for its first seven hundred years. This changed abruptly at the end of the sixteenth century, once effective English control over the whole island was established. The twelve subsequent chapters explore the four centuries of Dublin as capital city up to the year 2000.

By stopping at the year 2000, we gain some small space and distance from recent events, but I am very much aware that historical judgements (and historical fashion) are influenced by the writer's environment at the time of writing. This exploration into Dublin's history was conceived when it was indeed a 'tiger town' attracting global interest, but the book has taken shape in the shadow of an intense economic depression that has led many to question older verities. However, I am fortunate to have been surrounded by fellow students of history who share my belief in the virtue of taking the long view, whether it is to discover unexpected patterns repeated over the generations, or to confirm the notion that there is nothing new under the sun. Either way, drilling deep is a great antidote to present discontents.

❧

I would like to acknowledge my debt and appreciation to the following institutions for their support in the course of this project: Dublin City Libraries (notably Mary Clarke and Máire Kennedy), the Department of

Early Printed Books, Trinity College Dublin (notably its former Keeper Charles Benson and the late Vincent Kinnane); the National Library of Ireland; the Royal Irish Academy Library; the Public Record Office of Northern Ireland; and last but not least the now completed *Dictionary of Irish Biography* project (directed by James McGuire). Among the many individual scholars who have helped me, I would like to record my thanks to Juliana Adelman, Johanna Archbold, Sarah Arndt, Toby Barnard, Tom Bartlett, Charles Benson, Andy Bielenberg, Sparky Booker, Ciaran Brady, Maurice Bric, Terence Brown, Andrew Carpenter, Lydia Carroll, Christine Casey, Aidan Clarke, Howard Clarke, Catherine Cox, the late Maurice Craig, Anne Crookshank, Catriona Crowe, Louis Cullen, Bernadette Cunningham, Mary Daly, Anne Dolan, Rowena Dudley, Seán Duffy, Anastasia Dukova, Myles Dungan, Tony Farmar, Paul Ferguson, the late Desmond FitzGerald, Susan Galavan, Larry Geary, Patrick Geoghegan, Raymond Gillespie, Lisa-Marie Griffith, Peter Harbison, Richard Harrison, David Hayton, Brian Henry, Kevin Herlihy, Jacqueline Hill, Susan Hood, John Horne, Arnold Horner, Stefanie Jones, Dáire Keogh, James Kelly, Colm Lennon, Magda and Rolf Loeber, Breandán MacSuibhne, Eve McAulay, Ian McBride, Ruth McManus, Edward McParland, Ivar Magrath, Martin Maguire, Anthony Malcomson, Patrick Maume, Kenneth Milne, Gerald Mills, John Montague, Fergus Mulligan, Timothy Murtagh, Aidan O'Boyle, Gillian O'Brien, Niall Ó Ciosáin, Mary O'Doherty, Cormac Ó Gráda, Eunan O'Halpin, Jane Ohlmeyer, Séamus Ó Maitiú, Ciaran O'Neill, Micheál Ó Siochrú, Jacinta Prunty, Peter Rigney, Ian Ross, Edel Sheridan-Quantz, Alan Smyth, Bill Vaughan, Kevin Whelan, Ciaran Wallace, Patrick Walsh and Christopher Woods. I would also like to thank generations of graduate and undergraduate students who have worked with me on Dublin history over very many years, and whose ideas have woven themselves into this narrative in countless ways. I am indebted to Matthew Stout for his masterful map-making and to Georgina Laragy for her ever resourceful picture research. I would also like to record my thanks to the following for their very generous help in providing images, or in assisting in tracking down some of the pictures used here: Michael Barry, Brian Crowley, Chalkie Davies, Glenn Dunne, Paul Ferguson, Kieran Glennon, Thérèse Gorry, Tony Kinlan, William Laffan, Gordon Leadbetter, John McCullen, Raymond Refaussé, Angela Rolfe, Derek Spiers and Irene Stevenson. My warmest thanks are due to the Profile team, my most patient of publishers, especially my editor

Penny Daniel and my copy-editor Jane Robertson, remembering the late
Peter Carson whose idea this was and whose infectious encouragement
sustained me when the project could so easily have melted away. I would
also acknowledge the substantial support provided by the former Irish
Research Council for Humanities and Social Sciences at an earlier stage of
this project, and also that given by the TCD Arts and Social Science Bene-
faction Fund, the Grace Lawless Lee Fund, and my own TCD Department of History in a variety of ways. Finally, my profound thanks to my
family, but especially to my wife Bridget who has supported me in this
long journey through Dublin in so many ways that only she knows.

LIST OF
ABBREVIATIONS

AIB	Allied Irish Banks
ASRS	Amalgamated Society of Railway Servants
B & I	British and Irish Steam Packet Company
CIE	Córas Iompair Éireann
DHAC	Dublin Housing Action Committee
DMP	Dublin Metropolitan Police
DSER	Dublin and South-Eastern Railway
DUTC	Dublin United Tramways Company
DWWR	Dublin, Wicklow and Wexford Railway
ESB	Electricity Supply Board
FAI	Football Association of Ireland
GAA	Gaelic Athletic Association
GDA	Greater Dublin Area
GNRI	Great Northern Railway (Ireland)
GPO	General Post Office
GSR	Great Southern Railways
GSWR	Great Southern and Western Railway
ICM	Irish Church Missions
IDA	Industrial Development Authority
IFSC	Irish Financial Services Centre
IPP	Irish Parliamentary Party
IRA	Irish Republican Army

IRB   Irish Republican Brotherhood
ITGWU   Irish Transport and General Workers Union
IV   Irish Volunteers
MGWR   Midland Great Western Railway
MP   Member of Parliament
NBA   National Building Authority
NUDL   National Union of Dock Labourers
NUI   National University of Ireland
RDS   Royal Dublin Society
RHA   Royal Hibernian Academy
RIC   Royal Irish Constabulary
TBP   Temple Bar Properties
TCD   Trinity College Dublin
TD   Teachta Dála (Member of Dáil Eireann)
UCD   University College Dublin
UIL   United Irish League
WSC   Wide Streets Commissioners

DUBLIN TOWN AND THE FIRST THOUSAND YEARS

If the Roman legions had arrived in Hibernia and conquered the Irish lowlands, their likely point of entry would have been somewhere along the sixty miles of friendly coast between the Wicklow Mountains and the hills of the Cooley peninsula. The rivers Boyne and Liffey offer natural pathways into the interior, even though neither river is navigable for more than a few miles from the coast. The more northerly river makes an unobtrusive connection with the Irish Sea, but the Liffey flows out into the great amphitheatre of Dublin Bay, which has always charmed sailors, only to trick them with its sand bars, hidden shallows and peculiar currents. But two millennia ago the masters of the many vessels that filled the seaways of Roman Britain would have had no particular difficulty manoeuvring into either the lower Boyne or across the estuary of the Liffey. And entering on a high tide across the mud shoals of Dublin's inner waters would have led the eye to an elevated gravel ridge overlooking the south bank which extends westwards for a mile and more. To a Roman centurion, the ridge would have been a tempting location for a fortress, but Roman soldiers never came closer than Holyhead, and there was to be no scaled-down version of *Londinium* on the Liffey – or the Boyne.

The ridge's early history was not as a fortress but as a meeting point for travellers, fishermen and farmers. The southern prospect from the ridge was across a landscape that had been settled and farmed since Neolithic times, a district particularly rich in prehistoric monuments, with the wooded Dublin/Wicklow mountains filling the skyline. The northern prospect was across the Liffey and Tolka valleys, the borderland between two of the principal kingdoms of eastern Ireland, that of Laigin (Leinster), which lay to the south-west with its ceremonial centre the hill-fort of Dún Ailinne near Kilcullen, and that of Brega, associated with the southern Uí Néill, with centres at Knowth and Lagore in modern County Meath. Brega included the Hill of Tara, the prehistoric meeting-ground supposedly shared by all the Irish kingdoms, but by the sixth century it seems to have been abandoned. Embedded within these regional kingdoms were large numbers of dynastic territories or sub-kingdoms, one of which lay between the rivers Liffey and Camac to the west and the Dodder valley to the south, which was associated with the Uí Fergusa. It was a modest swathe of land that included all of the original urban settlement, but about the Uí Fergusa clan we know almost nothing.

The ridge was the final meeting point of several long-distance tracks that crossed the interior of Ireland and converged on the east coast, one from east Ulster, one from across the Irish Midlands and two from the south. They are of uncertain antiquity and their precise trajectory remains in dispute, but their convergence on the site of Dublin before the town even existed is suggestive. The ridge rises at most fifty feet above the river, which at that point is fully tidal, and two millennia ago the full tide transformed the Liffey into an expansive waterway more than 200 metres wide, shallow but treacherous. A spring tide could shrink the flow to a small channel, perhaps no wider than five metres. There were several points where it was regularly forded at low water, but the favoured crossing was some distance upstream near Usher's Island, where the challenge of wading across the muddy river-bed was made easier by the installation of sheets of hurdle under the water – by whom it is not recorded. This gave the nearby settlement on the ridge its first name, *Áth Cliath*, the ford of the hurdles. Yet, according to the Irish annals, despite the hurdles a small army was caught by the tide in 770 and many were drowned making their crossing, victors after battle.[1]

The muddy banks provided an embarkation point for the tiny vessels venturing out into the Irish Sea, some to fish, some to make the hazardous crossing to Wales. These and other landing places around Dublin Bay and along the coast northwards to the Boyne may well have been known to Roman traders, and Roman Christianity certainly penetrated the region very early. By the eighth century there were probably two small churches on the hill, one the precursor of the surviving medieval church of St Audeon's. A short distance downstream is the modest river mouth of the Poddle as it enters the Liffey. Nowadays its north-eastward trajectory is an invisible feature of the city, safely hidden underground, but then it was a vital waterway, more manageable than the Liffey but still liable to flood. Near its mouth was the dark pool, *Linn Duib* or (as it was later called) *Dubh Linn*, which acted as an antechamber between tributary and river. It seems that close to the pool an early church, possibly the monastery of Dubh Linn mentioned in the annals, was established in the seventh century, but precisely where remains a matter of archaeological debate: the earliest attested Christian site in the neighbourhood is in the Great Ship Street/Chancery Lane area where some 272 burials have been located, laid to rest in the Early Christian Irish manner and dated between the eighth and the eleventh centuries. These burials have been linked to the nearby church-site of St Michael le Pole, which may indeed have been the original monastic site. This first chapter in Dublin's history is still very opaque, but what is clear is that there were several nodes of settlement, one on the ridge, one across the Poddle, and, as Howard Clarke has shown, such duality is not untypical of many embryonic towns in the Europe of the Dark Ages. But there was certainly no street plan, no marketplace. Indeed, without any suggestion of coinage there is little to suggest the existence of commerce beyond what would have been involved in supplying the material needs of ecclesiastics and travellers. The *Dubh Linn* monastery, wherever it was located, was certainly not as rich or as famous as the monastery at Kildare, which was closely associated with the kings of Leinster, or the monastery at Swords to the north, but taken together, this pre-urban cluster south of the Liffey was becoming a busy point of transit and, perhaps also, a place of relative safety.[2]

Norse state

The first horror stories about barbarian pirates appearing over the northern horizon are likely to have been spread in 797 after the sacking of a monastery on Church Island, some twenty miles north of the Liffey mouth and close to present-day Skerries. In the following decades there was a string of such incidents, including the capture of 'a great prey of women' on Howth in 821. But then in the late 830s much larger fleets of longboats began to beach near the mouths of the Boyne and the Liffey. The *Dubh Linn* and Clondalkin monasteries, together with other local churches, seem to have provided the first pickings for the visitors, the Vikings. They erected seasonal camps along the rivers, which were larger and far more formidable than any previous type of settlement. And from 841, according to the Irish annals, these Norsemen began to over-winter on the Liffey, building huts and erecting a stockade, a *longphort,* to protect their boats. Just where they did this has been much debated and several possible locations have been championed. Linzi Simpson, one of the band of urban archaeologists who have transformed our knowledge of the Norse and Norman town, has suggested that the earliest Viking settlement may not have been beside the Liffey but to the south-east of the pool (to the west of modern South Great George's Street), to judge by some very early warrior burials discovered there, and that the original *longphort* may have been located there. But on balance it seems likely, as Andrew Halpin has argued, that the Vikings' fortified base from the 850s was on the eastern end of the ridge overlooking the Poddle/Liffey confluence (i.e. running from Dublin Castle north towards the river, east of the Werburgh Street/Fishamble Street line), where signs of late ninth-century Viking settlement show up strongly. But, wherever their first base, the impact of the newcomers was immediate. Within a generation of their initial settlement they controlled a small hinterland, perhaps from Donnybrook in the south to Clondalkin in the west and northwards to Finglas, and they may also have had settlements on the coast from Dalkey north to Lusk. The indigenous inhabitants within that zone, not least the churchmen, seem to have continued to live with some measure of Norse protection.[3]

Irish sources speak of huge numbers of Viking longboats, rich in booty, resting at Dublin in some years (no fewer than 200 in 871), and throughout the ninth century the settlement served primarily as a springboard for piratical raids conducted elsewhere around the Irish Sea, some of which penetrated deep inland, both in Ireland and lowland Britain, to a quite extraordinary degree: in the 860s and 870s an extended network of warriors closely related to Ívarr and Hálfdan of Dublin seized the military upper hand over a vast swathe of British territory (far more than the Vikings ever held in Ireland itself), capturing York in 867. In David Dumville's recent assessment, by 878 'the Dubliners exercised hegemony or direct rule over a solid block of territory from the Clyde to mid-Wales and had a significant stake in the conquest of all England'. But with the appearance of Alfred of Wessex, their ambitions across the water were progressively contained. As in all predatory societies, the predators regularly fell out among themselves, which in time gave opportunities to their enemies. In Dublin itself this was the background to the attack in 902 by the king of Leinster, working for once in alliance with the men of Brega, when the settlement and all its appendages were comprehensively destroyed. Most of the inhabitants, it seems, were expelled, many to Anglesey and the Wirral, from where they attempted but failed to capture Saxon Chester.[4]

The Liffey and its attractions were not forgotten. Hiberno-Norse warriors returned from their English wars and their principal base in York a decade later. It was probably a more ethnically mixed army that came back, and the later characterisation of them as *Ostmen*, men from the east, is only part of the story. In a series of land and sea campaigns in the south-east in 914 they captured (or possibly recaptured) Waterford, and three years later repossessed Dublin. The shock effect of this return of the Scandinavians was evident in the Irish response it triggered: the formation of an unusually large fighting force led by Niall Glúndub, the Uí Néill high-king, drawing men from all the northern Irish kingdoms, which swept down on the Norsemen in September 919, only to suffer a terrible rebuff a mile or two outside the town at the battle of Islandbridge. Niall and a string of accompanying Ulster kings were killed. That bloody defeat marks the beginnings of a true Norse urban community at Dublin and confirmed them as a naval and territorial power. Indeed, they subsequently tried to dominate a much larger Irish hinterland and to operate within a huge maritime space encompassing the north Irish Sea, southwest Scotland, the Western Isles and the northern seas to Orkney; they also had links in the west with what was in effect a new Dublin colony, Viking Limerick. Over the next two decades there was a clear attempt by Dublin-based forces to carve out a Scandinavian kingdom in east Ulster along the lines of what had been achieved in the north of England centred on York. But the resistance of the Ulaid and the Uí Néill eventually scuppered that plan, and soon the Scandinavian control of York was lost too. Norse Dublin, however, remained strong in its own right, and its kings were endlessly involved in Irish dynastic conflicts that in the long run worked against it. After 951 it rarely engaged in offensive raiding within Ireland, and the town was itself attacked from land on at least seven occasions between 936 and 1015, on two of these with great losses. Despite this, the site was never again abandoned. In the later tenth century, between times of war, it enjoyed a growing maritime trade and became an increasingly fortified place.[5]

Given the technology of the era, fortification meant strong earthen banks up to three metres high, crowned by post-and-wattle fences. In Halpin's model, the ninth-century site expanded westwards along the ridge, its limits following the future north/south line of Winetavern Street and Nicholas Street, with a bank surrounding the whole site, protected on three sides by the Liffey and the Poddle. The defensive strength of the compound, to judge by excavations on its north side, was enhanced around 950 and again c.1000, each rebuilding coming in the wake of military assault. The site, it seems, had a formal layout from the beginning, and within it lay the embryonic Castle Street, Fishamble Street, Werburgh Street and Skinner's Row – the area of the modern city that lies close to the east end of Christ Church Cathedral. Then, at some point in the eleventh century, the enclosure was extended westwards once again, along the future High Street and taking in part of the putative site of *Áth Cliath*. The street lines within the enclosure picked up fortification lines and older routeways, probably those of the long-distance paths of the prehistoric era. But the ecclesiastical buildings lying eastwards across the Poddle in *Dubh Linn* remained unfortified, while *Dyflinn,* as Norse/Ostman sources called their place, became a citadel of some thirty acres, the densest settlement occurring along Fishamble Street and on the north-facing slope above the river.[6]

For over eighty years, between 952 and 1036, one Norse family dominated that community: Olaf Cuarán and two of his sons. Olaf's ambitions had been to rule both Viking York and Dublin – and be a regional warlord extracting tribute from neighbouring kingdoms. But during their ascendancy, Dublin's power on the Irish political chessboard actually diminished while its economy strengthened. The battle of Tara (980) marks the end of Dublin's regional military ascendancy and of its control over what later became Kildare and Meath. Shortly afterwards, Olaf's reign ended abruptly when Máel Sechnaill, the king of Mide and occasional high-king, took the town after a three-day siege and released vast numbers of slaves and prisoners. Stories in the Irish annals about the extraordinary treasure carried out of the town gave a hint of its dazzling reputation. Máel Sechnaill besieged it on two further occasions, extracting a promise of permanent tribute in 989 and removing the 'ring of Thor' and other communal treasures in 995. But then in 997, as part of an island-wide share-out, he ceded overlordship of the town to Brian Bóruma, king of the Munstermen.

This was resisted in Dublin, but Brian defeated a mainly Norse army in 999 and thereupon sacked the town and extracted heavy reparations. The famous early twelfth-century tract, *Cogad Gaedel re Gallaib* ('The war of the Gael and the foreigner') spoke of the rape and mass enslavement of the civilian population after the Munster victory as just revenge for what the Vikings had inflicted – but this was a highly partisan account. Recovery again came quickly and in 1013 the Dubliners and the Leinstermen once more challenged Brian's ascendancy. Aided by Norse forces from the Isle of Man, the Hebrides and Orkney, the *Dyflinn*/Leinster forces met Brian's army at Clontarf in the following spring. They lost in the great Good Friday battle beside Dublin Bay and, despite what later generations thought, this was not so much a great Irish national victory over the Vikings as a bloody contest on an unprecedented scale between ever more powerful regional warlords, an unstable contest in which the Liffey townsmen had a major stake. Although they were on the losing side, the death of their nemesis Brian Bóruma on the battlefield temporarily restored Leinster's and Dublin's autonomy.[7]

As Howard Clarke has emphasised, perhaps the most remarkable survivor in *Dyflinn*'s history was Sitriuc Silkbeard. As one of Olaf's surviving sons, he had been installed by Máel Sechnaill as king in 989, but had moved out of the latter's orbit and managed to shift allegiances over the following forty years. Marrying at different times into the families of both Máel Sechnaill and Brian Bóruma, Sitriuc and his city-state survived repeated pillaging to become a pivot of trade in the Irish Sea, and his intimate links with Wales, Anglo-Saxon England and his Viking allies far to the north suggest a figure of rare energy and guile. He minted the first Irish coins in 997 ('SIHTRIC REX DYFLINN') and oversaw the strengthening of the town's fortifications after Brian's sacking of the place in 1000. The symbolic focus for his people was the Thingmót, a great mound to the east of the settlement and near the tidal limit (adjacent to modern College Green), 'where kings presided and law-makers pronounced', or possibly a building beside it on what became Hoggen Green. Indeed, here are the likely origins of corporate municipal government, even though we have no explicit documentary evidence how it might have operated, nor the area it controlled. The wider region dominated by the town was known as *Fine Gall*, the land of the foreigners in Irish sources, *Dyflinnarskíri* in Norse, the territory from Dublin northwards to Skerries and west to Leixlip. This district was both the bread-basket and the nursery of fishermen for a hungry town.

But despite its growing wealth and populousness, the city-state was now dominated by the regional dynasties jousting for the high-kingship. For about forty years at different times in the eleventh century the kingship of Dublin was assumed by the kings of Leinster, by the Ua Briain kings of Thomond or by one of their sons. Sharp divisions between the descendants of the original Dublin royal dynasty and the Hiberno-Norse mac Ragnaill dynasty in Waterford opened the door to such outside control; the longest such intrusion began in 1052 when Diarmait mac Mail na mBó, king of Leinster, drove out Echmarcach mac Ragnaill and left his own son in charge – not, it seems, an unpopular move and an arrangement which lasted for nearly twenty years. Just how much power resided in those who carried the kingly title is quite unclear, but it is striking that the descendants of the foundation dynasty of Ívarr of the 850s, labelled in the Irish sources as the *Dubgaill*, managed to return to recover the kingship on perhaps five occasions between the 990s and the 1140s. Yet the complete absence of internal documentation on this constantly evolving Hiberno-Norse state makes the identity even of some of its kings rather speculative.[8]

By contrast, modern archaeology since the 1960s has revealed an extraordinary volume of information about the material culture of this community. Indeed, much of what we now know about the insular Viking world comes from the Dublin excavations: nearly half of all Viking-age burials found in Britain and Ireland in modern times have been in the Dublin area, some of them pagan, some Christian burials. The town had a simple street system and single-storey post-and-wattle houses of a remarkably standardised design, with a typical floor area in the dominant house-type of about 40 square metres. Their roofs were of thatch, and they were usually set back from the street. The vast bric-a-brac of everyday urban life, from Anglo-Saxon coins, keepsakes of metal and bone and traces of textiles to their domestic detritus, have come to light in over fifty years of investigation by Breandán Ó Ríordáin, Patrick Wallace and their many successors. Botanical evidence has revealed much about the diet (wheaten and oaten bread, porridge, hazelnuts, berries and ale, some beef, shellfish and herring), in all likelihood a far more diverse fare than was then normal outside the town. It also points to the heavy demands by townspeople on nearby vegetation, both for heating their hearths and for building (evident in the ubiquitous traces of hazel woven into domestic walling and fencing, and of vast amount of ash timber turned into posts). Pre-Viking evidence

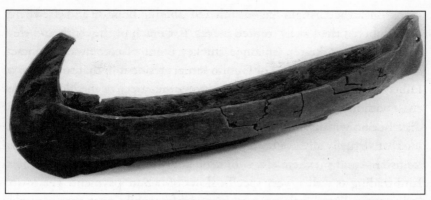

1. The wooden model of a Viking longboat, one of two found in excavations at Winetwaven Street, close to Wood Quay, which have been dated to the twelfth century. This was probably a child's toy. It would have had a single mast and the manoeuvrable square sail that was a standard feature in the hundreds of full-size longboats belonging to the Norse town.

of the town's material culture has been far less abundant, but that may reflect the sites that have been investigated to date. Numerous excavations in the Wood Quay and Fishamble Street neighbourhoods, and along the banks of the lower Poddle, have exposed the diverse material culture of a small but militarised trading community, expanding in size and commercial complexity over more than 300 years. Wallace has discerned some degree of occupational segregation from the archaeology: the merchants and well-to-do around the old site of Fishamble Street, 'Dublin's comb-makers concentrated in High St., the metal-workers in Christchurch Place, the cobblers in High Street ...', with some like the blacksmiths and the boat-builders probably outside the defended area. Some of the exposed street alignments of late ninth- and tenth-century dates mark out property divisions that, quite remarkably, have persisted down to modern times.[9]

But one of the most striking revelations as riverside sections of Viking Dublin were being excavated in the 1970s – the Wood Quay site – was evidence of the exotic range of luxury goods present in the tenth- and eleventh-century town: traces of Asian silks and gold braid, amber jewellery (made in Dublin), walrus ivory, gold and silver ingots, coins from possibly as far as Samarkand. This was, it appeared, both an entrepôt and a place where there was a local demand for luxuries. An upswing in wholesale commerce is suggested by the growing output of silver coin minted in Dublin during the first half of the eleventh century but, judging by the specie unearthed, Anglo-Saxon coins (of Chester, London and elsewhere) outnumbered the locally minted pieces. For much of the tenth and eleventh centuries Chester remained the key point of commercial contact, and there is some evidence of Dublin settlers resident in that town, and of Hiberno-Norse involvement in improving the safety of the North Wales coast with fortified quaysides and navigation aids. Judging by the regional distribution within Ireland of coin hoards dating from the era, it is striking that virtually all have been discovered in the northern half of modern Leinster – and nowhere else – hinting at a particular pattern of hinterland trading as well as very specific flows of tribute payment. The town's indigenous shipping fleet, small but highly mobile craft that routinely engaged in cross-channel movement, remained its strength, and access to high-quality Wicklow oak for building the boats may have been a strong comparative advantage over towns elsewhere in the Norse world. The key to understanding Dublin's commercial ascendancy was something that does not show up in the archaeology: the trade in slaves. This had been an element of Irish Sea commerce throughout the first millennium, but it reached a peak in the eleventh century: Dublin became an international slave market with prisoners of war being traded in both directions across the Irish Sea, captives from warfare within Ireland that were sold in Dublin by the victors, and slaves from Wales, England, Normandy and perhaps even outside western Europe (given the fleeting references to 'blackmen'). Poul Holm has suggested that the wholesale transmission of prisoners of war into slave markets may have begun as a Norse practice, but that from the late tenth century it was copied on a grand scale in the escalating conflicts between Irish kingdoms, particularly in eastern Ireland, with the slaves, young males and females, being disposed of in Dublin. The scale of the traffic is unknown, but it only subsided in the early twelfth century when the Norman ban on slavery and quieter times within England reduced both English demand and supply. The fate of the generations of slaves traded through Dublin is quite obscure, but presumably their owners were wealthy and their tasks were principally domestic.[10]

In his final years, Sitriuc copied King Cnut and went to Rome, travelling with the king of Brega (while their respective heirs went to war in their absence). Although Christian practices had been common in Dublin since the ninth century, Sitriuc was himself a convert. He went on to create a major endowment, the great church at the western end of the fortified compound near the highest point of the ridge, Holy Trinity Christ

Church. Its foundation *c.*1030 may indeed have been the catalyst for extending the town's defences westward. It seems to have originally been a timber-framed structure, the largest of the town's proprietary churches, but later in the eleventh century it became a great stone temple, perhaps coinciding with the period when it became a cathedral and Dúnán was installed as its first bishop. While Dúnán and nearly all his successors were Gaelic Irishmen, Christ Church's links were always with Canterbury, whose archbishops from the 1074 consecrated the Dublin bishops. Furthermore, its rule was Benedictine as in the English cathedrals, and its early relics, which give a hint of devotional preferences, were principally English or continental, notably the prized bones of the patron saints of seamen familiar across the Scandinavian world. With such influences from across the water came the development of territorial parishes within the town, something that was quite alien to the Christianity of the Irish countryside. This cultural hybridity – Norse, Irish and English – so evident in matters of religion, was increasingly the story in Dublin's trade and crafts as well, reflecting the coming and going of small numbers of skilled English artisans and the growing economic power of the West Saxon kingdom. Nevertheless the lingua franca of the town and the immediate hinterland remained Old Norse, although traders would have needed some knowledge of Leinster Irish.[11]

During the eleventh century, as the urban site expanded westwards, the newly enclosed areas around High Street, Nicholas Street and Back Lane were built upon. Sophisticated craftsmanship and the spread of ecclesiastical foundations indicate an affluent urban society in the making. By 1100 the walls protecting the enlarged town on the ridge were rebuilt using rubble masonry, and by then there were probably three substantial gates and an inner citadel, as well as a royal hall or ceremonial centre for the kings (though no evidence of this has come to light). The stable population may have exceeded 4,000, as the settlement was spilling outwards beyond the walls. In the early twelfth century, new churches proliferated around the perimeter, especially on the south-eastern side across the Poddle, a pattern of suburbanisation unknown in other Hiberno-Norse towns. By 1170 there were at least eight churches inside the fortified area and perhaps seven immediately outside it, to the south and east. North of the river and linked by a timber bridge (the dating of which remains obscure) were two religious foundations and a parish church.[12]

Yet despite its wealth and ecclesiastical profile, Dublin remained a subordinate power. Whatever its local autonomy under Norse sub-kings and their control of the coast, the town and its fleet of ships often seem to have been little more than prize chess-pieces deployed in the wider contests for the Irish high-kingship, mainly between the chief dynasties of Leinster and Munster. But that perhaps underestimates local agency: a price could usually be extracted when Dublin's naval power was being hired by Irish, Manx, Welsh or English kings in support of military campaigns, with cattle or slaves being on occasion paid over as a trade-off. The Hiberno-Norse world remained in essence a maritime one where power was widely dispersed geographically, and which was constantly adapting to the changing military pressures from the shore-based kingdoms. Even as late as the 1140s Dublin was briefly drawn back into the Hebridean sphere when Óttar of the Isles seized the kingship.[13]

A battle over Dublin's diocesan status in the twelfth century revealed emerging political tensions: when reformed territorial dioceses were agreed by the Irish bishops at the synod of 1111, Dublin was brought within the metropolitan province of Cashel, but where now lay Canterbury's role in the appointment of the bishops of Dublin? Most (not all) of the townsmen wished to continue the English link, but in 1121 Armagh pressed its claims of primacy over Dublin and indeed sought to secure the post. It succeeded in the former but failed in the latter. But the undisputed fact was that Dublin now mattered in all national contests. Even the Connacht men needed the prestige of Dublin: in 1166, when Ruaidrí Ua Conchobair organised his public inauguration as high-king, it was to take place in the east-coast town. Dublin – not Tara – had now symbolic as well as economic power.[14]

The King of England's town

Meanwhile Anglo-Saxon and Danish England had fallen to the Franco-Norsemen, the Normans, in 1066, and this stunning shift in power in the most developed parts of the neighbouring island threatened to draw in the men of Dublin. Links between the Uí Chennselaig kings of Leinster, with their base in modern Co. Wexford, and the leaders of Wessex in the English south-west had been strengthening over the previous generation; King Harold Godwinson, before winning the English throne, had spent time in Ireland during the 1050s. Such friendships strengthened the links between the trading communities in their respective spheres of influence – Dublin and Bristol. Bristol was still a modest Mercian town that had thrived on the slave trade with Ireland, and Dublin shipping at that time was involved around the Irish Sea and beyond, caught up in the turbulent intrigues convulsing England and the North Sea kingdoms. This element of Dublin's history was brought back to life in the 1960s with the discovery in Danish waters at Skuldelev near Roskilde of the skeleton hulls of five Norse vessels, one of them a 30-metre long warship. The oaken timbers of this vessel have subsequently been proven to be Irish and probably date from the 1040s, and the assumption is that this great vessel was made in Dublin. With space for some sixty rowers, it was a formidable weapon of war, and it is assumed that it worked the Irish Sea before journeying much further afield. And there may be a link to the events of 1066.

After Harold's death at the battle of Hastings, two of his sons fled to Leinster where they negotiated the loan of Dublin's ships from Diarmait mac Maíl na mBó, king of Leinster. In 1068, this fleet sailed up the Avon and attacked Bristol (the *Annals of Winchester* suggests fifty-two ships took part, which may have flattered them), but they were repulsed. Then the Irish force made a successful landing in Somerset and drew off plunder; a larger expedition to Devon the following year had mixed results, but was also pushed back by a Norman force. In the wake of all this, Harold's sons left Ireland and sailed away for good to the court of their uncle, the king of Denmark. It has been suggested that the 'Skuldelev 2' vessel was their means of escape. Whatever, the whole episode is noteworthy not just as one of the more serious after-shocks of the Norman Conquest but as almost the last intervention of Norse Dublin in English history. Dublin shipping and mercenaries, however, continued to be involved from time to time in north Wales until the 1160s, both as allies of the Welsh princes resisting Norman expansion, then in 1164 when acting in support of English forces. They were oars for hire to the end.[15]

The vigorous military consolidation of the Norman regime across all of England was felt in Dublin in many ways, not least in church affairs. On the north bank of the Liffey, the first of several religious houses associated with the continental reform movement was established in 1139, some distance downstream of the bridge: thus began the formidable St Mary's Abbey. Within a few years, this house was attached to the Cistercian order and placed under the care of a Shropshire abbot. Even further downstream and on the exposed south side of the Liffey, a convent and an

Augustinian priory were established in 1146 and 1162. Here the sponsor of both is well known: Diarmait Mac Murchada, great-grandson of Harold's Irish ally and the king of Leinster for some forty years. His territorial ambitions and violent conflicts with regional rivals became notorious in Irish history, but they mask a risk-taker and a wily survivor, a military tactician and a political reformer. He had successfully recruited Dubliners to aid him in his expansionist ambitions in the 1130s, was instrumental in breaking the town's revived Hebridean links in the 1140s, and greatly increased his control *c.*1162 when in one document he was referred to as *rex Dubliniae*. Apart from grants of land inside and outside the town that he made to dower his new religious houses, he engineered the promotion of his brother-in-law Lorcán Ua Tuathail to the bishopric of the diocese (who subsequently reformed the cathedral and made it an Augustinian establishment). But perhaps his greatest coup was in securing the necessary political support at the synod of Kells (1152) to secure the elevation of the Dublin diocese to become one of four metropolitan Irish archdioceses (on a par with those created in 1111, Cashel and Armagh), its new ecclesiastical province being more or less coterminous with Diarmait's kingdom of Leinster. The logic was clear.[16]

But in 1166 Diarmait's enemies beyond the province, led by Ruaidrí Ua Conchobair, king of Connacht, seized the initiative: the Dublin townsmen, or at least the leading families, disowned Diarmait and switched their allegiance. He was forced to flee southwards, and was subsequently banished from the country while Ruaidrí was elevated to the high-kingship. Diarmait sought help from as far afield as France and the Anglo-French empire builder, Henry II. He returned to south-east Ireland the following year, having received permission from King Henry to recruit Norman-Welsh soldiers. With these mercenaries he captured Wexford in 1169. Then, with the arrival of a much larger contingent of new-style soldiery in 1170, he began a rolling campaign to recapture his kingdom. His new military assistants seized the Norse town of Waterford with unprecedented violence, and from that point they began to take the initiative. Diarmait had a coalition of enemies who now expected his mixed force to attack Dublin, but they did not anticipate the route he chose that autumn – through the woods and upland tracks of the Wicklow Mountains. When his small force surprised the town, his kinsman Archbishop Ua Tuathail sought to negotiate. But after three days of haggling, several young Norman knights took matters into their own hands and, with superior weaponry, seized the town. On so doing they handed over control not to Diarmait but to the leading Norman knight and now Diarmait's son-in-law, 'Strongbow', Richard de Clare. It was one of the less violent coups in Dublin's early history, but it changed everything.[17]

Diarmait continued his military campaigning into Meath, apparently with ambitions to make himself high-king, but it seems he may have already been a sick man. He died in the spring of 1171. His Irish enemies kept their focus on Dublin in the belief that it was key to defeating the Norman interlopers, and they were determined to retake it. But the Norman knights with their superior archery and some local Irish help just about held their position over the next year. Ascall Mac Turcaill, the last Norse/Ostman sub-king of Dublin, returned the following spring with some sixty ships, and attacked the town from the east (at Dame's Gate). But this was unsuccessful, Ascall was captured and publicly beheaded. Then in the summer the town was besieged by Ruaidrí and five other Irish kings, with the armies of three provinces, camping west, north and south of the town, and they were supported on the river by Norse ships from the Isle of Man and the Hebrides, the common aim being to starve the garrison into surrender. After two months of privation and disapproval from England, they sought to make terms with Ruaidrí, but he overplayed his hand. A small Norman force broke out of the town by stealth and surprised the Irish camp near Castleknock, with devastating results. The wider siege was lifted.

These startling victories by small numbers of mercenaries led by Strongbow raised the prospect that a great Cambro-Norman fiefdom could now be created within the country – as long as Dublin could be held. And it was this novel prospect, following the power vacuum left by the death of Diarmait, that drew Henry II's attention away from his multiple concerns elsewhere. It forced him to focus on Dublin in order to prevent an autonomous Irish lordship being created, out of which his future enemies might emerge. So, for the first time, an English ruler in full command came to Ireland; he landed near Waterford with a small flotilla of 400 ships and some 4,000 fighting men, and then hurried via Cashel towards Dublin. On his arrival, a huge wattle tent was erected on Hoggen Green for the Christmas entertainment of the Irish kings, who came in number to offer fealty to the 'emperor'. It was just as well, for it was an exceptionally bitter winter.[18]

What happened to the defeated townsmen in all this? According to Giraldus, writing a generation later, some 'went on board ship, taking their most precious belongings, and sailed off to the northern isles'. Some may even have gone to the extremities of the Norse world. Certainly Dublin as a naval power was no more. But Norse/Ostman landowning families survived in the Dublin hinterland (some like the Harolds and the Archbolds accommodating themselves very effectively to the new regime), and we can assume that most non-elite citizens survived – the merchants and clergy, the craftsmen and sailors – although it seems that many, perhaps most, had to leave the walled town and to settle on the north bank of the river around St Michan's church, which became known as *Houstemanebi* (in later English, Oxmantown), absorbing a pre-existing north-side settlement that was probably two centuries old. In the archaeological record there is sufficient evidence of continuity in Dublin building methods to caution against assuming any dramatic change in craft methods or in the craft population itself; tellingly, an active involvement in the prized business of shipbuilding continued. A comparative analysis of skeletal remains (specifically the crania from 126 bodies) recovered from Norse and high medieval burial sites within the urban area has been carried out by Barra Ó Donnabháin and Benedikt Hallgrímsson, and this points in the same direction: their study strongly implies that genetic diversity within the Norse town was quite wide, and that this pattern of diversity was surprisingly similar to that found in nearby thirteenth- and fourteenth-century skeletons. Thanks to the near total absence of women among early Norse invaders, genetic and probably cultural mixing was taking place from the ninth century onwards, albeit the result initially of slavery and coercion; the gradual shift in focus in religious practice from Thor to the Christian deity was probably achieved through the influence of female partners. But we now have scientific evidence that Norse Dublin had been a hybrid mix, and that despite the huge changes in store it would remain so, a place where Norse and French, Irish, Welsh and the Saxon dialects of England would all be regularly heard on the street.[19]

The shape of the new order became much clearer after Henry II's six-month visit to Dublin in the winter of 1171–2. Dublin and its coastal hinterland (together with Waterford and Wexford) were declared to be royal demesne, leaving the rest of the kingdom of Leinster to Strongbow. The kingdom of Meath (including what had been Brega) was granted to Hugh de Lacy, Henry's custodian and constable of Dublin (in effect the first viceroy); a little later de Lacy's son established the town of Drogheda near the mouth of the Boyne on his vast lordship. Most but not all Irish and Norse dynasties holding land close to Dublin lost out completely, with many of Strongbow's circle receiving grants of land in south Dublin and de Lacy's men receiving lands in Meath and north Dublin. Only on the (very extensive) properties of the religious houses and the archdiocese in Dublin and Wicklow was there significant continuity of landholding. And the jurisdictional boundaries of Dublin itself, its 'liberty' of six square miles, were defined at this time: they included the town and its suburbs, plus a swathe of countryside from Blackrock in the south-east across the lower Dodder and the lower Poddle to the tidal limits of the Liffey at Islandbridge, then north-eastwards across the escarpment above Oxmantown to the mouth of Tolka, with a sliver of shoreline running beyond it along the north side of Dublin Bay. The royal exchequer and treasury were to be located in Dublin itself; as a consequence the place was to be fortified in the king's name and its citizenry attached as directly as possible to the Crown. But the properties held by the pre-existing religious houses and the diocese were confirmed to them. Christ Church was unaffected and Archbishop Ua Tuathail continued in office even as the process of Normanisation began. He was the crucial intermediary in laying the ground for the treaty of Windsor in 1175 that recognised Ruaidrí Ua Conchobair as high-king of that part of Ireland outside the territories in Norman hands, and he secured strong papal support to buttress his defence of the local church's property and privileges against mounting royal pressure. But the archbishop died suddenly in 1180, and the king managed to get John Cumin, a cleric from Bath and royal protégé, duly elected in his place.[20]

The town's first 'charter' (the tiny parchment still survives) was issued in 1171, and in it Henry opened up Dublin to the inhabitants of Bristol and spoke of it as being a gift to them: the freemen of the West Country town who had faced Dublin mercenaries at their gates a century previously were now promised that all the urban privileges they then enjoyed could be transferred to Dublin and they were given licence to settle there. But just how far this was a tangible endowment remains obscure. The charter may have had some effect on short-term migration insofar as surnames associated with the Severn Valley show up strongly in the thirteenth-century Dublin freemen rolls, but such links were there already. However, as Seán Duffy has pointed out, in Dublin's first real charter in 1192, 'an extraordinarily generous concession', there is almost no reference to Bristol, and in it the existing inhabitants were given control over 'all tenures within and without the walls ... by the common assent of the city', thereby encouraging reclamation and a jump in municipal revenues arising from the rent

2. *The bronze matrices of the city's first common seal. This was commissioned around the time of Henry III's charter issued in 1229, the first that permitted Dubliners to elect a mayor to govern their city. A unique seal was required to authenticate formal documents issued in the name of the city. One side of the seal depicted a small trading vessel at sea, the other the great gate of Dublin Castle, complete with musicians, archers and the heads of Irish enemies or felons.*

accruing from such land. The charter was obtained opportunistically at a time when the future King John was desperately trying to strengthen his position. Then, in 1215, in the wake of Magna Carta, John granted the fee-farm of Dublin to its citizenry, meaning that they were removed from the jurisdiction of the county sheriff and could retain their own taxes as assessed by their elected officers. In 1229 they were granted the right to elect a mayor, by which time, it seems, a council of twenty-four 'principal men' was meeting regularly. This incremental growth of fiscal and legal privileges, to be enjoyed by all free citizens but not by strangers, did not happen by accident, but was a result of the successful extraction of grants and concessions from a beleaguered monarchy and usually at a price.[21]

The physical impact of the decision to make 'the king's city of Dublin' capital of the Norman lordship of Ireland was evident quite quickly. The walls were immediately strengthened and a strong 'New Gate' at the east end of Thomas Street was built. St Thomas's, the Augustinian abbey founded in 1177 some distance west of that gate, was the object of special royal favour and the burying place for the Norman elite, and in its size and political importance it became something of a counterweight to the wealthy St Mary's on the far side of town. Thomas Street itself, a 'great new street', was a twelfth-century creation that pointed westwards towards

Strongbow's religious house beyond the Camac, the preceptory of the Knights Hospitaller at Kilmainham which he founded *c*.1174, gifting it a riverside estate along the Liffey and land at Clontarf.

On the north side, outside the walls, a series of streets and lanes, including Pill Lane and Broad Street (the future Mary's Lane), were laid out with a surprising degree of regularity, covering the space between Oxmantown Green to the west and St Mary's Abbey to the east, and bisected by Oxmantown (i.e. Church) Street. By the end of the thirteenth century, the north side's particular association with markets, slaughter-houses and ironworking was already evident, by which time it equalled the walled town in area, if not in population. However, much of its old-fashioned housing was consumed in the great fire of 1304 that started in Bridge Street and then spread northwards across the bridge. One of the institutions to suffer was St Saviour's, the Dominican priory built in the 1220s on the river just downstream from the bridge. The 'black friars' were the first of the mendicant orders in Ireland, ahead of the Franciscans who a few years later established their friary just outside the walls on the south-west side. These two Dublin houses were critical to the subsequent success and impact of the regulars, the wandering preachers, across thirteenth-century Ireland.[22]

The south side was, however, always pre-eminent. King John's decision in 1204 to build *de novo* a strong royal fortress in what had been a corner of the Norse town was crucial in this. John's long-serving arch-bishop, Henry de Loundres, oversaw the completion of Dublin Castle, the compound dominated by massive circular corner towers, unlike anything previously seen in the country. He may also have devised the ingenious re-routing of the Poddle, which meant the fortified quadrangle was now surrounded by water on three sides. The construction cost appears to have been shared between citizens and the royal treasury. Military threats to the town lessened in the early Norman era, although the massacre of large numbers of civilians on Easter Monday 1209 as they relaxed in Cullens-wood to the south of the town was a terrible warning. The background to this attack by Wicklow Irish swordsmen is obscure. Shortly afterwards an extramural gate, St Kevin's, was built on the south-east approaches to protect the southern suburbs, and Cullenswood was commemorated until the late seventeenth century as a reminder of the eternal threat from the mountains, but in reality there was little enough threat in the early days. Indeed, there was something of a hundred-year peace between Normans,

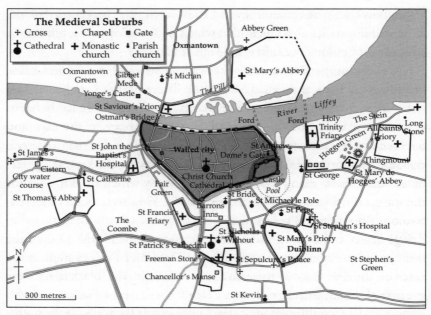

Map 1: Dublin city and its suburbs c.1250.

Irish and Ostmen landowners in south Dublin and across the wooded valleys of Wicklow, and land values close to the urban area were by the mid-thirteenth century quite high, even by English standards. But from the 1270s an intermittently violent and inconclusive three-hundred-year war commenced between the Irish dynasties based in upland Wicklow and Norman authority in Dublin.[23]

Archbishop Henry de Loundres completed the process begun by his predecessor of transforming one of the extra-mural churches on the Poddle, St Patrick's, into something very different. The initial idea had been to create a collegiate church for training English clergy for service in Ireland, but Henry secured permission *c.*1214 to elevate the church into a cathedral. In contrast to the arrangements for Holy Trinity Christ Church, which had become an Augustinian priory (dominated, for a long time, by Irish clergy), St Patrick's was conceived of as an orthodox English cathedral, its chapter canons to be secular clergy. Henry planned an entirely new building, heavily influenced it seems by Salisbury, and organised colony-wide fund-raising. But it was his successor, Archbishop Luke (in post between 1228 and 1255), who was actually responsible for building what Howard Clarke has characterised as 'the most elegant and most expensive ecclesiastical manifestation of the colonists' creative drive' and, at over ninety metres in length, it was by far the most formidable building in medieval Dublin. Its decades-long construction presumably swelled the number of immigrant stonemasons as they shaped the yellow limestone, shipped over from Dundry near Bristol. The carpenters may also have been migrants, but at least some of the cathedral's great oak beams came from near at hand (although more than a century later when the choir roof was being reconstructed in the 1360s, the oak came from northern, possibly Antrim sources, suggesting either the exhaustion of local supplies or the dangers by then of Wicklow woods). The overall stability of the building, lying beside the Poddle, gave recurring trouble, but even in the worst of times it was always repaired.

The senior clergy of the cathedral provided the royal government with key administrators over many generations, and Dublin archbishops acted as justiciars (i.e. viceroys) on at least six occasions between 1221 and 1503. The cathedral's relations were always more intimate with the Castle than with the established townsmen. Archbishop Bicknor, who was a divisive figure during his many years in office (1317–49), championed plans to establish a college of higher learning attached to the cathedral, with faculties of theology and canon law similar to the Oxford model, but whether anything came of this – Dublin's first university plan – is doubtful. The lands around the cathedral were among the first parts of town to become a distinct private jurisdiction, a 'liberty' within Dublin's urban boundaries, with separate courts to adjudicate and to punish beyond the writ of the mayor and the civic courts (establishing such a privilege was probably Archbishop Henry's work). Immediately to the south of the cathedral liberty was the archbishop's palace, St Sepulchre's, built in the 1180s, and the manor attached to it spanned a huge swathe of the nearby countryside.[24]

It is now possible to speak of Dublin as a *city*, for by the later thirteenth century its population nearly trebled its pre-1170 peak. It had become ethnically far more English and more closely aligned to Chester and Coventry, Bristol and London. Norse names do occasionally appear in the early municipal records, and there is a hint of a Gaelic Irish presence too, but the dominant impression is of a new urban elite entirely in charge, economically, politically and culturally, with a new legal system and a jurisprudence that owed everything to developments in the Anglo-Norman world outside and nothing to indigenous legal traditions. Traders and craftsmen were all members of a common association, the

Guild Merchant, its establishment in the late twelfth century being one of the many borrowings from Bristol. It soon had its hall in Winetavern Street and a side-chapel in Christ Church. We know nothing of its internal history until the later Middle Ages, but membership rolls survive from c.1190 to 1265 and indicate the overwhelming dominance of new names in city trade. Even around 1250, at least half of the newly enrolled names came from outside the city, and the great majority of these from across the water. However, there are hints that a guild 'of those coming from overseas' and a guild 'of the Irish' may have had a shadowy parallel existence at mid-century. The actions of the city assembly were not regularly recorded until the fifteenth century, or at least no documents survive, but a 'common house for executing laws' existed in the thirteenth century, and this was replaced c.1300, when a 'new tholsel' was erected beside the central crossroads on the ridge, a building that in due course was shared with the Guild Merchant.[25]

The site of the walled town expanded rapidly in the early Norman years, now enclosing about forty-four acres. That included the Liffeyside marshland lying between the north walls of the old Norse town and the high-tide mark, the area lying north of modern Cook Street and Essex Street which was systemically reclaimed c.1200, thereby creating Wood Quay and Merchant's Quay. It seems that these quays were always open to the river and that defences were not built on the water's edge. Upstream the old bridge, probably only passable to pedestrians and animals, was replaced by a more solid structure. John de Courcy has suggested that the new bridge had a timber superstructure resting on stone foundations, with perhaps twelve spans, not unlike London Bridge; it lasted until 1385. The old post-and-wattle method of house construction slowly gave way to a more robust carpentry, with oak replacing ash; two-storey houses, part timber, part stone, were appearing near the quay (and perhaps elsewhere), with the stone being in general quarried locally. But it was the scale and architecture of the two cathedrals that bespoke Dublin's new wealth and the spread of suburbs around the monastic houses north, south and east of the walled core that reflected its new scale of commerce. Water from two of the smaller southside rivers, the Poddle and the Dodder, was diverted to give a regular supply to the growing town in the 1240s, and coal (probably from near Chester) began to be imported as supplies of local timber for the hearth first came under pressure. There was a massive growth in number and size of watermills close to town, many of them on the Liffey's tributaries but some sited within the new monastic compounds in the city. These were primarily used to grind wheat and oats. Murphy and Potterton have estimated that it may have required more than 100,000 acres of arable ground within the manorialised hinterland of the city to supply the raw material for its food and drink. Pottery, which had previously been wholly imported, was from the late twelfth century manufactured using local clays, principally in Crockers Street outside the west gate (initially it was coarseware, but glazed fineware dating from the late thirteenth and fourteenth centuries has been found, both in city excavations and at rural sites).

An annual city fair was established in 1204 beside the western wall. It was held each May (later each July) for fifteen days, and overseas merchants buying wool and hides were among those who patronised it. The fair was the commercial hub of a trading network of far greater sophistication and extent than any system of exchange in Norse times, and in the first century of the Norman lordship new fairs and markets, roads and bridges were created across lowland Leinster, some of which were the nuclei for future towns. Waterford and New Ross became the principal ports for Irish exports, with Dublin only fifth as measured by export custom duties *c.*1300, but in the following century it became the largest importer of French wine and was always the main centre of demand for raw materials within the country, having the biggest concentration of urban craftsmen, reflecting its very well-endowed monasteries and cathedral chapters. Wheat was now the preferred cereal for bread, oats for ale, and in some years grain was exported to Chester or sent out to provision the king's armies in Scotland and France. Dublin's limitations as a port, with the shallow and treacherous approaches to its modest quays, may have begun to work against it and favoured the south-eastern ports when it came to receiving larger trading vessels. By the fifteenth century Dublin vessels were far less prominent at Bristol than were those from Wexford, New Ross and the south Munster towns, while at Chester many of the small vessels engaged in Anglo-Irish trade were based in Rush, Malahide and Howth – not just Dublin.[26]

The first 'parliament' of nobles was held in 1279, and although such meetings with king or justiciar were often held in the provinces, more than half of those held over the next two centuries were in Dublin, usually in the refectory of Holy Trinity Christ Church (although the canons of St Patrick's were far more heavily involved in the actual proceedings). We know little about the hierarchy of trades that supported church and state, but the everyday proximity of royal officials and wealthy clergy sustained a constant demand for a great variety of services and craft products. We know even less about the women of the town, other than that they enjoyed some legal rights (they could hold property and make wills, they could instigate legal proceedings and they could be members of the guild on the death of their husbands), and they appear to have been very active within the informal economy in malting, brewing and inn-keeping. That said, the archaeological evidence is more sombre: some of the medieval female skeletons analysed reveal distressing signs of arduous manual labour and the regular carriage of heavy weights. But, all in all, for Dublin residents it was an era of prolonged peace and urban consolidation, and apart from occasional trouble in parts of Wicklow its large hinterland was *terra pacis*, a land of peace. As a consequence, its own defences were allowed to fall into decay. From the time of the Norman takeover in 1170 (and excepting the Cullenswood massacre) more than a century passed before any major trouble returned.[27]

By the 1290s, however, there was a growing sense of insecurity in the immediate Dublin area, and a citizen-watch system was introduced about that time. But it was the Scottish invasion of Ireland in 1315–17 that firmly put an end to the long cycle of expansion. This coincided with the beginnings of a generation of extreme weather events, disastrous harvests and famine conditions internationally. Edward Bruce, who was crowned king of Ireland at Dundalk in 1316, approached Dublin the following spring and with his brother Robert threatened to lay siege. There was panic, St Patrick's Cathedral was looted, and in order to pre-empt the city's capture the mayor took extreme measures: the western suburbs (including Thomas Street) that could easily be burnt were knocked down, and St Saviour's priory north of the bridge was demolished, all with the aim of strengthening the city's defences. The siege was lifted quite quickly, but the losses were huge.[28] John de Pembridge, the leading figure in St Saviour's for many years, has recently been identified by Bernadette Williams as principal author of the 'Annales Hiberniae ab anno Christi 1162', a chronicle that gives tantalising glimpses of life in the fourteenth-century city. A (highly partisan) preaching friar, he exalted the generous patrons of his order and noted the horrific fate meted out to malefactors, most notably Adducc Dubh O'Toole, accused of claiming that the sacred scriptures were only fables; he was found guilty and burnt at the stake in Hoggen Green on Easter Monday, 1328 (a trumped-up charge against the head of the O'Tooles of Fercullen and Imaal, manufactured, it seems, by the Dean of St Patrick's). The Bruce invasion and the sharp reversals of fortune of powerful men, both in Dublin and far afield, caught much of Pembridge's attention, but natural disaster also featured: the terrible famine of 1315–17 (which affected much of Europe) led him to report that graves were being robbed for food and mothers were eating their dead children; and the extreme winter of 1338–9 that led to the freezing of the Liffey, allowed citizens to dance, feast and play ball on the ice. He himself was probably a victim of the next crisis, the Black Death, for his quill fell silent during 1348, the year when bubonic plague reached the city.[29]

Pembridge's generation had witnessed the beginnings of the long-drawn-out contraction of the Anglo-Norman lordship. Population in the heartlands of the colony was falling from around 1300, if not earlier, and the downturn had a particularly marked effect on Dublin. Its population before the Bruce invasion may have reached 12,000, not far short of that of Bristol, and forming nearly 1 per cent of Ireland's probable total population at its medieval peak. That figure for Dublin would not be surpassed for 300 years. The subsequent progressive weakening of royal power and exchequer revenues, the economic decline of the hinterland, and the catastrophic effects of plague and famine over several decades reduced Dublin's population to around 6,000, not far above its Norse maximum. John Clyn, the contemporary Franciscan chronicler based in Kilkenny, claimed that during the four months after the plague pandemic reached Dublin and Drogheda in August 1348, 14,000 died in Dublin alone ('*xiiii milia hominum mortui sunt*'), and that '*ipsas civitates Dubliniam et Drovhda fere destruxit et vastavit incolis et hominibus*' (Dublin and Drogheda were almost destroyed and emptied of inhabitants and men). Both the archbishop and the mayor were among its victims.[30]

Hard quantitative evidence to calibrate the disaster does not exist at the local level. Clyn knew Dublin well, but his figure is unlikely to have been based on a head count. Taking it at face value, it implies that the urban population was completely wiped out. This certainly did not happen, although Dublin was probably one of the places worst affected in the country. Archbishop Fitzralph of Armagh, who had returned to Ireland (presumably to Drogheda) in the year of the plague, informed Pope Clement VI a year later that the greatest toll had been among those living near the sea and particularly mariners and fishermen. As in all pre-industrial mortality crises, it would have been quite normal for large numbers to flee the towns at the onset of an epidemic, and on this occasion such a response would have been entirely rational, for the impact of the plague was far more severe in confined and congested environments where rats (or whatever actually was the vector of the deadly bacterium *Yersinia pestis*) could breed and move freely around. So it is quite plausible that there was a temporary emptying of the town.[31]

Seen in the longer run, it is clear that life in the post-plague era was utterly different from that of a century previously. Population both in city and hinterland continued to fall long after the crisis, buffeted by the return of bubonic plague in 1361 (and later) and by war. Dublin's wine imports from France had by the late fourteenth century plummeted (although the Hundred Years War was a factor here), and suburbs both to the south of the walled town and north of the river contracted as once busy urban tenancies reverted to agricultural use. Other Irish coastal towns shrank in size too, but Dublin's decline seems to have been starker. Its citizenry came to depend more on the monastic institutions and their proprietorial economies than on the business generated by Dublin Castle and the attenuated arms of royal government. The other Anglo-Norman towns now only rarely had recourse to the royal courts in Dublin. And it was telling that it took forty-three years to rebuild the single bridge across the Liffey after it collapsed in 1385, and that it was the abbot of St Mary's Abbey, not the justiciar or the merchants, who eventually oversaw the construction of what was the first fully stone bridge. St Mary's, ever conscious of its privileges under the Crown, continued to add to its huge properties in the fifteenth century and eventually controlled more than 17,000 acres in Co. Dublin and 3,700 in Co. Meath. Indeed, church institutions were critical to the town's survival: the cathedrals, parishes and religious houses between them owned a very large proportion of the agricultural land of Co. Dublin, and it was their cereal-producing tenants who were critical in provisioning the town, whatever the weather.[32]

The characterisation of Dublin as an endangered bridgehead protected by families of pure English descent against the king's enemies dates from this era, but in reality there were numbers of Gaelic freemen in fifteenth-century Dublin, acculturated and intermarrying on a limited scale, and much of the working population even in the inner hinterland was Gaelic in origin, even if English in dress and bilingual in speech. However there was evidently a shortage of labour and this may have increased the number of craftspeople and town labourers who in appearance, family name and deportment were Irish, not English. From the 1450s there was a series of attempts to exclude Irishmen from any city occupation and from marrying into city families. The motivation behind such restrictions is complex and the impact unknown, although the village of Irishtown near the mouth of the Liffey estuary may well have been established as a result of the ordinance of 1454. Whatever the muddy reality, the image of Dublin as an undefiled community of Norman/English families who had settled in the twelfth century, married amongst their own and upheld English law, customs and orthodox religion, was a compelling story. The urban community was certainly completely English-speaking by the mid-fifteenth century, when the Corporation began to keep its records in English.[33]

But by then there was something of a cultural shift underway, with laymen becoming more involved in running parish churches and local fraternities, religious houses no longer managing their own property, and with the church at large ceding ground to civic institutions in shaping the life of the urban community. Civic rituals, albeit heavily woven into the religious calendar, became more prominent; indeed, a civic officer, the Mayor of the Bull Ring, was appointed to oversee them. Corpus Christi pageants, where biblical dramas were played out on carts that were wheeled through the streets, were becoming a great summer event attracting outsiders, but it was increasingly the civic leaders who regulated them (festivities on Shrove Tuesday and St George's Day were also subject to civic management). The pageants were actually organised by religious fraternities or craft guilds, of which there were seventeen when processional rules were drawn up in 1498. The tailors were apparently the first craft guild to establish a separate identity outside the all-encompassing Guild Merchant. Some of the other guilds listed in 1498, such as 'the haggardmen and the husbandmen' who were 'to bear the dragon, and repair it on St George's Day and Corpus Christi day', were merely ephemeral bodies, but there were nearly a dozen craft associations in the Corpus Christi procession, which then or later became chartered bodies and as such an integral part of municipal government. Such differentiation below the merchant body may reflect the sharply improved economic status of craftsmen relative to those who controlled property in the century after the Black Death. This shift was an almost universal legacy of the great fall in population across western Europe, bringing about improved living standards, at least in the more advanced economies, and the possibility of new forms of economic conflict. But in Dublin the heightened sense of proximate danger from the hills and the periodic raising of citizen bands to go out on campaign must have been a powerful countervailing factor tending to strengthen communal solidarity.[34]

Signs of late medieval economic recovery are elusive. We learn very little about the material culture of the town from the archaeological record, since post-twelfth-century soil strata were destroyed in the making of seventeenth- and eighteenth-century cellars. However, it is evident that stone was being used on a larger scale, not least on the quays, notably Arran Quay where Alan Hayden has also discovered abundant evidence of late medieval processing of deep-sea fish (ling and cod), presumably for local consumption. The trade with Chester probably remained the most important business throughout the fifteenth century, and vessels from Dublin competed with Drogheda in the trade in hides and fish eastwards, salt and cloth homewards. The Guild Merchant association became more directly involved in bulk buying and selling in this era, and there was considerable friction in the 1460s between indigenous merchants and English (presumably mainly Chester) traders resident in Dublin, with the English seeking royal support for a scheme to exclude Irish shippers from the cross-channel trade. But Dubliners at that time had a strong foothold on the other side: in 1474, at least six of the seventeen traders entering the Chester Guild of Merchants were from Dublin. The relative prominence of Irish shipping at Chester, so evident in the mid-fifteenth century, fell away noticeably and, for whatever reason, English and Welsh shipping controlled the sea-lanes to the Irish east coast by 1500, with the minor Co. Dublin ports also becoming more prominent. Indeed, the evidence of Dublin's late medieval commercial wealth lies not within the city but outside, in the castellated warehouses and castles built by Dublin merchants at Dalkey and at the tiny deep-water harbour at Bullock nearby, which was used by long-distance shipping to offload high-value goods. Signs of commercial success can also be found in the fragmentary evidence on landholding in the wider region, which indicates that there was a steady growth in merchant families investing in land at a distance, particularly on the great church estates and the royal manors, their intermittent presence helping to create a fortified landscape of castles and tower-houses across the hinterland.[35]

As elsewhere in northern Europe, population levels remained low throughout the fifteenth century. Dublin's suburbs were very slow to be rebuilt, and even the construction of several great extramural gates (two

on the north side in Oxmantown *c*.1470, one at St James Gate to the west
c.1485) was not a positive sign of growth, more a response to the night-time
sense of danger felt in the surviving suburbs close to the city walls. The
walls themselves were far more formidable by the end of the medieval era:
in Sir John Perrot's survey of 1585, most sections were 16 to 22 feet high,
with parts of the south-side walls even higher. The mountains were not
far away, and for townsmen once they crossed the arc from Carrickmines
round to Saggart, the badlands began. Throughout the fifteenth century,
citizen bands were trained to march out in support of the justiciar against
the king's enemies, both in local and provincial campaigns, and James
Lydon has suggested that the 500-strong Guild of St George, created in
1472, was 'the first real standing army in medieval Ireland'. But the king's
writ was effective in only a small territorial enclave, a hinterland of peace
some thirty miles along the coast and rarely stretching more than twenty
miles inland. This was 'the Pale', a term only introduced in the 1490s when
landowners who 'mireth next unto Irishmen' were legally obliged to erect
a continuous line of earthen dyke – to hinder human movement into the
king's territory and cattle movement out of it. Murphy and Potterton have
concluded that 'some significant sections of the boundary were completed
but the envisaged enceinte never materialised'. Before the building of the
Pale dykes, a constellation of small castles, defensive tower-houses and fortified parish churches had been erected along the skirts of the hills and in
the upper Liffey valley.

Thus throughout the late medieval period, English royal authority
was with brief exceptions quite enfeebled, and this in itself was a factor
in Dublin's relative economic stagnation. The only safe communication
lines were maritime ones, along the east and south coasts and across the
Irish Sea. Parliaments sat, royal visitors very occasionally came and went,
but the most eloquent sign of the eclipse of English power was the manner in which the Kildare FitzGeralds, the greatest of the Anglo-Norman
magnates of the Leinster hinterland, emerged from relative obscurity in
the fourteenth century and came to assume utter ascendancy in both the
affairs of the town and of Dublin Castle, finally controlling the Lord Deputyship itself. Nevertheless, when Henry Glendower was changing English history at Bosworth Field in 1485, Garret Mór, 8th earl of Kildare, was
heavily committed to the defeated Yorkists, and two years later he oversaw
the coronation in Christ Church of a pretender, Lambert Simnel, to the
English Crown.[36]

Garret eventually made his peace with Henry VII, and Geraldine power survived almost half a century after that fiasco, a sign of early Tudor disinclination to invest scarce resources in re-establishing royal power in Ireland. The Maynooth-based FitzGeralds were by now in the first rank of wealth even by English aristocratic standards. But their fall – when it came – was dramatic in the extreme. Garret Mór's son, the 9th earl, was reared at court and held the Lord Deputyship from 1513 to 1519 and twice thereafter, moving in and out of royal favour as he conducted proxy war with the other great dynastic house, the Butlers. Something of a Renaissance potentate, with a taste for silver, gold and printed books, he was feared in Dublin and resented in London for standing in the way of greater royal control. Reluctantly he obeyed a summons to return to London in 1534, leaving his youthful heir, 'Silken' Thomas, Lord Offaly, to act as his deputy. The son, fearing for his father's life and determined on a show of strength, renounced his allegiance at the Council table in St Mary's Abbey, returning a few weeks later in force to capture Dublin Castle, the first direct assault in its history. He used light ordnance, while the Castle itself was defended with a 'great gun of brass', some much lighter firearms, and 'wildfire' (a flame gun of sorts). Spurred on by news of his father's imprisonment (and later death) in the Tower of London, Silken Thomas marshalled huge support both inside and outside the Pale, and left his followers to mount a somewhat lacklustre siege of the Castle while he campaigned elsewhere. But when the Corporation moved from tacit acceptance of Geraldine military operations inside the walls to outright opposition to him, he returned and mounted a general siege of the city, which lasted three months in all. The water supply was sabotaged and the south-western suburbs torched. By September Thomas's allies controlled most of the country, including the Pale. However, when English military relief eventually reached Dublin in October, the revolt moved away from the city and Thomas's support began to melt. But the conflict dragged on for another year before he surrendered and was sent to London as a prisoner. There, together with five of his uncles, he was executed in 1537. Their nemesis has always been taken to mark a sharp divide in Dublin's history.[37]

A Reformation in all things

In June 1541, on the Sunday of the Corpus Christi octave, solemn mass was as usual sung by the archbishop in St Patrick's Cathedral. Then an Act of the Irish Parliament, passed during the previous week declaring Henry VIII to be king of Ireland, was proclaimed 'in [the] presence of 2,000 persons, and [the] Te Deum sung'. The Corpus Christi pageant was used to celebrate the news and prisoners were released. The elevation of Ireland from lordship to kingdom came seven years after the fall of the over-mighty Geraldines, five years after the Tudor monarch had been rec-ognised in the Dublin Parliament 'as supreme head in earth of the whole church in Ireland', four years after the drive to assert royal control over its monastic wealth, and two years after the commencement of a campaign to sweep away relics, images and shrines out of every church.

However, this first wave of Reformation principally affected prop-erty, not doctrine, and took the form of the dissolution, first of some, then of all abbeys and priories, friaries, convents and shrines, together with the disposal of their abundant material assets. It was a very untidy affair, but in Dublin it was more or less complete by 1540. Many of the religious founda-tions in the city had not been in good shape and their members accepted being quietly pensioned off. The great days of the monasteries, even of St Thomas's and St Mary's, were a distant memory, and although the abbot of St Mary's lobbied Thomas Cromwell, no Dublin house actually resisted its dissolution. St John the Baptist's, a hospital foundation outside New Gate in the hands of the Crutched Friars, was alone in still performing a significant welfare function, providing some fifty beds for the sick poor, but Edmund Redman, a surgeon, was already the lessee and seems to have continued to provide a service in diminished form.

Lay opposition to monastic dissolution was greatly weakened by the enticing prospect of a flood of premium property becoming avail-able from the Crown on favourable terms: St Mary's alone had revenues more than five times those of the city treasurer. And so it was: venerable landed dynasties were reinvigorated and Dublin merchants also became very active in the land market, both locally and in the north Midlands. Crown office-holders had some of the choice pickings, notably William Brabazon, the carpet-bagging Vice-Treasurer; among the many acquisi-tions he secured were the lands of St Thomas Court and the manor of Donore, the well-watered premium land on which the family's city estate (universally known to later Dubliners as 'the Liberties') would be built. But there was open conflict over the fate of the cathedrals: the first plan was to dissolve Christ Church insofar as it was still an Augustinian priory.

3. A conjectural reconstruction of Dublin c.1500 by Howard Clarke, built by Dan O'Brien, which indicates just how small and congested the walled city was in the late medieval period. The building that towered above everything was the ancient Holy Trinity Christ Church, which was both physically and symbolically the focal point of the city, with Dublin Castle (left) the great citadel.

Outspoken civic opposition to the prospect of losing the mother church of the city – 'a great desolation and a foul waste and deformity of the said city' – proved effective. It was converted into a secular cathedral, and the city aldermen, despite their private views on Reformation, contributed generously to its repair when a large part of the nave collapsed in 1562, and continued to do so for decades. It was, and it was to remain, the Corporation's church. Meanwhile official attention had turned then to St Patrick's.[38]

As the prestigious centrepiece of the diocese, the case for St Patrick's dissolution was simply on the grounds that if Christ Church was to survive, one cathedral for the city should be sufficient. And St Patrick's, as all knew, was exceptionally well endowed. So, five years after that dramatic proclamation of the king, the great cathedral was closed by the recently appointed Dean, its chapter suppressed and its lands alienated. And yet this building, more than any other, had served as the focal point of the English lordship in Ireland, its *lieu de mémoire* and place of pomp and spectacle. Even if its archbishops had invariably been English-born, its chapter canons and vicars choral were drawn from hinterland families, the sons of the well-born of the Pale. Its dissolution was, if not the first step, one of the primary factors in sundering the ancient bond between that community and the servants of the Crown in Dublin Castle.

As it turned out, St Patrick's was resurrected: during Mary's five-year reign and the Catholic restoration, the decision of 1546 was overturned in 1555, and the chapter and lands were restored under the approving eye of Archbishop Curwen. And when the pendulum swung again in 1558 with Elizabeth's accession, there was something of a critical time-lapse: Curwen survived, as did St Patrick's with its still crypto-Catholic chapter. It was only a decade later, after the muscularly Protestant archbishop Adam Loftus had taken the reins, that things began to change. But because the state was committed to using the inherited diocesan structures and legal forms of the old church, in Dublin as elsewhere, things in the diocesan engine-room changed quite slowly, so that the St Patrick's chapter was only operating as a Protestant institution from the late 1570s. As James Murray has shown, this really mattered. First the offensive destruction of St Patrick's as an institution, then in Elizabethan times its reluctant preservation, greatly affected the reception of the Reformation in Dublin and its hinterland. The well-connected diocesan clergy set the tone for their people, the 'Old English' (although the term had not yet become current), who shared a profound sense of pride in the civilising, ordered, canonical Catholicism of the church in Dublin, a sentiment that was coloured by ancient hostility to the Gaelic clans on their doorstep and by a new hostility to the doctrines on church government and religious belief sweeping in from a changed England. Nowhere was that sentiment better captured than in the early writings of Richard Stanihurst, whose 'Description of Ireland', written in the early 1570s, displayed an intimate knowledge of his unalloyed Old English world centred on Dublin and its historic superiority over Irish Ireland, and of a town that was superior to all other towns 'in martial chivalry, in obedience and loyalty, in the abundance of wealth, in largeness of hospitality, in manners and civility'.[39]

St Patrick's curious history affected the Dublin Reformation in another respect. From the first talk of its dissolution in the 1540s, religious reformers picked on it as the ideal setting for a 'godly college', a centre for educating a reformed ministry. It was, in other words, to be a university, adapting Archbishop Bicknor's failed initiative of two centuries earlier. In the 1570s, plans to harness some of the cathedral's resources for a college

were revived with support from Lord Deputy Sidney, but hostility, mainly
from within the cathedral, managed to scupper this. There was in fact a
critical half-century delay in providing a training ground to supply clergy
for the royal 'Church of Ireland', during which time the old tradition of
sending sons of wealthy townsmen and Pale gentry for a foreign education
took on a new purpose. Yet there was swift movement in the production
of the new liturgy for local use: the Edwardian Book of Common Prayer
was the first book printed in Dublin, produced in 1551 by command of
the English Privy Council by an immigrant printer, Humphrey Powell, in
his house in Winetavern Street. This, though, was a mere token of intent.
Far more important was royal sponsorship for the translation of the New
Testament into the Irish language and seeing it through to publication.
However, this was far from swift, as there was a troubled thirty-six-year
gap between sponsorship and the printing of 500 copies in 1602, far too
late to have had any strategic impact.[40]

Apart from the huge delay in creating a seminary to supply Protestant
clergy and the impolitic handling of the local clerical elite, more covert
factors may have helped to put a brake on religious change. The monastic dissolution gave wealthy laymen in and around Dublin unprecedented
control over parish revenues and discretion as to how these were spent.
And the dissolution also, and quite surprisingly, left untouched a number
of property-owning religious guilds and fraternities in the city. These two
factors had the effect of weakening the power of the state to build up a religious infrastructure in the capital, and of making possible the financing of
a shadow clergy. The Guild of St Anne based in St Audeon's was a striking
case in point: despite legal attempts to dissolve it, it remained quietly in
existence until 1695, complete with its own chapel attached to the parish
church, its 'singing men' who seem to have been its recusant clergy, and an
income from property for other Catholic purposes.[41]

There was a strange contradiction in Elizabethan Dublin: on the one
hand there was a slowly maturing civic opposition towards the moderate
Protestantism of the state religion; on the other, the strong partnership
between royal government and city corporation through the many years
of war and rumours of war. This partnership involved emergency loans,
recurring local investment in city defences, active participation in some of
the military operations and logistical support in most, particularly during
the Nine Years War (1594–1603). The combat zones were far away in Munster and Ulster, but for Dubliners war meant unprecedented numbers of

English soldiers quartered in town whom the citizens had to feed and accommodate. Prolonged warfare elsewhere also hit Dublin's inland trade. But the other side of the coin was the considerable enlargement of urban privileges, beginning with the 1548 charter (which established the city of Dublin as a county borough, clarified the judicial powers of mayor and sheriffs, and strengthened their role in policing public markets). Then there were the very favourable amendments of 1577 (confirming the exclusive privileges of the Trinity Guild), and the 'golden' charter of 1582 (which affirmed 'admiralty' jurisdiction over a long coastline from Skerries to Arklow, eliminated charges on goods coming through Chester and Liverpool bound for Dublin, and gave Dublin traders an unprecedented primacy in Chester's trade with Dublin).

One effect of this strengthening of the Corporation was increased social distance between the board of twenty-four aldermen chaired by the mayor, which met every Friday, and the Commons made up of younger merchants and spokesmen for the other guilds, which met once a quarter. The mayor was now expected to be a man who could entertain on a grand scale: Patrick Sarsfield's term in 1554–5 was remembered as an exemplary demonstration of such hospitality, 'his house [in High Street] was so open, as commonly from five of the clock in the mornings to ten at night his buttery and cellars were with one crew or another frequented ...'; three barns of corn and twenty tun of wine were, it seems, consumed during the mayoral year. As Colm Lennon has shown, this buttressing of the city's legal status contributed to a concentration of power among the wealthier merchants, the families from whom aldermen were recruited. In other words, the craft guilds who had had a considerable share in municipal government in the fifteenth century had by the late sixteenth very little influence on office-holding or decision-making, and had weaker representation in the Commons, even though they remained an integral part of its ever more complex constitution. As for the aldermen themselves, Lennon has found that in the period 1550–1620 only a quarter had unimpeachably city origins, with 46 per cent originating from the four Pale shires, most of them with a property-owning background. But, tellingly, nearly half of the aldermanic wives were the daughters of aldermen.[42]

These city leaders were, however, profoundly divided on the issue of religion. The Anglican religious settlement of 1560 required that all subjects of the Crown conform visibly to the established church, but even in the city, where loyalty to the English Crown was central to civic identity,

The South front of *Donnibrook* Castle 1ᴹ from *Dublin*, *demolished in 1759*.

*4. Donnybrook Castle as sketched by Thomas Ashworth shortly before
its demolition in 1759. The castle was one of the sixteenth-century
homes of the Usshers, lying a mile from the walled city and close to the
Dodder. Its unfortified appearance and impressive scale suggest a new
sense of security and the conspicuous wealth of the Usshers, who were
one of the leading civic dynasties and clients of the earls of Kildare.*

there was evidence of discomfiture, even in the 1540s, at the removal of
shrines and images from the city churches, the plain painting of church
walls, the use of the vernacular and the new centrality of preaching at
divine worship. Lennon has suggested that by the early Elizabethan period
a few of the leading families in the city were enthusiasts for reform (notably the Balls, Challoners, Forsters and Usshers), a few opposed religious
change with equal passion (notably the Brownes, Fitzsimons, Sheltons and
Sedgraves), and a majority outwardly conformed for a while, reassured by
seeing the same clergy as of old officiating in the same parish churches,
following more or less the same religious calendar, and perhaps still using
some Latin in the liturgy. But the families who took a strong position on
their religious loyalties tended to marry within their own sub-group, a

real pointer as to the social ramifications of the new divisions. Meanwhile those in the middle, the majority of aldermanic families, were progressively alienated from the new religion, a sentiment very much in line with their country cousins around the Pale.

There are only a few hints as to attitudes among the wider city population. There was resentment no doubt at the cancellation of religious holidays, most obviously the Corpus Christi pageant in the 1560s, but little sign of either greater or lesser hostility than among the elite to the changes underway. Doubtless some of the regulars displaced by monastic dissolution and some of the parish clergy who refused to take the necessary oaths in 1560 were busy in the town as teachers and unattached priests. But there were several *causes célèbres* that must have had a deep public impact, notably the five-year imprisonment of the Catholic archbishop of Armagh, Richard Creagh, in a Castle cellar during the 1570s (before spending another dozen years in the Tower of London), and in 1583–4 the nine-month imprisonment and torture of Archbishop Dermot O'Hurley of Cashel, fresh from the Continent and politically compromised, which culminated in his covert execution in Hoggen Green. Although there was no public reaction to his fate, his grave in St Kevin's churchyard became an immediate place of veneration. Neither of these men had any prior connection with Dublin, yet their presence seems to have had great exemplary effect. O'Hurley met his fate in the wake of Spanish and papal support for rebellion in Munster and also, or so it appeared, in the Pale – where James Eustace, Viscount Baltinglass, a patrician Oxford-educated Palesman with a castle in Monkstown, had launched his hapless religious crusade from the Wicklow mountains, raising the papal flag against the new heresy. He had been profoundly affected by a long stay in Rome and was enthused by the early Counter-Reformation, but his rebellion was largely a Wicklow affair and an Irish war, his role that of 'a religious zealot ... instrumental in channelling Gaelic resentment against the government in the name of Catholicism'. But Lord Deputy Grey did not read it like that, and presumed the existence of a far-reaching conspiracy across the Pale. He led a witch-hunt which culminated in the execution in 1582 of twenty Old English peers and gentry, including the former Chief Justice of Common Pleas, Nicholas Nugent, against whom there was the thinnest of evidence. But the residual strength of the city's constitutional status was spectacularly demonstrated the following year when two aldermen (one of them the son of Christopher Sedgrave, the largest lender to the Crown in Ireland) were imprisoned on suspicion of involvement in the Baltinglass rebellion and then, even though they faced a charge of treason in the Crown Court, they were released from the Castle into the hands of the city, and shortly afterwards allowed to go free.[43]

Grey was one of several Elizabethan governors who combined a radical Protestant faith with a professional soldier's belief in the efficacy of exemplary blood-letting. His secretary, the young Edmund Spenser, was also new to Ireland in the early 1580s and shared much of this. He shaped his allegorical vision of a virtuous Christian kingdom under 'the fairie queen' Gloriana during his time spent in Dublin (and there may be echoes of it in his imagined city of 'Cleopolis'), a kingdom secured by educated knights who could only triumph over evil if allowed to act without restraint. It was a shade more subtle than Grey's view of things, but they and the other 'New English' who increasingly dominated Dublin Castle found their dire imaginings translated into fact in the final bloody years of the century.[44]

This leads us back to the fundamental reason why the state-sponsored reformation had made so little headway: the antipathy that had built up among the English-Irish of the Pale towards the Tudor state and the political and financial strategies it had chosen, albeit with many policy shifts along the way, to regain effective control of the country. The wider context was Tudor England's increasing economic power and military capacity, against which Ireland stood out both as a military challenge and as an opportunity for the stronger projection of that power. But this could only be achieved with far tighter control from the administrative centre. Tensions can be traced back to the Geraldine era and the short lieutenancy of the earl of Surrey in 1520 (it was the first direct involvement by the English Crown in Irish government in seventy years): reacting against the pervasive influence of Butlers and FitzGeralds in all things Irish, Surrey had recommended in effect a new conquest of Ireland, to be secured by a fresh wave of English colonisation. Nothing came of such radical thoughts then, although Surrey did strengthen Dublin Castle's defences, anticipating the events of 1534. And in the wake of that rebellion, Thomas Cromwell's man in Ireland, William Brabazon, had similar ideas, envisaging the clearing of all the Gaelic Irish clans from Leinster and the establishment of military colonies. But they were exceptional. It was only from the 1560s, as Anglo-Spanish tensions flared up, that the dangers of a too loosely governed Ireland really focused Whitehall's attention, and this can be seen in the particular strategies of Sussex and Sidney as powerful lord deputies. Although there was no consistent reform policy, the different strategies all involved greater intervention and the placing of new men in Dublin Castle without local loyalties or local patrons, men who in the nature of things would seek to enrich themselves as they served the Crown. The corollary was the eclipse of the Crown's ancient partners in the mission to civilise Ireland, the citizenry of Dublin and the Palesmen, a process that began *before* religious loyalty was an issue, and only developed into comprehensive exclusion in the next century, in large part because of their rejection of the new state religion.[45]

Yet there was always a minority among the urban elite who thought differently, and it was a measure of their temporary influence that the Corporation agreed in 1591 to lease the former priory of All Hallows – the city's compensation half a century earlier for the losses suffered during the Geraldine rebellion – for a new educational initiative. There, east of Hoggen Green, a fresh attempt was made to establish a university and this time it was successful. The resulting corporation, Trinity College Dublin, received its first charter in 1592. Its chief patron and first provost was the ever formidable Church of Ireland archbishop, Adam Loftus, who was then also Lord Chancellor and from time to time a Lord Justice. The citizens, lay and clerical, who had been the main promoters of the scheme, believed that the college could serve at least two worthy purposes: a humanist one, of bringing Ireland into the mainstream of European learning, and a religious one, in that it would try to recover lost ground and reignite the Reformation project within the country through the production of an Irish-born clergy, both Old English and Gaelic. But was it too late to halt the Counter-Reformation? Loftus privately believed it was.[46]

Compared with the Anglo-Norman conquest of lowland Ireland four centuries earlier, the Tudor reconquest involved much larger armies, was geo-politically far more complex, and in the end was far more comprehensive. The climax of that reconquest in the late 1590s came at a time of Europe-wide food shortage, probably the worst food crisis since the mid-fourteenth century. By 1597 the killer epidemics associated with hunger were rife in the city. And in the middle of this time of troubles the careless handling of 140 barrels of gunpowder on Wood Quay, on their way to the war in Ulster, led to a catastrophic explosion in March of that year. One hundred and twenty-six people were killed, seventy-six were Dublin residents, fifty 'strangers'. Between twenty and forty houses, from prominent merchant residences near the riverside to smaller houses up on the ridge along High Street, were destroyed – and the town had to bear the main cost of the huge reconstruction.

It was in this most distressful environment that the localised conflict over religious practice was played out. The polarisation between royal authority and the urban community was something new and this kind of cold war would be replayed, albeit in very different contexts, in the centuries ahead. But Lennon has suggested how in another respect the 1590s mark a great discontinuity: the quayside explosion marked the beginnings of a shift in Dublin's centre of gravity eastwards, with trade and high-status residents beginning to search for more salubrious quarters east of the Poddle, both on land that was yet to be reclaimed and on the slopes above the estuary where Norsemen had buried their notables seven centuries before. After a century or more of inertia over the problems of the harbour, the first signs of action were now evident with plans to dredge the channel and extend the quays. The erection in c.1585 of a prominent tower at Ringsend on the spit at the harbour entrance marked the start of a series of massive interventions spanning the next two centuries that would eventually conquer the natural dangers on the maritime approaches. But the eastward drift spelt the end of the walled city: within little more than a century the great stone curtains would almost all be gone, or rather seamlessly recycled into the city fabric in invisible ways.[47]

In 1600 the small town of Dublin, insignificant in the history of European urbanisation up to this point, was about to commence its ascent to become the second city of the English-speaking world and a place of some global significance. In its first thousand years it had been emptied and refilled on several occasions, whether by force of arms or by natural disaster, yet there were continuities through it all. It had remained the bridgehead and primary conduit through which outsiders, whether Norse, Norman or English, had sought to influence or control much or all of the island. It had also been a magnet for traders, craftsmen and the displaced from within Ireland, so that its population from the earliest Norse era was a mix, a genetic and cultural melting-pot, to a greater extent than anywhere else on the island. Attempts to restrain such mixing in the later medieval period only underlined the continuing power of the process. Yet the long view reveals a cyclicality in the first thousand years of Dublin, less clear in the complex ebb and flow of the Hiberno-Norse town than in the stark contrast between the thrusting Anglo-Norman town of the thirteenth century and the stagnant and embattled place a century later. But each high tide left a few indelible marks on the place, both physically and culturally. It remains to be seen in the era after 1600, when Dublin's scale and social complexity were to be utterly transformed, whether some of these older patterns and traits would reveal themselves again on what was to be a far larger canvas.[48]

1

THE FASHIONING
OF A CAPITAL:
1600–1647

In 1611 a small map of Dublin, a bird's-eye view of the town and its sub-urbs, was published in London (see plate 1). It formed part of John Speed's great atlas, *The theatre of the empire of Great Britain*, and the Dublin map was one of four Irish town plans, tucked within a larger map of the province of Leinster. Plans of almost seventy towns in England and Wales were included in Speed's volume, which was presented in celebration of the three kingdoms now united under James VI and I. Nearly all of Speed's town plans drew on maps and surveys that had been drawn or carried out in the previous century, and they were augmented in a majority of cases by Speed's own observations. But for the Dublin map there was no precedent to draw on and, as far as is known, the Cheshire-born Speed had never visited the city. Brimming with topographical detail and correctly aligned to magnetic north, the map was a dramatic step forward in the documentation of Dublin, a snapshot at a crucial moment. Yet its origins and authorship remain a little mysterious.

Internal evidence suggests that fieldwork for the map was done five or six years prior to publication and before the reclamation of the mud banks at the mouth of the Poddle just east of the city wall, for this is not shown. There is a strong possibility that the original mapping was carried out around 1605 under the direction of Sir John Davies, the Irish Attorney General, who was then emerging as a key figure in the Dublin government. Whoever was responsible, it is likely to have been a newcomer's view of the city, drawn a year or two after the end of the Nine Years War and before any peace dividend was visible. The scars of war are indeed hinted at in the area close to the 1597 explosion: around Wood Quay one can detect a number of telling gaps in the streetscape. Some of the houses on the map may have been emptied by bubonic plague in 1604, which could still strike terror and with reason: possibly up to a third of Dubliners had died in the visitation of 1575. The 1604 episode was, however, much milder.[1]

In total, Speed's map depicts about 254 houses within the city walls and some 400 outside them. All are represented as two-storeyed gable-fronted buildings. But in 1605 the actual house total would have been much higher: John Andrews has argued that the map can be taken to be a good guide as to where built-up streets existed, but not as to the number of individual houses standing in any particular street; if the typical width of houses within the walls was between fifteen and twenty feet (and recent archaeological investigation would broadly confirm this), it would suggest that in reality there were around 760 houses inside the city and perhaps 1,200 in the suburbs, north and south, implying an early seventeenth-century community of between 8,000 and 10,000 permanent residents.[2]

A time traveller from 1300 would have found Speed's Dublin very familiar in its physical layout. The buildings standing in 1605, especially those in the suburbs, may have been fairly recently built, but most houses stood on plots and sites that had been first developed more than three hundred years previously. Streets east of Church Street on the north side and to the west and south-west of the city walls were not so much new suburbs as suburbs reborn. But what is striking about the image of Dublin depicted by Speed is the sense it gives of an open town, with dense but unprotected ribbon developments along the suburban roads (notably Church, Patrick, Francis and Thomas Streets), old city walls, and a castle lacking the attributes of a fortified citadel. Admittedly, several of the extramural gates were still standing at the outer extremities of the suburban roads, but the absence of associated defence works hints at the function of such structures – that is, to restrict the movement of undesirables and to toll the trade of strangers.

This image of an open town reflected reality up to a point. Despite attention given to the city's defences in the 1590s and the regular array of a citizen's militia, Dublin was still a vulnerable town. The Castle's ancient walls would not have withstood modern siege artillery and the city walls, despite Tudor improvements, were little better. In addition there was the constellation of new and unprotected developments outside the walls – the College, the Bridewell prison, the lawyers' inns on the site of St Saviour's, and that unprotected sentinel on the southern approaches, St Patrick's Cathedral. Together these suggest that in Speed's 'theatre', Dublin was being exhibited as a zone of civility and order, not a fortress town or an Irish Calais. Nor was there any hint in this image of the great disharmony within, of the gathering political battle over the autonomy of the city between the Castle government and the municipal authorities in the Tholsel. That conflict was to turn into a prolonged virtual siege in which walls and fortifications would play no part.[3]

Chichester's prospect

One public building highlighted in Speed's map was 'the Hospital', located near the College on Hoggen Green and close to the river. This building had been financed by Sir George Carew, President of Munster, and erected towards the end of the Nine Years War, apparently to accommodate some of the many maimed and infirm soldiers. But with the coming of peace it was used to house the king's four courts, before permanent accommodation was found for them in the outer precincts of Christ Church. The hospital building then passed into the hands of Sir Arthur Chichester. He was the dominant figure in Irish politics from his appointment as lord deputy in 1605 until his departure in 1616. One of the most prominent New English survivors from the 1580s and a veteran soldier-adventurer, he became the greatest beneficiary in the massive land confiscations in Ulster in and after 1610. Around that time he moved down from his unsalubrious apartments in the Castle to the 'large mansion, with a gate-house, a garden and plantations' on Hoggen Green. This became Chichester House, and it became in effect an extension of the Castle, the focal point of Irish politics during his deputyship and a centre for constant courtly entertainment: 'If the Lord Deputy should but withdraw himself but for two years together into any other part of the country, the greatest part of the citizens of Dublin would be ready to beg ...'[4]

Chichester made little lasting contribution to the life of the city, but his long regime turned out to be of huge importance for Dublin's future. He was, if not the architect, at least the engineer of the Ulster Plantation, and the ramifications of that exercise in large-scale colonisation had a profound effect on the city's later history. Chichester was also responsible for elaborating the county assize system of royal justice and extending it to all thirty-two counties; this served to reinforce the position of Dublin as centre and pinnacle of that system, the city remaining the exclusive location for the higher Irish courts and the place where Crown judges invariably resided. One indication of the expansion of legal activity was the marked acceleration in the number of decrees handed down by the Court of Chancery and in the volume of cases heard in the three common-law courts. In 1613–15 Chichester oversaw the first sessions of the Irish Parliament of the century; all of these were held in Dublin – in the Lords and Commons chambers within the Castle precincts. But if he was remembered in Dublin it was because of his attitude to Catholicism. Throughout his years in power, Chichester and his circle pursued a singularly aggressive religious policy, most of the time having to overcome reservations and countervailing pressures from London. Tensions between Dublin's leading Old English families and the Castle, intensifying since the 1570s, now came to a head, and Chichester's determination to destroy the structures of the Catholic Church managed on at least one occasion to convulse the streets of Dublin.

The defining moment in his pursuit of religious conformity came late in January 1612 with the trial of Conor O'Devany, the octogenarian Catholic bishop of Down and Connor, and of a younger priest, Patrick O'Loughran. O'Devany was a Donegal man who had been closely associated with the Ulster lords during and after the wars, and he had no particular connection with the city; he had remained a fugitive in the North until his capture the previous year. Despite almost ten years of peace, the two clerics were tried for treason, found guilty and sentenced to be hanged at the gallows on George's Hill overlooking the northern suburbs. By this exercise in exemplary punishment Chichester hoped to concentrate the minds of the Old English recusants on his doorstep. However,

> divers citizens (whereof some that were of good sort and fashion) as the bishop passed by, fell down upon their knees in the dirt and mire, craving his fatherly blessing and benediction ... He was followed with troops of citizens, both men and women, and not of the inferior sort alone, but of the better, and amongst the women, of the best men's wives within the city of Dublin, that kept such a shrieking, such a howling, and such a hallowing, as if Saint Patrick himself had been

going to the gallows, they could not have made greater signs and shows of grief and sorrow.

Rather than weakening public support for Catholicism in the city, the hanging and quartering of the venerable Ulster cleric seems to have created an instant martyr:

> the same night after the execution was done, they flocked together afresh both men and women, with holy water, holy candle: and congregating themselves at the holy gallows, in the place of execution, they spent the fore part of the night in heathenish howling, and performing many popish ceremonies, and after midnight, being then Candlemas day in the morning, having their priests in a readiness they had Mass, and as some say Mass after Mass ...[5]

This was the first open collective display of support for the old religion in the city and stood in contrast to the muted public response to Archbishop O'Hurley's execution in 1584.

The 1612 executions were seen by many as political. They revealed the intense frustration in Chichester's circle at Catholic clerical resilience on their own doorstep, and their determination to weaken upper-class Catholic morale prior to the long-deferred parliamentary elections. But what is perhaps most revealing about the incident was the strength of the public reaction, the Old English burgher families apparently at one with the keeners from a different cultural tradition. The executions were the culmination of nearly a decade of overt religious persecution in the city – or rather of a battle between Chichester and his allies, and the predominantly Catholic aldermen. Government policy had been to target prospective municipal office-holders on the assumption that an enforced wave of religious conformity in 'the lantern of this kingdom' would intimidate those far outside it. But to the Catholics in the Corporation, the government's actions were seen as part of a broader attack by agents of the Crown on the city's liberties, its charter rights and its financial privileges, as well as on the private freedom of conscience of the citizenry at large. In this battle, foreign-educated Catholic clergy played a significant if covert role in emboldening the civic body. There was, for example, more than a hint of clerical choreography in the public response to O'Devany's execution.[6]

Continentally trained clergy, all of them Palesmen, had begun to appear in the city in the mid-1590s, notably a handful of socially well-connected Jesuits whose energy and self-confidence marked them out. The most celebrated was Henry Fitzsimon, scholar, controversialist and son of a city alderman who, in Bernadette Cunningham's words, was:

> renowned as a persuasive preacher. He conducted his ministry in an open, demonstrative manner, celebrating the first solemn high mass held in Dublin for forty years in 1598. He established a sodality to foster piety, promoted participation in confession and holy communion, and actively sought to attract converts to Catholicism ... His ministry may have been principally among the social elite; he reputedly never dined without six to eight guests, and rode through the countryside with three or four gentlemen as companions.[7]

Arrested in 1599, he spent the rest of the wars a prisoner in the Castle, busy at his books, before being deported to Spain in 1604. But there were others in the Fitzsimon mould, alert to the Counter-Reformation, active in education and catechesis, who were only too willing and able to give theological advice and pastoral succour to their patrons. During the wars the political loyalty of the Corporation had been vital to the Crown, not least because the burden for organising civic defence and for provisioning countless English soldiers in transit to the battlefield had fallen on the citizenry. Yet the peace was hardly signed when seven aldermen were placed in jail after they refused to attend public worship and were left there for several weeks; in 1604 the Catholic mayor-elect John Shelton was debarred from office by a commission headed by the Lord Chancellor, Archbishop Loftus, for his refusal to take the oath of supremacy. He was fined a massive £300, after which the government oversaw the election of a more junior but conforming alderman. This set the precedent for recurring if intermittent Castle interference in the business of the city, and specifically in the choice of city mayors. The government sought, not always successfully, to reserve the office for those willing to attend official worship in Anglican Christ Church and, at least outwardly, to conform.

Jacobean religious policy was, however, anything but consistent. In 1605, the year of the Gunpowder Plot, all Catholic clergy were ordered by royal proclamation to quit the kingdom and all laity to attend divine worship in the official churches. Chichester followed this up with orders given personally to leading members of Dublin Corporation that they must attend divine worship or face heavy punishment; detentions and fines for non-appearance became commonplace. But there was also a growing *esprit de corps* among the Catholic civic leaders; one alderman, Patrick Browne, resisted a *douceur* to conform by observing that he 'would not take money and lose my share in this persecution'.[8] This pattern of coherent and spirited resistance by a majority of the aldermen, supported by Old English lobbyists in London, brought relief from Whitehall and an end to this campaign, but the Chichester years were in general marked by a souring of relations between the government and the majority of aldermen, who not surprisingly distanced themselves from that old centre of civic public life, the ample spaces of Christ Church Cathedral. Protestant aldermen and guildsmen of course observed the civic rituals there, but they were a minority within the municipality and, unlike the pattern half a century earlier, few Dublin merchants from within the pool of patrician families switched allegiance and fully conformed to the state church at this time of growing harassment. The cynical old soldier Barnaby Rich mocked those who tried to go halfway:

> I will never believe him to be an honest man that will first swear obedience to his Prince, and then will submit himself to the service of his Pope; that will go to church openly, and hear a mass privily; that will listen a little to the preacher when he is in the pulpit, but will never come near a Communion.[9]

Chichester's frontal assault on Catholic activity did not receive full support from London, and the O'Devany execution in particular was criticised. So in such an uncertain climate, recusant religious practice remained discreet rather than covert. Rooms in the private houses of the wealthy and warehouses in and around High Street were fitted out for the regular celebration of mass, and by 1620 a serious attempt was being made to reinstate a Catholic parish structure in the city. Thus Father Luke Rochford, parish priest of St Audoen's from 1624, used a large room in the Bridge Street house of his cousin, Alderman Thomas Plunket, to say mass, and nearby he opened a classical school, an embrionic seminary. Rochford was a prominent figure in the city, publishing tracts on moral decay and religious laziness, and was a vigorous defender of diocesan authority which he saw being challenged by the footloose friars – who were perhaps less than respectful of the Old English world from which he himself was drawn.[10]

With the accession of Charles and his Catholic queen Henrietta Maria in 1625 there was a frisson of expectation of imminent religious tolerance, and in the following years extended negotiations took place between Old English notables and the king over some kind of pact in which religious concessions ('the Graces') would be traded in return for special payments to the Crown. Patrician families in the city, so many of them with hybrid or ambiguous religious loyalties, looked forward to easier times. This was the moment for a striking Jesuit initiative. Father Robert Nugent secured a lease for a large site in Back Lane – just inside of the walls – from his cousin the Countess of Kildare, and a college was quickly established there. The centrepiece was a magnificent chapel, which some compared to a cathedral, others 'to the banqueting house at Whitehall'. It was intended to serve as a Jesuit university in embryo, and functioned as such for about two years. The priests, it was noted privately, 'assume the dress of seculars and go about as merchants or physicians, some gird on the sword, and assume the character of noblemen ...' [11] But to the New English hardliners on the Irish Privy Council, intensely hostile to the Graces, this was a provocation too far. The Irish government secured clearance from London in April 1629 to suppress all Catholic religious houses, both in the city and outside it, and in particular to remove this offence on their doorstep. On St Stephen's Day that year, a confrontation occurred when the mayor, assisted by the Church of Ireland archbishop and the Lords Justices, attended a raid on a Franciscan chapel in Cook Street. But after carrying out pictures and other fittings they had to make a tactical retreat when they were attacked by members of the congregation. There is evidence that this 'suppression' was designed to provoke a public response, thereby shaming the Corporation into accepting the quartering of the army on the citizenry, a move previously resisted on the grounds that Dublin had long enjoyed royal exemption from the billeting of soldiers on the civilian population. In the event, sixteen city religious houses were closed, some of the buildings (including the Franciscans' chapel) were levelled, and the fine Jesuit 'university' was disbanded.

The motives for opening such an institution only a musket shot from the Castle are a little puzzling. Since the 1590s the sons of quite a few city families had travelled to continental universities and to the new Irish colleges in Spain, the Spanish Netherlands and France. The latter were intended principally as seminaries for the Irish mission, the former as stepping stones to professional careers within Catholic Europe. All such migration had been outlawed in 1610, but this was unenforceable and was ignored. There was of course the new university by the river, slowly taking collegiate form. But both its sponsors and its early fellows were very much in sympathy with the muscular Calvinism of Chichester's circle, so it was an uninviting place for the sons of those Corporation families who remained Catholic. Trinity College's strongly puritan ambience meant that its local appeal was limited to a small group of committed Church of Ireland families. This religious ambience was reinforced by William Temple, the Cambridge-trained provost from 1609 to 1627, an able philosopher, a nimble politician and a superb administrator whose success in securing vast landed property for the university created the resources necessary to sustain a lively scholarly community. The greatest scholar was James Ussher, one of the first graduates whose career reveals much about the early Trinity College: his background was entirely local and his cousins mainly Catholic, but from his student days he was an abrasive advocate of the reformed faith. He was also an exceptional biblical scholar and theologian, determined to make the college a laboratory of learning through the establishment of a fine library, a passion shared by his father-in-law, Luke Challoner, the first vice-provost who had got the infant institution off the ground. Such was Ussher's European reputation by the 1620s that even his religious adversaries respected him and, by extension, the institution which had produced him. In the first thirty years of Trinity College, students with Gaelic patronymics outnumbered those with Old English names, although both were outnumbered in turn by the sons of the New English, drawn from across the country and across the water. With fewer than 100 students in the 1620s the college's impact on the city lay in the future. However, as the one local institution enjoying the full patronage of government and the state church, its future seemed relatively secure.[12]

By contrast this was a time of troubles for its parent body, the Corporation, as the Crown and its agencies sought to undermine inherited procedures and civic privileges. This was part of a much wider story, both Irish and English, as Stuart monarchs sought to whittle down the financial and jurisdictional freedoms of chartered towns, large and small. Their motives in Ireland were more complex, with short-term political concerns weighing on the Privy Council (how to manufacture a Protestant and pliable House of Commons when the boroughs were still controlled by Old English Catholic families) and private agendas (how to profit from the legal vulnerability of 'old' money) often to the fore. In the case of Dublin, the state's assault on municipal privilege was certainly coloured by a determination to make aldermen and office-holders conform in matters religious. But there was more to it than that, for much of the legal and political energy invested in the early defence of municipal and guild privileges was the work of indigenous *Protestant* aldermen. Central to the struggle was the Castle's claim that customs dues collected and held by the city were rightfully the Crown's, even where these had been assigned to the city in previous centuries. Linked to this claim was the asssertion that the original merchants' body in the city, the Trinity Guild (the old Guild Merchant), had usurped its powers and had no right to regulate city trade. The Corporation of course bitterly resisted the threatened resumption of customs duties and the cancellation of the Trinity Guild's monopolies on many grounds, not least because this would greatly diminish civic revenues and remove at a stroke the valuable tax exemptions traditionally enjoyed by freemen over strangers in foreign trade.

Six years of legal argument and discreet advocacy in Dublin and London ended in 1612 with a string of defeats for the city (and for the other Irish corporations) on nearly all counts. The privileges of admiralty jurisdiction from Skerries to Arklow were cancelled, and the port of Dublin was in 1613 included in the first national customs collection scheme, with the privileges and exemptions enjoyed by freemen seriously eroded. Nothing so eloquently demonstrated the changed relationship between the Old English towns and the state than this forced resumption of customs: once strategic allies in protecting and extending the English interest, the merchant communities were now being treated by the state as recalcitrant sponges to be squeezed hard – in the name of religion and the Crown's prerogative. The new arrangements meant a substantial net transfer of income from merchants and municipalities to the Crown and to its tax-collecting agents. And even though Irish customs collection was outsourced to various (mainly English) syndicates over the next seventy years, the revenues derived from the taxation of maritime trade became crucial in sustaining the Irish exchequer. Indeed, over the next two decades they became the prime source of Crown revenue in Ireland. Maximising those revenues meant that local privileges and traditions, not least those relating to the monopolies that excluded strangers from trading in their own right, found little support in Dublin Castle.

Old wealth and new

The city's centuries-old commercial links with the Continent had become tenuous during the time of troubles in the 1590s, when demand for luxury goods had slumped. The local currency had been severely debased, Crown loans had been forcibly levied, and a vast and under-resourced land army had been constantly in motion through the city. Trade took time to recover, but when it did it seemed likely that the old patrician merchants would continue to be in control, and to invest in maritime ventures even if there was the threat of intermittent religious harassment. For generations there had been a very strong overlap between the aldermanic council of twenty-four, the merchants' Trinity Guild, and the two or three dozen most active traders in the city. There seems to have been little to distinguish the business activities of conforming aldermen like Sir James Carroll or Richard Barry from those of Catholic aldermen like Patrick Browne or Edward Arthur, or at least there is nothing to suggest that they were different. They were all involved in conventional types of business, the export of wool, salted fish, tallow and hides, mainly destined for Chester, Bristol or the ports of southern England, with the shipment of live cattle and sheep beginning to feature during the 1610s and soaring in the 1620s. By 1626 some 12,000 lean cattle were making the journey annually across the Irish Sea from Dublin, perilously tethered in exposed single-masted vessels, destined mainly for the Dee estuary and the Chester market. This was an unsophisticated business – organised by butchers, not merchants – but the related and more sophisticated export trades in tallow, hides, barrelled beef and wool were controlled by the larger traders (although the expansion of tallow chandling, and with it the manufacture of candles and soap, seems to have been associated with new money, notably the first wave of Dutch merchants). Grain from the east Leinster hinterland was also exported in the years of plenty, for sale in European ports or as far afield as the Canary Islands.

In 1611, Robert Cogan, one of the architects of the new customs arrangements, put the total value of the city's exports at a modest £20,000 p.a., the same as that for Cork and somewhat ahead of the value of exports from the other Old English strongholds – Drogheda, Waterford, Limerick and Galway. But it was a different story with imports: Cogan estimated the value of goods entering Dublin at £80,000 p.a., a far greater sum than for its provincial rivals. His reasoning is revealing: 'the state of the whole kingdom is continually resident here, and the four [law] terms are kept here, all the kingdom resorts hither, by which means the trade is far greater than [in] any other port ...' [13] This exaggerated the pulling power of Dublin in 1611, but the trend was moving in that direction. A bewitching variety of consumer goods arrived seasonally from the London and Chester fairs – fine textiles, exotic foods and spices, worked objects in metal and leather, books, and from further afield, wine and salt, mainly from France, and grain from the Polish Baltic in years of depleted harvest. A small but evolving group of merchant shopkeepers, some working on commission for London principals, controlled the sale and distribution of these goods, specifically through the provision of credit to bulk purchasers coming from outside the city. Dublin merchants were already playing a major role in lubricating inland trade and were also giving short credits to minor dealers on their doorstep like the city's butchers.

There are contradictory pointers as to the capital resources of these merchants. There was the famous case of Nicholas Weston who from small beginnings rose to the mayoralty in 1596–7. At that time and with full government connivance he was trading with the enemy (both with Spain and with Hugh O'Neill). He proved a highly resourceful supplier of provisions for the English army in Ulster during the wars, and his sea-borne ventures ranged from Danzig to the Newfoundland cod banks. But a string of disasters – weather, privateers and the currency debasement in 1603 – forced him to the edge of bankruptcy and demonstrated that trading on such a scale was a gambler's game. As a Protestant member of the Corporation, he was a controversial figure, but in the long run his ambitions to be a great land speculator in Ulster brought him the enmity of Chichester. Still, it seems he died a wealthy man. No one sought to emulate Weston in the years after 1600, and for a long time there was not a single ocean-going vessel owned locally. In a register of wine imported into the various Irish ports in the twelve months from October 1614, eighteen vessels were listed as landing wine at Dublin (principally from French and Dutch ports), but only one of these was a Dublin vessel. By contrast, four-fifths of the wine entering Waterford that year was landed on Waterford boats. Almost a decade later, a London-based Irishman noted that 'Dublin, the head city of that island, cannot challenge property in one ship', and complained of 'the sluggishness of the native merchants, who adventure no further than London for their commodities ...' [14]

From the start of the new customs arrangements in 1613, revenue

collected in Dublin was much the greatest in the country, the city contributing just under 20 per cent of Irish customs income between 1615 and
1619. Two decades later, in the years 1634–5 to 1639–40, that share had
more than doubled to 41 per cent of national revenure.[15] Even allowing
for considerable distortion in the data arising from changing collection
methods, this points to a radical readjustment in the commercial standing
of Dublin. Although the town's contribution to customs yields continued
to rise later in the century, at no time in the future was there a comparable
shift in Dublin's share of foreign trade, and it was all the more striking in
occurring at a time when overall customs yields were growing markedly.
Dublin's ascent was built upon the relative decline in cross-channel and
foreign trade coming out of other east and south-east coast ports, notably
Drogheda and Waterford. By the 1630s there were also signs of structural
changes in the organisation of inland trade, with Dublin-based merchants
now dealing and trading far outside their traditional hinterland of the Pale
and north Leinster, while at the same time benefiting from the increasing resort of the wealthy from all four provinces to the city. To take two
cases among many from the loyalist depositions of 1641, John Eddis, a city
merchant, was able to provide a huge list of petty commercial debtors
spread across no less than thirteen counties in all four provinces, while
the stationer-printers John Crook and Richard Sergier were carrying, after
five years in Dublin business, debts 'from ministers and other customers
of all professions throughout the kingdom'.[16] We can also get some indication of Dublin's growing importance as the centre of business from the
transactions recorded in the city's 'statute staple', an ancient corporate
institution that was in essence a municipal registry of wholesale lending. The amount of money borrowed through the Dublin staple nearly
quadrupled between 1597 and 1636 with landowners, office-holders and
merchants making regular use of it. Long pre-dating the private banks and
the emergence of promissory notes, the staple allowed those with accumulated surpluses to lend on landed security; government office-holders and
Dublin merchants featured prominently as creditors, but fully two-fifths
of those lending money on bond had addresses outside Dublin, and quite
a few came from across the water. Of the merchants, few could rival Alderman Robert Arthur who by 1637 had lent out over £15,000 in twenty-two
transactions recorded in the staple.[17]

    This was the tip of a growing iceberg. During the forty-year peace, the
merchants in all the old port towns became deeply involved in property

investment within their hinterlands: Robert Arthur is known to have made land acquisitions in at least six counties in Leinster and Connacht.[18] The main reason for such activity was the escalating indebtedness of most old and many new landowning families, which forced them to mortgage land, generally to the monied men they already knew in the larger towns. And in what was an era of rising prices, appreciating land values and – critically – a legal system that was able to enforce contracts, such secured loans were attractive to those with idle funds at their disposal. In the case of Dublin, most aldermanic families and many lesser traders and craftsmen acquired out-of-town leasehold or freehold interests, usually with usufruct possession during the life of the loan, often leading to the outright purchase of the collateral. For some, land in the country was a practical resource in uncertain times: 'there is not a citizen in Dublin (that is of any ability worthy to be spoken of) but he hath a farm in the country, that yieldeth him corn, both for bread and beer, enough to find [i.e. supply] his own house,' claimed Barnaby Rich in 1610.[19] But for those of larger ambition, land acquisition was a low-risk investment, perhaps to secure a jointure or portions for younger children when a marriage contract was being negotiated. Urban involvement in rural land was of course not new, but the scale and geographical reach of Dublin investment reached unprecedented levels by 1640: 'the merchants here in all the cities of the kingdom do as they grow into wealth withdraw themselves into the country and there settle upon farms and neglect their trade of merchandize in which they were bred.'

This may oversimplify matters; even those who built fine residences on the land they had acquired (such as four-times mayor Sir James Carroll, who in 1635 was completing a 'stately house' on the Slaney near Ferns while serving out his last term) were well able to mix city business with a rural retreat. In such an environment where rural land investment was so inviting and where Dublin merchants were well aware as to where the best bargains might lie, it may have been perfectly rational behaviour for them to have put rural property investment ahead of ships, and to have resisted the lure of venturing at sea.[20]

The physical evidence for this commercial transformation has long vanished. The first royal Custom House was opened in 1621 and lasted less than forty years. It was built on a 106-foot-wide plot between Dame Street and a new wharf on the river. The choice of location, west of the Poddle but outside the walls, was indicative of the downstream thrust of commercial activity. Merchants were, however, still very fond of Cook

Street – midway between the old spine of High Street and the quays – for their shops and warehouses. Other central places held in high regard were Skinner's Row for its proximity to the courts, the Tholsel and the mayor's house, and Castle Street, its eastern extension, which was still a narrow thoroughfare but admirably located for wealthy custom, lying close by the entrance gates of the Castle. On the corner here, beside the Tholsel, was the most prominent private house in the city, Carbery House, the earls of Kildare's old residence, divided in the 1630s between Robert Arthur and another wealthy Catholic merchant of the Brown clan. But the private residences of office-holders and of New English magnates tended to be further east, and by the 1630s there was a scatter of aristocratic residences along Dame Gate down to Hoggen Green. The future Dame Street was to be Dublin's answer to London's Strand. Buildings within the walls were still overwhelmingly half-frame in construction, but brick and stone were making an appearance in both city and suburbs, first in chimney stacks (with the outlawing of other materials in 1612), then in the load-bearing walls of new buildings. Carpenters had once greatly outnumbered all the other building craftsmen, but now there was a perceptible growth in the numbers of guild masons, bricklayers and glaziers.[21]

Everything points to an acceleration in the city's population between 1610 and 1640. There were recurring complaints in the Corporation from about 1620 of a breakdown of controls over strangers, whether petty traders from the country who were infiltrating the retail trade and setting up 'open shops and inward shops', alehouses and livery stables, or the unfree bakers who 'every day of the week sent their servants to private houses within this city furnished with bread'. There was also palpable resentment among the trade guilds over the immigrants appearing from England and the Low Countries who stood accused of lending money at 'extreme interest and usury', or of cheating the city by circumventing municipal charges, notably the coterie of Dutch merchants settling in the Archbishop's and Thomas Court Liberties.[22] The Dutch, it was said in 1632 with a little exaggeration, 'so swarm in Dublin ... that they [have] eaten out all our native merchants and mariners'. There were in fact about twenty-five Dutch or Flemish merchants trading in or near the city by 1639, all it seems Protestant and most of them short-stay factors acting for Dutch-based merchant firms. A few, however, put down local roots, notably Christian Borr. He became naturalised in 1618, marrying into an aldermanic family and settling in Butter Lane (now Bishop Street). He became a partner in many

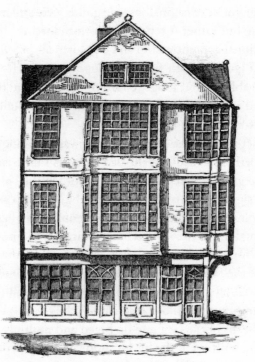

5. The landmark house that stood at the corner of Castle Street and Werburgh Street, which was demolished in 1812. It was the last example of a once-common type, the late medieval and sixteenth-century 'cagework' house, favoured by generations of well-to-do merchants and office-holders.

maritime ventures and was an owner of tanneries at Wicklow.[23] In a long-drawn-out legal battle between the Corporation and the Dutch traders led by Borr over whether as 'unfree' traders they should have to pay the municipal charges from which all freemen were exempt, the case went all the way to the English Privy Council. The Dutch eventually lost the battle, but they were soon to help in winning a bigger war. With strong trade and personal links back at home, they occupied a privileged economic position and they seem to have dominated the fledgling trade in bills of exchange between Dublin and the centres of international settlement, London and Amsterdam.

By contrast, the vast majority of new Dubliners had come to the city with very little, and had even less prospect of civic freedom than the Dutch. By the mid-1630s it was assumed that unfree heads of household were for the first time in a majority in the city: this, however, was not the result of religious exclusion, for trade guilds were still mainly Catholic in composition, but rather it reflected a forlorn attempt by the guilds to preserve traditional apprenticeship and employment practices at a time of unprecedented growth, both from interloping factors from outside Ireland who were able to offer longer credit than locals, and from provincial apprentices and tradesmen whose influx threatened to undercut conventional piece-rates.

The character of migration into the city was changing in the last decade of peace. Perhaps because of the bad harvests in the late 1620s or the disruptive effects of the 'sheep-walks' in parts of Dublin's hinterland, there were ominous signs of a squatter population building up around the edge of the city. Because of the presence of 'large numbers of beggars out of all parts of the kingdom' in 1629, a detention centre (or 'house of correction') was spoken of for Oxmantown, and in the meantime the Lords Justices used the site of the former Cook Street chapel for detaining out-of-town beggars – to little effect. In 1634 the Corporation noted that vagabonds 'do most presumptiously build cottages upon the commons and the highways of the suburbs of the city, and do breed and multiply ... many of the said cottages are built upon the lord bishop's liberty and other pretended liberties'. The authority of the Lord Deputy was sought to demolish such beggar settlements and havens of thieves and receivers of stolen goods.[24] No follow-up is recorded, but a statute was passed in the 1635 session of Parliament for the establishment of houses of correction in every county. A variety of other adminstrative measures were considered in order to deal with the growing signs of lawlessness, culminating in the government decision in 1641 to give all city aldermen the status and statutory powers of justices of the peace.

The new immigrants had little impact on the religious composition of the city before the last years of peace. Barnaby Rich maintained in 1610 that there were ten times as many Catholics as Anglican conformists in the city. Twenty years later, when the Church of Ireland archbishop surveyed the congregational make-up of the city's parishes, he found that Catholics were in a large majority in all but two parishes; the exceptions were St Werburgh's, skirting around the northern and western perimeter of the Castle, and St John's, immediately to the north, between Christ Church and the Custom House, and the location of the best, or at least the newest, commercial streets in the city.[25]

Wentworth's court

Since Chichester's period in office, the actions of particular governors did not impinge heavily on the city until the arrival of Thomas, Baron Wentworth, as Lord Deputy in 1633. Unlike the New English planters who had become such a potent influence in the Castle through the years of peace, the new courtier politician from Yorkshire had a more 'secular conception of politics' than many of his contemporaries and came with a determination to purge the private interests, New English and Old English, which in his view had weakened the Crown, the established church and the army. In so doing he had no scruples in advancing his own wealth and career at court.[26] Based in the city for much of the next six years, he developed a complex political strategy, playing off opponents and building up the status of the viceregal office. Deporting himself as the prince meant choreographed public displays and vigorous expenditure within the Castle: 'I trust to make this habitation easeful and pleasant as the place will afford. Whereas now by my faith it is little better than a prison.'[27] He created the office of Master of the Revels to oversee Castle entertainments and supported the holder of the office in a project to develop the city's first public theatre. It opened in 1637 beside the Castle in Werburgh Street. Wentworth also built but did not complete a palatial viceregal retreat near Naas, Co. Kildare ('a removing house of fresh air'). When John Howell, a much-travelled Welshman, reached Wentworth's Dublin in 1639, he was taken aback:

> Here is a most splendid court kept at the Castle, and except that of the viceroy of Naples I have not seen the like in Christendom, and in one point of grandeur the Lord Deputy here goes beyond him, for he can confer honours and dub knights, which that viceroy cannot ... Traffic [i.e. trade] increaseth here wonderfully, with all kinds of bravery and buildings.[28]

The economy was at its strongest in the Wentworth years to judge by the surging customs returns. Resolute naval action against piracy both in the Irish Sea and the southern approaches in 1634 had certainly helped, but strong demand from England for cattle, wool and fish underpinned the prosperous years. Wentworth had a major stake in this prosperity, drawing nearly two-fifths of his gross income from a share in the Irish customs contract of those years. He justified this on the grounds that at his own cost he was spending in the king's name on a lavish scale; where his predecssors had a personal troop of forty horses, he kept a hundred, and at the Castle he had built a 'gallant stately stable' fit for sixty horses. The spending associated with court life filtered down, and indeed was greatly augmented by the fraught but generally well-attended parliamentary sittings in 1634, 1635 and 1640. The sharp rise during the Wentworth years in the number of city freemen enrolling in the luxury crafts (such as goldsmiths, saddlers and mercers) and the spurt in the numbers of tailors, plasterers and brick-makers were indeed no coincidence, and Wentworth boasted how he had trebled the number of Protestants in the city. But visitors complained that with this boom, 'every commodity is grown very dear'.[29]

Wentworth's strong government and arrogant behaviour made him many enemies – most famously Richard Boyle, earl of Cork, the greatest of the parvenu New English who was obliged to disgorge some of his vast acquisitions to the established church and, in a symbolic humiliation, was forced to remove the huge monument he had recently erected in memory of his wife in the chancel of St Patrick's Cathedral. Sir James Carroll, mayor of the city for the fourth time in 1635, was swept into prison by Wentworth and barred from future office on the grounds that he had been profiteering in a coal contract. Even though there was no general religious persecution, Catholic interests resented Wentworth's duplicity on the Graces (the suite of concessions to the Old English that had been tentatively offered by the Crown), and his pressure on the Corporation to give civic freedom to new Protestant merchants and craftsmen settling in the city. There was indeed a dramatic growth in the number of grants of city freedom between 1638 and 1640, most noticeably in the craft guilds, and many of the recipients were newcomers. Among them were the first Dutchmen to be made free, a merchant and goldsmith, who became citizens in 1638, fully two decades after the first Dutch traders had appeared on Wood Quay.[30]

Retribution

Wentworth's final years were back in London as Charles I's counsellor, and he became part of the greater drama playing out in England. But long before 'Black Tom Tyrant', fall-guy for a bitterly unpopular king, met his nemesis and execution in 1641, things had taken a darker turn in Dublin. The covenanting crisis in Scotland had spilled over into Ulster and this, coupled with exceptionally bad harvests, depressed trade and falling rents, began to expose the brittle foundations of Dublin's prosperity. That, however, was as nothing compared to the crisis ahead. On 23 October 1641, the Lords Justices received credible information about an Ulster Catholic plot to seize Dublin Castle just hours before the planned event. The context for this extraordinary plan was the constitutional crisis in England, the dramatic weakening of royal authority and the widespread alarm that religious conflict in the three kingdoms was imminent. The plot on the Castle was a pre-emptive move. It arose directly from Catholic fears that the king's enemies in Westminster, gripped by anti-papist sentiment, were about to subvert the remaining liberties that Catholics enjoyed, and from their belief that this could only be halted by physical force. It was a desperate strategy and in the long run it cost the Catholic interest in Ireland very dear.

An attack on the Castle was completely unexpected, even though with huge stocks of ammunition and ordnance it was a prime military target, as was evident from the great cannon quite visible on the top of the ancient towers. But the value of its capture would have been principally political, given that the Castle was the ancient and defining symbol of English royal authority in Ireland. The wider plan was that in tandem with this coup in Dublin, a group of Ulster Irish lords (including landowners, army officers and Members of Parliament) would launch a military strike against New English power in Ulster, ostensibly in the name of the king and against the pretensions of the English Parliament. Despite the interception of the Dublin plotters, the northern rising exploded into life in the same week, but the rebel leadership quickly lost control. It soon became a collective assault on the infrastructure of the Ulster Plantation and on the thousands of English and Scottish settlers in the province. The public declarations of loyalty by the first rebels may have been for external consumption, but their fervent rhetoric of deference to an embattled king, combined with the visceral anti-Catholic reaction of the government in Dublin, helped push the Old English lords of Leinster to parley with the Ulster Irish leaders. Five weeks into the crisis there was an unexpected victory for the Ulster rebel army south of the Boyne at Julianstown as it edged towards Dublin, and this convinced the wavering Old English of the Pale that their only choice was to take up arms in defence of freedom of religion and against the king's 'evil' representatives in Dublin Castle.

6. Old Bawn near Tallaght, built c.1635 by Archdeacon William Bulkeley.
It was one of several dozen pre-rebellion mansions built near Dublin,
each with gardens, woodlands and perhaps (as here) a deer park. Old
Bawn was badly damaged in the rebellion but completely restored.
Shortly before the house was abandoned c.1900, the original stucco
fireplace and oaken staircase were given to the National Museum.

The Catholic citizenry of the city were caught between a frightened and divided administration in the Castle, holding limited military
resources, and the local representatives of the Protestant settler community now under massive attack across the country. In the winter of 1641–2,
one of the coldest winters of the century, the situation in Dublin must
have been not unlike that in German towns caught up in the horrors of
the Thirty Years War. In the first weeks of the rising, thousands of Protestant refugees poured into the town, diseased, hungry and fresh with their
atrocity stories. These were soon refashioned (and inflated) as the printing
presses in Dublin, but more especially in London, got to work. Sir John
Temple, the provost's son, in an eye-witness but deeply polemical account
of the rising (first published in 1646), recalled

> the daily repair of multitudes of English that came up [to Dublin] in
> troops, stripped and miserably despoiled, out of the North ... some
> over-wearied with long travel, and so surbated [i.e. foot-sore], as they
> came creeping on their knees; others frozen up with cold, ready to

give up the ghost in the streets: others overwhelmed with grief, dis-
tracted with their losses, lost also their senses. Thus was the town,
within the compass of a few days after the breaking out of this rebellion, filled with these most lamentable spectacles of sorrow, which in
great numbers wandered up and down in all parts of the city, desolate,
forsaken ... like living ghosts in every street.

He conceded that many were accommodated in barns, stables, outhouses
and under stalls, and 'the meaner sort' crowded into the churches, but he
claimed that the Catholic citizenry had failed to help, so that 'the greatest
part' of the female and child refugees sheltering within the town eventually perished.[31]

Temple's angry prose exaggerated, but did not fabricate, the extreme
state of Dublin. An official estimate spoke of more than 7,500 refugees
in the city by the summer of 1642, and this is plausible. The impact on
food supplies and on the hygiene of this human flood was traumatic for
a city where the resident population cannot have been more than 20,000
(allowing for Dubliners who had already made a prudential exit). Many of
the refugees who could afford to travel (or had cross-channel connections)
did not linger, but probably a majority of those who survived remained
on in town (notably many Ulster English). Temple's 'ghosts' continued
to haunt the streets and death rates seem to have remained very high for
a year or two.[32]

Thanks to the initiative of Henry Jones, a young Church of Ireland
clergyman, son of a bishop and nephew of James (now Archbishop)
Ussher, the refugees' stories of Catholic violence and how it had affected
them, their families, their houses and their stocks were systematically collected in a quasi-legal process. The purpose behind the project was firmly
political, but it operated at a number of levels. Some of the atrocity stories
crossed the Irish Sea and quickly appeared in print, principally in London,
where they helped to stoke the fires of rage against Irish papistry in all
its forms. But there were deeper purposes: to document Protestant losses
with a view to future compensation, to establish a record of who should
suffer retribution when the tables were turned, and more fundamentally
to demonstrate that the rebellion was a grand conspiracy to massacre the
Protestant population of Ireland, what in later times would be classified as
genocide. These depositions were gathered at different times and places,
but a very substantial part of the submissions were recorded in Dublin

between 1642 and 1644, and they would profoundly affect the future reading of the 1641 rebellion.[33]

Some, notably the young earl of Ormond, commander of the royalist Irish army (such as it was), had wished to take on the Ulster rebels immediately after the rebellion broke out and before the flames could spread to Leinster. But his more Puritan-inclined colleagues in Dublin Castle were inclined to hold back, not least in order to expose (as they saw it) the disloyalty of the Old English leaders in Leinster. Sir William Parsons, the senior Lord Justice, prioritised the protection of Dublin over all else, and drew provincial garrisons into the city. When the Leinster lords threw in their lot with the Ulster Irish leaders (in December 1641), the government, now palpably weak, waited for military support from England. The first military reinforcements only reached Dublin Bay at the end of December, more than nine weeks after the outbreak of the rising. Then, in the early months of 1642, Dublin-based (and largely English) forces sallied out and recaptured much of the inner hinterland of the city – at great human cost. In the initial quite small campaigns, a string of Co. Dublin villages (including Clontarf, Santry and Swords) were burnt down by government soldiers, and there were recurring reports of the wholesale slaughter of Catholic civilians and, most infamously, the torching of a refugee camp of women and children near Naas, Co. Kildare, and of the massacre of possibly hundreds of civilians after the capture of Carrickmines Castle in south Co. Dublin. These incidents were only documented most obliquely in Jones's depositions of loyalist sufferings.[34]

In the early months of the rebellion, Dublin was militarily isolated. The 'Catholic army' had besieged Drogheda, captured Lambay Island and threatened cross-channel shipping. But against the odds, troops loyal to the Dublin government held out in Drogheda, and by the summer of 1642 the Irish government managed to retake a large section of east Leinster. However, Dublin itself did not recover its capital functions that had been lost in the early weeks of the rising. The royal courts atrophied, trade seized up on land and sea, and credit and the circulation of coin were virtually halted. There were recurring if muffled threats to public order in the city, whether from unpaid and ill-equipped troops, disaffected citizens or distressed refugees. Food supplies were a particular problem in the early months; the government's attempts to commandeer food from within a ten-mile radius of the city misfired, and there were serious food shortages during 1642, only partially relieved by an abundant flow of fish from

Bullock harbour and imports of grain from Wales, the south of England and Holland.[35] With so much of the recent building activity having taken place outside the city walls, emergency action was taken during 1642 (as in 1317) to destroy some of the low suburban buildings, particularly in the earl of Meath's Liberty, and to throw a protective mantle around the whole urban site. An earthen rampart on the south side of the river was built to enclose an area roughly twice the size of the walled city, and north of the river a smaller district from west of Church Street across the St Mary's abbey lands was marked out for protection. To veterans of continental siege warfare (and there were many in the Confederate armies), Dublin's new ramparts must have seemed puny enough, their function no more than to give some protection from enemy cannon in the spaces outside the ancient walls and the fragile gate-towers.[36]

In the early months of the crisis, many citizens with English links bolted across the Irish Sea to Chester and beyond, while many Catholic merchants and gentlemen joined their country cousins in arms. In April 1642 two aldermen and nine Trinity Guild merchants, deemed to have joined the rebels, were expelled from the Common Council. Yet it seems that most trading Catholics stayed on in the city, at least in the earlier stages of the war, desperately trying to keep a toehold in the Corporation. In what was a poisonous atmosphere of religious hatred, they were marked men and many, even the wealthiest like Robert Arthur, spent long periods under house arrest or in prison. But Protestant as well as Catholic wealth, real and personal, was decimated in a civil war which ebbed and flowed until the truce of autumn 1643, the 'cessation', one of the reasons for which was the desperate state of the enclave of Dublin.

Through the course of the first English Civil War, Dublin remained in royalist control, ambiguously so in its early stages, then more firmly thanks to the growing authority of James Butler, marquess of Ormond. His determination to hold Dublin for King Charles led to the eclipse of the Puritan lords justices and then to their imprisonment in the Castle. By no small irony, the rival centre of power, the Supreme Council of Confederate Catholics, was in Ormond's own town of Kilkenny. While neither civil authority in the country exerted effective power over their respective spheres of influence, Kilkenny managed for seven years to develop a better claim to be the political capital of an island at war than did Dublin. Yet possession and control of Dublin, which as all knew had never been taken by force in five hundred years, remained the ultimate prize.

Ormond and his entourage were for several years a dominant presence in the city; from early in 1642 they controlled most of Counties Meath and Louth. Economic activity recovered there more quickly than in Counties Kildare and Wicklow. Ormond struggled for a wider peace, and through a series of precarious and intricate negotiations with the dominant faction of the Confederates, he transformed the truce of 1643 into a draft peace in 1646. This, however, came to fruition too late. The eclipse of the royalist cause in England, the military ascendancy of Owen Roe O'Neill in Ulster and the radicalisation of the Confederates undermined the Ormond Peace and with it Ormond's standing. Instead, the Confederates determined to bring the war to Dublin and capture the royalist outpost, not least because of the danger that it would pass into parliamentary hands. Ormond responded in the autumn of 1646 with a rushed drive to strengthen the defences of the city. A joint Confederate force of some 10,000 men, including O'Neill's army, arrived to the west of the city and faced a garrison of some 4,000. There was, it seems, no attempt to test the new defences with artillery, and with sixteen vessels laden down with parliamentary soldiers hovering off the east coast, the city seemed about to become a battle-zone. On this occasion Ormond was lucky: the Confederates' supplies were low – and the noose was lifted.

Early in the following year, Colonel Michael Jones, Henry's younger brother, was directed by the English Parliament to take over as governor of Dublin. He arrived in Dublin Bay at the beginning of June 1647 with some 2,000 English and Welsh troops. A Trinity College graduate himself and familiar with Ormond and his circle, Jones had a reputation for personal bravery and tactical intelligence, first in Ireland and latterly in England as governor of Chester. Now, in the name of Parliament, he forced Ormond to surrender the city or, as the latter characterised it, persuaded him to let Dublin fall 'rather to the English rebels than the Irish rebels'.[37] This handover, welcome to some of the Protestant veterans in the town, was the moment of truth for royalists and, more importantly, for the remaining Catholic citizenry.

2

COURT CITY:
1647–1690

Commonwealth rule

In a perverse way the marquess of Ormond's surrender of Dublin into Puritan hands in 1647 can be seen as the start of a process that led, two decades later, to the town emerging as a centre of upper-class display and to Ormond's return as its first great patron. For Governor Michael Jones laid the foundations in Dublin for the Cromwellian reconquest and the ensuing revolution in the country's property structure, a process that dominated the 1650s – and the survivors of that revolution would eventually make Dublin their home station and their playground.

Such a prospect was hardly imaginable in the summer of 1647. Pre-war prosperity was then all but a memory, much of the Leinster hinterland was unsafe for any form of commercial transaction, and ships crossing the Irish Sea remained at the mercy of privateers, particularly of the Confederate seamen based in Wexford. The business of tax collection, litigation, indeed all the facets of civil government which had driven Dublin's recent growth, remained almost completely in abeyance. Customs returns in 1647 were no more than 3 per cent of their pre-war peak.[1] Many of its peacetime citizens had vanished, some for ever.

Only Dublin's status as a military centre remained. It was thanks to its tough raggle-taggle soldiery rather than the quality of its fortifications that the town escaped destructive attack during the 1640s. After 1642 a sufficiently large force was kept in waiting to ward off surprise attacks and subdue any internal subversion. This imposed a very heavy burden on the surviving citizenry, who once again had to play host to soldiers and to compete with the garrison for food and fuel. The able-bodied unemployed were conscripted in the early days of the rebellion, and in the crisis of 1646 all male citizens were co-opted into militia companies to serve under the mayor. The large military presence kept trade ticking over, helped as soldiers' pay began to improve, and a few bigger merchants with access to English or Dutch commercial credit remained in town and made the provisioning of the royalist army their main business.[2]

Few among the civilian population are likely to have welcomed Colonel Jones's regime in 1647. Public worship according to the formularies of the Church of Ireland was immediately prohibited and, despite protests, Presbyterian forms of worship and church discipline were introduced. For Catholic residents, things were particularly ominous; before surrendering the town Ormond had secured assurances from Jones as to the safety of the remaining Catholic population, but these were soon set aside. In September 1647 no fewer than fifteen merchants and thirteen guildsmen were expelled from the Common Council – on the grounds of absence and presumed adherence to the rebels; about half of them bore Old English surnames and most had up to now enjoyed Ormond's specific protection.[3] The purge of the Council came a few weeks after Jones's unexpected but stunning success against the army of the Leinster Catholic Confederates at Dungan's Hill near Trim, a terrible bloodbath for the defeated army which immediately altered the regional balance of power. But Puritan Dublin was still fearful of an attack from the North, and there was a brief moment in November 1647 when Owen Roe O'Neill took his vengeance on Jones in a whirlwind of destruction across the Fingal countryside, which was still the principal granary of Dublin. One night, observers from St Audoen's steeple in Dublin counted around 200 fires burning across the north of the county.[4]

The war brought about drastic changes in the religious make-up of the city. In June 1642 it had been claimed in Westminster that there were still 10,000 Catholics in the town – an implausibly high figure as Catholic numerical dominance had slipped even in the first weeks of the rebellion. In a head count, possibly made in August 1644 or somewhat later, Protestants for the first time formed a majority of the then much shrunken urban population: 68 per cent of the adult total of 8,159 inhabitants (this did not include soldiers, which would have pushed the Protestant share considerably higher).[5] The town had obviously lost a great many of its peacetime citizens, but the Catholic exodus by the mid-1640s was part of a constant turnover of all types of resident, evident even in a wealthy parish like St John's.[6] Yet despite the summary expulsion of Catholic traders in 1647, large numbers of their unfree co-religionists hung on.

Jones consolidated his military ascendancy in the Dublin region, but the future was in doubt in 1648 following developments both in London (the rise of the Independents and the New Model Army, the purging of religious moderates at Westminster, and the trial of Charles I), and within Ireland (the new pact between Ormond and a majority of the Confederates). In the light of these changes Ormond decided to make a bid to recapture the town that he had surrendered only a year before. The new drive against Jones's enclave came to a climax in June 1649 when a coalition army of about 8,000 men, headed by the marquess, set up camp outside Dublin, the intention being to squeeze the town into surrender by obstructing both maritime and land access, and by ensuring that the surrounding pasture land became too dangerous for the town's horses and cattle. The success of the tactic depended on whether or not Jones would receive substantial military reinforcements from England before the noose tightened again. It was known that a very well-equipped English expeditionary force was being prepared to assert parliamentary control over Ireland, with Oliver Cromwell its commander in waiting, so it was a race against time for the besiegers.

However, some weeks earlier, the Wexford privateers, who had done so much to keep Dublin in near-isolation since the beginning of the war, were overwhelmed by the Parliamentary navy. As a consequence, English troops and supplies could now be shuttled across the Irish Sea without danger. Meanwhile, Jones put Dublin on a war footing; he 'cleansed' the walled town of *all* suspect residents, so that 'great multitudes of Roman Catholics, whereof most were aged men, women, and children' were driven without warning out of the gates. They promptly set up a vast camp in Finglas parish. Jones then authorised the destruction of all suburban housing lying outside the defensive earthworks that had been erected in 1646. Meanwhile Ormond, now the besieger, moved his main forces to the south and south-west of the town (stretching from Drimnagh to Rathmines), and (like Silken Thomas) cut off the town's water supply. With perhaps twice as many men under his command as were available to Jones, Dublin seemed destined to pass into royalist/Confederate control.[7]

7. When Cromwell and his army landed at Ringsend in August 1649 they received a fulsome welcome, totally unlike the reaction in other Irish towns under the control of Royalists or Confederates. Peter Stent's engraving appeared as frontispiece in A history or brief chronicle of the chief matters of the Irish warres *(London, 1650), the officially sanctioned account of Cromwell's victorious military campaign in Ireland, even though the war was by no means over at that stage.*

Ormond decided on a covert operation to fortify the still-formidable Baggotrath Castle that lay close to present-day Baggot Street bridge, an operation to be carried out on a single night. The intention was then to dig a series of trenches northwards over the marshland towards the Liffey in order to prevent Jones's forces from moving between Ringsend and the town, either on land or water. The plan seemed an ingenious way of throttling Dublin without damaging its infrastructure. But it failed – through a mixture of Confederate incompetence at Baggotrath and Jones's dexterity in response – and the threatened siege was transformed next morning into a running battle on the southern approaches of the town, through gardens, meadows and ploughed fields. The upshot was that Ormond and the Confederate forces were driven into a disastrous retreat, with large numbers of them surrendering to Michael Jones. This, the so-called battle of Rathmines of 2 August 1649, was the last military conflict in the precincts of the town until 1916, and it was probably more costly in terms of human life than the later conflict. Jones claimed (with some exaggeration) that 4,000 of his enemies died that day and that he had captured great numbers of genteel prisoners, as well as some 200 draught oxen and 500 tents.[8]

This extraordinary episode prepared the way for Oliver Cromwell's armada of small merchant vessels, 12,000 redcoats, abundant supplies and some serious artillery, which arrived at Ringsend a fortnight later. Cromwell's decision to begin the 're-conquest' of Ireland in Dublin had been based on the assumption that Ormond and his army would still be camped thereabouts. To have inflicted a knock-out victory near the capital would have suited the English general only too well. In the event, Cromwell did not linger more than a few days before commencing a forty-week campaign across two provinces. It was to be a war of sieges and feints, during which some of the extreme ruthlessness evident in Jones's military engagements was played out on a grander scale in Cromwell's dealings with the royalist/Confederate towns of Drogheda and Wexford. Had Dublin been successfully taken back by Ormond before Cromwell's arrival, it too could have suffered biblical levels of civilian slaughter.

❧

As the New Model Army began the three-year reconquest of Ireland, Dublin festered. The constant circulation of ill-kempt soldiers and displaced civilians was now combined with a half-forgotten hazard – bubonic plague. This swept through the town in three waves over five years; the first in the summer of 1650 was the most lethal. It was later claimed that 1,300 residents per week were dying at its peak. There are widely differing estimates as to the overall urban death rate, the most conservative modern one suggesting that around 10 per cent of Dublin's population may have died from plague or fever in 1650 alone (this was still far lower than the death rates in the fourteenth century or in 1575). Two bad winters, the highly unsanitary state of the soldiery, the general disruption of food supplies during the Cromwellian campaigns, all contributed to soaring fatalities among every class of citizen; one victim that year was the provost of Trinity College. The Corporation had to resort to emergency loans to fund poor relief and the cost of burying the dead.[9]

But busy as Dublin's burial grounds were, the shortness of its siege spared it the kind of apocalyptic destruction and devastating mortality that occurred in parts of the south and west of the country. When one burgess asserted in the town's quarter-day Assembly in June 1651 that ten years of war and plague had meant that 'at least one half of the number of houses that were therein [have since been] pulled down and destroyed, and the houses that remain are very much decayed and ruined ...', the Common Council modified this claim, stating more conservatively that 'well near the one half of the houses that were therein [have since been] pulled down, ruined and otherwise destroyed ...', a hint that some were perhaps too ready to exaggerate their losses. That said, the destruction of property since 1641 had been colossal, with most timber- and clay-walled housing near the Castle walls and in the suburbs sacrificed at different moments during the crisis.[10]

After 1649, the main theatre of war was far from Dublin and east Leinster, although it drew in many of the Protestant citizenry to serve in the Parliamentary army. Indeed, with the town often denuded of armed soldiery during the campaigning season, there were repeated rumours of imminent attacks from the hills, rumours that were fed by the mysterious rustling of a hundred of Dublin's horses from meadows within sight of the southern ramparts in September 1651. But the wars for Dublin were over. Insofar as any event marked the end, it was the arrival in March 1653 of the pathetic figure of Sir Phelim O'Neill, the premier spokesman for the Ulster Gaelic lords in 1641. He was promptly tried, executed and quartered. By then the Commonwealth administration was firmly in charge across the country, having at great cost annihilated Catholic and royalist military forces. It was now a wholly English administration with an agenda more radical and more ambitious than that of any Elizabethan government in Dublin. The mission was to expropriate all Catholic and royalist landowners across the island who had stood out against Parliamentary forces and, most controversially, to uproot and roll back the whole Catholic populations of Leinster and Munster across the Shannon, in so doing destroying the institutional Catholic Church and creating a godly commonwealth.

Protestant Dubliners, old and new, were complicit in these revolutionary Commonwealth plans, but the agenda remained an English one and the momentum, such as it was, came from England. Actual decisions touching on religious policy, military strategy and the expropriation of the estates of Parliament's enemies reflected the shifting political balance in London, but implementation rested with the English office-holders on the ground in Dublin. Admittedly, in the 1640s several influential Dubliners – notably Sir William Parsons and Sir John Temple – had contributed to the belief in London that all Irish Catholics bore a collective blood guilt, given their (supposed) intent in 1641 to murder all Protestants, and that therefore they merited collective retribution. But the confused evolution of that policy of retribution was primarily an English story, not a Dublin one. Reflecting the political eclipse of Dublin authorities came the decision in 1653 that there should be a de facto union of the three former kingdoms, and that Ireland should send thirty representatives to an expanded Westminster Parliament. But in this as in other matters, the many Irish-born Protestants who had supported, or at least come to terms with, the English Parliament in the 1640s were now sidelined by the Model Army leadership and by the religious radicals that followed in their wake.

For Dublin Corporation it was a case of new wine in old bottles. In September 1649 the ceremonial 'riding of the franchises' around the city limits took place for the first time in ten years, but it was a Dutch-born trader and goldsmith, Peter van den Hoven, who was one of the two sheriffs superintending the parade. He was part of a small group of Dutch families – the Wybrants, Verschoyles, Westenras and the Franco-Dutch Desminières – who had been bitter adversaries of the pre-war Corporation but who now formed a powerful faction within the Board of Aldermen. Four Dutchmen were to be elected mayor over the next twenty years. Family contacts and international credit-lines gave them decisive comparative advantage over longer-established Protestant families, and several traders of English birth who had been outside the aldermanic circle before the wars also rose to prominence: Richard Tighe, one of the merchants who had kept Ormond's war going before 1647, was a major money-lender in the 1650s and after; twice mayor in the 1650s and MP for Dublin in 1656–8, he was an astute lobbyist on commercial matters. Daniel Hutchinson, Tighe's associate, had a slighter longer history: a tallow chandler in the 1630s, he had helped provision the town at its time of greatest extremity; by the 1650s he was a monied merchant in Winetavern Street and a leading creditor of the Corporation. Like Tighe, he was an Independent in religion, served as mayor (in 1652–3) and as an MP (in

1653 and 1654). He became Deputy City Treasurer and a revenue commissioner. Hutchinson was succeeded as mayor by John Preston of Skinner's
Row, even more of a parvenu trader but one of the greatest dealers in the
Cromwellian land settlement. These men and their fellow Cromwellian
aldermen chose to live in the very neighbourhoods that the men whom
they had displaced from civic office had recently resided – around Bridge
Street, High Street and Wood Quay.[11]

It was the Cromwellian government's policy to open up corporate
freedom in all Irish towns to Protestant strangers in the wake of the general expulsion of Catholic traders and craftsmen. In 1651 Dublin Corporation formally opened its doors for three years and offered civic freedom
for a modest payment to 'manufacture men' who were English and Protestant 'to replenish the said city with able and fit inhabitants'. But not surprisingly there were mixed views about the wisdom of diluting corporate
privilege. Existing freemen still championed the rights of the guilds and
valued their control over access to civic freedom.[12] In the event, the open-
door policy had limited impact; the highest number of new admissions to
freedom came in 1649 before the offer was actually made, and very few of
the leaders of Cromwellian Dublin were new to the town, a situation that
contrasted quite sharply with the wave of arrivals in the 'cleansed' towns
of Cork and Waterford.

What was new in Commonwealth Dublin was the religious climate.
From the time of Jones's takeover in 1647, rival church communities with
competing models of church government – Presbyterian, Independent,
Baptist and later Quaker – jostled to establish themselves, the first three
enjoying civil and military support at different times over the following
decade.[13] The supporters of episcopacy did not go away, but their places of
worship, the cathedrals and the old parish churches, were taken over in this
new reformation. Samuel Winters, initially chaplain to the Parliamentary
Commissioners, was the most distinguished of the preachers throughout
the 1650s: an Independent minister based in St Nicholas' church (next
door to the Tholsel), he drew strong support from the new aldermen who
clustered around Hutchinson. Winter also became provost of the university in 1652 and was a reforming spirit there, reviving teaching, introducing the formal study of medicine and making the case for a second college
in town. John Rogers, one of the most radical of London preachers, built
up a congregation in Christ Church itself: most of his adherents were new
to Ireland but some were veterans of 1641. Common to nearly all such

Cromwellian ministers was a messianic zeal to convert the unreformed masses through preaching and education, in other words to achieve in Ireland what the Anglican episcopacy had so signally failed to do over the previous century. In this they had state backing: Charles Fleetwood, chief governor from 1652 to 1655, supported the Baptists, while Cromwell's son Henry, in effect governor during the Protectorate from 1655 to 1659, supported the Independents before switching his patronage to the less radical Presbyterians.[14]

The voice of Catholic Dubliners during the 1650s was almost silent. A proclamation of 1653 simply outlawed all Catholic priests, and within the precincts of the town it seems that the church ceased to function in any way. Large numbers of priests from the region were held in captivity, and there was talk of those detained in Dublin being despatched to Spain, then it was to be Barbados.[15] But despite this purge, lay Catholics still abounded – in the markets, in the suburbs, even among the freemen (although there were attempts to curtail the rights of non-Protestant guildsmen). Nevertheless the Cromwellian authorities remained jittery and in 1655 they prohibited 'Irish people' from residing within two miles of the town, announcing that the town itself was to 'be cleared of papists and superfluous Irish, [and] cabins and other noisesome places [to] be demolished'. Such orders were rarely implemented and were probably of little relevance for working civilians. Two years later a petition to the city Assembly complained that 'there is Irish commonly and usually spoken, and the Irish habit worn not only in the streets, and by such as live in the country and come to this city on market days, but also by and in several families in the city ...'[16] The Corporation's response was tepid: markets had to be supplied. But for rural Catholics arrested in the town as vagrants it could be a different story; unknown numbers were despatched, together with prisoners brought from outside Dublin, to the Caribbean islands – a trade conducted on local vessels and organised by local merchants.[17]

Fleetwood was the principal architect of the plan for mass internal transplantation. It boded ill for Catholic Dubliners but, whatever it meant elsewhere, it had little or no effect locally and did not alter the religious demography of Dublin, either in the town or the county.[18] However, the wholesale confiscation of Old English estates – as punishment for 1641 – did matter a great deal, and the dispossession of Pale gentry and city landowners touched nearly every Catholic family of substance. The huge task of expropriating the real estate of everyone associated with the Confederate cause only began in 1653, and the administrative process dominated public life for the next six years. Dublin-based surveyors, lawyers, money-lenders and the small battalion of dealers in the unwanted land grants of English soldiers and bond-holders all stood to profit greatly. William Petty, army physician turned surveyor, was a key figure and a massive beneficiary in this process, and behind him there were dozens of other functionaries who flourished in what was the most concentrated transfer of title deeds to land in Irish history. The impact in County Dublin was quite small, however, as the established church had been the dominant landowner in the county in 1641, and in any case forfeited lands in the county were reserved by the state. But in Meath, Kildare and Louth massive changes in local landownership were underway when the Commonwealth regime imploded in 1660.

From the mid-1650s Dublin began to enjoy a peace dividend of sorts as the slow improvement of the economy brought business back to town. This coincided with a swing of the political pendulum. Fleetwood and the radicals had overreached themselves, both politically and administratively, and in Dublin there were hints by 1655 that the moral policing of the community was breaking down. Sabbath day observance was being challenged with the survival of 'disorderly' taverns, and public decency was being compromised by the behaviour of students of the College, some of whom scoffed 'at the profession of godliness'. Reported profanities such as the raising of the maypole at Ringsend suggested that underneath the rhetoric of reformation an earthy plebeian culture still continued.[19]

By the end of the decade we have a much clearer picture of the religious make-up of Dublin from a survey taken just after the collapse of the Commonwealth government during the summer of 1660. The surviving abstract enumerates adult residents in most Irish counties and divides them into 'English' and 'Irish'. For Dublin, it indicated that 'Irish' (meaning Irish-born Catholic) householders were present in every Dublin parish; in some they were small minorities of the total (a fifth or less), as in the walled parishes and in St Andrew's immediately to the east, in others they formed a quarter – in parishes south and west of the walls. They constituted over a third of households in the south-west Liberties, and very nearly half in St Michan's parish, north of the river but within Ormond's earthen ramparts. And in the satellite villages of Ringsend, Irishtown, Baggotrath and Kilmainham, the 'Irish' were in the majority. Cromwellian Dublin must therefore have been a far more mixed community than the formal record suggests.[20]

After the death of Oliver Cromwell in 1658, the English republic lost support in each of the three kingdoms. There were several constitutional crises in 1659 and a slow-motion collapse of the regime in the spring of 1660 that occurred without violence. Much of the Irish part of the story was acted out in Dublin and involved the interplay between powerful 'Old Protestants' and the more recent arrivals who had accumulated land and office. During the deputyship of Henry Cromwell, many pre-war landowners from the regions had moved back into positions of influence, but during 1659 their position was threatened once again as power in England reverted first to the Rump Parliament, then to the Army. In response to this, a group of Irish-based army officers (including Theophilus Jones, Michael's youngest brother and his understudy) seized Dublin Castle on 13 December 1659, imprisoning the English Parliamentary Commissioners. Meanwhile their allies took control of provincial garrisons. It was a brief two-hour episode, the first and only successful coup in Dublin Castle's history. Dublin aldermen were privy to the plan and two militia regiments with some 2,000 men were immediately mobilised by the Corporation, ostensibly to pre-empt any move by Catholics to exploit the 'unsettledness of the present times', but primarily to head off any radical counter-coup. A ruling council of officers was established later in December and, despite bitter internal divisions between army factions, they summoned a national convention, a plan some said was hatched by Dublin's mayor and aldermen.[21]

One hundred and thirty-eight representatives duly met, parliament-style, in the Four Courts building beside Christ Church at the beginning of March 1660. More than two-thirds of these men were 'Old Protestants', the others more recent arrivals. They managed to display a unity of purpose, expressing support for the restoration of the Westminster MPs who had been purged in 1648 and reminding the English Parliament that it had no right to impose taxation on Ireland ('the right of having parliaments held in Ireland, is still justly and lawfully due and belonging to Ireland').[22] Such talk was driven by economic resentment at the arbitrary imposition of Protectorate Parliaments, and it played particularly well with over-taxed Dubliners. Events across the Irish Sea were, however, moving too quickly for the Convention, and it exerted very little influence on the sequence of events in England. The fully reconstituted Parliament in Westminster became increasingly royalist in sentiment, leading to the monarchy being formally restored in May 1660.

The prevailing concern among those who had attended the Dublin Convention was to protect the Cromwellian settlement, with or without a Stuart restoration, both legally and, if necessary, militarily. Some relished the prospect of monarchical restoration, others felt seriously compromised by their actions over the past dozen years, but all were determined to obstruct any further debate on the recent land settlement. Catholics, absent of course from the Convention, were as equally determined in the opposite direction, expecting that their loyalty to the house of Stuart, evident most visibly during Charles II's long exile, would be rewarded by the cancellation of the Cromwellian forfeitures and by full liberty of conscience (i.e. religious toleration), as promised by Charles before his restoration. Someone would be disappointed.

The king was restored without terms. Confirmation of the news in Dublin produced a mix of great pageantry and street theatre, culminating in the 'funeral of a certain monster they called The Commonwealth, represented by an ugly mis-shapen body without a head, but with a huge insatiable belly, and a prodigious rump. The deformed corpse ... was carried to the grave without expectation of resurrection.'[23]

Most assumed that the key to any revised settlement for Ireland was held by the great survivor and favoured courtier, James, soon to be 1st duke of Ormond. Despite surrendering Dublin in 1647 and failing so spectacularly to recapture it in 1649, Ormond had enjoyed a growing reputation during the intervening years of exile, helped by the celebrity of his wife Elizabeth, a wartime resident in the town up to 1647, who had returned to Ireland in 1654 to live in Co. Kilkenny. Summoned for interrogation by the Parliamentary Commissioners in 1659, she received an extravagant welcome when she came into town. It was claimed that she was met by sixty coaches and that shops were closed while she was detained inside the Castle. There was certainly an Ormond party in the capital.[24]

The aldermen were good trimmers. Some who had been heavily associated with the Commonwealth regime faced an awkward future, but most managed to move with the times. The close involvement of townsmen in the 1659 coup and in preparations for the Convention provided ample opportunity for turning the coat. A few had never made their peace with the Commonwealth, men like the goldsmith and proto-banker Daniel Bellingham of Castle Street, who had kept in contact with the Stuart court in exile, or William Smith of Wood Quay, wartime mayor three times during the 1640s and one of those selected to represent the city at Charles II's formal entry into London. But for such natural Ormond supporters, two long years passed before their hero returned, finally reinstated as Lord Lieutenant.[25]

Ormond's town

The great survivor arrived in Dublin in July 1662 and for the next seven years was the dominant influence both in Irish politics and in Dublin's development. After another absence he returned in 1677 for a third term as viceroy until Charles II's death in 1685. Lord Steward of the King's Household and an intimate of the king, Ormond brought tangible prestige to Dublin by his very presence. But his influence can be overstated. It is important to remember that his political fortunes were closely tied to the state of court politics in London and (in the 1660s) to the standing of the earl of Clarendon; the latter's disgrace in 1667 prefigured Ormond's own eclipse. Furthermore he was frequently absent from Dublin, leaving one or other of his sons, the earls of Ossory and Arran, acting as deputy in the 1660s and 1680s. And, most importantly, his wealth was not what it seemed; the family's finances, which had been grievously affected by wartime losses, worsened progressively as they were weighed down by his sumptuous lifestyle. It seems Ormond had to borrow money, horses and clothes for his magnificent entry into Dublin in July 1662.[26]

The character of Restoration Ireland was by then becoming clear. The initial hopes of the Convention leadership for a broad church settlement had been dashed once the king's own religious preferences became evident. The full powers and privileges of the episcopal Church of Ireland were restored, Protestant non-conformity was disadvantaged, and the religious toleration that Catholics had sought was formally denied, albeit with considerable ambiguity as to what this might mean in practice. Ormond – in the two years before his return to Ireland – had been crucial in shaping Irish religious policy. The new dispensation was sealed in quite dramatic fashion when in January 1661 no fewer than ten bishops and two archbishops gathered at Christ Church Cathedral and from there walked to St Patrick's where they were consecrated in a single ceremony. The Church of Ireland was now a reinvigorated church that, within the city at least, had a new sense of mission.[27]

Unambiguous Anglican orthodoxy was a price most Protestants were prepared to pay if it meant that the land settlement of the 1650s would not be radically unpicked. It was altered, but not fundamentally so. The Restoration adjustment, which was secured after two difficult sessions of the Irish Parliament (in the Acts of Settlement of 1662 and of Explanation in 1665), was a very uneven compromise and it left discontents reverberating across the political spectrum. In the end, Cromwellian land grants were confirmed to all but a few, but acreages were reduced by a third and 'innocent' or otherwise deserving Catholic proprietors were promised allocations from this pool of surrendered land. To implement such a legal quagmire, two Courts of Claims were necessary. The courts held marathon sessions in the King's Inns in the years between 1663 and 1669 and arbitrated on thousands of cases, 'an affair rather of policy than justice'. The first year of the court's proceedings brought a 'great confluence of the country' into town and kept the taverns busy.[28]

The land settlement had huge local implications. It led to the partial restoration of many Old English dynasties in east Leinster, far more than elsewhere in the country. During the 1650s many of the plum Catholic properties close to Dublin had been granted or leased to men close to the Cromwells or to other government office-holders. These figures were now dead or in disgrace, and the cancellation of such grants and their restitution to the old proprietors was much less problematic than in the great majority of provincial cases where adventurers or ex-soldiers were in possession. In addition, there had been a particularly active network of Co. Dublin exiles who had kept in touch with the Stuart court and with Ormond and his circle on the Continent, and who could now call on powerful patrons in Whitehall and Dublin for redress. There were also a few Catholic proprietors, notably the Fitzwilliams of Merrion, who had managed to keep in with the Commonwealth and had somehow never lost their patrimony. But all in all, even in the city and county of Dublin, the 1660s saw a very partial restoration and one in which larger old-established proprietors were far better treated than those with little influence. Excluding churchland and other institutional property, 69 per cent of the acreage of Co. Dublin had been in Catholic ownership before 1641; the figure in 1670 was 48 per cent.[29] Ironically, one of the Cromwellian grantees adversely affected in the restoration process was Theophilus Jones. Complaining that 'the Irish are all restored to their estates on the west side of Dublin', he had to vacate the Sarsfield estate at Lucan, albeit receiving full compensation. The decisions, particularly those of the first Court of Claims, enraged many Cromwellian veterans, as was demonstrated in May 1663 when there was a harebrained attempt by an alliance of ex-Cromwellian officers and Presbyterian ministers to seize Dublin Castle. They had the support of at least eight MPs, their declared aim being to restore 'liberty of conscience' and 'the Protestant religion in purity', as well as the Cromwellian land grants as they had stood in 1659. Thanks to a timely warning, Ormond was well prepared. The source of that warning, Colonel Edward Vernon, was rewarded with confirmation of his title to the small estate of Clontarf.[30]

The Restoration land settlement was the final chapter in the decline of a class of minor Catholic proprietors, ancient families of local standing, many of them of Gaelic origin in the counties around Dublin. It consolidated freehold ownership in the hands of a predominantly Protestant gentry class for whom the foundation of their wealth and future standing were the two Acts of Settlement passed in the Dublin Parliament. These Acts were in a sense their *magna carta*. They and their descendants would look to Dublin, its law courts and Parliament, its social and cultural institutions, as their focal point and their social stage. In sum, the Restoration settlement brought together the conditions to make Dublin an aristocratic capital city, with Ormond its first and reluctant prince.

Three months after Ormond's arrival, theatre reappeared. John Ogilby, the pre-war impresario, returned with a royal monopoly and built the city's first purpose-built playhouse close to the river on Smock Alley, fitting it out with galleries, boxes and a loft for musicians. It opened in October 1662 and ex-Cromwellian soldiers, royalist gentlemen and upper-class women mingled together in the audiences for the earliest productions. It was the most visible sign of the return of courtly manners and continental tastes to the city. Smock Alley's early success was tied to viceregal patronage, functioning as 'a sort of court theatre attended by the public', its clientele overwhelmingly genteel and aristocratic. The staple was heavily Shakespearean, but room was also made for French drama and a handful of local scripts. Remarkably, one of the offerings that first winter was an adaptation in translation of Corneille's tragedy *Pompey* by the poet Katherine Philips (she was one of the many long-stay visitors to the city involved in the Court of Claims). Her play had uncomfortably contemporary resonances, her theatrical efforts being championed by the earl of Orrery.[31]

Smock Alley was a well-chosen location for it was the epicentre of a zone of large private houses. In 1663 there were sixty-three residences in the city containing ten or more hearths, and just over half of these were concentrated in the parishes of St John's, St Werburgh's and St Andrew's. Fashion still hugged the old city and these large houses functioned as venues for private entertainment. Peers resided in ten of them, office-holders and other landowners occupied about thirty of the rest. Albert Jouvin, a French visitor c.1666, observed that along Merchants and Wood Quays stood 'les plus beaux palais' of the city, but that it was the extramural neighbourhood to the east (around Dame Street) that now formed 'un grand faux bourg qui est à present la meilleure partie et la plus grande de Dublin'.[32] Jouvin was less struck by developments north of the river, yet the suburbs 'over the water' were then emerging as an alternative choice for upper-class residence by such prominent peers as Marcus Trevor, Viscount Dungannon (Ormond's ally and future Marshal of the Irish Army), who purchased a house with ten fireplaces in St Michan's in 1661, and the young earl of Roscommon, Wentworth's nephew and Ormond protégé (who supplied the prologue for Katherine Philips' play). A soldier and poet, Roscommon was almost a caricature Cavalier with his reputation for gambling, duelling and rootless energy, and his north-side residence had a fourteen-hearth house. A near neighbour was John Clotworthy, Viscount Masserene, veteran Presbyterian politician and Antrim magnate, with a house of fifteen hearths; among other claims to fame, he had been a key witness in securing the conviction and execution of Roscommon's uncle Wentworth two decades earlier.[33]

The focus for this new interest in the north side was Oxmantown, specifically the largely undeveloped part running west from Church Street which was still owned and controlled by the Corporation. The common land thereabouts had been used for cattle fairs, military training and great public occasions, but the decision to enclose part of it for a tree-lined bowling green and banqueting hall shortly after 1660 was indicative of new demands. With a huge bowling green, 'perhaps the finest in Europe', it functioned as a secure space for social display not unlike the theatre; it 'so fans the nobility and gentry of both sexes every day that no immoderate heat offends them nor putrifies their blood'. The initiative here had been taken by Richard Tighe, the Cromwellian mayor whose financial power more than made up for his now diminished political influence. There was a well-defined cluster of high-status families in residence thereabouts by 1665, at which point the Corporation decided to enclose a T-shaped bloc at the eastern end of the common, dividing it into ninety-six building lots with a preference being given to freemen. Most of the plots were to open out onto 'King' or 'Queen' Streets or onto a new piazza where horses and cattle would be sold – Smithfield. And linked to the project was the decision to present Ormond with a green-field site of seven acres at the western end of Oxmantown, the aldermen hoping that he would build a palace on the city's edge. Ormond, on the other hand, was constantly in motion, content to populate the houses of state with his extended retinue, but he did not build.[34]

The duke's expansive conception of the viceroyalty did, however, have one huge bonus for the city. Ormond was directly responsible for the creation of Dublin's royal park two miles north-west of the walled city. Since the sixteenth century Irish governors had enjoyed the use of the demesne of the former Kilmainham Priory that straddled the Liffey, using it for both sport and food. Alienated by the Crown *c.*1610, these grounds were reacquired in 1618 after a great mansion, Phoenix House, had been constructed on a bluff overlooking the Liffey. With its superb panorama of Dublin, the house became the summer residence for governors and Lords Justices up to 1641. From Viscount Falkland's time (he was Lord Deputy from 1622 to 1631), a herd of deer adorned the surrounds. The house survived the wars and both Fleetwood and Henry Cromwell resided there and extended it. On his return to Dublin, Ormond decided to refashion the thirty-hearth house and make the surroundings a setting fit for the king's representative. This involved a vigorous programme of land acquisition east and west of the house, and by 1669 some 1,200 acres had been bought on Crown account. Even though about 200 acres south of the river were subsequently cut out of the scheme, the main park emerged to become a unique open space with its seven miles of wall enclosing a large population of deer. Budgets were ignored, and with over £40,000 committed to the project by 1670, it gave the viceroy's enemies plenty of ammunition. Ormond lost interest in Phoenix House itself and switched his enthusiasm to the newly acquired Chapelizod Lodge, set on the Liffey's banks on the edge of the park, which he extended and refurbished. This became the preferred country retreat for viceroys until the mid-eighteenth century. But despite waste and mismanagement, the Phoenix Park survived to become Ormond's great legacy to the city. It is hard to imagine such a park being successfully created at any other time in the city's history, for it required the coincidence of a depressed property market, the drastic simplification of land titles, and the presence of a Cavalier viceroy with access to the royal purse and a love of the hunt. All these factors were briefly present in Restoration Dublin.[35]

The other municipal initiative of these years was on the south-east side of town: the enclosure of the commons that carried the name of the medieval leper church of St Stephen. There is no direct evidence of the viceroy's hand in this project. Indeed, the catalyst for it was wholly financial – the weight of the city's debt built up during the wars and the armed peace. From the 1650s the city had been raising funds by issuing long reversionary leases to city tenants in return for lump-sum payments (in effect transferring the benefit of future improvements in rental value from landlord to tenant). In 1665 the Assembly agreed on further measures: the introduction of a water charge for those linked to the city pipes, and the dividing up of segments of the city commons into development plots. St Stephen's common was the first to be chosen, followed shortly afterwards by Oxmantown. Compared to the nearest contemporary piazza in London – Bloomsbury Square – St Stephen's Green was much the larger, but initially its development was not considered as a 'square'. A more direct influence may have been the new Mall beside St James's Palace, for the idea of tree-lined promenades had suddenly come into fashion. There may have already been an idea to manicure this rough space on the city's edge, while at the same time the basin on Dublin's west side was being landscaped and a fine pathway built around the water.

The St Stephen's Green site contained some sixty acres. The outer rim was divided into ninety building plots, nearly all of which were to have very generous 60-foot frontages onto the Green. Large free-standing houses were envisaged. But unlike Oxmantown or the early London piazzas, it lacked an aristocratic anchor resident. The first tenants were all city freemen, albeit high-status ones: a quarter of them had been, or were to be, mayors of the city. Daniel Bellingham, Ormond's banking friend from Castle Street and the first to hold the title of Lord Mayor, was probably the driving force behind the initiative. A creditor of the city, he had acquired fourteen lots by 1667. Development came slowly however; after a dozen years, houses had been completed on only a third of the sites and there was a considerable turnover of lessees; some like Francis Brewster

built quickly and sold quickly. A few of these early houses were imposing structures with ten or more hearths, some were very modest, some
on the west side mere taverns. The Corporation stood back and played
no part in building development after the 1660s, the tenants enjoying
ninety-nine-year leases with few restrictions. But it did retain control of
the park, encompassing it with a rough stone wall and building a landscaped gravel pathway by 1680. It became the site for militia parades and
for the city's regular May Day entertainment that was introduced in 1675,
as a prelude to (and from the 1690s a substitute for) the ancient Easter
Monday bean-feast at Cullenswood. But apart from that, the park's future
was as a controlled space for polite society, not as a popularly accessible
city playground.[36]

The building material for the houses on the Green had to be brick,
stone or a mixture of the two, a regulation hastened by the shocking evidence from London's great fire of 1666 when over 13,000 houses, most
of them constructed from combustible building materials, were destroyed
in three days. Thatch had already been outlawed from new buildings in
Dublin after a fire, a 'woeful spectacle', in the western suburbs in 1660, and
a proclamation a decade later insisted that all existing thatch in the city
was to be removed within a year; it also specified that new houses should
be made exclusively of brick or stone and be roofed with slate or tile, and
that their façades be vertical without protruding windows 'for prevention
of some danger by fire and for ornament'.[37]

Initially the west side of the Green saw most activity. It was next door
to the first private speculative development in the city's history, in which
Francis Aungier, 1st earl of Longford, played a key role. An Ormond ally
and powerful office-holder in his own right, Longford extended the family's existing Whitefriars estate south-east of the Castle by means of aggressive freehold acquisition. On a twenty-acre site he laid out a series of new
streets, widened existing routeways (notably the renamed Aungier Street)
and demolished the city gates that led into the new matrix. He let substantial building lots to master craftsmen in the construction trades and
to other petty merchants, who on completing the houses transferred their
leasehold interests to the eventual householders. With Longford's prestige
and connections and the estate's proximity to the Castle, it became a fashionable neighbourhood for a generation.[38]

Longford, like a number of other key players in Restoration Dublin,
had been a major beneficiary of the wider land settlement, accumulating

*8. 'Dutch billy' houses, c.1700, Great Longford Street. With the adoption of
brick earlier in the century, 'Dutch billies' became the common house-type,
with gable-fronted facades, cruciform roof ridges, shallow windows without
sashes, tight stairwells, small halls and floor-to-ceiling panelling, more elaborate
houses displaying curved or stepped front gables. Fashion and design changed
in the 1720s: linear parapets and parallel roof ridges became the new norm.*

very extensive estates in the 1650s in the north Midlands. Many of the first
men in the Green had done similarly: Daniel Bellingham had acquired
extensive properties in Co. Louth, John Preston in Meath and Queen's
counties, Daniel Hutchinson in Down and King's County, Richard Tighe
in Carlow, Westmeath, King's and Queen's Counties. Another multiple
tenant on the Green was Sir Francis Brewster. He had acquired very large
properties in north Kerry and was a junior associate of William Hawkins,
a London merchant in the 1640s and leading 'Adventurer' in Irish loans,
and one of the greatest beneficiaries in the 1650s. Having briefly served as
Commissary General for Provisions for the Cromwellian invasion force,
Hawkins went on to acquire rich pickings in Munster and in Ulster, retaining control in the Restoration settlement of over 20,000 acres in south

Down alone. Hawkins's local importance was that he became the driving force behind the reclamation of riverside land between Dame street and the Liffey. Holding both Trinity College and city leases, he funded the construction of some 450 metres of double riverside walling east of the Custom House, thereby protecting Hoggen Green and the College from tidal incursions and creating new development land. The first sign of this was along Lazers Hill (the future Townsend Street), the road to Ringsend strand, where on part of the recently reclaimed land a ribbon of houses faced the estuary in the 1680s, 'well-built and inhabited [by] merchants, common brewers, maltsters'.[39] Hawkins, Brewster, Sir Alexander Bence and other old London associates worked together and largely beyond the legal reach of the Corporation in exploiting the potential for eastward development of the city. They were the first to raise the possibility (in 1671) of a downstream bridge across the Liffey, far below the existing crossing, 'near Lazers Hill'. Brewster (who alone among this group became involved in municipal politics, securing the mayoralty in 1674) employed the English surveyor Andrew Yarranton to draw up a plan for an entirely new port district incorporating Lazers Hill and the marshes that lay between the College and the Dodder mouth at Ringsend, which would incorporate a dry dock, a canal and a relocated Custom House in what would have become a miniature Amsterdam. Such ideas were more than a century ahead of their time.[40]

These commercial speculations down-river were conducted by men with little weight in Ormond's court. Their influence was a little stronger in the 1670s during Ormond's absence, when the most extraordinary property development of the century got underway north of the Liffey and east of Oxmantown. Here the main mover was Humphrey Jervis, a Cromwellian immigrant who had married Alderman Robert Walsh's daughter and become one of the city's biggest overseas merchants in the 1660s. He diversified into urban property development in a way never seen in the city before. Securing one very long lease from the earl of Tyrone for twenty acres of the old St Mary's Abbey lands (on which there was a mainly pauper population), and a lease from the Corporation for a 1,200-metre-long strip of tidal marshland on the north side of the Liffey opposite Hawkins' new intake, Jervis invested very heavily in reclaiming the ground that lay between the future Upper Abbey Street and the river.[41] Having accomplished this, he cleared the Abbey lands, widened existing lanes, and adopted a symmetrical grid pattern for a series of new streets incorporating a 'great square or market place' (St Mary's Church was later built on that site). The longest and broadest street was given the family name of the viceroy who patronised and protected him – Arthur Capel, earl of Essex – a prudent move as Jervis was not short of enemies. His new estate was let out in twenty-eight large lots to tenant-builders (many of them master craftsmen), and its success seems to have undermined the Corporation's Oxmantown project further west. (The Corporation did, however, manage to attract one entrepreneurial tenant, William Ellis, who in 1682 undertook to reclaim and develop the ground between Oxmantown Green and the river – before becoming a key office-holder in Tyrconnel's government, and after that a very long exile in France.)[42]

Jervis's trump card was to link his estate and its new main street at one end to the road to the North, and at the other to the south side of the city by means of a new bridge. Any new crossing threatened to change the magnetic field of the city and affect vested interests, yet it had been obvious even before the wars that the 'Old Bridge' was congested and in poor repair, and that the ferries had their limitations. Shortly after the Restoration, the Corporation spotted the danger that new proprietors of land on the eastern side of the town (over whom it had little control) might choose to bridge the Liffey downstream, thereby altering trade patterns and upsetting property values.[43] However, the first new bridge was upstream, a wooden structure erected across a narrow neck of the river and designed to link Oxmantown with the west end of the city. It was built, claimed the city Assembly, 'against the general sense of this city, which had occasioned great evils'; certainly it undermined the revenues from one of the ferries. Young journeymen and apprentices (encouraged by whom it is not recorded) set out to demolish the structure on two occasions during the summer of 1671; conflict with the main guard led to arrests, an attempted rescue and the loss of four lives. The bridge survived, but the Corporation was deeply embarrassed by the rioting, which may explain why plans from the Hawkins consortium for a Lazers Hill bridge later that year were not publicly contested.[44]

Humphrey Jervis and his plans were another matter; his project was to drive a bridge from Capel Street south to the Custom House, channelling maritime access to the city's ancient quays via a narrow opening controlled by a drawbridge. Losing his initial partners but with the award of the city's toll revenues for seven years, Jervis went ahead and completed the part-stone bridge by 1678. It carried Essex's name on it, but by then the viceroy had been replaced by Ormond, returning for his third posting to Dublin.[45]

Meanwhile, east and west of Essex Bridge the north bank of the Liffey was transformed by Jervis into an elevated 457-metre quay as 'the old walls, stones and rubbish belonging to ... Saint Mary's abbey' were carted the short distance 'to wall in' the strand and narrow the channel. This became Ormond Quay, a particularly appropriate designation since the old Cavalier had expressed a strong preference for a broad riverside street with buildings restricted to the landward side 'for the greater beauty and ornament of the city'. Ormond supported Jervis's ambitions, securing his election to the lord mayoralty in 1681 and 1682. Jervis's second bridge was a more modest wooden structure which linked Winetavern Street with Pill Lane and the western edge of his estate. But, despite being dedicated to the viceroy, 'Ormond's bridge' was denied city funds and declared a 'public nuisance' by his enemies, whose real objection seems to have been the damaging effects his whole development would have on the old city, 'lest their rents for lodging for gentlemen when they came from town [*sic*] should fail'. During his double mayoralty Jervis was associated with three other initiatives for promoting the north side: the removal of some of the city's open markets from Fishamble and Thomas Street across the river to what became Ormond market (this was only partly successful); secondly, the transfer of the high courts from beside Christ Church to an unspecified site north of the river (this caused a storm of complaints and got nowhere). And thirdly, what must have seemed fanciful even to his own supporters: the reclamation of the vast tidal flats to the east of his new estate, the North Strand as it later became. This was surveyed during his mayoralty in 1682 and then, using the lottery method once again, the city let out 152 lots to freemen for a nominal sum. The 'North Lotts' scheme, like a Yarranton's plan for the south strand, was far ahead of its time. It was abandoned in 1686 because of 'great disorders' in the allocation.[46] Ormond left office for the last time in 1685, and it was no coincidence that Jervis's schemes ran into trouble at about the same time. He was embroiled in a suit with the city that was heard before the Privy Council. It concerned the Essex drawbridge and the houses adjacent. Jervis was briefly imprisoned for contempt of the Council and his business reputation was severely damaged by false rumours. His later years were a complex tale of misfortune, but his great project for the north side endured.[47]

Jervis was a Protestant non-conformist in religion. This does not seem to have coloured his politics but it allowed him to play religious patron in providing sites for the first two Presbyterian meeting-houses in the city. One of the legacies of the Commonwealth upheaval in Dublin was a strong dissenting presence in the city, fragmented in their denominational loyalties but sharing a common hostility towards the Restoration religious settlement and maintaining a solid presence inside the city guilds and the Common Council. Apart from Jervis there were at least two other dissenting mayors during the Restoration period and a larger grouping of aldermen whose political loyalty was suspected by enthusiastic royalists to lie in that direction. On the unresolved issue of the status of Catholics in the city, Protestant dissenters generally took a harsher stance than the Ormondites, who for family or factional reasons supported informal toleration. These differences came into sharp relief during the short vice-royalty of Lord Berkeley (1670–72). Apparently a closet Catholic himself and with a secretary who was openly so, Berkeley caused consternation within Dublin Corporation by attempting tighter governmental control over mayoral appointments and a limited promotion of Catholic freemen. This was very much in line with the king's private wishes, but Berkeley's heavy-handed interventions encouraged the Lord Mayor to attempt an ill-judged purge of dissenters, involving the dismissal of the city recorder (the key judicial officer) and seven senior aldermen who supposedly constituted a Presbyterian faction, including Hutchinson, Tighe and Brewster. Their exclusion was overturned judicially shortly after the arrival of Berkeley's successor, the earl of Essex, but the divisions inside the Council chamber reverberated for several years. Religious, political and personal tensions echoed the furious factionalism of English politics at the time and fractured relationships at the higher levels of the Corporation, which had the unintended effect of allowing less wealthy guildsmen an opportunity to become involved in city politics and gave courtiers and merchants additional room to pursue their private agendas within the city.[48]

There was, however, one group of dissenters who were completely excluded from political life and who were subject to recurring harassment in Ormond's Dublin: the Quakers, a radical network of believers that had emerged during the religious ferment of the Commonwealth and had won considerable support among military and civilian immigrants in the 1650s. Lacking a formal ministry and abhorring the state church to the point of refusing to pay tithes, Quakers, the Society of Friends, faced harassment and imprisonment in the 1660s. But the tightness of their communal discipline, their remarkable commitment to mutual support, and their belief in personal modesty and material restraint gave them a potent advantage as a trustworthy social network that stood apart. In Dublin, the Friends established a meeting place off Bride Street in the 1660s and a burial ground exclusively for their members on grounds west of St Stephen's Green. They were to remain a small but highly distinctive element in the city, innovative in business but inward-looking. Dublin was chosen as location for the national half-yearly meetings, and their first purpose-built hall was completed in Meath Street in 1684.

Anthony Sharp, who arrived as a young migrant from Gloucestershire in 1669, set the precedent for Quaker success in Dublin trade. In a career spanning nearly forty years and much adversity, he used his west-of-England family links to become a highly successful dealer in wool, woollen yarn and cloth-making, a master manufacturer and an exporter employing by 1680 around 500 people in spinning and weaving within the city. He lived most of his life just west of the walls in New Row, but his imprint was greatest in the Liberties. He was one of a group of traders and builders who became heavily involved in developing the Thomas Court district, the open ground and gardens bounded by Thomas Street, Francis Street, the Coombe and Pimlico on the Brabazon/Meath estate. This was the location for workshops and manufacturers' houses, easily drawn there by the ready access to water for industrial processes, the lower local taxes, and the partial exemption from guild regulation. The district's association with 'dirty' industry was indeed very ancient: a medieval tannery near the Poddle with almost 200 pits (half of them in use in the seventeenth century) has recently been excavated beside New Street, near the aptly named Blackpitts, and a small-scale brewery around Thomas Street also has medieval origins. The craft character of the whole district was well established before 1641. But with a more active estate policy by the Meath estate in the Restoration period and the granting of a patent for new fairs and markets in 1674, 'the Liberties' took shape as the pre-eminent craft district, thanks both to the energetic estate management of the Brabazons and the initiative of important tenants like Sharp who settled on the estate. Sharp himself owned about thirty houses by the mid-1680s, most one assumes let to weavers, combers and dyers, interspersed with leather workers, tallow chandlers and maltsters, who in religion were then overwhelmingly Protestant. By that time Sharp, like a number of other Quakers, was absorbed into the corporate structures of the city, first as a city freeman, then as an active member of a trade guild – whatever reservations he may have had about the feasting and raucous convivality of guild life.[49]

Spreading acres

The vigorous colonisation of the green spaces around Restoration Dublin – the gardens of Thomas Court and Donore, the meadows of Oxmantown, the commons of St Stephen's Green, the sloblands along the river estuary – was unprecedented, taking the city far beyond pre-war squatter zones or the furthest extent of thirteenth-century suburbs. A semicircle of satellite villages, Finglas and Drumcondra on high ground to the north, Kilmainham and its mills to the west, Ringsend and its seamen to the east, were showing the first signs of growth.[50] The dimensions of this physical expansion are fairly clear, but the scale of its population growth remains opaque. That population was rising rapidly between the 1650s and the 1680s is not in doubt, but despite the survival of a variety of statistical returns at parish level (relating to house numbers, hearths, baptisms and burials, recorded for posterity thanks largely to Sir William Petty's inveterate curiosity), the trend and timing of Dublin's population spurt remains speculative. R. A. Butlin suggested many years ago a population total in 1663 of between 22,000 and 28,000, and for 1682 a figure in the range 55,000 to over 74,000. The conservative assumption would be to accept the higher figure for 1663 and one at the low end of the range for 1682; that would imply a doubling of population in twenty years and allow for some further growth up to 1686. But there is a strong circumstantial case for assuming a city population in the early 1660s well in excess of 30,000 (assuming strong recovery since the nadir of 1650), and a peak in the mid-1680s of between 60,000 and 65,000, a doubling certainly, albeit from a higher base. But Petty's statistics remain tantalisingly inconclusive.[51]

In the pre-industrial world, urban demographic trends were always dependent on the level of immigration – from the near-at-hand countryside or, in the case of court cities and regional capitals, from much further afield. Immigration remained crucial because of lower replacement rates within urban communities, reflecting the greater proportion of adults unmarried (or rather not yet married) relative to the countryside and the particularly high levels of infant and child mortality: 57 per cent of recorded burials in the city in 1683–4 were under sixteen years of age. Dublin's old catchment area was of course the Pale counties, with early seventeenth-century Wicklow becoming for the first time an additional source of humble migrants and [O']Byrne the most common Irish surname in the city in 1660.[52] From that time there were several streams of migrants contributing to Dublin's expansion, some seasonal, some permanent, some highly visible in the historical record and some invisible. Visible and largely seasonal were the wealthier county gentry, coming to regard a stay in Dublin during the law terms as essential for social and political advancement and for legal security; some based themselves in city inns or rented lodgings, the wealthier beginning to settle their families and establish pieds-à-terre around the town. A little less conspicuous were the military and the office-holding functionaries with their families. Then there were the small numbers of migratory young traders who arrived in the city to try their luck, given the openness of the municipal regulatory environment. Behind them were the much larger stream of the educated youths from the hinterland, getting on the first rung of advancement by securing apprenticeships in trade or handicraft. After the wars most of the migrants in these categories were Protestant and many were first-generation migrants, principally from England. We cannot tell what proportion came directly from across the sea to Dublin, but it seems likely that most of the 'English' migrants did not in fact come directly from England to the city, unlike most of the immigrants from the Low Countries and France, who probably came to the capital first.

It is likely that this wave of newcomers populating the city in the second half of the seventeenth century was the largest infusion (in relative terms) since the late twelfth century. What is far less visible in the historical record is the stream of Catholic and Leinster-born migrants, male and female, coming into the Restoration city with modest resources, some securing entry to the burgeoning trades and crafts, many more swelling the informal sector – in petty retailing, porterage, general labouring and domestic service. William Petty suggested (in his back-of-the-envelope way) a more than doubling of the numbers of Catholics between 1671 and 1682. With the city emerging as a vital place of resort for the upper classes and as a pre-eminent commercial hub for an expanding export economy, there was an acceleration in the growth of artisanal employment in traditional fields such as baking, brewing, tailoring and leather-working. But distinctly new types of employment were emerging as fashion, upper-class lifestyles and aristocratic business acted as a catalyst for the growth of cabinet-making, perfume- and wig-making, and for the introduction of new lines in fine cloth-making, cloth-finishing and glass-making by immigrant masters, Dutch, Italian, English and French. Printing in general and the local production of books in particular, which had been of marginal importance before the wars, grew noticeably from the late 1670s.[53]

The guilds adapted to meet the changing economy: coopers broke away from the old carpenters' guild in 1666, and felt-makers and hatters were incorporated as a guild in the same year. Bricklayers and plasterers broke free of the carpenters' guild in 1670, and St Luke's guild (incorporating cutlers, painters, paper-stainers, stationers and printers) received its charter the same year. The old tallow-chandlers and allied trades guild was reincorporated in 1674, and the saddlers' guild was recast in 1677 to embrace coach-makers and upholsterers. These new creations were by royal charter, reflecting the approval, if not the active patronage, of Dublin Castle, and their formation brought added prestige to these crafts. Guilds continued to accept Catholic brothers in the 1660s but when the state policy swung away from toleration, their status became precarious, and in many guilds (notably the newer ones) both Catholic and Quaker master craftsmen were given second-class status as 'quarter brothers', paying a regular fee to enjoy some of the privileges of guild freedom. In the large Weavers' Guild, quarter brothers seem to have outnumbered full brothers in the late 1670s, although the position had reversed by the mid-1680s. In the Corporation at large, some hundreds of indigenous Catholic traders and craftsmen had been restored to full civic freedom in the 1660s, but thereafter the numbers of new Catholic freemen being sworn seems to have been small, so that access to council and municipal office, despite good prospects in 1671–2, remained illusory.[54]

Freedom was both a political issue reflecting status and family reputation, and an economic one: although quarter brothers secured some of the benefits of membership of the body corporate (such as freedom to trade and reduced toll charges), only full freemen enjoyed the 50 per cent discount on the new charge for municipal water. That was abandoned in 1675, from which time all of the 300-odd houses connected to the pipes had to pay the stiff one-pound-a-year charge. Water provision was the one utility that remained an exclusively Corporation business (although management and tax collection was regularly subcontracted). The growth of water connections can be seen as an indicator for wider urban growth:

there was a 4 per cent p.a. growth in connections between 1680 and 1705, which considering the intervening political crisis is quite telling. By 1705 there were in all 758 connections in fifty-two streets and evidence of occasional severe water shortages. Cheaper water in the Liberties was the trump card for the earl of Meath and his head tenantry in trying to attract tenants, and the absence of a water supply to St Stephens Green until after 1700 may have held back its development. Jervis brought water pipes over the Liffey in the 1680s and by the time of his death houses north of the river (and largely on his former estate) were contributing over a quarter of the city's water revenues.[55]

Water provision was a fairly discreet aspect of Corporation activity. Two Restoration building projects overseen by the city provided a more public expression of civic identity. Dublin's existing municipal hall was cramped, decayed and no fit place for a lord mayor. In Amsterdam, the centre of the trading world, the magnificent Stadhuis, six storeys high with a façade of nearly 150 windows, had just been completed. The straitened state of Dublin's finances meant that there was no danger of even a pale imitation, but a new Tholsel was built between 1676 and 1685 – a two-storey block, located quite deliberately within the old city walls at the intersection of Nicholas Street and Skinners Row. It was a baroque public space, the ground floor 'an exchange for the public meeting of all merchants and strangers' and the city court, and upstairs a municipal space for the assembly and civic officers. But it had a baleful effect on the city's finances and its limitations were soon recognised. The London bookseller John Dunton found it in 1698 'scarce big enough for the company that comes on it at high change, which is at half an hour after twelve', but it continued both as a trading centre for merchants and the stage for wholesale business deals for nearly a century.[56]

More striking visually was the new municipal school, the King's Hospital (1670–73), built amid the city's Oxmantown development. It had a curious inception: the original public fund-raising in the late 1660s had been to build a refuge for the poor and infirm adults of the city (and thereby hold back the flood of out-of-town beggars), at which time a small and under-funded school for the sons of freemen existed in Back Lane. But thanks in large part to the enthusiastic patronage of Ormond's heir, the earl of Ossory, the project for a great school took precedence and in effect absorbed the Hospital; with its chapel, great hall and 'four large school-rooms', it was seen very much as the academy for the sons of

9. The modest fourteenth-century civic hall continued to function until its demolition in 1676. The elaborate replacement accommodated a merchants exchange on the ground floor and municipal business upstairs. By the time James Malton sketched the building in 1791 it was in very poor shape, its tower gone and its archaic design ridiculed by latter-day connoisseurs of the neoclassical.

freemen. It opened in 1675 and catered for sixty children, including four girls, and was (eventually) adequately supported by the Corporation. The head rents from both Oxmantown and St Stephen's Green were diverted in perpetuity to the school.[57]

To the west of the city a far greater building project was then underway: an infirmary and home for old soldiers, the Royal Hospital (1680–86), strikingly sited on the south-bank ridge near Kilmainham and opposite Phoenix House. It cost over £23,500 and was financed primarily by a levy on soldiers' pay. Although not originally Ormond's idea, it was thanks to him that the project received royal backing and as a result of his taste for the magnificent that its scale was palatial and its decorative finish quite so dramatic. For Ormond, military leader before he became a courtier, the reconstruction of the Irish army as a royalist and generally dependable force had been one of his achievements in the 1660s, and he maintained an almost proprietorial relationship with the 1,200-strong Regiment of Guards based in the city. This elite force had been set up in

1662, officered by his family and old allies, and it was quartered in various postings around the city from Lazers Hill to Thomas Street, some in the old gate-houses, some in inns and alehouses. A scheme was mooted to construct a vast star-shaped citadel on the swamps of the future Merrion Square (de Gomme's plan in 1673 envisaged covering an area larger than the walled city), and this would have accommodated 700 soldiers, but with the ending of Anglo-Dutch hostilities the idea came to nothing and there was no talk as yet of a purpose-built barracks in the city.[58] So the idea of a grand military infirmary for the whole country, inspired by Les Invalides in Paris, was both a response to practical need – how to weed out disabled and infirm soldiers from the ranks in a way that would allow quartering to continue and not affect military morale – and a symbolic statement of the importance of the king's Irish army. It was also a powerful demonstration of the military's centrality in the affairs of Dublin. The quadrangular design by the Surveyor-General William Robinson, with its echoes of the College, sprouted above the western approaches, and the exceptional quality of its exterior and interior detailing, notably the wood carving in the chapel by the Huguenot immigrant James Tabary, made it an immediate object of public wonder. But for all its vast spaces and lavish capacity (it could comfortably hold about 300 veterans), the Royal Hospital would find itself, soon after its opening (like the workhouses of another age), overwhelmed by catastrophe – the return of war in Ireland.[59]

Peace unravelling

Late one night in April 1684 the city was disturbed by a huge fire and multiple explosions within the Castle compound. The fire had begun in the state dining room on the south side and threatened the whole ramshackle site. Ormond's second son, the earl of Arran, was in residence and, fearful of a repeat of 1597, he authorised the creation of a firebreak to protect the ammunition store in the north-east corner of the Castle compound. This inevitably led to the destruction of several sets of buildings, including the long gallery 'borne upon pillars in the nature of a *piazza*', which had been erected in the 1620s and had been the first intrusion of classical idiom into the medieval fortress.[60] Arran was praised for his prompt action and selflessness (in that a vast amount of valuable Ormond furniture, pictures and hangings was also destroyed), but the loss may have been made a little easier by the fact that successive viceroys had thoroughly disliked the Castle. The buildings were a hotch-potch of old and new and quite cramped, despite the various additions of Falkland, Wentworth, Essex and Ormond himself. The role of the Castle was also changing: the Parliament House on the west side of the quadrangle had been burnt down in 1671 and not rebuilt, and the Privy Council now regularly met outside the Castle in a 'large house' in Essex Street, following the construction of chambers beside the Custom House in the 1660s. Ormond and Arran had toyed with the idea – before the 1684 fire – of securing royal support for disposing of the Castle altogether and building elsewhere, or alternatively acquiring extra land on the perimeter, demolishing the curtain walls and making 'four fair streets into the Castle'. The fire made the future of the Castle a matter of wider debate, but the chances for wholesale reconstruction were poor.[61]

The improvement of the Castle turned out to be a very slow business, spanning the next quarter of a century. Its fitful progress reflected the wider turbulence, political and military, that plagued the city once more. Conventionally, this era began in February 1685 when a new king was proclaimed in the city, Charles's brother, James II. Ormond resigned, leaving Ireland for the last time a few weeks later. But English politics had been in an extremely volatile state since the early 1670s, with most attention focused on the religious affiliation of the heir to the throne after James's espousal of Catholicism was publicly confirmed. The effects of this had been somewhat muffled in Dublin, as no Irish parliament was summoned after 1666, and Ormond and Essex had a generally moderating influence at times of English volatility. But the surging anti-Catholicism associated with the Popish Plot of 1678–80, whipped up in England by those opposed to a Catholic succession, caused a local chill and forced Ormond to defend himself against charges of crypto-Catholic sympathy. There was a sharp crackdown on Catholic bishops and friars, specifically the arrest of the Dublin archbishop Peter Talbot on fairly dubious grounds. Despite Ormond's private views of his innocence, Talbot was held in the Castle for two years before his death there in 1680. Jervis's patron, the earl of Essex, was a victim on the other side: on returning to English politics from Dublin, he became an opposition leader, was imprisoned in the Tower and ended up committing suicide in 1683, apparently fearful of being implicated in the Rye House plot against the king.

How quickly did these rarefied dramas impinge on the city? The public burning of an effigy of the duke of Monmouth in Francis Street in July

1685 provides a tantalising clue: Monmouth, natural son of Charles II and Protestant claimant to the throne, had launched an abortive rising in the West Country against his uncle, and this celebration of his defeat in battle was the first local sign of Catholic elation at the tables being turned.[62] The choice of Francis Street is itself intriguing. Lying between the walls and the earl of Meath's Liberties, it was an area of residual Catholic influence; the adjacent Franciscan chapel, built *c.*1680, was one of four regular centres of Catholic worship in the Restoration city and the Catholic archbishop Patrick Russell ('a good man but … no politician') lived on the street. Clerical numbers in the city had oscillated with changing levels of formal toleration; perhaps fifty were present in the city at the best of times. The great majority of them were regulars, Dominican or Franciscan friars who were mobile, trained on the Continent and good preachers; and Francis Street seems to have had a particular concentration of friars.[63] The resilience of the Catholic Church at moments of Restoration toleration struck Protestant observers forcibly, even if those seasons of tolerance opened up bitter clerical divisions among Catholics between the *politiques*, anxious to regularise church/state relations, and those who saw any diminution of papal authority as a theologically slippery road. Russell had come to office in 1682, but he only acted in public after James II's accession, holding a council of Leinster bishops in July 1685 and chairing a succession of synods and conventions over the next four years. The main purpose of these was to try to impose Tridentine discipline on a divided and disordered church, with city Catholicism being positioned to take the lead in this.

Full and formal religious toleration was not granted until April 1687, but long before that the civil restraints on dissenters and Catholics had been swept away. Governance of the city remained in Protestant hands for the first two years of James's reign, but as early as November 1685 a group of Catholic merchants, led by the wealthy overseas trader Thomas Hackett, demanded their civic freedom. The Corporation baulked at reopening the door to Catholics, until they were forced to do so by the earl of Clarendon, Ormond's successor as viceroy, the following summer. But Catholic freemen still remained in a minority, albeit a rapidly growing one. Clarendon was then replaced at the beginning of 1687 by Richard Talbot, Lord Tyrconnel, brother of the recently deceased archbishop and long-time confidante of the new king.

Tyrconnel had already secured effective control over the Irish army, cashiering a large proportion of its Protestant manpower and encouraging

Catholic officers to drum up recruits from across the country. The flood
of raw countrymen milling around the city soon attracted ridicule from
Protestant citizens – inspired perhaps by the sentiments of the *Lillibulero*
march – and invited some bloody retribution.[64] But once Tyrconnel took
control of civil government as well, the pace of Catholicisation accelerated,
extending to the magistracy and the bench. Determined to secure corporate boroughs loyal to the new religious policies, Tyrconnel persuaded the
king to agree to what became a hugely controversial policy, the wholesale
cancellation of the existing charters of all Irish towns and cities. In the case
of Dublin this act of the royal prerogative was seen as an outrageous slur
on the city's centuries of loyalty to the Crown. The Corporation appealed
to the dying Ormond to save the city's liberties, but the tide was now rip-
ping the other way. A new charter and a new Corporation followed, with
fifteen of its twenty-four aldermen Catholic, plus a sprinkling of dissenters (including Anthony Sharp), and they took control in November 1687.
From then until the battle of the Boyne in 1690, Catholics controlled the
Tholsel. Hackett got his revenge by becoming the first lord mayor under
the new charter.

A Protestant challenge to the Jacobite regime in Ireland was slow to
materialise despite profound fears for the future, and it only really began
to take shape after the birth of a Catholic male heir to the throne and
rumours that William of Orange was preparing an English invasion. Its
genesis was in Ulster not Dublin, and in contrast to the great crisis of
the 1640s, the collapse of economic activity in the capital happened in
slow motion – indeed, it is only true to speak of a war economy from the
summer of 1689 – and, again unlike the 1640s, the military phase of the
crisis when it came was (for Dublin) relatively short and quite decisive. It
is true that from 1686 there were endless rumours of massacre and conspiracy, but the eclipse of Protestant Dublin and the departure of many
of its citizens across the Channel was a long drawn-out and partial process. From the time of Clarendon's recall and Tyrconnel's elevation, the
Protestant citizenry became deeply unsettled, moving assets where possible to England and contemplating their own departure. But it was not
until December 1688 – almost two years later – that this became a flood,
at the moment of the Williamite takeover in England. Over a three-
day period on the eve of a rumoured national massacre of Protestants,
some thirty vessels left Ringsend, shuttling women, children and goods
to north Wales. And when that panic passed, an outflow – notably of

menfolk northwards to the 'liberated' Williamite territory – continued for many months. But it seems that about two-thirds of the city's pre-war Protestant population, notably the older and the poorer, remained in place.[65]

Dublin, a Protestant city in a Catholic country and now with a Catholic government, was in a highly anomalous situation. Tyrconnel, a man in a hurry, never seems to have been comfortable in the city. His day-long celebrations in July 1688 of the birth of a Catholic heir – leading a vast procession from the Royal Hospital to High Mass in the Castle, placing wine in the public conduits, hosting a state dinner at Chapelizod and receiving supper in the Tholsel while fireworks were set off on the river – were something of an overstatement.[66] He saw fifth-columnists everywhere, and even as late as January 1690 he believed that a Protestant putsch in the city was imminent. Yet the Church of Ireland, with its profoundly monarchist instincts, was never going to lead a challenge to James's Irish governors and was seriously divided in its responses to the crisis. Anglican parish churches remained open and were indeed generally unmolested until the last weeks of the Jacobite regime. Only the chapel of the Royal Hospital was taken over, with Mass also being celebrated from time to time in the Castle, the Tholsel and the old King's Inns. The one symbolic reconsecration was that of Christ Church Cathedral, commandeered for Catholic worship in September 1689. Trinity College was closed down at the same time, to be used variously as an army camp and a detention centre for Protestant prisoners. But Anglican worship otherwise continued more or less openly, despite the detention of the Dean of St Patrick's, William King, who was held for five months as a state prisoner on the suspicion (subsequently confirmed) that he had been a regular conduit of information to the Williamite court. It was only ten days before the battle of the Boyne that Protestant churches were actually closed: 'not a bell but mass bells to be heard, and all people kept house that Sunday'. The Jacobite government had, however, engaged in the repeated disarming of Protestant civilians and in searches of their houses, churches, tombs even, and intermittently in the confiscation of their horses. Finally a night-time curfew was placed on all Protestants and large numbers were arrested, 'even beggars themselves'.[67] Much of this was driven by military necessity, but arbitrary internment and the forced recycling of firearms from Protestant to Catholic citizenry was hardly conducive to civic calm.

The year 1689 was in several respects an *annus mirabilis* for the city. It witnessed the first visit by a reigning monarch since 1399; it was the year in which an Irish Parliament, largely Catholic in composition, annulled the 1662 Act of Settlement – against royal wishes – and thus put a stop to the massive land confiscations of mid-century; and Dublin became the nerve centre and rallying point in the mobilisation of Tyrconnel's new Catholic army.

James made his entry into the capital on Palm Sunday 1689: after a triumphal cross-country journey from Kinsale he was greeted outside St James Gate by Lord Mayor and Corporation:

> there was a stage built, covered with tapestry, and thereon two playing on Welsh harps, and below [were] a great number of friars, with a large cross, singing; and about 40 oyster-wenches, poultry and herb-women, in white ... dancing, who thence ran along to the Castle by his side, here and there strewing flowers. Some hung out of their balconies tapestry, and cloth of arras; and others, imitating them, sewed together the coverings of Turkey-work chairs and bandle-cloth blankets, and hung them out likewise on each side of the street ...
>
> As he marched thus along, the pipers of the several companies played the tune of, *The king enjoys his own again*, and the people shouting and crying, *God save the King*. And if any Protestants were observed not to shew their zeal that way, they were immediately revil'd and abused ...

At the Castle Gate the king knelt for a blessing from the Catholic arch-bishop, who was accompanied by four bishops holding up the blessed sac-rament under a canopy and 'a numerous train of friars singing'.[68] In the king's party were the first of a huge contingent of French diplomats and soldiers, whose disdainful attitudes to their Irish allies and to the city at large were soon to be bitterly resented.

James II's Irish Parliament, a predominantly Catholic Old English assembly, sat for over two months that summer in the King's Inns. James spoke at its opening of liberty of conscience, the promotion of trade and the relief of those who had suffered in the Acts of Settlement, but Tyr-connel and his allies were focused on a more radical objective: complete repeal of the Restoration land settlement. This, it has been argued, was the final domino pushing Protestants into unambiguous support for the Williamite cause.[69] There were, however, many city Catholics whose families had invested in, or won back, real estate since 1660 who must have regarded the prospect of a new Court of Claims with some anxiety.

The war on Irish soil began that summer and spanned nearly two years, but it directly affected Dublin for less than one. Although there was a sustantial Williamite army in the north of the country from August 1689, and French reinforcements for the Jacobite army on Irish soil from March 1690, the principal contests took place during the following summer. The build-up of Tyrconnel's Irish army, begun in 1686 with the progressive disarming of Protestant officers, was largely achieved by 1689; there are widely varying claims as to the numbers of soldiers stationed in and around Dublin in the latter part of that year, ranging up to 30,000. Many of the complaints from Protestant citizens related to the economic burden this placed upon them, the forced requisitioning of food and goods for export, and the destruction of property by ill-disciplined levies; Alderman Ram's trophy house on St Stephen's Green was ransacked in September 1689, his books and money taken and his servants expelled.[70] Food supplies were increasingly precarious by the autumn, the scarcity exacerbated by price inflation that followed the vast minting of brass and other base metals. Fuel supplies were hit by a blockade of the Cumbrian coal boats through the winter. As a result, trees, hedges and even uninhabited houses in and around the city were ravaged by the soldiery.

Yet accounts of Dublin in this strangest of times suggest an air of reckless living for the moment. The king spent the winter in Kilkenny, but that did not dampen the social life of Dublin. John Stevens, an English Jacobite, recalled the drunken excesses with distaste:

> Oaths, curses and blasphemies were the one-half of the common familiar discourse ... The women were so suitable to the times that they rather enticed men to lewdness than carried the least face of modesty. In fine Dublin seemed to be a seminary of vice, an academy of luxury, or rather a sink of corruption and living emblem of Sodom.

Even Lent, he claimed, was ignored.[71] Equally striking was the very modest investment in the defence of the city by the Jacobite authorities in comparison with the efforts made in the 1640s. The suburban spread of the city, far beyond Ormond's ramparts, perhaps made such a task impossible, but it seems strange that there was only a token attempt to protect even the bridges. The prevailing view in the early part of the war was that the

Williamite army in Ulster could be defeated in the field and that Dublin was not at risk. When it became evident in the spring of 1690 that Prince William was himself coming to Ireland with a much enlarged force, that assumption was discarded. And as the Williamite juggernaut began its southwards advance out of Ulster in June 1690, there was a huge risk for Dublin, but as Tyrconnel told James's queen, this would mean a battle north of the city, 'for if we be driven from it and this province lost, there will be little hope of keeping the rest for long'. Yet ten days before the Boyne, and inconsistent as always, he seemed prepared to sacrifice Dublin if it meant not committing everything in a single throw of the dice. But for ordinary citizens, Catholic or Protestant, the prospect of a sudden Jacobite retreat or of outright defeat put them in immediate jeopardy. Rumours had circulated for months that if the Jacobite government had to be relocated, the capital would be burnt in the process: 'it would be done by fire-ball which were ready [sic], and if it should be four or five days a burning it could not be quenched till reduced to ashes'.[72]

Hours after the great battle at the Boyne on 1 July 1690, James arrived in the city ahead of his defeated forces, announced that the game was up for Jacobite authority in Dublin, and ordered that his army in their westward retreat should not destroy the city. Yet for almost a day after James's rapid departure for France, Jacobite cavalry and dragoons continued to make their dishevelled way through the city. The Castle was quietly abandoned, the prisons left unguarded. Robert Fitzgerald, younger son of the earl of Kildare, 'with a slender guard of Protestants', managed to get his hands on the keys of the city and the Castle, liberated the prisoners, and secured the stores. Then, 'with other persons of quality', he managed to establish control of the city and suburbs and to halt 'the rabble [who] fell to disarming the Roman Catholics'. Ormond's grandson and heir arrived two days after the battle with a small detachment of cavalry, the first signs of the victorious army. As one Protestant diarist memorably put it, 'we crept out of our houses and found ourselves as it were in a new world'. But the terrified Catholic citizenry feared that 'they would all be put to the sword' when the Williamite army arrived. But, no thanks to the dilatory William of Orange, the city was spared a pogrom and its physical fabric emerged from another war almost unscathed.[73]

3

INJURED LADY:
1690–1750

Among the frightened Protestant crowds who took flight from Dublin in the winter of 1688 were two young men, St George Ashe, recently appointed as professor of Mathematics in Trinity College, and Jonathan Swift, his former tutorial student and a recent graduate. Ashe, the younger son of Cromwellian settlers in Roscommon, had already made his mark in the Dublin Philosophical Society, a fledgling intellectual salon that had begun to meet in 1683, its handful of members sharing a broad range of interests and a common dedication to the Baconian approach to scientific inquiry, 'instead of words and empty speculations, ... things and experiments'. Ashe kept a weather log, including daily barometric readings, for two years, and he acquired a telescope and established a small College observatory (which seems to have been destroyed during the Jacobite occupation of the campus). In exile, he became chaplain to the British ambassador in Vienna for over two years before returning to Dublin with his scientific horizons much broadened; later he became provost of the College.[1]

For Swift it was a different journey. Born in St Werburgh's parish in 1667, he had more precarious beginnings. Fatherless, he spent his early years with a nurse in Cumbria before being sent to boarding school in Kilkenny; it seems he met his mother for the first time since infancy after he fled to England. His first literary attempt, *Ode to the king on his Irish expedition* (1691) gave little indication of the future. Ordained in 1694, he

moved between patrons in London and Dublin for a decade, only finding space for his restless ability in the political hothouse of Queen Anne's
London. Associating strongly with the Tory parliamentary world and
their defence of the established church, he became the most successful literary partisan of his generation. His first great work, *A tale of a tub* (1704),
included the superb satirical essay 'The battle of the books', which debated
the relative merits of ancient wisdom and modern learning. Unlike Ashe,
Swift displayed a profoundly subversive view of the presumed superiority
of contemporary knowledge.

Swift was perhaps too gifted for his own good; he was squeezed out
in the hunt for promotion in London, securing only the deanery of St Patrick's, which he took up in 1713 with the proximate collapse of the Tories.
He carried home to Dublin a burning sense of disappointment at his
patrons' inability to protect their supporters and at their failure to prepare
for the Hanoverian future, as well as a contempt for the immorality of
his political enemies, be they Whigs, dissenters or worse. This dystopian
world-view was to be recreated a decade later in the pages of *Gulliver's
travels*, with its multiple layers of allegorical meaning.

Swift and his extraordinary career have been seen as the unifying
strand in Dublin's history spanning the fifty years after the battle of the
Boyne. Such claims have been based on Swift's remarkable celebrity within
the city in later life and his impact on the development of the public sphere
in Dublin, but his earlier writing introduces another trope of even broader
application. *The story of the injured lady* was composed in 1710 but not published until after his death; it was his first critique of Anglo-Irish relations.
In the allegory, Ireland is cast as the female mistress rejected by England in
favour of the charms of Scotland. The status of Protestant Ireland within
such a parable, and the implications of the Williamite reconquest, were
left unresolved. But more importantly, the sentiments running through
The story – disappointment, breach of trust and betrayal of the weaker
party – became pervasive elements in Irish public discourse for more than
a generation. In the wake of the reconfiguration of power in London post-
1688 and the Glorious Revolution, different parties in Dublin bore different scars and harboured their own, sometimes competing, resentments.
Indeed, the articulation of unredressed grievance was the hallmark of the
era, an era that nevertheless turned out to be entirely peaceful.

Departures and arrivals

Strategic dynastic uncertainty, a shift in the centre of gravity of London politics from court to Parliament, and the escalating costs of continental war formed the backdrop to Dublin public life in the decades after 1690. With neither William of Orange nor his sister-in-law Anne leaving heirs, the possibility of a Jacobite resurrection remained a real threat in most people's minds up until 1714, and a recurring hope for some others long after that. This uncertainty, coupled with the ever-present fear of French military power, shaped domestic and municipal politics for a generation. With only a brief interlude between 1697 and 1702, war impinged on Dublin's maritime trade and its local politics, indeed, on nearly every aspect of social life. The pressing demands of the land war in Europe had allowed the Jacobite leaders in 1691 to extract unexpectedly good terms from William's negotiators at the siege of Limerick. But the civil terms of the ensuing treaty and its promise of a substantial level of religious toler-ation for Catholics stirred up profound hostility among Protestants, who felt that they had won the war in Ireland and that others acting in their name were losing the peace. Bitterness over the soft peace terms led to calls for comprehensive anti-Catholic legislation that would destroy for all time the economic and institutional foundations of Catholic power, the resilience of which had been so startlingly revealed under Tyrconnel.

These inflamed feelings found an outlet in the Chichester House meetings of the Irish Parliament which from 1692 took place more fre-quently, the result of the government's pressing need to get the Treaty of Limerick ratified and to secure additional revenues for military defence. But with the rise of increasingly regular parliaments in College Green came enormous pressure for ever more comprehensive anti-Catholic legis-lation, whether building on earlier discretionary and temporary measures ordered by the Irish Privy Council, or adapting older English anti-Catholic laws. Between 1695 and 1709 an untidy bundle of statutes were passed in College Green – only later were they seen as a unitary 'penal code' – which limited the capacity of any Catholic to hold real estate, to inherit landed property, to practise law, to have children educated whether abroad or at home, or to bear arms (a small number of Catholic gentry across the country were personally exempt from the ban on arms, almost 30 per cent of whom were resident in Dublin city or county).[2] The institutional church was torpedoed with the 'Banishment Act' of 1697, which sought to expel all Catholic bishops, vicars-general and members of religious orders and, most ominously, it placed a bar on the re-entry of anyone who had received a foreign education, including seminarians. 'By these acts', wrote John Dunton, the credulous London bookseller resident in Dublin in 1698–9, 'I think it will appear plainly enough that the Romish religion is on its last legs in Ireland ... the next age will have few people inclinable to any more rebellions against England'.[3]

The Williamite parliaments were entirely Protestant and the House of Commons, now swollen to 300 MPs, was composed overwhelmingly of rural gentry and their connections. The city MPs of the time blended in easily. Of the six who sat for the city between 1692 and 1713, three were lawyers and three were aldermen (each of whom had served as Lord Mayor), but most if not all of these also owned substantial rural property. The majority of city MPs were active on parliamentary committees and one became Commons speaker (John Forster, 1710–13); four of the six were Whiggish in their politics and therefore hostile to the ratification of the Treaty of Limerick – which passed in diluted form through the Irish Parliament in 1697 – and so were natural supporters of tighter anti-Catholic legislation. But there is no evidence that the city actually championed the introduction of any penal law.

The Corporation as an entity was in a strange position: English legislation, passed in 1690, had ruled that all borough charters issued since 1683, including that issued to Dublin in 1687, were null and void, and this regularised the status of Protestant ex-aldermen who had seized civic control of the city after the battle of the Boyne and restored 'its ancient Protestant government'. Many Catholic traders were held in detention for several months until they were prepared to swallow 'the pill of allegiance', and in September 1690 the reconstituted Assembly expelled all papist freemen 'who ... combined together to take away the city charters and to turn the several Protestant magistrates, officers and freemen of this city out of their places and freedoms', an ambiguous formulation which seems to have allowed a few Catholic freemen to retain their status (but in some cases only for a few years). However, the Assembly closed the door to further Catholic applicants in 1692, ruling that all prospective freemen must take both the oath of allegiance and a new Westminster oath declaring (*inter alia*) the mass to be idolatrous. Later in the decade harsh penalties were imposed on freemen who employed Catholic apprentices, and in 1699 the Assembly ruled that even its most menial employees must take the Protestant oaths.[4] Catholic freemen had of course made retribution more likely by their actions when the boot was on the other foot: property of many Protestant freemen had been seized after the great exodus at the end of 1688, and there were reports of at least one Jacobite alderman saying that if King James were defeated, the city should be burnt.[5]

Some Catholic merchants managed nevertheless to get back into business. In some trades, notably in food preparation and the retailing of alcohol, Catholic traders remained predominant. But in overseas trade they were a shrinking minority. There was a revealing episode in 1696 in a row over the continued use of Cork House yard as a merchant exchange in preference to the Tholsel: nine men were named in the Assembly record as defying the Corporation; six of these were freemen (three of them Hugue-nots) and they were threatened with disenfranchisement, and three were unfree Catholics who were threatened with criminal prosecution in the court of King's Bench. The disparate group had presumably been trading in commercial bills of exchange (and the Corporation's threats seem to have closed down their exchange).[6] Then there were the resilient Cath-olic booksellers, led by the rugged figure of James Malone, bookseller and freeman since 1672, a Jacobite alderman and King's printer, who was dis-enfranchised in 1696; he too managed to survive and was quietly restored to free status by his guild a couple of years later, although he was never far from the margins of legality (being imprisoned in 1703 for publishing the *Memoirs of King James II*, and in 1708–9 for printing Catholic prayer-books). But he remained a formidable presence on High Street until he retired from business in 1718.[7]

The status of Catholic traders and craftsmen in other Irish cities was at least as precarious as in the capital, but Dublin must have seemed par-ticularly hostile given its devotion to King William: dinners to celebrate his birthday (from 1690), a monument in the Tholsel (in 1692), a hugely expensive livery collar in gold for the Lord Mayor (ordered in 1697) and, most famously, an equestrian statue of the king (commissioned in 1700). Later times interpreted this as emblematic of Protestant Dublin's triumphant loyalism and its pungent anti-Catholicism, but this is mis-leading. William in the later stages of his reign was not uniformly popular in Protestant Ireland (both because of the Treaty and his promotion of foreign favourites), and he became distinctly unpopular in England, given the massive burdens of the war and his personal charmlessness; no English city moved to celebrate William in his lifetime in the way that Dublin did.

The splendid golden collar seems to have been an initiative of the then Lord Mayor, Bartholomew van Homrigh, the last of the city's great Dutch merchants, but the commissioning of the statue is more puzzling. Agreed almost as an afterthought in the Assembly in January 1700, the commission was given to the top sculptural workshop in London, that of Grinling Gibbons. The first plan was that it should grace the new Corn Market in Thomas Street, but in July 1700 it was decided to mount the metal statue on a plinth in the street outside Chichester House (with the stone taken from a demolished city gate). A year later it was unveiled. During that time Chichester House was home not to the Irish Parliament but to parliamentary commissioners appointed by Westminster to re-possess and sell the Jacobite forfeited estates, which in the 1690s had been given by the king to sundry favourites and clients. Most of these had been sold on to Irish purchasers – who now stood to lose their bargains. Their discomfiture was part of a wider resentment in Dublin at the ever more assertive English Parliament in Irish affairs. We can assume that the statue's unveiling, by design or coincidence, was something of an embarrassment to the powerful knot of Englishmen at work in Chichester House who sought to undo the king's largesse.[8]

Among the counsellors representing the threatened Irish purchasers of forfeited estates was Sir Toby Butler, the former Jacobite Solicitor General, one of the authors of, and a beneficiary from, the Treaty of Limerick. Like others protected by the treaty, he continued to function as one of the most prominent and successful barristers in the city – until he was excluded from court work by the Popery Act of 1704, which he had courageously sought to halt by appearing as one of the petitioners at the bar of the Commons. Butler died a wealthy Catholic in 1721, but there were many in his social world, notably men trained for the bar, who for prudential reasons began to conform to the established church after 1704 (including his son and heir; Viscount Fitzwilliam of Merrion; and one of the Jacobite Lord Mayors, Sir Michael Creagh).[9] The *converso* lawyers, Protestant but with a large Catholic cousinage and generally Tory in their instincts, became one of the distinctive new ingredients of the eighteenth-century city.

Despite the banishment of the higher clergy in 1697, there was, it seems, always a Catholic bishop resident in or around the city from 1694. Their presence was necessarily discreet: Archbishop Byrne (1706–23) went into hiding on at least four occasions and was arrested twice, albeit for short periods when there were invasion scares or rumours of plots, but at other times he made 'publicly his visitations with his chaise and retinue, without any question or interruption'.[10] The Catholic Church in the city continued to function in a pastoral capacity, strengthened by several intellectually able and continentally trained clergy, notably Cornelius Nary (parish priest of St Michan's for forty years) who enjoyed de facto toleration and even some access to the political world. However, the status of the Catholic Church and of its higher clergy was hugely compromised from 1691 by their unwavering association with the exiled Jacobite court, and the existence of this link sustained the parliamentary appetite for additional penal laws until at least the 1720s. Even more damaging for the urban infrastructure of the Church was the eclipse of its lay patrons in the city, as Catholic merchants, lawyers and gentlemen lost ground or changed their religious allegiance. The most famous such case was the merchant and banker Sir Thomas Hackett, the wealthiest Catholic trader before the wars and Lord Mayor in 1687–8. He was outlawed in 1689 and lost all his personal estate and business as a result. The disposal of his large landed estate, spread across three counties, was a tortuous affair, but its knock-down sale for £15,000 in 1708–9 gives some hint of his former power.[11]

The post-Jacobite city was a more emphatically Protestant town than at any time since the 1650s. The refugees who fled in 1688 seem to have returned fairly quickly, and there were other processes at work reinforcing the city's Protestant character. First, the more intense discrimination against Catholics widened opportunities for the younger sons of Protestant families coming from outside the city to take up trade apprenticeships or to enter the higher professions, particularly in those sectors of the urban economy which benefited from upper-class patronage. The more frequent sitting of the Irish Parliament, the growth in legal business and the anchoring of a large and comparatively well-paid military population in the city generated a very substantial growth in the demand for those goods and services which were now mainly controlled by Protestant merchants and masters.

Secondly, there was now a re-energised established church, led by Narcissus Marsh, the former College provost and archbishop of Dublin from 1694. Aware of the acute challenges to the status of Anglicanism in England and its eclipse in Scotland, Marsh became the most purposeful church leader in the city since Cromwell's time. Thanks to him, legislation was passed in 1695 to tighten up sabbath observance, and he encouraged clergy to expand their ministry in the city with more frequent services, more regular visiting of all households, and an active policing of sabbath practices by all citizens – inconveniencing not least the bakers, the tavern-keepers and their clients. Following a London precedent, there was something of a moral crusade for several years, orchestrated by a group of about ten Protestant 'sodalities'; these communities busied themselves in prosecuting cases involving public swearing, sabbath recreation and prostitution. Anglicans and dissenters were involved in this sudden reforming impulse, coloured as it was by the war and their sense of providential purpose in its outcome. But as the crusade turned to the policing of religious opinions, it splintered the ranks of non-conformity, the most startling instance coming in 1703 with the prosecution of Thomas Emlyn, minister of the Wood Street Presbyterian congregration, for blasphemous libel (a common-law offence), on the grounds that he had questioned the doctrine of the Trinity in print. Two archbishops joined the court of Queen's Bench in his trial, which culminated in a thousand-pound fine (later remitted) and some two years in jail. The foreman of the jury (to his great discomfiture) was the old Presbyterian Humphrey Jervis.[12]

Thirdly, there was the Huguenot influx. Nearly all the French and Walloon-speaking Protestants who settled in the city were part of *le grand refuge*, the last and largest diaspora of French Protestants that had begun in the 1680s as tens of thousands left Louis XIV's increasingly repressive regime. The earlier trickle of Huguenots reaching Dublin had generally consisted of merchants and their families, but as the flow expanded in the early 1680s, crafts people arrived, usually coming via London and encouraged by the offer of civic freedom. The trickle became a flood after 1691, with army veterans and their families and a diverse range of skilled artisans arriving from a variety of European resting points, but most originating from southern and south-western France. The post-Boyne surge came about for several reasons: a consequence of the large Huguenot representation in the Williamite army in Ireland; the statutory concession by the Dublin Parliament in 1692 (ahead of England) of freedom of worship 'in their own several rites' to non-conformist 'Protestant strangers'; and the emergence of the Huguenot general, Henri Massue, marquis de Ruvigny, the hero of the Williamite campaign in Ireland and the king's favourite Frenchman. He was appointed commander-in-chief in Ireland in 1692 and created earl of Galway in 1697, becoming then – in effect if not name – viceroy of Ireland. Galway's power and influence in the last years of the century facilitated and sustained the migration of his countrymen, although his prominence does not account for its sheer scale and diversity. Raymond Hylton has estimated that Dublin attracted roughly half of all Huguenot settlers in Ireland, and that from a pre-war peak of somewhat over 400 in the city, there were over 2,000 by 1700 and perhaps 3,600 by 1720 – which would imply that well over 5 per cent of the city's population were culturally French in the early eighteenth century.[13] Almost as remarkable as the scale of this settlement was the fact that it happened so peacefully. There had been some tension before the wars, notably on May Day 1682 when a gathering of 300 apprentices west of the city had to be broken up by the Royal Guard before they attempted to 'turn out the French Protestants', but there is no evidence of trouble in the 1690s.[14] Part of the explanation is the very diversity of the immigrants, from high-status *rentiers* and pension-holders to grocers and watch-makers. Also it is clear that there was very considerable disunity among the francophone settlers, not least between the conformist and non-conformist congregations (there were four in all by 1700). And while the modern belief is that Dublin's Huguenots were mostly silk-weavers, living mostly in the south-western Liberties, neither assumption is true: by 1700 Huguenots were spread across the city, featuring most strongly in the south-east neighbourhoods, and relatively few were involved in textile manufacture. By contrast, their supposed association with gold and silver is indeed borne out: over a fifth of all the masters of the goldsmiths' guild in 1706 bore Huguenot names.[15]

The Huguenot inflow bears comparison with the surge of New English settlers in Wentworth's time sixty years before. Whatever the difference in absolute numbers, on each occasion there were two distinct groups of new arrivals: high-status households *and* the attendant craftsmen and providers of luxury services. As we have seen, the upper-class households that had first made their mark in the 1630s reappeared and expanded in complexity in Restoration Dublin, but what was new about the 1690s was the concentrated demand from an essentially aristocratic network of displaced families who sought the specific goods and services to which they were accustomed. The purchasing power of this *noblesse d'épée* came, initially at least, from their army and royal pensions and from whatever rental income they were able (covertly) to have remitted from the French properties that they had abandoned.

The prolonged duration of war in Europe in this era solidified the French community in Dublin and allowed some of them to make a real impact on the city. Elie Bouhéreau, a Huguenot pastor from La Rochelle and the earl of Galway's political secretary, was the first to achieve local prominence when he took charge in 1703 of a remarkable institution that had just been completed in the shadow of St Patrick's Cathedral and was subsequently known as Marsh's Library. The initiative and funding of a library for 'public use, where all might have free access' had been Narcissus Marsh's idea, his ambition being to create a more educated clergy and Protestant laity, and in appearance and design the library pointed to Oxford, Marsh's alma mater, as its inspiration. But it was thanks to the much-travelled Bouhéreau, his book collections and his organisational skills, that the library was successfully established as an independent centre of study, strong in recent continental scholarship across the disciplines, a sanctuary where even the likes of Father Nary could work in peace. It became the most tangible expression of the new learning associated with the Dublin Philosophical Society.[16]

Bouhéreau, like most high-caste Huguenots, became an integral part of the local established church. David Digges La Touche (1671–1745), younger son of a minor aristocratic family, had an impact of a different order. Pensioned off after a short military career in 1697, he settled in Dublin under Galway's patronage; within a very short time he was acting as the financial agent for Huguenot officers, Huguenot charities and propertied refugees, skilfully managing to transfer assets into and within Ireland with such success that his reputation for probity and efficency became firmly established. In parallel to this he became a manufacturer and wholesaler of silk and woollen cloth, and was prominent enough by 1708 to be offered (and to refuse) mastership of the Weavers' Guild. His trading activity extended into manufacturing and it is likely that he recruited Huguenot silk-weavers in London. The silk industry, thanks in part to French influence, expanded and prospered in the first decades of the new century, but direct Huguenot involvement did not endure. La Touche's claim to fame rests not on his silks but on his success as a banker and on the speculative uses to which he put his later wealth.[17]

Poverty confronted

Francis Place, a Yorkshire gentleman with unusual talents as a topographical draughtsman and engraver, spent some time in Dublin in 1698–9. His
remarkably crisp ink-drawings of civic buildings are striking in themselves,
but a series of panoramic sketches of the city from the south (near Donnybrook), the west (near Chapelizod) and the north give a unique impression
of the skyline, 'the looming towers, spires and cupola forming a fascinating
mélange of the medieval and the modern'. A Norfolk clergyman, John Verdon, visiting the city the following summer, noted 'the buildings brick and
stately, the streets generally broader than those of London', and reported
that 'all come thither that are able to [afford to] live there, and many come
thither who can live no where else', referring to the Huguenot inflow. Vernon was particularly struck by Lord Galway: 'though a Frenchman, ...[he]
is much valued as an extraordinary govern[or], daily hearing complaints
without difficulty of admission and answering with justice and without
delay ...' What Place's serene drawings and Verdon's comments did not
register was the highly unsettled political atmosphere in the city, the Parliament having just been dissolved and its future status in doubt. One consequence of the progressive encroachment of the English Parliament on
the royal prerogative was the increasing willingness in Westminster to see
the Dublin assembly in firmly subordinate terms.[18]

The political flashpoint came in arguments about the textile trade:
woollen cloth was still England's principal export earner, but the industry
was in some trouble during the 1690s. The blame for depressed overseas
markets was placed (mistakenly) on the success of Irish cloth exporters
(based in Dublin and the Munster ports), and as a consequence there
was a parliamentary groundswell in England to shackle the Irish export
trade. There were, of course, the precedents for such cross-channel legislative intervention going back to 1642 and the Adventurers Act, and to
the Navigation Acts of 1671 and 1685 which had excluded direct Irish
(and Scottish) access to the most profitable trades in the English New
World colonies; English legislation of 1663, 1667 and 1680 had regulated,
then halted, the import of Irish live cattle, and this had had a particularly
severe impact on Dublin at the time.[19] By the 1690s Irish merchants were
exasperated at the progressive erosion of their liberty to trade within the
king's dominions, a process that reflected the superior power of English
lobbies in London to have their way. Total prohibition of Irish woollen

exports now became a real threat and into these troubled waters entered William Molyneux (1656–98), a Dublin lawyer, natural scientist and one of the original architects of the Philosophical Society. An office-holder and MP for Trinity College, he was an insider in the political village of College Green and one of its most respected voices. But his short political essay, *The case of Ireland's being bound by Acts of Parliament in England, stated*, published in Dublin, caused a sensation. It put forward legally grounded arguments to demonstrate that Ireland was no colony but an independent kingdom under the English Crown, an arrangement based on ancient consent, and that the Irish Parliament was thus co-equal with that of Westminster. Such arguments were resented and misinterpreted in London, and they greatly embarrassed his friends. He died suddenly later in the year, yet the arguments were not forgotten. The essay was reprinted nine times in the course of the next century, ensuring that his ideas continued to provide a bracing counter-narrative to the dominant imperial interpretation of Ireland's constitutional status. It was also the first locally produced example of what became a standard form of political debate for a hundred years and more, the relatively cheap octavo or duodecimo pamphlet, often rushed into print, that drew in an ever larger readership.[20]

In the short run, the campaign in London to restrict Irish woollen exports gained momentum, and English and Irish legislation was enacted in 1699 to end the trade. Writers then and thereafter spoke in almost apocalyptical terms of the impact of this action, but in reality the effect on Dublin's economy was modest (the areas more heavily affected were the south Munster towns and their largely Protestant artisans). But because the Acts came just ahead of a very depressed run of years for the whole Irish economy, they were believed in retrospect to have wiped out the post-war recovery. These were years of intense food shortage abroad, especially in Scotland and France, and this had a knock-on effect on local food prices so that there was an upsurge of visible poverty on Dublin's streets. The years of scarcity were the catalyst for the founding in 1704 of the first substantial institution to cater for the poor, the city workhouse. Its establishment was the culmination of a century of haphazard experiment in dealing with poverty.[21]

In the turbulent growth of the seventeenth-century city, poverty had come in many forms, yet the Hobbesian end results were all too similar. From the perspective of the wealthy, great importance was attached to differentiating between the categories of poverty and the gradations of social obligation: freemen in reduced circumstances, their widows and children, had first call on the compassion of the Corporation, just as parishioners in distressed circumstances had first call on the charity of their co-religionists. Other city residents hit by illness or accident had a lesser claim on the consciences of the rich. Abandoned infants were in a special category, even as abandonment became a far more common event. Locally resident beggars – made up of the infirm, the aged and the disabled – were also within the pale of charity. But 'strange' beggars, whether homeless or based in temporary dwellings on the suburban margins of the city, were the dark and frightening side of poverty, the supposed source of petty crime and the actual source of disease at times of rural distress.

Apart from periods of full-scale warfare and siege, the city had coped fairly well with its indigenous poor, but when waves of 'vagrants' entered the city at times of rural food shortage or in the wake of settlement disturbance and plantation, the strangers provoked something approaching panic among the settled citizenry. A sudden inflow had occurred at least once in every peacetime decade during the seventeenth century, each triggering a small flurry of institutional action, but when the crisis passed, things reverted to low-key provision. This involved a variety of approaches: plate money collected at church services was distributed to nominated local paupers (a practice linked to the licensing of known beggars by means of badging); unlicensed beggars were discouraged, sometimes arrested and detained; 'houses of correction' where 'idle' beggars were put to work were established; and small refuges or 'hospitals' to contain the infirm poor and the sick continued a shadowy existence. Welfare activity along these lines could be found in most pre-industrial cities, but what was distinctive in Dublin was the degree to which policies were shaped (or rather restricted) by the latent pressure caused by waves of *rural* paupers – at this stage the poor from the surrounding counties and those displaced by the agrarian changes underway in the hinterland.

The first post-medieval inrush of rural poor into Dublin appears to have been in the first years of the seventeenth century, and between 1603 and 1608 there were several moves to establish houses of correction for beggars and a parish badging system (adapting English precedents). Then, in the wake of the disastrous harvests of the 1620s, there was another burst of energy with three, possibly four, small houses of correction opened in town, two of them on the initiative of the Privy Council. In 1634, the year when the first Irish Poor Law required a house of correction in every county, there was a radical government proposal to establish a 'marshal' with ten armed assistants who would have free range to patrol across the city and suburbs in order to detain and expel beggars. At that time there was still one old refuge for the sick poor, St John's on the western walls, dependent presumably on private benefactions. There is little evidence for the actual operation of any of these initiatives, and all were subsequently overwhelmed by the events of 1641.[22]

A generation later, pressure to tackle begging in the city and to stem the inflow from the countryside prompted Ossory's very ambitious plan in 1669 for a large Corporation hospital and school in Oxmantown but, as we have seen, from the time of its opening the functions of the King's Hospital were restricted to education. The old Jesuit college in Back Lane acted as a hospital for the poor at this time and vagrants were detained with other criminals in the patched-up prison at Newgate on the walls and in the new Bridewell jail in Oxmantown. But the wretched harvests of 1673–4 (when reportedly there were hundreds begging on the streets and many dying) revived former debates. The poor in 1680 were said to 'swarm in the streets and do daily come out of the country p[re]tending themselves to be poor of the city', and in the following year, when Humphrey Jervis was Lord Mayor, he initiated a search for a suitable site for a city workhouse and ordered the parishes to reintroduce badging.[23] In the wake of the great frost of 1683–4, the Corporation agreed to build 'a workhouse and infirmary for the sick, to relieve the city of beggars'. But, tellingly, it was Tyrconnel's government that moved things forward, securing a site south of James Street for a workhouse, strategically located beside the busiest traffic artery into Dublin. It was a gift from King James and the earl of Limerick to the city.[24]

The project languished during the 1690s as ownership of the site became caught up in the legal battles over the forfeited estates, but there were recurring calls from the city Assembly for action against the waves of beggars. In 1703, parliamentary funding was finally secured to build on the James Street site. The preamble of the enabling act spoke of 'the necessities, number and continual increase of the poor within the city of Dublin and liberties ... [which] are very great and burdensome for want of a workhouse to set them at work and a sufficient authority to compel thereto'. The focus of the new institution was to be the marginalised, indigenous, able-bodied population, and there was the promise of 500 places and supervised work for all. Much of the capital costs of the project was raised in a flurry of philanthropy led by the viceroy's consort, the duchess of Ormond, in what was probably the first instance of female leadership of a major charity. City parishes, guilds, the nobility, the higher clergy and 'many hundreds' of others subscribed around £5,000 to the enterprise.[25] Yet when the building was partially opened in 1706, only 124 vagrants could be accommodated; they were joined a year later by some 200 'parish poor', consisting of destitute children over the age of five and of aged and infirm paupers who were on the lists of city parishes.[26]

Less visible than the workhouse but more important in dealing with poverty on the ground were the Church of Ireland parishes, for once Protestant householders became demographically dominant in the city, parish structures – the vestry, the church-wardens and other parish officers – assumed powers and functions theoretically in the control of the Corporation (operating through 'ward' units). Statute law strengthened the powers of the parishes to tax all householders, and in 1665 the east-end parish of St Andrew's secured statutory power to rate its inhabitants for the upkeep of the poor, adapting a central element of the English Poor Law. Other city parishes acted along the same lines as St Andrew's but without enabling legislation, combining their 'cess' income with collection dues: Rowena Dudley has calculated that in St John's parish between 1659 and 1696 38 per cent of its budget for the poor went on weekly doles, 18 per cent on the nursing of abandoned babies and a massive 26 per cent on salaries. In St Bride's parish, the vestry actually built a small poorhouse. Then, in 1695, there was a concerted effort by all city parishes to extend the St Andrew's law nationally, but despite their petition and the involvement of city MPs in drafting enabling legislation, nothing came of it.[27]

It is not clear how far parochial welfare was 'colour blind', or whether alms and institutional support were overwhelmingly directed towards the Protestant poor. It seems likely that at parish level poor Protestants were far better protected than Catholics, but there were no formal denominational restrictions on parish charity or workhouse provision, and Catholic Dubliners featured on some parish poor-lists. In addition, most of the abandoned infants maintained by the parishes and many of the orphaned children entering the workhouse had Catholic parentage (although the workhouse had a subsidiary religious requirement to put the children in its care into service with Protestant artisans).

James Street was soon recognised as a failure. With the able-bodied within it only a minority from the beginning, its mission to become a centre of coercive employment for the work-shy was lost sight of, while among the infirm poor the institution soon gained a notorious reputation. The need for a repository for destitute children and the aged infirm was so pressing that its capacity to accommodate able-bodied paupers was severely restricted. There was much friction between the parishes and the workhouse once its limitations became apparent, with parishes delaying the payment of their share of the workhouse tax. From the early 1720s there was a palpable sense that, once again, beggars, local and rural, had taken over the city's thoroughfares. There were a series of legislative amendments during that decade that modified the workhouse and increased its revenues, but they were replaced by a radical Act of 1730 that obliged the workhouse to accept all infants delivered into its care, to oversee their despatch to wet-nurses, and to take responsibility for their care when they reached two years of age. The legislation followed severe pressure from parish vestries in the city which were struggling with the number of babies abandoned locally.[28] Thus began the Foundling Hospital, an institution that for most of its century-long history was grossly mismanaged and under-funded. More than three-quarters of the thousands of infants that were passed into its care over the next half century perished within its walls or with its nurses. In an era when general infant mortality, especially in urban environments, was itself huge, the massive loss of those in institutional care was far less shocking than it appears in modern retrospect. That said, the litany of criticism directed at the Foundling Hospital later in the eighteenth century reveals the beginnings of a less fatalist attitude towards the city's benighted waifs.[29]

A new bridewell was built next door to the Foundling Hospital in 1730, thus bringing adult vagrants close to but separate from the unwanted orphans. The well-tried methods of local control – the distribution of parish alms (collected from the Sunday plate or after set-piece charity sermons) and the badging of local beggars – were still strongly supported, sometimes with obvious success as in St Patrick's Liberty where Dean Swift was an enthusiast for badging, more often as a stopgap measure in an urban landscape where begging, particularly female begging, was now ever-present. But the capacity of the older parishes to shoulder *any* kind of social responsibility was declining by the mid-eighteenth century because (apart from the burgeoning growth of indigenous pauperism) the wealthier residents of these parishes were beginning to leave and their Catholic character to reassert itself.[30]

*10. The quadrangle of Dr Steevens' Hospital. The hospital was opened
in 1733 with eighty-seven beds, and was the largest medical hospital in
eighteenth-century Dublin. Like nearly all city hospitals of the era, it was
philanthropically funded. The initial building costs were met by the estate
of Richard Steevens, a wealthy late seventeenth-century practitioner.*

But by that stage there had been a quite remarkable transformation
in the range of medical support for poorer citizens. Beginning with the
Charitable Infirmary established in Cook Street in 1718, there were six
comparatively large and philanthropically supported institutions in existence by 1750, all of which put down deep roots: Dr Steevens' hospital
opened not far from the workhouse in 1733; Mary Mercer's hospital for
the sick poor in 1734; the Exchange Street hospital for 'incurables' in 1744;
Dr Mosse's maternity hospital in George's Lane in 1745; and St Patrick's
hospital next door to Dr Steeven's, funded by Swift for the care of the
insane, in 1749. Greater disposable wealth in the city, the pervasive Anglican belief in the centrality of charity in the pursuit of virtue, and shifts
in cultural attitudes towards illness are part of this story, but the failure
of local *public* institutions – at parish, civic and parliamentary levels – to

respond to the periodic collapse of public health within the city or to cope
with the social challenge of swarming vagrancy kept pressure on the well-
to-do to act philanthropically in their own self-interest.[31]

The sinews of trade

The workhouse was designed by the Surveyor-General, Thomas Burgh. A
military veteran with a mathematical turn, he had been Sir William Robinson's understudy since 1697, and there were echoes of the Royal Hospital
in the appearance of the James Street building.[32] Burgh went on to become
the mastermind behind nearly all of the city's public building projects over
a quarter of a century. His largest assignment, and the one that established
his reputation, was the vast complex of buildings that came to be known as
the Royal Barracks. These were constructed on a twenty-acre site west of
the old bowling green between 1703 and 1708, much of it on land that had
been gifted to the 1st duke of Ormond and was now sold by his grandson
and viceroy to the Treasury. The new military campus consisted of four
squares, three of them open towards the river – in all some 300 metres of
unadorned ashlar terracing. Their vertical monumentality created a new
north-western boundary for the city, but they were built with none of the
architectural élan of the Royal Hospital, their purpose being simply to
house two troops of cavalry and two of infantry, some 1,500 men.[33] The
decision to create such a huge military complex that was open both to the
city and the river is at first sight puzzling. There was no equivalent development in any English city, and on the Continent purpose-built military
housing was only constructed within fortified citadels. If such a large military force was required in Dublin, why leave it so unprotected? Part of the
answer is that there was indeed a plan for its protection: the great star-
shaped fortress begun on the duke of Wharton's initiative in 1710, creating a 27-acre enclosure just inside the Phoenix Park overlooking both the
western approaches and the Barracks, was it seems intended primarily as
an impregnable arsenal. The earthen banks of the giant fort were built, but
in 1711 the project was abandoned on cost grounds (a much more compact
Magazine Fort was built nearby in 1734).

However, the principal reason why the Royal Barracks were never fortified was simply that their role was not primarily defensive, but rather it
flowed from the political agreement between Westminster, King William

and the Irish Parliament back in 1697 with the coming of peace. At that point there had been huge pressure in England for rapid demobilisation (both for financial and political reasons), a policy fiercely resisted by the Crown. The compromise was the (English) Disbanding Act of 1699, which placed most of the burden of maintaining an (English) peacetime army on Ireland, and so for the next seventy years Irish taxation paid for a regular military establishment of some 700 officers and 12,000 men in all. Some of these regiments were 'Irish' in that internal control was in the hands of Irish-based colonels, but even in these many of the non-commissioned ranks were recruited from outside Ireland, and until the 1790s all were nominally Protestant. But the whole military establishment was billeted, except in wartime, on Irish soil, with whatever economic and security benefits that might bring. It was this military arrangement that precipitated the great barracks-building programme, and for logistical simplicity much of it was concentrated on the larger towns. Dublin did best of all: the Royal Barracks, which by mid-century had been expanded to hold up to a third of the 12,000 army, created a new micro-economy in the surrounding district to service the needs of man and horse. The Barracks strengthened the role of Smithfield as the great livestock and provender market and stimulated a huge growth in taverns, whiskey shops and prostitution in and around St Paul's parish. But in the longer run the Barracks weakened the attractions of the north-west side of the town for fashionable housing. Stoneybatter became 'a receptacle for wickedness and a harbour for varlots', and even a premium location like Montpelier Hill became inextricably linked with the dubious world of the Barracks. But the officers stationed in Dublin, particularly the Irish-born, fraternised with the genteel classes in their public and private entertainments, and left their mark: it seems that freemasonry was introduced to Dublin in the 1720s by the military, but its appeal widened almost immediately.[34]

Thomas Burgh, as he struggled to complete the Barracks project, was also busy in the heart of town. The Revenue Commissioners had employed him to rebuild the Custom House on its existing confined site, and he produced an impressive four-storey building that seemed to float above the warren of nearby shops and warehouses and to dominate the skyline along the river. Immediately south of the new building stood the large Privy Council chamber, where viceroys and deputies were formally sworn in, and the Treasury offices, where public records were housed. This building (of which we have no image) was entirely destroyed by fire in

April 1711, with great archival loss, and Burgh was immediately employed to construct new quarters for the Council and the Treasury inside Dublin Castle, thereby leaving Essex Street to the merchants.

The new Custom House was also home for the Revenue Commissioners, much the largest arm of civil government since the 1680s when the sub-contraction of tax collection had ended. The Commissioners met there three times a week and, more closely than anybody in the Castle, they monitored the state of the country and in so doing controlled a vast patronage network of over a thousand posts.[35] Irish governments attached huge importance to the business of customs as it constituted the main component of exchequer income, generating far more revenue than property-based taxes or excise, and duties levied specifically on imported goods were the principal element. Insofar as Dublin was the leading point of entry for Irish imports, the policing of the port and its quays became strategically important, the responsibility in the first instance resting with the Collector of the port. This was not a sinecure, and when the politically well-connected Sir John Eccles, a leading Dublin merchant, former Lord Mayor and Collector, got into financial trouble in 1720, even he was promptly dismissed by the Commissioners. At that time there were nearly a hundred men on the Customs payroll in the city, another seventy officers and boatmen based at Ringsend (who oversaw ship movements in the Bay and the trans-shipment of goods between sea-going vessels and lighters), and a further thirty or so along the coast to Dalkey. Judging by the surnames, all but the boatmen were Protestant.[36]

Merchants generated the commercial traffic on which the state depended for its income – and Dublin's merchants were at this stage not particularly wealthy. A few came from families that had been trading for two generations or more, but most were first-generation residents, operating without local partners and doing much of their business on the account of overseas traders, their profit coming from commission charged on the purchase or sale of an agreed stock of goods. But the distinct status of a 'merchant', the wholesale trader who dealt beyond the seas, was universally recognised: most were freemen of the Guild of Merchants, but neither the guild nor the Corporation acted in the name of the merchant body as had once been the case. There were two reasons for this growing divergence: the complete exclusion of Catholic traders from full guild membership after 1692, and the progressive exclusion of Presbyterian, Baptist and Quaker merchants after the Test Act of 1704. The number of Catholic merchants involved in overseas trade was by this time quite small, but the number of non-conformist traders had mushroomed: Joseph Damer and Humphrey Jervis were still around to see their Presbyterian co-religionist Thomas Bell become lord mayor in 1702–3, and also to see him surrender his place as City Treasurer and alderman a year later after his refusal to take the new sacramental test. Benjamin Burton, banker, dissenter and Lord Mayor of the city in 1706–7 was similarly debarred in 1709.[37]

There were perhaps 150 to 200 merchants who had regular business in Burgh's Custom House when it first opened. By the mid-eighteenth century there was about double that number. Within this large group were some specialists, but the age of wholesale specialisation lay in the future. Small firms with one or two principals, a string of apprentices and a few book-keepers would have been the norm, many with limited capital, a short business life and a vulnerability to the huge vagaries of uncertain markets, unrecoverable debts, fraud and uninsured losses. Each merchant house built up an expertise in certain lines of foreign trade and, more crucially, a small portfolio of trusted correspondents beyond the horizon, often relatives, marriage connections or simply co-religionists. It was appropriate that the one exclusively merchant-run association to emerge at this time, the Ouzel Galley Society, playfully adopted the nomenclature and accoutrements of a trading vessel (it had come into existence *c*.1700 to resolve a dispute over an insured galley lost in the Mediterranean, which inconveniently reappeared some years after the underwriters had paid out). The Society survived for almost two centuries as an informal agency for dispute resolution within the merchant community at large.[38]

Merchant firms grew in number as the scale of Dublin's overseas trade grew. Taking the decennial average, the recorded tonnage of vessels discharging at Dublin during the 1740s was rather more than double that of the 1700s, a growth rate of just under 2 per cent p.a. This was probably ahead of population growth in the city and it came at a time when many other Irish ports were in the doldrums. War and the Restoration Navigation Acts (which had prohibited direct Irish importation of tobacco and sugar from the colonies) had had a disproportionate impact on smaller ports like Galway and Belfast, and only Dublin and Cork enjoyed sustained growth in customs revenue between the 1690s and 1750. In the case of Cork, the port's prosperity rested on its huge export trade in beef, butter and woollen yarn, whereas in the capital's case the focus was the importation of higher value goods (ranging from fashion fabrics, wines and tobacco to industrial raw materials like silk thread, hardwood and unrefined sugar), and it was this import-led commerce that gave Dublin such an ascendancy. Most of the high-value imports were now coming the short journey from English and Scottish west-coast ports – Glasgow, Liverpool, Chester and Bristol – and in addition there was the huge coal trade from Whitehaven and the Ayrshire ports which was also focused on Dublin and its domestic needs. Aggregate customs returns give us the best long-run perspective on these processes: back in the late 1630s, as we have seen, Dublin's share of national customs climbed to around 40 per cent of the Irish total; in the 1660s the proportion was almost identical; by 1681–2 it had fallen back somewhat. But after the Jacobite war Dublin's dominance became even more pronounced: in 1700, 46 per cent of the national customs duties were collected in Dublin, and for the first quarter of the eighteenth century it averaged 55 per cent, stabilising around that point for another fifty years.[39]

The first step towards such commercial dominance had been Dublin's emergence as the undisputed centre of internal Irish communication. This can be seen in several ways: in the 1660s, a rudimentary postal service had been established, linking a network of post-houses in the main towns with a post office in Dublin's High Street as national hub. In the later seventeenth century the city achieved a near-monopoly in the provision of wholesale financial services, specifically in offering a market in bills of exchange 'on London', the means whereby funds (e.g. rents) could be remitted to England and beyond, and external commercial debts and credits settled. Restoration goldsmiths, money-lenders, and speculative merchants like Abel Ram, Thomas Hackett and Joseph Damer, had been critical in the early days, but their kind of trade was becoming archaic by 1700, their place being taken by specialist bill dealers, i.e. 'bankers' in a narrower sense, who first emerged in the 1690s (with Burton and Harrison, William and Alexander Cairnes, and Thomas Putland among the earliest). And although there were separate bill trades between Cork and London, the Dublin–London axis grew much stronger from the beginning of the eighteenth century.

From that time there were up to eight banking businesses in Dublin regularly creating and dealing in bills of exchange, so that provincial traders and the out-of-town estate agents of absentee landowners saw the capital (via its nexus with London) as by far the most reliable and usually the cheapest place in Ireland to negotiate the transfer of internal

Irish, Anglo-Irish and foreign debts and credits. The turbulent and often depressed economic conditions of the early eighteenth century helped cement Dublin's financial status, and to be 'as safe as Ben Burton' became the conventional compliment in trade – until his bank collapsed in 1733.[40] By then the main Dublin banks, operating from fixed premises, were issuing their own promissory notes when discounting bills of exchange. Indeed, the huge growth of paper money issued against the credit of a small number of apparently powerful individuals appalled the likes of Swift and Bishop Berkeley, and Swift more than once savaged the MP and banker Sir Alexander Cairnes. It did not help in their estimation of banks and banking that nearly all the Dublin money-dealers had the strong smell of religious dissent about them. In addition to old Joseph Damer, Ben Burton and his partner Francis Harrison were dissenters, the Huguenot David La Touche's partner Nathaniel Kane was a Presbyterian, as were the Cairnes brothers Alexander and William; Hugh Henry was son of the minister of the Capel Street congregation, and Joseph Fade and his banking partners were all Quakers. The opening in 1728 of a very handsome six-bay Presbyterian meeting-house in Eustace Street near the Custom House served to emphasise the wealth and new self-confidence of city dissent, with its strong northern flavour.[41]

Northern influence in the city was growing sharply, with an Ulster mafia of traders first evident in the 1690s. The importation of French wine, for example, came to be dominated not by Huguenots or Catholics but by Protestant merchants with strong Ulster links who built up family connections in the Charente.[42] But the principal pathway of northern influence was the linen trade. From the time of Wentworth and the 1st duke of Ormond to the viceroys a century later, sponsorship of flax cultivation and linen production had been the *idée fixe* when creative thinking on Irish economic development was required. Back in the 1660s there had been one highly ambitious project to develop linen manufacturing near Dublin when Richard Lawrence, the Baptist entrepreneur who became Ormond's confidante, built a Dutch-style manufactory at Chapelizod, but this was a hothouse initiative entirely dependent on official contracting. There were signs of a more sustainable linen industry with export prospects emerging in rural east Ulster before the Jacobite war, but the critical development was the removal of English customs duties on Irish linen in 1696 (at a time when tariffs on rival continental linens were being raised). This handed Irish producers a strategic advantage within the English market and opened the way for linen to become the great industrial success story of eighteenth-century Ireland.

Dublin contributed to that success in several crucial ways: it became the unrivalled national marketplace for whitened linen in the 1690s and held that position for almost a century, during which time exports from the city rose from less than half a million yards p.a. to nearly 22 million in the 1790s. This found physical expression in the Linen Hall, Thomas Burgh's final public assignment constructed during the 1720s at the behest of the Linen Board Trustees, a parliamentary body established in 1711 to promote and regulate the linen trade. Burgh's vast quadrangular trading hall, which eventually contained over 500 small rooms, 'like cells in the gallery of a convent', was constructed on a green-field site on the northern edge of the city beyond Capel Street. It created another micro-economy on the north side embracing a network of new streets – their names, Bolton and Dorset, Lisburn and Lurgan, Coleraine and Derry, are indicative – and there the needs of myriad dealers and carters who flocked to the Hall were amply catered for. Subsidies were given towards the construction of a number of linen bleaching and printing yards on well-watered suburban sites (there were at least a dozen textile printing yards in an arc around the city from Ballsbridge to Drumcondra). Several of these printing yards remained active for decades, producing fashionable drapes exclusively for the Irish market. By contrast, the thousands of webs of plain white linen that passed through the Hall were mainly destined for export – to Chester, London and the colonies beyond. This business was choreographed from Dublin, not because of the Linen Board or statutory interventions, but because it was Dublin credit and Dublin merchants who underpinned the various transactions in the trade, involving the importers of flax seed, the vast country trades in yarn, brown linen (sold by weavers to Ulster bleachers), and the whitened linen sold to Dublin merchants and exporters. The practice grew up for the Dublin dealers to give seasonal credit to the Ulster bleachers, allowing them to make cash purchases in the brown linen markets, and this facility endured for most of the eighteenth century, giving the city substantial leverage over the Ulster economy. That said, most of those Dublin dealers were themselves originally northerners or had strong personal connections with the North. The success of the linen trade helps explain the pervasive influence of Ulster on eighteenth-century Dublin.[43]

Contests and shadows

Another Protestant Ulsterman, William King, dominated the city in a different sphere. After thirteen years as Church of Ireland bishop of Derry, he succeeded Marsh as archbishop of Dublin in 1703 and held the position for a quarter of a century. A formidable administrator, he was also a great political survivor, ever vociferous in the House of Lords and the Privy Council, a conservative rather than a partisan figure. In later years he regularly served as a Lord Justice during viceregal absences. His importance for the city lay in his relentless determination to strengthen the primacy of the established church within public life and to defeat those that would subvert it, specifically Presbyterians, lay and clerical. A disciplinarian with no desire for personal enrichment, he was a combative force in church and state. He engaged in an unprecedented building programme, claiming credit in his first ten years in Dublin for seventeen new or rebuilt churches across the diocese and for the repair of a similar number. New churches in the city followed the creation of additional city parishes, first after the division by his predecessor of St Michan's on the north side into three units in 1697 (creating a new parish of St Paul's to the west and St Mary's to the east), then a decade later a new Liberties parish, St Luke's, and two new parishes in the south-eastern quadrant of the city carved out of St Peter's – St Ann's and St Mark's. Civil as well as ecclesiastical units, the new parishes gave delayed recognition of the changing geography of the city. King championed the statutory strengthening of the civic powers of the parish unit through the medium of the vestry (in theory the taxing authority representing all cess-paying parishioners), and he searched ceaselessly for funds, both private and public, to improve the stock of churches and the tithe income of the incumbent clergy.[44]

St Mary's, begun in 1700, was the first of several fashionable northside churches, on a par socially with St Ann's (a stone's throw from St Stephen's Green) that was begun *c.*1710. Larger urban estate-owners helped (not least for commercial advantage), Jervis in the case of St Mary's, Joshua Dawson in the case of St Ann's, but where landlord support was not forthcoming, as in the case of St Mark's (which spanned the south quays and the Lazers Hill district), it took almost half a century to complete the parish church. King also oversaw the reconstruction of two of the most prestigious old parish churches, St Michan's and St Werburgh's. Thomas Burgh was responsible for the latter, designing a heavy, almost

Roman, façade with a tall incongruous steeple. King was anxious that his churches should pierce the skyline, but he 'was no connoisseur' and for all his prodigious energy the buildings he left behind were incomplete, some-times ungainly, and no match for the sublime chapel at Kilmainham.[45]

During King's long episcopacy, Dublin was more than ever dom-inated by the Parliament in its midst. During Anne's reign, Westmin-ster issues became Dublin issues – how was a Protestant succession to be guaranteed and the lurking threat of Jacobite revival to be countered; how was the succession of interminable European wars to be brought to an advantageous conclusion; how were the depressed economies in the three kingdoms to be stimulated; and which of the two party coalitions, the court-favoured Tories or the 'patriotic' Whigs, would dominate in the years ahead? The feverish state of high politics had a perceptible impact on the fledgling public sphere in the city. This was evident by the appearance shortly after 1700 of a number of partisan newsletters. Locally generated print was for the first time carrying political controversy from the narrow sphere of Parliament into the new coffee-houses, and newspaper printers had for the first time to protect themselves from the wrath of Parliament.[46] The city after 1710 became directly enmeshed in the 'rage of party' when the Castle was in Tory hands, the Commons increasingly Whiggish and Dublin Corporation similarly disposed. For some, memories of Jacobite times were revived as Constantine Phipps, the Lord Chancellor, 'running about like a roaring lion ... devouring the liberties and privileges of the city', deployed the law to try and silence his Whig opponents.[47] The flashpoint was in 1711 when a dispute began over the succession to the lord mayoralty, after the refusal by the (Tory) Privy Council to accede to the choice of the aldermen, invoking powers from 1672 and 'the new rules'. It was a bruis-ing battle that ran for nearly three years, and was marked by weak com-promises, interventions from London and finally a complete breakdown in city government in 1713–14 when the Tory Lord Mayor continued by default in office for a second year. The Tholsel courts were suspended for months, there was no oversight of municipal markets and other city ser-vices collapsed. Then a general election was called in the autumn of 1713, the government expecting a more malleable Commons. For the city it was probably the first public contest for Parliament and it was ugly: there were violent scuffles at the Tholsel during the poll, and the Whig sheriffs had to summon military assistance. There was one fatality. The Whigs dur-ing the election had caricatured the government's supporters as papists and Jacobites, the Tories abusing their opponents as 'sectaries', Puritans or Commonwealth men. There were significant numbers of Catholic free-holders registered to vote and one well-known Cork Jacobite, James Cotter, was centrally involved in the Tholsel riot, but the electoral significance of Catholics was exaggerated. And, despite the efforts of the government's allies, the outgoing Whig candidates, Ben Burton and the former Speaker John Forster, were re-elected.[48]

The succession of George of Hanover in August 1714 passed off peacefully, however. Dublin's aldermen had backed the right horse, and for the next generation they basked in a generally comfortable relationship with Parliament and Castle. As champions of a Protestant monarchy and the supposed liberties associated with 1688, the Corporation commissioned an equestrian statue of George I in 1722, placing the bronze sculpture on a stone pier midstream in the Liffey and attached to Essex Bridge ('a masterstroke' of location, allowing the king's image to oversee the port area). Most Protestant citizenry who cared to consider the matter accepted the Hanoverian succession, the Tories amongst them suffering loss of status or worse, while all but the most *politique* Catholics retained some measure of allegiance to James III in exile. But the news in 1715 that the recently departed viceroy and military hero, the 2nd duke of Ormond, had fled London and joined the Jacobite court in exile probably caused the greatest frisson. His long exile (he died in 1745) was a pathetic end to the dynasty.[49]

The early Hanoverian viceroys were birds of passage who made little mark on the city. It was a time when many of the high offices of state – on the bench and in the Church of Ireland – went to English-born appointees, some arriving as part of the Whig clear-out of Tory areas of influence, some because of a compromised political past in England. Spokesmen for Irish landowners were not slow to bemoan this evidence of London's strengthening control over Irish patronage as plumb positions in the various spheres of Crown service passed to new faces. But against this, a most intriguing figure came to the top as one of the power-brokers within the Irish Parliament: William Conolly, an Ulsterman of Catholic background, a barrister, land speculator and MP for almost four decades. Conolly, like Archbishop King, was a compulsively energetic 'man of business' who by his own guile and industry became one of the wealthiest landowners in the country by the 1720s. Most of his life was spent in and around the city, in the Four Courts, in Chichester House and within his palatial quarters at the north end of Capel Street. He was close to the Presbyterian world, well represented in that quarter of town, but he remained an Anglican. His political star had risen when the Whiggish duke of Wharton had been in the Castle (1709–10); he had then become a Revenue Commissioner and one of the strong men in the Commons, only to become the enemy of Phipps and the subsequent Tory government. After 1714 he emerged again and (together with the Cork-based Alan Broderick) was chief 'undertaker' of government business in the House of Commons, heading a phalanx of northern MPs. He became both Speaker of the House and principal figure in the Revenue Commission. Among his many property acquisitions was land to the south of the city, Rathfarnham Castle, and west of it at Celbridge, where in the 1720s he set about the largest domestic building project in Irish history, Castletown House.[50]

Unlike many in his circle, Conolly did not involve himself in city land speculation. Yet in his final years he profoundly changed the look of Dublin by securing funding for a new Parliament building. The decision to demolish Chichester House, given its congested and decayed state, and to hollow out the site behind neighbouring houses on College Green, was hardly controversial. But the scale of the project (it eventually cost about £30,000), its design and the materials used were quite startling. Nothing in the heart of the city, associated with the Castle, the courts or the Crown was remotely comparable. Edward Lovett Pearce, a young and well-connected half-pay officer and MP, displaced the ageing Thomas Burgh in securing the commission, helped not a little by his friendship with Conolly. The new Surveyor-General, unlike his predecessors, was an artist in stone. He still awaits a biographer, but we know that he toured extensively in northern Italy earlier in the decade, carefully examining some of the canonical buildings of the Renaissance landscape and that, back in Ireland, he aggressively sought the Parliament project. With the assistance of a superb draughtsman and understudy, Richard Castle, he brought the building from a foundation stone in 1729 to occupancy thirty-two months later, employing, it seems, a mix of indigenous and English craftsmen in the process. Precisely because it was such a delicately constructed building and so informed by architectural theory, it was in aesthetic terms a revolutionary event. As Edward McParland has observed:

> Here, in the Parliament House, was the novelty of an Irish architect justifying his design with explicit appeals to Vitruvius and Palladio.

*11. Although this early view of the principal front of the Parliament House is
attributed to the architect Edward Lovett Pearce, this is unlikely as in several
respects it is inaccurate (notably in misplacing the site of King William's
statue). But it does suggest the dramatic impact that Pearce's new building
must have had, both by its precise application of classical architectural
principles as then understood, and by its sheer monumentality.*

Here was the first external free-standing colonnade in Dublin ... and
the first marriage of [English] Portland stone and [Irish] granite which
was to become the characteristic medium for monumental Dublin
architecture into the nineteenth century.[51]

It was indeed an old man's commission and a young man's building. Inside,
the layout centred on the octagonal Commons chamber, with seats for over
90 per cent of its 300 members, and the main vista closed by the Speaker's
chair. The Lords chamber by contrast was a much smaller and more intimate space. Conolly had a direct say in this elevation of the Commons, truly
a riposte in stone to the notorious English Declaratory Act of 1720 (which
had formally articulated Westminster's right to legislate for Ireland and
to act as a court of final appeal in Irish civil litigation). The Irish Parliament had now acquired a building of great symbolic power, unarguably
the finest secular building in the kingdom. Its scale, visual impact and aesthetic success, at rest on its great open site in College Green, played a part,

at some level, in fostering the gentry-dominated political culture of civic patriotism that emerged in the next generation. But by the time the new Parliament House opened in 1731 Conolly was dead, and before it was fully completed its progenitor Pearce had also died. He was still in his thirties.[52]

The new building had been conceived at a time of pervasive negativity, at least in public discourse about the state of the country. It is possible that one of Conolly's motives for such a great project in the heart of the capital city was to stimulate the economy, just as his great palace at Castletown was regarded as much a great public-works initiative as it was an exercise in conspicuous personal consumption. The 1710s had brought some good years for the city, but the 1720s were grim: credit crises (the side effects of the South Sea Bubble in 1720), intermittent bad harvests, severe floods in 1725–6, recurring problems in the money supply, and unprecedented bouts of unemployment, most tangibly affecting the city's thousands of woollen weavers.[53] There was now mounting evidence that the growth of the economy was having markedly regressive effects on income distribution in the countryside. This gave rise to a gathering sense of social unease which found expression in some of the century's most perceptive writings by disparate members of the political class. The writer with far and away the greatest impact was the Dean of St Patrick's, Jonathan Swift. His pamphlet essays, from the *Proposal for the universal use of Irish manufacture* in 1720 to his *Modest proposal* in 1729, contained a surfeit of witty conceits and ironical, often scabrous assaults on English commercial legislation, on the follies of the Irish rich (both male and female), indeed, on the iniquities of all who held power. And while Swift's writings may have lacked economic insight, their allegorical language shaped the humour of the times.

It was most evident in the battle over the small-denomination copper coinage. This was introduced in 1723 by the Irish government, ostensibly to address an acute shortage of small change, but the move was characterised by its critics as no more than an ingenious way for a royal mistress in London to profit at the expense of the Irish public, forced to use debased small coin supplied by a Birmingham iron-founder, William Wood, who had paid generously for his patent. The ensuing controversy split Irish-based supporters of the government but united most of the parliamentary world, and it was a seminal moment for the city in at least two respects. It is the first time that we can see a print-driven public controversy emanating from Dublin and attracting attention across the country; folk in

Cork waited to hear of the latest developments, and the Dublin newspapers became heavily involved. The most remarkable intervention (if perhaps not quite as critical to the outcome as has often been claimed) was that by 'the drapier', the honest Liberties cloth-dealer, whose voice Swift assumed in his seven letters on the coin. There was a scurry of excitement as each of his letters came off the press; members of the Privy Council were reduced to getting copies from hawkers inside the Castle. It was probably the first occasion when the outcome of a policy dispute was determined by forces lying beyond the control of government or the parliamentary power-brokers – the Conollys, the Brodericks and their allies. Opposition to such a tangible thing as base money was of course relatively easy to mobilise, and it was not until the 1750s that extra-parliamentary hostility welled up again.[54]

City printers in the 1720s and 1730s produced a stream of pamphlet essays written by members of the parliamentary world, which debated the economic malaise and the failures of public policy. A few of these were very widely read, including Robert Molesworth's *Some considerations for the promoting of agriculture and employing the poor* in 1723, and Samuel Madden's *Reflections and resolutions proper for the gentlemen of Ireland* (1738). The scarcity of coin in circulation and the pervasive problem of rural poverty were the principal matters of debate, and apart from the conventional belief in the idleness of the lower classes, writers tended to focus on political explanations – the mercantilist trade policies of Westminster and the constitutional downgrading of the Irish Parliament. But others pointed to the rise of predatory landlords profiting from the export boom in cattle and sheep products at the expense of their tenants, or simply negligent landlords living far away from their estates. In this context, Madden, a south Ulster cleric, argued that 'even living in Dublin is a custom that has many ill consequences ... it is ruinous to moderate fortunes and hurtful to the greatest, if we take their children into account'. While not as economically damaging as residence in England, living it up in Dublin, he argued, had all the negative social effects of absenteeism. Urban prosperity in any form was represented in negative terms. Bishop Berkeley was the most provocative here, linking conspicuous consumption with poverty, holding up the folly of importing sugars and silks, wines and fine coaches into a land where the basic food supply was precarious, thanks to the depopulating effects of pastoralism. Urban poverty was not the primary issue of these writers, although several pointed to the growth of unemployment among weavers affected by the apparent surge in English imports. But the complete dependence of Dublin on English coal to heat its citizenry and on English hops and increasingly English beer to sustain its lower classes seemed further evidence of a world out of kilter.[55]

These ideas took practical form after the wretched harvests and food scarcities of the later 1720s. A group of fourteen men, six of them past or sitting MPs, established an association to debate practical ideas for agricultural and wider economic reform, to publish these ideas aggressively, and to lobby for their implementation. The association became known as the Dublin Society; it was a busy, relatively apolitical group, adept at using print to publicise their ideas, and it survived to become part of the institutional landscape of the city, thanks in large part to the self-belief and perseverance of a core group behind the idea, notably a small Midlands landlord, Thomas Prior, and Samuel Madden. Despite the initial focus on rural reform, its name was not misleading: it remained an entirely city-based group close to and sponsored by the parliamentary establishment, and in its second generation it championed city economic improvement more directly, notably in textiles, brewing and the plastic arts.[56]

Out of the malaise of the 1720s also came two transport initiatives of long-term significance for Dublin. Following English precedent, Parliament placed the public roads to Kilcullen and to Navan in 1729 in the hands of trustees with powers to levy tolls in return for bearing the responsibility to maintain and improve them. This led to the first of dozens of Turnpike acts over the next century; tolling the main roads improved their standard and facilitated the transit of wheeled-goods traffic to and from the city. It also marked the beginnings of the commercialisation of passenger movement; the first scheduled stagecoach services began in the 1730s (twice weekly to Drogheda, Kinnegad and Kilkenny).[57] More importantly, it now became public policy to try to wean the country, and specifically Dublin, off English coal. North Kilkenny, east Tyrone and the north Antrim coast all offered prospects of an alternative supply for the urban consumer and the only barrier seemed to be transport costs. The aim was to undercut Whitehaven coal, extracted beside the Cumbrian coast, even if this meant the construction of artificial waterways. Thus the idea was born of a canal from Newry to Lough Neagh to bring Tyrone coal to the hearths of Dublin, followed shortly after with the first plans to drive a canal south-westwards from the city to tap the supposed riches of the Castlecomer plateau. The Ulster canal was duly built with public money between 1729 and 1742, its construction initially overseen by Edward Pearce and then by Richard Castle, but plans for a Leinster canal stretching towards Kilkenny did not begin until 1756, and the first Castlecomer coal only reached Dublin by canal boat around 1780. Both projects failed in their primary objective – to end Dublin's dependence on imported coal – and that was because the anthracite coals of Kilkenny were never suitable for the domestic hearth, and the Tyrone colliery was little more than a chimera.

So why were scarce public resources over the decades pumped into canal-building? There were several reasons: contemporaries were aware of instances, notably in the Dutch Republic and later in England, where canal construction had brought demonstrable economic benefits, both in the movement of bulk goods and of passengers. There was a sense that the prosperity of Dublin was held back by the fact that its river was not navigable beyond the western suburbs, which an artificial navigation would compensate for. And insofar as the argument centred on fuel supplies, there was the general belief in the 1720s and 1730s that the shortage of coin and high cost of Anglo-Irish exchange was somehow tied up with the capital's utter dependence on coal from across the sea that was paid for with coin. Lastly, the boisterous skippers of the little coal-boats, none of them Irish, were resented (fairly or unfairly) by everyone in the city as manipulators of supply and architects of scarcity in order to maintain quayside prices, and such resentment was never stronger than in the bitter winters of the late 1720s. An Irish coal supply would break their power.[58]

The most reflective author of new economic ideas in these years was the much-travelled Bishop Berkeley, who returned to Ireland in 1734. Of his many claims to fame, it was in his role as librarian of Trinity College that he had the greatest physical impact on the city. As a young and very precocious fellow of the College in Queen Anne's time, he had charge of the library and its motley collections that had survived the Jacobite occupation of the campus. It was on his watch that the decision was taken in 1711 to fill the southern side of a new post-war College quadrangle with a vast library building; it would far exceed the university's needs. How far Berkeley's advocacy was required for such a bold project is not recorded. Thomas Burgh was involved from the beginning; indeed, this was to be his longest assignment and his greatest achievement. The College was basking in the patronage of its Chancellor and Lord Lieutenant, the 2nd duke of Ormond, when the foundation stone was laid, but after the Hanoverian

12. Joseph Tudor's 1752 panorama stretches from Burgh's library block to the isolated peninsula of Ringsend and a busy Dublin Bay. The library stood on poorly drained land, which is probably the reason why most of the ground floor was arcaded and left open. Beside it (to the right) was Burgh's Anatomy House and laboratory, the site for the very limited practical education offered to medical students.

succession Trinity was initially seen as a dangerous bastion of Tory, even Jacobite, sentiment. Provost Pratt was hustled off by the new government to a northern deanery in 1715 and his deputy, the firmly Whiggish Richard Baldwin, was given full charge of the College. He was to dominate it for nearly four decades, and to help buttress Baldwin's authority Parliament released funds for the completion of the library on a generous scale so that the resulting Long Room was saved from being just another barracks-like bloc. It was fitted out with a fine interior but was only completed *c.*1732. At over £20,000 the final cost was nearly treble the sum estimated by Burgh in 1711.[59]

Despite such a strong statement of intellectual intent, Trinity College was quiescent during that era, little scholarship appearing in print since its ablest fellows resigned after a few years to take up more lucrative careers in the Church of Ireland. The number of students entering the university peaked at around a hundred per annum in the 1720s, but fell back over the next thirty years by more than a third. By then the Dublin Philosophical Society with its close College connections was a distant memory. An awareness of the intellectual fashions in the world outside was far more likely to be found in the informal circles of sociability in the city, many of them of course involving graduates of the College. Two such groups are well documented, the circle of friends associating with Swift – Thomas Sheridan Snr, the Delanys, George Faulkner his publisher, the Pilkingtons – and a very different circle patronised by the former diplomat, Whig partisan and ideologue, Robert Viscount Molesworth, who returned to Ireland and his Swords estate in 1719. He was the champion at different times of Catholic architects, Presbyterian divines and maverick free-thinkers. Local Presbyterian clergy were publishing philosophical material in the *Dublin Weekly Journal*, a weekly paper that in its original format ran for seven years and has some claim to be the city's first literary periodical. One of the Molesworth circle publishing in the *Journal* was Francis Hutcheson, a young Presbyterian cleric. His seminal philosophical work, *An inquiry into the original of our ideas of beauty and virtue* (1725), was composed in Dublin while he enjoyed Molesworth's patronage. For almost a decade Hutcheson ran an academy on Drumcondra Lane, which prepared Presbyterian boys for entry into Glasgow University (an institution in which he was soon to become famous). His essentially optimistic reading of human nature and his belief that innate qualities of altruism and public virtue could be drawn out by education stood in remarkable contrast to the morbid world-view of the author of *Gulliver's travels*, whose allegorical masterpiece was being brought to completion in the same year in the same town.[60]

Noble spaces

Molesworth, the only child of a Cromwellian Dublin merchant and land speculator, had been able to pursue a somewhat maverick career in English politics, thanks to abundant Irish wealth, principally his properties in the city and county of Dublin. These included the Molesworth fields, a block of land lying between St Stephen's Green and Trinity College. On his death in 1725 his sons secured a private Act of Parliament to alter the terms of their inheritance and break it up for development, mainly by means of a new broad street that would point eastwards towards the sea: Molesworth Street. This was soon realised, but not as a tightly controlled development, as a variety of lessee-builders were involved. The street's unusual width copied, indeed slightly exceeded, the longer street running at right angles to it at its western end. That became Dawson Street, the initiative of an

Ulster landowner-cum-officeholder, Joshua Dawson, Under-Secretary at Dublin Castle from 1699 to 1714. On land he had recently acquired, Dawson planned an avenue to follow the rising gradient from the side of the College grounds up to St Stephen's Green, and he secured the legislation to establish St Ann's parish, with its church to lie midway up the avenue and near to his own residence. Building leases were taken up fairly quickly, but come 1714 the Tory Dawson lost office and his official status. He sold his fine house to the Corporation the next year for a princely £3,500. Following London precedent, the city had been seeking a house for the Lord Mayor where the first citizen could entertain court and Parliament in style, and in 1715 they got their mansion.

The Molesworths and Joshua Dawson were part of a small group of ground landlords who profited from the demand for upper-class residential property, first evident in Restoration times but far stronger by the 1720s. Some, like the Molesworths, the Temples, the Fitzwilliams and the earls of Meath, chose to exploit the land they had inherited; others acquired fresh property and actively planned its development. Dawson was in the latter category, but a more dramatic example was the Huguenot banker and trader, David Digges La Touche. Throughout his banking career he was involved in urban property development, first on streets east of the Custom House, then along Grafton Street (at that stage a narrow lane paralleling Dawson Street to the west), but most energetically on the Aungier/Longford estate west of St Stephen's Green, where he was involved in over a hundred transactions between 1720 and 1735. La Touche's preferred method was to lease out carefully demarcated plots to craftsmen-builders (mainly carpenters and bricklayers), then to buy back the lease on completion of the shell and reset the property at a full rent to a residential tenant for a long term of years. Deep pockets were required by such developers to finance the initial acquisition of blocs of development land, to facilitate loans to the craftsmen that might be essential to secure timely completion, and to ensure that the disposal of the completed houses was done in such a way as to maintain rent levels and not flood a weak market. Men in a hurry rarely made a profit in property.[61]

La Touche's counterpart in large-scale development was a Dubliner, probably of Liberties origin, Luke Gardiner. With a rare skill in accounting, a lucky break as secretary in the new Ballast Office (set up by the Corporation in 1708 to oversee the scouring and maintenance of the tidal channel from the Bay to the quays), and a marriage far above his station (in

1711), Gardiner rose to become the key office-holder in the Irish Treasury in 1725 as Receiver and Paymaster-General, which position he secured on the understanding that he would sort out the huge financial mess left by his predecessor. He held this office until his death thirty years later. He also managed to be a Castle Street banker for several years in the 1730s and become the leading urban developer for a generation. Gardiner's power was manifest yet discreet, and his enormous impact on city development was achieved with guile, subtlety and none of the fireworks associated with Humphrey Jervis before him or John Beresford later in the century. He was a property speculator from the time of his marriage, but his major investments only took place when he enjoyed personal control over the idle balances of the state.

He had begun by purchasing a speculative Corporation lease for riverside ground east of Lazers Hill in 1712, his Ballast Office knowledge no doubt an asset. After other small-scale acquisitions, he acquired by means of three strategic purchases nearly the whole of the old St Mary's Abbey estate between 1722 and 1729, including already developed portions where several new streets had been laid out on what was now the north-east side of town. He shared the largest bloc, the Moore/Drogheda estate, with a partner, but was able to buy him out in 1730. Gardiner was the sole initiator of what was the most ambitious north-side development of the era, a new street on rising ground beyond Bolton Street, laid out on a green-field site and close to the small Bradogue river: Henrietta Street. This plan was far more dramatic than the Molesworths' street on the south side. Individual site sizes were much larger and landlord involvement more intimate. Construction of the first houses began *c.*1729, just at the moment when the new Parliament House was beginning across the river (and Pearce was involved with at least one of the Henrietta Street designs). It took more than twenty years for Gardiner's bold plan to be completed, but by the time of his death, two giant terraces of massive houses faced each other, their brick-faced façades (some as broad as sixty feet) in precise alignment, their flat parapets emphasising the cliffs of brick, and their vast interiors displaying a level of architectural and decorative sophistication that established new standards and novel fashions. They were quite unlike the gable-fronted, brick-faced houses with fixed windows that had been the standard type of modern house erected in the city over the previous sixty years, and stood in utter contrast to the 'many old timber houses' with frontages of less than fourteen feet that were still to be found in the more ancient parts

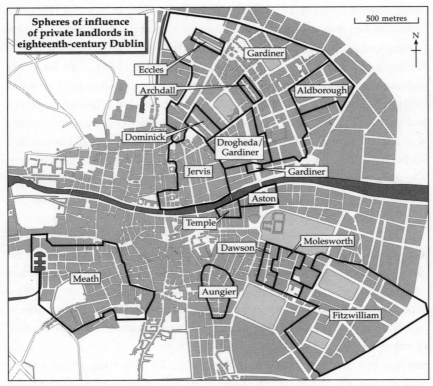

Map 2: Spheres of influence of private estates in eighteenth-century Dublin.

of the south side. Henrietta Street, with its superb views across the city and an elevation above the dirt and stink of the nearby markets and shambles, was shrewdly chosen. Eight of the original houses were financed directly by Gardiner and four by his Treasury deputy, Nathaniel Clements. Gardiner started by building his own house at the highest point of the street and persuaded Archbishop Hugh Boulter to take a plot directly opposite. Over the years, the most powerful parliamentary clans gravitated to 'Primate's Hill', creating by the early 1750s a remarkable concentration of political power and factional rivalry within a small physical space.[62]

It was indeed a coup for Gardiner to get an anchor tenant such as Boulter. Wealthy, Whiggish and very much a metropolitan insider, Boulter had arrived in Ireland in 1724 amidst the 'Wood's Halfpence' controversy. As a Lord Justice and dominant figure in the Privy Council for the next eighteen years, he was proverbially suspicious of the Irish political elite and its waywardness, seeking to assert London's control over the apparatus of the Irish state; his public reputation in the city was, it seems, intensely hostile.[63] Yet he was supportive of men like Gardiner and Clements who undertook the financial business of the Treasury with discretion and efficiency, and had a well-developed belief that office-holders had a social obligation to tackle the poverty in their midst. He was a strong supporter of the Ulster canal (it would help the economic development of his diocese) and of the 'charter school' movement (in which large-scale proselytism of the poor was a central but not overriding objective). Boulter's willingness to intervene was best demonstrated in 1740. At the beginning of that year the whole country, in common with most of northern Europe, entered a period of extreme cold weather without known precedent. The Liffey froze within a few hours, mills ground to a halt, coal supplies broke down, the city went dark as the street lamps failed to burn, ships were immobilised and 'a house, which stood at the extremity of the ... North Wall, was entirely cover'd over with a cake of ice which when the sun shone on it, made a very splendid appearance'. It was a seven-week crisis of great intensity, decimating even the wildlife: 800 of the 2,000 deer in the Phoenix Park succumbed. Wealthier households on the east side of town subscribed funds that allowed vestries on the west side to procure meal and coal for immediate free distribution (following the precedent of the 1729 famine). Nevertheless human death rates in St Catherine's and St Peter's parishes trebled during the weeks of the frost, and it is likely that hypothermia and respiratory infections took a similar toll elsewhere. But after the frost lifted, weather patterns remained bizarrely out of the ordinary for more than a year: a summer drought in 1740, devastating storms, snows and floods that autumn, another bitter winter and then a wretched spring.[64]

The effects of all this on the city's food supplies were severe: the near-total loss of potatoes during the frost started a chain reaction, exacerbated by a drought-induced harvest failure later in 1740. Meal prices soared and the size of the fixed-price common loaf shrank. Drawing on the experience of market protests in earlier years of scarcity (notably in the hungry spring of 1729), huge crowds sacked and looted grain stores and bakers' premises in the Thomas Street area and attacked suburban mills. The main guard killed several civilians and the Corporation sought to intervene in the markets, but prices remained stubbornly high and indeed rose to new heights in the autumn.

It was only in December 1740, after further intermittent disturbances and as ice floes could be seen passing down the Liffey, that the government acted – or rather Boulter in his capacity as a Lord Justice

responded to the pleadings of the Lord Mayor, Samuel Cooke. Flour
and oatmeal had just reached the highest price levels ever known, and a
scheme was set in motion to provide free meals at the Foundling Hospital, first for around 2,000 Dubliners, rising to over 4,000 by May 1741,
initially on a daily basis, then limited to several times a week.[65] It is not
clear whether the doles were for households or individuals, but the effect
was to moderate markets and to restore a measure of calm in the city.
The free-food scheme was funded through philanthropy, and was led by
Boulter himself, but many others got involved. However, it was only in
the spring of 1741 that prices fell back when substantial supplies of American flour reached the city. By that stage, 'famine fevers' were sweeping
the hinterland and inflicting the worst loss of life of the century across
many Irish counties. Typhus and dysentery ravaged the city jails but, perhaps surprisingly, the wider citizenry escaped relatively lightly, thanks in
some considerable measure to robust civic action and the pushiness of
the archbishop.[66]

The quiet minority

In February 1744, rumours of a new Anglo-French war circulated. Dublin
Castle ordered that Catholic chapels in all towns be closed immediately as
a precaution against Jacobite fifth-column activity. Temporary premises
were used by some of the clergy, including an old house on Pill Lane near
Ormond Market, where the flooring collapsed, killing ten people, including a priest. The government response to the accident was to permit the
reopening of all regular chapels shortly afterwards on grounds of public
safety. But the war came, and in the autumn of 1745 news of a full-scale
Jacobite rising in Scotland transfixed the city. A new Lord Lieutenant,
the earl of Chesterfield, took a calculated risk and ignored pressure for
another bout of religious repression, believing that there was no internal
military threat. Such a measured response marked changing times. Catholic worship was never again suspended in Dublin.[67]

The image of the teeming 'mass house' on Pill Lane is suggestive on
a number of levels – of the poverty of Catholic Dubliners of course, but
also of a growth in their numbers faster than the Church could provide
accommodation for, or, more precisely, faster than it dared expand its public presence. The Catholic share of the city's population, which had fallen

sharply in the 1690s, began to recover almost immediately, and although Catholics were still in a minority in the city in the 1740s, in absolute terms they were present in greater numbers than ever before. The prevailing view in the Irish Parliament was that the penal legislation passed at the beginning of the century against unregistered clergy and the religious orders had been too soft and there were unsuccessful attempts to place extreme sanctions (such as the face-branding or castration of unregistered priests) onto the statute book. But even those who thought in such barbaric terms regarded the penal laws against Catholic clergy as a means of Damoclean control rather than an excuse for a new persecution. There had been recurring threats of Jacobite invasion from France or Spain since the first years of the century and these usually led to the temporary closure of city chapels, but by the 1720s official toleration of religious worship in the city and of unregistered parish clergy officiating there was an everyday reality. That said, bishops and friars were discreet in the extreme, fearful of giving their enemies any handle. Several unsavoury bounty-hunters had acted as 'priest-catchers' in the 1710s, leading in 1718 to the slightly embarrassing arrest of Archbishop Byrne. Seven years previously, 'some hundreds of the popish inhabitants' had been involved in a running riot in Fishamble and Werburgh Streets as they pursued another 'priest-catcher' into the care of the military.[68]

In 1731, early in Boulter's career as primate and possibly at his instigation, the House of Lords initiated a national survey of the number of Catholic chapels, priests and 'popish' schools. Increasingly brazen displays by what were presumed to be Catholic crowds in the city had contributed to a sense of insecurity. These included disorderly celebrations every year on the night of James III's birthday that took place around St Stephen's Green, destructive attacks on dissenting meeting-houses, and fracas involving soldiers, civilians and students. Much of this violence was little more than recreational excess by young journeymen organised in neighbourhood groups and looking for a fight, the instigators being Protestant artisans or College students. But fear of 'popish mobs' was an easy call to make and there was sometimes a real political edge to it. The violent sacking of the Quakers' meeting-house in the Liberties in May 1720 came only days after the hugely controversial execution of James Cotter in Cork, the Tory hero of the election riot at the Tholsel in 1713 and one of the few openly Jacobite gentry still in circulation. Cotter was charged with the rape of a Quaker: his execution was seen as a political sacrifice and a ballad lamenting his death was 'sung in our open streets, under the very nose of the government'.[69]

The 1731 inquiry revealed the extent to which the Catholic Church in Dublin was rebuilding itself. Well over 100 priests were active in the city (perhaps treble the number present immediately after the 1697 Banishment Act), with a rough balance between diocesan clergy and friars or other religious, officiating in fifteen chapels (plus two attached to convents). Most of these chapels were on side streets, recessed in alleys or in courtyards. It was also reported that some forty-five Catholic schoolteachers were active.[70] What was striking about these returns was the concentration of chapels, clergy and teachers in certain parts of the city, as – apart from one location, the converted stables of Lord Ely's house in Hawkins Street – there was no Catholic church in any of the southeast parishes of the city and only four chapels (including a private one in the Channel Row convent) on the burgeoning north side. Catholic activity was grounded in the western side of the old city, notably in the corridor running from Francis Street northwards across the High Street to the Cook Street neighbourhood, where many of the fifty-odd clergy were regulars: Franciscans, Carmelites or Dominicans. In this sector, chapels had been recently extended or refurbished, and galleries, confessionals, pews, pictures and sacristies were becoming standard. But south-west of this 'Catholic' district were the Meath Liberties, where at the end of the seventeenth century estate policy had been hostile to Catholic tenants. There was still, it seems, no chapel or resident priest on the Meath estate, although the chapel opened by the Carmelites in Ash Street off the Coombe in the late 1720s showed they were not far away.[71]

The civilian population of the Liberties was by the 1730s quite mixed religiously. There were eleven 'popish' teachers listed there in 1731 (six of them women). One of them was 'Thaddeus Norton', Tadhg Ó Neachtain, based in Earl Street. His father Seán, of Roscommon origin, had also been a teacher and they were at the centre of a small but intriguing circle of men, a few of whom were Catholic clergy and many of them descendants of hereditary literary families who were now earning a meagre living by teaching and carrying out scribal work in the Irish language for patrons, Catholic and in a few cases Protestant. Tadhg Ó Neachtain made a list of his twenty-six literary friends and acquaintances in 1726, sixteen of whom can be linked to surviving Irish-language manuscripts – either transcriptions or original compositions, which were historical, linguistic, poetic, devotional or, in one or two instances, fictional. Seán Ó Neachtain's text, 'Stair Éamoinn Uí Chléirigh' ('The history of Éamonn Uí Chléirigh'), is an apparently autobiographical account of a migrant from the West who comes to Meath and Dublin, tries to earn a living by teaching but is brought low by drink and denied the woman he seeks; in the end, he is redeemed by an honest and compassionate friend. In its multilingual punning (in Latin, English and Irish) and linguistic hybridity, the memoir catches something of the transitional yet cabalistic cultural world of these teachers, for apart from their own circle very few in the city could read such material.[72] Yet in no sense were they isolated. With sermons being preached in both Irish and English, we can assume that the Catholic quarters of the town, overflowing with new migrants from outer Leinster and beyond, were now strongly bilingual. Furthermore, they had some contact with the world of high learning in the city, notably in the friendship between Tadhg Ó Neachtain and Anthony Raymond, a Meath Church of Ireland cleric, a friend of Swift and former fellow of the College, thanks to whom old Irish treasures in the Trinity library, notably the Book of Ballymote, were lent out to Ó Neachtain. Nowhere else in the country was there such a network of Gaelic literati at this time, and their busy presence in the capital points to the 'cover' that the city provided those whose skills might compromise them elsewhere, but also to the fact that only in the city was there a ready demand for their special mix of skills.[73]

There were controversial attempts by Church of Ireland clergy, notably in the 1710s, to publish Irish-language religious materials (for pastoral and proselytising purposes),[74] but there was no patron with the resources to turn the manuscript productions of Ó Neachtain's circle into print and no public market for them if they had. As the author of the only local bilingual printing of the period (a 1723 almanack with the Irish words spelt phonetically) observed, 'not one in 20,000 can either write or read their own language, even though they can write English. No shopbook was ever kept in that tongue, nor any agreement for a bargain written down, nor a receipt given, nor a letter written by the post.'[75]

There would also have been palpable dangers: one of their number, Aodh Buí MacCruitín/Hugh MacCurtain had published a restrained defence of pre-conquest Ireland (in English in 1717) and was briefly imprisoned (although the circumstances remain unclear).[76] But whatever the literary milieu out of which the 'popish' schoolmasters may have been drawn, their everyday business, like that of the free schools linked to the

Church of Ireland parishes, was the provision of elementary literacy and numeracy skills in English for what would still have been a minority of the city's children, although most of the offspring of skilled craftsmen were now receiving such an education.[77] In the Catholic diocesan statutes of 1730, priests were required to ensure that every parish had its school-teacher who would provide (*inter alia*) elementary catechesis for all children and servants, and insofar as this religious formation was achieved, it was probably delivered through the medium of English.[78]

The reading public

John Harding of Fishamble Street has gone down in history as a martyr for press freedom. One of the few printers to pose as an unreconstructed Tory in the early Hanoverian city, he ran the risk of imprisonment for several years. Chosen by Swift to print the *Drapier's letters*, he was charged and imprisoned in November 1724 in connection with the inflammatory fourth letter, detained through the winter in Newgate while the city grand jury refused to convict him, and released at some point in the new year after the prosecution case had been abandoned. Much weakened by imprisonment, he died the following April. Swift assisted Harding's young widow Sarah to resume the business, which she did with some success.[79] In the case of both Harding and the many printers who suffered the lesser fate of temporary imprisonment and heavy fines, the prosecution was initiated in Parliament. The first Hanoverian parliament in 1715 had helped to silence the Tory printers, and long after that time senior politicians displayed a generally hostile attitude towards the unsettling power of the press. Contempt of Parliament was a charge repeatedly used against politically obnoxious printers, yet despite dozens of prosecutions the resilience of the press was clear for all to see, its capacity to enlarge the public sphere and to reshape the reading habits of the city well proven by the time of Swift's death in 1745.[80]

Between the 1690s and 1760 the number of booksellers in Dublin more than trebled and the number of master printers grew by more than ten-fold. Since the sixteenth century Dublin had been the conduit for nearly all printed matter entering the country, but by the 1720s it had become the second largest centre of book production in the English-speaking world, still a minnow compared to London with its printing monopoly in Britain, but a reflection of the accelerating demand within Ireland for works of scholarship, devotion, entertainment and education; initially it was a Dublin market, but by 1750 island-wide. Since the 1670s upper-class and clerical demand had laid the foundations for local book-publishing, and Ireland's exclusion from the English copyright regime (after 1710) had encouraged the regular reprinting of London titles at lower cost, both for the Irish reader and (illegally) for the British market. Printing remained essentially a workshop activity, attracting little invest-ment and making few fortunes. But with the low cost of entry and rela-tively light regulation, ease of access encouraged a long wave of growth. A sign of the times was the launch of the first commercial 'circulating' library in the city *c.*1737, one step in widening the pool of readers as print became cheaper and was geared to a greater range of tastes and uses.[81]

The rise of the Dublin newspaper was a striking case in point. It evolved from a handful of ephemeral news-sheets in the 1690s to the appearance in the 1730s of rarely less than five competing titles, usually twice a week on Tuesdays and Saturdays to coincide with the post-days to the provinces. Their circulation was still predominantly within the dis-tricts of the capital, some readers committing to subscription, some buy-ing from newsboys in the street, many using the copies supplied to city coffee-houses and taverns. With the highest frequency of cross-channel packet-boats operating across the Irish Sea, Dublin usually obtained news, rumour and print from London (and the world beyond) before anywhere else, and the first Dublin newsletters naturally capitalised on this advan-tage. But newspapers only became profitable with the growth of commer-cial and personal advertising in the first three decades of the eighteenth century; by the 1730s most papers consisted of four large folio pages, much of which was taken up with advertisements set in an ever smaller point size. News was almost by definition foreign, and the column inches devoted to Irish intelligence, commercial or incidental, remained very modest until mid-century. Most of the 165 newspaper titles launched in Dublin in the first half of the eighteenth century failed fairly quickly, but the few that survived did so by specialising.[82] Before 1714 the divisions were fairly marked between Tory-supporting (and supported) papers and those whose politics were Whiggish. By the 1730s the evident distinctions were in the kind of advertising they attracted – in Pue's *Occurrences,* rural estate sales and lettings; in Dickson's *Dublin Intelligence*, importers and city wholesalers; in Carson's *Dublin Weekly Journal*, the book trade. By then, the paper with the largest circulation, approaching perhaps 2,000 copies, was George Faulkner's *Dublin Journal*, with at times up to ninety advertisements per issue. Faulkner, like many periodical publishers, was also a stationer, printer, bookseller and 'publisher' – indeed, his fame rested then and thereafter on becoming Swift's Irish publisher for *Gulliver's travels* and much else. Faulkner's partner in the 1720s, James Hoey, 'compiler, writer, corrector, and author', was unusual in being the only Catholic publisher of a newspaper at this time. Newspaper readers were also predominantly Protestant, but as every decade passed that became less emphatically the case.[83]

Book publishing in Dublin during this period has been the subject of much scholarly investigation, not least because of the survival of a large sample of the end product, but it is a rather uneven sample. We know most about the work of Faulkner, because anything associated with Jonathan Swift has borne a premium ever since, and least about the chapbooks and cheap devotional material run off by those working for the 'country' trade. Their wares have largely vanished. In Mary Pollard's classic study of the Dublin book trade, some of the myths about the industry have been disposed of, in particular that the Dublin trade was essentially an offshore parasite, thriving entirely on pirating London editions and smuggling the books back to England to undercut the legally copyrighted product. This did indeed happen, but its importance was greatly exaggerated, for Dublin printers depended primarily on the Irish market, producing shorter runs than London (perhaps averaging 500 copies by mid-century), but as well as reprints they published a substantial amount of original copy. Of 109 Dublin titles for which subscriptions were raised in the 1740s, 39 related to literature (ancient and modern), 24 to history and biography, 15 to religion and philosophy, and 13 to medicine and science; two-thirds of these were original titles, one-third had previously been published in London (at a higher cost). The implication is that the capital contained a small but active book-buying community.[84]

Among the original literary titles were two substantial volumes of poems by a teacher of mathematics living beside Merchants Quay, Laurence Whyte, published by subscription in 1740 and 1742. Whyte was a well-known figure in town and attracted some 700 subscriptions for his second volume. Artless as much of his poetry may have been, their simple stanzas drew on his rural background in Westmeath and on the tavern-centred city around him. One of the poems, 'The parting cup: Or the humours of *Deoch an Doruis'*, an evocation of old-style rural life in the face of an abrasive land market, is perhaps the most evocative comment on the malaise of the 1720s and 1730s.[85]

Probably an even better known citizen, Laetitia Pilkington, published the first of a three-volume set of her memoirs in 1748. She was daughter of Dr Van Lewen, physician and *accoucheur* of Molesworth Street, wife of the curate of St Andrew's and a friend of Swift and the Delanys. She had caused scandal a decade previously through marital infidelity and a flight to notoriety in London. Pilkington's text turned out to be a remarkably frank revelation of the vulnerability of a high-status woman to a scheming and unscrupulous husband and to the prevailing moral and legal conventions that led to summary expulsion from her home and to the utter loss of her reputation. But having been earlier moulded by the literary 'triumfeminate' of poets in Swift's circle – Mary Barber, Constantia Grierson and Elizabeth Sican – Pilkington found in her own poetry both personal solace and an economic lifeline through ghosting and by working in her own name. This brought her back to Dublin, to limited security and social acceptance before her early death. She too was in every sense an 'injured lady', spurned even by Swift and his friends, but she was able to rescue herself through the printing press and the reading nation, and in publishing her memoirs she secured a measure of revenge and redemption.[86]

4

'THIS NOW GREAT METROPOLIS': 1750–1780

Capital places

The settled population of Dublin stood at approximately 125,000 people in 1750, perhaps double the total of fifty years before. By this reckoning the city was now the ninth largest in Europe and the fifth largest north of the Alps, more populous than Madrid or Berlin, about the same size as Milan, a little smaller than Lisbon. But of Europe's ten biggest cities, all bar Dublin were capitals of sovereign states. Given Ireland's peripheral location, this ranking for Dublin is at first sight very puzzling. Its relative size in the hierarchy of European cities has probably never been so high, before or since.[1]

Such numbers would suggest that Dublin must have had many of the attributes of a capital city. But what were those attributes, and why did they make political capitals the largest cities of pre-industrial Europe? Richard Cantillon, the Kerry-born observer of the French economy, was perhaps the first to recognise the distinctive role of capital cities; writing in 1735, he characterised the dynamic elements present in a capital: a prince in residence, the nobility settling close by 'and enjoying agreeable society', and a large proportion of the nation's wealth being spent in the city.[2] Yet capitals in the four corners of Enlightenment Europe were drawing in the nobility and *rentier* elites for more than public entertainment and intellectual stimulation (although there was the universal sense among the spending classes that life in the capital would always be more exciting). Cantillon recognised the importance of the higher courts of law being anchored in the capital, and there were the unique services (personal and legal), the luxury supplies that were only readily available in a capital's shops and stores, the opportunities to have children 'polished' in metropolitan academies and, more generally for men, the chance to build personal connections and networks of friendship through membership of exclusive fraternal associations. Such connection-building was essential for every propertied family in their constant search for places and promotions within the patronage system of the *ancien régime*. But central to a great deal of this social activity, from formal balls to domestic entertainment, was the imperative for the unattached of both genders to engage in social display in their search for optimal marriage partners. In Dublin's case the city had been an upper-class marriage market since Restoration times, and although the very wealthy were now more peripatetic, Dublin was still an elite village which every year gave hundreds of wealthy young women the critical opportunity to come, literally, to market, whether by promenading on the gravel walks of St Stephen's Green or by occupying the boxes at command performances in the Theatre Royal. And for newly-weds the fashion continued. The expenditure of Robert French, a major Galway landowner and MP, over twenty-nine years has been reconstructed by Toby Barnard: his trips to Dublin were longest and most costly in the years immediately after he married his Armagh bride (and before he became an MP); in one of those early years of marriage, more than 35 per cent of the family's household expenditure was spent in Dublin.[3]

Cantillon also observed that a capital 'is the centre of the fashions which all the provinces take as a model'.[4] But who set the fashions? The 1st duke of Ormond and his family had certainly played the role of trend-setting princes, but none of his Dublin successors had either the inclination or the financial extravagance to try and emulate them. And since 1714 all the viceroys and their entourage were English-based, limiting their time in Dublin to the parliamentary session – five to eight months in every twenty-four. The Lords Justices who acted in their place at other times rarely entertained in an official capacity or indulged in public display. The arrival of the viceroy every second autumn – at Ringsend or Dunleary – was still a moment of great display: the mounted cavalcade, formal and informal, taking up to four hours to reach the Castle, and the presence of a viceroy with deep pockets or easy creditors greatly energised business.

But the faltering modifications to Dublin Castle in the decades after 1714 tell their own story.

Cantillon did not mention two institutions that infused Dublin's sense of metropolitan importance. The first was the university, now surrounded by the town on three sides, its buildings extended and modernised at mid-century, most noticeably with the façade beside the Front Gate being rebuilt on a more massive scale. Like the great monastic foundations of the medieval city, Trinity drew in wealth from its vast estates which then circulated within the town, and drew in the families of some of its students who chose to winter in the city *en famille* during term. But real as its civic impact was, the College was as nothing compared to Parliament, which attracted the political classes to town every second winter, creating a court-like social world within the city. Some secured lodgings, some rented by the month or the quarter, those with sufficient resources and ambition leased a townhouse, and some bought outright. The prospect of a parliamentary session encouraged high-class retailers to build up their stocks in anticipation. But in fact many from the rural propertied classes came to Dublin *every* winter: the city's drawing power was not limited to the seasons when the viceregal court and Parliament were live. A comparison of advertisements in *Faulkner's Dublin Journal* in the 1760s and 1780s relating to plays, assemblies, balls, charity sermons, club meetings and concerts suggests little difference in the number of events held during parliamentary sessions and those held when Parliament was inactive. It would seem that the law and university terms helped impose a firmly annual pattern on the movement of the propertied classes between town and countryside, with a long summer lull in social events in and around the city every year.[5]

The social worlds of the peerage and the parliamentary commoners were by now almost one and the same: the 'upper class' who wintered in Dublin were not, in other words, a legal caste, and landed wealth, connections and political influence were the things that mattered in the tortuous negotiations that surrounded strategic marriage alliances. A peerage was of course an enormous social asset and membership of the upper house was prestigious (about thirty-five titled families, or about a third of the total eligible, were regular or occasional attenders in the House of Lords in the 1760s and 1770s). Promotion within the peerage could also become a consuming ambition for men like James FitzGerald, whose eventual achievement of a dukedom (of Leinster) probably mattered more to him than all his great house-building.[6]

The social spaces inhabited by the parliamentary elite – the fashionable east-end parish churches, the coffee-houses, the respectable taverns and, principally, the great domestic spaces in the townhouses – provided abundant opportunity every winter for new modes of dress, behaviour and consumption to take hold, a world about which we have a great deal of anecdotal evidence, some of it over-coloured. By the 1750s, upper-class social life during the season was relentless, with mixed card-parties ('drums') every weekday night, private balls and assemblies that involved dining and heavy drinking, and an abundance of possibilities for male fraternising in clubs and Castle levées. There was as always a hierarchy in the fluid world of masculine sociability, whether in dining club, masonic lodge, charitable society or gambling den. For women of whatever class, landed or bourgeois, sociability in the town was more restricted. Thomas Campbell, perched on the edge of high-class society, claimed in 1778 that Dublin women had an abiding passion for dancing and that they 'say that the social pleasures are more easily obtained here than in London ... public amusements being less frequent here, domestic entertainments are more in use'. Perhaps so, but with the commercialisation of leisure underway there were new opportunities for women, and their presence in Castle receptions and the theatre audience had always set the tone.[7]

It is the history of these 'public amusements' that provide us with the best evidence on the changing dynamics of fashion. The Restoration playhouse in Smock Alley was where it all started. As we have seen, the theatre began as an extension of the court, its fortunes greatly affected by the presence or absence of viceregal patronage. Its survival as an institution was helped by the quite exceptional continuity of its management: Joseph Ashbury, a young participant in the seizure of Dublin Castle in 1659, moved from soldiering into acting and ran the playhouse for forty-five years until his death in 1720. Working with a troupe of around thirty actors, he was always able to offer a large if fairly conservative repertoire each winter. Ashbury knew his audience's tastes well, but he was constantly bringing forward new faces. Indeed, he developed a fine ability to spot young talent, so that a stream of actors and playwrights whom he blooded in Smock Alley went on to acquire celebrity in London, usually without losing their links with Dublin. He weathered occasional church disapproval, and when John Dunton, the London bookseller, visited in 1699 he noted that 'no church was half so crowded as the playhouse', and that it gave 'entertainment as well to the common man as the greatest peer'. However, despite the lively participation of servants, students and middling families in the upper gallery, Ashbury's clientele were emphatically patrician, if often badly behaved. At times this reflected the political excitements outside, most spectacularly on King William's birthday in 1712, when the city's first theatre riot took place between Whig and Tory partisans over a disputed prologue. It survived into calmer times, 'that plain house [which] is the fountain of all our love, wit, dress, and gallantry'.[8]

In the mid-1730s a second commercial theatre was opened (in Aungier Street) and Smock Alley was itself rebuilt. Each winter the two venues offered an ever-changing mix of Shakespeare and comedy, similar to but not identical with London repertoires; some Drury Lane successes did not travel, others like the ballad operas caught on in Dublin almost immediately.[9] In the quiet months of summer the two Dublin troupes toured the provinces, one developing a regular circuit to Kilkenny and the Munster cities, the other to towns in Ulster, bringing in effect London fashion moderated by Dublin taste to provincial audiences congregating for the county assizes. After several years of severe competition, the two companies were amalgamated in 1745 under the precocious management of Swift's godson, Thomas Sheridan Jr. The next nine years were something of a golden age for Smock Alley, notably in those seasons when Sheridan enjoyed strong patronage from the Castle. He championed a professionalism that he had learnt in London, a broader cultural conception of the importance of theatre for sustaining 'liberty' and an intolerance of the older rowdyism of the pits. This led to a bizarre episode in 1747 when he disciplined a College buck who had invaded the stage and threatened to rape an actress. The shaming of the intruder in question, Edward Kelly, kept the printing presses of the city busy, some defending the reputation and status of a gentleman who had been undercut by a mere player, others backing Sheridan and the moral standards of the city against the upstart Galway youth with his Catholic gentry friends.[10]

Sheridan's self-confident defence won the day in 1747, but in March 1754 the worst theatre riot in the city's history took place in Smock Alley. A largely male audience, made up of supporters of the parliamentary opposition at the time of the Money Bill dispute, saw Sheridan as a creature of the Castle, and they took it as an insult when (as they believed) he halted the recitation of a partisan prologue to the night's offering, Voltaire's *Mahomet*. This trivial spark led to the near-destruction of the theatre in six hours of mayhem but, strangely, there was no intervention by magistracy or military. Smock Alley reopened later that season, but Sheridan was gone, and he relocated permanently to London and to a career in acting.[11] On the surface, theatre retained its central place in city life in the 1760s and beyond, with two playhouses once again struggling for ascendancy. But after Sheridan's departure the links between Parliament, court and theatre became more distant, reflecting a step-change in city politics between the 1740s and 1760s and a dramatic broadening of the social constituency that interested itself in political controversy. The political role of theatre remained, but for the wealthiest in the city a partial withdrawal was underway – from public to private theatre and from a socially mixed environment to closed and more congenial spaces.

By contrast, the public performance of music did not begin as an extension of the court. Since the Reformation, choral events had been associated with the larger Anglican churches of the city, notably the two cathedrals with their professional choristers, fine organs, abundant space and the funds to attract and maintain singing talent. On the occasions when Castle ceremony required formal music, the 'master of the state music' was able to call on the resources of the cathedrals. Smock Alley also had its musicians from the 1660s, but there was no non-religious space for public musical performance until 1730. Then the Crow Street Music Hall was opened as a commercial venue for Ridotto balls (which usually involved dances in masquerade) and other forms of 'Italian music'.[12] From that point there was a remarkable flowering of musical activity in the city. Even the chapel of the Dominican nuns in Channel Row was attracting patrons from outside the denominational fold for concerts by Italian musicians. Performing societies proliferated, their public mission being usually philanthropic, and they used the press to publicise fund-raising events – whether for the new hospitals (none of which were publicly financed) or for the release of imprisoned debtors. For the musicians – a mix of gentry and professional players – the making of music was of course an end in itself.[13]

What seems to have been the first such body was the Charitable and Musical Society, which made the freeing of debtors from city prisons its principal objective. It had begun as a tavern-based club in the Christ Church/Fishamble Street area around 1710 and, according to Laurence Whyte, one of the founder members, music was a great leveller:

... tradesmen there gave no offence,
When blessed with manners or good sense;
Some gentlemen, some lords and squires,
Some Whigs, and Tories and Highflyers;
There Papists, Protestants, Dissenters,
Sit cheek by jowl at all adventures,
And thus united did agree
To make up one Society.

To begin with, a pioneering musical publisher and instrument maker, John Neal, and several former Jacobites (the printer James Malone and Boyne-veteran Patrick Beaghan) seem to have been the moving force, but by the 1720s (as it moved from tavern to tavern in the locality) its philanthropic side became more explicit as 'many noblemen and commoners of high rank' joined in. So successful had the society become by 1740 that Neal's son William, already dabbling in property development, undertook to build a great hall in Fishamble Street and commissioned Richard Castle to design it. It turned out to be a great success.[14]

Later philanthropic music societies were distinctly upper class from the start, and probably all the more successful in promoting charitable concerts to help fund one or more of the city hospitals – the Incurables, Mercer's, Dr Steevens's or the Charitable Infirmary. In 1741, thanks it seems to an initial prompt by the incoming Lord Lieutenant, the duke of Devonshire, London's great court composer George Frederick Handel was invited to Dublin to produce and perform in a series of mainly charity concerts during the following parliamentary season. He stayed nine months, comfortable in Dublin society and impressed at the technical standards of local musicianship. The highlight was of course the first performance of the *Messiah* in the Fishamble Street hall. There, 700 fortunate ladies and gentlemen crushed into the venue in April 1742 and seem to have immediately recognised the bravura nature of the oratorio that he had composed for his visit. The scale of the performance was modest by later standards, the orchestra led by the master of state music with the cathedral choristers providing the choir. But in the two years after Handel's visit the Charitable Society was able to pay for the release of some 490 city debtors and an equal share of the funds from the concerts went to the Charitable Infirmary and to Mercer's. Not surprisingly, Handel's popularity lingered in Dublin long after it faded in London.[15]

Music as spectacle always attracted the wealthy. Sheridan risked insolvency in 1748 when he established a resident orchestra with no fewer than thirty professional musicians in Smock Alley. But the most spectacular demonstrator of the bond between upper-class sociability, musical performance and philanthropy was his contemporary Bartholomew Mosse, a Dublin-trained surgeon with real entrepreneurial flair. After a short period as a military surgeon abroad, he turned to midwifery, studied it in Paris and returned to Dublin to practise around the time of the 1740–41 crisis. Indeed, it seems he may have been moved by the horrors of that year to establish a small maternity hospital for poorer citizens to try and cut the levels of neo-natal and maternal mortality. In 1745 he converted an abandoned pocket theatre off George's Lane into a ten-bed maternity facility, the first in Ireland or Britain, funding it initially through charity concerts in Fishamble Street. The wives and widows of craftworkers and soldiers featured strongly in his early admissions, all being drawn from the 'deserving poor' with no distinction as to religion; three-fifths of mothers in the first year came from the south-west quadrant of the city.[16] After twelve years in operation and some 4,000 births, he had kept neo-natal mortality at around 10 per cent and maternal mortality at around 1 per cent. That in itself was quite an achievement (and indeed the infant survival rates were far lower than in the following twenty years).[17] But Mosse had restless ambition and started to plan for a fifty-bed hospital that would be located in a zone of upper-class development. His initial idea seems to have been to fund this move by lotteries and concerts, but he seized on a far more ambitious plan: to develop a suite of fashionable leisure facilities adjacent to the future hospital which would generate all the necessary revenue.

Mosse was both clever and lucky, securing a site that precisely matched his needs at a moment of economic confidence. In 1748 he leased from William Napier a four-acre site on rising ground that fronted onto Great Britain Street in the north-east of the city; it contained a few thatched cabins and a small bowling green, and was almost completely surrounded by undeveloped parts of Luke Gardiner's great estate. Despite strong opposition, he pushed ahead. He extended the bowling green, laid out gardens, planted some 600 elms and by the summer of 1749 was ready for the paying public.[18] Open-air concerts were already popular in London at the Vauxhall Gardens, and locally at the nearby Marlborough Street bowling green. For the next decade, Mosse's gardens and Marlborough Street competed in their musical attractions, with concerts being held on most weekdays from

May to September in one or other venue. Mosse achieved a gradual ascendancy, helped by the provision of an octagonal coffee-room and other new facilities – and despite having a great Palladian structure under construction right beside the gardens, the 'Hospital for Poor Lying-in Women'.

This was opened in 1757, aided on its way by a variety of lotteries, parliamentary grants (to the hospital and to Mosse himself), and a royal charter – which established a fashionably large board of upper-class governors. Very little of its cost was met by direct philanthropy, yet charity lay at the heart of the project. One of its most remarkable features was the large chapel containing some of the finest stucco work in the city by Flemish artist Bartholomew Cramillion. With Mosse's father, brother-in-law and later his son serving as Church of Ireland clergy, the centrality of the chapel might imply a strong evangelical purpose to the whole maternity enterprise. Mosse did have plans for developing an industrial school involving Protestant masters, and he instructed that all the hospital staff were to be Protestant. But he was in truth a hard-living man of the town who saw the chapel's role as primarily a magnet for the fashionable, on whose philanthropy the hospital's future would depend.

Mosse died in 1759, financially in trouble and his great project incomplete.[19] But the governors followed up his revenue-generating ideas, helped by further parliamentary largesse, and shortly afterwards they commissioned a large indoor space, the Rotunda hall, complete with an organ. The precedent here, with which Mosse would himself have been familiar, was the Ranelagh Gardens in Chelsea which opened in 1742 and were a huge commercial success, and included a vast round room (to house evening and wet-day events). Dublin's circular space – with an indoor diameter of eighty feet – was about half the size of that at Chelsea, but for a while it was quite large enough to accommodate demand.[20]

The Rotunda and the adjacent gardens became the unchallenged hub of city fashion, the sixty summer concerts often drawing annual gross receipts in excess of a thousand pounds. The liberal use of coloured lights and fireworks made the gardens a night-time spectacle and a popular place of resort, notably on Sunday evenings when the playhouses were closed. But music remained central to the financial success and lasting reputation of the venue. Its governors spent liberally in securing a succession of conductors, singers and soloists from London for the summer season, and they remained 'the foremost and most consistent promoters of regular concerts' in the city for more than forty years.[21] This linkage of upper-class

*13. Thanks to her forceful character, long widowhood and comparative wealth
Lady Arabella Denny was perhaps the most influential woman active in the
public sphere in the second half of the eighteenth century. She was unusual and
highly effective in getting political support for social reform, but was also successful
in assisting the city's silk weavers achieve direct contact with retail customers.*

sociability and welfare provision for the poor continued to work well.
Despite rising neo-natal fatalities in the 1760s and 1770s, the hospital
was able to admit increasing numbers of women, and from the 1780s the
death rate was reduced to unprecedently low levels. Unlike many other
eighteenth-century public institutions, the hospital really did provide the
service it claimed to offer.[22]

Mosse's supporters had been overwhelmingly male but one exception
was Lady Arabella Denny, a childless and very well-connected widow (she
was Sir William Petty's granddaughter), who at this time was associated
with a string of philanthropic initiatives in the city. Following a parliamentary exposé of the dire state of the Foundling Hospital in 1758, she became
the driving force behind reform of the James Street institution, which was
now handling over 800 infants per annum. She part-funded the extension

of a hospital wing and and tried to tighten up the regulation of country wet-nurses. In consequence, the appalling death rate of infants abandoned at the hospital was for some years greatly reduced. This involvement led her to try to copy London's Magdalen Hospital: it had been set up in 1758 as a refuge and residential reformatory for 'contrite' young prostitutes and had quickly become one of the city's most fashionable charities, its chapel and preachers drawing royal patronage and prurient public interest. Denny's Magdalen Asylum was opened in Leeson Street in 1766 and was much smaller (being restricted to Protestant girls), but it was on its own terms a success. Being championed by such a formidible society figure and managed by fifteen governesses meant that it had a very different tone to the male-dominated London institution. And, once again, it was the chapel that became the chief source of revenue, the 'Magdalen' for many years attracting a high-status congregation, female and male. This 'coming out' of women as applied philanthropists was, however, not just an upper-class phenomenon – Teresa Mulally's charity school and orphanage for the poor Catholic girls in St Michan's parish also began in the 1760s – but in the years ahead the distinctive role of women in social institutions was to have a more strongly religious dimension.[23]

Great estates

Bartholomew Mosse's Lying-in Hospital helped create the north-east quarter of the Georgian city. Its dominant architecture and unrivalled social facilities became 'the greatest asset of the Gardiner estate', and set in train the upper-class development of the surrounding properties.[24] But the decisions of Luke Gardiner, ground-landlord of a vast swathe of the north-east side, had far greater impact. At the very moment that Mosse was forming his plans, Gardiner had decided to redevelop a large section of the nearby Drogheda Street as an upper-class boulevard, broadening it to 46 metres, inserting a promenading space down the centre of the street and rebranding it as Sackville Street, commemorating a viceroy who, in his two stints, was the longest to hold the office since the 1st duke of Ormond. Whether Mosse and Gardiner acted in concert remains unclear. At first sight it would have seemed logical that the great hospital building should have closed the vista at the north end of Gardiner's new street, rather than lurking just out of sight to the west. But Gardiner, by keeping clear ground to the north, left open the possibility of projecting the line of Sackville Street up to Drumcondra Lane (or, as it was soon to be rechristened, Dorset Street), and southwards towards the river. Did Gardiner intend to create a closed quarter, protecting it from the quays and the markets, or was there the hope that sooner or later a new link across the Liffey downstream of Essex Bridge would be built and that Sackville Street would then replace Capel Street as the prime north–south artery as the city centre moved eastwards?

There was indeed a move in the Irish House of Commons in 1749 which could have led to the building of such a bridge. A parliamentary committee of which Gardiner's elder son Charles was a member gave strong support for the idea. This suggests that Gardiner had in fact hatched a daring strategic plan in which the creation of Sackville Street was only the first move. However, there was a predictable storm of opposition from property-owners, upstream traders, Liberties manufacturers and the Corporation itself at any proposal for a downstream bridge which would only serve 'the convenience of the quality [sic] in frequenting drums and music-meetings, or the advancement of the rents of one or more very rich men ....'. Plans for the bridge were voted down in the Commons in 1750 and again in 1752 and 1753, but it was to remain a frozen possibility for another forty years.[25]

So in the medium term the development of Sackville Street was an end in itself, not unlike Henrietta Street a generation earlier. The scheme once again involved the leasing out of large plots to accommodate terraced houses, with façades in alignment and some diversity as to plot width and height. Oliver Grace published an engraving of an apparently fully built Sackville Street (c.1750) but this seems to have been a promotional exercise. It took more than twenty years for the last of the forty-odd houses as projected by Gardiner to be completed, but once again large numbers of politically active families chose to live on a Gardiner development. The forging of a new neighbourhood meant a new parish: St Thomas's was carved out of St Mary's, and in 1762 a Church of Ireland church was opened at the south end of Marlborough Street.[26]

In contrast to the torrid early years of Henrietta Street, the late 1740s and early 1750s were an optimum time for an upper-class housing scheme, a period of international peace and marked economic bullishness within the city that reflected rising rural land values and rental incomes, cheaper money and easier credit. Gardiner's deputy in the Treasury and office-holder extraordinary, Nathaniel Clements, was approaching the peak of his financial and political influence, and many of his family connections and friends, military, political and financial, were associated with Sackville Street. Indeed, as Gardiner was now an old man (he died in 1755), Clements's role in the early success of the street may have been critical. Something of an amateur architect, Clements erected three houses there (one became his townhouse), and including his old house in Henrietta Street these were together valued at £12,000 in 1759. In the same decade he completed a Palladian villa deep inside the Phoenix Park, which thanks to his position as Ranger of the Park was built at public expense. His mentor had already many years before constructed a bolt-hole on the north-western edge of the Park, Mountjoy House. Thanks to the earl of Chesterfield's gesture in 1745 in opening the Park to the public, it evolved rapidly from being a closely protected deer park to becoming a patchwork of great spaces for the city's horsemen and private enclaves for the well-connected.[27]

Associated with Gardiner and Clements, with Mosse and with many other public men, was the intriguing figure of Richard Castle, architect, surveyor and engineer, who died suddenly in 1751. Raised in Dresden and much travelled before settling in Ireland in the late 1720s, he had overseen the completion of the Parliament House after Pearce's death and had established a reputation for being a superb draughtman and outstanding project manager, a problem-solver and a clever architect, sensitive to clients' tastes and the potential of particular sites. He was a private man who disguised his Jewish background, but was nevertheless prominently involved with the Dublin Society and a champion of canal-building. His public works included designing and overseeing the Newry–Lough Neagh canal, but through the 1730s and 1740s he secured a string of great house commissions in the countryside, including Powerscourt and the Kildares' great house at Carton. In the city, his private work included Tyrone house in Marlborough Street, Doneraile house in Kildare Street, Bishop Clayton's and the Montgomerys' houses on St Stephen's Green (nos. 80 and 85). These latter two great houses transformed the dowdy character of the south side of the Green, and each was an architectural tour de force. The treatment of the entrance door on Montgomery's house, 'flanked by free-standing columns and set immediately within a semi-circular or elliptical arch', introduced what became one of the most distinctive elements of eighteenth-century Irish domestic façades. Castle also received a string of

institutional commissions in the city – the Printing House and the Dining
Hall in the university (the latter however collapsing shortly after construction), the Fishamble Street Music Hall, and Mosse's hospital (designed
by Castle but overseen after his death by his under-study, John Ensor).
Tyrone House, situated a block east of the future Sackville Street, was
completed c.1745 and is noteworthy for being the first completely stone-
built city mansion. Castle obtained most of the building stone for his
commissions from Irish quarries (notably Meath limestone from Ardbrac-
can, and Wicklow granite from Golden Hill near Blessington), and he
worked closely with the Darleys, stonemasons from Co. Down who controlled these quarries and who became one of the first building dynasties
in the city. Hugh Darley employed around a hundred men in the 1750s on
College building work alone; his nephew George was taking short leases
on Sackville Street plots in the 1760s, selling on the completed shells to
prospective residents.[28]

Tyrone House had been built for Marcus Beresford, 1st earl of
Tyrone, on exposed and low-lying ground overlooking the bay. Whether it
encouraged, or challenged, Gardiner to develop the Mall nearby is a moot
point. But what was undoubtedly Castle's greatest project in the city was
a south-side building that has always been credited with moving the epicentre of fashion. This was the urban palace known to future generations
as Leinster House, which he built for James FitzGerald, the young earl of
Kildare (and future duke of Leinster) in the late 1740s. The main structure
is a three-storeyed block of eleven bays which neatly closed the eastward
vista along Molesworth Street. Yet unlike any other city *palazzo,* it was
deeply recessed from the street, its forecourt protected by high walls and
its entrance via a (modest) triumphal arch. It was designed to be a Janus-
like building, the ornate western front facing the city, its stables and kitchens tucked away in an annexe to the south, and its eastern façade intended
to open out onto gardens offering an unrivalled maritime panorama. The
only problem was that the foreground of that panorama was in fact not
owned by the FitzGeralds but by the Fitzwilliams of Merrion.

There were parallels between Kildare House and the Lying-in Hospital – in their design and in their wider impact. They were both restrained
displays of neo-Palladianism, and in each case their rustic gardens came
to be overlooked by upper-class houses. But there was a big difference:
in the case of the hospital, the governors were entirely supportive of the
expansion of housing on the adjacent Gardiner estate, specifically on sites

that formed the three sides of the future Rutland (Parnell) Square, and
indeed Mosse was the first of several governors to be involved in building on the future square. By contrast, the earl of Kildare had a very testy
relationship with his neighbours, the Fitzwilliams, thanks to some very
unwelcome development on the perimeter of his palace. When the great
palazzo was getting underway *c.*1745, Kildare was still a young man, fresh
to the earldom and inheriting an income of some £15,000 p.a. At the
same moment he launched himself into Irish politics, displaying a full-
blooded pride in his Geraldine ancestry, an ambition to restore the family's political primacy and a taste for the extravagant gesture. Marriage
to Lady Emily Lennox in 1747 was a vital element in advancing these
ambitions, for with it he secured a link to the heart of Whig politics
in Westminster (Henry Fox became his brother-in-law), and a partner
of rare insight and sophistication who oversaw both the completion of
the country palace at Carton and the fitting out of Kildare House. The
family only began to use the townhouse in 1753, and work on its interior
continued for more than twenty years. Indeed, it was only after Kildare's
death in 1773 that the great picture gallery was completed by Lady Emily
and the gardens fully planted. Kildare had intended the house to rival
the Castle as the hub of Dublin fashion, and insofar as this ambition was
for a time achieved, it was thanks primarily to the women of the family. But the huge building programme left Kildare's heir with a severely
diminished income.[29]

The nearby Fitzwilliam estate was paradoxically the main beneficiary
of all this. Against the odds, the Old English family had avoided confiscation in the seventeenth century and fragmentation in the eighteenth, and
by the 1750s the estate was singularly well placed to rise in value as the south-
eastern extensions of the city edged towards it. The estate comprised over
2,300 acres of open ground, running eastwards from St Stephen's Green
and Kildare House across Baggotrath to the Dodder, down to Irishtown
and Ringsend, with a second block beyond Donnybrook bridge, arcing
south-eastwards to the coast; several miles from the city another segment
linked the settlements of Blackrock, Mount Merrion and Booterstown.
Part of this estate was of limited value – the coastal dunes at Sandymount
were subject to destructive flooding – but its overall potential was self-
evident by 1750 as the first fashionably large houses in Upper Merrion
Street were being completed, much to the annoyance of Kildare (who was
himself a tenant to Viscount Fitzwilliam for most of his garden ground).

Retaliatory action by the earl – the construction of a wall across Clare Street that blocked access to the Fitzwilliam estate from Nassau Street – appears to have forced a compromise, but the prudent decision by the Fitzwilliams to leave most of Kildare's eastward prospect open may have been the germ that prompted the idea for a great rectilinear development that would stretch out towards Dublin Bay, with Kildare House as its noble backdrop. The plan for such a huge development, a Merrion Square, was hatched in the 1750s and elaborated by the Fitzwilliam estate's surveyor, Jonathan Barker, in 1762. Such a scheme was now possible because the Fitzwilliams had managed to resume control over all the land that would be required for such a square. The rectangle as eventually built was somewhat smaller than what Barker had envisaged, but it became nonetheless one of the wonders of the city, with ninety-two houses being constructed around three sides over a thirty-year period.[30] They were somewhat smaller than the premium houses on the Gardiner estate (or the few mansions built around the corner in Upper Merrion Street), and were generally three-bay façades with three storeys over a basement. They were uniformly aligned to the street but varied considerably in their doorcase design, their plot width and their parapet height. The earliest and most substantial of the houses were erected on the north side of the square, with the later east- and south-side ones displaying more standardised brick façades.

The evidence of estate archives makes it clear that the impetus for this development did not come, as might be expected, from the ground-landlord, the 6th Viscount Fitzwilliam (d. 1776). He was largely an absentee, his political connections in Dublin being very limited, and his estate agents largely Catholic. Rather, it was the builder-speculators, the master carpenters, the bricklayers, coach-makers and architects, who leased groups of plots at a time on which to build. It was their decisions, anticipating the preferences of upper-class clients, which shaped the final look of the square, not any prescriptive estate plan. Yet although Merrion Square was very much a market-driven development, the estate was actively managed and its agents busied themselves in preparing roadways and sewers, securing boundaries and devising leases that would incentivise the early completion of buildings and enhance the long-term reputation of the estate. Regulations concerning house design, building materials and end-use were initially quite loose, but they had become much tighter by the time the square's last houses were being built. One of the factors that ensured its completion was the ease of access that builders had to the prolific brickfields in Sandymount and to building stone from quarries elsewhere on the Merrion estate.[31]

Rocque's view

In November 1756 a new map of the city was published, the first since Charles Brooking's less than satisfactory prospect of the city in 1728. Presented as an *Exact survey of the city and suburbs of Dublin*, the map was in several respects without precedent. Published in four folio sheets, it was entirely based on a fresh survey of the city, carried out over two years by its publisher and chief engraver John Rocque, a Huguenot who had already made his reputation in London with a series of town and county maps that had culminated in a twenty-four-sheet survey of London. Rocque stayed in Dublin for about six years, publishing during that time a variety of smaller city maps, a string of provincial town surveys and a four-sheet map of Co. Dublin. He was also employed by several landowners to produce detailed estate maps, his largest commission coming from the earl of Kildare.

Rocque's *Exact survey* of the city was an extraordinary achievement: working with a small team of Huguenot and Irish assistants and without any official sponsorship, he set out to triangulate the layout of the city and to plot every building within it. In the published version, individual houses were precisely delineated, more than 10,000 of them. This was a far more detailed treatment than in any of Rocque's other city maps and unlike any Dublin map before the Ordnance Survey eighty years later. Even if there was some imprecision in the representation of the poorer courts and lanes, this is only a problem at the margin, for the cartographic accuracy of Rocque when tested against modern surveys is of a very high order. His enterprise provided later generations with a unique window into the rapidly changing mid-eighteenth-century city, identifying new secondary lanes and alleys, non-official places of worship (notably Catholic chapels), port facilities, commercial warehouses and industrial premises (such as glass-houses, china works and sugar-houses). And with his background as an engraver of garden plans, Rocque revealed the diversity of urban open space: from Mosse's elaborate gardens to the unmanicured vastness of St Stephen's Green, from the sandpits on the Gardiner estate to the intimate formal gardens behind some of the established great houses.

There were over 400 subscribers to the first printing – the great, the

14. Interior, 20 Lower Dominick Street. The large terrace house, built c.1760,
contains behind its plain brick façade a spectacular display of Irish stucco work.
It was built by Robert West, one of Mosse's stuccodores, and West was at least
partly responsible for the bravura rococo work for which the house is famous.
West was the first indigenous stucco artist to reach the top of his profession.

good and a handful of builder-developers. The maps kept selling – in several altered states – before a new edition was published in 1773. Rocque revealed the city to its citizens in a novel and exciting way, its layout depicted with an unimagined level of accuracy. The faint traces of the long-demolished city walls were evident in his streetscape, the disparity between the closely packed old city and Liberties districts and the generously spaced east side. Also the clutter of the south-side quays and nearby streets were shown in striking contrast to the grid-iron layout of the Jervis estate and the uninterrupted passageway that now ran along the north quays for nearly 1,300 metres. Rocque's motives for producing such an exceptional level of detail can only be surmised: in the early stages of his project there was talk of a rival map being published, coming from the hand of the city surveyor, Roger Kendrick. It never appeared, but it may have spurred on the ever-resourceful Frenchman.[32]

Rocque's *Exact survey* did not capture developments beyond the edge of the city, but his smaller-scale *Survey of the city, harbour, bay and environs of Dublin* (1757) and his county maps of 1760 documented landscape change beyond the outskirts. In these later maps, several features stand out: the mushrooming of several hundred detached villa residences, all within easing riding distance of the city, 'delicious mansions of content' which stretched northwards from Clontarf to Coolock, Santry and Swords, westwards along the Tolka valley from Glasnevin to Blanchardstown, and on a few favoured locations overlooking the Liffey from Chapelizod to Leixlip; on the south side, isolated developments were springing up from Rathfarnham to Dundrum, Stillorgan to Monkstown, so that the countryside around the bay seemed to be 'spangled with white villas'.[33] The Fitzwilliam estate was first to respond to this demand for villa accommodation by laying out the lengthy Merrion and Cross Avenues in the 1750s, fine new roads that lay above the coast and were four miles from the city centre, and other owners with ample demesnes and sea views like the earl of Carysfort at Stillorgan copied the Fitzwilliam example. Most of the villas were summer retreats, but some became the main residence for families, 'free from the noise and bustle that attends/A life of business, in the nauseous town'. Blackrock, 'a long village by the shore', became both a service centre for the villas and a particular beneficiary of the tentative fashion for sea-bathing.[34]

A second tendency evident in Rocque's county maps was the rapid growth of mills upstream along the Liffey and dotted along both the Dodder and Tolka. Where once water-power had been chiefly used for grain-milling for local consumers, now it was being harnessed for a diversity of textile, iron, rapeseed and paper-making processes, polluting the rivers but giving substantial employment, and the first mill-villages were already appearing at Ballsbridge, Templeogue and Palmerstown. But the greatest change plotted by Rocque was downstream of the city and outside the harbour. Since the beginning of the eighteenth century the city had tried to tackle the problem for shipping caused by the great sand bar in Dublin Bay and at the same time to minimise silting along the narrow channels approaching the quays, and their efforts had focused on the construction of 'the Great South Wall' that ran from Ringsend point eastwards into the bay, the intention being both to provide additional shelter and to alter tidal patterns and the resulting sand deposits. The Great Wall was almost half a mile long by Rocque's time, and it continued to engage the attentions of the Ballast Office, a standing committee of the Corporation, until its completion in 1778. Navigation problems in the Bay remained into the next century, but the landmark wall was both a symbol of the taming of the elements and the first major step towards reducing the hazards for shipping outside the harbour.[35]

Word power

At the beginning of July 1753 the earl of Kildare, the twentieth to hold that title, arrived in Dublin to extraordinary acclaim. He had gone to London with the publicly declared intention of petitioning the king for the dismissal of the Lord Lieutenant, the duke of Dorset, an unheard of gesture of defiance towards the viceregal office. During his first period in office (1730–37), Dorset had been celebrated for his expansive hospitality in the Castle, but he and his lieutenants, in place again since 1750, were now deeply resented by many Irish MPs. He presided over a series of extremely fractious parliamentary sessions which culminated in the Money Bill dispute of 1753, and he was associated with one of the two parties to the dispute. Overweening personal ambition, poor political judgement, a succession battle among Irish parliamentarians as to who in future would manage government business, were all ingredients in this polarisation of parliamentary life, but tectonic shifts in Westminster politics at the same time exacerbated local rivalries. Families (including the Gardiners) were divided, and friendships (notably of close neighbours in Henrietta Street) were sundered, but the final outcome in 1755 was a compromise: the installation of a new generation of patronage managers (specifically the Ponsonby family from Kilkenny) and the pensioning off of older faces (notably Speaker Henry Boyle). Kildare as the senior resident peer and impetuous as ever, epitomised the opposition to Dorset's government and in so doing borrowed the language of patriotism to mobilise support for the Speaker's cause, in opposition to the gaggle of supposedly corrupt 'English' placemen. As with the Wood's Halfpence dispute thirty years before, second-order issues ignited a political fire which was then sustained by a huge pamphlet and newspaper war. But the fire was broader, the language richer, the participation greater than in the 1720s, and for one reason in particular: the upheaval that had recently occurred in Dublin municipal politics.

The Corporation, with its cumbersome representative structure drawn from the twenty-five guilds, had hardly altered since the Hanoverian succession. The city had grown, new trades appeared, new wealth generated, but aldermanic control of the Assembly had remained in overwhelmingly Anglican hands, politically Whiggish of course, commercially representative of the bigger merchant houses, but to those outside the charmed aldermanic world it seemed increasingly oligarchic and exclusive. There had been grumblings in the 1730s, but the first real challenge had arisen in the early 1740s when two names came to the surface – Charles Lucas, a young and prolix apothecary originally from Co. Clare, and James, younger son of David Digges La Touche, who ran the silk manufacturing side of the family's multiple interests and who had sponsored the new Weavers Hall on the Coombe.[36] Both had at different times served as guild representatives in the Tholsel but Lucas was the more unrestrained critic, first of slack aldermanic practices, then of aldermanic corruption and the unconstitutional denial of the chartered rights of the Common Council and of the free citizenry. From his earliest pamphlets Lucas positioned himself as the champion of the trade guilds and their members, initially with little result. But the golden moment came in August 1748 when one of the sitting MPs for the city died and Lucas, despite his intermediate social status, decided to test his popularity among the city electorate of freemen and freeholders, which then stood at over 3,500. With no by-election until Parliament reassembled more than a year later, it was to be a very long campaign. At first Lucas and La Touche competed for support against one of the more orthodox aldermanic candidates, but after the death of the second sitting MP in May 1749 the pair came together on a joint ticket.[37]

Their campaign, its methods and ideological content, reshaped the practice of politics in the city. Canvassing went on for over fourteen months. The masters and wardens of a majority of the guilds mobilised support among their members and organised meetings and resolutions. Lucas and La Touche directed their appeal, literally and metaphorically, to the free tradesmen of the city, whether at boozy hustings or in printed essays. With the two aldermanic candidates vigorously contesting the pitch and well able to call in multiple debts of friendship and obligation from freemen, it was a highly adversarial campaign and its bruising longevity strengthened the sense of fraternal solidarity within many of the guilds.

The visible legacy of the campaign was a huge outpouring of print from the 'popular' candidates – mainly from Lucas himself who produced some twenty election addresses and ten other tracts. In June 1749 he launched a weekly newspaper, *The Censor*, which was the city's first exclusively party political newspaper. Lucas shaped his campaign around a Swiftian attack on both city and national governance, applying his earlier critique of the city fathers to the Castle, the king's ministers and their tyrannical denial of Irish liberties. Lucas was never a systematic thinker and his ideas derived from an eclectic reading of Molyneux, Swift and Country Whigs in England, but in the excitements of 1749 his supercharged rhetoric and vivid representation of a free and ancient constitution corrupted by modern vested interest brought the Dublin workshop into the world of politics.[38]

With the reassembly of Parliament in November 1749, MPs were encouraged by the Castle to pursue Lucas as an 'enemy of his country', with the intention that he should be charged and imprisoned on the authority of Parliament. However, he fled before he could be arrested. La Touche was elected to one of the city seats but was quickly disqualified on the spurious grounds that he and Lucas had used 'undue influence' to mobilise electoral support. The alderman candidates therefore took the two seats, Lucas's newspaper was closed down, and it seemed that College Green was quite impervious to 'guild power'. But it was a pyrrhic victory. Many of those who had supported the challenge to what was seen as the city's golden circle continued to act informally as the 'Free Citizens', influencing municipal and (in 1756) a parliamentary by-election when they endorsed a Presbyterian alderman, James Dunn. He won the seat and was not prevented from entering Parliament, despite making a strong commitment to municipal reform. Prior to this advance, the 'Lucas affair' had indirectly but quite clearly influenced the conduct of politics within the Irish Parliament itself. The 'popular' and 'patriotic' arguments that had circulated so freely in 1749 were taken up four years later by the scribblers and writers supporting Kildare and Boyle in their struggle with the duke of Dorset and his Irish allies. And there was the new willingness by the Boyle party to co-opt the street in order to demonstrate to London the unpopularity and incapacity of their opponents.

It was a dangerous game, as events in 1759 suddenly revealed. Shortly before the reassembly of Parliament that autumn and midway through the Seven Years War, rumours circulated in Dublin that the Crown was about to introduce measures to prepare the way for a permanent dissolution of the Irish Parliament and an Anglo-Irish union. No one in power was actually canvassing for such a momentous change, but the rumour

gained credibility 'in coffee-houses and all places of resort [and was] proclaimed by the minor orators of societies; sung at corners of streets; and
commented upon by coal-porters'.[39] It culminated one Monday afternoon
in early December when a menacing demonstration took place outside
the Parliament House at the time that MPs were entering it for business.
Since the 1720s there had been many instances of city riots between territorial gangs, perhaps picking up on much older neighbourhood rivalries. These gangs were composed principally of journeymen, and the riots
occurred sometimes in the streets, sometimes at the seasonal fairs at Donnybrook and Oxmantown. The earliest were between young artisans in
specific craft occupations, but the great confrontations in the 1730s and
1740s were between the 'Liberty Boys' and 'Ormond Boys', the former
group Protestant and linked to the textile trades, the latter mainly Catholic and associated with the slaughter yards and tallow chandleries north
of the river around Smithfield. Every few years there was a flare-up, and
an alarmed response by the city authorities. But the violence was limited,
stylised and geographically contained, and the contests were recreational,
not political. December 1759 was different.[40]

Several thousands assembled that day in College Green, and in the
excitement the precincts of Parliament were breached and dozens of peers
and MPs manhandled. The Lord Mayor was decidedly slow to call for military assistance, and it was only on the initiative of the Lord Lieutenant
that the main cavalry guard were sent in to clear the streets around Parliament and to arrest protestors. There were several hours of disorder in the
Dame Street area and some reports claimed fatalities. A French plot was
immediately suspected in Whitehall, but contrary evidence was supplied
to William Pitt by the Lord Lieutenant, the duke of Bedford, who discounted any Jacobite-style conspiracy and put the blame firmly on Protestant artisans from the Liberties, although conceding that the Catholic
poor had swelled their numbers. There was indeed a strong suspicion in
the Castle that the riot had been orchestrated, possibly by College students, that men in College livery had beat the drum in the Liberties and
harangued a crowd in Weavers Square, leading them via the Coombe and
Patrick Street towards Parliament, picking up extra numbers all the time.
But the scale and intensity of the ensuing demonstration suggests that if
there were indeed organisers they had found a willing audience, alert to
the significance of Parliament and the implications of its closure. There
were peaceful precedents: a political crowd from the Liberties had been

spotted in 1753 when it was claimed that 2,000 men with green boughs in their hats had marched into the city in support of the earl of Kildare during the Money Bill dispute. As one writer suggested in the wake of the anti-Union riot, since the election year of 1749 'our Dublin citizens ... have been so wrong-headed as to talk of national rights, of liberty, of worthy representatives, sensible and faithful constituents, and free and uninfluenced electors ... They now read newspapers and even the votes of the House of Commons ...' And by 'citizens' the writer included 'the lowest tradesmen'.[41]

The most tangible legacy of the riot was, perhaps surprisingly, a victory for the city reformers. Dunn and a few allies had forlornly tried to get support for a statutory change of the municipal constitution, but the debacle of December 1759 made their task a great deal easier. The duke of Bedford was deeply embarrassed by London criticism of the riot and was supportive of more representative local governance within the city and of enhanced powers for the city officers that would allow them to have authority as magistrates to enforce the criminal law across the whole city and Liberties. Within weeks the Corporation Recorder, James Grattan, drafted a compromise measure that would allow the guilds a complete say over their representatives to the lower house and a far stronger say over the election of sheriffs, Lord Mayors, and the filling of vacancies in the upper house, but which also gave the city officers magisterial power in the Liberties. This received government support and became law as the 33 Geo. II, *c.*16. It was to be the only constitutional change in the city's governance between the New Rules of the 1670s and the wholesale changes of 1840. By later standards it was a modest shift, not affecting the exclusively Protestant character of the civic community. But in making the Corporation more responsive to the Protestant craft world, the 1760 Reform Act began to weaken the authority of the upper house, and in the longer run (from the 1790s) it helped make the Corporation a bastion of plebeian Protestantism within a changing city.

After the accession of King George III in 1760, Charles Lucas returned to Dublin – with two medical degrees and a martyr's reputation – and took part in the first general election in more than thirty years. He was elected for one of the city seats and was welcomed into Parliament by a band of younger, richer and better connected admirers. They went on to form a ginger group of 'patriot' MPs who in the course of the 1760s managed to exploit the political instability in Westminster and the rapid turnover of viceroys, and drew inspiration from John Wilkes's radical crusade in Middlesex in a campaign to strengthen the constitutional position of the Irish Parliament. They were closely associated with a bi-weekly paper set up in 1763 and soon known universally by its sub-title, the *Freeman's Journal*. It was printed in an old mural tower beside St Audeon's Gate by Phoebe Bate, one of the widow-printers who featured so often in the eighteenth-century book trade. Its patrons were a shadowy 'committee for conducting a free press', and its 'editor' in the first years was Henry Brooke, playwright, author and long-time supporter of Lucas. Thanks to Brooke, it became the city's most popular weekly reading with its mix of reformist political opinion, original news and philosophical commentary, and in so doing helped sustain the new prominence of politics in the public life of the city. The 'patriot' MPs were the beneficiaries of the *Journal*, but the superintending 'committee' of nine were made up of the new type of guild-based politician, who of course attracted the scorn of their betters:

> That low, malicious, motley tribe;
> That puritanic, vile committee;
> The pest and scandal of our city,
> Who slander virtue, libel station,
> And trumpet faction through the nation.[42]

It inspired short-lived opponents, notably *The Mercury*, produced between 1766 and 1773 by the Catholic printer James Hoey Jr., which mixed government advertising with satirical attacks on city patriots and their malevolent anti-Catholicism.

Less controversial but no less ambitious was a monthly periodical, *The Dublin Magazine*, launched in 1762. It was not the first literary journal produced in the city; indeed, the publisher, Peter Wilson, had tried something similar in 1744 (with *The Meddler*), and the model of a monthly journal of essays, philosphical and political, had been well established in London with Addison's *Spectator* half a century earlier. Leading Dublin booksellers (notably Edward Exshaw) had been publishing Irish editions of the London monthlies since the 1730s, and the specialist bookseller Jean-Pierre Droz had promoted some of his French literary imports in the *Literary Journal* (1745–9). But Wilson's *Dublin Magazine* was distinctive, with its strongly Irish content and local historical interests. The first item in the first issue was a reproduction of John Speed's 1610 map of the city, with an accompanying note by 'Philohibernicus' who suggested that contemplation of antiquity should be left to others and that readers should share his pleasure in 'considering my native city, as having arisen, in little more than a century and a half, from the lowest ebb of wretchedness and contempt, to almost the summit of elegance, extent and magnificence'.[43] Over the following three years Wilson supplied his readers with a stream of essays and letters, engravings of new city buildings and distant exotica, reviews of Rousseau and designs for improved coaches. One MP, stung by a harsh judgement of his literary talents, had Wilson committed to prison for a month in 1763, but the business thrived. Yet, despite sales of up to 1,000 copies, he closed the *Magazine* after three years, devoting himself in old age to easier publishing challenges. The baton was taken up in 1771 by Thomas Walker (a former Exshaw apprentice), whose monthly *Hibernian Magazine*, less adventurous than the *Dublin Magazine*, ran without a break for forty years, albeit with a variety of owners.

One of Peter Wilson's other innovations was a directory of the city's traders, published with their addresses. He produced his first alphabetical list in 1751, a second in 1753, with the *Directory* appearing annually from 1755, complete with a city map, lists of lawyers and physicians and updated information on Corporation, guild and parish officers. In the first edition, some 925 traders were listed, the great majority being sole traders, and the number grew in every edition. By the end of the century the list included more than 5,000 wholesale traders, master manufacturers and shopkeepers, but the minor service trades, the street traders and hawkers, the public houses and whiskey shops remained invisible. 'Merchants', 'wine merchants' and sugar refiners made up a quarter (238) of the 1751 list, but by the end of the century wholesale importers and other 'merchants' formed no more than 10 per cent of a greatly expanded commercial listing.[44] The directory was primarily a tool for merchants and wholesalers in identifying their clients, enforcing debts and measuring opportunities, but its perennial appearance was a sign of the complexity and scale that Dublin's business world had reached, for apart from London no other city in the British world saw this kind of regular publication for some decades.

Directories, however, only listed the masters in a trade and this can be misleading. For instance, in 1760 only nineteen booksellers and three printers were listed, hardly suggesting a dynamic sector. Yet we know that in the course of the eighteenth century there were at least 24,000 books, pamphlets and paper titles printed in Dublin, a reminder that at any stage behind the small numbers of bookmen listed in the directories there were probably fifteen times as many actually employed in the print trades in the city, including irregular booksellers, journeymen printers and a small army of apprentices, and not including the growing numbers in paper-making, engraving and type-founding. The continued ability of Dublin printer-publishers to supply the Irish market with local reprints of London titles more cheaply than the imported product depended on their success in keeping costs down, specifically in finding ways to control wages of their lowly employees.

Relatively little of international note was first published in Dublin, apart from works with an exclusively Irish focus. Two such titles related specifically to the city: Walter Harris's *History and antiquities of the city of Dublin* (1766), and John Rutty's *Essay towards a natural history of the county of Dublin* (1772). Harris's posthumous work was antiquarian confetti, drawing principally on unpublished late seventeenth-century investigations and providing a suitably Whiggish gloss on the early history of 'this now great metropolis'. Rutty, who like Harris was sponsored by the Dublin Society, produced work that, if equally eclectic, was far more original. A Quaker physician with a large but unremunerative practice, he spent most of his life in Pill Lane, writing and experimenting and publishing. A key figure in the local Society of Friends (of whom there were then about a thousand in and around Dublin), he was one of a coterie of city doctors trained in the rigorous Leiden medical school. Like many of them, he had a lifetime fascination with the natural environment – botanical, geological, meterological – and how it interacted with human health, and his home was something of a primitive laboratory. He was a relentless pattern-seeker and a systematiser, but his science was informed by a huge respect for ancient medical knowledge and a powerful but private religious faith. Although never in the limelight, he was a central figure in Medico-Philosophical Society, a scientific salon that met monthly from 1756 for many years. Several of his fellow members practised in what by then was the largest of the city's hospitals, built from the estate of a much wealthier doctor, Richard Steevens, and opened on the city's western edge in 1733. It also received a legacy from another Leiden alumnus, Edward Worth, who had practised for many years in Bride Street and was one of the city's most active book collectors. Worth's horde of some 4,400 books, a third of them medical and scientific, was bequeathed to the hospital to inform and enlighten the medics of the new foundation. The exquisite

Worth Library remains a time capsule revealing the boundless intellectual curiosity of an eighteenth-century Dubliner.[45]

Capital credit

The twenty-five years running from the late 1740s to the early 1770s were a time of more or less continuous expansion of the city's trade, both inland and overseas. The character of wholesale trade established in the late seventeenth century was little changed, however. Dublin held onto its position as national warehouse and, less confidently, as national workshop. Many of the leading luxury dealers and manufacturers played a dominant role in fitting and furnishing the country seats of the gentry, many of which were rebuilt or extended in this period. For example, John Houghton, 'the most eminent carver in Dublin' in the 1750s, not only worked for the Castle and leading city institutions, but had aristocratic clients from Kerry to Fermanagh who drew on his skills in wood and marble, and his superb picture frames and mirrors were widely dispersed.[46] There was in this period an intensification of Anglo-Irish trade, linen exports soared, and Dublin forged an ever closer financial relationship with the city of London. Links with the port of Liverpool were now stronger than with Chester, reflecting strategic economic changes underway in the Midlands and north of England. But some erosion of Dublin's workshop economy was evident by the 1760s, thanks partly to growing provincial competition, partly to the penetration of English textiles, iron goods, china and even beer.[47] But in one respect Dublin had become less dependent on English imports: after bad harvests and very high prices in 1757, the duke of Bedford supported a proposal to use public funds to cover all the costs of transporting Irish grain and flour from any county outside Dublin to the city's markets. The 'inland bounty' scheme was credited with giving a huge boost to tillage across Leinster (although the shift in relative prices between pastoral and cereal farming may explain this rather better); certainly the bounty did help to shift the geography of Dublin's food supply, ending the partial dependence on cross-channel supplies and encouraging the construction of flour mills from Meath to Cork. The measure (despite many modifications) stayed in place for forty years; it was controversial but, helped by the ongoing improvements in turnpike roads and the opening of the Grand Canal linking the city with the grain districts of south Leinster, the bounty had a benign impact on the city and gave a new stability to its markets. There was no food riot recorded in Dublin after the 1740s. MPs wanted a quiet city.[48]

The most startling economic episode in this era was a series of bank failures in the 1750s. The first credit crisis in two decades came with the bankruptcy of the Catholic firm of Dillon and Ferrall in March 1754, but the real shock came twelve months later after rumours of multiple bank failures caused a public panic and the thousands holding private bank paper desperately sought cash. Fade's old Quaker bank in Thomas Street, now trading as Willcocks and Dawson and probably the most important source of paper credit in the whole country, ceased trading and their chief cashier absconded. Two days later the other Quaker bank, Lennox and French, also closed its doors and the partners disappeared: 'never was known in this kingdom so great a calamity ... an entire stagnation of trade and credit, and many families [are] ruined by the failure of the banks', reported one Dublin resident.[49] The political consequences were dire. A parliamentary inquiry blamed the city's merchants for mismanagement and for the reckless creation of credit without the capital to support it. Legislation was passed prohibiting merchants in the future from describing themselves as bankers. Not unconnected with this, Nathaniel Clements and his parliamentary allies entered the field in 1758 with an experiment in deposit banking, but to his great embarrassment the scheme had to be aborted in 1759, albeit without bankruptcy, and he survived as the key figure in the Irish Treasury. But Clements's bank closure helped to bring down two other banks, those of Mitchell and Macarell and of Alderman Dawson. This prolonged and multi-layered banking crisis was in many respects a legacy of the over-rapid growth in trade and business confidence earlier in the decade, but it was brought to a head by bad harvests, foreign exchange pressures and the dislocating effects of the Seven Years War (1756–63).[50]

The legislation of 1756 placing a barrier between involvement in wholesale trade and in banking caused much resentment in the city, and this was compounded by Clements's cavalier involvement in the business two years later: 'banks are absolutely necessary to put the whole credit-machine in motion' and only merchants could understand their function, protested one merchant pamphleteer.[51] When the 1759 riots erupted, many saw a link between Clements's financial excesses and the troubles on the street. This was probably not true, but frustration at the seemingly untramelled power of the great office-holders and the perceived weakening position of the Corporation and the Guild of Merchants coloured the 1761 general election. Shortly afterwards some leading merchants decided to form a lobby group, a standing Committee of Merchants. Its declared purpose was to influence government and the legislature in 'the defence of trade against any illegal imposition, and the solicitation of such laws as might prove beneficial'.[52] This innocuous-sounding manifesto disguised the significance of the initiative: while many of those involved were established members of the Guild of Merchants, the new committee distanced itself from 'corporate bodies' and constituted itself on 'liberal principles ... no regard being had in it to any difference of party or opinion, but merely to consideration in trade or capacity, and active disposition to be useful'. This was code for a membership that would be religiously mixed: around seven of the twenty-one merchants were Protestant dissenters and four were Catholic. The inclusion of men such as Anthony MacDermott of Usher's Quay and Michael Cosgrave of Abbey Street was indeed a political risk and indicates where the impetus for the initiative lay. And the 'illegal impositions' that upset the Committee were emanating not just from Parliament and the city's big men, but also from below, from the turbulent artisan world. The growing incidence of direct action by weavers, butchers and other craft journeymen against the free movement of goods was threatening the interests of the men of capital.[53]

The Committee's real claim to fame was as progenitor of one of the finest classical buildings of the city, the Royal Exchange. The background to this project brings us back to the matter of bridges. One of the arguments of Gardiner's friends in 1749 when advocating a new downstream crossing had been the woefully congested state of Essex Bridge as a result of increased wheeled traffic, a problem to which the Liffey ferries could offer no solution. But of course, were any such a bridge to be sanctioned, the Custom House and much of the commercial activity in the Temple Bar district and along the higher quays would be drawn eastwards, undermining property values in the centre and west of the city. It became a well-rehearsed argument, but in the short term this fear was the catalyst for pre-emptive action: Essex Bridge, already much damaged, was rebuilt *de novo* without totally blocking the flow of traffic crossing over it in a little over two years (but one casualty in the process was George I's statue, so little regarded that it retired to a crate in Aungier Street for many years). The new bridge, 15.5 metres broad, was far wider than any existing crossing and when it opened in 1755 it was regarded as a triumph of civil engineering, thanks not least to the spirited self-promotion of its architect and clerk of works, George Semple. The Semples were long established in the various branches of Dublin's building trades, but George was the first to describe himself as an 'architect', reflecting an unusual enthusiasm for book-based research into diverse plans and projects that allowed him to ruminate on both technical and aesthetic issues. He seems to have been the first to sketch out plans for a new south-side street, equal in width to the bridge, that would extend the line from Capel Street across the bridge to the edge of Dublin Castle (a printed version of his plan exists from 1757).[54]

The attraction of such a project was evident to all those anxious to undermine the case for a new downstream bridge or the transplantation of the Custom House, and Semple's idea gained surprising political momentum. An enabling Act in 1758, 31 Geo. II *c*.19, had the limited objective of facilitating such a development. But as Dublin's first 'Wide Streets' act, it set in motion a series of initiatives that over a forty-year period changed the city. Some uncertainty remains as to the prime movers behind this legislation, but Speaker John Ponsonby, the greatest beneficiary of the parliamentary turmoil earlier in the decade, supported it. Gorges Howard, a literary-minded attorney who had held a string of Crown and parliamentary appointments, claimed that the idea for the street arose from a dinner conversation in a local chophouse with a Revenue Commissioner.

This was unfair to Semple, but it was probably Howard who drafted the legislation and, as treasurer of the scheme, was certainly key to its implementation. Creating the new street involved the compulsory acquisition of a honeycomb of commercial properties close to the Custom House and, although funded by a generous parliamentary grant, it was a fraught process. With the threat from some of the tenants in residence challenging expropriation, Howard later boasted how he had employed a force of labourers at night, 'ready with ladders and other instruments' to strip the slates off those houses where legal resistance was threatened, driving 'several of the inhabitants … directly from their beds into the streets, some of them, in their fright, conceiving … that the city had been taken by storm'.[55] The legal process was completed and sites auctioned in 1762, the builders being obliged to clear their sites, build in brick and observe tight standards of elevation and alignment. Such restrictions were of course similar to those already being enforced by Gardiner, Clements and other private owners of east-side land. But where the latter generally sought gentry tenants, here the plan was to attract fashionable shopkeepers and warehousemen from older and more congested locations. In the event, 'Parliament Street' was a great success, with booksellers, silk mercers and lace-men opening businesses in the early years. The wily Philip Crampton, bookseller, property speculator and a former Lord Mayor, was a particularly active builder on the street. Knowing the Temple Bar neighbourhood intimately, he was perhaps crucial to its early success.[56]

Semple had also reflected on how this new commercial development could help open up the Castle. When first imagining Parliament Street, he had proposed an open piazza on land acquired by the commissioners south of Cork Hill and abreast the north-east corner of the Castle, suggesting the erection of a suitable monument at its centre. Others, it seems, touted the idea of a new viceregal chapel on the site. Thanks to Chesterfield's initiative in the mid-1740s, major improvements had been ongoing inside the Castle for a decade (including most of the great rooms that became the State Apartments), and the duke of Bedford, who sponsored new work in the upper Castle area, may well have been tempted by such schemes (one variant of Rocque's *Exact survey* rashly depicted the bijou square as a reality, bearing the name 'Bedford Square'). But certainly none of Bedford's short-stay successors in the early 1760s interested themselves in anything so permanent. Thus, as the new street took shape, the fate of the Cork Hill site remained in abeyance until the Committee of Merchants came along with an alternative idea: to use it for a great merchants' exchange, something worthier of the city's scale and wealth than the congested ground floor of the ageing Tholsel or the poky dealing rooms in Crampton Court behind the Custom House. The Committee first advertised their plans in November 1765. Within weeks the Guild of Merchants began a rival move with the same end in view. Parliament eventually gave financial support for the scheme, albeit after imposing a compromise: the site was to be assigned to trustees made up of representatives drawn equally from the Committee and the Corporation, and they were to assume responsibility for financing, design and construction of the new exchange. Predictably, it was the Committee men who did most of the work.[57]

The site, once the location of Cork House, was a challenging one: on rising ground beside the Poddle, it closed two vistas, that eastwards from Castle Street and southwards from Capel and Parliament Streets. The trustees' plan was to build on a scale that would proclaim the centrality of commerce in the city, even if the resulting edifice overshadowed the

*15. Painted in 1791, Malton's view across Essex Bridge and along
Parliament Street, with the vista closed by the Royal Exchange,
brought together in a single composition three of the most
important eighteenth-century building projects in the city.*

Castle. For the first time, an open competition to design a public building
was held; sixty-one entries were received, more than half coming from
England. The winner was an unknown young London-based architect,
Thomas Cooley, and his design took some ten years to realise. It was
funded in part by parliamentary grant but mainly by a series of lotteries. The resulting structure with its white Portland stone, soaring Corin-
thian columns and stunning interior was (unusually for Dublin) admired
from the very beginning. The very high quality of construction and chaste
neo-classical finish in stone and stucco contributed to its lasting impact.[58]
Yet in two respects the project was a failure: the vastness of the rotunda
assembly room implied the existence of a community of merchants that
were regularly engaged in face-to-face dealing, as in the great bourses of
seventeenth-century Europe. However, the character of trade was changing and by the time the Exchange opened its doors the attraction of a
great trading room for dealing in international bills of exchange was fast
diminishing. Anglo-Irish commerce was becoming more standardised
and financial services more specialised. More fundamentally, the expectation that the Exchange would permanently anchor wholesale trade to that

quarter of the town was dashed within a few years of its opening when plans for a new downstream Custom House finally got the go-ahead in 1780.

The merchants who planned the Exchange were primarily wholesale merchants, much of whose business was international. Far more numerous were the less capitalised traders who were to be found scattered through the market districts and in the old heart of the city. In High Street, for example, where brick buildings and ancient cagework houses, displaying their plaster walls and exposed oaken beams, still cohabited, the mix of traders shared one thing in common: they all depended on out-of-town custom, some of it wholesale, much of it retail; the printers of Catholic devotional material were based here, as were numerous shoe-makers, tailors, pin-makers and sadlers. There were also some two dozen woollen drapers trading in the street, the majority of whom were Catholic. The Hendricks, a Church of Ireland family, traded at the sign of the Sun and were employing two 'shop servants' in 1758 at a time when their stock in trade was valued at £5,080. Such a figure gives some indication of the variety and high quality of fabrics that would have been on display to dazzle the rural clientele. Drapers still sourced much of their cloth locally and in some cases became large-scale employers of Liberties' weavers, but with a growing volume of fashion cloth coming from English suppliers tensions between these great warehousemen and the weaving community were building up. Back in 1733 Dean Swift had been part of the first controversy over large-scale importation when seven drapers, 'seven vile citizens', were named and shamed for importing English woollens and silks, and the following spring Liberties' weavers ransacked one of the named drapers (Richard Eustace of High Street) before the army was summoned and one weaver was killed in the scuffle.[59] The most successful of the High Street woollen drapers at mid-century seems to have been Robert Lawless, who avoided trouble and ended up as one of Dublin's really wealthy Catholic traders. In old age he conformed to the established church, as did his son Nicholas a few years later. Robert had gone into banking in partnership with the Quaker John Dawson Coates in Thomas Street, and Nicholas extended this side of the business; his success as a banker was powerfully evident from major land purchases in Limerick and Kildare, his entry into Parliament in 1776, and in 1789 a peerage as the 1st Baron Cloncurry. High Street could still be the stepping stone to greatness.[60]

The world of fashion was, however, gravitating eastwards by the

1770s. Castle Street still had its array of goldsmiths and printers, woollen drapers and sadlers, but the principal corridor for luxury shopping now ran from Parliament Street along Dame Street, College Green and into the sinewy recesses of Grafton Street. Along this line the best gunsmiths and booksellers, silk mercers and dealers in other fashion fabrics were to be found, operating beside many less prestigious traders. Broader front-ages, greater light and easier access differentiated the new commercial streets from the old.[61] Just how much of the stock displayed in these premium shops was locally manufactured remains a vexed question. In their newspaper advertisements many shops boasted of the freshness and distinctiveness of their imported stock, but since the 1730s they had also been careful to declare their commitment to Irish and specifically to Dublin suppliers. Events in the late summer of 1763 were a case in point; it was a season of very high food prices and rumours spread that Cot-tingham and King, the largest silk mercers on Dame Street, were about to abandon their thirty to forty local suppliers in the Liberties and to import Lyon silks to the value of £20,000. A black flag was hung above the Weavers Hall in the Coombe, and the Dame Street premises had to be protected by the military. After some days, a crowd of some 500 jour-neymen and apprentices, unable to get access to the shop, destroyed over 1,000 yards of fine silks and £454 worth of silk on the bobbin in their suppliers' premises at eleven locations across the Liberties. Benjamin Houghton, already the largest Liberties silk manufacturer (and a sup-plier to the Castle), was blamed for stirring this up, but after a nine-hour jury trial he was cleared of the charge. Meanwhile Cottingham and King claimed in a parliamentary petition that the intended French imports had been worth a tenth the amount rumoured (though that was still very substantial), and that their object had been 'to obtain the newest patterns' to copy. They received generous parliamentary compensation for their losses but shortly afterwards left the business. One upshot of the affair was the move by the Weavers' Guild to secure Dublin Society patronage for a retail warehouse where Liberties' producers could avoid the tyranny of middleman mercers. Two years later the 'Irish Silk Ware-house' was opened with much publicity and aristocratic endorsement in Parliament Street, where it survived for two decades and helped to protect a fragile but highly vocal manufacturing sector.[62]

Other trades like coach-making, cabinet-making and upholstery were only marginally threatened by luxury imports – as long as they kept abreast of English fashion. But the lure of London and Paris goods was always a challenge for the local producers of small-scale, high-value temptations such as perfumes, lace and fine silk, watches, silver and other plated goods. Alison Fitzgerald has suggested that by the 1750s nearly two-fifths of the plated goods being sold in Dublin were imported from England, presumably on local account.[63] Agents working for the new-style English manufacturers of Sheffield plate and Staffordshire ware also began to appear: in 1772 Josiah Wedgwood sent an assistant to open a shop in College Green, and for five years his relatively cheap, distinctive and immediately fashionable creamware pottery found a ready sale. This helped to extinguish the local Delftware business of Henry Delamain, whose workshops on the North Strand and at Palmerstown had employed 'several hundred' at their peak.[64] There was indeed little that was distinctive about locally produced luxury goods: one element in the longevity of leading firms like Calderwood, the goldsmith on Cork Hill, or William Moore, the Abbey Street cabinet-maker, was their success in closely monitoring cross-channel trends, aided by the growing movement of assistants, apprentices and pattern-books between Dublin and London.[65]

And yet, despite periodic protests about the inflow of English goods (whether from patriotic mercantilists or Liberties' manufacturers), it is likely that the diversity and range of pre-industrial craft manufacturing within the city was never greater than at this time. Wilson's *Directory* in 1763 listed around 125 distinct crafts and services in its list of traders, and no doubt it overlooked many low-prestige crafts in the informal sector. But the city's workshop economy was clearly vulnerable to being undercut at times of cyclical glut, and the terrifying ease with which public controversy could be stirred up about English, French or country imports testifies to the sheer size of the workshop sector and to its sense of insecurity.[66]

In terms of the quality of locally produced goods, whether printed fabrics or furniture, coaches or fine harness, it does seem that the standards in design and finish were rising in the third quarter of the eighteenth century. Wealthy consumers were now more fastidious, given the growing numbers who had travelled on the Continent and whose taste for fine things had been sharpened. Many more had been touched by French high culture via the printed image, the stage set or close sight of the latest objects imported from Paris, and a steady demand existed for the replication of rococo and neoclassical fashions at affordable prices. Even among the wealthy, the cachet of supporting Irish manufacture while keeping abreast of the latest fashion was becoming more evident.[67] Probably the involvement of the Dublin Society was the single most important factor sustaining the city's craft economy, both by the development grants it gave to import-substituting initiatives like Delamain's pottery, and more particularly by underwriting the costs of training of journeymen and apprentices in the techniques of drawing and design. The Society took over a successful private drawing school located off Dame Street in 1750 and the rooms were then 'furnished with several fine models in plaster imported from Paris'; it funded a series of part-time classes for promising teenagers, creating what became a highly successful training academy in the plastic arts which in its first twenty years admitted over 750 students. The original initiative was timely and practical, greatly helped by its French-trained first master Robert West, and almost immediately the school was seen as having real impact on the quality of worksmanship among carvers and engravers, cabinet-makers and coach manufacturers, launching many who went on to achieve distinction in a variety of fields. As John Turpin has argued, here was a clear case where without challenging the guilds, innovation was stimulated from above and where 'the intellectual Irish gentry who directed the Dublin Society clearly looked to France, not England, for guidance in educational practice'.[68]

West's greatest pupil was Hugh Douglas Hamilton, son of a Crow Street wig-maker. Even as a journeyman painter he had attracted the notice of the La Touches and their circle, but the best evidence of his precocious talent is a collection of sixty-six drawings of street life in Dublin which he executed in 1760, possibly intending them for publication as 'The cries of Dublin' (they were only published two and a half centuries later). The intimate and remarkably sympathetic portrayal of a variety of street traders and domestic servants, waifs and scavengers suggests a bustling outdoor world completely familiar to the young draughtsman, and a world that no other artist sought to capture – hinting at a diverse material culture of the poor using the recycled baubles of fashion (especially second-hand clothes), coarse earthenware and eating utensils, simple country goods and cheap print (see Pl. 10).[69] Hamilton, it seems, found no demand for such an exposé, and he went on to spend much of his life abroad, first as a success in London, then as a contented exile in Rome for fifteen years, before returning to Mount Street in the 1790s to become a disgruntled portrait painter of the top faces in the city.

For upper-class Dubliners, the grand tour to Italy was usually a much shorter affair, a rite of passage which for some proved educational and for a few an intoxicating exposure to connoisseurship and the art of collecting. Joseph Leeson, only son of the eponymous brewer of St Stephen's Green and the property developer who had earned Swift's sarcasm, was a spectacular example of the latter. Travelling to Italy in mid-life (after the death of his father), Leeson went to Rome in 1744 to purchase furnishings, paintings and antique statuary for his country house, then being built in west Wicklow and designed by Richard Castle. However his colossal collection of purchases was lost on the voyage home to a French privateer; he returned to Rome in 1750 and had more success. The result was the dazzling display of antiquity and rococo inside and outside his Palladian palace at Russborough, 'where artificers from most parts of Europe' were involved in decorating this 'necklace of glinting local granite'.[70] Leeson was accompanied on the second trip to Rome by his nephew Joseph Henry, heir to the great Presbyterian banker Hugh Henry; Joseph remained in Rome for eleven years before returning to Dublin and establishing in Sackville Street one of the better picture collections in the city.[71]

Among their close friends in Rome was James Caulfeild, Viscount Charlemont, a young Ulster peer whose family base had been in Jervis Street. His Mediterranean education spanned ten years (1746–55) and included an extended trip around the Aegean and through Egypt and Anatolia. Intelligent, well-tutored and with a strong visual sense, Charlemont was part of a group of wealthy young connoisseurs based in Rome that regularly fraternised with a network of gifted artists, several of whom were to shape neoclassicism in Britain in the next generation, in particular Robert Adam and William Chambers, the future architect of the king's works. Charlemont's easy sociability and artistic sensibility made him a central figure in this milieu, and when he returned to Ireland in 1755 he came with a trained eye and the friendship of some of the best architects and artists in Europe. Several of these, thanks to Charlemont, would leave their mark on Dublin.

Although it was many years before he decided to make Dublin his principal residence, Charlemont was soon involved in two major long-running architectural projects. First there was his new townhouse: he secured a double site from Luke Gardiner's son at the central point above Mosse's gardens, commanding views south-eastwards across the city and the bay. With designs supplied by Chambers, he commissioned a fine stone-faced mansion, certainly not the largest of city palaces but in the quality of its finish and attention to detail setting new standards. Unlike any other great house, it had a strong stylistic relationship with its neighbours, and the whole terrace of 'Palace Row' when completed was visually striking. As Robin Usher suggests, in this as in many respects it is comparable to Chambers's great mansion in Edinburgh built for Sir Lawrence Dundas. Charlemont was indeed an architectural enthusiast but a very poor financial manager, and three decades later parts of the house were still unfinished. However, from c.1770 the public rooms, designed to display Charlemont's collections of statuary, vases, coins and paintings, were complete, including the Library annexe in the back gardens. Charlemont House now became a magnet for all those who could secure entry, and in later years it was the natural rendezvous for Charlemont's political allies and friends.[72]

More homely and less resolutely masculine was the family base a mile north-east of the city, Marino House, where Clare-born Lady Charlemont held sway (a late marriage, brokered, it seems, by his physician Charles Lucas). But on its encompassing demesne Charlemont indulged his compulsion to build to even greater effect. There he erected an experimental 'Gothic' tower beside a small artificial lake to house a collection of vases, but the main project was the Casino, a Roman temple inspired by one of Palladio's great villas, La Rotonda, outside Vicenza, which he had once inspected. The Casino became a monumental essay in neoclassical precision in which Chambers and Charlemont cooperated very closely (even though Chambers never saw it or indeed any of his Dublin buildings). Deceptive, even playful in design, this secular temple dedicated to the arts perched on the skyline above the Clontarf road and marked the arrival of something quite new, with its oddity of purpose, ingenuity of design and superb quality of carving, stucco and fittings, all of which reflected Charlemont's fastidious fussiness and the artistic and managerial skills of Simon Vierpyl, a London-born stone-carver whom he had befriended in Rome and brought back to Dublin. Vierpyl oversaw the construction and internal decoration of both the townhouse and the suburban temple, on each of which close to £10,000 was spent in the nine years up to 1771. A small group of established Dublin master craftsmen worked on the two projects, and the skills that they honed in private work for Charlemont found public expression in the Exchange in the 1770s and in the new Custom House and other great public projects of the 1780s and 1790s.[73]

Charlemont was an enlightened spider, with many webs. Perhaps his most enduring one was an organisation created late in life, the Royal Irish

16. An 1860s photograph of the bronze copy of Giambologna's Mercury, *which Charlemont had commissioned in Rome. It stood midway along the corridor leading from Charlemont House to the Venus library and gallery at the bottom of his garden, all part of Charlemont's spectacular display of classical and enlightened connoisseurship, and open to visitors who came suitably recommended. The Venus library and gallery were demolished in the 1930s.*

Academy. There had been at least two attempts during the century to create a scholarly salon in the city, a meeting point for those with interests in history, science and 'polite literature'. The Physico-Historical Society in the 1740s had brought together such a group of clergy, doctors and gentlemen of the College, but it lacked strong patronage and faded away. A group attached to the Dublin Society had tried something similar in 1772, with a particular focus on Irish antiquities. But it was a measure of Charlemont's prestige and stature that his academy succeeded where others had failed. It received a royal charter in 1786 with terms of reference of sufficient intellectual breadth to attract almost every man of leisure with an interest in the sciences, mathematics or antiquities, and it became a fashionable assembly with nearly one hundred members and able to sustain a

vigorous publication programme. But its early success was more a reflection of existing intellectual interests than a sign of startling new thinking.
Slightly over half the original council of twenty-one were Anglican clergy,
befitting a project that, in one recent judgement, was 'the first concerted
attempt of the Anglo-Irish Ascendancy to colonise the ancient Irish past'.[74]

America

Charlemont, aristocratic patriot as well as aesthete, made a rare street
appearance in November 1771 when he acted as pall-bearer at the huge
funeral for Charles Lucas. And within a year, Vierpyl's apprentice Edward
Smyth was commissioned to produce a full-sized marble statue of the old
warrior for the Exchange (where it stands to this day). But by the time of his
death Lucas had become more a symbol of the struggle for freemen's rights
than an actual champion, and younger men were now extending his legacy
of raucous guildhall politics and patriotic rhetoric in Parliament. Two in
particular were just beginning long public careers. The first was Sir Edward
Newenham, a Revenue official who had first gained fame as the ruthless
enemy of the Rush smugglers; he married well, displayed an extravagant
love of all things American and eventually sat as MP for Co. Dublin for
more than twenty years (with the Liberties his main source of votes). Then
there was James Napper Tandy, his friend and factotum, who inherited an
ironmongery business in Cornmarket but tired of it, instead pioneering a
new kind of city politics. Tandy excelled as a public performer and committee politician but hardly published a single paragraph. Both were local
celebrities before they won elections – to Parliament in Newenham's case,
to the city Commons, the lower house of the Corporation, in Tandy's.[75]

   In 1771 the Irish government had for nearly four years been in the
hands of a singular viceroy, the miltary veteran Viscount Townshend,
whose remit on taking office was to extract from the Irish Parliament a
much larger financial commitment from Ireland to fund the imperial
army. In painfully achieving that goal Townshend broke the mould: gov-
ernment-sponsored legislation limited the life of parliaments to eight years
and in so doing Townshend stirred up political life in 'open' constituencies
like Dublin city and county. He set aside the old government alliances
with the Ponsonbys, the Boyles and the Kildare/Leinster clan, and instead
built up a firm body of 'Castle' MPs in the House of Commons, aided by

new landed alliances, notably with the Beresfords. And capping this was Townshend's decision (his own it seems) to reside permanently in Dublin while holding office. This had both symbolic and practical effects, bringing the reality of English power closer and more visible, and keeping political controversy more or less permanently on the boil. Townshend's colourful lifestyle and choice of dinner companions, male and female, diminished the status of the office, and with such a viceroy *in situ* the patriots had an enemy in the open. With his late brother a controversial figure in the British Cabinet and the object of profound hostility in colonial America, the patriots could see a pattern – the erosion of liberty by George III and his confidantes, and the insidious return of arbitrary monarchical government at a time of imperial crisis.

Townshend summarily prorogued the Irish Parliament at the end of 1769, closing it until such time as he could count on a working majority in the Commons. Over the following fourteen months there was a simmering threat of novel confrontation. When the Irish Parliament was eventually recalled in February 1771, plans for a large demonstration in College Green were met by a pre-emptive show of force, with infantry patrolling the environs and a cavalry charge down Dame Street, swords fully drawn. The 'augmentation' of the army was quickly agreed to by MPs, and the opposition press had some justification in talking darkly about 'military government'.[76]

Later that year Benjamin Franklin visited the city, taking his seat briefly among MPs in the House of Commons. He felt that those he met in Dublin (Lucas among them) were 'all friends of America' and perfectly shared his resentment at London's new assertion of metropolitan authority.[77] But this sense of commonality was something of an illusion. Despite the acrimony and suspicion and the greatly expanded news coverage of international affairs in Dublin's newspapers and magazines, the stuff of politics in the city remained local and personal, and in the contested parliamentary elections there was very little constitutional advance on the arguments of the 1740s. It was only with the approach of war that things began to change: the Society of Free Citizens, now a more formal body than the old dining club that had supported Lucas, campaigned for specific policies against corruption and in favour of making MPs accountable to their electors. It was controlled by a coterie of civic politicans led by Sir Edward Newenham, Napper Tandy and John Binns, partner in one of the larger Dame Street silk shops.[78] The Society developed the idea of holding aggregate meetings of freemen and freeholders to be convened by sympathetic sheriffs as a new weapon to challenge the Castle and its city allies. The first such meeting took place at the Tholsel in October 1773, where a proposal for new taxes was roundly attacked.

However, it was the crisis in America that really invigorated civic politics. When news of the first loss of life in New England reached Dublin in late summer 1775, one of the Free Citizens' dinner toasts summed up their feisty reaction: 'May the gates of Temple Bar be speedily decorated with the heads of those who advised the employing military force to enslave our fellow subjects in America'.[79] Sympathy for the American cause peaked quite early: at the behest of Tandy and the Free Citizens, the sheriffs summoned an aggregate meeting in October, despite the strong disapproval of the aldermen (a striking example of their gradual loss of influence over the city Commons and a legacy of the 1760 municipal reform).[80] Several hundred attended and an address to the king was overwhelmingly endorsed; it referred to 'that great community of which Briton, Hibernian and American have heretofore been all the happy members', lamented the prospect of 'civil war' and appealed for imperial reconciliation. The address was then circulated around the coffee-houses, and over the course of several weeks it received nearly 3,000 signatures. But shortly afterwards a rival address, firmly supporting government action in America, garnered over a thousand signatures around the city – not quite a draw. The government's position was strengthening, however, and the press became noticeably more guarded during 1776. A newly elected parliament was in session when word arrived of the declaration of American independence. It was a measure of the management skills of Townshend's successor, the earl of Harcourt, that the Commons remained relatively subdued and malleable.[81]

The impact of the American war on the citizens at large evoked other types of response. Relations between the army garrison (now around 4,000 at full complement) and their north-side neighbours had become very tense in the early 1770s, with a series of vendettas involving the scarring and maiming of soldiers and retaliatory attacks on the civilian population in the Ormond markets area. 'Houghing' incidents such as these were not unprecedented, but their upsurge in 1774–5 and again in 1777 was much commented on. The temporary employment of soldiers by master butchers to break a cattle-skinners' 'combination' in 1774 was probably the catalyst, but there had been a forty-year history of ugly sparring between soldiers and butchers. Vincent Morley has suggested that the intensification of army recruitment on the eve of war may have ratcheted up these tensions. Thousands of young men were impressed into naval service in the city and the port immediately before and during the war, and there was occasionally violent resistance.[82] But were the attacks on soldiers and press gangs in any sense political? The violent dinner talk of the Free Citizens was a long way from the butcher-boys on Arran Quay – or was it?

The Catholic archbishop of the city, John Carpenter, was much exercised by any suggestion of Catholic involvement in attacks on the military, and issued a sharp denunciation in April 1775. The son of a city tailor and appointed to Dublin in 1770 when in his early forties, Carpenter was quite unlike the elderly patrician prelates who preceded him. Educated locally by Tadhg Ó Neachtain, he had a lifelong enthusiasm for the Irish language, its literature and the early Irish Church, as well as broad scholarly interests (at his death he left a library of some 4,000 books in Usher's Island). He was an able adminstrator and through the 1770s began the long journey to re-energise Catholic practice in the city 'through the pulpit and the printing press'. Schooling was for another day.[83]

The slow détente between the Catholic Church and secular authority, which had begun during the Seven Years War with prayers being offered in city chapels for the new king and for success in arms against the French, moved more rapidly under Carpenter. Pressure from the Catholic laity, country gentry, city merchants and professionals to agree on a doctrinally acceptable oath of allegiance to the house of Hanover had perplexed the clergy since the 1720s, but with the diminished credibility of the Jacobite court and the growing stake of individual Catholic families in the status quo the search for an acceptable oath, desirable in itself and a necessary step to dismantling the penal code, had intensified since the 1750s. Part of this long process was the establishment of an informal Catholic Committee in 1756, a Dublin-based lobby group in which the key figures were a Roscommon gentleman, Charles O'Conor, a city physician, John Curry, and two substantial merchants, Thomas Reynolds of the Coombe and Anthony MacDermott of Usher's Quay. O'Conor was a gifted pamphleteer and a canny lobbyist, while Curry's contribution was in his historical scholarship designed to overturn the received wisdom on 1641, which culminated in his *Historical and critical review of the civil wars in Ireland* (1775). Curry's medical background is perhaps relevant here: medicine was one profession not directly affected by the penal code (unlike the law), and Catholics accounted for nearly a quarter of city practitioners listed in 1762. These men had all had a continental education and experience (at Paris and Rheims in Curry's case), all were economically secure, and presumably all had a clientele that extended beyond their co-religionists.[84]

The Catholic Committee was not directly involved in the high-level negotiations over an acceptable oath of allegiance that with some difficulty was passed into law in 1774. The Munster bishops were strongly supportive, but Carpenter, despite being entirely familiar with the politics of the matter, declined to recommend the oath until such time as Rome had determined that it was not doctrinally offensive. That only came in 1778, but the local reaction was then immediate, literally the coming out of the Catholic Church after nearly ninety years of total exclusion from civic and public life: on 9 November that year Carpenter, with seventy priests of the diocese, presented themselves in the Four Courts and took the oath of allegiance to George III, their example being followed by hundreds of other bourgeois Catholics (all male).[85] This of course was not happening in isolation but midway through the (for Britain) disastrous American war, and in the year when the French joined the colonists in that war. It also came some months after the first practical relaxation of the penal laws, the 17 & 18 Geo. III, c.49, which reopened the land market to Catholic speculation for all those who took the new oath; full land purchase was however not permitted until 1782.

The relief measure of 1778 was introduced into the Irish Commons by Luke Gardiner, grandson of the first Luke with whom he shared more than a name. Thanks to an English education (Eton and Cambridge) and a politically advantageous marriage, Luke II built up excellent connections in London and with the Beresfords in Dublin before being elected MP for the county in 1773. As ambitious as his grandfather but less self-effacing, he courted immediate unpopularity with his peers when he introduced the bill for Catholic relief in his own name. The earl of Buckinghamshire, Lord Lieutenant since 1776, was unaware of his intentions, but Gardiner had support in London within the cabinet of Lord North (prime minister since 1770), and in due course the Castle MPs fell into line and duly supported the bill, while the patriots, almost to man, opposed it.[86]

It was not the first case of quiet London support for Catholic relief. Indeed, this had been somewhat less subtle in Townshend's time when there had been huge pressure from the Dublin guilds and other Irish corporations to secure a statutory basis for the quarterage system, the assertion by all guilds of a right to charge recurring fees to non-members, in effect a licence fee to practise their trade or craft locally. A Catholic legal challenge to obligatory quarterage had started in Munster, but it was Dublin which led the fight back. Lucas and the patriot lobby agitated for more than a decade for legislation to secure the chartered rights of (Protestant) freemen. Heads of bills were repeatedly passed in the Irish Parliament but were then overturned, either in the Irish or the British Privy Councils. This failure to get quarterage onto the statute book was an omen.

The factors driving political movement on Catholic relief in the 1770s were much broader – Britain's imperial crisis and the search for new sources of military manpower, the precedent of Catholic relief in Quebec, and the powerful advocacy of English-based politicians, not least the young political adviser of the Rockinghamite Whigs, Edmund Burke. One of the striking features of this first stage of Catholic relief is that those who welcomed it locally were associated with the eastward extension of the city – not just Gardiner and some of those around him (like Michael Stapleton, the Catholic stuccodore and property developer) – but also the newly inheriting 7th Viscount Fitzwilliam, an absentee crypto-Catholic working through his Catholic estate agent, Barbara Fagan, in overseeing the great south-eastward extension of the city. By contrast, the Society of Free Citizens, instinctively hostile to Catholic claims, had their businesses and their dinners in the older parts of the city.

This tectonic shift in the public status of Catholics came at a time when the urban economy was suffering a more than average recession. Depressed linen and agricultural prices led as always to a sharp fall in demand for Dublin manufactured goods, and then an imported credit crisis in 1778 brought down Mitchell's bank, contributing to a sense of impending crisis. Reinforcing this were the rumours of French (or American) attack on the Irish coast, sustained by the appearance of enemy privateers in the Irish Sea (although some of these were in reality enterprising smugglers based in Rush in north Co. Dublin, which, as in previous wars, became an international entrepôt for maritime contraband).[87] In this charged atmosphere, and with a very large exodus of Irish-based regiments to fight in America, there were repeated calls for a militia to be mustered. These calls were ignored by the Irish government, which was in trouble financially as well as being politically inept. The result was the spread during 1778 of a country-wide move to establish territorial 'volunteer' corps, initially with an entirely defensive purpose in mind. In October 1778 the first such corps was embodied in Dublin under the command of the duke of Leinster, and a string of other corps were established in the city over the next two years, some linked to the guilds (the Merchants, the Goldsmiths, the Weavers corps), the professions (the Lawyers), or to other high-status institutions (the Linen Hall corps, the Dublin Revenue Volunteers). Leinster's Dublin Volunteers corps soon had around 200 men under colours, Newenham's Independent Liberty Volunteers 140, but most of the city's thirty or so corps were much smaller and short-lived. A further fifteen were formed within a six-mile radius of Dublin, nearly all to the north or the west. City corps were made up of merchants, shopkeepers and master manufacturers and their officers were rotated, but the county corps, like the vast majority of provincial ones, were controlled by gentry patrons. Every corps had a distinctive uniform (each volunteer having to pay for his own), and the emphasis in many of them on bespoke and sometimes quite extravagant plumage acted as a spur to competitive emulation and as a means of social exclusion.[88]

By the autumn of 1779, with the rapid spread of volunteering across Protestant Ireland and an enfeebled government facing a new parliamentary session, politics and militia became interwoven at a moment of deepening imperial crisis. The parliamentary opposition won an early victory in determining how the formal reply to the Lord Lieutenant at the opening of Parliament should be worded; the agreed Commons text demanded quite simply 'a free and unlimited trade' for Ireland. As Newenham explained to his son,

> we have, at length, overcome the court and the placemen, and carried the most important questions that ever came before parliament since the days of King James the second ... The Patriots were so numerous that the counties [representatives] were forced to give way, and we addressed his Majesty for a free trade. It must be granted, for otherwise the Crown will not get any money from us to pay a standing army. So glorious a sight was never seen in Dublin, as the Volunteers lining the streets, when the House of Commons went up with the address to the viceroy. We were five hours under arms, all trained and fit for the field, able and willing to face an enemy.[89]

The background to this crisis had been the massive build-up of support, in Dublin and nationally, for a major measure of commercial relief from London in response to the recession and the wartime collapse in local textile employment.[90] Commercial concessions had been offered, then cancelled by North's government in 1778, and the rallying cry of 'free trade' was adopted in response. The term itself meant a repeal of all the accumulated (British) legislation restricting Irish access to imperial waters and preventing Irish merchants from directly importing sugar, tobacco and the other emblematic goods associated with the colonial prosperity of Liverpool, Bristol and Glasgow. It also assumed the repeal of the various restrictions on Irish textiles export, most notoriously the 1699 Woollen Acts. The campaign for free trade began in April 1779 and moved quickly from a local agitation to a political and almost national movement. Dublin was only part of the story but it was thanks to its opposition newspapers that a far more combative political discourse came into currency.

Within the city, two groups were critical in the free trade movement: a cabalistic political club of some fifty barristers and patriot MPs (later known as the Monks of the Screw) which began to meet weekly at a house in Kevin Street, and insofar as any group developed and sustained a national political strategy over the following months it was this group; and the very public Society of Free Citizens.[91] The Society built up support in the city Commons and held a public meeting to launch the boycott of British textiles. The agreement to *associate* (the word carried new potency) in a trade dispute drew on local precedent, but it carried additional menace in its echo of recent American example. Non-importation was adopted in many counties and generated quite strong provincial support. However, its success in Dublin, the principal entry-point for English textiles, was critical. The dirty business of naming importers in print was revived, individual drapers were threatened with dire punishment, and there was a string of violent incidents involving large gangs of weavers during the summer and autumn, albeit without loss of life. The campaign had the support of at least two city newspapers, and most Volunteer corps made it a point to wear only Irish-made cloth. Not surprisingly, cloth imports at the Custom House for the year 1779–80 were down by more than three-quarters on the 1776/7–1778/9 average.[92]

This was the background to the Volunteer parade at King William's statue on his 4 November birthday in 1779. Since the fiftieth anniversary of the battle of the Boyne in 1740, the Lord Lieutenant, a selection of peers and a regiment of the garrison had always marched from the Castle to College Green on that day to acknowledge William's legacy. But in 1779 they were upstaged. A cavalcade of ten Dublin Volunteer corps, over a thousand men under light arms, assembled in St Stephen's Green and arrived at the statue ahead of the viceroy's official party, where they fired several elaborate fusillades, the Goldsmiths discharging two cannon, and placards were hung from the statue with simple messages: 'The relief of Ireland', 'The Glorious Revolution' and, most famously, 'Short money bills – a free trade – or else'. The event was celebrated (in a sanitised version) by the visiting English painter Francis Wheatley. His great canvas conveys a sense of orderly carnival and communal brinkmanship.[93] But all this may overstate the importance of the capital's Volunteers in achieving political change, for the source of the agitation, in Dublin at least, was the city guildhalls and the informal networks that had been organising the various aggregate meetings. Volunteering merely reflected that. The inchoate energy of politicised grievance was starkly revealed nearly a fortnight later when a far more disorderly crowd of thousands surged down to College Green. The old Liberties' artisans were at it once again, some with light arms, threatening and harassing any MP thought to be a government supporter, some of them carrying a startled Newenham into Parliament. But tellingly, it was the prior circulation of a printed handbill that had encouraged this demonstration. By now a division was emerging between the aristocratic Volunteer leadership, engaging reluctantly in orchestrated street theatre outside *their* Parliament House, and the small manufacturers and artisans encouraged and abetted by Kevin Street barristers and guildhall politicians. Ironically, it seems that it was the untidy mid-November demonstration that particularly unnerved Dublin Castle and helped force the issue in London, where Lord North's government was coping with a raft of other disasters.[94]

News reached Dublin shortly before Christmas 1779 that imperial 'free trade' would indeed be conceded for Irish shipping and merchants, and that the century-old restrictions would now be lifted. All the familiar elements of civic celebration – bell-ringing, banners and fireworks, candles and illuminated transparencies – appeared, but in addition the major public buildings were lit up. It was a rare case of Dublin Castle competing with its local opponents to capture a moment of excitement and imperial unity, an occasion when it seemed, uniquely, that everyone in the capital could feel a winner.[95]

5

PATRIOT TOWN:
1780–1798

Freedoms

As Lenin apparently said, 'sometimes decades pass and nothing happens; and then sometimes weeks pass and decades happen'. There was a sense of this in Dublin in that transformative autumn of 1779 as exuberant Volunteering and official panic opened doors that had seemed so firmly sealed, leading to the achievement of 'free trade' and the promise of major constitutional reform at a moment of existential imperial crisis. This complex political melodrama impressed itself on every citizen who could read, and was reflected on the Smock Alley stage, in the print-shop window and the ballad-monger's offerings.[1] The acute crisis passed, the loss of the American colonies became a fact and patriot ambitions for the liberation of the Irish Parliament from subservience to Westminster were painlessly achieved in 1782. But for those who experienced the radical excitements of 1779, they were a taster of what was in store in the 1790s when politics would again invade life on the street, and revolutionary events abroad would threaten to tear open and inflame the social and religious divisions that smouldered below the city surface.

A precondition for this transmission of political debate to an enlarged public sphere was the relatively unregulated circulation of print. As one writer in the *Hibernian Journal* put it in 1778, 'the liberty of the press is one of those invaluable blessings which the malevolence of those in power has not been hitherto able to deprive us of'.[2] Irish governments had intermittently harassed opposition printers since 1714, usually by charging them with seditious libel, and Parliament had hounded and even imprisoned city printers deemed to have violated its privileges by making rash statements in pamphlet or newsprint. Defence of 'the freedom of the press' was a potent opposition rallying call from the 1750s and despite legal threats, occasional prosecutions and the introduction of stamp tax on newspapers in 1774 the range and diversity of newspapers broadened decade on decade. There were about fourteen Dublin newspapers in the early 1780s, only one of which, *Faulkner's Dublin Journal*, was a survivor from the 1720s and the early days of combative journalism.[3]

Advertising, both commercial and domestic, still competed for dominance with foreign and British news, and service information (commodity prices, exchange rates on bills, port movements), and Irish news, parliamentary, social and criminal, rarely occupied more than part of a single page, although the patriot papers, notably the *Freeman's Journal*, had somewhat changed things with their inclusion of greater Irish political content (original essays and letters) and their greater care in the choice and presentation of news. Papers appeared between one and three times a week and print-runs remained small; the new *Dublin Evening Post* claimed an output of 2,500 to 3,000 copies in 1779, making it the largest by some distance. Robert Munter has estimated that altogether about 45,000 newspapers were coming off the Dublin presses each week in the early 1780s, most for sale in the city and district. In the decade between 1774 and 1783, official Dublin newspaper sales were relatively stable, possibly because of the sharp growth of provincial newspaper sales. However, much of the news content in the country papers was lifted from the Dublin press, thereby conveying the capital's political concerns to a new set of readers.[4]

Was it then a free press? Until the American Declaration of Independence, there had been no shortage of American material and of intensely sympathetic comment in the opposition papers, but there was a telling example of self-censorship when the *Hibernian Magazine*, reprinting Tom Paine's great pro-American essay *Common Sense* in 1776, chose to paraphrase his scathing remarks on monarchy. However, by 1779 the boundaries were being pushed out again, nowhere more than in the letters of 'Guatimozin', published weekly in the *Freeman's Journal* from mid-April. Inspired by events in America, the author lamented the negative effects of the British connection and the possibility of Irish 'emancipation' as a result of the non-importation movement. The author later revealed himself to be Frederick Jebb, 'a young gentleman of fine parts', who had trained in obstetrics in Paris and was then master of the Lying-in Hospital. Such radical political speculation was highly unusual, but a year later Buckinghamshire, the Lord Lieutenant, managed to 'turn' this latterday Swiftian into a critic of the patriots. Nevertheless, the government shared a pervasive sense of powerlessness in the face of a rampant press; an appeal for 'secret service' funding to help control things in Dublin was made directly to Lord North, the prime minister, in 1781. It met with no response.[5]

The short Dublin career of Mathew Carey (1760–1839) revealed the limits of press freedom. The son of a well-to-do Catholic baker in Cook Street, Carey served his apprenticeship with Thomas McDonnell, co-founder of the *Hibernian Journal* (an unusual venture in that McDonnell was a Catholic printer and his partner Michael Mills a Protestant). Fearless, well-read and naïve, Carey drafted a pamphlet late in 1781 calling for 'the immediate repeal of the whole penal code', and promoted it with handbills distributed around the city. The Catholic Committee, at that point in private contact with the government over further Catholic relief, was appalled at the prospect of such a provocative publication that directly invoked the American language of rights as a reason for changing the law (why, Carey asked, should Catholics deign to support political reform, when they were 'taxed and governed without representation, whether their taxers and tyrants be English or Irish'?). Fearing the Protestant reaction, the Committee disowned the pamphlet before it appeared and prevented its publication, and his father made sure that Carey left town quickly.[6]

The young printer spent time in France before reappearing to launch another opposition paper, the *Volunteer Journal,* in October 1783. This broke other taboos: drawing on the separatist sentiments of Guatimozin he attacked the Irish House of Commons ('the den of thieves') and threatened individuals in government and government supporters with street justice, his verbal attacks taking visual form in April 1784 when he published a cartoon depicting the Chancellor of the Exchequer, John Foster, hanging lifeless from a gibbet in College Green, a just punishment for resisting local demands for tariff protection. The incident marked a caesura in press freedom: Carey was arrested and detained, but managed to flee for a second time (now disguised as a woman), making his way to

Philadelphia and a long and hugely successful career as a publisher and bookseller there. But despite Carey's exit, Foster drafted a swingeing press bill, and although it was only passed in modified form it led to a sharp hike in newspaper stamp duties and to a parallel growth in the government's use of the courts to harass editors and printers. All in all, this curbed the uninhibited defamation of the rich and powerful that had been building up for a decade. By 1784 the government had also begun to use other means of control – selective official advertising (mainly of proclamations) and the payment of secret pensions to favoured publishers. The strange transformation of the *Freeman's Journal* from stalwart champion of guildhall values to shrill government advocate (which occurred in 1783–4) was one such case, achieved by the quiet co-option of its new owner, Francis Higgins. Like no other, Higgins, the 'sham squire', demonstrated how profitable an energetic pen for hire could be, even if it meant earning a popular reputation as a duplicitous and oleaginous hack.[7] Yet despite this new animus of government towards a free press, the opposition newspapers, even if they became more careful in their criticism of government, remained commercially far more successful than Castle-supported journals. Prison and the threat of huge financial penalties did not smother political debate and the market for Dublin-produced print – political, polite or improving – continued to expand.

In his unpublished pamphlet of 1781, Carey had complained that 'some [Volunteer] corps, even in this city, admit not Catholic members. Fie on such illiberality! It would disgrace the darkest ages of bigotry'.[8] By then Volunteering was in its fourth year and had come far from its innocent beginnings. Large summer military reviews in the Phoenix Park were as colourful as ever, but after the stirring events of November 1779 divisions had emerged within and between city corps – over whether or not to use the movement to extract constitutional concessions from Westminster, whether or not to widen the social base of Volunteering and, closely related to that, whether or not to admit Catholics, despite the legal ban on Catholics bearing arms. The duke of Leinster distanced his Dublin Volunteer corps from any further political agitation. Tandy challenged him and was expelled from the corps, thereupon transferring his energies to the Dublin Independent corps. Other Volunteer colonels like Luke Gardiner played a waiting game. Of the city aristocrats, only James Caulfeild, Viscount Charlemont, saw a further political role for the Volunteers, and he emerged as the national figurehead of the movement to secure the 'constitutional claims'. His status was confirmed when he was elected by the Dublin corps, over Leinster and Gardiner, to act as reviewing general for the 4 November 1780, and the numbers parading around College Green that day were even larger than in 1779. The motley Liberty corps was probably the largest unit but the Independents were the most prestigious, their colonel being Charlemont's protégé, Henry Grattan (1746–1820).[9]

The disinherited son of a former Dublin city recorder, Grattan had risen during the 1770s from struggling young barrister with a taste for political debate to become the man of the moment. Charlemont had secured him a parliamentary seat in 1775, but it was not until 1779 that he began to stand out from his peers. His tactical political judgement and superb set-piece oratory made him a scourge of government in the Commons and the apparent embodiment of public sentiment in the world outside. Invoking, with great emphasis, 'the people' as both the source of legitimacy and a weapon of strength against Westminster, he drew politics even more emphatically out of the Parliament chamber. From April 1780, when he delivered his 'declaration of the rights of Ireland', Grattan ensured that his stirring words were projected via the printing press far beyond the capital, especially northwards, and it was Volunteers corps in Ulster more than those in Dublin who inaugurated the final push for constitutional concessions in the spring of 1782. But Grattan seized the rhetorical high ground in Parliament and gained unanimous backing for his declaration of the patriot position on Ireland's co-equality with Britain under the Crown. Within weeks a new Whig government in London moved (despite strong misgivings) to repeal the notorious Declaratory Act in Westminster and to support the cancellation of Poynings's law in College Green. Gone was the hidden control of Irish and British privy councils over Irish legislation and restored was the status of the Irish House of Lords as a court of final appeal. Grattan became the national hero *sans pareil*, no one demurring when the Commons voted him £50,000 for the purchase of a landed estate.[10]

The patriot victory in spring 1782 overshadowed the passing of two further Acts of Catholic relief, the first restoring Catholic freedom to acquire land, the second removing restrictions on Catholic education. Both were once again sponsored by Luke Gardiner, but unlike the bill in

1778, they do not seem to have been prompted by London, and they now attracted patriot backing. The supporting rhetoric spoke of enlightenment, toleration and a new age of civic inclusion. However, Carey's rash advocacy of full political rights for Catholics received no public support at this stage. Some city Volunteers had already sought Catholic members, but even within the Liberty Volunteers this was a divisive issue. Only one rather obscure corps, the Irish Brigade, became mainly Catholic.[11]

For two years after 1782 the 'reformation of Parliament' emerged as the new big issue for opposition politicians, by which was meant legislative action to weaken aristocratic control over parliamentary representation and to strengthen the influence of the freeholder vote in constituencies with large electorates (like Dublin city). These were objectives which many Volunteer corps were happy to support. But when 'reform' was extended to embrace the widening of the franchise and the inclusion of Catholic freeholders, that divided the ranks, as was first evident at the great Volunteer Convention held in the Rotunda in November 1783 under Charlemont's nervous superintendence. It was even more apparent during the following summer when the more advanced Dublin and northern patriots made strong efforts to recruit Catholics into their Volunteer corps and to enlist open Catholic support for a national Reform Congress.[12] Tandy, John Binns and other veterans of the Free Citizens pursued this new departure in the long summer of 1784, and several Catholic Committee members joined the initial city committee (this was the moment when John Keogh, another of the wealthy silk merchants of Dame Street, first appeared on a political platform). However, for the Catholic hopefuls 1784 was a false dawn. When an open meeting was held outside the Weavers' Hall on the Coombe in October to select representatives for the Congress, drawing an attendance of many thousands, the chairman (Newenham) managed to ensure that there was no reference to voting rights for Catholics. Even before the National Congress held its somewhat anti-climactic first meeting, the tide was turning.[13]

A key ingredient in the turbulence of 1784 was severe economic recession. Despite the promised benefits of 'free trade', the early 1780s had offered little solace to the city's poor. Wretched harvests in 1781 and 1782 had led to soaring food prices and the arctic winter of 1783–4 ended with the worst city-centre flooding in decades. At least one household in five that winter was jobless, cold and hungry, with the proportion in St Catherine's and the Liberties parishes much higher. The depressed home market

*17. City weavers had a fearsome reputation for punishing cloth-importers
and tailors at times when trade was depressed – if the latter ignored their
declarations outlawing the imported product. The cartoon borrows from
a recent incident in the Tenter Fields in the Meath Liberties to make the
point that plebeian patriots had 'tar enough for the whole tribe' of 'mock
patriots' who had failed to help the 'thousands of starving manufacturers'.*

for Dublin goods meant that workshop employment, especially for those
involved in textiles, was far below pre-war levels. James Kelly has suggested
that by February 1784 around 20,000 citizens were in receipt of some kind
of charity, official or private, and that it was only this mobilisation of relief
and the intervention of both the Castle and the Corporation in sourcing
overseas grain that prevented large-scale mortality.[14] Compounding all
this was a run of post-war commercial bankruptcies and a particular crisis
in the silk industry, where direct employment, which may have topped
8,000 before the war, was at half that level by 1784. The appearance of
cheaper fashion fabrics, such as muslins and chintzes made of cotton or
mixed fibres, was undermining the long primacy of silk.[15]

Extreme levels of distress were the prologue to the final non-
importation campaign which commenced during the winter of 1783–4.
The object was now to nudge the Irish Parliament with its new legislative
autonomy into protecting the domestic Irish market for fine cloth against
cheap English imports by introducing significantly higher tariffs. A city
campaign against traders who ignored the embargo reached new levels of

intimidation, and there were several notorious instances of tarring-and-feathering. However, there was a separate upsurge of journeyman attacks on masters over other issues (the hiring of country apprentices at cheaper rates and the importation of new types of machinery). So tense was the situation that in July 1784 the Corporation had to request a military guard in the Liberties and at the Tholsel. Street politics, born in hard times, now seemed to be passing out of the control of guildhall politicians.[16]

Parallel to this, a series of demonstrations had begun in early April in which two issues came together: anger at the failure of the House of Commons to support protection, and resentment at the prospect of a new paving tax and new statutory authority to oversee street maintenance (an initiative of Parliament, not the Corporation). This, the new Paving Board, came into existence with very wide powers; it took over responsibility for Dublin's street lighting, street cleaning and sewerage, in addition to road maintenance and the provision of twenty public fountains, all of which spelt higher taxes. College Green protests ended with another occupation of the Parliament House and a mock debate in the Commons' gallery as to whether Foster, the opponent of protecting duties, should be hanged. The military calmed matters without loss of life, but an upper-class fear of the mob persisted that summer. Everyone knew what had happened in London in 1780 when the mob had taken control of large parts of the city, and order was only restored by the roughest of military counter-measures. Many feared that the verbal excesses of Carey's newspaper had broken down social restraints. Outlandish stories circulated among government supporters of foreign plotters at work in the city (supposedly involving Tandy and Newenham).[17] So when Tandy and his friends enrolled Catholic support in public calls for parliamentary reform, it allowed those opposed to reform to warn of the danger of pandering in any way to Catholic political ambitions. Many leading patriots privately agreed that Catholic relief had gone far enough in 1782. Among those were Newenham and Charlemont, who still believed that 'popery' was always subversive of 'liberty' (in the sense of a refined constitution where property and power were in perfect alignment) and that accommodation of even wealthy Catholics would be a prelude to democracy, which Charlemont saw as 'in effect no other than a fluctuating despotism' and the antithesis of liberty. The modest entry of city Catholics into the public political debate had therefore the unintended consequence of creating a temporary alliance between government and opposition figures.

Protestant fears of Catholic ambitions were reignited and the social status of some of the new 'popish' politicians was ridiculed, a tactic that helped put 'the Roman Catholic business ... asleep', at least for a few years. It also meant that support within College Green for radical reform ebbed away.[18]

The junto

The covert involvement of key officials in Dublin Castle in such a campaign is at first sight surprising after the quiet support for Catholic relief evident in Whitehall since the 1760s. But what had changed was not so much attitudes in London as the emergence at the centre of government in Dublin of a group of Irish-born office-holders in 1783–4. They became the informal and much-valued cabinet serving successive viceroys for the next fifteen years, and their authoritarian instincts helped define the character of Irish government for nearly a generation.[19] The permanent members of this 'office-aristocracy' or 'junto' were John Foster, John FitzGibbon and John Beresford. They were all Dublin University graduates and all had been called to the bar, but they differed in family background, personal attributes and political priorities. At times reluctant allies, they were united in a highly jaundiced view of patriot politics, whether of the Charlemont or the Tandy variety, in their common resistance to Catholic political concessions, and in their belief that the institutions of the Irish state could and should be reformed from the top down (and indeed that they in their separate spheres of responsibility were uniquely equipped to be the agents of reform). By their own lights they were 'clean' politicians with a contempt for the 'jobbery' of their class, but their political enemies were convinced otherwise. A memory of the Castle's intermittent loss of control (over both Parliament and city) haunted them, and this goes some way towards explaining the energy they devoted to reforming the disordered capital city. Their apprenticeship to power came during the short viceroyalty of the earl of Carlisle (1780–82), and in particular in their relationship with his very able and ambitious Chief Secretary, William Eden.[20]

John Foster (1740–1828), or 'Jacky Finance' as Mathew Carey christened him, was the hate-figure in the summer of '84, but his impact on the city was actually the most tangential of the three. His private passions were rural, botanical and horticultural, and appropriately his main urban legacy was the Dublin Society's National Botanic Gardens at Glasnevin, for which he secured public funding in 1790 and 1797, and actively supported Walter Wade in its creation.[21] Foster's wider impact arose from his commanding knowledge of the Irish economy that long predated his brief stint as Chancellor of the Exchequer in 1784–5, and which continued during his sixteen years as Speaker of the House of Commons. With a Co. Louth base, he had a direct interest in extending both the grain and linen trades; he introduced a workable scheme of price subsidies on Irish grain exports that was calibrated to market prices ('Foster's corn law'), the effect of which on Dublin was to soften the annual fluctuations in the cost of living. And as the defender of linen as the great export staple, he ensured that the Irish government would oppose any move to protect silk or woollen textiles if the purpose was only to keep Dublin workshops in business. As a palliative, he championed the use of parliamentary, Dublin Society and Linen Board funds to subvent new processes and products using flax and cotton (or exclusively cotton), particularly favouring Irish manufacturers who sought to introduce labour-saving modes of spinning cotton, and/or new techniques of textile printing.

There was a sub-text to Foster's support for these innovators: funds were specifically offered to those investing in new spinning and/or printing works who agreed to establish rural colonies of hand-weavers recruited in Dublin. In 1783 a parliamentary fund was set up to encourage the establishment of integrated textile enterprises located at least ten miles from the city, and landowners in the north of the county (at Balbriggan and Malahide), north Kildare (at the new settlement of 'Prosperous'), and west Wicklow (at Stratford) entered into partnerships with city drapers or manufacturers to produce mixed cloths, using new technology and employing relocated city weavers. The logic for this rustication policy was partly economic, to reduce the cost of living for weavers and by extension their wages and the competitiveness of the end product, and partly social, to weaken the turbulent and whiskey-soaked world of the Liberties and to break the power of the journeyman associations. But despite the scale of public grants and loans and the actual movement of many hundreds of families, these new enterprises had a short and anaemic history. However, one legacy was the remarkable growth on the edge of the city of textile printing (both in the numbers employed and in fixed capital), producing fashionable patterns onto cotton, linen and mixed fabrics for the home market. Several of these enterprises, dotted beyond the city's edge, became the largest employers of industrial labour by the 1790s.[22]

But it was also on Foster's watch that the Dublin Linen Hall began to lose its century-old dominance of the white-linen business; northern producers were now developing direct commercial links with English importers and exporting a growing proportion of Ulster linen via Newry and Belfast. Some 12,000 tons of linen were still being brought into the city by road each year, and around twenty-two million yards of cloth were being exported, but the city's share of Irish linen exports fell to 47 per cent in the last quarter of the century. The unique role of the city in financing Ulster rural industry was drawing to an end.[23]

Foster was also one of the instigators of the Bank of Ireland. The case for a public bank had been made repeatedly since the 1720s, and as recently as 1780 Charlemont's cousin and financial manager Annesley Stewart proposed establishing a national bank as a logical corollary to the granting of free trade. Foster was a supporter of the idea, but it got nowhere. However, in the final weeks before Lord North's government fell in March 1782, legislation was introduced in the Irish Parliament to establish such a bank, and despite strong misgivings within the merchant body it passed into law – at a time when larger constitutional questions were attracting everyone's attention. Foster and William Eden, the outgoing Chief Secretary, were central to this initiative, and although some saw the bank's creation as part of the new constitutional settlement, the truth was more complex. Since 1770 Irish governments had been running significant deficits, and the servicing of this debt lay at the discretion of Parliament. One route to a more secure and sustainable system was the establishment of a joint-stock bank regulated by statute and modelled on the now venerable Bank of England, one that could act both as a broker for state borrowing and as a custodian of state funds. But what was important at the time was that such an institution would offer safe cover to those private Dublin bankers heavily involved in lending to government during the war, and among the bankers particularly keen on the idea were the La Touches.

The key man here was David La Touche (1729–1817), grandson of the founder of the Dublin dynasty, whose private bank in Castle Street was by now the leading firm handling the movement of landowners' revenues, and also offering deposit facilities. La Touche, his father and his two brothers subscribed altogether £40,000 of the Bank of Ireland's original capital of £600,000 (much the largest family bloc among the 228 subscribers to the Bank), and the family's distinctly conservative outlook

shaped the early history of the institution. From the time it first opened
its doors to business in June 1783 (in Mary's Abbey, off Capel Street), the
Bank had a strong commercial side, offering Dublin private banks a facility
to discount bills of exchange on which they had paid out, in other words
greatly enhancing their liquidity. Tested immediately by the highly turbulent state of the economy in 1783–4 (and a destructive banking collapse in
Cork), the Bank's exclusive position gave Dublin one further advantage in
its role as national financial hub. But the Bank's very restricted governance
(excluding Quakers and Catholics from its board of governors), which
bears the mark of Foster and La Touche, only added to the polarising tendencies within the merchant community that had been first evident in
the row over the Royal Exchange.[24] It was no coincidence that in the same
year as the Bank opened, a group of merchants associated with the patriots
relaunched the Society of Merchants as the Dublin Chamber of Commerce. This was religiously open where the Bank was closed, and it elected
as its chairman Travers Hartley, a long-established and reform-minded
Presbyterian merchant who had shot to political prominence in 1782
when he won one of the city parliamentary seats at a by-election. Apart
from an intimate knowledge of the linen business and of the exchange
trade with London, Hartley had little in common with Foster.[25]

John FitzGibbon (1748–1802) enjoyed a higher profile in the city. He had
a Munster background not unlike his kinsman Edmund Burke. Both had
fathers who had conformed to the established church and become successful lawyers. But FitzGibbon inherited much greater wealth, had family connections with the Beresfords and (unlike Burke) never saw political
or philosophical merit in Catholic relief, only constitutional danger. And
he was always more interested in upholding the authority of the Crown,
the British connection and the rule of law than in buying peace or popularity. Regarded as a precociously brilliant courtroom lawyer before entering Parliament, he served as Attorney General from 1784, but he was still
a surprising choice, given his age and Irish birth, when he was appointed
Lord Chancellor of Ireland in 1789 and created earl of Clare. He was not
afraid to flaunt his wealth in entertaining at his superb Dublin home, Ely
House, set back from St Stephen's Green, or in travelling through the city
in his extravagantly appointed official coach. He stirred up a storm of

protest in 1784 when he sought to challenge the legality of aggregate public meetings in the city, and the violent disorders of that summer led him and Thomas Orde, then Chief Secretary, to draft a radically new policing system for Dublin. It was presented to Parliament two years later and was an intricate and hugely controversial proposal.[26]

The parish-based system of policing which they found wanting had operated under legislation dating from 1715 and 1723. It had been relatively cheap, leaving the primary responsibility for the safety of the citizen and good order on the streets to the Lord Mayor, aldermen and sheriffs, whose duty it was to oversee the parish arrangements. The watchmen were generally elderly and unarmed, anchored to their watch-houses during night hours and overseen by unpaid parish constables. The system had not coped well with the growth of the city, and tax revenues in some of the small western parishes were too small to support a viable watch. Furthermore, the system did not operate outside the city limits, so Liberties parishes remained the responsibility of estate officials. One writer in 1765 complained that the city's watchmen were entirely lacking in training or discipline and that their numbers were nearly a third below strength; four of the wealthier parishes had by then raised voluntary subscriptions to help maintain the local watch, and were it not for some 'hawk-eyed constables' most street robbers, he believed, would escape undetected.[27] When it came to daytime trouble and the threat of crowd disorder, the legal powers of the Lord Mayor, sheriffs and aldermen to maintain the peace (acting in their capacity as magistrates) were considerable, but their ability to enforce that peace rested on a combination of bravery and bluff when they had to face down angry crowds. City magistrates were reluctant to summon aid from the garrison (who could only intervene on the street if directly summoned by the Lord Mayor), and they often left it too late (as in 1759 and 1784). But in hard seasons 'many times heretofore, when evils from robbers have run high ... the city hath solicited aid, and found it, from the army patrolling at night'.[28]

The persistence of recreational but highly disruptive faction-fighting in the west of the city had in earlier times shown up the weakness of municipal policing, and more recently the irregular but increasing incidence of industrial crime – the periodic attacks on the importers of foreign goods and the violent enforcement of trade rules by journeymen associations on their peers and their masters – had led to a variety of half-measures of reform. Legislation in 1778 grouped the parishes into wards and installed aldermen to oversee the watch committee in each ward. Then in 1780 the excess energy of several Volunteers corps in the city was harnessed when they became involved in night-time street patrols. Several MPs, including members of the patriot group, had pressed for a general statute to criminalise journeyman clubs and trade combinations, and the passage of such a law through the Commons in June 1780 (with almost no political opposition) triggered a mass demonstration by journeymen in the Phoenix Park, one week after the end of the Gordon riots in London. The demonstration was remarkable for its scale and the absence of violence. It dispersed quietly after a petition had been drawn up for presentation to the Lord Lieutenant, requesting him to block the bill, but large numbers of Volunteers were mobilised that night just in case. Despite this unprecedented show of disciplined artisanal protest, the bill passed into law. The ban on combinations was, however, so sweeping as to be unenforceable, but by removing all statutory restrictions on the number of apprentices a master (whatever his religion) might now keep, the Act made quarterage obsolete and added further distance between masters and journeymen.[29]

The threat of journeyman disorder and the high levels of property crime kept city Volunteers actively involved in policing. Five corps divided responsibilities across the city and Liberties in the winter of 1780–81, and there was a parallel growth of parish and/or territorial 'peace preservation' associations in more than a dozen districts. In some cases they were very busy for a short period, such as the Essex Street association, which harried brothel-keepers, 'fences' and the criminal flotsam in the riverside neighbourhood for nearly a year; others like the suburban Blackrock Felon Association lasted for more than a decade (it instigated night-time patrols on the suburban high roads, paying for constables and furnishing them with a 'police station' in Blackrock village). But part of the problem was brazen upper-class delinquency: a set of young bucks known as the 'pinking dindies', many of them connected with Trinity College, became notorious for extorting and roughing up brothel-keepers, gamblers and 'single men and citizens who neither wore fine clothes [n]or swords'. One of their leaders was Richard Crosbie, whose gang trashed the Drogheda Street premises of Mrs Leeson, the city's most reputable courtesan (a few years later he achieved celebrity of a different kind when, watched by tens of thousands, he ascended from the Ranelagh gardens to become the first Irish hot-air balloonist before touching down in Clontarf).[30]

Thanks to the vicarious interest in crime of one or two Dublin newspapers, it becomes possible to get a more rounded picture of city crime and its consequences in the 1780s. Brian Henry's analysis of the press reveals a casually violent city with easy access to offensive weapons – pistols and blunderbusses, swords and knives – used principally in connection with theft. It seems that the majority of property-related crimes took the form of outdoor robbery. Theft could be a hanging offence: over four-fifths of those executed in the city or at Kilmainham between 1780 and 1795 were being punished for property offences, not for homicide or crimes against the person. Measured against large English cities, Dublin was somewhat more violent at this time and a lot more likely to witness capital punishment.[31] The assumed number of public executions for city and county peaked in this era at thirty-three in 1785, but a disproportionate number of these sentences were handed down at the county quarter sessions at Kilmainham (which had of course jurisdiction over the Liberties). This profligate use of capital punishment for theft and burglary was a reflection of the fragility of law enforcement and of the desperately overcrowded state of 'new Newgate', the city jail in Green Street that had only been opened in 1780. The high-level platform on the front façade of Newgate became the ghoulish venue for city executions, after the old gallows hill beyond St Stephen's Green was finally abandoned; Mary Fairfield, strangled and burnt at the stake in 1784, was the last victim of capital punishment on that site.[32]

The new arrangements for policing Dublin that FitzGibbon drove through the Irish Parliament in 1786 were closely modelled on plans for a London force that had been rejected in Westminster the previous year. They marked a radical departure in many ways: there was to be a force of 440 men – fit, young, Protestant and uniformed; all were to be armed, they were to patrol the streets and to operate day or night, with powers of entry and arrest far beyond those of the old constables and their geriatric watchmen. Initially there was also a mounted force of forty constables. The city was divided into four neat divisions, with a central police office in William Street, and the Liberties for the first time were fully integrated into the scheme that included the whole area inside the Circular Roads.

The police were to be funded by a sharply increased house tax and by the income from licences, the collection of which it became directly responsible for. Its creators sought to establish an agency of social control equipped to do what traditional authority had signally failed to do, that is, to regulate and tax all forms of street trading (including porterage, second-hand clothes dealing and pawnshops), to enforce the licensing of all premises selling alcohol and to restrain apprentices, journeymen and servants from 'drinking, tipling or gaming at unseasonable hours', with the threat of immediate detention. Prostitutes, beggars and unruly festive gatherings were also targeted. The police were responsible for traffic management, licensing hackneys and carts, and had powers to control speeding and reckless driving. But perhaps most controversial at the time was its governance: command of the force was to repose in three commissioners – aldermen and therefore magistrates, but they were salaried appointees not of the Corporation but of the Castle. In addition, the other 502 paid positions (divisional justices, constables and police) were to be in the gift of government. Such a policing system lacked the restraints of the old arrangements with their ponderous accountability to parish and city, and Grattan and his allies saw the new scheme as having more than whiff of Parisian absolutism and as a massive erosion of the liberties of the citizen ('no measure', he claimed, 'ever excited discontent so strong or so general as this abominable establishment'). Quite simply, it grossly offended basic Whig and patriot principles in that it subverted common law and chartered rights. By enlarging ministerial powers and patronage, it threatened a creeping despotism, and by offering the aldermen-commissioners large salaries, it threatened to break the independence of the Corporation.[33]

The force was recruited quickly (in part from the youth of King's Hospital) and it took to the streets in September 1786 under the command of Nathaniel Warren, merchant, alderman, Volunteer and recently elected MP for the city. His was a political appointment and he did little for the popularity of the new police force when he chose Wilton carpets, fine mirrors and other symbols of affluence to fit out his headquarters. There was no doubt about the commitment and ambition of Orde and FitzGibbon to make a success of the new police, but were they successful? Under political pressure, police numbers were gradually reduced, and there were repeated occasions when the new constables were overwhelmed on the street and had to be rescued by the military. Thus, when Newgate jail was taken over by its inmates in July 1790 (leading to the escape of forty prisoners), the police were swept aside and only military intervention calmed matters. A lingering sense of lawlessness was felt in the suburbs: on Lord Charlemont's demesne around the Casino, one visitor was given an armed guard in 1792 as the old Volunteer and his lady had been 'repeatedly robbed ... on open day'. Yet the trends in reported crime suggest some impact: assaults between 1780/85 and 1787/95 fell by a third, and prosecutions for theft soared more than threefold. But the average number of city homicides only fell from twenty-five per annum in the years 1780–85, to twenty-four in the years 1787–95, and the average number of executions fell from around sixteen to around thirteen a year. The verdict is therefore unclear.[34] But success, such as it was, came at a price: police costs were initially treble those of the old watch system, and discipline and training were seriously defective. In an extraordinary move, some 7,000 householders petitioned Parliament in 1788 to restore the old system and there was a chorus of petitions from guilds and parishes over the next three years. But FitzGibbon was not for turning, declaring in 1789 that the police had dealt 'a fatal blow to the mobocracy of Dublin'.[35] Repeal of the Police Act remained a hugely emotive issue in the city, even in the changed political landscape of the early 1790s, and in 1795 Camden's government sought to build allies in the city by agreeing to repeal 'that monstrous, burdensome and ineffectual institution, the police'. The elaborate structure was partially unpicked and an unarmed parish nightwatch was restored, albeit now firmly controlled by the Corporation.[36]

Yet the impact of the new police was enduring. A Dublin Police Act of 1799 restored many elements of the original police force and this framework was adapted and elaborated in the decades following. The innovation in 1786 had been to draw government directly into the business of policing Dublin, weakening and eventually eliminating the role of local agencies in law enforcement. With this went the growth of more systematic intelligence-gathering by the Castle, not exclusively focused on Dublin, but the security of the city – from without and within – became a huge and recurring concern from the early 1790s. The government's experience learnt in running the first Dublin police force helped to keep the lid on the city in the era of Jacobin revolution, and for long afterwards.

FitzGibbon also showed his single-mindedness in a determined reform of the Chancery, his high court. From the time he became Chancellor in 1789 he accelerated legal process, took delight in exposing oppressive conduct and was unique among the judiciary in opposing the extension of combination legislation in 1792 (against journeymen carpenters). His singular contempt for Whig pieties about liberty and a sturdy belief that equity must inform all legal processes made him a difficult enemy to pin down.[37] And his visibility to friend and foe was reinforced by the fact that the two great institutions he dominated in the 1790s – the

Court of Chancery and the House of Lords – were newly built, as if timed for his coming, though that was largely a happy coincidence.

Beresford's Dublin

Of the three members of the Castle Cabinet, John Beresford had the wealthiest connections. Younger son of the 1st earl of Tyrone, he grew up in the family's great house in Marlborough Street, close to river and port. Like Foster, he was a lifelong MP – in College Green from 1761 until the Act of Union, then making the move across the water. Viscount Townshend had picked him out early in his viceroyalty as a Castle ally and when management of the Revenue service passed back to full Castle control, he made Beresford a Commissioner in 1770. An unusually energetic administrator, he governed the Irish Revenue service for thirty years and in so doing benefited public revenues but not, he insisted, his own pocket (taking such charges to the duelling field in 1795).[38] He was regarded as a uniquely powerful figure situated at the centre of a web of connections, political, administrative and ecclesiastical, enjoying the total trust and support of London and specifically of William Pitt (prime minister from 1783 to 1801, and from 1804 to 1806). Unlike his colleagues in the Irish government Beresford was something of a connoisseur. This was evident in his approach to public issues and in the friends he chose, notably Luke Gardiner II, whose wife and Beresford's second wife were sisters – two of the three 'Irish Graces' celebrated in Sir Joshua Reynolds' painting (commissioned by Gardiner in 1773). The third 'Grace' became the now departed Townshend's second wife.[39]

The year 1773 also saw Beresford beginning the long battle to relocate the Custom House. The first argument made by the Revenue Commissioners to the Lord Lieutenant was that a new downstream bridge was inevitable, therefore the Custom House must be moved. But subsequent arguments focused on the limitations of the existing Custom House and how it compromised revenue collection and clogged traffic on land and river. Advocates highlighted the fact that only about one-sixth of all vessels entering the port actually discharged at Custom House Quay (principally those with wines, spirits, sugars, tobacco and high-value goods), and that all the city's exports were shipped from the lower quays.[40] There were, however, divisions among the commissioners and by championing the move Beresford exposed himself to huge unpopularity outside Parliament. Everyone assumed that such a move would affect land values and the viability of countless businesses in the west of the city. With his own family's townhouse on the eastern edge of town, Beresford risked accusations of private advantage, reinforced by the coincidence of his new marriage link with the Gardiner clan, who, as everyone knew, had been lobbying for a new Liffey bridge since 1749. With full support from Harcourt, Beresford brought the matter to the Commons in 1774, and the committee hearings threw up contradictory predictions as to the effects of relocation, the Corporation and many merchants expressing strong disapproval. But his parliamentary support held and legislation was passed authorising the purchase of land for a new Custom House on the North Wall, close to that part of Bachelor's Walk where exporting merchants had long enjoyed the privilege to lade their goods.[41]

Unexpectedly, the bill was vetoed by the British Privy Council, an outcome repeated in 1775 and 1776. The obstacle in London was Welbore Ellis, a self-important member of Lord North's cabinet who had inherited his uncle's Oxmantown estate back in 1738. In taking this line he was quietly supported by his Irish nephew and heir James Agar, who had secured a seat on the Irish Revenue board a year after Beresford. The Ellis estate extended back from Arran and Ellis quays (between the third and fifth bridges upstream), and as it had not been fully developed its commercial prospects seemed likely to be adversely affected by shifting the Custom House three-quarters of a mile downstream. However, Thomas Burgh's old building was very dilapidated and some action was essential. To Buckinghamshire's fury, Ellis held out for terms – the delay, he argued, 'besides being a great inconvenience to trade, loses many thousands of pounds to the Revenue'. But thanks to Beresford's prolonged lobbying in London, Ellis finally agreed to the plan in 1781. The price was an Irish government commitment to move the old Four Courts from beside Christ Church, not eastwards to College Green as a parliamentary committee had recommended, but north across the river to Inns Quay. This site was unattractively close to the markets district, but it already housed the partially completed 'public offices', designed to accommodate state records. More importantly, though, it was adjacent to Ellis's ground-rents.[42]

The Revenue Commissioners had initially hoped to secure the services of Charlemont's friend and architect, Sir William Chambers, for a new Custom House, but the latter's interest in Irish commissions had now

waned. But also in London was his 'old pupil' James Gandon, who had
come out second in the Exchange competition a decade previously and was
known to Charlemont and other prospective Irish patrons. One wealthy
young Irish peer, Viscount Carlow, persuaded him to come to Dublin for
work and subsequently put him in touch with Beresford. Gandon came
to the city in April 1781, but he had to remain incognito for four months
until the Revenue Commissioners got possession of the North Wall site.
The first months of work there turned out to be technically challenging
(with major problems with the water table) and personally hazardous for
the architect. The Corporation made a brief legal challenge, and Tandy's
supporters occupied the site on at least one occasion. Indeed, the ensuing
public controversy was reported back to London and led Lord North to
check whether the project should not 'on mature reflection' be halted.[43]

The decision stood. Gandon's alchemy slowly transformed the tidal
marshland: an elongated white palace twenty-nine bays wide, resting in part
on a massive floating timber lattice, began to appear close above the water-
line. With its four neoclassical façades, it stood as detached from the city to
the east as the Royal Hospital a century earlier had been to the west. It began
to be used from 1787, although it took a full decade to complete, the bill
running to over £200,000 (nearly four times that of the Royal Exchange).
Initial funding for the project had been allocated by the British Treasury
from hereditary Crown revenues that lay outside the discretion and oversight of the Irish Parliament, but parliamentary oversight increased and full
accounts were presented to a highly critical House in 1791.[44]

How was it then that the plans of 1773 for an 'elegant but simple
building' that would combine 'convenience, solidity and proper economy'
had been transformed into the great 'temple of taxation' a decade later,
complete with lavish apartments for the chief commissioner in the north-
west pavilion? Had Dublin's trade grown so much in the interim, or were
over-exuberant expectations as to the impact of 'free trade' responsible?
Apart from coasting vessels (and they were always plentiful), there was
an average of about five ship movements a day at the port in the mid-
1780s, no more than in the early 1770s, although merchant vessels were
getting noticeably larger. Liverpool, London, Whitehaven and Greenock
remained the principal ports doing business with Dublin – and colliers
made up the majority of those ships – and the great hopes of 1780 for
an Atlantic commercial renaissance were not apparent as the new building took shape. There were the long-established direct trades with more

distant markets, with the ports of Bordeaux, Rotterdam, Cadiz and Philadelphia being the most important destinations, but, compared to the global reach of Liverpool, Dublin's trade was still largely contained within the Irish Sea and there was little sign of that changing.[45]

One factor explaining the Custom House must be Gandon's lofty ambition to produce a masterpiece comparable to the work of the English great architects – Wren, Vanbrugh and Chambers. McParland has traced how Gandon managed to bring an already well-developed set of plans drafted in London all the way to completion without significant compromise, a process greatly helped by the sharpness of his judgement in selecting building materials and choosing reliable local contractors. But Gandon was lucky to be able to call on some truly gifted craftsmen, whose spectacular sculptural work proved critical in bringing together the vast façades of the building; the most famous was Edward Smyth, some of whose carving Gandon declared was 'equal to Michael Angelo'.[46]

But the scale of it all is still puzzling. Beresford's terrier-like commitment to what became such a lavish project was critical. Never swept up in the patriot wave, he persisted in bringing to Dublin a palace of commerce that no English city could rival. Was there an element of provincial pride here? Anthony Malcomson has suggested that for Beresford, 'matters personal to himself were the only things he felt strongly about', so that the successful completion of the project would have been sufficient reward for all the pain and subterfuge.[47] But apart from being a man of well-developed architectural taste who doubtless took pleasure from his creation, Beresford may also have had more material reasons for encouraging this architectural tour de force. Its construction set the tone for a whole district that had lacked any defining central feature, and while Beresford did not himself profit from the immediate impact on local land values, his family and his Gardiner connections undoubtedly did benefit from the surge in demand for sites in the 'cabbage-garden' lands east of Marlborough Street and northwards of the North Wall (one critic in 1790 maintained that the rent for building ground on the Gardiner estate thereabouts had more than doubled in recent times). But one also gets a sense that the monumental audacity of the project was for him an answer in kind to the rabble-rousers who in the 1770s had challenged the state and the constitutional authority underpinning it. The allegorical statuary which adorned the building – Britannia and Hibernia in embrace, Irish rivers juxtaposed with distant continents – was open to a variety of patriotic and imperial readings, but we know that Beresford himself had nothing but contempt for the populist patriotism of the Napper Tandy brigade. Assailed by the city sheriffs and random protestors at the very start of the project, Gandon was comforted by Beresford in a telling message: 'prevent all opposition, and laugh at the extreme folly of the people'.[48]

The related project of a new downstream bridge was a long time coming, with rearguard opposition still alive and viceregal support lukewarm. The go-ahead was finally given in 1789. Beresford's determination to get the bridge built and, related to this, to transform the management of the lower port is evident from two moves on his part. He ensured that the bridge, its site, design and financing, should become the responsibility not of the city (which might very well refuse it), but the Revenue Commissioners. Secondly, in something of a coup in 1786, he staged a parliamentary takeover of the Corporation's Ballast Office and, with it, responsibility for the lower quays and walls, the port, pilotage and outer harbours. The old body had run up heavy debts and was an easy target for administrative reform, and by relieving the city of responsibility for the Office's debts, Beresford established the new Ballast Board with little controversy. But his reform was driven by a determination to make the Custom House in all its parts a success.[49]

The location of the new river crossing, midway between old Luke Gardiner's Mall and College Green, had been decided in 1782, and Gandon was soon preparing designs for a triumphal bridge. But after the seven-year delay in getting the go-ahead, his final version was a great deal more sober. Taking four years to complete, Carlisle Bridge (commemorating the viceroy who had made it all possible a decade earlier) only opened to carriage traffic in 1795.[50] We can see that this bridge was really the crucial element tying together some six planning decisions taken by related agencies between 1782 and 1785: 1) that the length of Gardiner's Mall should be doubled and taken at its full width (46 metres) south to the river, to terminate at a new but narrower bridge (18 metres wide); 2) that to the east of this, Lower Abbey Street be widened, its trajectory changed and, in parallel, a new quay created, the future Eden Quay (out of that came plans for a new crescent that would face the north side of Custom House); 3) that a new street should be driven south from the bridge to College Green; this was later adapted to allow a second street of equal width to run south-eastwards from the bridge to the end of Lazers Hill (Townsend Street); when built, these streets were narrower than Sackville Street (each

27 metres wide), but they were still very wide; 4) that a new street beginning one block north of Sackville Street, beyond Mosse's gardens, be laid
out, reaching up to Dorset Street and thereby completing a new axial
route from the North into the centre of the city that would rival Capel
Street/Parliament Street; 5) that the fifty-year-old Parliament House be
extended and opened out, both on the east side to create a formal entrance
to the House of Lords, and on the west side to expose the Dame Street
approaches to the great building; and 6) that Dame Street itself be reconstructed to a new uniform width of 80 feet. Taken together, this package
(or as William Eden called them, 'our great plans ... for the improvement
of Dublin') represented perhaps the most important set of decisions ever
made to reshape the centre of Dublin. Over the next quarter of a century,
a total of nearly £700,000 was spent on these projects by the Wide Streets
Commissioners alone.[51]

Beresford was the catalyst, but there was a great deal more to the
story, or rather a series of overlapping stories. Carlisle and Eden, while
fully backing Beresford's eastward strategy, made efforts to sweeten the
pill by keeping the widening of Dame Street a high priority, although it
is striking that (unlike in the 1750s) no priority was now given to opening up the environs of the Castle.[52] Before they left office during the fateful spring of 1782, they agreed to a strengthening of the powers of the
Wide Streets Commissioners. This was critical. In the 1750s and 1760s
the Commissioners had been exclusively concerned with opening up
access to Essex Bridge and its surrounds and, as we have seen, they were
entirely controlled by political interests opposed to the eastward move.
The body then became almost inactive, with only William Burton, Townshend's aide-de-camp and a Commissioner from 1772, championing the
widening of Dame Street, but not convincing Townshend. But a decade
later, with new powers, new finance and new members, the Commission
was transformed by 22 Geo. III, *c.*15. With a remit to widen Dame Street
'and other ways', the Commissioners were now in receipt of a healthy revenue flow from a city coal tax, as well as specific parliamentary grants. Its
membership was widened to include Beresford, Foster, Gardiner, Carlow,
La Touche (the banker), Frederick Trench (MP and amateur architect),
and Andrew Caldwell (Presbyterian landowner and art collector). Both
Trench and Caldwell were close friends of Gandon from his London days,
and through them his architectural influence was continuously felt.[53]

Here then was, in Edward McParland's much quoted words, a

'combination of enlightenment and power', an assemblage of men with differing priorities and enthusiasms, each of whom at different stages used the Commission to advance their particular interests (public and/or private). The uneven pattern of attendance at meetings reveals how far members' participation was narrowly tied to individual planning issues. Most of the Commission's work involved the painstaking business of overseeing the surveys of new street lines, the compulsory purchase of affected properties and their valuation by jury, the servicing of plots and auctioning of leases, together with the monitoring of the builder-developers to ensure that the new façades met the Commissioners' increasingly exacting specifications. With strong political backing, healthy revenues and growing borrowing powers, they maintained momentum through the 1780s, although it was less than some anticipated.[54] By 1792, much of the south side of Dame Street had been widened, its unified symmetrical façades and ground-floor shop-fronts startlingly different from the old and ill-assorted variety of gable-fronted buildings they replaced. And to the north-east of College Green, Gandon's triumphal portico now announced the entrance to FitzGibbon's bailiwick – a resurgent House of Lords, which had been completed under Lord Carlow's direction. Sharply rising land values were pushing up the costs of compulsory purchase, and this held back the laying out of Lower Sackville Street until the early 1790s. Indeed, the plans for the northern spur to Dorset Street (the future North Frederick Street) and for the two great avenues on the south side (the future Westmoreland and D'Olier Streets), fanning out from the south side of Carlisle bridge, were only partially agreed in 1792, by which time the development costs for Westmoreland Street alone were estimated at £95,000. Major construction of the latter only began in 1799 and took nearly a decade to complete. The loss of momentum in completing these great streets, agreed in principle in the early 1780s, reflected the much harsher fiscal and economic climate beginning in 1793 with the return of international war. In addition, competition between the Bank of Ireland and other possible builders on the island site between Westmoreland and D'Olier Streets placed a further brake on plans. The avenues, when completed, were nevertheless the best examples of the Commissioners' work, their 'uniform elevations ... structurally daring and typologically advanced'. The superintending architect, Henry Aaron Baker, was Gandon's well-trained understudy.[55]

James Gandon remained a highly controversial figure in the city, resented for scooping up plum public commissions and for being so close

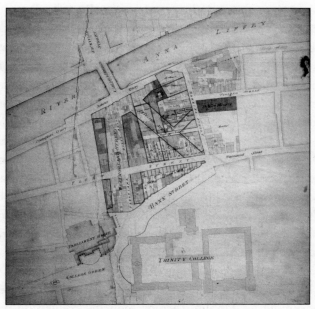

*18. One of the many maps of the Wide Streets Commissioners that highlights just
how radical their interventions into existing street alignments could be. Plans
for a street extending southwards from the new downstream bridge were first
considered in 1782 – the genesis of Westmoreland Street, with plans for D'Olier
Street added later. This map, setting out the fully developed V-plan, dates from
c.1799. Houses on the two boulevards were constructed over the next dozen years.*

to the patrician Beresford. Even among the Commissioners, neither Foster nor Burton were comfortable with Gandon's artistic ascendancy. The Four Courts project on Inns Quay, isolated from the other metropolitan works, revealed these tensions. The plans for the new courts (integrating the public offices) received strong viceregal approval in 1785, but Gandon's plans generated heated opposition from among some of the government's supporters. However, the challenges of the site were surmounted and the nay-sayers proved wrong when it opened for business in 1796, having cost £114,000. The domed pantheon with its airy courtrooms and great public hall was an appropriately cavernous space, effortlessly accommodating the increasing flow of legal traffic within its walls. Externally it was a very muscular building that immediately dominated the upper quays.[56]

Gandon's principal adversary in this project was William Burton (from 1781 known as William Burton Conyngham), antiquarian extraordinary and energetic sponsor of improvement projects in town and

country. A veteran cavalry officer and former Barracks Board commissioner, he was exercised by the implications of the new Four Courts for
the free movement of the military along the quays. Indeed, as the government had purchased two villas in the Phoenix Park in 1782 as suburban retreats for the Lord Lieutenant and the Chief Secretary, uncluttered
access between Castle and Park was now a priority. Burton Conyngham
was also the main advocate among the Wide Streets Commissioners for
widening of the western approach road to the city between Islandbridge
and the Barracks, and in 1786 he persuaded the viceroy, the duke of Rutland, to cede a small part of the Phoenix Park near the river and paid the
costs of acquiring the section east of the Park himself. The result was the
Parkgate/Conyngham Road boulevard, which not only improved military mobility westwards but strengthened the link between the north and
south sections of the 'Circular Road'.[57]

This road had been sanctioned by legislation in 1763 (3 Geo. III
c.36) and had been intended to link the four toll roads and twelve other
routes converging on Dublin, thereby reducing congestion within the
city itself.[58] The Act settled on an oval-shaped route for the north- and
south-side circular roads but, despite the fact that it was almost entirely
through 'orchards and gardens', only the south-side section, arcing from
the Donnybrook road (the future Leeson Street) westwards to the Cork
road, across Kilmainham Common and down to the river at Islandbridge,
was built in the first ten years, and it took a series amending acts to complete the north-side arc from the North Wall across to the Phoenix Park
and downhill to Barrack Street.[59] Some sections of the six-mile circular
roadway became quite busy, but the overall impact on traffic was modest,
its importance more in 'furnishing a convenient airing', and as 'a broad
walk ... much frequented by the better sort of people, on foot, on horse-
back, and in carriages'. It also became a marker of the natural limits of the
city. As we have seen, it defined the jurisdiction of the new police force
in 1786 and also that of the landmark planning act of 1790 (30 Geo III,
c.19), which required all landowners to submit plans for any new street
to the Wide Streets Commissioners for review and approval (their remit
was extended in 1792 to include ground lying up to half a mile *beyond* the
Circular Roads).[60]

This oval route, chosen almost casually in 1763, exercised a strong
influence on two specific developments. In the north-east, it provided
an urban boundary for the expansion of the Gardiner estate, and on the

*19. The view north from Sackville Street into Rutland Square on a summer's
morning c.1791 includes the Rotunda building on the left (opened in 1764),
its elegant new entrance hall, and the Assembly Rooms (unfinished at the
time of Malton's visit). In the distance the vista is closed by the west end of
Gardiner's Row, and beside it the new link to Dorset Street and the road to
the north, North Frederick Street, then at an early stage of development.*

south-west, it influenced the route of the Grand Canal. The younger Luke
Gardiner's ambitions for an accelerated infilling of the Gardiner estate
were evident from the time he inherited in 1769, beginning with Gardiner's Row in the 1770s, Summerhill and Temple Street a decade later, and
the completion of what in 1784 was renamed as Rutland Square (modern
Parnell Square). That year, the Rotunda's governors decided to quadruple
the covered space available for dances and other types of upper-class recreation in order to boost income for the maternity hospital; they commissioned a suite of ballrooms and supper-rooms (designed by Frederick
Trench) to open onto Cavendish Row north of the Rotunda itself. A new
tax was sanctioned by Parliament in 1785 to be levied on the owners of
sedan-chairs in the city and thanks to this charge on the very wealthy (and
to some vigorous borrowing) the Assembly Rooms were soon in operation. This renewed the square as the epicentre of high fashion and helped
drive demand for the new terraced properties to the east and north of
the square. However, unlike the developments associated with Gardiner's grandfather, those of the 1780s and 1790s were entirely the work of

speculative builders and their approach was to produce fairly standardised three-bay units. There were a few showpiece neoclassical gems like Belvedere House in Gardiner's Row, the product of their owners' enthusiasm and deep pockets. Others following in the Gardiner slipstream, like Nicholas Archdall, owner of what became North Great George's Street in the 1780s, also played a permissive but relatively passive role in the transformation of their properties.

Existing routes and contours influenced Gardiner's plans for further streets to the north-east, but everything was compressed within the encompassing Circular Road. A key decision was the creation of an entirely new street, running three-quarters of a mile from Gandon's Custom House northwards towards the Circular Road. This became Gardiner Street, and was more or less aligned with older streets to the west. Its centrepiece, set on the highest ground, became Mountjoy Square. Initial designs in the 1780s envisaged palatial terraces with integrated façades for the square and a new parish church at the central point, but these proved fanciful. When building began in 1790, controls had to be relatively light in what soon became a cooling market. Indeed, much of Gardiner's plan for the north-east remained on the drawing board, or was only very partially realised, by the time its progenitor died at the battle of New Ross in 1798.[61]

On the opposite corner of the city, the long-heralded Grand Canal had begun commercial operations in 1779 with a handful of boats operating out of the small harbour located just east of the City Basin. When the idea of constructing an artificial waterway to link the Liffey and the Shannon had first been seriously canvassed in the 1750s, the principal justification for committing public money to such a project had been the likely impact on Dublin fuel prices given access to Castlecomer coal, but it was assumed that a canal would also boost inland grain production and give greater security for Dublin's food supply. Almost a quarter of a century elapsed between the initial parliamentary grants for canal-building and the opening of the first inland section. In the intervening period, Dublin Corporation had had to rescue the project, overseeing the construction of sections of the canal closest to the city, including the west-end harbour. The Corporation's motives for getting involved were quite simple. By the early 1760s there was a water crisis; the ancient sources supplying the City Basin from the Poddle and Dodder rivers, augmented since the 1740s by Liffey water scooped up by a wheel near Islandbridge, were proving quite inadequate for the burgeoning demand.[62] The potential of a canal to solve the problem and boost the water supply entering the Basin seemed a god-send for the city, but everyone involved in the 1760s underestimated the engineering problems that would be encountered in the bog country of north Kildare. The scheme would have stalled a second time but for the establishment of a joint-stock venture in 1771–2 with a capital of £100,000 (the city subscribing 10 per cent); investors were promised a fixed share of net revenues from the city's water taxes, once canal water began to flow into the pipes. With stronger finances and better technical expertise, the first twelve miles of canal were opened in June 1779, but the link-up with the Barrow at Athy was not completed until 1791, and nirvana – access into the River Shannon – was only achieved in 1804.[63]

The commercial case for building the canal was always rather dubi-ous, and as it turned out the investors in the 1771 company were poorly rewarded for their enthusiasm. But the canal did have real commercial impact: brick, stone and other building materials filled the incoming boats from the start, to be joined by grain (especially barley and flour), potatoes and turf. Kilkenny anthracite appeared a little later. In reverse, the canal's great service to the city was in helping to dispose of the ever-present curse of 'night soil', animal manure and other waste from the city, finding a ready sale for such effluent along the canal, particularly among those small-scale producers of potatoes in north Kildare working for the city market and lacking ready access to other fertilisers.[64]

From the first years of the Corporation's involvement, the canal's potential as 'a pleasing recreation as well as a salutary walk' close to the city was recognised: the first of thousands of elm trees, thirty-foot high, were purchased in 1766 to adorn the canal banks, and the view from the Chinese bridge on the City Basin out along the canal was celebrated. This issue of amenity arose again in the 1780s when the extension of the canal down to the River Liffey was being mooted. The initial idea was to extend the water-way by a series of deep locks and enter the river opposite the Barracks. But this plan was scuppered because of the scale of the technical challenge and a concern that access to the port might be compromised by future bridge development. The alternative was to construct a much longer branch across the south-side of the city to a deep-sea dock, either opposite the Custom House or far to the east of the new works. Richard Griffith and John Macartney, the largest investors in the company, championed the latter idea and in 1785 the Wide Streets Commissioners were lobbied to support a route that would hug the South Circular Road for much of its length before crossing the meadows behind Sir John Rogerson's Quay, reaching the sea just short of the Dodder's exit.[65] This three-mile waterway was duly built in the early 1790s, loosely following the course of the Circular Road. It terminated in a huge L-shaped dock, capable of accommodating 150 sea-going vessels that was cut into undeveloped ground beside the river. This south-side canal and the new docks together cost almost £180,000; they were built at a time when investors in canal stock were at last enjoying huge capital appreciation. But it was an extreme example of ill-planned public expenditure, a vanity project that brought public acclaim for its two champions – the Kildare nabob Richard Griffith and John Macartney – as was evident when the viceroy opened the docks in April 1796 before a vast crowd. But nemesis followed only a few years later when the Grand Canal Company became insolvent, Macartney spending his later years as a bankrupt on the Isle of Man, Griffith as postmaster in Holyhead.[66]

A second private canal scheme, taking a more northerly route from Dublin to the Shannon, received limited parliamentary support in 1789, and despite severe engineering difficulties an eighteen-mile section of the 'Royal Canal' was opened in 1796 running from Kilcock to an elevated harbour in the north city at Broadstone, where it overlooked the markets district. There was a strongly Whig/patriot flavour to this project, with Tandy and John Binns among the early backers and the duke of Leinster a key supporter. But its commercial prospects were even more limited than those of the Grand Canal: it did eventually reach the Shannon north of Lough Ree in 1817, although huge construction costs wiped out the original company so that its completion placed a hefty charge on the Exchequer. But the lure of Leitrim coal turned out to be even more of a mirage than Kilkenny anthracite. A relatively short city extension from the main line was carried eastwards down to the river, exiting through the marshes half a mile east of the Custom House. This was executed on a far more modest scale than the city extension of the Grand Canal (see Map 4).[67]

These 'wide streets of water' spelt huge private loss for most of their investors, but they did provide a tangible public amenity. Indeed, the tree-lined landscaping of the Grand Canal helped promote recreational passenger traffic (the service began at the Portobello hotel on the road to Rathmines), and even more importantly the canal helped frame the ambitions of the blossoming Fitzwilliam estate. In a rough development plan of 1789, with Merrion Square almost completed and the idea of Fitzwilliam

Square in the air, possible new developments running towards the South Circular Road and the canal were pencilled in: these became the future Baggot Street, the two Mount Streets and Grand Canal Street/Artichoke Road. By 1797 each of these had a designated canal bridge with an impressive lock nearby, offering leafy prospects along the track-way. Admittedly, the infilling of the Fitzwilliam estate, even within the canal, took fifty years to complete, but the ground-plan had been sketched out just as the canal was being excavated.

Bastille to Back Lane

The intervention by Dublin Corporation in the early 1760s had probably saved the Grand Canal project. That was to be its last strategic act for a very long time. All the new agencies by which the city was now to be managed – the Wide Streets Commissioners overseeing planning, the Revenue Commissioners and the Ballast Board dealing with the port, the 1786 police force overseeing law and order, traffic and street trading, the Paving Board of 1774 (and remodelled in 1784) – were created by Parliament and answerable to it, and collectively they diminished the powers of the Corporation within the liberties of the city (although in some instances they extended the jurisdiction of the city magistrates outwards).

Yet an observer of Dublin in 1790 might well have thought otherwise. Two great victories for city patriots were notched up that summer, first the triumph of Grattan and Lord Henry FitzGerald in the general election for the city, a campaign 'exceptional in its ostentatious populism', which was choreographed by Tandy and his allies to be a devastating rejection of Castle influence in the city.[68] Tandy was now at the height of his popularity and the victory emboldened him to lead the city Commons in a four-month battle, first with the aldermen and then with the Irish Privy Council, over the right of the lower house (drawing on the 1760 Reform Act) to veto a mayoral nominee if it so wished. With rugged determination, the city Commons blackballed the nomination of a series of aldermen who had been tainted by service as police commissioners. There was a real threat that municipal government would grind to a complete halt. But the Commons got their way and an untainted (and reformist) merchant, Henry Howison, was put forward and accepted as mayor, to the Lord Chancellor's chagrin.[69] There was an unlikely sequel to the affair: the previous year the Corporation had authorised the expenditure of £1,200 on a new ceremonial coach for the Lord Mayor, and a leading Dublin coach-maker, William Whitton, was completing the commission when the earl of Clare's striking new state coach arrived from London in autumn 1790. Not to be outdone, the Corporation seems to have instructed Whitton to go one better, which at a final cost of £2,691 he did: their gilt state coach, drawn by six black horses, first appeared in the procession marking William III's birthday in 1791, its bare-breasted goddesses glistening in the rain as they attested to Hibernia's fortunes rising under Dublin's protection, and, on the richly painted door panels, the crown of Ireland, the Parliament House, Trinity College, shipping in the port, all crowded together. It was a somewhat extravagant celebration of the city's claim to greatness.[70]

It was also quite misleading. The power of the mayoral office had declined greatly since mid-century and the reputation and standing of the Corporation in the eyes of most Dubliners was about to be deeply compromised by the new turn of politics. The coach with its unifying themes, albeit with a strongly Williamite flavour and its boundless optimism, would soon be strangely anachronistic (it was subsequently only brought out at the annual swearing-in of the Lord Mayor before the Lord Lieutenant). Two other aspects of municipal life gave a truer indication of affairs: the riding of the franchises and the eclipse of the Tholsel. The former, the triennial ceremony in which the Lord Mayor and the guilds ('about fifty [men] to every corporation') paraded in ceremony around the city limits, had survived huge political changes since its late medieval inception, and was a day of loud street-theatre for masters, journeymen and spectators, a time of carnival and excess. It included a sham battle at the entrance to the Coombe where the city met the Meath Liberties. But the event became dangerously disorderly and craft journeymen in most trades had now at best a tenuous connection with their respective guilds. The last attempt to hold the event was in 1785; it was abandoned after rioting along the Coombe and military intervention, leading to three deaths.[71] A second sign of corporate decline was the Tholsel: so dangerous had the city hall become that in 1791 both the quarterly Assembly and principal committees were relocated to a modest building in South William Street that had been built in the 1760s for the short-lived Society of Artists. There the Corporation was to remain for sixty years, despite grand plans to build a new Tholsel on Essex Quay. It was no place for great public meetings, so the Royal Exchange and its expansive curtilage became the prime site for open gatherings from the 1790s.[72]

To complete this process, the city courts moved from the Tholsel across the river to the new Sessions House in Green Street, next door to Newgate jail, which opened in 1797. Green Street already had bad associations. In July 1790, at the height of the mayoralty dispute, the city authorities, as we have seen, had lost control of the jail. The gaunt building was holding well over 200 prisoners when they overpowered their guards and threatened to destroy it. It was retaken by the army that night without loss of life, but a Bastille-like fall of Newgate had for some hours seemed likely.[73] The extraordinary events in Paris twelve months previously and the gradual implosion of the *ancien régime* in France now formed a backdrop to every public issue. This arose from the unique prestige of French civilisation and the constant appetite for French ideas, goods and fashions, ranging from prized sets of *L'Encyclopédie* to the translation and local publication of current French writing, political and philosophical.[74] Then there was the explicit use, again and again, of French prototypes for architectural innovation and interior design that had been so successfully mediated through the Dublin Society schools. The lustre of things French was strengthened by the high visibility of Huguenot wealth in the city, and the French language was now more widely understood by those with formal education than ever before (with evening classes offered in French since the 1770s and a French-language boarding school on the Donnybrook Road since 1788). Many in the city had received their professional education in France, including a large handful of the city's Catholic clergy and Catholic physicians. Thus the unfolding of the Revolution had a shocking and compelling immediacy for many Dubliners, some fearful as soon as they read Burke's dire warnings in 1790, most welcoming what seemed like France's constitutional rebirth along lines marked out by Williamite England a century previously. In the final weeks of 1789 the two city theatres were offering rival representations of the fall of the Bastille on stage. In both cases the scripts were highly approving of 'the revolution', the Theatre Royal publicity characterising it as 'that glorious struggle which gave birth to national freedom'. French events again dominated the Dublin stage three years later but the tone was very different: the locally composed verse play *Democratic rage* expressed horror at a revolution that saw the execution of the king and queen, the spread of a 'levelling' political ideology, and the outbreak of a new war against Britain and its allies.[75]

Those three years were a watershed in public life. Events in France brutally exposed latent divisions within Dublin society, and sectarian discord that was to be such a feature of the nineteenth-century city took its modern form at that moment. Fractures were evident at several levels: among those who had defined themselves as Whigs, patriots or simply opponents of government, among the ranks of the politically active Catholics, and among the artisanal masses. And a key part of this fracturing process was the contagious effects of democratic political debate, spreading from guildhall and tavern to whiskey shop and Catholic chapel.

In the case of the Whigs, divisions emerged over how to interpret the events in France, thanks to Edmund Burke's inconvenient denunciation of the Revolution. In 1789, Leinster, Charlemont, Grattan and the Ponsonby faction had formed the Whig Club and with it the makings of a parliamentary party, in opposition to the Castle's parliamentary group. Somewhat later, the Free Citizens, riding high after the election victories of 1790, rebranded themselves as the Whigs of the Capital. Tandy was quick to grasp the political potential when Burke's adversary Tom Paine published his *Rights of Man* (part I) in London early in 1791. Its brutally mocking attack on the pretensions of aristocracy and hereditary rights, its plain-speaking celebration of equality and the sovereignty of the people was inspired by the *Déclaration des droits de l'homme et du citoyen,* and chimed well with the language of city hustings. But its almost messianic sense of the dawning of 'an age of revolutions' went considerably further. Paine's tract was serialised in three Dublin newspapers and printed in several full-priced Dublin editions before the Whigs of the Capital produced a subsidised print-run of some 20,000 copies, offered for sale at sixpence a piece. Paine was the public hero when on the evening of Bastille Day 1791 several Volunteer corps paraded through the streets to St Stephen's Green behind a great lantern on which was inscribed 'The Rights of Man', whereupon a cannon and two field pieces were discharged. The Dublin Whigs had been trying to revive Volunteering since 1790, and although the numbers mobilised were small by former standards, the Tandy party enjoyed surprising freedom to develop a democratic political movement complete with military trappings, not that these trappings implied a pathway to violent confrontation. The revolution when it came would be peaceful, and their defiant public posturing was helped by the unwillingness of parliamentary Whigs to disown them.[76]

This changed when the Catholic issue forced itself back to centre-stage.

The guarantee of freedom of thought and of religion in the 1789 *Déclaration* began the movement for a similar end to civil disabilities in Britain and Ireland, but to many Whigs the prospect of Catholic political emancipation (the phrase was new) remained a step too far. Charlemont's private view in 1791 was typical of many reformers: the full admission of Catholics to the constitution would make Ireland a Catholic country, obliterating Protestantism and the current social order and leading 'to one of two, by me detested, consequences either to separation or to union'.[77] Some Whigs who baulked at Catholic relief in 1791 subsequently changed their views, but there were other Protestants who championed Catholic relief from 1790, both as a political strategy to secure parliamentary reform and as an end in itself. The quite disproportionate role played by Presbyterian activists since the 1750s in the push for political and religious reform is striking; Travers Hartley, the old linen merchant first elected an MP in 1782, was only one of many in the 'New Light' (mainly Unitarian) congregation of Great Strand Street who associated with Tandy. William Drennan, who arrived from the North in 1789 to practise in the city as a 'man-midwife', was one of its more patrician members; thanks to the survival of the vast and intimate correspondence with his sister Martha McTier in Belfast through the 1790s, we have an insight into the highly politicised world of dissent binding Dublin and Ulster, as well as his very personal commentary on the flux of politics within the city. Long before coming to Dublin, Drennan had been an ardent advocate of bringing Catholics into a Volunteer-led campaign for political reform, and in Dublin he championed the idea of a secret club, 'a plot for the people' that through a revival of Volunteering and cooperation between dissenter and Catholic would engineer a French-style transformation of Irish public life.[78]

Quiet since the early 1780s, the Catholic Committee (still a heavily Dublin-dominated body) was re-energised by events in France and the prospect of Catholic relief in England. Triennial elections to the Committee at the start of 1791 weakened the influence of the moderates (led by Viscount Kenmare and supported by Archbishop Troy) and emboldened Tandy's friends John Keogh, Thomas Braughall, and the great sugar-manufacturer Edward Byrne. They brought in new money, notably Randall MacDonnell, who had built his first fortune in Spain.[79] The Catholic 'democrats', assisted by supportive noises from dissenters, north and south, resolved on a public campaign to petition Parliament for political concessions, and they also gained unprecedented political access. Chief Secretary

Robert Hobart, in a private meeting in November 1791 with Byrne, Mac-Donnell and two other Catholic merchants, was left in no doubt as to their frustrated sense of civic exclusion: 'we stand in an inferior situation to men much below us in trade and opulence'.[80] They refused to disown the *Declaration of the Catholic Society of Dublin*, the work of a ginger group of radicals (its president was the veteran merchant Thomas Braughall and its membership included Mathew Carey's elder brothers). This *Declaration* referred disparagingly to 'the liberty of Ireland [which] to those of our communion is a calamity', oppressed as they were by a 'thousand inferior despots', and it demanded the prompt abolition of the entire penal code.[81]

Shortly afterwards, the Catholic Committee had a bitter split as to how to respond to the *Declaration*. The moderate minority, who disowned it, seceded. City Catholics were, however, firmly behind the majority, and Lord Kenmare, 'Lord Lickspittle', was burnt in effigy. Meanwhile there were rumours that Pitt's government was shifting its position on the Catholic question and prepared to give ground. When this was privately confirmed there was something close to executive rebellion in Dublin Castle. Pitt's plans were shelved and a relatively modest relief bill emerged, allowing Catholic access to the legal profession.[82] Fears within the Protestant world of an imminent restoration of full Catholic political rights and anger among Catholic activists at the power of the Dublin Castle to block their emancipation dominated public life through the long and sulphurous summer of 1792. Dubliners of all parties were central to this drama: in January, with the first move by the Corporation in Assembly, sending an address to the king and praying that he would defend 'Protestant Ascendancy', meaning the confessional constitution; in February, with the Catholic Committee petition to Parliament, seeking relief, and the scathing rejection of this in the House of Commons, with those involved ridiculed as 'turbulent men, shop-keepers and shop-lifters';[83] in March, with the publication by the Catholic Committee of a declaration of Catholic principles that was subsequently circulated nationally and signed by tens of thousands; in the summer, with plans for a national representative convention of Catholics, which eventually went ahead in every Irish county despite the government's severe disapproval; in September, with the 'Letter to the Protestants of Ireland' published by Dublin Corporation that warned the Catholics of Ireland to press their case no further and, in more coded language, warned London of the limits of Protestant loyalty; in October, with a statement by Catholic Dublin 'householders' attacking the Corporation and asserting that it was a source of their oppression; and culminating in December, with the meeting of the Catholic convention that squeezed into the largest of the guildhalls, the Tailors in Back Lane. After the meeting a small delegation of Catholic leaders was despatched, not to Dublin Castle but to St James's and an audience with the king, which in the early weeks of 1793 prompted the drafting of 'political relief', a bill to admit Catholics to the parliamentary franchise, the magistracy, grand and petty juries and the university, and to bear arms. The Act passed all stages in April.[84]

These extraordinary events occurred at a time of gathering international crisis and of unprecedented internal challenge to the state from democratic enthusiasts, rich and poor. Other Irish cities, most obviously Presbyterian Belfast, were swept up in the public politics of 1792, but Dublin provided the leadership and the venues, both for the Catholic campaign and for the conservative counter-attack. Kenmare and his supporters, it is true, came mostly from Munster, but his episcopal ally was Dublin's Archbishop Troy – until the canny Dominican saw which way the wind was blowing and endorsed the convention. He attended both its opening and its ending. Dublin printing presses played their part in securing country support for the Catholic leadership in Dublin – with print-runs of 10,000 sanctioned for half a dozen essays and declarations. Sentiments, rarely voiced previously, now achieved a formal status, as in the published proceedings of an October meeting of Catholic householders which quoted Swift's fourth Drapier's Letter and included the memorable aside from Thomas Ryan, a radical doctor from Arran Quay: 'six hundred years we have been a wretched, debilitated people; despised by other nations, because we despised one another; a resting spot for birds of passage, and a banquet for birds of prey'. No longer were Catholic arguments to be framed in language comfortable to Protestant ears.[85] There were many country voices, gentry for the most part, raised in the Tailors' Hall in December, but just over half of the 284 delegates at the Catholic convention were Dublin-based businessmen or professionals, many representing counties or towns with which they had personal or commercial links. The whole occasion provided powerful evidence of the arrival of a network of wealthy merchant families who were determined to translate economic power into political influence. Its choreography was the achievement of Keogh and Braughall, who with long years in trade and with fine houses symbolised a new Catholic affluence, but they were helped by their newly appointed secretary, Theobald Wolfe Tone, son of a Protestant coach-maker and a Catholic mother, barrister, Whig Club scribbler and joint architect of the Dublin Society of United Irishmen. His journals give the most graphic account of that week-long assembly.

Democracy and discontent

Tone was one of many who publicly attacked the Corporation for its rousing defence of Protestant ascendancy. Both Burke and Grattan saw the hand of the Castle in their posturing, and indeed there were men like William Cope (a silk merchant in partnership with John Binns) and John Giffard (now editor of *Faulkner's Dublin Journal,* well fed with government advertising and in the city Commons since 1790) who may have acted as intermediaries. But there seems to have been an unprecedented shift in political attitudes within the Common Council and the guilds in reaction both to the sudden uncertainty about their exclusive civic status and to the new abrasiveness of Catholic public utterances. The evident danger of levelling philosophies imported from France doubtless contributed too. In other words, many of Tandy's foot-soldiers of 1790 could now give Ascendancy rhetoric an enthusiastic hearing in 1792 as they warmed to the idea of Protestant dominance as an ancestral providential birthright, a birthright to be enjoyed by all Protestants and not just the well-born, and something of such intrinsic importance that no authority could cancel it.[86]

Tandy's weight within the Corporation was fading, but in November 1791 he emerged as secretary of a new political club, the Dublin Society of United Irishmen. This emerged from the grafting of Drennan's idea of a secret brotherhood onto the somewhat battle-scarred Whigs of the Capital. Meeting first in the Eagle Tavern off Dame Street and later in the Tailors' Hall, it was too large to operate in secret (unlike the Ulster United societies), attracting a regular attendance at its peak of about 200 members. The Society's public rhetoric was filled with French allusion and libertarian symbolism, but the philosophical basis for its reformism still owed much to the civic patriot tradition, and its professional members had many links with the Grattanite Whig opposition. Its denunciation of the pernicious effects of English influence and its industrial protectionism built on the rhetoric of 1779, and its great objective, an equal representation of the people in Parliament, harked back to the early 1780s. But the

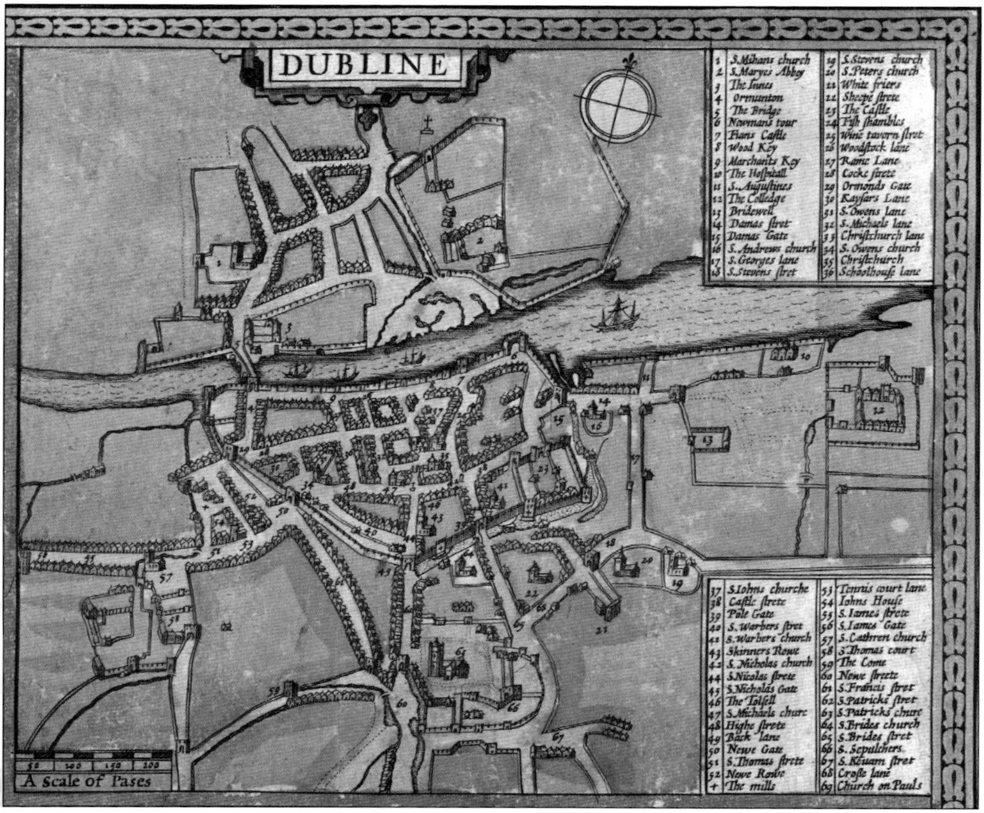

1. This view of the city at the beginning of its post-medieval cycle of growth was no more than a detail within the composite map of Leinster that appeared in John Speed's *Theatre of the empire of Great Britaine* (London, 1611). Over the next two hundred years this Dublin map was re-engraved on at least seventeen occasions for books published in London, Cologne, Amsterdam, Paris, Nuremberg, Frankfurt, Venice, Leiden and Dublin itself.

2. James Asser, *A drawing of His Majesty's park the Ph[o]enix*, c.1775. Although parts of it were now open to the public, the Phoenix Park contained half a dozen residences built by Crown office-holders, and the open spaces continued to have a strong military character.

3. The Dublin-born actress Peg Woffington (*c.* 1720–60) is reputed to have begun as a child street-singer, but for nearly two decades she was the most popular figure on the Dublin stage and also took many leading roles in London. She was celebrated both for her comic performances and Shakespearean roles, her art and intelligence entirely offsetting the obscurity of her origins.

4. Erskine Nicol, *Donnybrook fair*, 1859. Although it had been a commercialised carnival for generations and was now very heavily policed, Donnybrook's celebrated excesses remained to the end and were deeply offensive to reformers, both Catholic and Protestant. The annual fiesta was eventually suppressed in 1868.

5. James Malton, *Lord Charlemont's Casino …, 1795*. Completed more than twenty years earlier, Charlemont's neoclassical gem was now being shaded by the advancing woodland vegetation.

6. Alexander Williams, *Old clothes shop [near] Patrick St.*, 1885. The view along
murky Plunket Street is closed by the imposing landmark of St Nicholas
of Myra. The mid-nineteenth century parish church in Francis Street had
replaced the rambling Catholic metropolitan chapel on that site.

7. The extraordinarily rich barn-like basilica of the University Church, St Stephen's Green, was created by the John Henry Newman to the designs of J. H. Pollen, his professor of Fine Art in the short-lived Catholic University, in 1855–6. The church's antique Roman ambience was unique in the city, its warm sensuous colours culminating in the sumptuous apse that may have seemed at odds with the pulpit homilies delivered to generations of students.

8. Harry Kernoff, *Davy Byrne's pub from The Bailey, 1941*. Kernoff's is the central figure caught as a reflection in the pub mirror. Social and socialist, Kernoff was a permanent fixture in the city's literary landscape for more than three decades between the 1920s and 1950s during which time he produced a flow of woodcuts and paintings in various media that provide a unique record of street-life, industrial work and casual recreation.

Society's central commitment to Catholic relief and to a union of creeds was new, and the priority given to developing a detailed blueprint for constitutional reform and to the mobilisation of public opinion to secure these objectives was also fresh. Recent success in the mass circulation of the *Rights of man* pointed the way: mobilisation meant a relentless process of publication, public meetings and demonstrations, and new forms of propaganda.[87] But the Society was monitored from the beginning by Edward Cooke, the Under-Secretary. Detailed reports were regularly despatched by Thomas Collins, a Parliament Street mercer who had fallen on bad times, via Francis Higgins to Cooke's desk in the Castle.

The Society grew rapidly in the charged atmosphere of 1792, but with the coming of war in February 1793 this slackened considerably. Over its two-and-a-half-year history, more than 400 men joined: about an eighth were from outside Dublin and most of them were gentry, notably the Unitarian Archibald Hamilton Rowan, but its membership was for the most part made up of city professionals, merchants and shopkeepers, with the latter two categories far outnumbering 'law and physic', and with those linked to textiles most in evidence. Many but not all of Tandy's reformist allies of the 1780s were early members, but it was the barristers and those with university links who dominated proceedings and chaired the committees. The involvement of men like Thomas Addis Emmet, son of the State Physician and a highly successful young barrister, Simon Butler, son of a peer and a senior member of the bar, Whitley Stokes, a newly elected fellow of the College, and John Ashenhurst, public notary, stockbroker and secretary of the Dublin Insurance Company, gave initial prestige to the Society, but the ascendancy of an inner professional circle came to be resented (although how much so is not clear).[88] Some of the wealthiest merchants were also involved, notably Malachy O'Connor, partner in the largest Catholic firm trading to the Caribbean and the Mediterranean, John Sweetman, the Francis Street porter brewer, Oliver Cromwell Bond, a major woollen draper in Bridge Street, who 'made £6,000 a year by his business', and Henry Jackson of Pill Lane, Bond's father-in-law and the greatest ironmonger in the city (and the first merchant to use industrial steam-power). Bond and Jackson were both Presbyterian (and more worldly-wise than Drennan). Printers and booksellers, Catholic and Protestant, were also strongly represented, notably Patrick Byrne, the great Grafton Street bookseller/publisher, and John Chambers, the wealthy Abbey Street printer and stationer. Builders and the construction trades were almost completely absent as, it seems, were those 'middling Catholics, who had idle money, [and] so soon as they could take satisfactory leases, ran into house building' in the 1780s after Catholic relief. Overall membership in the early days was well balanced between Anglican, dissenter and Catholic, but the composition became more mercantile and more Catholic over time. The Society's programme of reform took more than two years to emerge because of sharp divisions as to how far the franchise should be widened and whether or not any religious restrictions should operate. In the end, the programme was indeed very radical – adult male suffrage, annual parliaments, salaried MPs, constituencies of equal size – but by then many of the moderates had departed.[89]

About fifty of the delegates to the Catholic convention in Tailors' Hall and some of the most prominent ones there became United Irishmen, playing as their enemies saw it a double game – toadying up to Pitt's government and also flirting with the Dublin democrats. But at the very moment of success for the Catholic Committee, pressure on the Society intensified as war with France loomed. Repeated attempts to regenerate Volunteering, now as a French-style citizen militia, were smothered by legal action, and Butler, Drennan and Hamilton Rowan among others faced trial for seditious libel over an ill-judged *Appeal* to the Volunteers to re-arm themselves.[90] Each had been a high-profile member of the Society while retaining the respect of their social peers. But for Tandy it was downhill from the first days of the Society in 1791: unambiguously supporting full Catholic relief, he found that his vaunted popularity among fellow freemen slumped, and thereafter his judgement repeatedly failed him. He tangled with the Solicitor General, ducked a duel and fled town to avoid arrest in September 1792, then was slighted by the Catholic Committee in December. He became briefly involved in the final efforts to revive Volunteering but did not challenge their suppression in January 1793. He capped all this by taking a 'Defender' oath in Co. Louth and, fearing a capital charge, fled the country at the outbreak of war.[91]

The Society, despite strong pressure from Belfast that it should become a private organisation, remained open and 'uncovered' until the Jackson affair – a 'sting' that provided evidence of the willingness of some of the leadership to communicate with France and contemplate French intervention. In May 1794, the Society was suppressed. That was not of course an end to the matter. Some United Irishmen disappeared out of opposition politics completely, but a sizeable fragment of the constitutional society became involved over the next three years in revolutionary conspiracy. And there were a few who had only been tangentially involved before 1794 but who now emerged into leadership positions, notably the duke of Leinster's youngest brother, Lord Edward FitzGerald.[92]

By the time of the Society's suppression there was a palpable animosity towards both government and Parliament within the city, and such sentiments were now more firmly rooted than in 1779 or 1784. Apart from the long apprenticeship in crowd politics, there were other factors causing this deeper alienation of a large swathe of the city's unenfranchised male population. The cumulative effect of United Irish propaganda through newspapers, handbills and pamphlets was part of it, but this wave of print was perhaps more influential in bringing the Painite message to the world outside Dublin than into the city's courts and laneways. Admittedly, the many artisanal reading clubs that sparked briefly into life between 1792 and 1797 (the pioneer was the 'Sons of Freedom') presumably brought Jacobin and *sans-culotte* ideas a great deal closer to the apprentices and young journeymen involved. The Philanthropic Society, established by the failed College student John Burk in 1794, was the longest lived of these societies and, despite its bland externals, it was unambiguously revolutionary and republican in its objectives.[93] But such clubs were marginal. Larger influences were at work which better explain this surging politicisation in the early 1790s.

First there was the very sharp economic recession that began to bite in the autumn of 1792. This had spread from England, but the slump in credit and business confidence was exacerbated by the local political crisis and a sudden halt to speculative building activity. A wretched harvest compounded matters. By the following spring the construction trades were idle and the weaving community seething. Bakers in the Liberties were attacked in May 1793 and there were marches and demonstrations in the centre of town. In the same month there was 'a dreadful earthquake on the mercantile world' when the largest firm in the cotton industry, Comerford and O'Brien, employing a large workforce in the city and in Balbriggan, suspended payment, and there was a wave of lesser bankruptcies. Well might the radicals try to link the outbreak of a bad war with the painful collapse of household incomes.[94] Things did improve somewhat over the next two years, but as indirect taxes began to rise it soon became evident that the regressive effect of wartime inflation on wage-earners was not going to be reversed.

A more pervasive influence shaping lower-class politicisation was the now very large number of artisans who were sworn members of journeyman combinations. Some of these associations had a city-wide membership, others were defined by proximity to a particular meeting place (usually a public house), and all were occupation-specific. A few could claim great antiquity – journeymen tailors had operated a friendly society outside guild control in the 1670s, and ephemeral societies had existed in the clothing trades from the 1720s (when the first anti-combination legislation was introduced). In their structures and practices they were similar to, and probably influenced by, journeyman clubs in London and the larger English cities. In the expansive 1750s and 1760s there seems to have been a real growth in the capacity and durability of these combinations, notably in the printing and building trades. A carpenters' society, founded c.1761, negotiated a scale of piece-rates and wages that was to operate within a ten-mile radius of the city; by 1781 there were some 1,900 names on its registers. Its industrial strength may explain the attempt by master builders in 1792 to tighten the legal controls over journeymen in the building trade, a proposal that (as in 1780) brought out thousands of craftsmen from a multiplicity of trades to gather in the Phoenix Park and march to College Green, and this set in motion the subsequent failure of the bill. Employers who came fresh to the city like James Gandon were taken aback at the strength of the journeyman societies and the control that they had secured over the terms and conditions of work. Gandon was particularly struck by the 'fellows ... called orators' in the skilled building trades, paid to move around between workplaces 'to keep up a perpetual ferment, rendering the men dissatisfied with their employers'.[95]

Full-time 'orators' were fairly rare, but by the 1790s most if not all journeyman clubs did have a committee structure, a stock of records and a 'house of call'; they inducted new members by oath and required a regular payment of fees; they offered some level of social insurance (funeral costs at least), and operated a well-defined set of rules to protect employment and incomes (preventing masters from expanding the number of apprentices hired, setting out piece-rates, outlawing the hiring of 'strangers' or unapprenticed labour). They were also on occasion prepared to sabotage machinery that threatened employment. So although the general Combination Act of 1780 may have increased the formal power of masters and of magistrates to intervene, the law was always chasing developments on the ground. Journeymen skinners, bakers, sawyers, tailors, hosiers, linen weavers, and above all the shoe-makers, achieved notoriety in the 1780s and 1790s for taking industrial action against masters who challenged their rules (and it is striking that most of these were trades where guild structures had become ossified). There were occasional acts of extreme violence: in 1789 an enforcer group, the Liberty Light Horsemen (echoing Volunteer nomenclature) was involved in ugly incidents in the Liberties, and in July 1790 two of its members (both journeymen sawyers) and a linen weaver were executed. Why this apparent growing conflict? Fergus D'Arcy has suggested that real wage levels of both skilled and semi-skilled wage-earn-ers in the Dublin building industry were under pressure by the 1790s. There are other possibilities, such as the unsettling effects of the rapid growth of unapprenticed labour (in cotton-weaving and textile printing for example), the economic eclipse of masters as more and more capitalised middlemen became their employers (in the silk and fine worsted trades, as well as in construction), and a general sense that the old discipline which a master had enforced over his apprentices was disappearing with 'the abomina-ble custom adopted by the masters of keeping only outdoor apprentices'. Whether or not there was an erosion of social control over youthful work-ers, combinations now operated as powerful social networks within the city, pathways for the transmission of news and new ideas.[96]

Defenderism was in a sense a new idea. A phenomenon of the south Ulster/north Leinster countryside, it first came to notice as a rural move-ment in 1791. It was organised into lodges and its members were bound together by secret oaths that were strongly sectarian both in format and in their declared objectives. The new assertiveness of the Catholic Com-mittee and the mobilisation of Catholic congregations across much of the country in 1792 sparked tensions in religiously mixed districts, among them north Co. Meath, and this hastened the spread of Defender lodges. How far the movement was coordinated at a regional level remains unclear, and whether or not it developed realisable political goals is debat-able. We know that it reached Dublin by 1793, and from that time there were reports of Defender meetings and lodges, particularly in the north-side markets district.[97]

After the suppression of the United Irish Society in 1794, some of the committed radicals maintained a shadow organisation that got its name from a favoured 'hole-in-the-wall' meeting place, the Struggler's Inn in Cook Street. Jackson and Bond, wealthy republican traders with close ties, politically and commercially, to Presbyterian Ulster, were the key figures, and Pill Lane (now Chancery Street) was reputed to be their centre of support. Pill Lane was a great retailing thoroughfare, running eastwards from Church Street towards Abbey Street and it lay immediately north of the Ormond market and contained the only wholesale market for fish. By the 1790s its many businesses were split fairly evenly between Catholic and Protestant names, with textiles featuring more strongly than elsewhere north of the river. Jackson's foundry at the west end of the street was the biggest employer, and his workmen who were strongly politicised by their employer fraternised in the George and the White Cross taverns nearby. The latter was 'the principal place where the northern carmen [i.e. carriers] received their lodging'.[98]

John Burk was briefly associated with these Jacobins of Cook Street and Pill Lane, but the covert artisan clubs that he and other democratic enthusiasts sponsored around the city were rather different. They were youth groups which were more revolutionary, utopian and accommodating of Defenders and their profound if inchoate hostility to Protestantism. These artisan clubs were overwhelmingly Catholic in their membership, but were happy to declare their loyalty to the Revolution, with Bastille Day bonfires outside their drinking places even in 1795. Meanwhile, in the Meath heartland of Defenderism, the belief seems to have developed that Dublin, citadel of the enemy, must be captured, and that Dubliners must be involved in such an enterprise. Some overlap in membership between Defenders and Burk's Philanthropic Society had certainly occurred by August 1795 when there was a series of arms raids close to the city and a small garrison mutiny. This prompted a run of arrests after which Defender activity in the city subsided, especially following the trial and execution of two city Defenders in 1796. Both were teenagers.[99]

Desperate remedies

By 1796, three years into a long war, there had been a political roller-coaster in Dublin. The Relief Act of 1793 had allowed municipal corporations and guilds to admit Catholics on equal terms if they so wished, and counties to open membership of their grand juries to Catholic gentlemen. There was now no religious bar as to who could be registered as a forty-shilling freeholder and thereby be entitled to a vote in city and county parliamentary elections. But there was no obligation on corporations to admit Catholic freemen, and in Dublin only six of the twenty-five city guilds chose to admit Catholic applicants in 1793, and none of those admitted as guild freemen were confirmed as freemen of the city. Even Valentine O'Connor, newly accepted into the Merchants' Guild and nominated for city free-dom by the aldermen, was voted down in the city Commons by a large majority. No further Catholic application for any class of civic freedom was received for many years.[100] The registration of freeholds for electoral purposes could not be spiked in the same way and Catholic registration proceeded in the city and county, albeit slowly. Later in 1793 a follow-up Convention Act placed a legal ban on all delegate assemblies for the future and a Militia Act opened the way for a religiously mixed national mili-tia force. This was to become the reserve standing army for Irish defence, organised in county and city regiments for deployment within Ireland (but never in their own localities). The subsequent raising of the militia was not particularly controversial in Dublin (unlike in many parts of the coun-try); indeed, it was credited with soaking up many unemployed weavers. But when the first Catholic-dominated militia regiments were stationed near the city, some were quick to question their loyalty. Indeed, the battle for the hearts and minds of the militia became a lasting preoccupation.[101]

The Catholic Committee continued to maintain an informal exist-ence after the heady days of 1792, despite agreeing to stand down. Over the next two years there was a growing sense of emancipation unfinished, and internal disputes over strategy split the Catholic leadership. They were saved by events in London – the creation of a war coalition involving the Portlandite Whigs. Integral to that agreement was the appointment of a reforming Whig viceroy for Dublin.[102] Both Catholic politicians and most Irish Whigs expected great things when this was finally settled late in 1794. Earl Fitzwilliam, a Whig magnate (with no connection to the lords of Mer-rion), arrived in Dublin in the first days of the new year; he was fired up with ideas for a Burkean reform of Irish government and the construction of a new governing consensus, one that would fully reintegrate propertied Catholics and create an alliance in arms to face down the social challenge from below. The degree to which he had discretion to determine Irish pol-icy was, however, unclear, and this would soon lead to terrible trouble.

A final Catholic Relief Act was to be part of this grand programme and therefore, encouraged by Grattan, Catholic leaders organised a new round of petitioning for emancipation even before Fitzwilliam's arrival. Dublin led the way and the city's petition, when duly signed, was brought to the

Castle followed by a convoy of a hundred carriages. In order to achieve Catholic relief and to reform Irish affairs, Fitzwilliam was convinced by his Irish friends that he must dismiss the supposed font of corrupt and divisive government – John Beresford and the backroom officials in the Irish government, Under-Secretary Sackville Hamilton and Edward Cooke. This he did, and Grattan and the Ponsonbys were elevated to form a de facto cabinet, whereupon Grattan set about drafting a new Catholic relief bill.[103]

Beresford's growing unpopularity had been heightened by a long-running inquiry in the House of Lords over a dubious land deal in the centre of the city. A large block of property that had been acquired by the Wide Streets Commissioners between Abbey Street and Eden Quay had been leased to Henry Ottiwell back in 1792, but without the usual auction process, and Beresford's son and newly established banker, John Claudius, was heavily involved with Ottiwell. The defence, that the Ottiwell lease had been agreed at a time of falling land values when prospective bidders were colluding, was probably true, but by this stage the whole metropolitan improvements programme had become tainted in the eyes of Beresford's many opponents (including by this stage John Foster), and the Abbey Street transactions were seen as self-serving and corrupt.[104] Beresford's disgrace in 1795 was hugely popular.

The Fitzwilliam government was, however, a very short melodrama. The dismissal of London's loyal Irish allies outraged the prime minister, and his Whig allies were uncomfortable about the new religious policy. So Fitzwilliam was quite sensationally recalled in mid-February. For anyone who had seen merit in the settlement of 1782, his recall revealed the hollowness of Irish parliamentary independence, for Fitzwilliam would almost certainly have commanded majority support in the Irish Parliament for his legislative programme. But that was not the issue. Catholic opinion was outraged at his departure, seeing it (wrongly) as exclusively related to the proposed Catholic bill. The Grattanites were dismayed after their momentary taste of power. And the Corporation and conservative opinion generally were quietly jubilant. The rhetoric of Catholic leaders shifted perceptibly: 'the people of Ireland are never more to look up to the cabinet of England for protection or relief', one speaker told a packed meeting in Francis Street chapel in April, held after further Catholic lobbying in London had been rebuffed, and this sense of self-righteous anger and betrayal led some of the Catholic leaders to become more receptive to the idea of foreign intervention.[105]

Fitzwilliam's successor, the earl of Camden, arrived swiftly, and after Privy Council formalities in the Castle there was a series of coordinated stonings – on the Chancellor in Grafton Street and on his house; on Foster's Molesworth Street house; and on the Custom House apartments of John Beresford (his son Claudius fired on the crowd, killing at least one person). These attacks were choreographed by the Strugglers group and were, it seems, lubricated by free drink. They were intended as a display of strength and perhaps as an assertion of Pill Lane's primacy at a time when opposition politics were in complete flux.[106]

Perversely, the Dublin police was disbanded later that spring (it was a measure that Fitzwilliam championed and it survived on Camden's agenda as a sop to the city). The Corporation now resumed control over the appointment of aldermanic police magistrates; the uniformed force of constables was cut down to fifty; and the old parish watch was revived.[107] Yet as things turned out, the city became more overtly militarised over the next three years. Police magistrates worked more closely with the Castle secretariat in the drive against political subversion and the old office of Town Major was redefined: Henry Sirr, whose father had held the post as a sinecure, took it over in 1796. Already a well-travelled veteran turned wine merchant and recently elected to the city Commons, Sirr emerged to become the coordinator of civil and military decision-making in the city, in effect the chief of police, whose intelligence successes and high-profile arrests soon made him notorious. The strategic defence of the city now became a matter of pressing attention: the military garrison was extended and a large camp, primarily accommodating provincial militia corps, was established eight miles south of the city at Loughlinstown. Then, early in 1798, Yarranton's old idea for a harbour fortress was revived: a hostelry at the landward end of the South Wall, 'Mr Pigeon's House', was acquired by government and transformed into a small fort and citadel, giving protected access to the sea.

The most important step in this cycle of militarisation was the creation of the yeomanry. Camden was forced late in 1796 to underwrite this new version of Volunteering in the face of escalating lawlessness in the countryside. Fitzwilliam had championed the idea of a non-confessional yeomanry, allowing all property holders to share in the burden of local defence, but the new force turned out to be a bleakly loyalist variant, with propertied Catholics seriously under-represented. Their initial absence resulted from a campaign by Catholic leaders to discourage any supporter from volunteering as a mark of their disapproval at the return of the junto, and when city Catholics later applied to join in (in the spring of 1798) their motives were open to question.[108] By June 1798 there were nearly 5,000 armed yeomanry in the city, distributed across twelve infantry and seven cavalry corps, and another twelve corps in Co. Dublin. Together they amounted to a sizeable fraction of the male Protestant citizenry, plus a sprinkling of well-to-do Catholics. Seven of the city corps were organised by district (including a new Liberty Rangers), seven were profession- or guild-based (with four connected to the law), and four had an institutional base (the Linen Hall, the College, the Custom House, and the Grand Canal). They constituted a vast, highly visible and overwhelmingly loyalist force, the enforcers of what many, perhaps most, citizens now regarded as a hostile political order.[109]

The rump of radical political activists, United and Catholic Committee men, who were prepared to contemplate an armed challenge to the state in 1795–7 did so in the expectation, or at least the hope, of French intervention. An exclusively Irish rebellion would, it was assumed, be a forlorn cause. Testing French promises of fraternal aid became the great game; the Catholic Committee's secretary Wolfe Tone, who had been lucky to escape imprisonment after complicity in the Jackson affair, reached Paris via Philadelphia early in 1796 with endorsements, if not instructions, to seek such aid. Following quite separate paths (in every sense), Lord Edward FitzGerald and the radical Cork MP Arthur O'Connor were also on the Continent for much of that year. Tone, however, was the crucial figure in persuading the French Directory of the likelihood of victory if they committed a formidable invasion force to Ireland. And so in December 1796 the great armada was despatched from Brest and, but for the appalling Christmas weather, it would have made a successful landing in Bantry Bay.[110] However, if a large French force had managed to establish a Munster bridgehead at that point, there would have been little that their supporters in the capital could have done to help. Neither the surviving United Irish clubs nor the radical Catholic leaders had developed any military capacity. The unreadiness of Dublin's radicals was in stark contrast to the situation in parts of Ulster, where since the beginning of the war the paramilitary capability of the United Irish movement had greatly increased – and there was an appetite in Ulster for pre-emptive action.

In the weeks after the abortive French invasion, the Catholic archbishop of Dublin took the political initiative for the first time since 1791.

Assembling many of his fellow bishops in Francis Street chapel for a solemn thanksgiving for deliverance from the French, Troy attacked Painite ideology, its 'wild ungovernable democracy' and 'the rotten tree of French liberty'. The clerical onslaught on regicidal France was of course nothing new to the congregation of 3,000, but the pungency of his attack on all things French was startling nonetheless. Troy was no longer the pliant sponsor of Tailors' Hall politicians as in 1792, but the cleric who with quiet diplomacy and quite against the odds had in May 1795 come to an extraordinary deal with Thomas Pelham, Camden's Chief Secretary, by which he secured a recurring state grant of £8,000 p.a. for a Catholic seminary in Ireland. In so doing he rescued another of Fitzwilliam's ideas from the wreckage of the viceroyalty, but on terms which gave Irish bishops more autonomy over their 'Royal College of St Patrick' than would have resulted from any deal with Fitzwilliam. Originally destined for the city, the seminary was opened within months of the deal in the more congenial location of the duke of Leinster's estate village of Maynooth.[111]

Catholic democrats like Richard McCormick and William MacNeven were unfazed by the episcopal attack. Indeed, they had the sympathy of a significant minority of the diocesan clergy in the city in abandoning the politics of accommodation.[112] Even before Bantry Bay, when the Belfast United Irish leadership had first encouraged Dublin activists to transform the jumble of subterranean and disaffected networks into a unitary cellular movement that would be oath-bound and passive until summoned, there was very little sign of clerical obstruction. That integrative process had, it seems, started in the Liberties where Belfast influence had previously been weak, but the financial and logistical centre of gravity remained Pill Lane, and the external trappings were United Irish. The early months of 1797 saw a flurry of activity. By May, Francis Higgins, the Castle's everbusy informant, was reporting how Pill Lane merchants had lately sworn in 'upwards of 700 persons in and about Ormond Market, butchers and their apprentices ... and they are now commenced swearing servants', that pikes were now being manufactured 'in numbers' in the iron-mills along the Dodder (presumably Henry Jackson's), and that overall 'not less than 10,000 of the lower orders and of working people are sworn'. Next month Higgins's reports included claims of military training taking place in the cloth fields in Phibsborough in the northern suburbs, and details of how three United men, a grocer, a toy seller and a tailor from the centre of town, 'went lately into different parts of the county of Wicklow, distributing their treasonable papers, delivering their books of constitution and swearing many deluded people'. But this was not, or not yet, an armed conspiracy – although it was claimed at that time that 'not a man in Pill Lane, Church Lane and all that neighbourhood [is] without one or two muskets'.[113]

The Dublin leadership came under strong pressure from northern United Irishmen to mount a pre-emptive rising in the spring of 1797, but this was resisted, apparently on the grounds of continuing unpreparedness, and Dublin's 'cowardice' rankled. Later in the year, however, Dublin filled the gap created by the violent closure in Belfast of the *Northern Star*, the dominant radical newspaper of the decade. Throughout the winter of 1797–8 John Stockdale, veteran United Irish printer in Abbey Street, oversaw the production of *The Press,* a punchy newspaper that combined anonymous political commentary (by O'Connor, the Emmets and most of the movement's Dublin leaders) with shrill exposés of army and yeomanry excesses. During its five months of existence, three of its nominal publishers were jailed, but 'the soul of the Dublin public' somehow survived until a squad of militia arrived with sledge-hammers. They promptly destroyed the presses and arrested Stockdale. But by then – March 1798 – the city's revolutionaries were finally posing a real military challenge.[114]

The bigger picture had changed greatly in a year. The United Irish movement in Ulster had been greatly debilitated during the spring and summer of 1797, its vast rural support hammered by a drastic 'pacification' policy that involved both magistracy and military. In Dublin there had been a brief return to constitutional politics early in 1797 as rumours of peace and the fall of Pitt's government animated the Grattanite Whigs and encouraged contacts between Grattan and the United Irish leadership. But after the collapse of such prospects, the Whigs withdrew from Parliament (aligning their protest with Foxite tactics in Westminster). Then in a subdued general election there was – for the first time in decades – no contest in the city constituency and Grattan went quiet. One of the two incoming MPs was John Claudius Beresford, now a politician in his own right. From the start he identified himself with a new loyalist movement, the Orange Order, which, like Defenderism before it, was imported into the city from south Ulster, mutating in the process. Its formularies were masonic but its local objectives in the city were to strengthen, protect and cherish Protestant control, both in the constitution and in the Corporation, part of a new assertion of pan-Protestant identity.[115]

The economic climate had also shifted. After adjusting quite successfully to the war economy in the mid-1790s, the city was hit by an even sharper credit crisis in February 1797, with the Bank of Ireland (following the Bank of England) forced to suspend the convertibility of paper for gold. There was a growing crisis in Irish government finances: the aftershocks of Bantry Bay and the spiralling costs of Irish military spending were the immediate problem, bringing about retrenchment and new indirect taxes, some of which (notably that on salt) fell directly on poorer consumers. Speculative building once again shuddered to a halt and artisanal unemployment soared. Thus, as in 1779, 1784 and 1792, we can sense a strong correlation between the onset of real economic distress and novel forms of political protest. The United message had little new to say on how urban life might be reordered – the leaders were after all employers or gentlemen – but it did offer access to the lottery of revolutionary political change.[116]

United Irish strength across the city was always uneven. Apart from the established hotspots in the old city and the Liberties and in the Church Street/markets area north of the river, there were distinct pockets in the east. The port neighbourhood along Lazers Hill/Townsend Street and Sir John Rogerson's Quay, involving shipwrights and the other organised trades of the river, had never featured in the old street politics, but now there were a number of radical cells and taverns. Its coastal trade links, with Rush in north Co. Dublin 'celebrated for smugglers and maiden ray, where there are more pigs than Protestants', with Wexford, east Down and west Cork, all took on a new significance in 1798.[117] One block away from the river was Trinity College: most of the professional United Irishmen before the war had been recent graduates, professionals who had got a first taste for politics in their student debating days, with Tone a prime example. In the early stages of the war, John Burk, founder of the first artisanal republican clubs, had learnt his adversarial skills in a fight with the College Board over his heterodox religious views. But from late in 1796, when the cellular oath-bound movement was developing outside, four undergraduate United Irish 'societies' were established within the College. Their full extent was only revealed when the Chancellor as College Visitor held a very public inquisition in April 1798: some fifty students (including Thomas Moore) were under suspicion for United Irish complicity and nineteen were expelled; the latter were more bourgeois than landed, more Munster than Dublin, with about half of them drawn from the new Catholic intake of students. They included the teenage son of John Keogh and the youngest son of the State Physician, one Robert Emmet.[118]

1798

The prospects for a successful Dublin-centred insurrection were always poor. With the state's abundant military resources on the city's edge, a half-loyal civilian population and control over communications on land and sea, the government – even in the midst of financial crisis and external threat – held the strategic advantage. Thus the reluctance of radicals to commit to military action in 1797, however bleak they viewed the political landscape, was entirely understandable. The intentions of the French Directory remained completely unknown. So in an effort to secure another French armada, the Dublin leadership supported Arthur O'Connor's plan to go back to France, but he and his party were arrested in Kent and tried there for treason. O'Connor was lucky to escape execution. With no clear signal of encouragement coming from Paris, why then was a full-blown attempt at city revolution made in May 1798?

United Irish volunteers in the city and suburbs had developed considerable military capacity, achieved through a haphazard process involving stolen firearms, purpose-made pikes and furtive training. Estimates of the total numbers given elementary training were tossed around, but we can take it that by May 1798 many thousands had access to the stockpiles of pikes in and around the city (Higgins guessed that despite seizures there were at that point '30,000 stand of arms concealed in the city').[119] Such military plotting reflected the call for action from below; the United Irish paramilitary organisation for Leinster, only settled in August 1797, rested on a command structure in which each cell had twelve members and was led by a sergeant; sergeants elected captains, captains their colonels, and they in turn came together as a county command, which was to send three delegates to the provincial committee. The reality may have been somewhat different – the election of colonels in the city was only completed in April 1798 and the papers of one of the colonels seized in May included a return of 234 'societies' or cells operational in the city, with the greatest number (69) and largest average membership (23.1) in the north-west quadrant of the city, the smallest number (26) and lowest average size (15.5) in the south-east quadrant. Such a cumbersome structure was hardly covert, but at least it ensured a high degree of sensitivity to the mood of those on the bottom rung. Fear bordering on panic became a potent factor in predisposing men towards violent action – fear based on economic distress, fear generated by the harsh actions of army and magistracy in the neighbouring counties, fear imagined of a pre-emptive Orange attack, and fear that the penal laws were going to be reintroduced. Blood-curdling rumours were now circulating in the *Union Star* broadsheets and in the United Irish songbooks, and this was a quite deliberate tactic to mobilise support. But as random acts of violence – against informers, prosecution witnesses and yeomen – became more common, with a matching pattern of military indiscipline, the pressure for action on those in command grew.[120]

But the decisive reason why Dublin became the centrepiece for a stand-alone rebellion was the sensational capture carried out by Major Sirr and his assistants of fourteen members of the Leinster provincial committee of the United Irish leadership in Oliver Bond's house in Bridge Street on 12 March, and the arrest of five national leaders immediately afterwards. The profile of the Dubliners arrested revealed the United Irish rainbow: three from the old Pill Lane leadership (Jackson, Bond and McCann), two veteran Catholic Committee leaders (MacNeven and Sweetman), and two well-connected Anglican barristers, Thomas Addis Emmet and William Sampson.[121] But the perverse effect of these arrests was to make a Leinster rebellion more rather than less likely, for Emmet and MacNeven had been resisting pressure for a rising without the French, on the grounds that such an insurrection would be both hugely destructive and unlikely to succeed, and a majority on the Leinster executive directory had supported this view. Arthur O'Connor and Lord Edward FitzGerald, both former MPs but with a greater appetite for risk, had championed the opposite view for many months, and had tried but failed to win over a majority of the city leadership. O'Connor was now out of the way, having been arrested in England, but Lord Edward remained a free man. A military veteran with some sense of how to conduct asymmetrical warfare, he was now able to push forward an insurrectionary strategy. He was author or part-author of plans for a staggered rising, which would begin with a surprise night-time attack in the city on key public buildings (the Castle, one of the banks, the Custom House, perhaps Newgate and the College), using United Irish volunteers from the city and surrounding districts in Cos. Dublin, Wicklow, Kildare and Meath, plus defectors from the militia. The non-appearance of mail coaches coming out of the city would be the cue to the counties in outer Leinster and beyond that the rising had begun in Dublin and that they should prevent troop movements towards the capital. In elaborating these plans and completing a military command in and about Dublin, FitzGerald had some excellent adjutants like Myles Duigenan, a Grafton Street grocer with a flair for logistics, and William Lawless, a Meath Street surgeon, but his real co-organiser was the veteran northern United leader Samuel Neilson, who had by now abandoned Belfast and thrown himself into tilling the fertile revolutionary soil of west and north Co. Dublin.[122]

Despite the Castle's network of spies and a flow of correspondence from all parts of the country reaching Edward Cooke's overburdened desk, there was no exact warning of the date and design of the United Irish coup. As a preventive measure the city was placed under martial law in mid-May, and cannon were positioned beside Newgate and outside the county jail at Kilmainham. Sentries were placed on both the Liffey and the canal bridges, and the yeomanry was deployed in large-scale pike searches, often involving the casual flogging of suspects and unrestrained house entry. The actual details of the plan to mobilise thousands of United men was not known in the Castle until almost the last moment. Indeed, the rising was nearly aborted by the violent arrest, five days before the chosen date, of Lord Edward, who had been hiding in a feather merchant's store in Thomas Street. Again this was Major Sirr's work. But on the evening of 23 May 1798, Samuel Neilson managed to assemble the fifteen city colonels near Church Street (including several drawn from outside the city) and allocate them their postings, but as Sir Richard Musgrave, first historian of the event and a witness that night recalled, 'the rebel drums were to have beaten to arms, an hour after ours ... if they had preceded us by ever so small a space of time, the fate of the city and its loyal inhabitants would have been decided'.[123] A last minute warning and the early arrest of Neilson (reconnoitring Newgate jail prior to launching an attack on it) led to the collapse of the Dublin plan, so that next day 'after sunrise the lanes and alleys to Smithfield and other posts were found full of pikes and muskets which [the rebels]... had dropped and thrown away in their precipitate retreat'.[124] The forwardness of the city yeomanry was generally credited with the near painless collapse of the rebellion within the city area, aided by the City of Cork militia who were stationed in St Stephen's Green. Outside the city bounds it was a somewhat different story, a scatter

*20. A somewhat theatrical representation of Lord Edward FitzGerald's
arrest in Thomas Street five days before the planned rebellion, it was based
on a large painting by Thomas Moore's friend James Dowling Herbert that
was later lost. The woodcut simplifies a complicated story of misadventure
but firmly identifies Town Major Sirr as firing the decisive shot that
wounded FitzGerald, who died a fortnight later in Newgate prison.*

of armed encounters on nearly every side of the city from Dalkey to Lucan
and around the north side to Santry, with reports of large groups mobilised and waiting for orders to enter the city and join the fray.[125]

Three of the four mail-coaches going down the country were stopped
that night, igniting a wider rebellion in Wicklow and Wexford, Carlow,
Kildare and Meath, which was far more prolonged and costly in human
life than anything in Dublin. The roads out of the capital were blocked by
rebel action, and the mails did not run again for a week. It was a time of
retribution, arms searches, the large-scale torture of prisoners (notoriously
under John Claudius Beresford's direction in the Tyrone House stables),
the courts martial of compromised yeomen, and executions. 'The common
people consider themselves as betrayed or abandoned by those of the more

respectable orders,' reported the Castle's best-placed informer, Leonard McNally, but the repression was biting: 'sullen, silent rancour and revenge will be a consequence ... Executions are now considered martyrdoms ...'[126] Rumours abounded that there would be another attempt in the city: 'the apprentice boys who are sworn and in great number are the most forward and determined for shedding blood in the city, and it is ... fear of not being joined by any other than clerks or shop-men which prevents them from rising'.[127] Fears of an attack on the city peaked as the Wexford rebel army moved northwards towards Arklow, and a rush for Dublin was anticipated when the town fell. But the south Wicklow town did not fall to the rebels and their defeat on 9 June removed that possibility.

The year 1798 was no re-run of 1641, to be sure, the military campaigns were fairly short-lived and Crown forces generally ascendant. Yet in the course of four summer months at least 10,000 lives were lost between the Leinster, Ulster and Connacht phases of the crisis. Many hundreds of Dubliners joined their country associates in the Leinster fighting – including seven of the city's United Irish colonels – and for two months the movement of men and materials between United Irish sympathisers in the city and rebel camps in the Dublin and Wicklow hills was maintained. In turn, the city became a refuge for men on the run from the counter-revolutionary violence in Wicklow and Wexford – and for frightened Protestant families from every quarter.[128] Almost immediately, once horror at the event began to subside, arguments began over the apparently religious character of the rising and the presence or absence of sectarian motives in the actions of United Irishmen and government forces. But apportioning blame for the crisis began at the very top, with the replacement of Camden as Lord Lieutenant in late June by an old veteran of India and America, Lord Cornwallis, who introduced an entirely new atmosphere to Irish government. The junto was effectively sidelined after his arrival, and government was now run from army quarters in Kilmainham, not the Castle. Cornwallis was in some respects nearer to Fitzwilliam than Camden in his political instincts: highly critical of the way the junto (and his predecessor) had managed affairs, he saw the abolition of the Irish Parliament and full Catholic emancipation as top of the civil agenda, and a de-escalation of hostilities on the military side. He halted extra-judicial punishment, reined back the holding of courts martial and insisted that the city yeomanry should be restricted to the city. He pursued a surprisingly conciliatory approach towards United Irish foot-soldiers, and when a weapons amnesty and conditional pardon was offered in August, 1,064 Dublin citizens (including nineteen publicans and eight blacksmiths) were among the many who availed themselves of the offer. He displayed a willingness to spare the rebel leadership capital punishment in exchange for full confessions as to the origins and course of the United Irish project, an offer they eventually accepted, in MacNeven's words, 'to save the country from the cold-blooded slaughter of its best, its bravest, its most enlightened defenders'.[129] News of a second, albeit modest, French flotilla on Irish shores at the end of August, and of General Jean Humbert's landing in north Mayo did not cause the panic in Dublin that might have occurred a few months previously. And Cornwallis's authority was soon enhanced after he had overseen Humbert's defeat at Ballinamuck.[130]

For most Dubliners the ghoulish horror of a civil war almost on their doorstep was an abiding memory, 'every public building a prison ... every street a Golgotha', lamp-posts used as gibbets and bridges across the river decorated with the trophy corpses of rebels. In the first days of the rebellion, two yeomen traitors had been executed on Queen Street Bridge; a Fingal colonel on the Old Bridge; and Thomas Bacon – master tailor, former member of the city Commons and an associate of Tandy, a member of the Goldsmiths yeomanry corps and a reputed United Irish colonel – on Carlisle Bridge. His corpse was joined some days later by that of Dr John Esmonde – a representative at the Catholic convention in 1792, an active yeoman but also a covert leader of the United Irish movement for Co. Kildare.[131] The spectacle of the Anglican Bacon and the Catholic Esmonde, both prosperous men and well regarded by their peers, on display in death amidst Beresford's great metropolitan improvements provided a barbaric coda to an era that had promised so much.

6

APOCALYPSE DEFERRED: 1798–1830

Union

Early in 1793 James Malton, one of James Gandon's former assistants, announced in London the publication of an engraving that gave a sidelong view of the portico of the Irish Parliament building, 'unequalled in Europe ... and among the many elegant structures that adorn that rising capital, the boast of Ireland'. A quite exceptional draughtsman, Malton had spent much of 1791 creating twenty-five views of Dublin buildings and streetscapes. These were exhibited as watercolours before he engraved the images for the press. They began to appear as aquatints from 1797 and were first published in London as a folio set in 1799, together with a brief history of the city. They were monochrome, though most subsequent impressions were hand-coloured. As consummate architectural drawings and as panoramas of eighteenth-century Dublin they have no rival and have never slipped out of fashion. The sunlit calm and 'arcadian clarity' they evoke helped to create the retrospective sense of pre-Union Dublin as a benign and self-confident capital in its golden age of parliamentary independence, a world captured just in time. It was deeply ironical that in the very year that his completed masterpieces went on sale, the death of the city was everywhere being spoken of. Malton's last work in Dublin, executed a year or two later, was a reworking of his sidelong view of the College Green portico: two views, one in its pristine state, one in its imagined future, a ruined broken shell.[1]

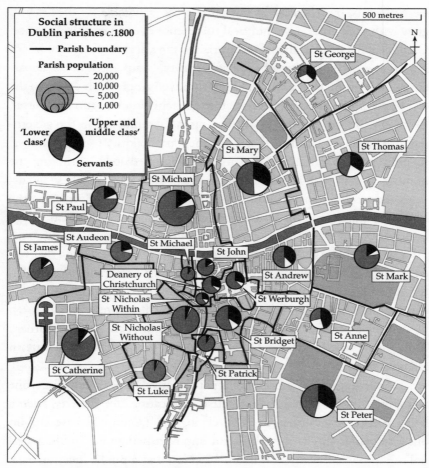

Map 3: The social topography of the city c.1800, based on the Revd James Whitelaw's Essay on the population of Dublin *(1805), which presented data he had collected in 1798 shortly after the rebellion. As Anglican rector of St Catherine's, he sought to highlight the extreme contrast in social conditions between the western and eastern districts.*

Fear of a union of parliaments and of the closure of the Dublin legislature was an old bogey. After the 1759 riot, guild politicians had on several occasions stirred things up with warnings of hidden plans for union – and with reason: the abolition of the Irish Parliament was something privately wished for by Pitt the younger and by several of his Dublin confidantes as the dangers inherent in the 'constitution of 1782' revealed themselves over the next fifteen years. The political difficulties in securing such a union were obvious, but the cost of postponing the inevitable, as they saw it, grew with each crisis – the political turbulence over regency in 1789 and Catholic relief in 1792, the financial crisis in 1797, and the brief civil war of 1798 that gravely threatened imperial security. Exasperated at the apparent failures of the Irish government, Pitt moved Anglo-Irish union to the top of the political agenda even before the rebellion had run its course.[2] Over an eighteen-month period starting in December 1798 the government struggled to build an Irish parliamentary majority for the proposal to unite the British and Irish Parliaments immediately (shrinking the number of Irish MPs by two-thirds in the process), and to phase in customs, monetary and fiscal unions over a longer period. But Cornwallis, the Lord Lieutenant, and his Ulster-born Chief Secretary, Lord Castlereagh, underestimated the political battle required to secure such an outcome. They were embarrassed by a parliamentary defeat in January 1799 that was engineered by John Foster, the first anti-unionist champion, after which the government deployed a variety of tactics over many months involving the unprecedented use of patronage and the printing press. The first step in securing a parliamentary majority for union was achieved in February 1800, the Act itself was passed in June, and the final parliamentary curtain fell on 2 August.

The struggle over union was a particularly Dublin affair. Everyone recognised that it would have negative implications for the city. Such a belief was long established and entirely logical. 'Union will leave Dublin but a splendid ruin ... the fallen and impoverished and crumbling capital of a province,' warned William MacNeven at a public meeting back in 1795 when the possible trade-off of union for Catholic emancipation had first been aired, and no one had dissented. The dire effects of the closure of the Parliament were presented in much greater detail in 1799 when one of Foster's allies carried out an audit of all upper-class houses likely to be vacated, with estimates of their post-Union fall in value and of the annual household expenditure that would be lost: 250 'of the best houses thrown on hands [i.e. surrendered by their lessees] would alone so overstock the market as to annihilate the building trade', and the houses of 'coach-makers, cabinet makers, woollen drapers, haberdashers ... who live by the consumption of people of fortune' would be abandoned; in short, he argued, 'Dublin must be a desert'.[3] City merchants and suburban manufacturers (sugar merchants, cotton printers, ironmongers) spelt out to a Commons' inquiry just how much they were now dependent on the creeping protection of the Irish market which had come about as a result of the hike in import duties during the 1790s (an unintended benefit of wartime budgets), and how catastrophic for their businesses was the prospect of free trade.[4] But the leading advocates making the case against union were lawyers. At least half of the anti-Union pamphlets came from a legal pen and the Dublin bar was quickest off the mark in organising public meetings against the proposal. The prospect of a legislature voting itself out of existence was offensive to the legal mind, but there were less principled factors explaining the stridency of the bar: legal and parliamentary careers had an incestuous connection, and a sharp diminution in the number of parliamentary seats and of related official patronage threatened to do great damage to professional opportunities. Furthermore, Dublin lawyers had played a central role in Whig-patriot politics over the previous forty years, and despite recent events this still applied. Pitt's measure was naturally seen in Dublin in party terms, just as in Westminster where it was opposed by the Foxite Whigs.[5]

Cornwallis remained steadfast in his commitment to secure parliamentary union, but for many months he remained disengaged from the political process, and in so doing made several tactical errors. By permitting open debate of the issue and consequently a full return of press freedom, he made it a very public process. But his conviction that the benign neutrality of Catholics was critical in keeping the opposition in check was borne out by events. Despite increasing signs of royal opposition, Cornwallis managed to hold the trust of the Catholic bishops and, like them, he expected full Catholic emancipation to follow parliamentary union.[6]

The old junto, now far less powerful, was divided on the measure. Beresford senior and FitzGibbon were in favour (of union but without emancipation), while lesser members of the old Cabinet joined Foster and worked (uncomfortably) with the parliamentary opposition. The anti-unionists were an unstable mixture from the start, ranging from those (like Foster) who had been implicated in the harshest treatment of the rebels a year before, to those Whig-patriots (like Grattan and Curran) who had sought to find common ground with the United Irish leadership in 1797. The proliferation of ribbons of green, orange and garter blue, and stirring rallying cries (along the lines that 'the Parliament is the birthright of the people; it gives a stamp of consequence to the kingdom, and is the only security which the nation can possess') temporarily united Orange partisans and radical barristers in the early weeks of 1799, and for a while it seemed as if Dublin's anti-unionism would generate an unstoppable national outcry. The Corporation began to publish a series of resolutions denouncing the Union and the methods being used to carry the measure, and it was supported by at least seventeen of the guilds. The Lawyers yeomanry corps also declared against the Union and appealed to other corps to come out in support. There was a sense that it had been the yeomanry, not the Castle, that had secured victory over the rebels the year before, and now London was attempting to dismantle the apparatus of *their* state. Such sentiments were certainly present in the three anti-Union Orange lodges in the city. But government control over the yeomanry was sufficiently tight to keep the lid on anti-Unionist feeling in that quarter, although some city officers resigned in protest at the government's policy.[7]

With its total dominance of the publishing trade, Dublin produced about 85 per cent of the 225-odd pamphlets produced on the controversy, the great majority of which were arguing for rejection.[8] From serious constitutional essays to scabrous ballad-sheets, all the luxuriant variety of local print culture was deployed. Cartoon images of a post-Union College Green overrun with grass and cattle appeared, and the teasing prophecy of *rus in urbe* became a catchword (mock parliamentary proceedings were reported from Pimlico in the Liberties, the true home of Parliament, as it faced the prospect of union with the old enemy, the Parliament of Oxmantown, all to strengthen the interests of the 'Dalkeyan empire', and these came out as a running serial). But it is doubtful if the tide of print had much impact on provincial opinion. Dublin Corporation's assertive opposition certainly did not have the intended effect. Unlike its clarion call in 1792 to defend Protestant Ascendancy, provincial grand juries and corporate bodies, especially those outside Leinster and south Ulster, were muted in response or took the other side. In the course of 1799, Cork and Belfast became centres of pro-Union sentiment, and provincial writers were not averse to seeing the promised new dispensation as an opportunity to take Dublin down a peg. As one northern bishop observed, Dublin had 'long drained the public treasury in jobs and schemes for its separate emolument, of no adequate use to the nation in general'.[9]

By the end of 1799, as government employed its patronage powers to an unprecedented degree (including the illegal use of secret service funds), the tide was flowing in favour of a union. But there were still fears of massive trouble on the streets of the capital. However, when the measure crossed the first of several parliamentary hurdles in February 1800, there were little more than scuffles. This seems surprising in view of all that had happened, doubly so when one considers that food prices reached unprecedented levels that winter and workshop employment, which had never recovered from the shock of 1797, was contracting even further. The ingredients for trouble were certainly there, but public passivity can be explained. The military command was now very much on the alert and, unlike in times past, took pre-emptive action against suspicious crowd activity. Furthermore there were considerable efforts by Catholic clergy to keep things quiet – in the expectation of an early political dividend from Westminster. But perhaps the strongest reason was that, despite all the rhetoric of the lawyers, College Green as an institution had been discredited, especially in the world of the Catholic journeyman and the small trader who were mindful that some of the strongest protests against union were coming from the firmly Protestant Corporation and from men with 'Orange' associations. The appeal to the yeomanry to defend their Irish constitution could easily be given a hostile interpretation.[10]

Aspects of the Union were subject to negotiation, particularly the commercial terms, and a delay in the lowering of import duties on vulnerable textile products was conceded, staggering the full customs union for twenty years. But this was secured by Belfast, not Dublin, lobbying and, despite much talk, the capital's politicians did not even try to secure deals for specifically Dublin sectors at risk. There was, for instance, no attempt to protect the publishing industry from the likely effects of an extension of English copyright legislation, or to secure a share of defence expenditure to compensate the construction trades for a probable decline in house-building. The fact that the Union did not directly affect two metropolitan institutions, the viceregal office and the four Irish high courts, was of course critically important for post-Union prospects, but neither of these had been under threat. The legal establishment actually thrived and expanded in the years ahead, and the Lord Lieutenant was to remain the executive representative of London government, albeit with much uncertainty as to his powers. After 1801 he was no longer Commander-in-Chief of the army in Ireland and was therefore shorn of control over military patronage. Indeed, army command in the Royal Hospital became for a few years a rival centre of authority to the Castle in security matters, with highly embarrassing consequences.[11]

Emmet's moment

Anglo-Irish union became a reality in January 1801, and the arrangement was to outlast the new century. But shortly after it came into effect, two events redefined politics for the next generation. The expectation that full Catholic emancipation would directly follow union was dashed within weeks when George III indicated his total opposition. Pitt's government, already riven by internal tension, promptly resigned and Lord Lieutenant Cornwallis and his Chief Secretary followed suit. It was a sign of changed times that Archbishop Troy, who had been the Castle's confidante in the delicate choreography during the Union struggle, escaped personal criticism for what had turned out to have been such a profitless strategy. But the wealthy Catholic leaders of the 1780s and 1790s were at this point silenced, compromised, exhausted or dead – MacNeven and Sweetman, like the other 'state prisoners', were still held in detention at Fort George in northern Scotland, McCormick was in France, Ryan the physician had died, Keogh had managed to make 'his peace, privately, with the government', and the ageing Braughall had withdrawn from public life after a lengthy imprisonment in 1798 and bitter legal battles in the wake of it. Yet after the furious switches of fortune over the previous ten years, it would have been natural to assume that the new delay in settling the Catholic issue would be a matter of at most a few years. That it took nearly three decades to resolve and dominated Irish public life for so much of the intervening time had the effect of intensifying the religious polarisation of the city that had already become so apparent in the 1790s.[12]

The second event was the 'sudden insurrection' of July 1803, usually remembered as 'Emmet's rising'.[13] The long conflict with France had been halted in spring 1802, leading to the release of the state prisoners and to their banishment. But the ensuing peace gave little more than a breathing space, for it collapsed in May 1803 with threats from Napoleon of a naval attack on Britain. The likelihood of new trouble in Ireland was not entirely discounted, even though the United Irish leadership was now either dispersed or deceased. But troop levels had been greatly reduced since 1799 and the yeomanry marginalised. There was, however, a continuing deployment of regular forces through the city in secondary barracks (on the south side, in the old Custom House, in James Street, in Newmarket, and in Cork Street; on the north side in Mary Street, and at the Pigeon House at the harbour's entrance), which compensated for the modest police establishment. As many as a quarter of the 3,000-odd urban garrison was now quartered *outside* the Royal Barracks. But new men were in charge in the Castle and intelligence-gathering in the city had been weakened as a result. Thus, when an attempt was made to capture key buildings in the city on the evening of 23 July 1803, it caught the government almost entirely by surprise. Communications between civil and military authorities were in chaos for some hours before order was restored. The element of surprise would never have been sufficient to swing the outcome, but the general intelligence failure, coupled with the revelation that sophisticated arms dumps had been built up within a few minutes' walk of the Castle, caused an outcry and forced a painful reassessment of policing and a drastic increase in government surveillance of the city.[14]

The 1803 rebellion was in military terms a modest matter, accounting for at most sixty deaths, yet it was a pivotal moment in the city's history. Robert Emmet, younger brother of one of the '98 leaders, was by any reckoning a luminous figure – intense, intellectually gifted and as strongly imbued with the universalist ideals of the American Revolution as any older radical. He was one of the nineteen expelled from Trinity College in April 1798 and had remained politically active. After several years in France, he returned to Dublin late in 1802 and collaborated on plans for a new *coup d'état*, adapting and improving Lord Edward FitzGerald's urban strategy, independent of but supported by French military action. While Emmet had been away, a diminished group of local United leaders, based mainly in the south-west of the city and of quite mixed economic status, had kept in regular contact with associates in Kildare, Wicklow and Wexford. As others fretted about the Union, this shadowy United Irish group drew support from the large cohort of local veterans who had seen action in the field and who shared a sense that the cause in the city had been let down in May 1798, both by poor leadership and by informers. The pre-'98 electoral structures were set aside and a far more covert system was built up, cemented not by formal oath but by unspoken trust between those who had been 'out' five years before. The discipline of the journeyman associations (surviving largely unscathed) may also have facilitated the rebuilding of an underground political organisation.[15]

Emmet's own intimates were a tightly knit middle-class group, notably William Dowdall, a Fort George ex-prisoner, Philip Long, a Crow Street merchant, and John Allen, son of a Liberties dyer. Many months before the resumption of the war with France, the decision was taken to mount another rebellion in the city, but it only began to take shape in March 1803. A major innovation was the establishment of two well-disguised depots in the city for the stockpiling of pikes and munitions and for manufacturing powder and rockets, one in Patrick Street to equip the Wicklow and Wexford men when the time came, one in Marshal Lane (near the James's Gate end of Thomas Street) for the men from Kildare and the Liffey valley. A number of other 'safe houses' were secured – from Irishtown to Smithfield. Emmet was appointed by his peers to be the General for Dublin, in the expectation that other counties would collaborate under independent commands. This nomination reflected his natural personal authority, his social class and his family connections. He soon displayed remarkable ingenuity – in developing new weapons for urban guerrilla warfare (beam bombs, hand grenades and folding pikes), in the art of concealment by designing secret closets in safe houses and in devising new tactics for a successful insurrection.

It was to begin with an attack on the Pigeon House to the east and on the Artillery barracks at Islandbridge to the west, and was to culminate in a two-pronged attack on the Castle, one group arriving at the main gate in a retinue of coaches, the other to scale the back walls with grappling hooks. The Castle was, of course, not a fortified complex (it was bereft of weapons), so its capture would have been almost entirely symbolic. The plans also envisaged the use of double chains to blockade particular streets, thereby hindering the movement of troops. All this was premised on the understanding that Wicklow and Kildare would supply men in their hundreds on the night of the rising, to be armed from one of the secret depots. Emmet oversaw the manufacture of pistols, ammunition, pike shafts and much else in these locations, the pike-heads coming from country forges in Kildare by canal barge. The costs were considerable: £15,000 was one estimate of what had been spent on the Marshal Lane equipment, with funds coming from the dwindling resources of the coterie around Emmet. Everything was to be paid for, but much that had been ordered from the ironmongers and gunsmiths failed to materialise ahead of the fateful Saturday, 23 July.[16] In the preceding months, only a handful of men were aware of the plan in its entirety, although there was vigorous rebuilding of passive support for a rising among journeymen and small traders, mainly in the Liberties. Here the unlikely figure of Jemmy Hope, Antrim weaver and former confidante of Neilson, was critical. Trading as a haberdasher in the Coombe, he was singularly effective in rekindling their enthusiasm during the spring of 1803. He reckoned that by May there were 5,000 men in the city ready to 'turn out' and there is no reason to think he exaggerated. By July, Emmet was counting on at least 2,000 to be poised and ready, in and about the city.[17]

The plan, for all its sophistication, failed utterly in its execution. The Patrick Street store was wrecked in an explosion a week before the rising; and the workmanship required to produce much of Emmet's sophisticated weaponry was beyond the volunteers' abilities, so neither rockets nor grenades were available in time. On the day itself, some of the Dublin-based leadership argued for cancellation, and the army of supporters from Co. Kildare, many already in the city, were summoned home when it became evident that, despite a mountain of musket-balls and cartridges, there were almost no muskets or other firearms available. The Wicklow men, for whatever reason, simply failed to show up as planned. And police suspicions about the Marshal Lane depot began to grow in the hours before the rising was set to start.

Lacking communication rockets, muskets or the expected manpower, Emmet drastically scaled back the original plan, but the intention to take control of the Thomas Street district, both as a rendezvous and to partially isolate Dublin Castle, remained. Capture of the Castle was still the strategic objective, the spark that would set the country aflame. Despite nearly everything going amiss, the unflappable Emmet marched out onto Thomas Street in his general's uniform two hours early, leading an army of between one and two hundred men, most of whom had been unduly fortified by the long wait in neighbouring taverns. They were joined by others returning from an unauthorised attack on the Mansion House in Dawson Street where they had liberated its small armoury of mainly ceremonial weaponry. The numbers thinned, Emmet's orders were disobeyed, and by the time he reached Patrick Street he had called it all off and fled southwards, leaving a leaderless crowd to exact revenge on any symbol of authority they could find. They soon came upon the Lord Chief Justice of the King's Bench, Lord Kilwarden, a minor member of the old junto, hurrying along Thomas Street with his family to the Castle. Kilwarden and his nephew were taken from his coach and piked to death; his daughter was spirited away to safety. There were several dozen other fatalities that night, but the death of a privy councillor created the greatest sensation.[18]

Emmet himself was arrested in Harold's Cross a month later and brought to trial by a special commission a month after that, one of twenty-two facing execution for treason. But it was these months after the rebellion

21. 'Louis Perrin ... greets and embraces Robert Emmet as he descends from the dock.' *Emmet had just delivered, or tried to deliver, an apologia at the end of his trial in the Session House in Green Street. He was taken from there to Kilmainham jail and the following afternoon, 19 September 1803, was executed in Thomas Street, close to where Lord Kilwarden had been assassinated two months earlier.*

that determined Emmet's destiny to become perhaps the most iconic figure in Dublin's history, thanks to the manner of his going and to the revelations about his character and his relationship with Sarah Curran. His story became the epitome of the tragic young hero, motivated by Enlightenment ideals of freedom and betrayed by fate and the timidity of those around him, and its extraordinary impact on the literary imagination of the romantic era was to endure far beyond that time. Emmet's impact was to some extent self-fashioned, evident in his careful choice of a general's uniform to sally out into Thomas Street, evident in the deeply reflective and carefully crafted language of the 'Proclamation of the provisional government' (which was only printed by Stockdale on the day of the rising), and evident most clearly in his extraordinary speech from the dock that was published in rival versions shortly after his execution in Thomas Street on 20 September. The Shakespearean force of his words to the court, their justification of his actions and repudiation of the low motives attributed to him, never lost the immediacy or the intense poignancy they first evoked in the Sessions House in Green Street as he finished with his most famous dictum: 'when my country takes her place among the nations of the earth, then, and not till then, let my epitaph be written'.[19]

For all his modesty, Emmet was a patrician figure and, like several of those closest to him in planning the rising, he was a Protestant. As he said to Thomas Russell, 'no leading Catholic is committed – we are all Protestants – and their cause will not be compromised' in the event of failure. Not quite true, but Emmet's utterly secular language was a reinstatement of the United Irish ideals of the early 1790s and a renunciation of the sectarian horrors of '98. A shortened version of the Proclamation, addressed specifically to the 'Citizens of Dublin' and also printed at the last minute, was apparently Philip Long's work: its harsher tone and threats of 'inevitable destruction' to Orangemen if they offered any opposition was perhaps closer to popular feeling at the time. But it was Emmet's loftier vision of Irish nationality in the extended Proclamation and the sentiments of his speech from the dock that were to be remembered and repeated.[20]

Fall-out

The multiple failures of the rebels were matched by security failure in the Castle, uncertain of its post-Union powers, and in Kilmainham, where General Fox, the newly appointed Commander-in-Chief, had signally failed to comprehend the accumulating evidence that another rising was being planned. Fox's prior determination to strengthen military control over law and order in the city left him exposed after the event to a torrent of criticism (some of it self-serving, for even Major Sirr had misread the warnings). Hardwicke, viceroy since 1801, survived the crisis, but the Chief Secretary, William Wickham, resigned, haunted, it seems, by guilt at Emmet's fate. With renewed threats of French intervention, habeas corpus was suspended for three years and hundreds of modest Dubliners were held in prison or on hulks in the Bay without trial, some for up to three years. Burgh's Corn Market in Thomas Street became a strongly fortified barracks, 'each window has a sloping cover, from which soldiers can fire without being annoyed by the mob'.[21]

The feebleness of Dublin's maritime defences was also finally addressed. Late in 1804 construction began on twenty-six small coastal forts, or 'martello towers', most of which were located on coastal promontories between

Balbriggan in north Co. Dublin and Bray on the Wicklow border, each supporting two cannon and some with separate batteries for heavier weaponry. This sudden programme of coastal defence-works (costing over £64,000) had no parallel elsewhere in Ireland and preceded a similar (but larger) project in Kent and East Sussex. Given the very small chance that any beach in the greater Dublin area would be chosen as a landing point if another French armada materialised, the project was a rather perverse use of resources and reflected something of the security panic in the wake of Emmet's rebellion. It served, however, as a statement in stone of the new resolve to defend the post-Union city, underlining Dublin's strategic military importance as the natural conduit to all parts of Ireland and the place where military resources (human and material) were most heavily concentrated. Even after Trafalgar in 1805 and the establishment of British naval ascendancy in home waters, the possibility of another French intervention was never totally discounted until almost the end of the Napoleonic Wars. Later in the decade, the Pigeon House on the Great South Wall and the Magazine Fort in the Phoenix Park were extended, and a large infantry barracks, the Richmond, was constructed beyond Kilmainham.[22]

But the principal legacy of 1803 was a major reorganisation of the Dublin police, which heretofore had done little 'towards the detection of treason or sedition'. Remarkably, this took five years to accomplish: in the immediate aftermath of the rebellion the city was divided up into fifty-three police neighbourhoods, with 'respectable citizens' in each division appointed to act as 'conservators of the peace' and report 'any secret plots or conspiracies'; shortly afterwards the number was reduced to twenty-one. It was only through the determination of Arthur Wellesley (the future duke of Wellington), Irish Chief Secretary between 1807 and 1809, that a more robust police force was introduced. The 1808 Dublin Police Act was a startling demonstration of the new order of things; it revealed the political irrelevance of the Lord Lieutenant and the crucial role of the Chief Secretary, both in the formulation and the execution of Irish policy. The new police force was Wellesley's doing and, although a Dubliner of impeccable Old English pedigree who had sat briefly as an MP in College Green, he viewed Irish security problems from an entirely imperial military perspective, seeing local concerns over the infringement of corporate rights as almost meaningless. Despite strong opposition from Dublin Corporation and from the two Dublin MPs, he resisted all amendments to the legislation during its passage through Westminster.

The Act extended the Dublin police district far beyond the suburbs to the whole area lying within eight miles of Dublin Castle, increased the number of police magistrates from three to eighteen and of higher constables from ten to twenty-four, and it restored a 200-man patrol force (police patrols on horse and foot had been abandoned in the reforms of 1795). It also strengthened government control over appointments, for although the new 'chief magistrate of police' still had to be an alderman, twelve of the eighteen magistrates were to be direct government appointees and the others, nominees of the Corporation, were subject to viceregal approval. The central police office was now to be located within Dublin Castle. Its proposed size (including the lowly watchmen) was almost double that of the existing ramshackle force, with the costs of the police component to be paid for by the central exchequer and the watch system continuing to be paid for by city taxpayers. To the government, its great merit was that it would relieve the military from having to act as the de facto police of the city.[23]

When the details of the 1808 bill reached Dublin, the city Commons voted 68 to 1 against the measure, but the aldermen welcomed it. The lower house then demanded (by a smaller majority) repeal of the Union in protest. But this was empty noise, for beyond its own representatives Dublin now had few champions in Westminster, and Wellesley's more elaborate version of the 1786 Dublin Police Act became law and was established within a few months. When the young viscount Palmerston made his first visit to Dublin that summer, he was struck by the continuing 'military look throughout [the city] that brings to one's recollection what things have happened, and proves that the argument most relied upon to secure the tranquillity of the people is the point of the bayonet'. But the first chief magistrate, Alderman Joseph Pemberton, a political conservative, proved efficient in establishing the new force and, in effect, civilianising security on the street. His deputy and successor in 1812, the great builder Frederick Darley, held office for over twenty years and, despite his political associations as a leading member of the Orange Order, was an able administrator. The new police force adapted quite quickly, allowing the city in the later years of the war to settle down to low crime rates and relative calm.[24]

Yet beneath the surface things may have been a bit different. The starkest evidence of the still-inflamed state of Catholic opinion comes from *The Irish Magazine, and Monthly Asylum for Neglected Biography*, a miscellany that ran from 1807 to 1815, which was published by Watty Cox, gunsmith and maverick radical who had been involved in fly-by-night printing in the 1790s (notably the *Union Star* news-sheet in 1797), before accepting government money and a passage abroad in return for his silence. It is not clear when he came back to the city, but he was well established before 1807, trying his hand in various business ventures, but none succeeded until the appearance of the *Magazine*. He produced much of the copy himself (although not, it seems, the startling political engravings, which appeared in nearly every issue), and he spent over three years of the *Magazine*'s life in Newgate prison after a conviction for libel (from 1811 to 1814). Yet he managed to produce the miscellany without fail and to hold a national circulation at around 5,000 per month, far ahead of its more respectable rivals. For Cox's *Magazine* was not respectable: it railed against loyalist politicians, yeomanry officers, city magistrates and the 'Orange' gentry who had been involved in '98 and its aftermath. His particular object of attack was John Claudius Beresford and he made repeated references to the vicious whipping of United suspects that had been carried out in the family's riding stables in Marlborough Street. That the miscellany continued to appear for ninety-seven issues – in the face of huge official disapproval – was fairly remarkable, and Robert Peel (Chief Secretary from 1812 to 1818) had to pension him off in 1816 on condition that he removed himself to America once again.[25]

The Irish Magazine was always well informed if highly partisan, wickedly satirical if sometimes obsessive. There was a colloquial, at times subversive, intimacy between writer and reader where much was left unsaid, but much that was said took the form of unrestrained personal attacks on Cox's political enemies. And throughout the biographies, obituaries and political commentary, a Manichean contrast was drawn between everything Irish, Catholic and national, and the coarse and corrupted opposite – English, Protestant or Orange. At times, in its bitter commentary, particularly on the Union and on the folly of those who had supported it, there was an echo of Swift. Cox's line on the Union was that it was an English plot, economically motivated to undo the benefits flowing from 'free trade' and 1782, allowing monopolistic English manufacturers to undercut and destroy Irish industry: Dublin, he declared in 1814, was now a city that 'has not built a ship or a sloop since the Union, a city that has not manufactured a cable, an anchor, or an oar, since the same fatal period, a city that has no intercourse beyond Liverpool or Whitehaven', and many of its so-called merchants were insolvent.[26] He saw the canals as a political story:

> projected in the days of our independence, the Royal Canal arose with the revolution of 1782; they were to promote the circulation of our domestic industry, and facilitate a commercial intercourse with our manufacturing towns, which were to appear in every direction. In this view they were to act as rivals to England; and to erase the danger, which England apprehended, the Union was resorted to: the expedient answered, our manufactures have disappeared, the canal is useless, only as a military road, and the proprietors are begging.[27]

Cox's bleak message was spelt out in text and image, constantly recalling the misdeeds inflicted by official Ireland on Catholic Ireland, and weaving into this a pervading sense of economic victimhood. Cox was clearly picking up something of the plebeian mood of the time, but he also helped to shape a master narrative of great potency – that Dublin was being destroyed by the Union. But was that really the case?

Consequences

Cox was certainly not alone in asserting that the worst was happening, but others were quick to counter. John Gamble, army surgeon and former radical, visited Dublin in 1811 for the first time since Union, and noted playfully that despite the political prophecies that the grass would grow in the streets of Dublin, 'I see nothing green in the streets, though I do [see] a number of geraniums in the windows, which give a delightful fragrance to the air'. Other visitors in the 1810s and 1820s commented on the wealth of new public buildings and made comparisons, often flattering, with the public spaces of central London. Sir Walter Scott, on his visit in 1825, found the city 'splendid beyond my utmost expectations'.[28] But as the condition of the post-Union city entered into fiction, different stories emerged: for Lady Morgan in *Florence Macarthy* (1818), desolation and decay was axiomatic; for Maria Edgeworth in *The Absentee* (1811), it was about redemption and improvability; while for Charles Maturin, who showed in *Women: Or, pour et contre* (1818) that he knew the city best, post-Union Dublin was an anxious city in flux. Thus Maturin captured the scene when the news arrived that the Allies had captured Paris in March 1814:

> the whole population of Dublin appeared concentrated in College Green. Carriages stopping by dozens before the [newspaper] placards, – horsemen rising on tiptoe in their stirrups above the heads of the crowd, to read them, – and the crowd, wedged head to head ... The demand for white lilies, and high French bonnets, rose every moment; the lilies were twined in the locks of every belle, and worn in the straw-hats of apprentices. The general sentiment was certainly that of joy. The appalling, supernatural greatness of Buonaparte had terrified even those who wished him well, and men seemed relieved, as from the spell of an enchanter.

The enchanter, of course, bounced back from Elba to meet his final nemesis, the duke of Wellington, at Waterloo. Plans to celebrate the former Chief Secretary's military successes against the French had begun in 1813, but it was only after Waterloo that the organisers decided to raise a giant obelisk to his honour in St Stephen's Green, its completion budgeted at £32,000. Many of the promoters of the project were non-resident peers, but the Corporation by a narrow margin opposed the idea. The Green was spared and became a private space for the surrounding residents, and the great granite monument was erected instead in the Phoenix Park, where it became the city's western landmark. But the money dried up long before it was completed, and the decorative cast-iron elements were only placed on the monument in 1861.[29]

Anti-unionists had made a number of distinct predictions as to how Dublin would be damaged in the long years ahead. The first prophecy was that property values would collapse and the construction industry would be severely depressed with the sudden withdrawal of peers, MPs and their families, whether to London or to their country estates. The private opinion in April 1799 of one of those directly involved in property development, Viscount Fitzwilliam's agent Barbara Verschoyle, is striking: 'the Union is the terror of everyone ... and if it is [passed] – even here in this delightful spot Merrion Square – we shall have grass where there should be new pavement ... I fear the present building[s] will fall into decay, or at least not be kept up in the style they ought ...'. But a few challenged the prophecy even at the time: William Stevens asked,

Are the inhabitants of the new streets and great squares of Dublin mere men of fashion, mere members of Parliament? I affirm they are not. Perhaps one-fifth of these inhabitants may consist of unemployed families, who live in Dublin, as a place where an elegant establishment is most cheaply supported. The remainder are men of profession, men in office, opulent merchants. How could their residence in Dublin be affected by the sitting of Parliament?

He suggested that most of those who regularly attended the Irish Parliament held public office that would still require an attendance in Dublin, and that the Dublin season

will continue exactly so long as persons, who require amusement, find here plays, balls and card parties, and not one moment longer ... the city will be recruited [sic] and extended so soon as our political squabbles are put to rest, by the return of our middling gentry, and by the additional number of merchants, whom the increase of trade will enable to live splendidly.[30]

Stevens was right – most of the tenants of the Fitzwilliams, the Gardiners and the Humes were not parliamentary families, and many MPs did not maintain Dublin houses. Indeed, only 56 per cent of them were listed in 1798 as having 'town residences' in Dublin.[31] And while building activity on the east side of town may have been depressed in the first years of Union (as it had been since 1797), public-works projects took up much of the slack for the construction trades, notably the Gandon-designed King's Inns building on Constitution Hill (begun in 1800), the elaborate conversion of the Parliament House to accommodate the Bank of Ireland (begun in 1804), the rebuilding of the viceregal chapel in Dublin Castle in *à la mode* Perpendicular Gothic (begun in 1807), and the construction of two prisons – the vast Richmond Penitentiary in Grangegorman (started *c.*1812), and the Richmond Bridewell near the South Circular Road (started in 1813). Here the key figure was Francis Johnston, an Ulster-born architect who had learnt his trade under William Cooley and Samuel Sproule (one of the principal architect/developers in Dame Street and on the Fitzwilliam estate), and he stamped his mark on the post-Union city. Johnston's restrained versatility, meticulous detailing and successful management of very large projects made him a worthy successor to Gandon, and as architect to the Board of Works from 1805 he dominated public architecture for a generation.[32]

Wide Streets projects were also reactivated. In 1799 the Commissioners found some of their old ambition when they were allocated the proceeds of fresh taxes, and although an application to the imperial Treasury in 1802 for a grant of £137,000 to complete outstanding projects was rejected (despite John Beresford's advocacy), a modest Treasury grant remained the largest single source of revenue for many years. Several avenues that had been laid out a decade or more previously were completed – Westmoreland Street by 1805, D'Olier and Lower Sackville Streets a little later.[33] This of course involved speculative activity on the part of those who had purchased lots from the Commissioners and was driven by a recovery in the market for commercial property. For new initiatives, the Commissioners concentrated on the quays, seeking to complete the riverside thoroughfares running along each side of the Liffey, and on the comprehensive opening up of the streets west of the Castle – around Christ Church Cathedral, along the old city spine towards James Street, and in the approaches to St Patrick's Cathedral. Because of falling Treasury grants and a heavy burden of pre-Union debt to service, this work had to be funded by new local taxes (legislation in 1807 allowed for this). And while such work proceeded at a slower pace and offered few opportunities for architectural display than earlier interventions on the east side of town, the public-health benefits from this kind of street clearance were likely to have been much greater.[34]

As for private building activity, despite the death of Luke Gardiner in '98, domestic building activity did recover on the Gardiner estate, notably on the unbuilt parts of Mountjoy Square and on the long extensions running from it. But the average width of plot frontages on the square shrunk from 30 to less than 25 feet, a telling indication of a changing market. The strongest indication of the estate's continuing vitality was the construction of the Church of Ireland's St George's church. Johnston's tour de force, this was placed in the centre of Hardwick Place, its Gothic steeple rising to become the tallest point in the city. It was built between 1800 and 1814 at a vast cost (reportedly 'upwards of £40,000'). Frederick Darley, the city's largest stonemason and builder of many houses in Mountjoy Square, was the contractor, and the suspicious cost overrun and consequent financial burden placed on all parish residents led eventually to complaints in Parliament.[35] On the Fitzwilliam estate, building activity

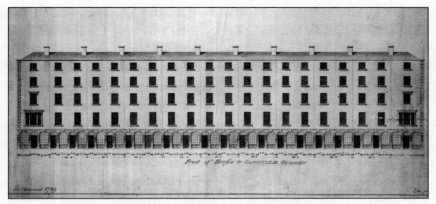

22. *Gandon supplied the original designs for what was one of the Wide Streets Commissioners' most eye-catching developments, the twin blocks that were to run north from Carlisle (later O'Connell) Bridge to Abbey Street. The plans had, however, been modified by the time Thomas Sherrard, the Commissioners' surveyor, drew this version of the west-side terrace in 1789. It was not until some years after the Union that the two terraces, with their strongly commercial character at ground-floor level, were actually completed.*

resumed on the streets between Merrion Square and the Grand Canal, also along Fitzwilliam Street. And elsewhere on the south side, much of Harcourt Street dates from these years. Nevertheless the fate of the two most distinctive residential developments of the 1790s shows the softness of the residential market. The 'Royal Circus' on the north side had been Luke Gardiner's pet project, designed to create a huge oval-shaped development of two facing crescents, to be built just east of the Royal Canal. The terrace façades were to be entirely symmetrical, their parapets decorated by giant vases. Building leases for most of the Circus were granted in 1792 and some ground work was done, yet nothing was built before Gardiner's death. Leases were renegotiated in 1808, but whether because of litigation over title or because of the rigidly controlled designs for the proposed terraces, it remained a chimera, still appearing on city maps in the 1830s as 'intended', and survived until the plan was abandoned with the disposal of the Gardiner/ Blessington estate in the 1840s.[36] Similarly, Fitzwilliam Square, planned c.1789 at the north-west corner of the Fitzwilliam estate, attracted its first builder-tenants in 1791, but with only four houses built by the time of the Union it also seemed still-born, despite a favourable location only a block away from St Stephen's Green. It was, however, fully realised, albeit slowly: by 1817 half of the sixty-nine houses planned for the square had been built, but the project was not completed until 1828. These were of course expensive and high-quality houses and the estate's building regulations were not relaxed, but there was no attempt to impose rigid uniformity on façade detailing. A measure of the prudent management of the development was that rent levels on newly issued leases in the 1820s were much higher (in nominal terms) than those dating from before the wars.[37]

Something of a two-tier market in high-status property was emerging. Demand for 'middling houses' on the east-side resumed quickly in the early years of the century, whereas there was no private demand for large townhouses. Visitors in these years spoke once again of growth, 'buildings ... increasing in every direction', pointing usually to the suburbs and the satellite villages. The hard evidence is more ambiguous: the private census of James Whitelaw (of whom more anon) from 1804 pitched the city's population at 182,370, and the first official census to be completed in 1821 returned a figure of 227,335. However, the latter included several largely rural parishes not included in 1804. The population of the city was certainly still growing, but at a substantially lower rate than before the wars.[38]

But with the top tier there was undoubtedly an exodus. It is hard to quantify the movement of a perpetually mobile class, but insofar as the directories are a guide they suggest a long decline in the number of townhouses maintained by aristocratic families. In 1798, eighty-seven lay peers had Dublin addresses (two-fifths of them on the Gardiner estate); by 1824 the comparable figure for the city was twenty-five. The process was more evident in some districts than others, with a marked shift in the relative status of particular neighbourhoods: townhouses that were outliers from fashionable districts – those in Henrietta Street, those close to the river like Moira House on Usher's Island, Aldborough House on the north Circular Road – were most at risk and provided early evidence that the demand for premium houses was contracting. But it was also evident in the city centre: six peers and eight MPs had Sackville Street addresses in 1800, but by 1810 no politician or peer of note resided there, their houses being generally let out rather than sold. There were of course special factors at work here: for example the impact on the old Mall of the opening of Carlisle Bridge and the decidedly commercial character of Lower Sackville Street from the beginning. By contrast, in St Stephen's Green at the end of the wars, some twenty of the houses were still occupied by peers or 'county' families.[39]

But townhouses in all locations were changing their function, from seasonal hubs of private entertainment to more public institutional use, or they were being divided up into smaller but still high-status domestic units. North-west of the city, the sale of Luttrellstown Castle in 1800 by the earl of Carhampton to the parvenu financial genius Luke White was the first sign of changing times. An elaborately choreographed visit by the viceroy and his party in 1803 to White's castle put a stamp of approval on the new order: 'great wealth does not get a man forward here as in London', observed Lady Hardwicke afterwards, 'the society is small and the individuals proud', but White in his yeomanry uniform and Mrs White, 'a very well-behaved little woman', proved an exception. However, it was the sale of Leinster House in 1815 to the Dublin Society (for £10,000, plus a head-rent of £600 p.a.) which really signalled the end of an era. The Leinster family had made relatively little use of the house since the death of the 3rd duke in 1804, but their exodus from Kildare Street still came as a shock. It occurred just before a second jolt to the top tier of the property market: the fall in agricultural prices after Waterloo, which was felt very quickly by the *rentier* class, and quite a few gentry families retired from Dublin after the wars, either to 'bacon and poultry' on their country estates or to restoration France, with its dramatically lower cost of living.[40]

However, those gentry who chose to give up their Dublin houses were not giving up Dublin. The winter season, the law, and the medical and educational resources of the city remained far superior to any Irish or English rival outside London. The city (like London) had to adapt to the upper-class's more peripatetic lifestyle and the growth of well-appointed hotels and gentlemen's clubs was symptomatic of this. By 1813 there were thirty-five registered hotels in the city, although it was not until the late 1820s that the Shelbourne (in St Stephen's Green) and Morrison's (at the bottom of Dawson Street) became established places of gentry resort. Gentlemen's clubs in dedicated buildings evolved out of the myriad of tavern-based dining-clubs. A move towards exclusive clubs was already evident by the 1780s and closely paralleled London developments. Daly's Club in Dame Street had started out inside a public chocolate house in the 1760s, but it became a mecca for gamblers and developed something of a hell-raising reputation. But it was well regulated and controlled its membership by secret ballot. In 1787 a former Chief Secretary led the drive for subscriptions to build grander premises on the site, and this was duly opened in 1791. Its fine façade, designed apparently by Francis Johnston's brother, formed part of a palatial terrace running between Foster Place and Anglesey Street. Its seven principal rooms consisted of a 'coffee-room, reading-room, writing-room, hazard-room and private dining-rooms', and it thrived on the site for over thirty years, holding onto 315 members to the end, but probably fewer than in the days when it functioned as 'the Parliament at play'. In the 1790s there were at least three other clubs with their own premises. The Kildare Street Club – with its strong links to the La Touche family – was a breakaway from Daly's, the Sackville Street a breakaway from the Kildare, and both of these were to have a long life. The Kildare Street Club had over 600 members, both in the 1790s and the 1820s, but by the latter decade many of these were country members for whom it acted as their social base in the city.[41]

Industry

A second prediction of the anti-unionists was that Dublin's artisanal industries would collapse once luxury crafts lost their upper-class clientele and local workshops were exposed to unfettered competition from more highly capitalised and technically advanced English producers. In the event, some of the luxury trades flourished in the post-Union generation (cabinet-making, silverwork, wallpaper manufacture), other luxury trades shrank, either because of tax changes or technical innovation (jewellery and watch-making for example).[42] But many of the Dublin manufacturers who had protested loudly at the prospect of free trade in 1800 (such as John Duffy, employing '1,200 daily' in his Ballsbridge print-yards; John Orr, who claimed to have recently spent £30,000 on cotton works in Dublin, Stratford in west Wicklow and Hillsborough in Co. Down; Edward Clarke with his Palmerstown business in west Co. Dublin; or John Anderson from Love Lane in the Liberties) went on to invest heavily in cotton printing in the post-Union years. Full protection on cotton goods was maintained until 1808, and more limited tariffs until 1824. During that period the big cotton print-yards survived and adapted successfully, attracting Lancashire investment, and textile manufacturing more generally did not succumb as feared. Raw cotton imports to Dublin peaked in

*23. John Duffy began as a modest dyer and cloth-merchant in Bridgefoot Street,
but with the backing of Edward Byrne, one of the wealthiest city merchants,
he greatly expanded his activities at a site in Ballsbridge during the 1790s. The
cotton-printing works there survived for more than half a century, most of its many
hundreds of employees in the later years being unskilled women and children.*

1808–10 and cotton yarn imports in 1820–22, on the face of it a healthy
picture.

But the reality was somewhat different. There was what can best be
described as a hollowing out of the city's manufacturing economy in the
post-Union years; it was a time of uneven contraction and declining fortunes for most craft workers, badly affected by the wartime rise in food
prices, excise taxes, window taxes and parish charges, punctuated by particularly bad years such as 1808–10 when the Continental Blockade led
British exporters to dump goods onto the now less protected Irish market, and 1815–17, when post-war depression and appalling harvests led to
soaring unemployment in most trades within the city. These sharp economic oscillations masked a long process of structural change, specifically a process of deskilling, in which the finer branches of various crafts
were undermined by changes in fashion and by a multiplicity of technical

innovations. Where strong journeyman organisations existed to hold up wages and enforce traditional practices, this could mean confrontation, 'lock-outs', emigration and the collapse of a whole sector, while in other areas a craft might survive but skilled earnings fall. Shipbuilding (controlled by the carpenters and sawyers societies) was an example of sectoral collapse; silk-weaving a case of the impoverished survival of large numbers of small workshops – where wages were regulated by Dublin Society arbitrators until 1826 – and of declining numbers of medium-sized specialist dealers. But while skilled silk-weavers in the Liberties district lost ground, the far less skilled business of cotton-weaving ebbed and flowed, there and elsewhere in the city. Apprenticeship controls broke down as women and adolescents were now regularly employed at the loom.[43]

What was even more striking during the war years was the growth of highly capitalised and vertically integrated 'manufactories', mainly in the suburbs, again employing large numbers of women and children and all trying to operate outside the control of guilds and journeyman organisations. In terms of plant size, the four long-established print-yards (at Ballsbridge, Rathgar, Love Lane and Islandbridge) were producing vast quantities of cheap patterned calico for the Irish market and were pioneers of this new type of employment. By the early 1820s, youths, women and children (some as young as seven years) made up a large part of their labour force; according to Duffy this had been a necessary response to the over-powerful combinations. Water, both as a source of power and as part of the dyeing process, determined the location for these enterprises. The harnessing of water for cotton-spinning, first tried at Balbriggan in 1782, had come a long way by 1815 when there were half a dozen spinning mills within a few miles of the city, but cotton in the Dublin region lacked the dynamism evident around Cork or Belfast. Given the high rental costs of premium water-power sites, large-scale operations were confined to Finglas and Greenmount. The latter, lying just south of the Grand Canal in Harold's Cross and close to the Liberties, was unusual in that steam-power was introduced quite early. The mill was taken over in 1816 by the Pims, one of the new Quaker dynasties in the city; power-looms were introduced there in the 1830s, and it remained as one of the very few large textile businesses in the city, surviving until the 1920s.[44]

The fate of the woollen industry was another example of the hollowing-out process. There were around 5,000 people employed in woollen manufacturing in the Liberties in the early 1790s, but no more than 700 by 1816, during which time the volume of fine woollen imports to Dublin had roughly doubled. Yet one branch of woollen manufacture actually expanded in that time, just beyond the city perimeter, producing coarse coating cloth and 'knap'. By 1816 there were around a dozen water-powered worsted spinning mills on the Liffey and the Dodder, the two largest of which (at Kilmainham and Celbridge) were financed and managed by west Yorkshire families, the Willans and the Houghtons. These traders also operated great wholesale warehouses in the city centre, some of their stock coming from their local mills, much of it from Yorkshire and other English suppliers. Large numbers of male hand-loom weavers worked in the immediate vicinity of these mills and, unlike the situation in the print-yards, they had some success in organising themselves into trade societies. There were several bitter disputes over wage-rates between 1810 and the mid-1820s. In both the English- and Dublin-owned mills (and in many other technically advanced workshops), there were by this time groups of English 'regular bred workmen' as part of the workforce – in 1821 roughly a third of Willan's men at Kilmainham were English, but (as Gandon had found out many years before) that did not prevent quick assimilation into the habits of Dublin artisans in terms of obeying the rules of the trade. But why did English entrepreneurs become involved in post-Union Dublin? In the case of this 'factory' woollen industry, the attraction was its tight integration into the city's wholesale cloth trade: most if not all of the millers were also running wholesale warehouses in the city, competing in the supply of vast quantities of cheap cloth to retail shops across the country. This had nothing to do with the upper classes, present or absent.[45]

Similar trends were evident in a number of other trades by the 1820s: despite the fading importance of linen in Dublin's economy, suburban water-powered flax-spinning took off in the later stages of the war, the coarse machine-spun yarns being used for sail-cloth and canvas. The first such mill was built at Glasnevin, but the Crosthwaites, one of the most prominent merchant houses in the city, made the deepest commitment, adding flax-spinning to their multiple involvements in flour, sugar, banking and shipping by fitting out a very large water-powered mill at Chapelizod and employing over 300 workers there by 1821. Paper-mills (recycling linen rags), which had at one time or another operated at nineteen locations close to the city, were now becoming larger in size and fewer in number, thanks, it seems, to the ubiquitous McDonnell clan who had been involved in paper-making since the 1740s. Their two large mills were at

Killeen near Ballyfermot and at Saggart on the Camac river, and they supplied much of the city's newsprint. And industrial-scale flour-milling, which had first developed in the countryside in the 1760s, was now being carried on at some of the best mill sites near the city, funded by the city's powerful flour factors and corn merchants. In 1802 there were eighteen flour mills in south Co. Dublin and seven in the city, three of which were equipped with steam engines.[46]

Other large-scale industrial enterprises in the region were city-based. This was particularly noticeable in the case of alcohol, an industry where excise changes had progressively favoured larger units of production since the 1780s so that capitalised breweries and distilleries became a dominant feature in the south-west of the city by the 1820s, a pattern that reflected the relative abundance of water and the convenience of the Grand Canal harbour. In 1824 only two of the city's twenty-six breweries were on the north side of town. But brewing, while capital-intensive, was not yet a dominant sector in the city economy, employing in 1821 no more than about 400 men, two-thirds the number working in the growing distilling industry. A stationary steam engine had been installed in Sweetman's Francis Street brewery in the mid-1790s, and Guinness's at James Gate followed in 1809 with the new technology, as did several of the distilleries during the war years. The output of breweries and distilleries fell sharply after 1815, providing a weather-vane of wider economic difficulty and of the huge competition from illicit cheap spirits.[47]

Iron foundries had also expanded since 1800, reflecting the increased affordability and application of cast iron. Henry Jackson's pioneering business in Church Street survived in family hands for only a few years after his banishment in 1798, but the Pill Lane/Church Street focus for foundry activity continued. By the 1820s the largest enterprise, the Phoenix Iron Works in Parkgate Street, was owned by another wartime English immigrant, Richard Robinson. His firm manufactured everything from steam engines to the hoops for casks, and employed over ninety men. Glass manufacture (of bottles and finer white glass) had a long but fraught history in the city, but by the 1820s there were three large enterprises employing many hundreds on the east side of town, one long-established one in Marlborough Street and two at Ringsend where the critical ingredient, coal, was cheapest. There were ten coach manufacturers and over fifty gig and jaunting-car makers offering their services by the 1820s, but one, Huttons of Summerhill, established in 1779, was by far the largest, employing over 160 adults by 1821. Using Irish timber but benefiting from easy access to English suppliers of a huge varieties of parts and trimmings that went into a top-class vehicle, Hutton was one of the many manufacturers who by 1820 saw real economic benefit if Union duties were completely abolished. The corn traders, the distillers and the brewers and the majority of those producing fashion goods all agreed, anxious to secure easier access to the English market or to secure imported parts on the best terms. Indeed, some, like the leading brewers and the flour factors, were already substantial exporters to the north of England. But for those who had sunk tens of thousands of pounds into industrial plant producing standardised products for the Irish market – the owners of the printing yards, woollen mills, glass-works for example – the retention of limited protection still mattered acutely in the early 1820s, and when the pre-Union tariffs were finally (and precipitously) ended in 1824, it was seen as a bad omen.[48]

The rustication of city industry, the weakening status of traditional crafts and the sharp fluctuations in the fortunes of many sectors had of course been driven by much deeper processes than the Union, for urban craft industry was in decay across southern English cities as well. But there were several cases of industrial collapse that could be traced back to the Union – the finer end of the book-printing industry for example, with the virtual end of the reprint trade after 1801 and the exodus of many journeyman printers (mainly to England) and several top publishers (who either retired, went out of the business, or transferred their operations to the United States, principally Philadelphia). However, the cataclysmic picture of a collapse of the book trade in 1801 should be qualified somewhat. Rising taxes on paper and economic uncertainty had seriously affected the book trade since the mid-1790s, but printing as an industry survived and changed character by going down-market. The actual number employed in the industry was almost certainly greater in the 1820s than in 1800, thanks to the growth of newsprint and of the institutional demand for cheap literature. Nevertheless the city's dominance within the Irish print trade was weakening by the 1820s, the number of book titles having fallen by at least a third and original fiction almost entirely gone to London. And when a sumptuous new history of the city by James Warburton, James Whitelaw and James Walsh finally appeared in 1818, published in London, there was no talk of an affordable Dublin edition to follow.[49]

Sugar-refining was a more dramatic case: there were around twenty sugar-houses in the city in the 1790s, refining raw sugar imported either directly from the Caribbean or via English and Scottish intermediaries. But with the end of tariffs on white sugar, refining disappeared within a decade, helped by wartime dumping on the part of London sugar-houses denied access to continental markets. Never a huge employer, Dublin's sugar industry had nevertheless been important in sustaining direct commercial links with the Caribbean ('sugars are in general returned for our own manufactures' it was said in 1800). Several Dublin families had shares in slave-operated sugar plantations, and refining had attracted many of the wealthiest city merchants (like Edward Byrne) a generation previously. It never revived, although vestigial links with the Caribbean remained.[50]

The vulnerable textile sectors had their moment of truth in 1826, in the wake of a severe financial crisis and recession in England and of food scarcity at home. It was the year when Irish coin (the Bank of Ireland's silver tokens) finally disappeared and Anglo-Irish monetary union became operational, the final act in the Union process. That was coincidental, but many believed otherwise. The below-cost dumping of English cottons, silks and muslin at a time of depressed Irish rural demand proved a tipping point, and the complete collapse in provincial demand for clothing fabric hit hard. By the summer of 1826 it was claimed that over 3,000 city looms were idle. But was this any worse for weavers than what their forbears had experienced in 1779, 1784 or 1797? Almost certainly it was, and for two reasons: many of those affected were already poorer before the 1826 crisis than had been the case a generation previously and, secondly, most of their employers, the petty-capitalists in the cotton and silk trades, now went into bankruptcy. There was an unprecedented flurry of relief activity and a public-works scheme employing over 1,500 artisans (including some from the industrial satellite villages) for several months, but after this there was no bounce, no revival of employment. Then, three years later, the opening of UK markets to French silks routed silk as a large employer in the city. As one insider reported in 1832,

> there never was a period of any distress in the Liberty of Dublin that lasted as it has now done since 1826 for six years, to the almost total extinction of its manufactures, the ruin of that part of the city where such manufactures exist, and the pauperism of so many thousands of its once prosperous inhabitants.

Most types of handicraft textile employment – in cotton and woollens

– vanished from the city, although it survived for a while around suburban
mills and down the country. It left in the city remnants of the silk industry, notably fine tabinet and poplin (the 'long celebrated' mixed fabrics
that incorporated worsted and silk yarns) as handicraft survivors, 'but the
young only find employment [in them], that branch of business requiring
good sight'. Here the patronage of the big wholesale houses was critical in
keeping a few hundred specialist looms alive.[51]

A quarter century after the Union, Dublin was therefore every bit
the national warehouse it had been for the previous two hundred years,
but the social benefits of that role were now greatly diminished with so
many of those wares shipped in from the industrial behemoth across the
water. James Bibby, the Liverpool ship-owner with a fleet of nine sailing
vessels constantly on the run to Dublin, boasted in 1821 about the 'always
mixed' cargoes crossing the channel worth 'fifty, sixty and seventy thousand pounds a ship', returning now with agricultural exports rather than
linen as of old. But that missed the more basic point that something similar was happening in London, Bristol and other older cities away from
the new coal-fired economy of northern England and central Scotland.
Dublin's partial de-industrialisation, severe and deeply impoverishing as it
was for so many, was not unique.[52]

New waves

A third prophecy of the anti-unionists in 1799 had been that Dublin's
civic, cultural and physical infrastructure would atrophy with the loss of
the Irish Parliament. There were solid grounds for such fears, given College Green's lavish support for the metropolitan improvements, for the
rebuilding of the university, and for a variety of 'national' institutions such
as the Dublin Society. However, the Wide Streets Commissioners, as we
have seen, continued far into the future, albeit with reduced exchequer
support. The university, with the completion of the neoclassical chapel in
1798, fell back on its own resources for the early nineteenth-century expansion into 'Botany Bay' and New Square, helped by a great growth in student numbers after the Napoleonic wars. The Dublin House of Industry,
with its mission to clear beggars from the city streets, had initially been
funded by private donations in the early 1770s, but the Irish Parliament
was soon forced to step in as the House became a working hostel for those

in distress and an asylum for the old and the infirm, rather than a penal repository for beggars. The first parliamentary grant of £3,000 had come in 1777; forty years later it stood at over £30,000 p.a. The original modest site off North King Street on the northern edge of town became the first stage in the colonisation of a great swathe of land deep into Grangegorman on which no fewer than five affiliated institutions linked to the House of Industry were built in the two decades after the Union (a fever hospital, an asylum for children, a surgical hospital, a mental asylum, and a hospital for incurables), with a total capacity of about 1,700 beds. Immediately to the north of this complex, the state acquired a portion of the Monck estate in 1812 on which to locate the Richmond Penitentiary, a huge new prison that was completed in 1816. This immense programme of public building was funded entirely by the exchequer, each initiative being taken by successive Chief Secretaries struggling with an increasingly sickly city and growing evidence of a deeper poverty afflicting both town and countryside, for which enlarged 'national' institutions located in Dublin became the only solutions available. By the 1820s, roughly half of the many thousands of needy people passing each year through the various House of Industry departments came from *outside* Dublin city and county, a proportion that tended to rise even higher in particularly hard seasons for the rural poor.[53]

The Dublin Society of the post-Union era also saw itself as a national institution, committed to the dissemination of scientific knowledge for practical ends and the promotion of industrial design, 'moulded by the very hand of the [Irish] legislature'. Long the beneficiary of parliamentary aid, its regular grant was protected under the terms of the Union for twenty years. In 1800 it received parliamentary aid to acquire and fit out large premises on Hawkins Street, complete with lecture rooms, a laboratory and exhibition space, and these were the venue for many public events, most memorably the lecture courses given in 1810 and 1811 by the Royal Society chemist Humphry Davy; in the latter year he attracted a paying audience of 525. Yet in 1814 the restless John Claudius Beresford (ex-banker and now Lord Mayor) persuaded the Society to purchase Leinster House, a move that made a potent statement of the Society's self-regard. With the establishment of a museum of geology and natural history (in 1792), of the Botanic Gardens in Glasnevin (in 1797), and a series of scientific posts (between 1795 and 1800), the Society appeared to be thriving as ever, expanding the geological museum and mounting a multiplicity of well-supported scientific lectures. But beneath the surface there were problems: the Society reflected the values of College Green, or at least of Speaker Foster who with General Charles Vallancey had controlled the Society's development agenda since the 1780s. With changing ideologies as to the economic role of the state, the Society also ran the risk of seeming dangerously out of date. The move from Hawkins Street proved a financial albatross for the Society, exacerbated when its state grant of £10,000 p.a. began to be pared back in a series of cuts starting in 1819. Its membership had grown in the early post-Union years (unlike that of the Royal Irish Academy), particularly around the time of the move to Kildare Street when ordinary membership peaked at 772 in 1816. But the predominantly landed and aristocratic membership of 1800 was becoming overshadowed by a more urban and professional, but still overwhelmingly Anglican, membership by the 1820s. In time the sheer spaciousness of the new site vindicated the move, and its potential to become a cultural quarter for the city began to be evident by 1830. The Drawing Schools, busy as ever, were relocated in the mid 1820s to a new building lying just north of Leinster House: equipped with an exhibition gallery, this was the genesis of what a generation later became the National Gallery. In 1828 some 3,000 people attended the Society's scientific lectures and almost 30,000 visited its museums; again, the first moves were being made towards establishing what was already being called 'the national museum'.[54]

Perhaps the greatest surprise in post-Union Dublin was the transformation of its transport and communications links. There were several elements to this: a huge investment by the state in improving maritime facilities in the Dublin region and, with that, a vast improvement in cross-channel postal communication; the revolutionary effects of the partial replacement of sail by steam on the Irish Sea; and parallel changes in inland transport. All of these processes helped ensure that Dublin remained the commercial capital, but they also helped to hollow out its industrial core.

The limitations of Dublin port, even with the completion of the Great South Wall to the Poolbeg lighthouse, remained a recurring issue. The completion in 1795 of a small harbour at the Pigeon House, one third of the way along the South Wall, gave new protection for cross-channel packet boats, but when Admiral William Bligh surveyed the Bay in 1800 he recommended the construction of a great *north* wall. This was opposed by several of the ocean traders on the Ballast Board and they promoted the idea for a new wall to run out from the Clontarf shore towards Poolbeg, and that became the Board's preferred policy. Yet it was not until after the wars that funding was secured to implement this idea – the 'Bull Wall', which was built between 1819 and 1824. Part embankment, part bridge, it proved to be the holy grail in that it finally tamed the notorious bar at the harbour's entrance, creating a pattern of regular tidal scouring (and the Board purchased several steam-powered dredgers *c*.1830 to consolidate their victory over nature).[55]

Long before this successful modification of the Bay there had been an appalling demonstration of its dangers. Late in November 1807 an easterly storm drove two outward-bound vessels overladen with army recruits, one of them a Parkgate packet boat (the *Prince of Wales*), the other a larger sloop (the *Rochdale*), back into Dublin Bay and onto the rocks near Blackrock with the loss of some 385 lives; at least two other small vessels were sunk on the same day. It was at that point the Bay's worst shipping disaster. One consequence was the placing of a floating light-ship over the Kish sandbank in 1811; another, the construction of the Baily lighthouse on the Howth peninsula in 1813. But the immediate reaction was a public campaign for the construction of an 'asylum harbour' for vessels in distress. Dunleary was the preferred location, possibly linking it by canal to the city. This was an awkward case to make; the government had only recently decided to build a new packet station *outside* the Bay on the north side of the Howth peninsula, a decision taken in the wake of the security panic of 1805 and based on a quite inadequate assessment of the site and its suitability. Howth harbour was supposed to replace the Pigeon House. It became a huge public-works project for the Ballast Office, running from 1807 until 1816 and employing up to 700 men, at a final cost of some £350,000. It only opened as the official packet station in 1819, and while this cut some nautical miles off the cross-channel voyage, the harbour on 'Ireland's Gibraltar' was never wholly secure from winter storms. The approaches were dangerous and its capacity was reduced by the uneven depths and a tendency to dry out at low water. Even before Howth began its short career as a packet station, the advocates of Dunleary represented the south-side harbour as the ideal all-weather refuge for every type of vessel traversing the Irish Sea. The visionary champion of the idea was a Norwegian-born sea captain and merchant, Richard Toutcher, but the scheme only got the formal go-ahead in 1816 when it was supported by Robert Peel as Chief Secretary, 'a work sufficient in itself alone to immortalise your administration'. And then John Rennie Sr, the Scottish civil engineer who had been involved in Howth (at a distance), threw his weight behind the idea of building two

24. *Howth was then beginning its short history as the main Irish 'packet station' linked to Holyhead. Thomas Telford and John Rennie Snr, the most successful civil engineers of their generation, had been involved in the costly construction project. But the natural limitations of the harbour were soon evident, and the packet service was moved to Kingstown (Dún Laoghaire) in 1834.*

'embracing protecting piers' at Dunleary. The project secured additional funds for the second pier in 1820, helped, it seems, by the Admiralty's recognition of the military value of the facility. The two piers, some 52 feet wide (each providing abundant space for a public promenade) were constructed on massive Runcorn sandstone blocks shipped over from Lancashire, with the higher levels built with the abundant local quartz granite quarried on nearby Dalkey hill. By 1822 around 800 men were employed, at which stage a funicular truckway with 250 wagons was operating from the edge of the quarries down to the new harbour. The combined length of the two piers on completion was over 2,650 metres, the eventual cost of the works by 1860 (including lighthouses and additional minor piers) coming close to a million pounds. The project's great moment was at the end of the royal visit of George IV in 1821 when the harbour and village were rebranded as Kingstown, an auspicious preparation for its role as the Irish Sorrento to which affluent local Neapolitans could escape.[56]

Maritime security was the rationale for the great harbour. But an equally pressing government concern, both in the war years and after, was the provision of fast and secure long-distance communication lines, especially between Dublin and London. The long sea journey from Parkgate on the Dee near Chester remained an option until after the wars, but with the introduction of mail coaches between London and Holyhead in 1785 and the unprecedented improvements in the north Welsh road system, journey times for official communication between Dublin and London fell to around sixty-five hours by the early nineteenth century, with the ferry at the Menai Straits and the limitations of Holyhead itself being the major remaining obstacles. These were resolved by the mid-1820s: the new route through the Welsh mountains became 'the world's fastest all-weather road', there was a major reconstruction of the harbour at Holyhead, and Thomas Telford's enormous suspension bridge over the Straits was built between 1819 and 1824, the effect of which was to eliminate several hours off the journey time from London. And parallel to these developments a new form of maritime motive power was under trial: the steam-paddle. Two small 'hybrid' vessels were purchased by a Dublin partnership in 1816 and these operated intermittently in 1816–17 between Howth and Holyhead, cutting the journey time to seven hours; the experiment ended in litigation among the partners. A second attempt was made with a new company and two larger vessels in 1820, and so impressed were the Post Office authorities in London that they purchased their own vessels the next year and forced the commercial operators to relocate to the city, leading to the inauguration of a hesitant Dublin/Liverpool service. Several parties, Dublin- and Liverpool-based, experimented over the next two years with new services and, after improvements in ship design, with much larger and faster vessels. The British Post Office authorities made the critical move in 1821, pushed by Sir Henry Parnell, the Irish MP and indefatigable champion of all these schemes, commissioning two ships specifically for all-weather operation on the Holyhead–Howth run. As a consequence, by the mid-1820s mail was being moved twice daily between London and Dublin in about thirty-six hours, a revolutionary foreshortening of distance.[57]

Three joint-stock companies, two Dublin-based and one, the St George, in Liverpool, were formed in 1822 in order to acquire larger vessels for regular operation on the Irish Sea and beyond. These second-generation steam-powered vessels were major capital undertakings, but the prospect of capturing existing commercial traffic and attracting new cross-channel business was alluring. Two local initiatives, the City of Dublin Steam Packet Company and the Quaker-dominated Dublin and Liverpool

Steam Navigation Company, seized the moment and competed fiercely with each other, principally on the critical Dublin–Liverpool route. Then the Post Office, much to the fury of these commercial operators, opened a Liverpool–Dublin mail service in 1826. Having to use larger vessels for the longer journey, Howth was simply too small for the mail-boats and thus began the first use of Kingstown as a packet station. For the private companies, funding the new steam-boats required new methods of raising capital. It had been standard practice in trading communities for centuries to divide up the ownership of merchant ships into small shares in order to reduce risk. There was a local precedent of sorts for a corporately owned shipping fleet – the Passage Boat Company formed in 1785, which for many years had operated six sailing vessels between Parkgate and Dublin, but ownership was restricted to the Wirral shipbuilders and the sailors involved. The capital required for steam-powered boats was of a different order. 'Anonymous' or sleeping partnerships had been allowed under Irish (but not British) law since 1781, and this had been the mechanism for those with money to invest to become involved in a venture without taking on its trading liabilities; it was widely used during the wars to fund mill construction and other advanced industrial undertakings. Anonymous partnership was used by City of Dublin Company to bring in its first thirty-two shareholders, but with the ceiling on a partnership set at £50,000, this was restrictive. There were a few publicly traded utility companies – the two canals, two gas-light companies, several speculative mining companies and four insurance companies – but these had all required specific legislation.[58]

The key man in the City of Dublin Company was Charles Williams, son of the long-serving secretary of the Bank of Ireland. Williams was a natural engineer, a canny trader and a good judge of risk. His vessels were the first all-weather vessels to carry general cargo, and he started a Liverpool–Dublin service with two paddle-boats in March 1824. His company went on to become one of the most successful businesses in the city's history, moving to a daily service in each direction from 1826 and operating fourteen large vessels by 1830, each costing in the region of £16,000, serving routes from Dublin to Belfast, Greenock, London and Bordeaux. The company was indeed lucky in the early years (even when two ships were wrecked in 1829, no lives were lost). After several years of fierce competition, it effectively took over the Dublin and Liverpool route in 1826, secured a private Act to increase the subscribed capital to £225,000 and

made a traffic pooling agreement with the St George, the main Liverpool
rival, and an understanding with the Post Office authorities that allowed
the latter to concentrate on the cabin-passage trade, leaving the City of
Dublin to develop freight, cattle and the 'deck trade'. Thus in its first six
years of operation, over 25,000 passengers were carried each year between
Dublin and Liverpool, 91 per cent of whom were open-deck passengers
– and it was these poor travellers (often harvest workers), livestock, eggs
and other perishable foods that filled the company's boats (and its coffers)
in the early years.[59] The company's initial shareholders were principally
Dublin merchants (all 32 in 1823, and 322 out of the 492 investors five
years later when its capitalisation was greatly enlarged). Yet despite the
local provenance of the company, the hulls and all the working machinery
were manufactured in Liverpool, 'which, if there had been any mode of
preventing combination', observed Williams, 'might have been expended
in Dublin', and the company's large repair yards were also in Liverpool.[60]

Howth, Kingstown and the lower city quays were all greatly affected
in this communications revolution. Despite strong political support,
Howth was the loser to Kingstown which, thanks to the far greater depth
and scale of its harbour, became the exclusive packet station for Dublin
in 1834. This came at a time when Dublin port itself was changing. The
cross-channel coal trade remained the principal business as ever, but commodity trade with the larger Irish urban centres, which had heretofore
depended primarily on coastal shipping, had now shifted landwards. Since
1800 there had been huge improvements in the main coaching roads, the
Grand and Royal Canal networks had expanded (reaching a maximum
mileage c.1830), and public investment in river improvement was at last
beginning to bear fruit. The City of Dublin Company invested in several small steamers to work the Shannon Navigation in conjunction with
the Grand Canal services, arranging for goods to be forwarded from any
part of the canal system or the Shannon to Liverpool via Dublin. And the
sheer volume of human movement on the roads had increased exponentially since the Union. Where in 1800 there had been four commercially
operated mail-coach routes (for post and wealthier travellers), linking the
city with Belfast, Derry, Limerick and Cork, and eight stagecoaches leaving the city, by 1830 there were thirteen mail-coach routes and twenty-two
stagecoach routes, with competition lowering prices and widening the
market. Only introduced in 1789, the mail-coaches quickly developed a
visibility and regularity; they were obvious rebel targets in 1798.

The volume of mail handled in Dublin rose rapidly, Irish postal revenue increasing by 94 per cent between 1804 and 1814, and the Post Office was substantially reformed when the earl of Clancarty (a confidante of Castlereagh) became Irish Postmaster General. Out of that came plans for a much larger purpose-built General Post Office: the foundation stone was laid on the centenary of the House of Hanover in 1814. The choice of Sackville Street for the new office was quite deliberate: with its great width and new hotels, the street offered better access for the mail-coaches than the congested termini outside the hotels further west. Johnston's palatial Greek Ionic façade, over 220 feet long in front of a hidden quadrangle where the mail-coaches were loaded, suggested an engine house for the new information age, its very scale staking a claim to be the new centre of the city, giving 'life and business to the very first of our principal streets'. The decision to create 'Talbot Street' *c.*1822, pushing east from Earl Street to the North Strand and out along the new coast road to the Howth packet station, reinforced this sense of the GPO as the new hub. No south-side avenue could rival the theatrical impact for a visitor arriving into Sackville Street, and not just because of the GPO or the array of new shops near the bridge, but because of the new monument at the Street's centre.[61]

Frozen promises

The great Doric pillar erected at the centre of Sackville Street in 1808–9 to honour the memory of the fallen hero of Trafalgar was not the earliest such monument (Glasgow had got there first), but it was the most elaborate of the era. William Wilkins' original design was modified by Francis Johnston, with mixed results: carved from Wicklow granite, its merits and choice of location continued to divide opinion for as long as it dominated central Dublin's skyline. Seen by many latterday Dubliners as a triumphalist statement of British imperialism, Nelson's pillar was not an official gesture. A century later, W. B. Yeats, no fan of its appearance, respected it as representing 'the feeling of Protestant Ireland for a man who helped to break the power of Napoleon', but even that was not quite true: three of the wealthiest Catholic merchants (MacDonnell, O'Brien and Valentine O'Connor) were on the committee of twenty who raised nearly £7,000 for the memorial, and the chair of the building committee, Luke White, had strongly Whiggish sympathies. On completion, it did not become a 'site of memory' for party displays like King William's statue in College Green, yet the alacrity with which Dubliners chose to commemorate Nelson and the monumental scale chosen is striking, hinting at powerful subterranean emotions stirred up by French naval defeat.[62]

Several years earlier, Valentine O'Connor had come forward with a loan of £5,100 to the Catholic archbishop for a nearby project, the purchase of one of several aristocratic houses on the market in 1803, the very amply laid out Annesley House on the west side of Marlborough Street. It was chosen as the site for a new Catholic 'metropolitan chapel' to replace the cramped St Mary's in Liffey Street. There had been a minor flurry of Catholic church-building since the 1780s (St Catherine's in Meath Street, St Paul's on Arran quay, and the Carmelite church off Clarendon Street, all before the Union, and the Gothicised parish churches of St Michan's on Halston Street, c.1811–14, and St Michael and St John's on the site of Smock Alley theatre, c.1815), but nothing remotely on the scale planned by Archbishop Troy. The genesis of the idea and its early history remain obscure; even the author of the design for 'a hybrid of the Greek temple with the Roman basilica' is unknown. The inspiration was clearly Parisian (specifically St Philippe du Roule), and both John Sweetman, the United Irish leader exiled in France until 1820, and the archbishop were directly involved in the design. It took five years of fund-raising to reimburse O'Connor, and another six years before sufficient funds had been raised to begin the new building, but the elderly Troy directed much effort in his final years to realise the project between 1814 and his death in 1823, by which time some £31,000 had been raised. The purity of the earliest designs had to be modified and the great portico was only completed, amid financial difficulties, in 1837 at a final cost of around £45,000, but its claim to architectural sophistication was never in dispute. As the first de facto Catholic cathedral in the post-Reformation city, its powerful Greek Revival character influenced St Andrew's Catholic church a decade later and its great portico was echoed in many of the city's Catholic churches of the next generation.[63]

When Archbishop Troy died in 1823, he had been in charge of Dublin for thirty-seven years. The funeral was held in the unfinished shell of the cathedral and with great pomp.[64] That was appropriate: Catholic Dublin in the twenty years since Emmet's rebellion was a strange mixture of unfulfilled ambition, new-found assertiveness, and a potent sense of confessional identity. There had been a marked growth in the number of affluent Catholic professionals since 1800, many with no previous connection with the city, who resented the glass ceiling that denied them access to high public office and entry into Parliament. Denys Scully and Daniel O'Connell were the leaders of this new generation, although few could aspire to follow them into Merrion Square, where both had homes by 1809. Their wealthy Munster family backgrounds and early success at the bar made them a bit dismissive of the Dublin merchants who had dominated Catholic politics up until then. The Cambridge-educated Scully's strength was his aristocratic friendships and law-book knowledge, O'Connell's his remarkable physical presence, rhetorical brinkmanship and tactical abilities, honed first in the courtroom. O'Connell had been one of the few Catholics in 1800 to argue publicly for the retention of the Irish Parliament, and the religious consequences of Union only enhanced his reputation. As he was the first to note, all Dublin administrations between 1801 and 1818 had been firmly Protestant in character (punctuated only by the Bedford viceroyalty in 1806–7, when the tradition of the birthday parade around King William's statue was brought to an end). But even in the becalmed state of Catholic politics after 1800, when older activists were fearful of alienating their Protestant allies, Scully and particularly O'Connell relaid the foundations for mass constitutional politics in the wake of the disasters of the 1790s.

The Catholic Committee exploited legal loopholes to reconstitute itself in 1804, but only began to organise country-wide elections for a new national committee in 1811 (once again to petition Parliament for emancipation), by which time O'Connell was very much in the ascendant. The government and the Catholic leadership engaged in legal jousting over the interpretation of the 1793 ban on delegate conventions, with neither side gaining a decisive advantage. The barristers managed to dominate the more risk-averse gentry, helped by their success in keeping the bishops negatively disposed towards any possibility of emancipation if it meant allowing government to have a veto over episcopal appointments. However, in 1813 the committee split on the veto question, with an upper-class minority seceding in protest over O'Connell's intransigent stance and his rough-house rhetoric. But the bishops also stayed in rejectionist mode. Meanwhile, with Robert Peel as Chief Secretary from 1812 to 1818, aided by William Saurin (Attorney General from 1807 to 1821 and a leading member of the city's Orange Order), O'Connell met his match: Peel was determined to use the law to smother Catholic political activity and silence the more outspoken parts of the Catholic press. But this was not before O'Connell's bravura performance in 1813 when, acting as defence counsel for the liberal newspaper editor John Magee, he attacked the corrupt partisanship of government (several office-holders including Peel were present in court) in a blistering four-hour tirade, humiliating Saurin in particular. He had, however, overreached himself and the government seized the initiative.[65]

The next ten years were quiet as far as the Catholic question was concerned, aside from one instance in 1815 when O'Connell attacked the Corporation for its ongoing opposition to emancipation and described it as 'beggarly', causing feigned insult and leading one naval veteran in the city Commons, John D'Esterre, to issue a challenge to O'Connell. The affair of honour, held on the Kildare border, became a public spectacle. D'Esterre was fatally wounded in the duel (to O'Connell's later mortification), but celebratory bonfires burnt in the city that evening. Of O'Connell's personal popularity among the Catholic citizenry there can be no doubt, and he enjoyed walking regularly to the courts as 'all the people turn to look after him'.[66]

The *annus mirabilis* was 1824, the year when a new Catholic Association, launched in Dublin the previous summer, defied all expectations by becoming a truly mass movement through the mechanism of an affordable membership of one penny a month, which every Catholic household in the whole country was encouraged to pay. The Association's success in terms of popular mobilisation and publicity drew on 1790s precedents, but by lasting the pace (despite legal suppression in 1825 and a tactical wobble by O'Connell in 1826) until Wellington's government conceded Emancipation in 1829, the movement triumphantly delivered on its primary aim. Yet in purely Dublin terms, the great political struggle of the 1820s was only one phase in what was to be a hundred-year-long contest over ultimate control of the city's destinies between predominantly Protestant interests and predominantly Catholic ones – in local government, business, welfare provision, education and high culture. And this struggle in the 1820s for emancipation was not a sectarian battle; O'Connell himself was ever-anxious to acknowledge the powerful Protestant support that came from Whig liberals, helped in the city by the enduring anti-unionism that remained a sentiment unifying nearly all political shades. Yet denominational loyalties were strengthening in this era of renewed evangelical purpose and Catholic revival, dividing social, medical and educational institutions across the city's public sphere into Protestant or Catholic categories. Most such institutions (voluntary and state-supported) were still strongly Protestant: of the 100 or so 'charitable institutions' listed for the city in *Pigot & Co.'s Directory* in 1824, no more than half a dozen had significant Catholic participation in their governance and only two, the very active Sick and Indigent Roomkeepers' Society and the Mendicity Association, made a virtue of their religiously balanced governance. There were at least twenty small Catholic charities operating at parish level before 1829, but their public profile was low.[67]

The prospects for Catholic emancipation without concessions had ebbed and flowed since 1815. The appointment in 1818 of a sympathetic Chief Secretary, William Grant, in place of Peel, coincided with the election of a reform-minded Lord Mayor, Thomas McKenny. Disowning the usual display of party colours and Williamite toasts, he chaired an aggregate meeting of Protestant citizens midway through his term which resolved that emancipation would be 'highly conducive to the tranquillity of Ireland', but in the general election the following year, emancipation was hardly mentioned. As in the four previous parliamentary elections, Robert Shaw and the venerable Henry Grattan were elected for the city. Since re-emerging into parliamentary politics in 1806, Grattan had made many attempts to find a formula to break the logjam on emancipation, but failed completely to broker an agreement. His sudden death in June 1820 forced a by-election where, for the first time, emancipation became the issue dividing the candidates – Henry Grattan Jnr and Alderman Thomas Ellis, a conservative lawyer. It was fought out as of old in the guildhalls and in the press, and the electorate was still overwhelmingly the freeman body (entirely Protestant despite 1793), and a very small freeholder group (many of whom were Catholic). But what was new was the way in which the unenfranchised Catholic citizenry at large followed the canvas, on occasion even met as trade groups, allowing it to become an Orange and Green combat. There was an usually high number of abstentions from the public poll, but young Grattan, despite the family name and anti-Union pedigree was defeated by nearly three to two, a result which shocked liberal and Catholic commentators.[68]

Thomas Ellis's victory helped reinforce a sense that the Corporation and nearly all its parts were now irredeemably anti-Catholic, its most visible aldermen, like Frederick Darley, the police commissioner, and John Claudius Beresford, in control of city markets and tolls, well-known

Orangemen. Since 1813 the city's ancient right to levy tolls on non-free-men and strangers entering the city and at the markets had been chal-lenged, both legally and by direct action. A universal toll-strike was hard to counter; O'Connell later claimed that 'at first the police interfered, but the government prevented the police from interfering, and insisted that the Corporation should try the right with the people [in court]'. By 1820 the Corporation had completely abandoned the effort, sacrificing an income of over £5,000 p.a., a strange admission of legal and administrative incapacity. The fact that the principal contractor to collect the disappear-ing tolls was none other than Beresford cannot have been coincidental.[69]

At the end of 1820, on the initiative of McKenny's guild (the Hosiers), an invitation was sent George IV, shortly after his accession, to visit Dub-lin. Apart from those who knew of his affections for the chatelaine of Slane Castle, Elizabeth, 1st marchioness Conyngham, the king's accep-tance was a great surprise, the first royal visit to Dublin since 1690. Given the unpopularity of the new monarch in Britain in the wake of bitter royal divorce proceedings, the auspices were not good and were made a great deal worse by the death of Queen Caroline only days before his arrival at Howth in August 1821. There was a surprising degree of cooperation beforehand. Unlike the exuberant celebrations of his father's jubilee in 1810, or of the centenary of the Hanoverian succession in 1814, which had been Protestant events with little or no Catholic input, now an organising committee of thirty-two stewards, half of them Protestant and half Catho-lic, was established with the active support of an Orange Lord Mayor and of Daniel O'Connell. The visit itself caused great excitement and almost no controversy, revealing a residual cross-party loyalism (which may have been helped by the king's unpopularity at home). The king made a formal entry into the centre of Dublin through a triumphal arch erected beside the Rotunda, and the state dinner included a large Catholic participation. Later during the three-week visit he met a delegation of Catholic bishops in their robes before his departure from Kingstown.[70]

To many commentators, the visit was 'a melancholy farce', but to others it was a practical demonstration of 'conciliation', realised with the subsequent appointment of Wellington's brother, Richard, 1st marquess Wellesley, as Lord Lieutenant, the first Irishman to hold the office in over a century and known for his pro-Catholic sympathies. Yet for all the social recognition that leading Catholics might now receive in the Castle, nei-ther the king nor Wellesley was disposed to concede the kind of deal that the more radical emancipists were seeking. The real importance of the thaw in 1821–2 was the way it provoked conservatives, wealthy and plebeian, to put themselves in the wrong, rejecting a move to make a number of wealthy Catholic merchants freemen and creating endless arguments over their entitlement to parade at William's statue in College Green. The culmination was the 'bottle riot' in the newly opened Theatre Royal in Hawkins Street in December 1822: the actors refused an invitation to toast 'the Glorious Memory', upon which fruit and a bottle were thrown at the stage and a watchman's rattle was propelled at the viceregal box. It was a tame affair by comparison with the riots that had marred the final years of Smock Alley in 1814 and 1819. But it was exploited superbly by the Catholic and Whig press and put Orange Dublin, not least Darley the police commissioner, onto the defensive. It marked the end of any official involvement in Williamite celebration and opened up divisions within the Orange Order, leading to a real slippage in the prestige and influence of the Dublin Grand Lodge over the northern heartlands of the movement. Then, in the following year, Grattan's humiliation in 1820 was reversed – in a Co. Dublin election: Sir Compton Domville, with estates scattered across the constituency, was defeated by the very deep pockets of old Luke White, who had himself contested the county seat in 1820 and now bankrolled his fourth son to victory – with muscular support from O'Connell. It was the first time that Catholic freeholders tipped the balance in a Dublin election, and there was a victory parade from Kilmainham to College Green which only ended when College students fired a fusillade of stones at the celebrants.[71]

In 1824 the new Catholic Association, working from above Coyne's bookshop in Capel Street, launched its strategy of constructing a mass membership through the penny rent. There was at least one Dublin precedent. St Michael's and St John's church on Exchange Street had been completed a decade previously 'by public contribution, in which the lower ranks of the population cheerfully bore a part by a voluntary subscription of one penny per week', and that can hardly have been unique. The nationwide spread of the Association was rapid, and this is conventionally attributed to three complementary factors: the end of infighting among Catholic leaders over the veto; the broadening of the agenda of the Association to include a cluster of other, mainly rural issues (so that it became in effect 'a Catholic protective organisation'); and the wholehearted cooperation of the bishops and enthusiasm of the parish clergy for the Association. Its stunning success by the end of 1824 transformed both its own ambitions and the perception of government as to its real agenda. Raising the 'rent' in the city itself was harder than expected, despite the appointment of dozens of collectors. And although Dublin city and county contributed 11.6 per cent of the £16,859 raised by March 1825, it was a relatively modest response. Did the promise that all manner of Catholic grievances from the 'Giant's Causeway to Cape Clear' would be aired by the Association resonate less in the city where multiple forms of redress were more available than elsewhere, or were parishioners already weighed down by contributing to the many parish causes and the building costs of a new cathedral? Did it simply reflect the fact that, in contrast with the 1790s agitation, none of the Association's leaders were Dublin-born or men of trade?[72]

The powder was kept dry in the 1826 general election in the city, for despite a great expansion in the number of Catholic freeholder voters, a conservative candidate and Grattan junior were returned unopposed. The headline events of the next three years lay outside Dublin – the defeat of the Beresfords in their electoral homeland of Co. Waterford in 1826, the mass parish-petitioning campaign of January 1828, and the game-changing parliamentary victory of O'Connell in Co. Clare in July (no one remembered that John Keogh had had the idea of running a Catholic candidate many years before). The aim of those around O'Connell, 'to keep the steam up to the original pressure, without risking an explosion', was achieved at least in part because of the Dublin press, eager and able to play a vociferous role in communicating the unfolding story nationally. At least four of the eighteen Dublin newspapers were supportive of the Association, notably William Conway's long-established *Dublin Evening Post* and Michael Staunton's new *Morning Register*. Staunton was unusual in employing a team of reporters concentrating on home news. The absence of tight press control (for most of the 1820s) and the unwillingness of government to smother the political mobilisation of the rural masses contrasted strikingly with the censorship and harassment of the 1810s, not to mention the crackdown in the 1790s. As Thomas Bartlett has suggested, Peel and Wellington, while committed to the preservation of the Protestant interest in Ireland, accepted the inevitability of emancipation several years before 1829, looking 'to O'Connell ... to provide them with that plausible crisis which would enable them to yield under apparent duress'. O'Connell's epic victory in Co. Clare provided them with just that.[73]

Aside from Emancipation, there was a tangible victory for Dublin Catholics in 1829: a Catholic cemetery. Up to then, their choice had been between interment in an overcrowded parish graveyard in the city (where obsequies, if any, had to follow the Anglican rite), interment in Bully's Acre, the paupers' 'wilderness of death' west of the Royal Hospital, or removal to a country graveyard (and little regulation). O'Connell had politicised the issue and secured statutory relief in 1824 with the Easement of Burials Act, but it was only with the opening of Golden Bridge in Kilmainham that a Catholic committee (a spin-off of the Association) took control of burial grounds. It was immediately apparent that something larger was required, so the 'Catholic Burial Committee' acquired nine acres in Glasnevin and opened 'Prospect cemetery' in 1832. This was not intended to be denominationally exclusive, but when Mount Jerome, a commercial cemetery on the south-west side of town, was opened in 1834 the city was divided anew: Mount Jerome became the resting place for most middle-class Protestants, Glasnevin the necropolis for Catholics of all classes.[74] The latter was tightly run and on its own terms highly successful, more obviously so than other Catholic-dominated initiatives like the Hibernian Bank or the National Bank, and its growing visibility on the north-west approaches proclaimed the resurgent Catholic character of the city.

The streets on a Dublin Sunday in the 1820s were filled with the sound of bells. Christ Church's 'deep tremendous toll', the carillons in St Patrick's and St Werburgh's, were joined by a multiplicity of single bells in most of the twenty parish churches and bells in the chapels of the university and the Castle. The first Catholic church bell since the sixteenth century in St Michael's and John's could now be heard along the quays – until the passing of the Emancipation bill, when it 'was rung so violently that it became cracked'.[75] It was an intensely Sabbatarian age, a time when the visible performance of religious duties was a compelling obligation for the respectable classes. This was universal across the English-speaking world, but in Dublin the evangelical revival had particular potency, first evident in the new 'proprietary chapels' (licensed by the Church of Ireland archbishop but independently financed), where huge congregations turned out for celebrity preachers (in the Bethesda chapel in Granby Row, Trinity

Church in Gardiner Street and St Matthias's in Adelaide Road). Religious observance, in the household and in public, was reinforced by a pervasive sense of confessional competition that was of course related to the new political environment and sharpened by deepening inter-denominational tensions, both at the elite and popular levels. In 1822, William Magee at his installation in Christ Church as archbishop of Dublin proclaimed that the established church still had a mission to evangelise the whole population of the country and spoke later of the Reformation only now beginning in Ireland. In so doing he drew unprecedentedly sharp rebuttals from several Catholic bishops. Magee's rallying cry was characterised as the start of a new religious war and a deliberately inflammatory response to the heightened sense of Catholic grievance.[76]

One of the great enthusiasts for bell-ringing was Francis Johnston. We know little of his political or religious sensibilities beyond the fact that he gave of his best in designing the Chapel Royal and St George's Church. The latter's magnificent (and costly) tower and spire reflected Johnston's enthusiasm for aural as well as visual impact. In 1828 he and his wife presented the parish with a peal of eight bells for the church and the inscriptions he chose for some of the bells are suggestive: 'GOD PRESERVE THE CHURCH AMEN'; 'PEACE AND PROSPERITY TO IRE-LAND'; 'WE REJOICE TO RING FOR OUR CONSTITUTION AND KING'. Some years earlier, he built an ecclesiastical folly at the bottom of his Eccles Street garden, incorporating a bell-tower and spire designed to accommodate the peal of twelve bells that he had acquired from the Theatre Royal, Crow Street.[77]

But Johnston's greatest gesture to the city was firmly secular. In 1821 he was listed as one of thirty-one citizens owning a major picture collection. Some of the other collections, like those of the Charlemont and La Touche families, had been built up over several generations but most, like Johnston's, had been acquired by their current bourgeois owners (in the great-house hinterland of the city only a few fresh collections of paintings or sculpture were now being assembled, notably in the new Lawless palace at Lyons on the Dublin/Kildare border). Because of the wars, most of the city's art collectors had, like Johnston, travelled very little (unlike their eighteenth-century forebears), but they had found other ways of acquiring art. There were a number of large art auctions as city houses were emptied and there was a well-established tradition of the public exhibitions in the city. The Society of Artists was re-established in 1800, and for several years they used the old House of Lords as an exhibition space, then occupied a part of the capacious Dublin Society's house in Hawkins Street. The Royal Irish Institution was established in 1813 for the display of Old Masters borrowed from private collections (some of which were being scattered with the spate of private sales), and it attracted strong upper-class patronage. For several years it also ran exhibitions in Hawkins Street until the disposal of the premises and in 1827 it opened its own premises in College Street.[78] But local artistic talent coming out of the Drawing Schools was clearly struggling for patronage after the wars, which led to a more robust initiative: the establishment of a Hibernian Academy, membership of which would be entirely composed of professional painters, sculptors, architects and engravers. After some delay the Academy received a royal charter in 1823, but no funds. Two masters from another age were invited to join – James Gandon, who refused on grounds of age, and William Ashford the landscapist, who accepted and was chosen as first president. But both were dead within months. The project faltered but was then rescued by Francis Johnston: he acquired a site for the Academy on an undeveloped part of Lower Abbey Street and designed a three-storey gallery, which was realised at an eventual personal cost of some £10,000. The first exhibition of Irish artists was held in 1826 during Johnston's presidency, with over 400 exhibits, and some years later his widow added a sculpture floor to accommodate Johnston's private collection. It is striking that despite the Academy's non-political character and real sense of national mission, all but one of its fourteen original members appear to have been Protestant. But at least one of these, William Cuming, was a strong supporter of O'Connell.[79]

7

A TALE OF FOUR CITIES: 1830–1880

Certain facts

Queen Victoria's first visit to Dublin was in August 1849; Charles Dickens' first was in 1858. The queen's exquisitely choreographed five days drew vast crowds and no apparent trouble, aside from a South Great George's Street pharmacist who erected 'on the top of his house a large *black* banner, displaying the crownless harp, and draped his windows with black curtains, showing the words *Famine* and *Pestilence*', which were forcibly removed by the Dublin Metropolitan Police (DMP). Victoria reckoned the Dublin she saw to be 'a very fine city', and the unexpectedly warm reception that she received 'a never-to-be-forgotten scene'. Dickens was surprised to find Dublin 'very much larger than I had supposed, and very much more populous and busy. Upon the whole it is no shabbier than London is, and the people seem to enjoy themselves more ... It may be presumed that it has greatly improved of late years.' The thousands who crowded into his readings in the Rotunda seemed little different from the English audiences he knew so well. All was pleasantly familiar.[1] But if either visitor had stayed a little longer they might have sensed the differences from London: the pervasive belief in a lost golden age, a middle class fractured by confessional rivalry, and an urban core where the degree of social inequality was extreme by English standards. Most contemporaries who wrote about Dublin either exoticised its street life, or had a political point to prove. No one wrote about its complexity.

By the 1850s there were at least four distinct social layers across the greater urban area – permeable layers – but each evolving rather differently within the wider transformation of the country. We can distinguish a professions-centred layer, still mainly Protestant; a 'respectable' world of the 'shopocracy', mixed in its religious affiliations; a Dublin of the productive working classes, predominantly Catholic; and the city of the destitute. From the 1830s there was a torrent of social, demographic and cartographic evidence collected and published by Parliament and state agencies which gave the opportunity to deconstruct this society and track its evolution. A small Dublin Statistical Society was formed in 1847, committed, like Dickens's Mr Gradgrind, to 'the collection and classification of facts' in the belief that statistical evidence was a superior form of social knowledge that must shape economic policy and social reform. But for all the earnest inquiries of its members into contemporary social ills, no one in the Society attempted a holistic analysis of the city in which they lived.[2]

The bedrock 'facts' that now became available were the great decennial censuses beginning in 1821, although the Rev. James Whitelaw's private census begun more than two decades earlier was used as a Union-era benchmark. Almost none of the raw material of these nineteenth-century inquiries survives, but the results as published provided a great leap forward in documenting the city. They appeared in the same era as the Ordnance Survey maps of the city (1840–7) and the first street directories (beginning with Pettigrew and Oulton's in 1834).[3] Whitelaw's census, begun in 1798, had been opportunistic (being drawn from the lists of residents which under martial law all householders were required to post on their front doors), and it was updated before publication in 1805. The first official census was begun in 1813 but was abandoned. The census of 1821 was broadly successful (though the mode used to present results is highly problematic); that of 1831 rather less so. All depended on the efficiency of local government. But later enumerations were conducted by the police, and the census template became far more sophisticated. The results published from the 1840s were highly detailed, reflecting in particular the ambition of the architect of the 1841 Irish census, the military surveyor Thomas Larcom, that it should be 'a social survey, not a bare enumeration', and that it should therefore supply evidence on literacy and occupational structure, disease and public health.[4]

Successive censuses revealed that Dublin was no longer a rapidly growing city and that as a consequence it was falling down the UK rankings – from the second most populous city in Whitelaw's time to the seventh by 1881. With the clear exception of the 1840s, the city's rate of population growth was declining. Population density, within the canals at least, was also falling, but the corollary of this was that the urban site constituting greater Dublin was expanding faster, at times much faster, than population. But as most of the new suburbs lay resolutely outside municipal boundaries until the twentieth century, the city's population growth appeared to be even more anaemic than it was in reality. City population within the canals totalled 224,317 in 1821, implying a growth rate of close to 1 per cent p.a. since the Union. But the population for the identical area in 1841 was less than 9,000 greater, suggesting a very tepid growth rate of 0.2 per cent p.a. However the picture changes when we look at growth across the fully urbanised area lying inside and outside the canals, *plus* the contiguous baronies: for this notional greater Dublin area, population was growing at 0.6 per cent p.a. between 1821 and 1841. The city's population then surged forward between 1841 and 1851, as did the population of every Irish town, the direct result of the Great Famine (1845–50). Many of the extra 36,631 Dubliners recorded in 1851 were crisis migrants, some of whom may have put down roots in the city but many were mere birds of passage in city institutions. After this, the pattern of slow growth, first evident in the 1820s and 1830s, reasserted itself in the post-Famine decades; growth in the city and contiguous suburbs averaged 0.7 per cent p.a. between 1841 and 1861, but only 0.2 p.a. between 1861 and 1881, by which time the city and suburbs returned a population of 345,052. If these suburbs are included, Dublin just about managed to double its population between 1800 and 1881, during which time Liverpool, its closest trading partner across the Irish Sea, grew eight-fold (and by 1881 was twice the size of Dublin), and even Bristol (like Dublin a commercial rather than an industrial hub) almost quadrupled its population over these eighty years.[5]

The great majority of Bristol and Liverpool's Victorian residents were migrants: Dublin's relative demographic calm meant that throughout the nineteenth century a majority of its citizens were natives of the city or county – some 73 per cent of the citizenry at the first reckoning in 1841. The non-native proportion rose sharply in the Famine years (only 61 per cent were Dublin-born in 1851), but the indigenous share recovered in subsequent decades and moved between 67 and 61 per cent for the rest of the century. Just under three-fifths of the 1841 migrants had come from within Leinster, with the old hinterland counties of Kildare, Wicklow and Meath leading the way, more emphatically so in the case of female migrants. And despite the coming of the railways and of heightened mobility, Leinster's role as the overwhelming source of migrants went unchallenged.[6] This was demonstrated tellingly when the question on language usage was introduced into the 1851 census. It revealed that even with Famine immigration the city was overwhelmingly anglophone, with only 1.3 per cent of the over-fives declaring a competence in the Irish language. This was in line with the very low levels of Irish-speaking across most of Leinster, evident since the late eighteenth century, but the absence of Irish from the streets of Dublin contrasted with the Munster cities (notably Waterford with 16.2 per cent) and the town of Galway (with 61.3 per cent), both of which had very different language hinterlands.[7]

The other side of this was the relatively high levels of elementary literacy in the city. When first measured in 1841, 74.4 per cent of the over-fives in the city could read and write, or read only, with 84.5 per cent literate in the best educated cohort, the 16–25 age group; about a fifth of this group could read but not write, with more of these women than men. The age profile of literacy was also revealed in 1841, demonstrating that reading and writing skills were long established among most men in the city, but that young adult women were somewhat more literate than their mothers.[8] With the state's growing involvement in funding elementary education, a huge amount of quantitative data on schooling began to be collected, yet it was private pay-schools, tutors and charity schools which, between them, had created a literate city long before the state entered the field with the National School system in 1831 (only a handful of the 167 city schools enumerated in the 1834 Commission on Public Instruction were linked to the new initiative). At that point there were 13,341 pupils on the rolls of the city's day-schools, but the 1841 census made the more conservative estimate that 26 per cent of the 6–15 age cohort were actually attending school at the time of the census. That figure had jumped to 39 per cent by 1851, contributing to the further rise in literacy levels for the over-fives to 81 per cent by 1861, after which there was little improvement for the rest of the century.[9] It is striking that school attendance was lower in Dublin than in any of the provincial cities, and the western half of the city seems to have been the outlier here where literacy levels were significantly lower than on the east: nearly one-third of the over-five Catholic population in the western wards were illiterate in 1861, compared to about one-fifth of their co-religionists in the eastern wards. The river was not yet an educational divide.[10]

Religious affiliation was not included in the census until 1861, but an elaborate effort was made in 1834 during the Public Instruction inquiry to calculate denominational strengths at parish level. The results for Dublin were intriguing but not unexpected: the city's Protestant majority was a distant memory in 1834, but the actual Protestant share was lower than some expected – at around 28 per cent. Protestant numbers were highest in the south-east parishes (which were 33 per cent Protestant overall), lowest in the north-west parishes (19 per cent Protestant), no parish had a Protestant majority (although St Ann's at 45 per cent was not far off), and no parish had less than 13 per cent of its householders Protestant (St Michan's having the least). The 1834 exercise confirmed the absence of religious segregation within the city but suggested a fairly strong east/west contrast in the religious balance. It gave a very low number for Dissenters (3,640, or about 5 per cent of the Protestant population), but this was a serious underestimate. In the more rigorous exercise of 1861, the overall picture was not very different – a Protestant share of now less than 23 per cent – but it indicated that Dissenters (more than half of whom were subscribing Presbyterians) made up almost 15 per cent of Protestant Dublin, a much more credible figure. As had been the case in the eighteenth century, Presbyterians were strongest on the ground in the north-east of the city, a fact proclaimed when the Mary's Abbey meeting moved in 1864 to the Gothic magnificence of the Abbey Church on the north-east corner of Rutland Square, funded by one of the several Scottish migrants who had risen to the top of Dublin business, Alexander Findlater.[11]

The censuses revealed a slow but fundamental shift in male occupations in the city, greater stratification, less workshop employment, and the rise of the service sector – but little for women. Taking Mary Daly's estimates, it seems that male professionals (broadly defined) formed 8.4 per cent of the city's male workforce in 1841, 11.0 per cent in 1861 and 12.8 per cent in 1881, and that transport-related employment for men rose from 3.0 per cent in 1841 and 11.7 per cent in 1861 to 12.4 in 1881. By contrast, the proportion of men employed in manufacturing declined from 33.4 per cent in 1841 to 27.2 per cent in 1861 and 23.9 per cent in 1881, and there was little change in the numerical significance of male general labourers, which hovered at just over a sixth of the total. For women 'productively employed', domestic service of course predominated, moving from 50.4 per cent in 1841 to 45.3 per cent in 1861 and back to 50.5 per cent in 1881, and remaining well ahead of female manufacturing jobs (34.4 per cent of those employed in 1841, 35.7 per cent in 1861 and 32.2 per cent in 1881), and of female dealers (11.8 per cent in 1841, 16.2 per cent in 1861, and 12.4 per cent in 1881). The overall profile was not unlike that of London, except that the decline there of manufacturing occupations was less pronounced, and the general labouring population was less than half the Dublin proportion.[12]

The correlation between income and distance from the old city became progressively stronger with the majority of the professional class living outside the city boundary, whereas only one quarter of general labourers in greater Dublin lived in the suburbs. This pattern of social seg-regation continued to intensify. Perhaps the most striking trend revealed was the progressive eclipse of the south-west quarter of the city, the Lib-erties parishes in particular. In Whitelaw's census *c*.1800, 42 per cent of the urban population living within the Circular Road was located in the south-west quarter; that proportion had fallen to 32 per cent in 1841, and to 25 per cent in 1881. Yet even with this decline, population density in the south-west remained the highest in the city – six of the eleven parishes still had over 200 persons per acre in 1841 – and as late as 1881 Wood Quay ward (which included the two old cathedrals) contained 152 persons per acre, at a time when the city average was 66.[13] The delayed revaluation of property in the older parts of the city meant that they bore a dispropor-tionate burden of local taxes, which only compounded their decline. The problem was recognised in the 1820s, and in a city-wide valuation com-pleted in 1828 the combined housing stock of the eleven old parishes west of Dublin Castle contributed only 21 per cent of the total city's valuation. However, it was more than twenty years before the revaluation gave any relief to the poorest districts. In the new city valuation *c*.1854, their contri-bution had shrunk to an insignificant 14 per cent, and their proportion of empty houses was the highest in the city.[14]

Whitelaw had presented his statistical survey of the city in 1805 to enlighten the citizens of the richer east as to the poverty engulfing him in St Catherine's parish, and in hopes of a change in public policy. But he was disappointed by its limited impact. William Wilde (Oscar's father), then a young doctor and budding polymath, took up the challenge in 1841, using the new census data to correlate housing quality, occupation and mortality across Dublin. His findings – that the death rate in 'third-class shop streets' north of the Liffey was now more than twice that in south-side 'private streets' – were controversial, but were largely borne out in later work. Yet despite such startling revelations and the huge expansion of 'useful' statistical knowledge, annually disseminated (from 1844) in the prodigious *Thom's almanac*, there was little evidence that knowledge of the 'facts' could force social change.[15]

The professional city

A few peers and a far larger number of physicians were among the many who met in the Rotunda in May 1830 to consider establishing a city zoo. It was two years after the opening of the zoological gardens in Regent's Park, and Whitley Stokes, former United Irishman and leading city physician, led the call for a similar initiative for Dublin. Thanks principally to Surgeon General Philip Crampton, a Zoological Society was indeed established within a year, and a corner of the Phoenix Park near the city was handed over by the Crown for the new venture. Plans to acquire exotic mammals, birds and reptiles were soon underway. In the history of public zoos, Dublin was early off the mark and (unlike in London) the enterprise was publicly accessible from the beginning (for a sixpenny fee, reduced to a penny on Sundays). The medical profession was central to its establishment, recognising its value for research into living and (especially) dead fauna, but it was also an immediate success as a place of public spectacle, aided by the recurrent attention given to the zoo in the innovative weekly paper, *The Dublin Penny Journal* (1832–6), where woodcuts of the zoo's more alien inhabitants filled its pages. Twenty thousand visitors swamped the zoo on a free day in 1838 that coincided with Victoria's coronation.[16]

The birth of the zoo touches many themes – the residual importance of aristocratic patronage, the latent public interest in the world beyond and in new discoveries, the power of print to fan that interest, and the prominence of the medical profession in civic life. The ascendancy of medicine was comparatively new: in the mid-1780s there had been around sixty physicians and a similar number of surgeons practising in the city, in an era when the former commanded larger incomes and higher status. But the early success of the Royal College of Surgeons of Ireland (established in 1784) helped raise the standing of surgery as a profession, and the escalating demand for military surgeons during the wars had encouraged the College's expansion and its move in 1805 to a purpose-built site on St Stephen's Green. By the mid-1830s the number of physicians in the city had doubled, but the 230-odd members and licentiates of the College of Surgeons living in Dublin amounted to almost four times the number of city surgeons back in the 1780s. Most of these had institutional affiliation, whereas physicians for the most part depended on their private clientele. There were four doctors resident in Merrion Square by 1836, but out of the large army of surgeons only Crampton had made it that far.[17]

Philip Crampton is important in another respect: attached for most of his professional career to the Meath Hospital, he was one of the pioneers of a style of bedside clinical teaching that achieved international notice. This technique was elaborated by Robert Graves and William Stokes, both of whom were physicians at the Meath for many years, and by Abraham Colles, the great surgeon in Dr Steevens's Hospital. Altogether a group of fewer than a dozen practitioners achieved fame as teachers, diagnosticians and champions of new medical instruments, not least the stethoscope, and on the strength of their reputation Dublin shifted from its old dependence on universities abroad for medical education (in Scotland, Holland and France) to becoming a centre in its own right. Over the course of their careers, the group had multiple connections with the College of Surgeons, the revamped School of Physic in Trinity, the Meath and Dr Steevens's Hospitals, and with many of the twenty-two other medico-surgical hospitals in the city, most of which were philanthropically funded and nearly all of which were Protestant-run. The extraordinary reputation that they had generated by the 1840s rested in the first instance on their exceptional personal skills of rigorous observation, forensic investigation and a humane patient-centred ethic. But the 'medical ecology' of the city helped too: operating beside the colleges with their formal systems of accreditation were a number of unregulated but highly successful private medical academies offering practical training. Crampton started one of the earliest ones in Dawson Street. And then there was the great array of hospitals within the city, ranging from the publicly funded military infirmary, the fever hospitals and the Lock Hospital for venereal diseases to the voluntary hospitals specialising in everything from diseases of children (Pitt Street) to diseases of the eye and ear (William Wilde's St Mark's hospital), from the old Jervis Street Charitable Infirmary, which catered for 'those who have received fractures and other casualties', to the new Sir Patrick Dun's hospital near Trinity, which was specifically organised to facilitate the teaching of students. Across the British dominions only London exceeded Dublin in such institutional diversity. In 1861 Sir Philip Corrigan estimated that the number of medical students training in Dublin, including those exclusively attached to the hospitals, averaged about a thousand, and that exclusive of the cumulative fees they paid (£15,000), they spent some £85,000 in the city each year. Dublin's international medical reputation had of course required good publicists: young Stokes was publishing on the stethoscope while still a student, and Graves, Stokes and Colles produced classic works on the heart, pulmonary diseases, joint fractures and fever which circulated far outside Ireland, and in some cases went into early translation. This exposure was helped after Robert Graves (with Robert Kane) launched the monthly *Dublin Journal of Medicine and Chemistry* in 1832, which provided an outlet for 'the Dublin school' to develop an international readership.[18]

In 1839 Henry Maunsell, a strongly Tory-minded medic, established the *Dublin Medical Press* and used it to argue that the profession must champion public health and that the 'disgraceful condition' of many parts of the city reflected badly on the medical profession, given their expertise. 'In no country in Europe is the treatment of fever [epidemics] so well understood as in Ireland ...' Graves had claimed in 1835. There had, it is true, been a large philanthropic fever hospital since 1804, located on a three-acre site beside Cork Street, which in the intervening years had admitted over 102,000 patients, and a smaller facility attached to the House of Industry on the north side, but while the symptoms and characteristics of typhus and relapsing fever that invariably appeared in the wake of food scarcity were well known to Dublin medics, the methods of treatment – ranging from blood-letting to cold baths, high-protein meals, fresh air, clean water and simple isolation – had changed very little over the decades. Only in the case of smallpox, which had its own epidemic cycle, was there a promising prophylactic: vaccination had become a standard precaution among most city families since 1800 and the incidence of smallpox had waned markedly. Fever hospitals did, of course, reduce fever mortality by containing those already infected (isolating the fleas and lice that were the main vectors of disease); they were also responsible for improving the general health of patients, overseeing a large-scale programme of whitewashing patients' homes, thereby momentarily improving standards of basic hygiene.

Medical expertise could do little to stem the epidemics of typhus, typhoid and dysentery which periodically overwhelmed poorer neighbourhoods – as in 1817–18, in what was the final act of the post-war crisis, when some 25,000 fever patients were admitted into city institutions over a twelve-month period, many of them recent migrants, and although deaths were held below 5 per cent, several thousands died during this episode. The relative impotence of the medical profession in 1817–18 moved a number of city doctors to advocate a new initiative to take beggars off the streets: following a Munich precedent, a Mendicity Association was set up in Hawkins Street the following year. This involved compiling a voluntary register of all street beggars and then allocating clothes, food and very basic employment as far as funds would allow, in so doing demonstrating the inadequacies of existing state-funded agencies like the House of Industry. Some 2,000 registered beggars were marched through east-side streets one day in September 1818 to shock affluent householders into supporting the 'Mendicity'. It was a successful stunt. In 1825 the Association secured a long lease of Moira House on Usher's Island, which for the next two decades became a daytime magnet for several thousand, mainly female, beggars, about a third of them drawn from outside the city and county. It struggled financially, but did manage to reduce the volume of street-begging – and there was no major fever epidemic during the period (although cholera made its first terrifying visit in 1832).

Then came the highly centralised new Poor Law in 1838 – 'labour, discipline and confinement' – with city and suburbs on the north and south sides becoming two of the 130 Irish Poor Law unions, each with its workhouse and ancillary facilities, with onerous new Poor Law taxes falling on every household. The North Dublin Union absorbed the House of Industry and the string of institutions that had grown up beside it in Grangegorman, and the South Dublin Union incorporated the Foundling Hospital and its large James Street site. This brought about a massive change in the scale of social provision, in governance structures and in financing. It hit voluntary institutions like the Mendicity, for the workhouses were there to tackle the able-bodied destitute, not 'the sick-poor' or the wider effects of a public health crisis. The medical profession was deeply divided over the new arrangements and many resented the increased interference of the state in the regulation and remuneration of medical services, notably when the medical remit of the Poor Law Unions was widened in 1843 to admit the sick poor suffering from fevers. But hospital wings were quickly added to the new workhouses and this increased the city's capacity to ride out another fever crisis.[19]

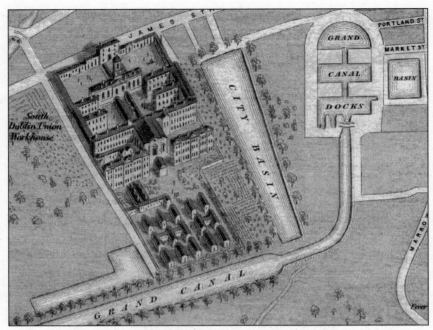

25. *The South Dublin Union Workhouse, the City Basin and Grand
Canal Harbour (detail from D. Edward Heffernan's* Dublin in 1861*).
The monumental south-side workhouse complex close to James Street
weathered the Famine years better than its sister institution north of the
river; several of the buildings shown here had been added since 1847.
Control of the South Dublin Union Workhouse remained in Conservative
hands, and the Union was much criticised by Catholic spokesmen.*

That crisis soon came. City doctors were among the earliest to warn
of the health implications of the new disease that afflicted the potato, the
mainstay of rural diet in autumn 1845, and long before the more serious
potato failure of late summer 1846, Irish government policy was being
advised by a Central Board of Health, where Crampton and Corrigan
were the key members. Indeed, for much of the Famine Corrigan *was* the
Board of Health (and as such was despised by many in the profession for
being too close to government). Against the wider history of government
misreading of the crisis and its ideologically blinkered definition of the
appropriate role of the state, the Dublin medical world was shrill in its
public criticism of Dublin Castle and massively involved in responding
to the five-year crisis. The city was of course fortunate in having a very
well-developed medical infrastructure in place by 1845, and on balance the

existence of two functioning and fairly well-managed workhouses, despite all their rigidities, saved many lives. Yet there was a rapid deterioration of the urban environment in the bitter winter of 1846–7, 'heaps of mud ... for a mile and a half ...' in the old city, as vast numbers of country beggars mingled in the trafffic. The most fortunate factor was the existence of an exit door for those tens of thousands leaving the land and entering the city during the crisis: if access to either British or North American ports had been denied to Famine refugees during the late 1840s, Dublin would have been catastrophically overwhelmed by those seeking institutional protection when their own workhouses became full or simply broke down. As it was, by the later stages of the Famine, an unprecedentedly large proportion of the paupers in city institutions were migrants: in the North Dublin workhouse by the autumn of 1850, 65 per cent of all admissions were non-Dubliners, and in the Mendicity Institute almost four-fifths of the 7,698 beggars passing through its doors in 1849 were strangers to the city.[20]

The practical knowledge accumulated in handling recurrent fever epidemics meant that the city's doctors and the support staff working in the greatly expanded fever hospitals just about coped, despite Treasury penny-pinching. Peak indoor numbers were reached in March 1847 when some 14,700 fever patients were being catered for in the course of that month, the largest facility being the 4,000 emergency beds created in the North Dublin workhouse. While the economic downturn of 1847–8 hit the city very hard, excess mortality in 1847 was probably less than in 1817. The worst came later, when cholera returned with a vengeance in 1849. Its mode of transmission by infected faeces (usually in water) was unknown, but this meant that its impact was puzzlingly uneven. Nevertheless, high case-fatality made it a source of popular panic, and some of this was directed at an uncomprehending medical profession. William Wilde, already the most prodigious scholar in the city's medical community, responded to the crisis by gathering together an extraordinary array of deep historical and contemporary medical data on epidemics and other mortality crises in Ireland, and this appeared as a supplementary volume to the 1851 census. Ignored at the time, it remains a remarkable social document.[21]

☙

John Gamble, the retired army surgeon, had remarked of the city in 1811 that 'the professors of law and medicine may [now] be said to form the aristocracy of the place'. A little premature perhaps, but he was right in placing lawyers ahead of the medics in the ascent to social primacy. A century later, in 1915, Stephen Gwynn reckoned 'Dublin has been and is more a city of lawyers ... than anything else'. Since the late eighteenth century, Dublin's abundant population of lawyers had continued to grow, albeit less dramatically than was the case for medicine, but with just over 2,000 practising lawyers in the city in the 1830s, a quarter of them barristers, they were a truly formidable presence. In the north-east quarter of the city there were nearly 900 solicitors (and despite the upstream location of the Four Courts there were almost no lawyers resident in the western half of the city). Barristers with their far higher fees made a stronger showing in the south-east of town, and more than a quarter of those who had taken silk were settled in Merrion Square by 1836.[22]

As with medicine, the professional formation of Dublin lawyers now took place within the country, and although the requirement on prospective barristers to 'keep terms' at one of the Inns of Court in London remained in place until 1885, it had become a formality long before that. Legal education was still essentially an apprenticeship in solicitor's offices, or in the Bar Library and the courts. Both branches of the law developed tight self-regulation, the Benchers (prodded by FitzGibbon) formalising governance of the Bar in 1793, the solicitors with the Law Society in 1830. And even though they took nearly forty years to complete, the striking cluster of buildings at the top of Constitution Hill that formed the new King's Inns made a very strong statement as to the clubbish affluence of the Bar. One maverick barrister, Tristram Kennedy, made a serious attempt to create a legal training academy within the Inns in 1839 (the Dublin Law Institute), and although it foundered after a few years, it pointed the way for the professionalisation of legal education. Numbers entering the two branches of the profession had grown strongly after the wars and peaked in the 1830s, after which there was no long-term growth. Despite a shared common-law system with England and Wales, the Dublin legal world was relatively inward-looking, its leading practitioners home-bred and its entry levels restricted. Those who sought a professional career in the world outside almost never returned. The other side of the coin was the intimate link between the Bar and parliamentary politics: until the mid-1880s there was a strikingly high proportion of Irish MPs, Protestant and Catholic, who had had a legal training, and the Four Courts remained a hothouse of party political division. But even a century after O'Connell had been

called to the Bar in 1798, the higher branches of the law remained disproportionately Protestant, a distinct world with a strong sense of its own
identity. This was much less the case in medicine, which was also more
cosmopolitan. Medics at the top had almost invariably picked up international experience early in their careers; they were aware of international
advances in their field, and an increasing proportion of those they taught
were destined to emigrate. Hardly any Dublin medics of this era entered
politics.[23]

This concentration of professional expertise in Dublin remained one
of the really powerful magnets drawing the well-to-do of provincial Ireland back to the city. And it was a two-way movement, notably with the
law: barristers surged out twice a year on circuit, while at least an eighth
of all Dublin solicitors also had a provincial address, some now specialising in estate management for large and distant proprietors, others as
national agents for cross-channel insurance companies. Peirce and David
Mahony, a legal partnership based for many years in Dame Street, have
some claim to be regarded as the first corporate lawyers in the city: from
a Protestant Kerry/Limerick gentry background, the brothers were the
registered Dublin solicitors for about ten public companies in the 1830s
– in life assurance, water, gas, mining and banking. Peirce, 'a self-taught
man', had been directly involved in drafting the 1825 banking legislation (6
Geo. IV, c. 42) which opened up joint-stock competition with the Bank of
Ireland, and was then a key figure in the launch of the Provincial Bank of
Ireland. With a large shareholder register and a preponderance of English
subscribers, the Provincial was the first company to develop Irish branch
banking, and although legally based in London to avoid infringing the
Bank of Ireland's fifty-mile monopoly, its shadow presence in Dublin was
overseen by the ever-resourceful Mahony. Despite his commitment to the
Provincial, he was deeply involved with dissidents in the Hibernian Bank
(founded in 1824), and represented some of the disgruntled shareholders
in the ill-fated Agricultural and Commercial Bank a decade later. With
his reputation as a skilled draughtsman, Mahony was parliamentary agent
for the Catholic Association in 1829 at the inception of Emancipation and
helped the first Irish railway promoters through the tortuous hoops to
secure enabling legislation in Westminster – the Dublin and Kingstown
Railway (for which he was solicitor), and shortly afterwards the Dublin and Drogheda Railway. Not unconnected with this, he became one
of the original residents of Gresham Terrace overlooking the harbour in

Kingstown (although he still kept his house in Merrion Square and a country home on the family estate in Kerry). In politics, Mahony was a Whig/Liberal, an ally after 1832 of O'Connell, and a strong supporter of 'reform'. The social world in which he moved was politically liberal and religiously mixed, best reflected in the make-up of the St Stephen's Green Club that he helped found in 1840. His obituarist noted how his home had 'for many years [been] ... the Holland House for the Irish Whigs'.[24]

The Mahonys' choice of the east end of Dame Street for their office in the 1830s was logical. The quarter-mile corridor running from Fownes Street eastwards to the College had become the city's central business district to the exclusion of all rivals. The process started when a group of merchants (led by Ouzel Galley members) raised £20,000 in 1796 to construct a quadrangular block on a site just west of Daly's Club. The aim was to create a convenient commodity trading centre with an abundance of offices for hire, the model being the (much larger) Linen Hall, and it amounted to a rejection of the Royal Exchange – being too public, too far west, too inflexible. With a coffee shop and facilities for a stock exchange, the 'Commercial Buildings' were an immediate financial success after 1799, and they long remained a hive of activity. Three years later the Bank of Ireland decided to purchase the Parliament House nearby (for £40,000), completing the move in 1808 after Johnston's structural modifications. The presence of the Bank set the seal on the neighbourhood, its pre-eminence and privileged financial status only strengthening during the following decades. By the mid-1830s more than a third of businesses in the eastern half of Dame Street and on College Green were 'new' – notaries and stockbrokers, life and fire insurance agents, or solicitors – reflecting the make-up of business conducted within the Commercial Buildings. The older types of trade – bookshops and high-end retail warehouses – were still there, but their numbers were contracting. However, located between College Green and Suffolk Street on the site of the old post office was Home's Royal Arcade, opened c.1819. Many of the early tenants of this novel venture were women – offering millinery goods, perfumes and fancy goods – but there was also military ware and an archery warehouse. Everything was on sale at a fixed price and most were imported goods.[25]

However, the Arcade, its ballroom, bazaar and card-rooms, its picture gallery and pocket theatre, were short-lived, all destroyed in a spectacular fire in 1837, but it was a harbinger of retailing to come. For in the wake of Anglo-Irish free trade, the revolution in cross-channel transport and new forms of commercial banking, the general wholesale merchant dealing in bulk all but vanished from the scene within a generation. The commanding heights of Dublin business came to be occupied by families whose wealth was a hybrid of new-style commercial and capital-intensive manufacturing activity, ranging from shipping, brewing, textiles, banking and building to the development of retail 'monster-houses'. Old money, where it had not been lost or completely sunk in property, was finding new outlets: there was the pronounced growth (as elsewhere) in 'blind capitalism', the rise of portfolio investment in shares at home and abroad and in government bonds. The Dublin Stock Exchange, informally established in 1793 and given statutory authority in 1799, thrived initially as a market for government debt, but had also traded in canal stock, Wide Streets, Ballast Office and other Corporation debentures, and then in the 1820s in mine, steam-packet, insurance and town-gas stocks. It weathered corporate bankruptcies – the Royal Canal Company in 1812, the St Patrick Assurance Company in 1829 and the two dozen-odd stockbrokers were a tight self-regulating group. But in 1845 the sudden widening of public interest in stocks and shares, fed by railway speculation, led to the opening of no less than three rival stock exchanges and some seventy unlicensed brokers advertising their services. The rival exchanges failed, but some of those involved challenged the official stock exchange's restrictions on professional entry, and from 1849 the government assumed responsibility for licensing new entrants to the exchange, thus breaking the golden circle. However, the real significance of this flurry of activity that erupted on the eve of the Famine crisis was its confirmation of the existence of a fairly large body of local cash-rich investors who were not risk averse. They were even more in evidence in the 1850s, when sights were increasingly set on investment opportunities outside the country.[26]

The Dublin Chamber of Commerce, riven by political tensions at the beginning of the century, had been revived in 1820. Its committee was solidly conservative, with a heavy imprint of the La Touche, Guinness and Crosthwaite families until the 1880s. Liberal, Catholic and dissenter businesses were always represented, however, and the make-up of the Chamber mirrored the evolving character of 'big commerce' in the city. Among its members in the 1830s were still a few European and inter-continental traders, dealing with New York and Quebec (the thriving timber and emigrant trades), Jamaica and Barbados, France and the Mediterranean and, after the relaxation of the East India Company monopoly in 1834, trading in

26. Foster Place was epicentre of the Victorian business district, the Bank of Ireland dominating one side, the Royal the other. Established in 1836, the Royal functioned as the bank for city business, its clients mainly Protestant and its early shareholders including many Quakers. It enjoyed close links with the railway and steamship companies, and was heavily involved in financing the cross-channel cattle trade.

Asian waters as far as Canton. But these firms were increasingly dependent on the services of local shipbrokers, for the 'merchant house' with its complement of ocean-going vessels was a thing of the past. Even in the 1830s the greater part of the city's external commerce was routed through Liverpool, and to a lesser extent through Glasgow and London, and this pattern only intensified later in the century (despite the far greater deep-sea capacity of the port). By the late 1860s the old trading links with the Caribbean and the newer ones with East Asia had disappeared. By then, about a third of the committee of twenty-five in the Chamber were large-scale industrialists (distillers, brewers, textile manufacturers, paper- and coach-makers), a third involved in foreign trade (with an emphasis on the import trades in timber, wine and tea), and the rest had a more local focus. Thomas Pim and later Frederic Pim were unusual in representing both manufacturing and maritime trade, with the family's great mills in Greenmount and their poplin works in Love Lane thriving, a wholesale and retail drapery warehouse in South Great George's Street, a leather warehouse in Drury Lane, a flour mill in the Grand Canal docks, and several of their vessels still trading to New York and beyond. But, the Pims apart, these latterday long-distance traders were far less important in the city's economic life than the wealthy families outside the Chamber who were engaged in financial services, in the higher professions and in the new transport companies.[27]

A decade after steam had revolutionised cross-channel trade, steam came ashore. In 1825, following excitements in England, there was a flurry of local interest in developing a steam-powered railway service between the city and Kingstown. James Pim Junior has traditionally been credited as midwife of this idea, but he was not involved at first. The son of a brewer and miller and cousin to the owners of the Greenmount mills, he first came to notice as a Dame Street stockbroker in the early 1820s, a time of hectic financial innovation in which his Quaker co-religionists featured prominently. In addition to the first attempts at joint-stock banking, these years saw the launch of a succession of Dublin-based insurance companies designed to compete with English companies for Irish fire, life and marine business: new skills were acquired, fortunes made and lost, and lessons learnt. Pim and his father were centrally involved in the Patriotic Assurance Company (set up in 1824); a little later he was active in the Grand Canal Company, building a financial stake and championing plans for a ship canal to run from the Grand Canal docks across to Kingstown harbour. Others supported this enticing project, but Pim switched his enthusiasm to the idea of a railway link instead, with the freight potential the principal consideration. He financed a survey to determine the optimum route and became a steady champion of the proposal – despite some full-blooded opposition. It helped that the prototype in everyone's mind, the Liverpool and Manchester Railway which opened in 1830, was commercially successful from the beginning, even though it was seven times the length of the proposed line to Kingstown and technically a far more challenging construction project.

Pim was lucky to recruit able allies – George Vignoles as surveyor (he had worked on the Lancashire railway), Mahony as legal adviser, and William Dargan (Telford's understudy on many road projects) as main contractor – and he also secured the full backing of the Grand Canal Company. As with steam-packet funding in the 1820s, over 90 per cent of the initial capital subscribed for the Kingstown railway was local and commercial, two-fifths of this being Quaker money. In contrast to the

27. *The promoters of the Dublin and Kingstown Railway chose a direct route from the city to Kingstown, and in so doing they had to build several long embarkments close to the high tide mark, as here beside Booterstown. It was a risk, but despite the rush to complete the line on time the foundations proved sufficient to weather winter storms.*

shipping companies, much of the physical infrastructure and some of the rolling stock was sourced locally. Part-funded by a government loan, the company spent £106,000 on construction and rolling stock. Managing the cash-flow in such a huge undertaking was not the least of Pim's achievements. It took some 2,000 men working for more than two years – in the quarries, the workshops and along the route – to create the five-mile line running from Westland Row through the low-lying Pembroke estate and the old brickfields of Sandymount, along the foreshore of the Bay, to the new asylum harbour, and despite very costly compensation battles with seafront residents in Blackrock, it was completed on time. Spectators applauded the first trains.[28]

This was almost two years ahead of London's first suburban railway to Greenwich, but the first engine-drivers on the Kingstown line were all English (they were all locals by 1841). Long before regular services began in December 1834, Pim and his backers realised that profit lay with sub-urban passengers, not with freight. A string of established villages and set-tlements along the coast from Booterstown to Dalkey had been gaining population since the wars, some of the residents seasonal, most permanent, and the proliferating villa population was far outnumbered by working families employed in the quarries and in construction projects, in the tav-erns and in domestic service. But it was a surge in the number of well-to-do residents and speculative investors in the Kingstown and Monkstown district that brought about the establishment in 1834 of a new township board, a body with limited powers of taxation over Kingstown residents. It established a precedent for the cluster of satellite townships that were created around the outer city area over the next forty-four years. One of those Kingstown speculators was Thomas Gresham, fresh from making a success of his hotel in Upper Sackville Street. He built the first terrace in the new town: nine four-storey houses with flat-roofed viewing prom-enades looking out over the harbour, neatly aligned with the nearby Hayes Royal Hotel which had been completed in 1828, its twelve-bay frontage 'like a range of lofty private houses'. Gresham was a major advocate for the new township.[29]

Pim's second achievement was in developing a train service and a fare structure that captured existing traffic from the road and also created new demand. Daily passenger numbers continued to climb during his steward-ship, doubling between 1840 and 1846 by which time it was carrying nearly 6,500 passengers per day with a half-hourly service from 6 a.m. to 11.30 p.m. Six per cent of the passengers were first-class travellers, 55 per cent second-class; and artisan and workmen on the third-class were encouraged to travel before 7 a.m. when the fare was halved. Traffic declined during the Famine years, and Pim's response was to cut fares. Record traffic in 1849 was the result. He stayed in charge of the company for two decades, and none of the other railway projects around Dublin matched his record for profitability or stable management. Admittedly, in adopting an untried 'atmospheric' technology for the short extension from Kingstown to Dalkey in 1844, Pim allowed his technical fascination in exotic engineering solutions to get the better of his business judgement, but it did not harm the company.[30]

After the early success of the Kingstown line and the speculative bubble in railway projects in 1836–7, a parliamentary inquiry (the Drum-mond Commission) was held to determine the optimal shape for a trunk network for Ireland and the form that state support should take to secure an orderly development of such a system. The inquiry generated fascinating information on existing traffic flows across the country, illuminating Dublin's trade hinterland in graphic form; it made sensible suggestions as to trunk routes and advocated massive state involvement to achieve such an outcome. But by the time of the next speculative wave in 1843–5 the report had been shelved, and state involvement was minimal during the seminal years when the trunk system actually took shape, government's role being restricted to the provision of the type of commercial loans that had helped the Dublin and Kingstown Railway get off the ground.[31]

By the time of Pim's death in 1856 there were four other railway termini in the city, all of them geared to capture long-distance traffic from the coaching services and the canals. Where Pim's city terminus was tucked neatly into the streetscape and overlooked by the new St Andrew's church, the other termini (taking their cue from English fashion) exhibited varying degrees of magnificence.[32] The Dublin and Drogheda, authorised in 1836, secured land on the North Strand not far from the Custom House, on which it constructed a high-level Italianate terminus in Amiens Street. Joseph Lee has shown that Lancashire capital was as important as Irish in the company's funding (more than a third of its early directors were Manchester men), and although there was the possibility of some commuter traffic (from Clontarf and Malahide), it was the potential commercial benefits for the port of Drogheda that were uppermost in promoters' minds. It opened in 1844, and although it triggered some suburban development (notably by James Fagan, a timber-merchant from Bridgefoot Street, who speculated heavily in houses and hotels in Malahide), the company singularly failed to copy Pim's success. But there seemed little prospect of extending this railway across the Boyne gorge at Drogheda, so other plans for a Dublin–Belfast route through Meath and Armagh secured parliamentary approval in 1844. That was one of Peirce Mahony's pet projects (after he had fallen out with the Drogheda company), but it stalled. He was also a leading advocate in the 1830s for a trunk railroad from Dublin to Munster, specifically to an Atlantic steam-packet base to be created in the far south-west. But a less ambitious project for a trunk line into the south Midlands eventually got off the ground, despite vigorous opposition from the Grand Canal. Once again English capital was critical, and the Great Southern and Western Railway (GSWR), launched in 1843, drew heavily on the London and Birmingham Company, both as a business model and as a source of outside directors. However, its first chairman was Peter Purcell, the veteran Irish mail-coach contractor who adopted a cautious approach to investment. It was only after English directors joined the board and the great paper manufacturer, Edward McDonnell, became chairman that the legal, financial and engineering problems of a direct route to Cork were overcome. The 165-mile railway was opened in 1849. Almost two-thirds of the initial capital was English, but by the 1850s this had been completely reversed in favour of Irish shareholders.[33]

The GSWR attracted sixty-five entries in the competition to design a terminus building on the western edge of the city, upstream of the new King's Bridge. The winning design by a young London architect, Sancton Wood, was a superbly disciplined classical palazzo, its glass-roofed interior drawing comparisons with the Crystal Palace. Location so far to the west avoided the development costs of running a line through the city, but in choosing such a site the company signalled the complete unimportance of potential commuter traffic. By contrast, the fourth enterprise, the Great Western (Ireland) Railway, was rooted in the city; the project was for a trunk line via Mullingar to the Shannon at Athlone, and to avoid a fight with vested interests the company bought out the Royal Canal Company in 1845. By acquiring the latter's property it secured a superb location for a railway terminus on Constitution Hill, beside the Royal Canal harbour. The Egyptian-inspired acropolis on the hill, completed in 1852, was arguably the most striking commercial addition to the city's architecture, but the Midland Great Western Company (MGWR), its final name, lacked the dynamism of its southern competitor. Its directors were reluctant to extend beyond the Shannon and only drove a trunk line across to Galway to spike the GSWR. Their failure to get the go-ahead for a new street from the river up to Constitution Hill was symptomatic.[34] The fifth terminus, at the south end of Harcourt Street, was for a railway to run towards Wexford, taking an inland route across south Dublin to Bray – what became the Dublin, Wicklow and Wexford Railway (and, much later, the Dublin and South-Eastern). There was no commuter potential along this route until the end of the century, and beyond Bray (reached in 1854) there were severe engineering problems; Wexford was not reached until 1872. The company agreed to lease the Kingstown line, a deal which the Kingstown directors tried to wriggle out of, but after much bitterness it was implemented in 1856, and a costly track was constructed around Dalkey Hill to link Pim's railway with the 'Harcourt Street line' north of Bray. Here, as elsewhere, English capital and expertise were necessary but not sufficient elements, for Dublin capital was crucial in all Dublin-based schemes. To a lesser extent Dublin money was poured into Munster-based railway projects, but not, it seems, Ulster ones.[35]

Much of the success of the city's first railway rested on developing a fare structure that would induce regular recreational travel from the city to the sea. But if the 'shopocracy' of the city were now willing and able to enjoy the parks, sea-baths and promenades, the first commissioners of Kingstown township wished to preserve their town as an enclave of fashion and respectability, playing on its associations with Admiralty and royalty. Two yacht clubs, the Royal St George and Royal Irish, built neoclassical club-houses within the harbour area in the 1840s. And even if very few of their members actually lived within the district, the summer regattas became a new element in the upper-class social calendar. Freehold ownership of the township was shared by two major Irish landed families, the de Vescis and the Pakenhams, earls of Longford, but the land with the most potential had been demised on long leases at the beginning of the nineteenth century, with the result that

> no system whatever has been observed in laying out the town so that it has an irregular, republican air of dirt and independence, no man heeding his neighbour's pleasure, and uncouth structures in absurd situations offending the eye at every turn.

Indeed, the physical development along the whole coast from Blackrock to Dalkey was carried out almost entirely by building speculators, many of whom came from the city. Once they became resident themselves, they dominated the boards of the townships as these came into existence. They made little of the fact that many of the earliest residents were poor: in the 1860s, upwards of a third of Kingstown householders resided in teeming courts and lanes, 'unlighted, unpaved and undrained', ideal for the spread of cholera and much else.

The largest single speculative development in the new suburbs was in Monkstown, just above the original terminus of the Kingstown railway: Longford Terrace. This consisted of two towering sets of four-storeyed houses over basements, twenty-five in all, which were erected between 1842 and 1856. Early residents included the Inspector-General of the Irish Constabulary, half a dozen high-status professionals (stockbrokers, barristers, solicitors and a banker), scattered among dowagers and half-pay officers. But the developer himself was Thomas Bradley, a timber merchant from Golden Lane in St Bride's parish (he was also very active on the Pembroke estate). To Longford Terrace he attracted other men whose money had been made in the old city, as well as a maltster and a bacon merchant from the Liberties and Henry Roe of the Thomas Street distillery.[36]

The early powers of Kingstown Township were modest. The first suburb to secure full control over local taxes lay much closer to the city, in the rural part of St Peter's parish which lay due south of the city and beyond the Grand Canal, and which became known (misleadingly) as Rathmines township. As in Kingstown, the ground landlords, in this case the earls of Meath, had leased out most of the land in large blocs decades earlier (mainly in the eighteenth century), principally for villas and demesnes, and therefore they played almost no role in the intense nineteenth-century development of the area. It comprised the old villages of Ranelagh, Cullenswood, Rathmines and Milltown, which in 1821 had a combined population of less than 400. But that was on the eve of a veritable flood of development – along Ranelagh Road and its offshoots (notably Mount Pleasant Square where Terence Dolan, an enterprising glover from Pill Lane, built sixty-two modestly proportioned houses between c.1808 and 1832), and up the Rathmines Road, which became 'one continuous line of elegant buildings, upwards of a mile and half in length, intersected by numerous terraces, with detached villas'. The combined population of these 'villages' had grown more than sixteen-fold by 1841, and reached 11,259 by 1861. For some of the new suburbanites it was an escape from high city taxes, for others a retreat to a healthier airy environment. Nevertheless, lying beyond the city boundary and the reach of the Paving Board, the area became notorious for its muddy roads and erratic water supply. The threat in 1844 that the city would secure statutory powers to impose a water tax across these southern suburbs and be allowed to assert its monopoly in the supply of water galvanised the south-siders to petition successfully against the measure.[37]

After a robust government inquiry in 1847, the case for Rathmines opting out of Co. Dublin grand jury control was conceded and, despite resolute opposition from the Corporation and benign neutrality from Dublin Castle, specific legislation permitting the formation of a Rathmines local authority was passed in Westminster, creating what became the most enduring and combative of the suburban townships.[38] The leading figure here was the English-born Frederick Stokes. He had made his name as a forceful Dame Street commodity broker, steamship director and insurance agent, and had become an early resident of Leinster Road, soon to be one of the finest avenues in Rathmines. For some years he ran one of the two companies offering a horse-drawn 'omnibus' service between the city, Rathmines and Rathgar (although he was not the first to do so, as an omnibus service had been introduced between Dame Street and Rathgar in the mid-1830s). Stokes became chairman of Rathmines township for twenty years and, like many of his colleagues, was an active property developer himself (in his case, on its eastern edges in the Leeson Park area). The commissioners justified their existence on the grounds of efficiency, lower taxes and an absence of political jobbery, always painting a lurid contrast with the deficiencies of Dublin Corporation and of the world within the canals. As Mary Daly has observed, 'the commissioners operated in a manner akin to the directors of a private company with large shareholders – i.e. property owners – being co-opted and commercial profit, symbolised by a rising valuation, an active building programme and few unoccupied houses being the principal ambitions'. There was an unspoken agenda to protect and develop the new Rathmines as a set of linked neighbourhoods that would be socially more homogenous and more 'respectable' than the city, but low rates meant a cut-price and defective water supply from the Grand Canal Company right up until 1877, the year that Stokes stood down.[39]

It was a different story further east in the suburban parts of the Fitzwilliam estate. Here a great swathe of territory lying between the Donnybrook Road and the sea had formed part of the historic city area until 1840 when, as part of municipal reform, boundaries were redefined and the area outside the canal 'was ... thrown out of the city'. The old village of Ballsbridge lay at the centre of this district, and at one point the Rathmines commissioners were hoping to 'capture' it. Nothing came of that and, somewhat hesitantly, the 'Pembroke' district secured independent township status in 1863. In contrast to Rathmines, there was a pre-eminent ground landlord and a long history of prudent leasing. After the Fitzwilliam estate had passed in 1816 from the unmarried seventh viscount to the very wealthy eleventh earl of Pembroke, there was little pressure on the estate's agents to promote new development. In 1837 the estate financed the long strand road creating a coastal rim for Sandymount, but speculative development was not it seems encouraged. Even the opening of the Kingstown railway which was permitted to carve its tracks through the estate was not exploited. However, Upper Leeson Street and the massive houses on Pembroke Road were built in the 1830s, Waterloo, Wellington Road and Lansdowne Roads in the 1840s, all with very generous frontages, ample street width and deep back gardens. But this was a response to speculative interest, not a worked-out estate policy. It was only with the appointment of John Vernon as agent in 1853 that the estate became proactive again and, even though he resisted the creation of a Pembroke township, Vernon (and his son after him) dominated its proceedings for decades. Between 1863 and 1879 the estate laid out more than ten major roads in the Ballsbridge and Donnybrook districts and installed some twenty-two miles of mains waterpipes, thereby facilitating a fairly steady programme of house-building and the growth of high net-worth tenants. The town commissioners themselves were in many cases the builders of these very large houses. The most successful such developer was Michael Meade, diversifying from his wholesale timber business in the city. He was the first to see the potential of the mile-long Ailesbury Road in the 1860s, running from Sydney Parade station on the Kingstown line up to Donnybrook, and he built an Italianate palace for his own family at a strategic intersection (latterly St Michael's College). He claimed that by 1879 he had laid out £30,000 in property development within the Pembroke township over the previous dozen years, and for the most part he retained ownership of the large properties that he developed (his son and heir James owned over 120 houses in the city and suburbs at the time of his death in 1900).[40]

The earls of Pembroke were a distant and ethereal influence, rarely visiting their Dublin property, the impact of their vast wealth being restricted to improvements in the estate's infrastructure. But there were two Dubliners of this era who did seek to use great wealth for a wider social purpose. One was William Dargan, the largest railway contractor in the country and dominant shareholder in the Wicklow and Wexford railway. By the 1850s he had a towering reputation as a resourceful but humane entrepreneur, employing several tens of thousands on railway and reclamation projects across the country. Like Pim before him, he recognised the creative possibilities of the transport revolution and invested heavily (too heavily) in property development and recreational facilities in Bray and in hotel development in Kingstown.[41]

He decided to underwrite single-handedly the cost of an industrial exhibition in Dublin that would build on the success of the extraordinary London event of 1851, and his action was lauded as a rare case of patriotic altruism. His belief in the untapped economic potential of the country to industrialise despite the appalling social crisis through which it had just passed was quite widely shared, but it was his credit-line that made things happen. The Dublin Exhibition of 1853 was organised by his confidantes and ran for nearly six months on the grounds of the (now Royal) Dublin Society (RDS), filling the great lawn that faced Merrion Square. Dargan was almost unique among his contemporaries in keeping his political opinions and religious beliefs entirely private, and his emollient ambiguity helped protect the exhibition from political controversy. The end result was spectacular (even if there was no palace of crystal), but it was poorly organised and its failure to stir up the anticipated level of international interest among exhibitors was telling evidence of just how marginal Dublin and, by extension, Ireland were now seen to be in the new international order. Admittedly it had to compete for attention with New York's better financed 'world fair'. But in the five specially constructed exhibition halls, Irish handicraft goods (lace, poplin and fine furniture), imported consumer goods (clocks, musical instruments and small arms), labour-saving devices (sewing machines and lathes), and steam-powered processes (printing presses and power looms) were all on public display, most of them startlingly new, and they competed with old masters and antiquities from the RDS and the Royal Irish Academy, and with official national exhibitions from a number of European countries. The French made the strongest impact, but there was great public interest in the display of Oriental arts and crafts, notably the Japanese exhibit provided by the Dutch government. But too much space and too little planning diluted the educational impact of it all. Admission prices were pitched too high and it was only in the final weeks (after prices had been slashed) that it was filled to near-capacity, helped by a royal visit midway through the event. The final cost to Dargan may have been no more than £18,000, partially recouped by additional traffic receipts on the railways in which he had an interest. But he was greatly feted for his sponsorship, exemplified by Queen Victoria's decision to visit his home at Mount Anville, his Italianate villa overlooking the city.[42]

The public legacy of the exhibition was the creation of a permanent home for the art exhibits, something that would not be exclusively controlled by the patrician RDS. Initial monies for this came as a tribute fund raised to acknowledge Dargan's achievement. It took more than a decade of lobbying and argument to realise the idea, but the 'National

Gallery' finally opened beside Leinster House lawn in 1864. More intangibly, the cornucopia on display at the exhibition and witnessed by its million or more visitors affected consumer tastes for novelty and exotica. The involvement of some of the city's textile warehouses and 'department stores' was not without the expectation of significant new business and, unlike the Great Exhibition, where male visitors formed the majority, women outnumbered men in Dublin by nearly two to one – to the organisers' surprise.[43]

Dargan's wealth, never as great as it appeared, was in serious decline by the time of the next Dublin exhibition in 1865. The focus on that occasion was more specifically the promotion of industry. The location was different – the Winter Gardens, south of St Stephen's Green – and the sponsor, Benjamin Lee Guinness, unashamedly the city's wealthiest man of business. Grandson of the original Arthur Guinness, he had taken effective control of the James Street firm from his father, Arthur Junior, in 1840 and oversaw its transformation from being the largest city brewery to the largest porter brewery in the world by the time of his death in 1868. In the mid-1850s Guinness had sold the family's private residence in Thomas Street and purchased on the south side of St Stephen's Green first one, then a second, townhouse, the former being one of Richard Castle's masterpieces. Guinness transformed the two houses into the kind of opulent Victorian palace not otherwise seen in the city, and it became the family's winter base. The motivation was at least in part to facilitate his greater involvement in city affairs. Always shy of politics while his father was alive, he made up for it in his sixties, running successfully as a Conservative candidate in the city election of 1865. This coincided with the planned exhibition, to be housed on the expansive site behind his property. He was a major shareholder in the company established in 1863 to provide there a permanent 'exhibition palace' for the arts and manufactures; it was to contain an elaborate assembly hall with concert rooms and galleries, which would open out into a gas-lit 'crystal palace' at the rear. This was duly built on the site fronting onto Earlsfort Terrace. The subsequent exhibition was deemed a great success (although attendance at 725,000 was down on 1853) but, as with the Merrion Square event, the sumptuous buildings and low level of follow-up activities forced the company into liquidation. Benjamin Lee's son, Sir Arthur, bought back the fifteen-acre site, but he leased it out for a third and less ambitious exhibition in 1872.[44]

A more enduring display of Guinness wealth was in relation to the

Church of Ireland and St Patrick's Cathedral. The palpable decline in the political leverage and financial health of Anglicanism in Ireland was evident from the 1830s, and Archbishop Magee's ambitions for a second Reformation back in 1822 were replaced by the 1860s by a defensive determination to protect its established status at all costs, whether from English Liberals or Irish nationalists. One dimension of this resolve was the effort to elaborate on Archbishop Ussher's old contention that the Church of Ireland, not the Roman Church, was the authentic heir of early Christianity in Ireland and to create a more rigorous historiography of the Patrician era. This was led by churchmen, many of them linked to Trinity College, notably James Todd (who published the first modern biography of St Patrick in 1864) and William Reeves. Such historical claims stood uneasily beside the utter dilapidation and neglect of the city's extra-diocesan cathedral, with its pre-Norman associations and its dedication to the patron saint, mouldering in a quarter of the city where the Church of Ireland numbers had shrunk most rapidly. With talk of disestablishment in the air, there was no prospect of major state support for its repair. But then Benjamin Lee Guinness came to the rescue in 1860, undertaking to restore St Patrick's to its medieval magnificence. During the next three years, he spent over £110,000 on a building programme that he personally directed, the object being to restore 'our national cathedral'. Along the way he encountered strident protests from professional architects at some of his more muscular decisions, but this did not distract him.[45]

A decade later, the owner of the leading south-side distillery, Henry Roe, came to the rescue of Christ Church Cathedral. However, he stood back and allowed the leading English architect George Edmund Street to restore the city's principal church with ingenuity and, for the most part, with architectural sensitivity. He also underwrote the commission to erect a national Synod Hall as a meeting place for the by then disestablished church on the adjacent site of St Michael's church, complete with a 'bridge of sighs' linking it to the cathedral. But the Roes overreached themselves, and this transcendent gift to the Church of Ireland, which eventually amounted to £220,000, destroyed the Roes' business.[46]

John Beresford's nephew, Lord John Beresford, archbishop of Armagh since 1822, had engaged in a similar gesture two decades earlier in funding the restoration of Armagh Cathedral; as chancellor of the University of Dublin, in 1851 he paid for the rebuilding of the great campanile located at the centre of the College's now fully open Front Square, its sculpture binding classical and Christian motifs, highly appropriate for an institution that was educating virtually all the Church of Ireland clergy. Indeed, those preparing for ordination (undergraduates and graduates) may at that point have accounted for almost half of all students on the books of Trinity. Seated figures, representing Law, Medicine and Science, cohabit the bell-tower with Divinity, but in reality they were junior partners in an institution where most fellows of the body corporate were still required to be ordained clergy. But another building project contemporaneous with the campanile was very different: the Museum Building. Taking the form of a Venetian palace in the Park, it was radical both in design and in purpose, which was to house the College Museum and the emerging applied sciences – civil engineering, chemistry and geology. The new disciplines shared at least one feature with Divinity: the growing expectation that most of their graduates would emigrate, whether they were ordinands, engineers or doctors. As the Rev. Samuel Haughton, professor of Geology, observed in 1868, university education had now become

> a necessity imposed upon the sons of the less wealthy middle class. The openings in life for young men of this class in Ireland are so very limited, that they must either emigrate, or rely on their talents and education, in pushing their way in the learned professions in England and the colonies.

The Museum Building was opened in 1857, the same year as David Livingstone helped the Royal Dublin Society launch its Natural History Museum on the edge of Merrion Square. At that point, both Trinity and the RDS, together with the Royal Irish Academy and the associated teaching hospitals, were enjoying an unprecedented level of international scholarly recognition, thanks to the presence of a coterie of outstanding and productive scholars across a range of disciplines. But the irony here was that the overwhelmingly Protestant character of these institutions was beginning to make them seem anomalous in an increasingly Catholic city. Admittedly, the sons of many prominent city Catholics, including two of Daniel O'Connell's, attended the university, and it was from among its graduates that some of the most radical critiques of contemporary politics emerged (notably the Young Ireland circle around Thomas Davis in the early 1840s). Therefore the decision in the 1860s to erect seated statues outside the Front Gate to two long-dead alumni, Oliver Goldsmith and

Edmund Burke, was shrewdly ambiguous, 'the best emblems the University could have chosen, the best sign board for the hostel' (but the sheer quality of John Henry Foley's craftmanship helped too). However, a real disjuncture had by then emerged between the university as a venerable civic institution, and its original sponsor and landlord, Dublin Corporation, where the political tables had been turned.[47]

Shopocracy

The great remodelling of Dublin Corporation spanned decades, but within that long process were two periods of acute crisis and dramatic institutional change, the first between 1835 and 1840, the second between 1847 and 1851. Seen in a fifty-year perspective, we can discern the slow ascent of a predominantly Catholic 'shopocracy' of publicans, small traders and retail merchants to the commanding heights of city government, but it was a strange journey. Between the 1790s and the 1820s the old Corporation had relished its role as national champion of the Protestant constitution and of chartered rights, during which time it had enjoyed an easy relationship with post-Union governments until its unabashed partisanship became more flagrant on the eve of emancipation. There were, it is true, rare occasions when the Lord Mayor and the Catholic archbishop could share the same platform, as at the annual meetings of the Mendicity Association, but even these were a little tense.[48]

By the 1830s, with the Whigs in power most of the time and a reform agenda in the Castle, the relationship between Corporation and Castle became far more fraught. The 'corporators' fought a rearguard battle to save the Corporation as a Protestant guild-based institution from a Whig government and its Irish allies, who seemed determined to push through political reform in every borough and to sweep away corporate privilege. The abolition of the city's archaic constitution based on the privileges of civic freedom became increasingly likely in the course of the decade, especially after 1835 when radical legislation to rationalise and remodel English urban government was passed in Westminster, with only the city of London, the old square mile, remaining untouched. Dublin Corporation lacked similar leverage to demand an equivalent exemption, but its defenders seem to have believed that its antiquity and inherited prestige would be sufficient to save it and that the House of Lords would block reform. Tory opposition in the upper house did indeed kill off a series of Irish municipal reform bills. Some hoped that the Whig administration would soon fall and be replaced by a Tory/ Conservative administration that would quickly abandon reform. But as others sought compromise, the champions of the old Corporation played the religious card in desperation, warning of the fatal dangers of giving control of Irish towns and cities to O'Connell's allies and thereby collapsing the Protestant interest.[49]

As Jacqueline Hill has shown, public opinion in the city became acutely polarised during this period of prolonged political uncertainty, old divisions within the freeman body between liberal Protestants and Orange diehards being overtaken by the common fear of what a Catholic takeover of the city might mean. Since 1823 the *Dublin Evening Mail* had provided a highly effective outlet for such views, but it was more than matched by the O'Connellite press. A litany of Catholic grievances concerning the Corporation – its inefficency, its self-serving corruption and its unrepresentativeness – were presented to the Whig-dominated parliamentary commission into Irish corporations in 1833–4 (published in 1835). The Corporation, according to John Reynolds (one of O'Connell's closest city allies), was generally regarded as 'an engine of insult and oppression by the respectable portion of the citizens', with a city Commons now composed almost entirely of 'most violent Orangemen ... [who give] all kinds of insulting political toasts at city feasts and elsewhere'. O'Connell himself sent mixed messages, at times signalling that the freeman body were potential allies in his new great cause – repeal of the Union – at other times talking darkly of how he considered

> the present members [of the Corporation] as usurpers, and would treat them as such, and proposes to remove them altogether; considers them as usurpers from their being only freemen by favour, and from the citizens at large having no voice in their appointment. Considers citizens and inhabitants as synonymous ...

There was simply no middle ground between such a radical view of the civic community and the contractual and confessional arguments that shaped the defence of the city's ancient constitution. All assumed that if O'Connell's views prevailed at Westminster, his faction would totally wipe the slate in Dublin. Not surprisingly, support among Protestant freemen for 'Repeal', once such a powerful sentiment in the guildhalls, ebbed dramatically.[50]

In tandem with this stand-off was an ongoing struggle as to who would represent Dublin at Westminster, fought out in no fewer than seven fiercely contested elections between 1830 and 1841. The Irish Reform Act of 1832 had enfranchised all household heads holding property valued at £10 or more, which had the effect in Dublin of reducing the number of freemen to less than a third of the city electorate. Management of the election register now became critical, and O'Connell was first to exploit this. Going forward with Liberal Protestant running mates, he won famous victories in 1832 and 1837 (but lost, after an appeal in 1836). During these years O'Connell remodelled the parish-based support networks that had first been developed by the Catholic Association, and for many years the Corn Exchange on Burgh Quay was used as a regular public meeting point, debating club and national nerve centre for 'his' MPs. But Tories in the city also became adept at electoral management, helped by financial support from England which was used to build what became in effect a Dublin Conservative party. Their moment of triumph came in the 1841 general election, by which point the registered city electorate was about 53 per cent Protestant. That was the election when the Conservatives under Peel swept back into power, and for Dublin it was the beginning of a twenty-seven-year period of almost uninterrupted Conservative control of parliamentary representation, resting on very tight voter management and on the continued inclusion of all past freemen on the register.[51]

But it was too late for the old Corporation. When a bill for Irish municipal reform reached the House of Lords in 1840, legal counsel for Dublin Corporation once again set out the political case for rejection ('you are constituting in Ireland a Catholic parliament'), but their pleadings failed. To the defenders of the old order, the passage of the 3 & 4 Victoria, c.108 amounted to a gross betrayal by Westminster, politically (in sacrificing the loyalist citizenry), socially (by enfranchising 'the very lowest classes of society'), and in a religious sense (by surrendering the 'bulwarks of Protestantism' to the old enemy with the handover of the property of the city and the twenty-five guilds to the newly constituted body). The city was promptly divided into fifteen very unequal wards, each of which were to elect four councillors to a unicameral council; the candidate with the highest vote in each ward was accorded the title of alderman and eligible to stand for election as Lord Mayor. Aldermen were to serve for longer terms than councillors, a third of whom were to stand down every year (one of the immediate criticisms of the Act was that it set in train a process of almost constant low-level electioneering). O'Connell was heavily involved in the first campaign and the result in October 1841 was only slightly below his expectations. 'Repealers' triumphed in twelve of the fifteen wards, gaining thirty-six of the sixty seats, plus eleven that went to his Whig allies; precisely two-thirds of the new council were Catholic. This was all the more impressive given that the municipal franchise was restricted to the £10 parliamentary threshold (not to all male ratepayers, as in reformed English towns). However, the occupational make-up of the new council was not so different from the old: lawyers were the largest group (about a fifth), just ahead of wholesale traders; about half a dozen were retail traders, there was one builder, a doctor and a handful of men of independent means, a very similar profile to the political activists behind O'Connell's contemporaneous Repeal campaign. When the sixty of them gathered in the Assembly Rooms on All Saints Day 1841, it was no surprise that one of the first items of business was the triumphant election of the sixty-six-year-old O'Connell as Lord Mayor. He relished the moment.[52]

The new arrangements gave Catholic Dublin control over the trappings of power, but as the corporators soon realised it was more show than substance. They had responsibility for the municipal courts, the markets and the water supply, but had almost no discretion over new taxation. The appointment of sheriffs and magistrates had reverted to the Castle (and sheriffs determined the composition of the city grand jury); more importantly, three venerable statutory authorities – the Wide Streets Commission, the Paving Board and the Ballast Office – were left untouched, as were the Dublin Metropolitan Police (DMP), established in 1836, and the city's two Poor Law Boards of Guardians, established in 1838. Both the new poor law and the new police were at a formative stage, the former with some accountability to ratepayers, the latter more firmly than ever answerable to Dublin Castle. Unlike the force created in 1808, the DMP was a trained and tightly regulated force of about 1,000 uniformed constables, patrolling the city by day and night, and was closely modelled on the London Metropolitan Police established in 1829. The Corporation had no direct say in its affairs, but continued to be represented on the Wide Streets, Paving and Ballast boards. Most commissioners on these bodies were of the old stamp, government appointees in the first two, self-electing members in the case of the Ballast Board. The Paving Board, with its manifold responsibilities to maintain 88 miles of street, 6,000 street lights, and 98 public fountains, as well as to collect and dispose of rubbish and 'night soil' across the city, actually sought to extend its responsibilities into water after 1840.[53]

'O'Connell's Corporation' had to struggle with bloated expectations and very considerable debts. Many office-holders from the old Corporation were dismissed (with compensation and some disruption) and political supporters were rewarded with office, albeit on reduced salaries. But most of the Corporation's difficulties were not of its own making, and it was entirely understandable that the Council chamber should become a platform for political argument. The memorable three-day debate on repeal in 1843, at which O'Connell and the young Tory barrister Isaac Butt engaged in a heroic verbal dual, set the precedent. Apart from political grandstanding, the Council focused its energies on winning back control over the statutory bodies, the public case being that there was duplication, maladministration and waste in having such a profileration of agencies, the private case being that these bodies were all in conservative and mainly in Protestant hands, pursuing a partisan agenda. Against the backdrop of the Famine crisis, the Corporation invested great energy and scarce resources between 1845 and 1849 in its attempt to get amending legislation to secure this. But even with the return of the Whigs to government in 1846, corporate penury and a grave public-health crisis in the streets, there was no movement. Rathmines got its township bill in 1847, while the Corporation tried and failed with three improvement bills. Early attempts to secure legislation that would have given it control over the DMP and the Ballast Board were abandoned, and it failed to secure government support even for a more modest consolidation. Conservatives inside and outside the Corporation were completely opposed to any strengthening of its powers, at least until the ward structure established in 1840 was reformed. The remarkably detached attitude of the earl of Clarendon (Lord Lieutenant, 1847–51) and a succession of Chief Secretaries as to the governance of the city stood in complete contrast to the Castle's interventionism half a century earlier. It implied that the civic concerns of Dublin were really not very important.[54]

The logjam was eventually broken and the government agreed to support a compromise structure which emerged as the 1849 Dublin Improvement Act. This brought the Paving Board, the Wide Streets Commission and the powers of the Grand Jury into the Corporation, but not before

the existing Corporation was dissolved, an autonomous local tax-collecting agency created, and a new ward structure devised. Fresh elections were
held in 1850, with all separately rated male householders now included as
burgesses – if and only if they had been on the register at that address for
thirty-two months. With that sting in the tail, the burgess population was
held for several decades within the 5,000–6,000 range, not in fact much
larger than the eighteenth-century freeman body, but socially far more
variegated. However, what was fresh about this second reformation of the
Corporation – it came into existence at the beginning of 1851 – was that
it was a distinctly more conservative body than its predecessor, and some
suggested that Protestant councillors, Liberals and Conservatives, actually formed a majority again. But more strikingly, it was the arrival of key
figures from the railway companies and the banks into the Corporation
that suddenly made it more representative of big business than it had been
for generations. How had this come about? It seems that there was a concerted effort by the Chamber of Commerce in 1849–50, in particular by
its secretary Francis Codd, 'to bury the hatchet of party'. A wealthy Catholic merchant in the malt trade who had failed to get the Chamber involved
in Famine relief measures in 1846, Codd was credited in later years as the
architect of detente in the city. The 'power-sharing' understanding that
the mayoralty should alternate between the religions dates from this
time, made manifest with the election of Benjamin Lee Guinness in 1851.
During his year in office, the administrative structure of the Council was
reorganised and three powerful standing committees created, the post
of city engineer established (Parke Neville, son of the old city surveyor,
was appointed), as was a quasi-public health officer (the Inspector of Nui-
sances). At last the Corporation could operate as a unitary authority over
most matters touching urban environment and public health. The new
spirit continued when next year the Council voted by a large majority to
exclude 'political or sectarian discussion' from their proceedings. But the
most tangible legacy of the Guinness mayoralty was the acquisition of the
Royal Exchange from its trustees on very favourable terms, allowing the
new Corporation to move during 1853 from William Street and acquire a
home, a real city hall, that was the full measure of their ambitions.[55]

The plans of Codd and the other Chamber men were however frustrated by the financial weakness of the Corporation and the failure of central government to underwrite any of the big plans. They had dropped
out by the early 1860s and the Corporation gradually reverted to its

factionalised character, its energies absorbed by national politics and its composition emphatically Catholic once again. By the 1870s, retail merchants, particularly licensed publicans, heavily outnumbered big business (although the Corporation's many critics liked to exaggerate the modest social standing of the councillors). Mansion House and City Hall could still on occasion provide a platform when big and small business was united – the massive opposition in 1863 to plans for an overground railway through the city linking the termini being a case in point (when the Corporation erected a dummy wooden bridge across Westmoreland Street to highlight the visual threat). But this became rarer: the bitterness over Gladstone's church disestablishment bill in 1869 spilled into the council chamber, and the 'power-sharing' agreement broke down for a year. It resumed in the 1870s, even though several of the Protestant mayors were latterday repealers. But by then there was a chasm once again between the elected representatives in City Hall and the patrician merchants who controlled the Chamber of Commerce and the Port and Docks Board (which had been created in 1867 when the Ballast Board was restructured). And the Corporation was becoming far more sensitive to retail lobby groups like the powerful Licensed Grocers and Vintners Association (formed in 1860) and to the concerns of the Catholic archdiocese than to matters of state a stone's throw away in Dublin Castle.[56]

But no one could gainsay the one big achievement of the reformed Corporation: a revolution in Dublin's water supply. As in many cities of this era, the search for purer and more abundant water at high pressure and unaffected by the seasons was the great challenge and, against the odds, Dublin despite its divisions and its economic problems was ahead of most larger British cities in graduating from a pre-industrial low-pressure system to a flexible and reliable high-pressure one. The city's public water supply had been more or less dependent on the canals since 1777, first the Grand and after 1809 on both canals, when the basins at Portobello on the south side and at Blessington Street on the north were opened. Thereafter the old city watercourse supplied no more than about an eighth of the city's daily needs. Supply improved with the laying of metal instead of wooden pipes in the 1810s and the service was gradually extended. But even in the 1850s an intermittent supply of running water was reaching less than three-fifths of the city's households, everyone else being dependent on the public fountains, wells or directly on the canals. By that time there were huge concerns about the quality of the water, its irregular supply and its adulteration – whether through industrial pollution, effluent or the general neglect of the basins – and the effect of all this on public health. Lurid accounts of the polluted north-side water supplied by the Royal Canal were particularly graphic.[57]

The new Corporation struggled to find a permanent solution at a time when demand, both industrial and domestic, was accelerating and a run of dry summers made the problem more acute. In addition, the long-term agreements with the canals were due to expire in the following decade. The process began in 1853 when the city engineer was instructed to investigate an alternative to the canals, and this lasted until a Royal Commission intervened in 1860, when to everyone's surprise the commissioner (John Hawkshaw, an English engineer) ruled that the Vartry, a distant river in central Wicklow, was the optimal (if most expensive) solution. The commission was the latest twist in a bitter controversy between proponents of a new (and economic) canal scheme, those who advocated an upstream Liffey scheme, and champions of a new Dodder supply. It was generally (but wrongly) presented as a battle between Conservative interests who wished to moderate local taxation and go for the cheapest solution, and Corporation interests who had grandiose and possibly corrupt motives for pursuing first a Liffey scheme and then Hawkshaw's choice of the Vartry. In fact, it was a financial crisis within the Grand Canal Company that drove its Conservative management to play tough with the Corporation (with which it expected to reach an agreement). Then, when it had overplayed its hand, the Canal Company tried to use its parliamentary connections in Westminster to undermine the Corporation's proposed legislation. The canal interest was supported by the larger railway companies, Trinity College and the Rathmines Commissioners among others, but the Corporation won the struggle for public opinion, and in the final battle in 1861 some 20,000 signatures were mobilised for the Vartry option, five times those of the opposition. The great champion of the new water scheme was John Grey, medical doctor, owner and editor of the *Freeman's Journal*, and a former protégé of O'Connell. His political acumen was vital in securing the enabling legislation and the finance for the mountain reservoir, the twenty-four-mile pipeline and a suburban distribution reservoir at Stillorgan. But the city was also well served by its engineer, Parke Neville, who (despite suffering a serious accident during construction) oversaw completion of the project. The new water arrived in July 1867, bursting old pipes and valves. The eventual cost of the scheme, £541,000 (far ahead of Hawkshaw's estimate) reflected the land compensation costs and the need to re-pipe much of the city. This was still relatively cheap by contemporary British standards, and revenues were increased by the decision of all the southern townships (except for Stokes' Rathmines) to buy Vartry water from the Corporation. The high-pressure supply brought water through 110 miles of pipes to all locations in the city, and attic cisterns began to replace the traditional basement tanks. But the luxury of a fully fledged bathroom and a ceramic flushing toilet was slow to reach even wealthier households, and the impact of the new abundance of water in poorer neighbourhoods was even less clear-cut. Until domestic and public sewers were improved, there was a hidden cost – the frequent saturation of subsoil and of house foundations from an over-worked sewerage system.[58]

The easy availability of clean water was nevertheless a prerequisite for basic domestic decency and for maintaining a respectable appearance to the world. By the 1870s the number of Dublin families with such aspirations had grown markedly since the 1830s. Marx may have been quite clear what he meant by the *petit bourgeoisie* when he belittled them in the Communist Manifesto, but the Irish census commissioners, in their analysis of occupations, failed to track the growth of the middle classes or to differentiate wage-earner from petty entrepreneur or salaried clerk, the cap from the hat. So the emergence of the 'lower middle class' is hard to measure, but as to its new importance there is no doubt.[59]

It came about for several reasons, but principally because of structural changes in the city economy from the 1830s, with the shift from manufacturing employment to commerce, and the re-emergence of Dublin as unchallenged national centre of wholesale trade. This is evident from the huge growth of trade passing through the port: ship tonnage volumes more than trebled between 1841 and 1878, a rate of growth faster than in Belfast, Cork or Liverpool and its outports. In 1869 Parke Neville estimated that 'the traffic through all the leading streets [and] the line of the quays etc. has been quadrupled since 1849', which he principally attributed 'to the trade created by the railways'. Indeed, the completion of the trunk railway system in 1853 reinstated the capital's pivotal position in Anglo-Irish trade and strengthened employment across a whole spectrum of service activities, traditional and novel. As we have seen, one-eighth of the male workforce by 1881 held transport-related jobs. Retail employment, large and small, was at least as important. The growth of Dublin's wholesale trade reflected the relatively favourable state of the wider economy in the post-Famine generation, which was increasingly dependent on the live cattle trade, and involved the heavy use of canals, railways and the steamship companies. Thus in 1862 the Corporation, faced with railway company plans to develop a great cattle market on the North Wall that would have undermined Smithfield, moved with unaccustomed alacrity and commissioned a new market on a ten-acre site near Stoneybatter. This, supposedly the largest such market in Europe, became the hub for the cattle trade for a century, and meant that the North Circular Road became the corridor for the hundreds of fattened bullocks and sheep that were driven down to the cattle boats every day in late summer and autumn. And while the live cattle trade created little skilled employment, the sheer scale of the business gave ample seasonal work for drovers and sales clerks, publicans and the retail sector generally in the depressed north-west of the city. A second and more general factor swelling the city's lower middle class was the secular expansion of clerical employment in every decade from the 1830s – in education and the police, in the prisons, hospitals and welfare institutions, in both civic and central government – with Dublin really benefiting from the high level of administrative centralisation in Ireland compared with Victorian Britain.[60]

The material consequences of this broadening bourgeoisie can be seen in two ways: changes in the kind of houses being built, and changes in the city's retail landscape. Small brown-brick houses, two bays wide with a single-storey over a basement, were something of an innovation when they first appeared west of Camden Street, for example in Heytesbury Street, a long road running southwards from Kevin Street towards Portobello Harbour (it had been laid out thirty years before the first houses appeared there in 1845). Their minimalist classical detailing, outside and inside, was copied by several local builders on contiguous streets in the 1850s, some of the houses having four, some six rooms. Here in embryo was a housing style that proliferated and evolved further west along the South Circular Road, and in the north of the city on the outer parts of the old Gardiner estate west of Dorset Street, and on side streets off the North Circular Road. Earlier houses stood back from the street and contained a back garden, but by the 1860s these small-scale brick terraces were built flush to the street, often with tiny backyards. Virtually all early residents were tenants, and many were birds of passage for whom such small houses were the first rung to better things; they were built for those who could afford to take a step up from lodgings in the typically 'small, inconvenient and often delapidated houses', or from the kind of tenement that remained the standard for most inner-city wage-earners. The resources to rent a complete house with a cut-stone fireplace, modern furniture and fittings, a servant, and the income to purchase new clothes for the family and educate one's children beyond the elementary stages: these were the markers of social advancement that were possible for families earning £150 to £300 p.a., but well beyond the earning power of the dependent wage-earner or the weekly paid craftsman. But it was not until the 1860s and 1870s that this small-scale building boom really took off, led by Frederick Stokes (in Portobello), and by James Fitzgerald Lombard and John MacMahon who between 1867 and 1879 opened up some thirty streets and built 'about 600 houses, large and small', some west of Heytesbury Street, many on the north side of the city between the North Circular Road and the Tolka; by 1879 they still had a land bank of about seventy acres. They saw the main attraction for tenants who rented such houses beyond the city's northern boundary as an escape from city taxes, now all the more enticing with the opening of a north-side tramway. Lombard and MacMahon took the lead in creating what was the last of the satellite townships, that of Drumcondra in 1879, where they had recently erected about a hundred houses.[61]

Lombard and MacMahon were not themselves builders but developers. Many of their houses were constructed by 'small builders and enterprising industrious artisans' on loans secured by Lombard and MacMahon, and then sold on to 'small capitalists, [and] also men with savings of £500 or £600, grocers and butchers ...' Some, it seems, were built directly by the City and County of Dublin Land and Property Company in which they had a dominant interest. Both men had diverse commercial interests: Lombard had first made his fortune in Cork and MacMahon had Limerick links. Lombard's sometime partner was the remarkable John Arnott, who despite investing on three continents never left his Cork base. This Munster coterie, mixed in religion and Liberal or Home Rule in their politics, were among the most nimble in the city in finding ways to exploit the social changes underway. They were involved in the Dublin Carriage Company (which managed some hundreds of horses, post vehicles, hearses and livery stables), and this led them into the tramway business. Following closely on developments in Britain, the horse omnibuses, unable to cope with the growth of city traffic, were replaced quite quickly in the 1870s by fixed-rail trams with a much larger capacity, greater speed and therefore lower fares. Between 1872 and 1879 eleven routes were opened by five companies, six of which ran from the city centre into the southern suburbs (to Sandymount, Donnybrook, Dartry, Rathmines, Rathfarnham and Harold's Cross), two into the north-side suburbs (Glasnevin/ Drumconda and Clontarf), and three east–west services (to James Street, to Parkgate, and from the DWWR terminal in Harcourt Street to the GSWR at Kingsbridge). The new network generally followed rather than created the recent web of suburbanisation, and not all were a commercial success. Lombard was the driving force behind Dublin Central Tramway Company, which opened services to Clonskeagh, Rathfarnham and James Street in 1877–9, and he was centrally involved with his son-in-law William Martin Murphy in the amalgamation of three of the tramway companies in 1880.[62]

Lombard was for a time Arnott's man in Dublin, and was associated with his drapery business in Henry Street, which by the 1860s was one of seven department stores trading in the city, four on the south side (McBirney Collis on Aston Quay, Brown Thomas and Switzer Beatty in Grafton Street, and Pims in South Great George's Street), and three on the north side (McSwiney Delany in Sackville Street, Todd Burns and Arnott's Cannock White in Henry Street). These institutions were very much a phenomenon of the age, mushrooming out of the older drapery stores, their economies of scale made possible by the railway and the steam packet, by new systems for the mass production of consumer goods, and by a burgeoning consumer demand for new fabrics, fashions and furniture. Without that expansion in the consumer base, there would have been a far slower evolution away from the old-style family-owned specialist warehouse. As Stephanie Rains has revealed, Dublin's cluster of great shops was particularly impressive, each of them having up to thirty separate departments and each a factory-scale workforce of at least 150 assistants. Home's Royal Arcade had been the precedent in the 1820s, then McBirney's on Aston Quay in the late 1830s. But McSwiney's purpose-built five-storey 'New Mart', with its plate-glass windows on the ground floor, was startlingly new. It opened for business on Sackville Street in 1853 to coincide with the Dublin Exhibition.

The physical expansion of these stores in the 1850s and 1860s caught the public eye, much of their growing custom coming from country business and (in the case of Arnotts at least) up to half the turnover from wholesale sales. But their core business lay in the city and the suburbs,

catering for middle-class female shoppers (even if there was some concession by opening on Saturday evenings to accommodate the artisan cus-
tomer). Their commodious layout was intended more for spectacle than
convenience, and the enticing displays and abundant availability of consumer goods with prices fixed and payment (for retail sales) on the nail
had a slow but massive impact on fashion and conspicuous display. In the
1850s there were intermittent protests against these monster stores – that
their stock was shoddy, that most of it was imported, and that they were
undercutting the smaller warehousemen and putting them out of business.
Some of this was true, but the apparently high level of profits recorded
in the 1850s told its own story. Three of the stores were later floated as
public companies and this allowed for extensive refurbishment. Arnotts,
in the year after it went public, reinforced its bourgeois appeal by adding
two public dining rooms and a luncheon saloon to its great Henry Street
premises in 1875.[63]

An adaptation of the department store was the purpose-built shopping mall, a scheme championed by the Pims to draw the centre of retail
gravity westwards from Grafton Street to their unfashionably narrow
George's Street. In the late seventies the South City Market Company
managed to obtain a large block of condemned properties, much of it
made up of abbatoirs, widen the approach streets and develop an English-
style shopping mall with a 112-metre frontage, 46 shops and 120 stalls. It
opened in 1881, and while the commercial value of surrounding properties
was greatly enhanced, the Market itself was a disappointment for investors. Much of it was destroyed in a spectacular fire in 1892. Shortly before
it was reopened, Arnotts was destroyed in an even more spectacular blaze.
But it too was fully rebuilt – a fireproofed giant on the city skyline.[64]

❧

The material trappings of social respectability were highly visible, but a
key ingredient of social status in the city was less tangible: schooling. The
city may have been largely literate by the early nineteenth century but
the opportunities at that stage for a more advanced education were very
patchy and mainly took the form of small private fee-paying academies.
In 1846 there were over 200 of these in the city. None of them had overt
denominational links but the religion of the owner played a major part in
the confessional make-up of pupils. A disproportionately large number of

these were Protestant-owned – perhaps half – and women were listed as managers in more than half (these were presumably for female students). About a quarter took boarders. Some 140 free-wheeling 'professors and teachers' also advertised their services, more than two-thirds of whom were music teachers or dancing masters. Below them, at least up to the 1830s, were the city's 'hedge-schools', where vast numbers of poor tutors gave elementary lessons and 'taught in private rooms'; they were compared unfavourably with country hedge-schoolmasters.[65]

Between the 1830s and the 1880s this informal sector was rendered almost extinct by (at elementary level) the coming of national education, and (at secondary level) the rise of the Catholic teaching orders, the expansion of Protestant post-primary schools, and the self-improvement lecture programmes and evening classes offered by, among others, the Museum of Irish Industry, the Royal Irish Academy of Music and the Mechanics Institute. One of the few exceptions to the trend was Rathmines School, owned and managed for the forty-one years of its existence (1858–99) by one man, a gifted teacher and Church of Ireland minister, Charles Benson: 2,190 pupils passed through his hands during those years, many of them rectory boys, and at least twelve of his alumni became bishops. That was a rarefied exception to the general trend. The Corporation's King's Hospital school, the original public school of the city, retained its Anglican ethos after 1840, its pupils being 'of very respectable parentage, one-half being the sons of gentry in reduced circumstances', but it was quite overshadowed by the Protestant fee-paying schools which emerged between the 1840s and 1890s: St Columba's College (1843), located in the Dublin foothills on the model of an Oxford College and 'conducted on the English public school system', Wesley College (1845), St Andrews College (1894), and the Diocesan Intermediate School (1896), each of which were attached to a quite specific Protestant tradition. Trustees were mainly clerical and the teachers predominantly lay. Other Protestant initiatives had broader appeal: an endowed school with an explicitly commercial orientation, 'highly regarded by the lower middle classes', operated for many years in South Brunswick Street and set the precedent for the larger and more exclusive High School (1870), 'a first class English [day] school for the middle classes' ('English' in the sense that the syllabus lent towards modern literature and the sciences). Alexandra School (1873) was something different: it was established as a feeder school for the eponymous college established in 1866 by the Quaker Anne Jellicoe, where the

28. *Founded in 1866 and inspired by Queen's College London, Alexandra
College pioneered advanced female education in the city. It catered primarily
for the Protestant community, but it encouraged the development of rival
institutions for Catholic further education. However, the battle by women to
gain full access into Irish higher education was not won until after 1900.*

immediate object was to provide prospective governesses with a modern
academic education and the longer-term plan was to give women full
access to higher education. Jellicoe was a quiet but determined revolutionary who allowed others (mainly Anglican clergy) to take the credit for the
success of 'Alex' – both school and college. But its very success (responding to the desire of 'middle-class parents that a girl should be brought up
to be independent') reduced the demand for governesses in middle-class
Protestant families, so that the college soon set its sights on greater things.
Jellicoe was also responsible for an academy in Grafton Street, the Queen's
Institute, which offered practical training to young women, among whom
were the first female public servants – a group of telegraph clerks hired in
1870.[66]

Protestant Dublin was therefore fairly well provided for in educational terms with this range of increasingly secular schools in the south
of the city. Catholic participation in superior education was somewhat

different. Their attendance at Protestant-run schools and academies declined rapidly from the 1820s, bringing about a near-total educational apartheid by the 1860s. This was in part a reaction to proselytism, past and present, but the belief, asserted with increasing warmth from every Catholic pulpit, that a Catholic child's attendance at a non-Catholic institution posed an ever-present threat to faith, was wildly overstated. But it was mainly because of the proliferation of Catholic schools and colleges after 1830, which almost without exception were in the hands of the religious orders or the parish clergy, and most of the advanced teaching was delivered by members of the regular orders. During the long episcopacy of Daniel Murray (1823–52), the initiative behind the growth of the religious in the city came from the creative energies of a generation of activists, women and men, who were warmly encouraged by Murray. Frances Ball, daughter of an affluent silk manufacturer, was a striking case in point. Educated at a convent in York, she was professed in 1816 and quite quickly managed to set up an Irish branch of the order in which she had trained; she used private wealth to purchase Rathfarnham House, and in 1823 opened there the first 'Loreto' convent school. By 1850 she had personally overseen the establishment of five other schools in the greater Dublin region (most of them former upper-class private houses converted into tightly run boarding establishments), and she facilitated Loreto foundations elsewhere in Ireland, England and across the empire from Calcutta to Toronto. The Dominicans, who had run an upper-class convent school in Channel Row since 1717, retreated into the suburbs, to Cabra on the north side (1819) and Sion Hill (Blackrock) on the south (1840). Cabra remained a boarding school, but for financial reasons the order opened a fee-paying day school in Sion Hill side by side with the boarding convent. Another French order of nuns, the Society of the Sacred Heart, acquired Dargan's great house, Mount Anville, and opened shop there in 1865.[67]

Catherine McAuley, like Ball, was a gifted social entrepreneur and with Murray's encouragement she spent a family inheritance on various charitable works before establishing a new religious order, the Sisters of Mercy, in 1831. Her mission was directed towards assisting poor women and her Baggot Street House of Mercy (already opened in 1827) became in time a great school, part primary, part vocational (training governesses and female national teachers). It served as the mother house for four other schools in the city and suburbs, and like the Presentation Sisters on George's Hill and the Sisters of Charity, the Mercy order gradually widened their operations. From the beginning, those educated by Ball's Loreto order, by the Dominicans and other French orders, came from middle-class homes (although there was usually a free elementary school annexed), whereas pupils in the 'Irish' orders were generally from poorer homes, their fees notional, their advanced classes much smaller. Yet the contrast can be exaggerated: in 1864, 133 of the Charity Sisters' 932 'poor' pupils in their Henrietta Street convent were teenagers able to avail themselves of music teachers and, even more remarkably, a sewing machine. Some claimed that convent schools were giving lower-class girls an entirely inappropriate exposure to middle-class gentility, but the huge popularity of the convents by the 1860s suggests otherwise: 'girls educated in the convent schools are in general easily recognised by their gentleness and modesty', it was claimed by one inspector, the schools themselves providing 'a model of cleanliness and order' for their neighbourhoods. The pioneering women who established the first convent network were strong leaders in their time, but Murray's successor, Paul Cullen, archbishop of Dublin from 1852 until 1878, had a sharper sense of the primacy of episcopal governance in all matters educational, and he asserted much tighter control over their successors and over all religious orders in the diocese.[68]

The social distinctions in the convents were even more evident in the case of Catholic boys' schools. The first large-scale initiative came when the Jesuits opened a boarding school twelve miles west of the city at Clongowes Wood in 1814, its 'system of education ... adapted to those who are destined for the universities or the learned professions', and it competed with Catholic public schools in England. Then in 1832 the Jesuits opened Belvedere College in the city, a somewhat less exclusive establishment. Murray encouraged the Vincentians to open a diocesan seminary, but the resulting Castleknock College was primarily for lay students and became a junior rival to the Jesuit schools. Something similar occurred in 1860 when the French Spiritans were encouraged to open a missionary college in Blackrock, only to find that there was a real demand for a French-style superior college in south Dublin, catering for lay pupils. And then there were the Christian Brothers: the order were first invited to open a city primary school in 1812, but their break came when O'Connell gave £1,500 from Catholic Association funds in 1828 to build a large premises in North Richmond Street, and 'the O'Connell schools' there became one of the most successful educational institutions in Dublin. The Christian Brothers' distinctive mission of cheap education for all comers within a tightly defined religious format took shape in the following decades, and by 1880 the Brothers had twelve day-schools and fifty-one teachers across the city, many built by 'the shillings and pence of the working classes'. These Brothers (with the help of pupil-monitors) were by then teaching 6,350 pupils, each of whom was required to pay a penny a week fee (though upwards of a third of all pupils failed to do so). Most Christian Brothers boys were in fact only primary pupils, but 'provision is made for giving more extended instruction to the advanced pupils and to those displaying special aptitudes', and there was a pronounced shift towards 'superior education' after 1880. One long-established brother observed then that 'many of the pupils had raised themselves considerably in life', and there was a sense that the Brothers' plain fare was highly popular because it provided a practical educational foundation at very little cost.[69]

Archbishop Paul Cullen, the champion of episcopal authority and papal infallibility, became the first Irishman to be appointed a cardinal in 1866. His early career was spent in Rome and throughout his later years in Eccles Street he remained a Roman insider while he micro-managed the local concerns of the Dublin archdiocese, captured control of the Irish hierarchy, and masterminded a remarkable growth of Irish influence within the Catholic Church across the anglophone world. His funeral in 1878 was one of the largest in the city since O'Connell's in 1847, but he was by no means the transcendent public hero that O'Connell had been. There were two great monuments to commemorate O'Connell in the city: the soaring round tower erected in Glasnevin Cemetery in 1861 and Foley's superb statue in bronze dominating the south end of Sackville Street (completed in 1882); the Corporation also erected a smaller statue outside the north portico of City Hall. Cullen's memory was, by contrast, celebrated by a single indoor marble statue within the Pro-Cathedral by Thomas Farrell (1882). Nevertheless, the archbishop's imprint on his adopted city was more enduring than that of O'Connell.

At first sight, the 'devotional revolution' in Irish Catholic religious practice, conventionally attributed to Cullen's leadership, is not the issue here, for most of the elements of that revolution – heightened levels of church attendance, the spread of lay confraternities, sodalities and parish missions, and a standardisation of devotional practice and religious observance – had been present in city Catholicism since at least the late eighteenth century. The 1830s had been the decade *sans pareil* for new landmark churches – St Paul's on the north quays, the Franciscans' Adam and Eve on the south quays, the Jesuits' St Francis Xavier's in Gardiner Street, St Nicholas of Myra in Francis Street, and the huge St Andrew's parish church, accommodating a standing congregation of 3,200, in Westland Row, plus five in the suburbs. Patrick Byrne had been the leading church architect of that era, but his last great work was under Cullen, 'the bold and beauteous dome of Our Lady of Refuge' that dominates the Rathmines Road. During Cullen's episcopate, two new city parishes were created (in the north docklands and on the South Circular Road), and over two dozen additional churches and institutional chapels were built or rebuilt across the city and suburbs. Now Gothic was preferred to the Graeco-Roman designs of the Emancipation era, and most churches boasted soaring spires and embellished interiors, causing considerable financial strain for most of the parishes involved.[70]

Was the city over-churched by the 1870s? David Miller's close scrutiny of the national data on mass attendance gathered in 1834 suggests that Catholic church observance in Dublin was at that point actually lower than in much of its Leinster hinterland, and that at least two-fifths of the Catholic population of the city did not attend mass on a weekly basis, despite the more ample provision of chapels and priests than fifty years earlier. We can only assume that there was a strong correlation between poverty, marginal literacy and irregular religious practice. But the existence of such a sub-group in the city, 'vulnerable' to the intervention of the state or Protestant agencies, helps explain Cullen's muscular support for a diversity of Catholic social initiatives within the city to deepen the piety of the less privileged so that, by his death, Sunday Mass and the regular practice of the sacraments were, in Mary Daly's judgement, 'almost universal in the city and suburbs'.[71]

Cullen's distinctive legacy had three strands: his elevation of clerical control over all branches of education involving the Catholic laity as a fundamental and non-negotiable principle, whatever the compromises on offer might be, and the creation of a cluster of Catholic educational institutions on the north side of the city to make that a reality; his patronage of the Catholic religious orders, assisting their expansion into state-funded welfare and medical institutions and into the voluntary sphere; and his use of the new power of the Church to marginalise and demonise political radicalism, thereby laying the basis for a modus operandi between the Catholic Church and Irish government in the aftermath of the disestablishment of the Church of Ireland.

The management of most state-funded national schools had already passed into clerical hands, Catholic or Protestant, when Cullen returned from Rome in 1850, although the denominational character of primary education was only formally endorsed by the Powis Commission twenty years later. Cullen was adamantly opposed to classroom compromise, demanding that education, even in the workhouses, should be strictly denominational. But the liveliest issue was university education and whether or not Catholic bishops would support the new non-denominational Queen's Colleges, designed as a counterweight to the Anglican ethos of Trinity College but all three of them located outside Dublin. Murray had supported the scheme; Cullen did not, and he secured a general episcopal denunciation of the 'godless' colleges at the synod of Thurles in 1850. Shortly afterwards, he launched plans for a denominational university in Dublin, to be funded by voluntary contributions nationally and run under direct episcopal control, which in time would utterly eclipse its rivals. In something of a coup, he recruited the English convert John Henry Newman as its prospective rector. The Catholic University opened its doors on the south side of St Stephen's Green in November 1854, with thirty-eight students but no royal charter. Newman's intellectually elegant vision of a great Catholic university for the English-speaking world where scholars and clergy would cooperate, which he first suggested in 1852, was quite at odds with Cullen's more pragmatic plans and the bishops became progessively disenchanted with the initiative, so that it was in financial trouble by the time Newman returned to England in 1858. His successor, Bartholomew Woodlock, a Dubliner and Cullen's willing understudy, had more circumscribed ambitions: the creation of a residential campus for 300 students in the suburbs. A thirty-four-acre green-field site in Drumcondra on the Gardiner/Blessington estate was secured, plans for a massive building project announced, and the foundation stone laid by Cullen in 1862. However, by a bizarre coincidence, part of the site was compulsorily acquired for a railway extension from the MGWR line to the north quays in 1864, thereby killing the plan. Whether it could ever have been funded without government support is doubtful.[72]

Nevertheless, Drumcondra was the location for two other highly successful Catholic institutions. The first pre-dated Cullen, the missionary College of All Hallows (1842), which was an autonomous collegiate foundation established to train clergy for the new Irish diaspora in the empire and the United States, the worker-bees for Cullen's episcopal network overseas. Woodlock was in charge there before he became rector of the

Catholic University. The second foundation, which was much closer to Cullen's heart, was Clonliffe; he was never an admirer of the national seminary at Maynooth, with its mixed governance and supposedly Gallican ethos, so he proceeded to establish a specifically Dublin seminary, Holy Cross College, on what became a thirty-five-acre campus on the Drumcondra edge of the city, its twenty-three-bay central block completed in 1861. He took pains to establish its early reputation as an impeccably Roman institution, reflected in the design of its very fine chapel, the interior an accurate reproduction of Rome's fifth-century Sant'Agata (which had been gifted to the Irish College during his time as rector). Meanwhile the trustworthy Woodlock managed to keep the modest Catholic University in the city centre ticking over in the 1860s and 1870s, its largely autonomous medical faculty in Cecilia Street being the only real success. No British government of any party colour was prepared to accede to Cullen's recurring demand for state support of a Catholic-controlled university, but a working compromise of sorts was eventually reached just after the cardinal's death with the creation in 1879 of the 'virtual' Royal University of Ireland, its only physical presence being the former exhibition buildings in Earlsfort Terrace which were used to examine all-comers.[73]

During Cullen's episcopate, there were no fewer than twenty-nine Catholic religious foundations established in the city and suburbs, run by eighteen religious orders, only four of which were male. The nuns, Cullen's 'excellent communities of ladies', were his dependable allies, nowhere more clearly than in the 'great hospital' on his doorstep, the Mater Misercordiae Hospital, that opened in 1861, nearly thirty years after the Sisters of Charity's hospital in St Stephen's Green had become the first Catholic-controlled general hospital. The Mater's nine French-trained nuns were supported by nine 'ward helpers', five surgeons and two physicians, and it soon became one of the largest general hospitals in the country.[74]

For Cullen, a recurring theme was the superiority of religious institutions over the secular Poor Law agencies, specifically the South Dublin Union, 'a model for badness in every respect'. Giving evidence to an 1861 parliamentary inquiry, he showered praise on the Mercy Sisters in Baggot Street for accepting seventy unmanageable teenage girls from the South Dublin workhouse, all apparently veterans of that institution; he reported that on arrival at the convent they had

threatened to throw themselves out of the window, roared and shouted at the people in the street, and played all sorts of antics; but after a time the Sisters of Mercy brought them generally to order, got them situations, and sent them into the country, and they are going on well.

It was indeed in the overlapping fields of the care of orphans, juvenile criminality, and child vagrancy that Cullen had lasting effect, being in charge at a time when the institutional response to children in trouble was shifting from workhouse provision to dedicated institutions, and from Protestant or state control to largely denominational management. The functions of the old Foundling Hospital had been absorbed by the workhouses in 1840, but by the mid-1860s this had changed: most abandoned or parentless children were now catered for by one of the two dozen Catholic orphanages or boarding-out schemes across greater Dublin, nearly all of these controlled by female religious, who were handling at any one time at least 2,000 children, outstripping the business in the half-dozen Protestant or mixed orphanages. Then there was the issue of adolescent children serving prison sentences in adult facilities, an old concern for penal reformers. Legislation to establish 'reformatories' was only passed in 1858, and denominational control was accepted from the start; two small Protestant reformatories were opened in the city, one for each gender, and a small one for Catholic girls. But deep in the Wicklow hills, the Oblate Fathers converted a disused barracks in Glencree into a large detention centre for Catholic boys. All of this helped to empty the city prisons of teenagers. A decade later, Irish MPs, with Cullen's encouragement, sponsored legislation to establish a network of 'industrial schools', state-supported institutions to cater for displaced and vagrant children under fourteen years (their scope was subsequently broadened). They too were firmly divided along the lines of gender and denomination. Of the five early industrial schools in the city, by far the largest was Artane Castle, established by the Christian Brothers. The city's Protestant Recorder painted a reassuring picture of its 700 inmates in 1877:

> happy, healthy and busy as bees ... its dozen trades taught in the best methods ... its youthful brass band playing national and imperial airs ... its one hundred or two hundred tiny knitters making socks for the large household instead of festering in the slums ...

Children as young as five were sent to these institutions until 1908, when legislation specified that the under-eights should be fostered. But even then there was little hint of their later notoriety.[75]

Cardinal Cullen did not, however, pass into Dublin history as a great welfare reformer, but as the scourge of the Fenians, the radical republican movement that seemingly emerged out of nothing in the early 1860s. By adopting a model of oath-bound secrecy the movement evoked intense hostility in the episcopal mind. Cullen's first shock came in 1861 with the disputed reburial of one Terence MacManus. A Fermanagh man, Mac-Manus had come to the city and worked in a drapery warehouse in the 1830s, moving then to Liverpool where he made and lost a small fortune. He had been an ardent supporter of repeal, then a Young Ireland leader in Lancashire. He was associated with their Irish Confederation from its founding in 1847 and was one of the quickest to contemplate the use of physical force to secure repeal in 1848. He was involved in the disastrous Tipperary rising that summer and was one of the Confederate leaders arrested and sentenced to death, but like the others he was exiled to Tasmania instead, from where he eventually escaped to California and moved out of politics. He died quietly a decade later. However, the San Francisco Fenians seized on the idea of exhuming his corpse and sending it back to Ireland for public reburial. When his remains eventually reached Dublin, Cardinal Cullen forbade the use of either the Pro-Cathedral or any parish church for the display of the coffin. But the Mechanics Institute in Lower Abbey Street, a firmly secular even contrarian enterprise, obliged and allowed the coffin to lie there in state for a week. There was a hidden struggle between various political groups as to who should deliver the oration; the shadowy Fenian organisation got its way. The subsequent 'funeral' cortège of perhaps 8,000 traversed the city for hours before reaching Glasnevin Cemetery in darkness, the coffin having been viewed by many tens of thousands. The cortège included representatives from thirteen trade societies. Public funerals had been used as political propaganda since 1771 and Charles Lucas's interment, but not since the 1790s had a truly subversive figure been accorded such public recognition. Ironically, the Dublin Fenians were privately contemptuous of MacManus's Young Ireland antics, seeing themselves as made of sterner stuff.[76]

The scale of the funeral was surprising and perhaps misleading. The surreptitious 'Irish Republican Brotherhood' (IRB), the Irish progenitor of Fenianism, had not as yet put down deep roots. The once-vibrant revolutionary republicanism which it invoked had been almost entirely absent from politics during O'Connell's long ascendancy, although there had always been more radical voices in the wings, as O'Connell himself never forgot. But the origins of the huge demonstration of sympathy for MacManus in 1861, in the teeth of strong clerical disapproval, lay in the mid-1840s in Young Ireland's public rejection of O'Connell and of his uncompromising commitment to moral-force politics. The 1846 split in the Repeal movement, a year before O'Connell's death, had many elements, but Young Ireland's refusal to abjure the possibility of physical force was the central issue. Sharp differences on strategy soon emerged within their breakaway organisation, the Irish Confederation. Those differences were aired in public – in rival newspapers and at a series of great rallies held in the Abbey Street Music Hall during the early months of 1848. Upwards of 3,000 attended some of these meetings, clearly exhilarated by reports of a new and largely bloodless French Revolution and of a provisional government in Paris that recognised a universal *droit au travail*. At the Abbey Street rally on 3 May, 'over the chair was suspended the tricolour flag (the staff surmounted with a pike-head), brought from Paris by Mr Meagher'.[77]

Reflecting French developments, the social make-up of the platform at Confederation rallies differed from the Repeal Association, whose Dublin leaders had been almost exclusively professional or commercial. On at least one occasion an 'operative', the shoe-maker Michael Crean, took the chair at a Confederation meeting 'as one of the representatives of the working classes in this city (cheers)'. A few days previously he had spoken about how city tradespeople 'felt themselves honoured by the success achieved by their brethren in Paris'. O'Connell had managed to marginalise local supporters of English Chartism and its call for universal suffrage, but now their demands were infiltrating mainstream debate. However, the nominal leader of the Confederates was the patrician William Smith O'Brien, MP, and the Dublin organisation was still controlled by bourgeois journalists, young lawyers and the well-connected. The protagonists were Charles Gavan Duffy and John Mitchel, both Ulstermen and key players in the commercial success of the *Nation* newspaper, one a non-practising barrister, the other a successful attorney. In their bitter falling out over tactics, Duffy generally held the upper hand, but it was Mitchel, mixing radical, then republican, rhetoric with Robespierrean menace, who became the popular favourite in Abbey Street: 'nothing short of an Irish republic and every man armed'. And in his own sensationalist paper, *United Irishman* (which ran for sixteen issues), he invoked 'the illustrious conspirators of Ninety-Eight' and called for national insurrection.[78]

There were, however, no arms, no external patron, and all the talk of forming a National Guard along the lines of the old Volunteers was platform talk. When pressed, Mitchel spoke of the primacy of 'passive resistance'. Yet for several months in 1848, before government controls on political association were re-imposed, young men were recruited by the hundred into 'Confederate clubs' in greater Dublin (and also in Munster and the south Midlands). They met not in taverns as in the 1790s but in dedicated premises where reading, lectures and debate were the main activities, the precedent being the reading rooms established by the Repeal Association in 1842. But the names of some clubs – 'Curran', 'Sheares' and 'Emmet' – suggested a decided departure from Repeal orthodoxy. The clubs provided an opportunity for male sociability in a new setting or, as Duffy put it, 'to homogenise the people ... to blend up class and class, to mingle creed with creed'. Some of the Confederate clubs developed a social programme, even sports (including rifle practice), and three published penny newspapers for short periods. Only one priest, the curate of St Michael and John's, came out in support, while Archbishop Murray warned publicly of the horrors of another '98. At the time of the first (and abortive) trial of William Smith O'Brien in May 1848, some 10,000 men, drawn from sixteen city clubs, marched behind him from Westland Row down to the Four Courts. O'Brien got off that time, only to be arrested in the wake of the Tipperary rising later in the year. But Mitchel was sentenced in May and was promptly exiled, before news arrived of the June Days and the counter-revolution in Paris. Mitchel's supporters continued to organise in the city and published two short-lived papers, the *Irish Felon* and the *Irish Tribune,* and the number of Confederate clubs grew to fifty-six in Dublin (and over 200 in the country as a whole). They were suppressed in July, many of them far more radical than the surviving Confederation leadership. In the tough subsequent clamp-down there were no executions, no martyrs, and a well-disciplined police. But a network of shadowy clubs (forming the Irish Democratic Association) survived in Dublin for a year or two, and there was a half-developed plot to kidnap the queen on her Dublin visit in 1849. But it all fizzled out as more moderate figures like Gavan Duffy were released from jail and re-assumed control. However, Mitchel, a distant but electrifying voice, was not easily forgotten.[79]

This all happened before Cullen's arrival from Rome, where he had witnessed the 1848 convulsions in the Papal States and the humiliation of Pius IX. It affected him profoundly. In his early years in Dublin he stood back from parliamentary politics, although he was blamed for quietly sabotaging the Independent Irish Party of which Duffy was one of the architects. During the 1850s, most Young Ireland veterans settled into a resolutely constitutional nationalist path, sharply distinguishing themselves from the democratic republicanism championed by Mitchel. The only visible sign of the latter was a new version of the *Tribune* (1855–6); two of its staff writers were Dublin Protestants who had seen action in '48, Thomas Luby and Philip Gray. Gray died young, but Luby joined several Confederation veterans, notably James Stephens, a Kilkenny man who had spent six years in France, to launch what became the IRB in 1858, most of them taking Luby's oath of allegiance 'to the Irish Republic, now virtually established'. The timing was prompted by the growing possibility of Anglo-French war that year. Stephens became the dominant personality in the new organisation and shaped a strategy predicated on Irish-American financial support and the utter rejection of parliamentary politics. Gone was Mitchel's idea of spontaneous popular revolution, instead the silent preparation of the initiated for an opportune moment to strike at British authority in Ireland, the object being a secular Irish republic to be established by force of arms. Stephens had an almost Leninist belief in the necessity to concentrate power at the centre and indeed in his person, and he displayed a ruthless streak when it came to sabotaging rival political activity. But he radiated mesmeric optimism and a self-belief that attracted many.[80]

However, it was a small core of Dubliners like Luby, Peter Langan, a lathe manufacturer in East Lombard Street, and James O'Callaghan, a department store salesman, who were critical in the build-up of IRB networks, both in the capital and in the southern counties. The numbers sworn in the city remained small until after the MacManus funeral, with real growth in 1864 and 1865, when the city was divided up into some two dozen 'circles', incorporating perhaps as many as 10,000 Dublin members by 1867. Shin-ichi Takagami's analysis of 474 Dublin Fenians who became known to the police points to some strong parallels with the 1790s: their youthfulness, their strong assocation with the western half of the city, the prominence of tailors, shoe-makers and, on the north side, metal-workers in the old Pill Lane area and the North Wall. New was the prominence of skilled wage-earners in the building trades and to a lesser extent in the gas and railway companies, and of employees in the north-side department stores, who were prominent as organisers and who (unlike most skilled craftsmen) were recent migrants to the city, single and free from family discipline. The skilled working class formed a clear overall majority of Dublin Fenians. The unskilled were almost entirely absent, nor were there now any professionals, business-owners or maverick members of the upper classes in the mould of Lord Edward FitzGerald.[81]

Late in 1863 the organisation launched a weekly, the *Irish People* – without quite owning up to its own existence. The paper, perhaps surprisingly, was permitted to pump out its radical nationalist message for nearly two years before being suppressed in September 1865. It was edited by two very able Tipperary men, John O'Leary (like Luby, a one-time Trinity student) and Charles Kickham, with the shadowy figure of Stephens lurking in Sandymount or on his travels to America. At least half of its 5,000–10,000 print-run was sold outside Dublin: IRB members actively promoted it in the provinces and among Irish communities in the north of England and the United States. As Matthew Kelly has argued, its caustic hard-hitting commentary projected a quite distinct perspective on public affairs – anti-clerical, anti-parliamentary, anti-imperial and against the old O'Connellite moral-force strategy. But although it suggested that 'the real Irish gentry' were those who populated the back lanes of Dublin, it set out little in the way of fundmental social reform. Its period of publication was precisely the time when the organisation in Dublin grew fastest, and when the DMP took notice. The *Freeman's Journal* and other moderate papers spoke darkly of hidden American influence and characterised Fenianism as an innately disreputable enterprise, contrasting it with the noble patriotism of Young Ireland and pointing to the low social status of its members. However, the *Irish People* relished its democratic credentials and the absence of gentlemen, poured scorn on the cowardice of the leaders of '48, and attacked the unmanliness of O'Connell's Repeal agitation.[82]

The *Irish People* was closed by the police in September 1865, its presses carried into the Castle and those involved arrested. This was the beginning of a long battle to snuff out the IRB. Stephens was himself arrested later in the year, but added to his reputation by being sprung shortly afterwards from the Richmond Barracks. Habeas corpus was suspended early in 1866, and hundreds of Dubliners were among those detained across the country. The IRB had become less a Dublin-controlled conspiracy, even though

29. *Fenian prisoners, November 1866. The camera was first used in 1860 to create a visual record of convict prisoners held at Mountjoy jail, but with the spread of Fenianism this was widened to a the systematic photographing of all political suspects, linked to the collection of biographical and biometric information. Of note here is [top right] the image of a confident Patrick MacDonald, described as 'Head Centre F[enian] B[rotherhood], Dublin', but despite this attribution little is known of him.*

plans for a Fenian rising in Ireland took it as axiomatic that Dublin would be centre-stage. There were several waves of arrests, the most successful in December 1866. Sharp internal divisions had damaged the organisation from the beginning, both in Ireland and America, and the arrests only worsened matters. Even those supporting Stephens's leadership lost patience with his temporising tactics. He was unseated at the end of the year, leaving the field open for those who sought an early rising – Irish-American veterans of the Civil War, whose local knowledge was severely limited.

In the event, the Fenians of Dublin came out on the night of 5/6 March 1867, with the government having late and incomplete knowledge of what was afoot. Perhaps 5,000 were mobilised, most of them with some sort of weapon but very few with appropriate military training. Details of the IRB master plan remain obscure, but it seems that some of the circles in the city were ordered to stay in town and await orders while others, some thousands of young men, assembled in darkness on Mount Seskin, south-west of the village of Tallaght, apparently as a decoy. There had been plans to sabotage railway communications into Dublin (an echo of '98 and the mail-coaches), but nothing came of this. Poor IRB communications and an unexpectedly robust response from the DMP barracks in Tallaght brought a quick end to the affair with few fatalities, although a Rathmines-based circle managed to attack three police stations in the south of the county. The Fenian rising revealed even more clearly than 1798 the futility of large-scale military action by lightly armed civilians at a time when the civil power had overwhelmingly superior police and military resources. This was all the more the case when it was free to deploy those resources at a time of international peace and when it could draw on considerable public support in stifling the conspiracy.[83]

Episcopal denunciation of secret societies in general and of Fenianism in particular resonated in every Dublin Catholic church through the 1860s. This weakened its appeal and gave clerically endorsed politicians an apparent ascendancy in Catholic public life. This was demonstrated most spectacularly in 1864 when, after two years of nationwide fund-raising, the foundation stone for the great monument to O'Connell was unveiled beside Carlisle Bridge. Church, nationalist aldermen and the press coordinated an extraordinary celebration of O'Connell's memory: police estimated that there were 45,000 men in the three-hour procession to the site and that half a million had filled Sackville Street and beyond, constituting at that point by far the largest crowd in Dublin's history. Thirty-nine trade societies, some appropriating the title of 'guild' but not 'trade union' as yet, marched with their banners, only one of which (the Grocers' Assistants) suggested a hint of sulphur ('Oh, for the swords of former times'). Those who organised this tribute may have been looking over their shoulder at Fenian shadows, but for the vast majority of participants, then and later, celebrating O'Connell and Catholic Emancipation was not an exclusive act. Much of the huge sympathy that Fenian prisoners attracted later in the decade came from a Catholic public whose nationalist sentiment was all-encompassing and undiscriminating, first evident in the huge campaign to reprieve the 'Manchester Martyrs' in 1867, then in 1869 in the vast rallies at Inchicore and Cabra pushing for an amnesty for all Fenian prisoners (which was achieved in 1871). The William Smith O'Brien statue, the first monument commemorating a 'physical-force' patriot which was placed in 1870 on the south side of Carlisle Bridge, was a further demonstration of constructive ambiguity: no facilities for the unveiling were allowed by the police and no clergy appeared. Yet the conservative Lord Mayor showed up (distancing himself from O'Brien's politics but praising the patriot), and once again large numbers of trade societies and local bands took over the thoroughfares to cheer the guest of honour, Mitchel's friend John Martin. With such latent support the IRB, though shaken by the botched insurrection of 1867 and by recurring infighting, managed to reorganise and to build up its local membership for several years. But in the longer run its strength as a secret society was to lie in the provinces and in the diaspora, rather than in the Liberties or Pill Lane.[84]

Fenian violence abroad (in England) had enormous impact, forcing British Liberals to search more deeply for a permanent solution to Irish discontents. Paradoxically, this was good for Cullen: the Church of Ireland was disestablished in 1869, and in the 1870s the prospects for securing the Catholic Church's social and educational reforms within the constitutional status quo seemed far better than before, and far better than within some kind of Irish republican experiment, or in Cullen's judgement, even with repeal. So when the next round of agitation for Home Rule began in 1870, he was profoundly unsympathetic – not least because its early leaders were not of his flock. For the three-day celebration of O'Connell's birth in 1875 Cullen sought to place all the emphasis on him as liberator of a Catholic people and on the huge Catholic advances since 1829. The absence of any reference to repeal in the parades and official speeches, and the near exclusion of Isaac Butt, former Tory, dogged defender of Fenians in the courts, and now head of the Home Rule party, exposed the fissure between Cullen's triumphant Hiberno-Romanism and the older civic-national traditions of Dublin politics, whether Grattanite or republican, Young Ireland or Fenian, that focused on the great unfinished business, breaking the union. Cullen's views prevailed in 1875, but the volatility of public allegiance was again in evidence two years later with the funeral of the American Fenian leader John O'Mahony, which had all the ingredients of 1861 – episcopal denunciation, clerical non-involvement, a circuit of the city, and huge crowds – albeit on a smaller scale. Two months before his own death and after long negotiations with a sympathetic Dublin Castle team (the duke of Marlborough and Sir Michael Hicks Beach), Cullen was party to a major political breakthrough, the 1878 Intermediate Education Act. Its passing opened the way for all superior schools to compete for significant state funding – whatever their religious governance, and *without* any state supervision of their internal arrangements. In its social consequences, the Act was revolutionary.[85]

The crafts

In the era of Cullen and the Fenians, what of material life in working-class Dublin? The Irish economy enjoyed something of Britain's mid-Victorian boom and Dublin, with its strengthened infrastructure and expanding service industries, was very well placed to benefit from this. But Fergus D'Arcy's longitudinal survey of wages in the city's construction trades suggests that the earnings of skilled craftsmen remained flat until the mid-1860s and only rose modestly in the following fifteen years, a time of increased building activity (to judge by timber imports) and of several bitter labour disputes. In the case of the more numerous building labourers, there was an uninterrupted rise in wages from a trough in 1840s, and this was quite pronounced in the 1860s. Levels in the 1870s were about 75 per cent higher than in the 1840s average. However, this improvement was from a very low base. More importantly, it spanned a period of general if modest inflation. If we use Liam Kennedy's national cost-of-living index, factoring in food and fuel costs, it seems that most of the nominal wage rise for the unskilled was cancelled out but that there was some small net gain, perhaps more evident in shorter working hours than in greater Saturday-night spending. To date, this is the only hard evidence we have on trends in working-class standards in this era and, as D'Arcy's work shows, pay rates varied very considerably between the particular large building projects for which evidence survives, and this evidence tells us nothing about changing levels of unemployment.[86]

There were some 6,500 men and 300 women employed in the building trades in 1871 out of a total city workforce of 129,181. Employment in the sector was highly cyclical, but its overall size remained fairly stable. Printing and its allied crafts formed another area of strong labour organisation and of relatively modest firm size, where sub-contracting was common and technical change cumulative rather than revolutionary. There were 2,362 printers and binders in the city in 1871, 27 per cent of whom were women (principally young bookbinders), but the organised crafts in the industry were resolutely male. And although there were now 220 working as booksellers in the city, the business of printing revolved far less around book production than in the past (and indeed, nearly all the fiction sold in Dublin, whatever its genre, was now produced in London). Educational titles, commercial job-printing, newspapers, magazines and yearbooks, popular aids to devotion: this was the bread and butter business, and some of the high-end skills once in demand mattered little. Wages, whether by the week or by the job, were sticky until the 1870s, and industrial disputes over apprentices, working time and wage levels never far away. One firm engulfed in a bitter lock-out in 1878 was that of Alex Thom, government printer since the 1830s and an old-style owner-manager who profoundly disliked organised labour. The Middle Abbey Street firm's output was highly varied, but its fame rested on the annual *Almanacs*, which grew in size to more than 2,000 pages by 1871. Even in the mid-1840s it was something of an object of wonder, requiring eight printing machines during the print run, powered by two steam engines with twenty-two men employed, assisted by twenty-four apprentices who served unusually onerous seven-year terms. For all grades in the Dublin printing trade, sixty-six hours had been the standard working week up to the 1830s. A sixty-hour week was gradually conceded (reflecting English practices), falling after 1872 to a fifty-seven-hour standard.[87]

The wider history of skilled employment in this era is dominated by the rise of a few very large employers, and by the emerging contrast between the working environment in new industries and older workplaces. In the new sectors there was a strong leavening of immigrants taking up skilled positions and little demarcation, whereas in the older crafts hard-learnt skills still mattered, apprenticeships were to a large extent still controlled by 'the trades', and the conditions of work fairly tightly regulated. Once the cost of living edged upwards in the 1860s, trade societies used the now-legal weapons of industrial dispute to renegotiate wages and lower working hours. Collaboration between journeyman societies went back to 1780 at least, but the Dublin United Trades Association, formed in 1862 by the main Bakers' Society and supported by twenty-four other societies, was the first to achieve any sort of permanency, and with this went increased social activities, greater public displays of bands and banners, and a heightened sense of craft identity. This came at a time when the links with trade societies elsewhere in Ireland and Britain became much more common. Those working in the precision end of the metal trades had been first to become attached to a well-organised UK-wide 'trade union' in 1851, the Amalgamated Society of Engineers, and within the year there were 104 members. Trade societies representing printers (the Typographical Association), tailors and coach-makers were also involved in tentative amalgamation. But when the British Trades Union Congress met for the first time in Dublin in 1880, the local organisers lamented the still fragmented state of organised labour in the city.[88]

Where major business consolidation occurred, the power of labour was weak. The giant department stores, for example, dominated if they did not actually own the surviving silk and poplin workshops, and they controlled the 'sweated trades' of tailoring and dress-making which absorbed vast numbers of low-paid workers, many of whom were based at home. Thanks to the exuberant complexities of middle-class Victorian fashion, 8,419 city women were employed as dress-makers, seamstresses, shirt-makers or tailors in 1871, in addition to 1,661 male tailors and 4,007 predominantly male boot- and shoe-makers. But a growing proportion of the dress-makers and milliners were regimented into large workshops equipped with new-fangled sewing machines. But even here much of the cutting, preparation and finishing work was done by hand; Sir William Wilde (who, among his other attributes, was a pioneering eye and ear surgeon) noted the toll on the eyesight of women in the city 'chiefly young women from eighteen to twenty-five, pale from watching, haggard from working sixteen hours a day ... nearly blind from stitching for the votaries of fashion'.[89]

There were around 7,500 transport-related jobs within the city in 1871, about half of them related to road traffic (working with trams, hack-neys, wagons, drays, livery stables and in coach manufacture). About a third held canal, port or maritime employment, and jobs with the railways the remainder. What was new by then was the scale and complexity of the leading railway companies: both the MGWR and the GSWR were by now operating island-wide rail networks, and both companies chose to site their engineering and repair shops in Dublin, the former at Broadstone, the latter opening up a green-field site in Inchicore west of Kilmainham in 1846. By 1880 there were some 600 men employed at Broadstone and double that number at the Inchicore Railway Works, which by then was a truly self-contained industrial suburb. The hundredth GSWR locomo-tive was completed in 1879, and nearly all the company's huge inventory of engines, rolling stock and sleepers continued to be built in Inchicore

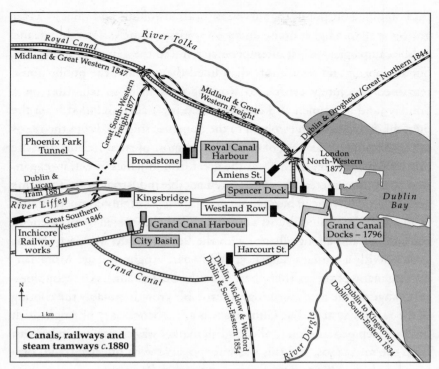

Map 4: Railways and canals in Dublin c.1880.

to standardised designs, produced by a diversity of precision craftsmen trained on site. Early managers were English, but both the workforce in Inchicore and the hundreds working in the traffic department of the company were recruited from across the GSWR's hinterland, a religiously mixed, hierarchical community. Dozens of them enjoyed company housing in 'New Kilmainham', and Inchicore became a small colossus. Independent engineering companies, led by Mallet of Capel Street, had thrived for a time on railway demand, both for large-scale iron castings and precision engineering. But these firms failed to find new markets once the Irish railway system was complete and as the operating companies became more self-sufficient.[90]

The supreme example of commercial consolidation was of course the Guinness brewery. In an age of falling transport costs and strong economies of scale, alcohol production became brutally competitive, favouring concentration and indeed cartelisation by the surviving enterprises. In 1836 there had been twelve distilleries in the city, by 1880 only seven of any size, nineteen ale and porter breweries in 1836, eleven by 1880. Yet the combined output of the survivors (both in volume and value) was far greater in 1880. Higher excise duties on spirits and the various church and public campaigns against intemperance reduced the demand for whiskey, but ale, porter and stout more than filled the gap, and the public house remained absolutely central to working-class male socialisation on a Sunday (and as women and children were invariably excluded from the pub, this helped confine women to the domestic sphere). From the 1840s porter became the alcohol of choice across most of rural Ireland, and the principal beneficiary of this was the great firm in James Street, its expansion across the nineteenth century a remarkable industrial story. The firm's genetic good fortune in having four generations of highly competent family managers, spanning almost a century and a half, assisted by an extended cousinhood and a long alliance with the Purser family, was part of their success, with a strong evangelical ethic (part Anglican, part Moravian) uniting many of them. Then there were the benign effects of technological change on the firm's seemingly inexorable growth, notably the coming of the railway system. But Guinness was a real beneficiary of Anglo-Irish union. Deep penetration of the English market was critical for its growth from the mid-1820s, and this was only possible with full free trade combined with the efficiencies of steam navigation. Then the conjunction of rising post-Famine farm incomes, a comprehensive Irish railway network, and a still functioning canal system allowed the company to build up an unassailable dominance of provincial Irish markets. By 1864 it supplied over half of all the beer sold in Ireland. Then, belatedly, Guinness conquered the capital itself, which it achieved by offering free delivery within a ten-mile radius and keeping an army of dray-horses busy.

The brewery broke out of its original four-acre site in the 1850s and expanded ten-fold in the next two decades, colonising a vast brownfield site between James Street and the Liffey. Edward Cecil, Benjamin Lee Guinness's youngest son, became sole proprietor in 1876 and oversaw the building of a second brewery in 1877–9; thanks to the pioneering use of electric light, it was built by shift work in record time. Yet for all its prominence, the brewery was a large but not dominant employer in the city. Granted, its workforce by 1880 was considerably more than the total employed in all other breweries and distilleries. At that stage its payroll stood at somewhat below 2,000, a majority of whom were classed as labourers; labour costs amounted to less than 5 per cent of the firm's total costs and the salaries of the brewers and clerks formed the greater part of this. Employment at James's Gate was however eagerly sought, the brewery offering somewhat higher pay rates, job security and from 1869 an expanding programme of employee supports – a free dispensary, medical attendance, sick pay and employee pensions for widows and the old (after compulsory retirement at sixty was introduced for general labourers in 1891). But although embedded in the south-west quarter of the city and close to the Liberties, the firm seems to have recruited widely for its staff in the periods of rapid expansion. It is revealing that in the 1860s there was virtually no trace of Fenian support within the plant. But what struck contemporaries most was the extraordinary capital growth of the firm from a valuation in 1869 of £80,000 to £500,000 in 1879, and at the time of its stock-market launch in 1886 ten times that sum again. Some of the family's enormous wealth was ploughed back philanthropically, and the multiplier effects of the company's presence – on the receipts of steamship, canal and railway companies, on tillage farmers and provincial maltsters – highly beneficial, but its overall effects on the city at large are harder to judge. Spence Brothers, the Cork Street foundry established in 1856, thrived on Guinness custom, not least in becoming the main supplier of steam engines for the railway system built within the works in the 1870s, but that synergy was unusual. Barrel manufacture for the wholesale distribution of porter was carried out on site in the company's vast cooperage and was subject to tight quality control, and the company kept entirely out of the retail side. None of the many small bottle-making firms that filled the gap managed to dominate the retail supply of bottles to publicans, and unlike the labour history of James Gate, the glass industry (mainly associated with Ringsend) experienced recurring industrial unrest.

One business dynasty whose rise to local celebrity did have a Guinness link was that of Alexander Findlater. In the 1830s, when the first Findlater was a young merchant exporting a variety of ales, porter and spirits, bottled Guinness featured very prominently in his overseas business. By the time of his death in 1873, Findlater was part-owner of the leading wine and spirit businesss in the city, of the Todd Burns store, and of the Mountjoy Brewery on the north side (which was the nearest thing to local competition that James Gate then had to deal with), and he left a huge porfolio of railway shares. Early profits in despatching Guinness overseas had served him well and established a household name.[91]

The city of rags

The Corporation, concerned with the effects of smoke pollution in 1864, discovered that there were no fewer than 120 stationary steam engines at work in factories and workshops across the city. Three-fifths of these were in the south-west quarter, principally in breweries and maltings, distilleries and bakeries. That area of the city was indeed a strange mix of busy enterprise and intense deprivation, an incongruity which eventually stirred the Guinness family into frenetic philanthropic action. But between the 1820s and the 1870s, the core of the old city and the Liberties was assumed to be synonymous with poverty, and specific streets like Skinner's Alley a by-word for prostitution, public drunkenness and petty crime. To outsiders, the sensory experience of this poverty was overwhelming: the sight of ramshackle old houses with broken windows and leaking roofs, of 'the stunted proportions and listless aspects of the adults, and the pale scrofulous faces, full of precocious knowingness, of the children', the smell of unwashed clothes, human excrement in open drains and oozing cesspools, and of pigs on and off the street. The Corporation operated a scavenging service during the small hours each night to keep the public streets clear, but yards and courts were not a public responsibility. For outsiders who penetrated a little deeper, the shock was the sight of gutted interiors and the lack of any solid furniture, the darkness of the rooms, the stale air, the near-absence of food (when the diet was cheap bread, potatoes and tea), and the lack of personal privacy. There were of course gradations of poverty and a natural tendency to publicise the worst black-spots such as Fordham's Alley, which had 'once resounded from one end to the other with the glad sounds of industry, but where now [1836] out of 700 inhabitants, not six families maintained themselves by their own labour'. But these black-spots were located in a sea of grey.[92]

The 1841 census revealed for the first time a level of overcrowding in Dublin quite unlike that in other UK cities: 46.8 per cent of all city families were living in one-room accommodation, principally in sub-divided parts of larger houses that were being rented out, usually by the week. In such circumstances, families moved frequently: in Hammond Lane in St Michan's parish two-thirds of the families moved between 1840 and 1845. This preponderance of one-room families only began to fall in the 1860s, but in 1881 they still formed two-fifths (41.9 per cent) of all families in the city. Within this huge group there were several major distinctions: first, between those where one or more in the household was a wage-earner, whether skilled or unskilled, and was therefore likely to be a paid-up member of one of the hundreds of friendly societies (in other words had some small measure of insurance to cover medicines, illness and burial costs), and those classified as destitute, broken families without resources, often ill or infirm, many headed by widows or abandoned wives, who were forced to beg, to resort to charity, or to engage in prostitution. 1,630 working prostitutes were enumerated by the Dublin Metropolitan Police in 1838, some of whom may have maintained precarious links with the world of privilege, but the vast majority were illiterate outcasts. In Fordham's Alley, the destitute and the outcast were in the majority, but the Coombe and Newmarket right beside it were socially far more diverse.

A second distinction was between those living in the court and alley dwellings (or cottages in some suburban ghettos), and those renting a single room in a larger house that had seen better days. The term 'tenement' was loosely applied, but it came to designate the latter type of residence. The relative importance of the courts and alleys had been much greater in the eighteenth century, but from the 1820s the tenementisation of larger street-facing houses became far more common, and indeed a move from a 'cottage tenement' to a larger house was regarded by the families concerned as something of an improvement. The transformation of many main streets of mixed commercial/residential character to a tenement zone could occur quite quickly once it commenced. House values were affected by the contagion effects of neighbouring tenements, a process hastened by the intervention of 'housejobbers'. These specialists in weekly renting, operating often on a large scale, were singled out from the 1850s and criticised by social reformers for their failure to maintain properties, pay water rates or discourage unsanitary practices. But the jobbers could plead that it was not in their financial interest to invest in ageing real estate when there was a steady demand from poor and undiscriminating room-tenants. In the Meath Liberties and in other old districts, where generations earlier house sites or house property had been leased out on very long terms, ground landlords had very limited legal powers to intervene in the process even if they had so wished.[93]

For all the contemporary commentary on Dublin poverty, the very poor are themselves almost voiceless in the historical record. Occasionally, when those of modest means fell down the social scale, their witness survives. The outstanding case here is James Clarence Mangan, son of a

Fishamble Street grocer who lost all after the Napoleonic wars in misjudged property speculation. Mangan attended at least four Catholic
pay-schools in the city and developed extraordinary literary and linguistic gifts, and for many years worked as a scrivener. He also wrote nearly
a thousand poems, from satirical to darkly metaphysical, nationalist to
nihilist, many of which appeared in the *Dublin University Magazine*, the
Nation and the *United Irishman,* the earnings from which helped support
his destitute family. Famous for his bizarre appearance and dark-green
spectacles, he became addicted to alcohol and probably opium, suffered
much ill-health, and in later years lived in a succession of one-room lodgings, 'a porter bottle doing duty for a candlestick, and a blanketless pal-
let for a bed and writing table', or he was out on the streets. He died a
miserable death in the Meath Hospital in 1849, but his unfinished and
somewhat allegorical autobiography (1848) captures something of the tor-
mented pauper genius. His literary contemporary, William Carleton, who
came to Dublin as a pauper migrant in 1818 and achieved sufficient literary
acclaim in the 1830s to become financially secure for a while, also left an
unfinished autobiography that included a striking pen-picture of his first
night in town spent in a Bridgefoot Street cellar where hordes of beggars
lodged on straw beds, 'the lame, the blind, the dumb and ... every variety
of impostor', a Dantean world unknown to the settled citizenry. [94]

Many, however, observed and wrote about the very poor, occasionally with great empathy. Asenath Nicholson, the Vermont 'penny-
philanthropist', who travelled the country in 1847, spent six months as
a penurious lodger in Cook Street during the peak of the Famine crisis,
dividing her meagre income between gifts of bread to all comers and the
hand-outs of fuel, rent and cooked gruel to the most desperate twenty
families she could find. In her account (published in 1851) she focused on
the individual tragedies she had witnessed, judging them as victims of a
cruel world, and concluded that Dublin 'is a city celebrated for its benevo-
lence, and deservedly so, as far as giving goes. But *giving* and *doing* are
antipodes ...' This was a harsh judgement, such was the range of religious
charities then operating. Mary Aikenhead, founder of the Sisters of Charity in 1816, had Nicholson's sense of mission, but also had organisational
flair – running a female 'house of refuge' from 1819, a city orphanage from
1822, and then in 1834 establishing the first female-run hospital, St Vincent's, in St Stephen's Green, which offered its services free to 'the suffering poor'. Margaret Aylward in the next generation was an even clearer

case of a strong-willed Catholic philanthropist. From a wealthy Waterford background, she settled in Dublin in 1846 and among her various initiatives in the following decade were a needle-factory for poor women and a boarding-out orphanage, St Brigid's, which liaised with the workhouses. By 1870 it was the largest rescue agency in the city, placing nearly 300 foundlings with Catholic foster-parents in the countryside each year. Aylward was not afraid to court controversy and even imprisonment to protect 'her' Catholic charges; in the 1860s she set up five 'St Brigid' schools for poor girls in the inner city, ostensibly to protect them from rival Protestant agencies, and these 'ragged schools' mirrored Christian Brothers' schools in many respects. In 1864 she established the Holy Faith order to formalise and extend this programme to 'save' the marginalised. Like Aikenhead she was driven far more by a sense of religious purpose than social reform and had little reason to diagnose or to publicise the condition of the poor other than as a means of extracting donations from the faithful.[95]

Dr Thomas Willis, an apothecary based on Ormond Quay, was rather different. He was a leading figure among the nineteen mainly lay Catholics who in 1844 established the Dublin St Vincent de Paul organisation. This soon became the largest voluntary provider of assistance to poor householders in the city, distributing food-tickets entitling the holders to rations of meal, bread, tea, even 'one sheep's head', and in the 1860s pioneering a highly successful penny-bank scheme. Willis's activism was based on rigorous observation: having been a guardian (i.e. board member) of the North Dublin Union for several years, he carried out a minute social survey of the artisanal population of his parish of St Michan's in 1844, publishing the results the following year. He was influenced by Edwin Chadwick, the first champion of public health reform in Britain, and believed that the 'miasma' of the city, the pervasive stench in many districts, was toxic, for 'all smell is disease' and only a re-engineering of the environment with proper urban drainage and abundant water could transform the health and life expectancy of poorer households. Personal dirt reflected a lack of water and Willis lamented that 'amongst the working classes, there is not a woman with a washed face in almost the entire district of St Michan's'. He was also influenced by Wilde's recent demonstration of the sharp differentials in city mortality, specifically of children under five, reflecting the huge differences in hygiene, nutrition and access to unpolluted water. Willis demonstrated that 51.7 per cent of the population in his sample of 3,000 working-class families (none of them actually destitute) died before their fifth birthday, giving a life expectancy at birth of 19.2 years, considerably worse than Wilde's estimate for the city at large of 25.6 years. Willis's working-class group, beside being obviously poorer than the city average, were also less rooted in the city: as many as 45 per cent of his heads of household were born outside Dublin and had spent an average of 9.3 years in the city. Despite his particular fascination with water and drains, Willis drew a general conclusion that resonated in all later debates on public health and poverty – without every city family being housed in 'residences fit for human beings', all other measures of reform would be a mere palliative. And, as it turned out, St Michan's suffered very severely in the years following: 27 per cent of the city's cholera deaths in 1849 were in this one parish.[96]

Despite the strengthened powers of the Corporation from 1849 and the economic upturn in the decade following, the material deficiencies affecting working-class living that were documented in such detail in the 1830s and 1840s stubbornly persisted in more prosperous times. A third of the city's housing stock within the municipal boundaries remained in tenements in 1861, and in a survey that year of 134 'of the worst streets' there was an average of 3.6 people to a room and 2.7 to a bed. One reform advocated by Willis, the ban on the use of cellars as tenements, was, however, followed up with by-law changes, and by 1864 over 3,000 below-street basements had been closed for human habitation. A city bath-house was opened in 1852, attached to the Mendicity Institute – a huge success for its overwhelmingly male clients, especially on Saturday evenings – but it was not until 1885 that the Corporation developed public baths. The policing of retail food markets greatly improved; thus in 1876 more than 90 tons of butchers' beef was condemned, beside much smaller quantities of mutton, pork, fish and goat meat, but municipal oversight of slaughtering only really began with the opening of a large public abattoir in 1882. Public urinals, one of the many reforms advocated by Willis, began to appear in the 1860s. Progress on sewerage was more limited: the hybrid drainage system of the city – some forty-two miles of street sewers – was systematically surveyed and examined in the 1850s, confirming the relative absence of main drains in the western half of the city. But funding a comprehensive sewage disposal system on the London model was decades away.[97]

The arrival of abundant Wicklow water was the first really tangible improvement, even if its impact on tenement Dublin was muffled. The Corporation gradually acquired statutory powers to monitor public health and enforce sanitary regulations: a part-time medical officer was appointed in 1864, a Public Health Committee in 1866 at the time of the last serious cholera epidemic, and in 1874 a small team of 'sanitary officers' was created (by direction of the new Local Government Board). This process was extended after the more comprehensive Irish Public Health Act of 1878, which inaugurated the 'Cameron era', the forty-year reign of Sir Charles Cameron as Chief Medical Officer. The background was the city's persistently high death rates; indeed, with better data after the introduction of civil registration in 1864, there was worrying evidence that rates in the 1870s were actually getting worse. However, fear of epidemic, specifically cholera scares (even as late as 1873), concentrated minds far more than statistical trends. But the central issue for most reformers remained the persistence of tenement housing into an age where this was becoming anomalous, if not scandalous.

The total number of tenements was actually falling from the 1860s, but compared with other major UK cities Dublin's housing statistics and its public health ranking were becoming quite out of line. Reformers were not united on the housing issue, a few still doubting its importance. The relatively large number of unskilled labourers, the relatively slow growth of the city, and the relatively weak financial position of the Corporation, its tax revenues compromised by the ongoing drift to the autonomous suburbs, were all a drag on the capacity of local government to intervene. And, as became clear in the next generation, there was a powerful lobby of house-owners, well represented in City Hall, who had simply no wish to see the Corporation transform the housing landscape. It did, however, make a tentative first step in 1877 by acquiring a four-acre site in the heart of the old Liberties off the Coombe for public housing. But realising this plan turned out to be far more costly and troublesome than predicted: 984 existing residents were bought out and the site levelled, whereupon it was leased on very favourable terms to the newly established Dublin Artisans' Dwelling Company. With great ceremonial, the viceroy earl Cowper laid the foundation stone in December 1880, and the company promptly erected 212 one- and two-storey cottages. The scheme was one of a number of projects it undertook to supply new-style working-class housing. Perhaps surprisingly, the company had almost no links with the Corporation, but it had a long credit-line and was strongly Protestant in

its make-up. The earl of Meath was one of the largest investors. Was this
move on inner-city housing a patrician epilogue, or a prologue to something better?[98]

8

WHOSE DUBLIN?
1880–1913

In Parnell's shadow

The results of the great remodelling of the Phoenix Park, begun in the 1830s, were well hidden to the casual eye half a century later. The beauty of the park's open spaces seemed natural and timeless. But they were an artifice, the legacy of London landscape architect Decimus Burton and his 'improvements'. He created the formal carriageway that bisects the Park and runs with Roman straightness from Parkgate at the city end north-westwards to the Castleknock Gate, providing thereby a series of superb panoramas: the Dublin Mountains across the city to the south and closer to hand the Wellington Monument and the three government residences, the 'lodges' of the viceroy, the Chief Secretary and the Under-Secretary. The 'Big Wind' of 1839 had destroyed much of the eighteenth-century timber, but Burton's ash, beech and lime trees were by now artfully framing these vistas. Burton had got to know the Phoenix Park when he was designing the layout for the zoo, and he went on to adapt for Dublin some of the improvements that he had planned for Regent's Park and other royal spaces in London. He transformed the visual quality of the Phoenix Park, managing to exhibit viceregal power in an understated way while enhancing public access. The Park had of course been a place of public resort long before Burton, particularly when military reviews were scheduled. The area had always possessed a strong military flavour, surrounded as it was by the Magazine Fort, the Hibernian Military School, the Ordnance Survey in Mountjoy House and the Royal Military Infirmary, and these buildings were supplemented in 1842 by the large training depot built for the Royal Irish Constabulary (RIC), to which a riding school was added in the 1860s. But despite this military 'necklace' and Burton's formal boundary walls and gate-lodges, the Park was no defensive citadel. Apart from the momentary frissons in 1848 and 1867, the houses and families of the three great officers of state were lightly guarded. Indeed, William Forster, Chief Secretary from 1880 to 1882, often walked through the Park on his way to work in Dublin Castle.[1]

The Castle, by contrast, remained its old ramshackle self, continuing both as the hub of an ever-expanding government machine and the ceremonial centre of viceregal entertainment, notably the daytime 'levées' and the evening 'drawing-rooms', which enjoyed something of a mid-Victorian revival. Several attempts were made in the course of the nineteenth century to abolish the viceregal office and with it the pageantry of the Castle (most famously in 1850), but such moves stung Dublin politicians, conservative and nationalist, into common outrage, prompting them to warn of the huge loss to the city if the office were abolished and the Castle abandoned to bureaucrats and policemen. However, it is doubtful whether abolition would have had much economic impact, for as time went on most of those who were summoned by the Ulster King-at-arms to the great formal events were resident public servants, army officers, plus an uncertain assortment of the city's bourgeoisie. At the first levée of 1881, a quarter of the 800-odd present were army officers, fifty were medics and a mere seventeen aristocrats. Much, of course, depended on the reputation and party colour of particular viceroys: entertainments held during the Liberal earl of Carlisle's years (Lord Lieutenant 1855–8, 1859–64) were reportedly packed by all sorts, but even conservative figures like the marquess of Abercorn (Lord Lieutenant 1866–8, 1874–6) could invest the post with great theatrical spectacle, memorably in 1868 when he took over the newly restored St Patrick's Cathedral for the installation of the Prince of Wales as a Knight of the Order of St Patrick. Such *ancien régime* events gave welcome springtime business to the many hundreds of dress-makers, wine merchants and pastry cooks, but these occasions were only the most rarefied of the many excuses for public wining, dining and display across the civic calendar.[2]

By comparison with the Castle, the official houses in the Park were semi-private spaces where there was only modest entertainment. But the Park itself had become a popular amenity, what with the success of the zoo and of the nearby Promenade Grounds (later the People's Gardens), the proliferation of middle-class sporting grounds (with the first of several cricket pitches in 1838, a polo ground in 1873, and briefly a golf club in the 1880s), and its choice as venue for large protest meetings. The great gathering of city journeymen in 1780 opposing the Combination bill had probably been the first such event, and the Park was used for mass meetings from time to time thereafter. There was huge controversy in 1871 when the Amnesty Association organised a meeting at the Wellington Monument to call for the release of the remaining Fenian prisoners. This was banned, but it went ahead nevertheless. A major riot ensued, the result of poor policing. The upshot was that Gladstone's Liberal government determined that there would be no further attempt to curtail the right of assembly in the Park. Other great causes, notably the battle for and against the Sunday closing of public houses, were championed at raucous meetings, but much the largest event was a rally in March 1880 in support of the National Land League, when a crowd of some 30,000 were led through the city by the usual trade societies and bands. 'Workers of Dublin! Your poverty is the result of a system which endeavours to degrade labour and to elevate idleness', declared the placards in advance, and Thomas Brennan, one of the speakers, gave a stirring socialist analysis of the interconnectedness of urban poverty and the ills of the land system, a task made easier by growing signs that the recent fall in agricultural prices was hitting urban employment and boosting numbers in the two city workhouses. Brennan was one of the founders of the Land League and an ex-IRB man, very close to his uncle Patrick Egan, who was also on the platform: they were city men and republicans, shareholders in the North City Milling Company in Phibsborough, and quite unusual in being men of capital *and* social radicals. The leading speaker that day was another founding member of the League, Andrew Kettle, a wealthy Fingal farmer, Home Rule veteran and close confidante of the new Home Rule leader, Charles Stewart Parnell.[3]

Parnell, despite inheriting an old Wicklow estate, had limited personal links with the city, his formal education having been outside the country. But he had important local allies whose role in the Land War tends to be overlooked. A number of city-based organisers of diverse origin were crucial in devising the 'new departure', the tactical link-up of Home Rule MPs with the politicised land agitation spreading from the west of Ireland and involving elements of the Fenian movement – where the sole agenda heretofore had been to realise the Republic. Egan, Brennan and their circle handled the national finances of the League (including a large inflow of funds from America), coordinated major meetings and provided legal support. They secured the backing of the still dominant national daily, the *Freeman's Journal* (holding out the threat that their very popular party weekly, *United Ireland*, might have to appear daily), and they helped shape the story for the international media, presenting the rent strikes and other actions as a desperate response to the greed of a parasitic landlord class and an outmoded property system. Thanks to the ferocity of the League's subsequent campaign across much of the country and to Parnell's guile in bonding and managing the Home Rule party that took it over, the power of the gentry was indeed cracked, but not quite broken, in the years ahead.[4]

One of the defining moments in the long war of attrition between the League and the British government came in October 1881 when Parnell, having denounced Gladstone and his reforms, was arrested in Dublin, as were most of the national leadership. In prison, they declared a national rent strike, as a result of which the League was declared illegal. The detainees were held in Kilmainham jail, now well established as the main repository for 'political' prisoners. The arrests led to serious rioting in Sackville Street and to accusations of brutality by the Dublin Metropolitan Police. The nationalist leadership was held in prison without trial for almost six months. A breakaway group of city Fenians, calling themselves the 'Invincibles', came together later that autumn with the intention of staging a high-profile political assassination. It seems that around thirty to forty members were sworn in by the English-based leadership, none of whom was directly connected with the Land League. 'Buckshot' Forster, the controversial Chief Secretary, was targeted and surgical knives were obtained in London. The plan, however, miscarried. Meanwhile Parnell negotiated a political deal with Gladstone ('the Kilmainham treaty') that promised to de-escalate the Land War, and in early May 1882 the League leadership emerged as heroes out of jail. A new and more reform-minded team, led by Earl Spencer, was appointed to take over the Irish government.

On the evening after Spencer's swearing-in, the new Chief Secretary, Lord Frederick Cavendish, and the long-established Under-Secretary, Thomas Burke, were walking home unaccompanied through the Phoenix Park. Unknown to the police, the latter had become the new target for the

Invincibles. Some ten members of the gang followed them, attacked Burke and killed him. Without recognising his associate, they dealt the same fate to young Cavendish, all in full view of the Viceregal Lodge. Their deaths were nearly instant, an act of demonstrative political violence unique in the city's history.[5] A midnight edition of the *Evening Telegraph* was the first to break the news, and 'by the light of street lamps men were everywhere seen reading aloud to others the details of the frightful affair'. All local papers, even *United Ireland,* denounced it roundly; American Fenians were the first suspects. The immediate consequence on the nationalist side was to strengthen Parnell's resolve to impose an iron hand on his heterogeneous political army, both at home and in Westminster, and with the establishment of the National League later in October he managed to harness the agrarian movement onto a new kind of centralised 'Irish Party'. He drafted in the Munster Land League veteran Timothy Harrington to help build a national electoral organisation, and by 1887 there were over 1,500 branches. But his erstwhile Dublin allies of a more radical turn, notably Egan and Brennan, were damaged by false rumours of links with the Invincibles and disappeared from the scene.[6]

For government, the imperative after the assassinations was to break the Invincibles, to punish those responsible, and to drastically improve state security. Here the role of the city police comes into prominence, for it was G Division, the detective section of the DMP, led by John Mallon, that faced immediate criticism for not anticipating the threat, and it was then censured for the slow progress in cracking the conspiracy. G Division was forty years old and was made up of around thirty plain-clothed officers, chosen from the general ranks on merit and political reliability. Mallon's background was the small-farm world of south Armagh and, like the vast majority of the force, he was Catholic; however, most of Mallon's fellow DMP officers were Protestant. There was considerable discontent over wages and working conditions in the ranks at that time, but the political reliability of the force was not an issue. Since beginning its operations in 1838, the DMP's numbers had hovered at around 1,000 men and, as Anastasia Dukova has shown, it was always a fairly tightly run organisation, its effectiveness strengthening over the decades with better training and discipline, as was evident in the relatively low general crime rates for the city in the later nineteenth century. For example, the number arrested for common assault in 1882 was less than a quarter of the 3,307 arrests made in 1850, and in 1882 there were only two murders recorded in the whole police district – other than the two in the Phoenix Park. Mallon's combination of dogged detective work, artful use of informers and 'a memory that never slept' cracked the Invincibles, but he was helped by emergency legislation that permitted the almost unlimited interrogation of political suspects.

Many believed that Egan, the Land League treasurer, was the godfather behind the conspiracy, but Mallon focused on the cigar-smoking James Carey of Cork Street, a bricklayer, master builder and owner of some eighty tenements. He had been a major IRB figure in the city for nearly twenty years before stepping down in 1878, apparently in disgust at the infighting. He was arrested two months after the murders, but then released for want of evidence. Some weeks later he capitalised on what was presented as police victimisation by winning a seat on the city Council, only to be re-arrested and tricked by Mallon into becoming a prosecution witness early in 1883. His evidence helped convict fifteen men, five of whom were executed. Their dignity and mildness in court helped soften public attitudes and stirred up popular sympathy. Carey was now seen as the shameful 'approver', his notoriety heightened when news came through of his murder in South Africa while travelling incognito under Crown protection. His effigy was promptly burnt in numerous city bonfires, eloquent proof that repeated use of informers gravely impaired public acceptance of the judicial process. A less obvious legacy of the Park murders was the birth of systematic intelligence-gathering by the government, both in Dublin and London, the Irish Crimes Special Branch becoming a fresh addition to Castle bureaucracy. G Division survived these reforms and the all-knowing Mallon remained in office for another two decades; overall DMP numbers rose by a fifth. One practical dividend of the crisis was the decision to build an elegant brick palace on the edge of the Park a short distance east of the Viceregal Lodge. On completion in 1892 this became the Marlborough cavalry barracks.[7]

The 1851 agreement that the lord mayoralty should alternate between Catholic/nationalist and Protestant/Conservative councillors was abandoned in 1883. Conservative numbers in City Hall had fallen considerably since the Indian summer of the 1850s, but it was the polarised political climate of the 1880s that brought power-sharing to an end. The breaking point came when George Moyers, conservative Lord Mayor in 1881, used his casting vote to reject a proposal to give Parnell and John Dillon, then in Kilmainham jail, honorary freedom, and this led the nationalist majority to abandon the conciliatory practice (even though the vote on honorary freedom was reversed three months later). During that tense winter, plans for a new industrial exhibition in the Winter Gardens had to be abandoned as the cross-party committee fought over whether or not to invite the queen to be its patron (a replacement exhibition in the Rotunda gardens had a strongly Irish focus, focusing on the promotion of rural Irish crafts and Dublin manufactures, and without any official patron). And it was from this time that the Lord Mayor and city officials declined all invitations to formal events in the Castle. There were to be few breaches in that frosty relationship for more than twenty years.[8]

Part of the Liberal programme of reform in the 1880s was a further widening of the parliamentary franchise across the UK. This was enacted in 1884 and was followed by a drastic redrawing of constituencies in 1885. Dublin city was divided into four single-seat constituencies, Co. Dublin into two. On the eve of Gladstone's reforms, the size of the city electorate had still been very restricted – with fewer than one in five adult males on the register – whereas in the momentous parliamentary election of November 1885 more than two in five males were able to vote, in what was now (since 1874) a secret process. The overall result produced a hung parliament and the very real prospect of Home Rule, but in Dublin city and county neither Tory nor Liberal candidates survived the democratic blizzard. Four Irish Party MPs were elected for the city, two of whom were leading newspaper proprietors (Edward Gray and Timothy Sullivan), and three of whom were part of the 'Bantry band' which dominated constitutional nationalism in Dublin during Parnell's ascendancy.

The nationalist stranglehold on City Hall was also intensified in these years (it was only in the southern townships and on the South Dublin Board of Guardians that the trend was resisted). Throughout the years of Parnell's ascendancy there was a rare unity among nationalist politicians in the city, reflected in the names chosen for new streets, a public endorsement of both constitutional and insurrectionist traditions: Isaac Butt, former head of the Home Rule party, was scarcely in his grave when the new swivel-bridge just above the Custom House was given his name; then the Corporation and the Port and Docks Board had a tussle over the renaming of Carlisle Bridge after its substantial reconstruction: the Corporation won out and attached O'Connell's name to the new structure, to coincide with the long delayed completion of his monument nearby. But when in 1884 the Corporation tried to rename Sackville Street in a similar fashion, most commercial property owners rose up in protest and secured a permanent injunction against the Corporation adopting O'Connell's name. However, City Hall retained a free hand in the christening of new streets. For the boulevard striking south from Butt Bridge that was opened in 1885, they made the safe choice of Tara Street, but for the corridor running from City Hall towards the precincts of Christ Church Cathedral and opened the following year, they returned to a more dangerous history, gracing it with Lord Edward FitzGerald's name. No one, it seems, protested.[9]

A crucial factor in this nationalist consensus was a marked shift in the attitudes among the Catholic clergy. After the death of Cardinal Cullen in 1878, the earnest under-study Edward MacCabe took his place, but was a far less effective leader. Predictably, he was no friend of the Land League with its Fenian patina and he was highly suspicious of Parnell. The city clergy were more or less kept out of politics. This restriction was resented at the time as other bishops were taking a more supportive position towards the Irish Party. But after MacCabe's death in 1885, his successor moved with the times: William Walsh, son of an Essex Quay watch-maker and president of Maynooth College at the time of his appointment, was discreetly supportive of Parnell from the beginning. He ran into trouble in Rome for his endorsement of the 'Plan of Campaign' – the renewed land agitation in 1886 – but this made him hugely popular in the nationalist press and helped cement the broad political front that was Parnellism.[10]

One of the new MPs elected in the Irish Parliamentary Party (IPP) landslide of 1885 was William Martin Murphy. He won in St Patrick's, the constituency for the old city and Liberties. Murphy was a Belvedere College boy from west Cork, and had returned to the city from the south ten years previously. That was the start of an extraordinary business career. Working with Lombard, his father-in-law, he created the Dublin United Tramways Company (DUTC) in 1880, a move that resulted in the near-total integration of horse-tram services across greater Dublin into a thirty-two-mile network, and he went on to manage it with great success. Passenger numbers rose from around ten million in 1881 to twenty-five million per annum in the mid-nineties – without the addition of further routes. And after witnessing the new tramcar technology in America, he switched from horse-power to electricity in the late 1890s, absorbing the remaining independent tram company and extending the company's system to some fifty-five miles. A relaying of the tracks to a wider gauge and the erection of a mesh of overhead wires were completed by 1901; by 1914 the company was carrying 58 million passengers p.a. and boasting that it was one of the finest urban tramway systems in the world, with capital invested exceeding £2 million. Murphy became involved in a myriad of other transport projects; in the 1880s he busied himself in light-railway construction (both as promoter and contractor), mainly in south and west Munster, then in the city where he was involved in the high-level 'loop line' linking the south-east with the north-side network in 1891 (at a very high visual price, the inelegant iron and steel bridge over the Liffey completely obscuring downstream views of Gandon's Custom House). Later in his career, his company was involved in tramway and light-railway projects in England, Scotland, Argentina and the Gold Coast. Outside of transport he invested in retail houses, hotels, newspapers, gas and electricity, exemplifying what for Dublin was an unfamiliar type – a restless, boundless capitalist who chose nevertheless to remain at home. He had first shown his appetite for commercial risk in the very depressed retail conditions of the early 1880s when he led a consortium that took McSwiney's great department store on Sackville Street out of receivership. It was rebranded as Clery's, but Murphy was the money behind it. It took some time before it became what he wanted, the city's most famous shop.[11]

Murphy's business career combined prescience, nimbleness and a single-minded toughness. His political career was far more chequered, at least from November 1890 when nationalist unity was sundered in quite spectacular fashion. Following the exposure of Parnell's liaison with Mrs Kitty O'Shea, the leader's private life became public property, his rejection by the Irish Party the price that the Liberals demanded if Home Rule was to remain their policy. And even though Parnell died within a year of this, the divisions so suddenly stirred up by the crisis continued to convulse nationalist politics for a full decade and gave space for other political creeds to emerge. In Dublin, there was a strange imbalance of forces: most of the Irish Party leaders in the city came out against Parnell and his continued leadership, as indeed did Archbishop Walsh and all the hierarchy, but the city at large did not. Murphy was quick to disown Parnell, and he played a powerful if discreet role in establishing and bankrolling a new party organisation, the Irish National Federation. But nationalist public opinion within Dublin remained predominantly Parnellite and anti-clerical, as was strikingly evident at Parnell's funeral in October 1891. After a short Anglican service in St Michan's and a lying-in-state at City Hall, around 100,000 joined the procession to Glasnevin, not a priest in sight and 'the mass of working men ... all grave and seemly, ... [which] gave to the event at once its substance and its solemnity ... the keening and clapping of hands of the women [was] frequently heard'. Thanks not a little to extravagant clerical endorsement of the new National Federation, anti-Parnellite candidates triumphed in the 1892 general election in most constituencies outside Dublin. But in the capital Murphy and his colleagues polled abysmally, securing less than one-fifth of the votes cast in the city. Harrington (who alone among the city-based politicians remained loyal to the Parnellite faction) was the only sitting MP to be re-elected that year. Both the *Freeman's Journal* and *United Ireland* had initially chimed with this metropolitan Parnellism, but an anti-Parnellite paper, the *National Press*, funded initially by Murphy, had far greater impact outside the city. A fortnight after Parnell's funeral, a small bomb exploded in the basement of this paper, the work, it seems, of a Fenian and former Invincible, Jim Boland. The paper was unaffected.[12]

The hub of news

The political excitements of the 1880s transformed newspaper sales, and the greatest beneficiary in the short term was the venerable *Freeman's Journal,* even though *United Ireland* had taken greater risks and suffered greater official harassment. Earlier in the century Dublin's papers, conservative and independent, had lost ground to English rivals, and the nationalist press had fragmented. Things began to change after the abolition of stamp duty in 1855; four Dublin daily papers took the plunge and slashed their prices to a penny an issue in 1859, including the *Freeman's Journal* and a new conservative business paper, *The Irish Times,* in hopes both of increased provincial circulation and advertising revenue. Gradually this paid off. After the 1850s, wholesale newspaper distributors, exploiting the trunk railway network, managed to get Dublin papers onto provincial news-stands every morning ahead of the post. The Abbey Street warehouse of W. H. Smith, the pioneer wholesale newsagents in both islands, was a hive of activity from 5 a.m. each day.[13]

Dublin's role as Irish news hub was enhanced by the revolution in telecommunications beginning with the establishment of telegraphic transmission with London, operational via the North Channel link from

1853, and this Morse-linked web was dramatically extended in 1866 with the opening of a successful transatlantic cable via Valentia Island, meaning that news from America could now reach Dublin as quickly as London. As the cost of electric telegraphy fell in the 1860s, its crucial role in the transmission of commercial information was established. By the 1890s there were thirty-five telegraph offices in the city from which telegrams could be despatched worldwide, most of them open twelve hours a day, with the Cattle Market service the first to open at 6 a.m. That said, it was the seamless operation of the postal service, which remained vital to the functioning of the urban economy, evident since the dramatic fall in postal costs in 1840 with the coming of the UK-wide penny postal service. This was crucial to the growth of firms like the Stewart and Kincaid, the first Dublin land agency to provide management services to a nationwide portfolio of landed estates. Postal volumes grew exponentially in the following decades. By the late nineteenth century there were six postal deliveries every weekday in the city, five in the suburbs. The speed at which transatlantic mail reached the city via Queenstown was a constant issue, and Dublin's slight advantage here over Liverpool occasionally counted.

Telephone communication came to Dublin c.1880. The first primitive exchange was located in the Commercial Buildings, and once a link with Belfast was established commercial interest developed quickly. By 1888 there were some 700 telephones in the city. Voice quality was very poor, but the technology inaugurated a subtle change in the character, first of commercial, then social, communication. A telephone link to London (via Scotland) was established in 1893, but it was only after the opening of the Crown Alley exchange in 1900 and the introduction of a direct and robust cross-channel link in 1913 that telegraphy was fully eclipsed by the telephone. By that stage, perhaps one house in twenty had a handset, and there were nearly a hundred public 'call offices' in the city. Other American technologies were beginning to revolutionise the production and processing of information: the office typewriter, first used in Guinness's in 1893, was soon joined in their cash office by a 'mechanical calculating machine'.[14]

The accelerating speed at which information could be transmitted had both positive and negative effects on Dublin's role as national cultural broker. The range and volume of news carried in the Dublin papers of the late nineteenth century was vastly greater than in O'Connell's time, and the fall in newsprint costs reduced the price of the dailies and encouraged the development of weekly editions of the major papers. The latter were particularly popular with new readers and with emigrant subscribers. The progressive fall in both printing and material costs also led to innovations in cheap book production. Full-length editions of out-of-print works by Gerald Griffin, John Banim and William Carleton became available at prices that had once been charged for monthly magazines, and the pioneer here was James Duffy. Initially he made his name by publishing huge runs of cheap Catholic devotional material, but he soon diversified into song-books and popular histories for Young Ireland, then into a succession of cheap monthly miscellanies. A Monaghan man originally, he knew the country market. From c.1840 until the turn of the century his firm was almost single-handedly responsible for the regular reissue of 'national' and Catholic fiction in a variety of formats and on a vast scale. For over twenty years he published a series of ever-cheaper magazines, with reportedly 100,000 copies of the *Illustrated Dublin Journal* (1861–2) being sold at a penny each. But so successful was their fiction list that Duffy's sons abandoned the magazine format and sought overseas markets for their publishing imprint. The firm's list was safe and derivative by nature, but there was no rival in the city and no one seeking out new fiction, whatever the genre, no equivalent of William Curry Junior, who in the 1830s and 1840s had done precisely that. London houses completely dominated the anglophone market for new fiction in the Victorian era, even Irish fiction. The Loebers' magisterial survey of Irish fiction has revealed that in the course of the 1890s, 656 works of fiction by Irish authors were published in London as against a mere twenty-eight in Dublin. London firms even had a financial stake in the expansion of Dublin's commercial lending libraries.[15]

Such dominance is perhaps not surprising, but the near-absence of Dublin-produced popular magazines in an era when these were proliferating, particularly for a female readership, is curious. As Louis Cullen has shown in his study of Easons (which started out as the Dublin branch of W. H. Smith), there was a late Victorian surge in the number of weeklies, cheap periodicals and serialised fiction being imported from London, which were distributed nationally by Easons and their Dublin competitors, with only a few local titles like *The Shamrock* (with strong Fenian links), the Jesuit-run literary magazine *The Irish Monthly* (from 1873), and the *Irish Builder* (far broader in its concerns than the title might suggest), rare indigenous survivors in a flood of English material. By far the most successful local magazine was the *Lady of the House*, which started in 1890 and ran for forty-five years. Its claim to be 'written by gentlewomen for gentlewomen' was misleading as its sole editor was male and its market was the diversity of potential consumers of female fashion. Originally the house magazine of Findlaters, the high-class grocery chain, it became the essential line of contact between the city's department stores and their female clientele. For older children, English comics poured in, without, it seems, any local imitation. But this ocean of cheap print eventually met a challenge, *fin de siècle* cultural nationalism. And that in turn opened a new phase in the capital's role in the remodelling of Irish culture.[16]

Protestant strength

But in the meantime, what of those in the city who rejected both Gladstone and Parnell and who opposed the radical reordering of power within the country? The old party divisions between Liberal and Conservative disappeared in the 1880s, with the collapse of one and the retreat of the other, as defence of the Union became the new rallying call after 1885. But despite the prominence of Ulster in the revulsion against Gladstone's policies, Irish Unionists still took their cue from Dublin and read the Dublin conservative press. Home Rule was defeated in 1886 and 1893 by events in Westminster, not Dublin, but Dubliners played their part in engineering the survival of the Union, notably the great Tory lawyers and Dublin University MPs Edward Gibson and David Plunket.[17] Less important but more noisy opponents were the city's twenty Orange lodges, their members meeting each year for fire-and-brimstone speeches in the Rotunda on the twelfth of July. Although well supported by some Anglican clergy, the Order lacked strong patrons in the city, but it was heavily involved with Conservative clubs in the dark arts of voter registration. As Martin Maguire has shown, the Protestant Working Men's Club in York Street, located beside an Orange lodge, was the most conspicuous point of resistance to Home Rule in the city, with its lavish display of loyal flags and banners, and it was the scene of serious rioting during the 1885 general election. Indeed, it says much for the agility of the DMP throughout the 1880s and 1890s that the provocative behaviour of both nationalist and Conservative supporters at sensitive moments in the political calendar was held in check.[18]

Working-class hostility to Home Rule was by definition almost always Protestant, but support for the Conservatives was not exclusively

Protestant, and of course Parnell was not without some, albeit limited, Protestant support. Tellingly, it was William Kenny, a Catholic lawyer, who in 1892 captured the parliamentary constituency of St Stephen's Green for the Unionists (thanks to the divisions within nationalist ranks). And in the same year, some of the electoral support in South Dublin for the Unionist Horace Plunkett, aristocratic champion of agricultural cooperation, was Catholic. The heartland of this Unionism was in the southern townships, particularly Rathmines. A decade earlier, the township had successfully resisted the appalling vista of boundary change and incorporation into the city, and confidence in its independent future was celebrated with a new town hall. Its striking bank-like exterior, constructed in Scottish red sandstone, was completed in 1899.[19]

From 1892 to 1900 Conservative/Unionist candidates took four of the ten parliamentary seats for Dublin city and county (including the two university ones), and they became the lone but vocal spokesmen for southern Unionism in Westminster. With their opponents now so bitterly divided, it was possible for Unionists to see the nationalist advance of the 1880s as little more than an aberration, the product of hard economic times and misguided Liberal policy. After all, the commanding heights of business and the professions were still firmly Protestant, perhaps even more so than at mid-century. Murphy and his friends may have controlled the tramways, but most of the banks, most of the public utilities, the insurance companies and other financial services, still had a firmly Protestant air. The management of the GSWR, despite a strong Catholic presence in its early days, now had the reputation of being a Protestant-run business. And the MGWR appeared to be the personal fiefdom of Sir Ralph Cusack, chairman for a quarter of a century and a man not averse to promoting his relatives. But in reality the railway companies, engineering firms and other advanced sectors were not practising religious discrimination per se, but enthusiastically headhunting talent from across the water and looking after their own. Nowhere was this more apparent than in the greatest success story: James's Gate. After the brewery's public flotation in 1886 (on the London, not Dublin, Stock Exchange) and the temporarily diminished role of Edward Cecil Guinness, the management became less Trinity and more Oxbridge, its growth markets British, American, even Australian. Yet in the world of Dublin Protestantism, the extraordinary success of the Guinness family was a source of intense pride, reinforced on a more modest scale by the rise of Cantrell and Cochrane, the UK's largest mineral-water manufacturer by 1900, and of the great biscuit-making firm of Jacob's of Bishop Street, which had also become an international brand, employing over 2,000, mainly female, employees by that time.[20]

The Jacobs had come from Waterford in the 1850s and, like the Pims, were exemplars of Quaker commercial success. Sir Henry Cochrane was a Cavan man who had come to Dublin via Belfast, and his firm remained a two-city venture. But the Guinnesses were unambiguously Dublin and Anglican. Benjamin Lee, as we have seen, was politically active as a reforming Tory in the 1850s and 1860s and his elder son Arthur Edward (created Baron Ardilaun in 1880) followed a similar path. After sharing control in James's Gate with Edward Cecil for nine years, he sold his share in the business and turned to politics and philanthropy. As Tory MP for Dublin (1874–80) he wielded discreet political influence, and his enormous wealth helped bankroll Irish Unionism in the following decades. This included the purchase in 1900 of the Tory rivals of *The Irish Times* – the *Evening Mail* and the *Irish Daily Express* – at a moment of Unionist division. But the importance of his political activities was far exceeded by his civic and private spending: in the late 1870s he financed the reconstruction of the Coombe maternity hospital (his grandfather had been involved in its establishment), and he oversaw the remodelling of St Stephen's Green, buying out the key-holders and turning it into an oasis of woodland and wildlife, before opening the gates and handing it into public ownership in 1880. Then there was the massive investment in the family's suburban bolt-hole off the Howth Road, St Anne's. This became an Italianate palace of Vanderbilt proportions, overlooking Bull Island, its French gardens and parkland spreading across nearly 500 acres (a handful of farms and villas being eradicated in the process). Ardilaun was intermittently active on the local front: he acted as one of the original commissioners for Clontarf when it secured township status in 1869, remaining formally involved until its demise in 1900, and he underwrote the cost of a new Anglican church, rectory and school for Raheny parish.[21]

But Ardilaun had strong rural interests (notably forestry and hunting), and he poured money into the family's estates in Galway and Mayo. Thus arose his interest in the Royal Dublin Society: late in life he became its president for sixteen years, helping it complete a transformation from its post-Union portmanteau role as national sponsor of the arts and sciences back to being the patrician champion of rural improvement. From the time of his involvement with the 1867 Industrial Exhibition he

30. St Anne's, Clontarf, c.1912. Much the largest mansion built in the suburbs in the later nineteenth century, Lord Ardilaun's house overlooked Bull Island, with exotic gardens and French-styled parkland to the rear. His nephew, Bishop Plunket, inherited in 1925 and spent years trying to offload the huge property. It was eventually purchased by Dublin Corporation in 1938, who developed the demesne as a public park. But the mansion was gutted by fire in 1943.

supported calls for a national museum of science and art along the lines of the cultural cluster emerging at Kensington in London. Conflicting interests, political and scholarly, stymied the idea, but as city MP he played a critical role in securing the passage of the compromise Dublin Science and Art Museum act in 1877 (40 & 41 Vict., c.234). This led to the London-based Department of Science and Art acquiring the whole of the Leinster House complex from the RDS; it leased back the main building to the Society rent-free but took over the Natural History Museum and the Agricultural Hall, the latter being earmarked as the site for the much-heralded museum. It also acquired the RDS library – and the librarian, William Archer, whose innovative ideas heavily influenced the superb National Library building. This was designed in tandem with its twin, the Dublin Museum of Science and Art (later the National Museum), by the Dublin architectural firm T. N. Deane and Son, and was completed in 1890. There was a gentle irony in the fact that it was a Tory government

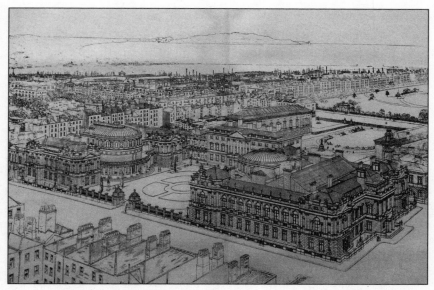

31. A birds-eye view of the new National Library and Museum. *By the early 1890s the four national cultural institutions, the Library and Museum, the National Gallery and the Natural History Museum, were open to the public, sharing the expansive grounds of Leinster House with the Royal Dublin Society.*

that set in motion the construction of two of the city's most distinguished cultural institutions, whose *raison d'être* was premised on the cultural distinctiveness of Ireland. Generous terms allowed the RDS to transplant its modest cattle and horse shows out of Kildare Street to a green-field site in Ballsbridge, and in purpose-built and far more ample quarters a new-style RDS Horse Show was first held there in 1881. This was a great success and, despite the troubled rural backdrop, attendance levels trebled in the course of the decade. By the time Ardilaun assumed the presidency in 1897, the Society's Horse Show Week, held then at the end of each August, drew high society from the three kingdoms, with all its attendant hunt balls and house parties. Also located in the new Ballsbridge facilities, the 'Spring Show' was another winner, becoming 'one of the largest, if not the largest, show of breeding cattle in the world' by 1900, scheduled towards the end of the old social 'season' and after what had become the other great spring occasion, Punchestown Races.[22]

Ardilaun's greatest impact on the city was as the first president and leading investor in the Dublin Artisans' Dwelling Company (DADC). Between 1877 and 1909 this enterprise constructed over 3,750 houses and apartments, most of them within the canals, ranging in size from two-roomed, single-storey cottages to six-roomed two-storey terrace houses, brick-built for the most part and nearly all of standardised design. The largest scheme was the Mount Temple project in the Manor Street/Arbour Hill district on the north-west side of town, where over 1,000 dwellings were constructed between 1901 and 1909 on twenty-eight acres. Board of Works loans helped augment the company's working capital, but throughout this period the DADC was a tightly run and profitable business, overwhelmingly Protestant in both ownership and management, including old ground-landlords and new business leaders (like the Kinahans, the Martins and the Findlaters). Its tenants were drawn from a cross-section of the city's skilled working class and above, 'a genuine elite' of securely employed householders. The company's 'overseers' (mainly ex-policemen or ex-soldiers) monitored the behaviour of the huge tenant population, handled rent payments and recommended house switching as family size grew or contracted.[23]

The DADC was not a charity and was not intended to rehouse the city's poorest. A related enterprise, associated with both Ardilaun and his brother Edward Cecil Guinness, *was* a charity and did have a social mission: the Guinness, later Iveagh, Trust. Edward Cecil's wealth far outstripped that of his elder brother, for he was the great beneficiary of the company's flotation (for £6 million) in 1886, and continued to draw huge dividends from his controlling stake in the firm. Prior to their separation, the brothers had begun in the 1870s to provide subsidised apartments for employees at Bellevue (beside the brewery) and at Rialto, but these were not popular. Edward Cecil's much more ambitious initiative was in 1889–90, when he established the Guinness Trust, ostensibly to fund new housing for 'the poorest of the labouring population'. By then, possessing three English as well as two Irish mansions, his focus, socially and politically, was on London, and it was perhaps not surprising that fully four-fifths of the Trust's funds were earmarked for the London poor, a move that eased his way to the peerage (as Viscount Iveagh). But during the 1890s the Guinness Trust's Dublin wing, working with the DADC, caused a stir when it financed the construction of three five-storey apartment blocks at the western end of Kevin Street, containing 335 family units. Despite their Dutch gables, they were more London than Dublin in their monumental scale.[24]

Later in the 1890s, Dublin once again became important for the new Lord Iveagh. He returned to the brewery's boardroom in 1897 and in 1902 resumed the chair, while Farmleigh, his suburban mansion west of the Phoenix Park that had been purchased in the 1870s, was now given a fashionable makeover. Coinciding with this, he financed two striking interventions in the heart of the old city, the first in 1897 when, with his brother and another partner, he secured legislation to acquire the three-acre block of land lying between St Patrick's Cathedral and Bull Alley, a low-lying ghetto of murky alleyways, condemned houses and street markets. The project involved the complete clearance of the block and the creation of a new park, both as an amenity for the neighbourhood and as an elegant foreground for the cathedral on which their father had spent so much. Lying mostly within the old Liberty of St Patrick's, the neighbourhood had a fairly earthy reputation for its brothels and its second-hand markets, and was notorious as 'a very nest of fever'. To compensate for the loss of the markets, Iveagh financed the construction of a huge indoor market-hall a short distance away in Francis Street (the Iveagh Market), providing numerous stalls for the old-clothes dealers at a cost of some £60,000. His second intervention came when he secured a Dublin Improvement Act in 1899, allowing him to acquire a similar-sized 'rookery' to the north of Bull Alley (including St Bride's church and graveyard) and 'to cover it all over' with new buildings, in part to house the population being displaced from the alleyways beside the cathedral. To administer this project and the earlier local housing initiatives, he established a specifically Dublin housing charity, the Iveagh Trust, in 1903, and assigned it a capital fund of £240,000. Unlike the DADC, the new Trust was by definition philanthropic, which meant that rent levels could be set closer to those in the tenements and that the occupants would have access to an unprecedented range of social facilities, bath-houses for men and women, a palatial hall and 'play centre' for all, and purpose-built shops. A night-hostel with 508 cubicles was also included. The Trust had the resources to commission buildings of a very high specification and these were designed by London architects specialising in artisan housing and included many decorative flourishes. But, as with the DADC, the Trust insisted upon the moral policing of tenants and would-be tenants. And while there was an upper limit placed on the income of prospective tenants and considerable variety in size, the apartments were not intended for the unemployed or the destitute (although some of those displaced from the St Patrick's Park were very poor). The Trust prided itself on being strictly non-sectarian and non-political (although when Lord Iveagh brought George V to visit the

32. St Patrick's Park, c.1905. *There was now no sign of the ghetto in the manicured spaces of the public park and gardens north of St Patrick's Cathedral. By this stage the park was overlooked by the recently completed Iveagh Trust buildings (on right of photograph).*

Buildings in 1911, the children were drilled to sing the National Anthem).

When set against the totality of Dublin's housing needs, Kevin Street and Bull Alley were little more than a token gesture – but they were quite a token. They certainly spurred on the Corporation's resolve to tackle the 'fearful slum' next door, the area north of the Iveagh Buildings. There the Corporation shadowed Iveagh's scheme, acquiring and demolishing the ancient rookery around Bride's Alley, dislodging and scattering its inhabitants, and over the course of a decade they built a cluster of five-storey blocks of striking external similarity to those of the Iveagh Trust, but which internally were actually superior in some respects. However, as some of these blocks were built over the underground course of the Poddle, the project became something of a financial nightmare, costing the Corporation just under £100,000. But by 1911, thanks to the combination of private unionist and public nationalist action, the urban landscape between the two medieval cathedrals was finally cleansed and utterly transformed.[25]

The links between the Guinnesses and the Church of Ireland operated on several levels: Annie, the only sister of Iveagh and Ardilaun, was married to William, Baron Plunket, Anglican archbishop from 1884 to 1897, and she focused her considerable philanthropic energies on the St Patrick's district as well. Her husband, the aristocratic leader of a now disestablished church, was an assertive evangelical, entirely comfortable in cooperating with the other Protestant churches. He was a veteran of the 'bible wars' in the West in the 1850s and had been heavily involved in the Irish Church Missions (ICM) there. The ICM had opened a second front in Dublin, using old and new methods to proselytise among the very poor of the city, and as a result there was a rash of minor sectarian attacks on people and property, mainly in the Liberties, in the late 1850s. These subsided, and the Dublin mission proved far more durable than those in Clifden or Achill, and Plunket became a powerful and unapologetic patron of its activities. By the time he was elected archbishop, there were twenty-one ICM branches in the city with teams of paid house-visitors coordinated from a hub in Townsend Street. At that location there were 'ragged schools', an orphanage, a training depot and a church. The Mission maintained some 600 children in its homes in the city and suburbs, and was feeding another 600 at its day schools. Plunket's ambitions were not restricted to Dublin: he campaigned for the recognition of Protestant congregations in Spain, Portugal and Italy, and this culminated in 1894 with his controversial consecration of a Spanish bishop in the Anglican rite. It was on his watch that the Dublin University Missions to China and to Chota Nagpur in India were established. Empire and its purposes were perhaps a more central concern in the Plunket household than in most: their eldest son (a diplomat) married a daughter of the marquess of Dufferin and Ava, the most influential Irish-born architect of empire, and viceroy of Canada and India. But by the 1890s, empire spelt opportunity for a great many Dublin households, and family success in the military and imperial public service, in civil engineering and colonial medicine was now a commonplace, to be celebrated in school magazines – and on church plaques.[26]

Protestant Dublin was, however, no monolith. There were at least seven autonomous Protestant denominations within the city, with non-Anglicans slightly under a fifth of the Protestant total in 1901. Presbyterians were particularly well represented both in the Clontarf area and in the inner south-side suburbs: Christ Church, the Presbyterian landmark in the centre of Rathgar, had opened in 1862 with seating for 400, but it had to be greatly extended in 1900 to accommodate another 160 seats. In all denominations, weekly church attendance, while not as high as Catholic levels, remained above urban levels in England. John Crawford has estimated that only 10 per cent of middle-class Anglicans were non-church-goers, with a higher (and it seems growing) proportion of absentees in working-class households. Within the Church of Ireland there were unceasing tensions, fanned from across the water, between High and Low church tendencies, between those who worshipped in ritualistic splendour at All Saints' (Grangegorman) or St Bartholomew's (Ballsbridge), and those who shared their Sunday afternoons with the Plymouth Brethren in the Merrion Hall. This 'cathedral' had been opened in 1863, its huge seating capacity by far the largest of the eight gospel halls in the city. The Brethren had been founded by a disaffected Dublin curate, John Darby, c.1830, and the sect became a cultural export across the anglophone world. Like Methodism in a previous generation, they attracted many adherents from orthodox Anglicanism, dividing families or splitting their loyalties.

But the visibility of the Church of Ireland was still striking: nearly sixty churches had been built or rebuilt across greater Dublin in the course of the nineteenth century, a majority before 1869 with state funds, but many by private subscription or bequest. The last church in the city attracting state funds, St Andrew's (completed in 1862) was the third post-Reformation church on the site, once the Parliament's and now the Stock Exchange's place of worship. The spread of church-based voluntary associations in the late nineteenth century like the Boys' Brigade, the Temperance Association, the Mothers' Union and the Church of Ireland YMCA, mostly English in origin, helped reinvent the city parish as a social unit and instil a sense of confessional community (the old formal status of the parish as a unit of local government, governed by a vestry, had withered away almost completely by mid-century). By comparison with such parish bodies, the importance of the Orange lodge in associational life was quite limited, its composition largely lower-middle-class and upper-working-class, city rather than suburban. Freemasonry provided a more effective fraternal network, overwhelmingly middle-class, liberally inclined and well resourced: the monumental Grand Lodge, opened in Molesworth Street in 1869, made this clear. Having a Lord Lieutenant as Grand Master (which was the case with the duke of Abercorn on his second tour of duty in the Viceregal Lodge), while having at the same time one of the brothers, Maurice Brooks, serving as a Home Rule MP for the city, indicated a broad church indeed. Freemasonry's strength in Dublin seems to have been growing around the turn of the century, not least because of its value as a passport for those who travelled the British empire. But Catholic masons were now an extreme rarity.[27]

The demographic decline of Dublin Protestantism nevertheless continued through the final decades of the Union, its make-up becoming more suburban, more middle-class and older than the average. There had been no Protestant ghettos for 200 years, and even in the most salubrious parts of Rathmines and Monkstown there were none now. The social distance from the Kildare Street Club to the Protestant Working Men's Club in York Street was still very great, yet other divisions within Protestantism were disappearing: access to St Stephen's, 'the Pepper Canister' chapel of ease, strikingly positioned east of Merrion Square, which had opened in 1827, was initially restricted to those who rented pews. Other east-side churches had strictly limited numbers of free pews. But such social apartheid was well gone by 1900 and the Anglican parishes and their churches were now socially mixed. Fissures remained, however, and politics revealed them in 1900 when the sitting Unionist MP for South Dublin, Horace Plunkett, stood for re-election. He had been intimately involved with the 'conciliatory' policies of the Conservative government, which had included the abolition of the grand jury system and its replacement by elected county councils in 1898, and also the introduction of district councils and the local franchise for women; the following year an Irish Department of Agriculture and Technical Instruction was established, extending further the complexity of devolved administration. Now there was talk of a final push to establish a state-financed Catholic university, an arrangement which threatened the intimate link between Trinity College and the University of Dublin. Many elements of this reform programme inflamed Protestant opposition in Dublin, and it was seen as nothing less than Conservative betrayal. Plunkett was associated with these conciliatory causes and his election campaign in 1900 exposed him. A strange coalition was mobilised to defeat him: TCD academics, Lord Ardilaun and the newspapers he now owned, and local leaders of the Orange Order. But ex-Liberals and business spokesmen came out in Plunkett's support. In the event, he outpolled his Unionist rival – but neither was returned. Instead Rathmines, Kingstown and parts adjacent were represented by John Mooney of the reunited Irish Party, with 43 per cent of the vote.[28]

Revivals and discoveries

Since the days of Smock Alley, going to the theatre had transcended creed
and softened social division. The dress circle and the sixpenny galleries
may have been worlds apart, but each could see and hear the other. This
was still true in the late nineteenth century when there was a much greater
choice of venue and repertoire. Ease of travel had allowed for a constant
circulation of performers and players across the Irish Sea and from further
afield. When the young prodigy Franz Liszt included Ireland on his hectic
British tour in 1840–41, he arrived (with his support team) in mid-winter
via the steam packet and the Kingstown railway to give six performances
in the Rotunda, and smaller ones in three provincial venues. The regular
visitors were Italian opera companies, who came to the city nearly every
autumn, appearing like a small army when they arrived. Their venue was
the massive Theatre Royal, the first major post-Union theatre that had
opened in Hawkins Street in 1821, its maximum capacity of 3,800 being
almost four times that of old Smock Alley. For decades the Hawkins Street
management was English, and as in the other theatres its offerings were
similar to those in English provincial venues, although after the huge success of Boucicault's *Colleen Bawn* in 1861, Irish melodrama came back into
fashion.[29]

Up to the 1870s Dublin theatres had maintained a resident troupe
of actors. But this changed when the Dublin brothers Michael and John
Gunn, whose father had prospered selling pianos and sheet music in
Grafton Street, opened the Gaiety Theatre in South King Street in 1871.
They operated it as a 'receiving house', hiring it out to an endless succession of touring companies. Michael Gunn was no passive *rentier*, however: while building up a highly profitable theatre business, he dabbled in
Buttite Home Rule politics (serving for some years on the Corporation),
and then taking a lease of the Theatre Royal as well. With extensive theatre dealings in London (notably with Richard D'Oyly Carte), he used
his two Dublin stages to bring over the latest London successes, ranging
from Gilbert and Sullivan to Wagner, as well as the standard classics. His
Theatre Royal was destroyed by fire in 1880, but he survived the setback
and built Leinster Hall on the site as a music venue (later opening the
first commercial gymnasium in an annexe). Then the Leinster was converted back to become another Theatre Royal in 1897 (although by that
time Gunn had disengaged and moved to London). During his regime

the competition had principally come from music halls and variety shows, notably from the Star of Erin in Dame Street (later 'Dan Lowery's', then completely rebuilt as the Empire Palace in 1897), and from the Queen's Royal Theatre in Great Brunswick Street (opened in 1844). The Queen's, under John Whitbread, its canny English manager, began to offer 'romantic subversion', much of it commissioned by Whitbread or even written by him, for the most part contorted romantic melodramas that were loosely based on Irish historical events, but well attuned to the charged politics of the 1880s, and he continued to pack them in for more than two decades. By creating a 'resident touring company' and sending the actors, after a successful run at the Queen's, to appear in provincial theatres in Ireland, Britain and the diaspora, Whitbread was able to transmit Dublin popular culture to an international audience at considerable profit. Ticket costs at each city theatre varied enormously, which meant that they remained as socially inclusive as cinemas were to become in the next century. Christopher Morash has estimated that in the early 1850s nearly 3,000 Dubliners would have attended theatre, be it opera or pantomime, on any one night; May Laffan in her fiction on Dublin street children in the 1880s imagined the waifs using the proceeds of a good day's begging to get into 'the Royal'. In Gunn's Gaiety there were times when over 600 people were left standing despite the provision of nearly 2,000 seats. The attendance of the police in Dublin theatres was a well-established practice – there to control audience enthusiasm or their disapproval – but despite such large numbers and mixed clientele they were safe and popular places.[30]

Musical literacy was commonplace in middle-class homes, thanks to the convent schools, the proliferation of independent music teachers and the increasing affordability of pianos (various forms of hire purchase were now well established). Music in working-class life was less structured, but the importance of a club band in any self-respecting branch organisation was always visible at public demonstrations and local ceremonial moments. More disciplined music-making in the public sphere was associated with the theatre pit and, even more so, with church. In the course of the century the number and quality of church choirs had blossomed, supported by ever more sophisticated organs. As in the past, those involved with Anglican cathedral music (notably the Robinson family) were the most prestigious figures in city music. But music-making, especially opera promotion, was a hard matter of business and was more predictably profitable than in pre-Union days. The 'Antient Concert Rooms' in Great

Brunswick Street and the Abbey Street Music Hall (both opening in the 1840s) were really large spaces, rented out for public meetings, recitals and a diversity of musical entertainments. However, by the late nineteenth century it was the career musicians associated with the Irish Academy of Music who dictated trends, the Academy becoming a more formidable body once the Corporation became directly involved in its governance in 1889. The remarkable professor of piano, the Neapolitan Michele Esposito, was a pivotal figure in Dublin music for more than forty years. In 1884 he launched the practice of regular chamber concerts in the RDS (in Leinster House), introducing Brahms and Dvořák, Debussy and Sibelius to Dublin ears. Then he oversaw the establishment of an auxiliary school (the Municipal School of Music) for working-class enthusiasts, embracing brass, percussion and wind as well as the more refined world of string. At the end of the 1890s he set up the Dublin Orchestral Society, which funded the first part-professional symphony orchestra in the city. It was not an unalloyed success, but some 200 concerts were held during its fifteen years of existence; the fact that they were generally scheduled for late afternoon suggests their limited social reach. The Feis Ceoil, an annual music festival, established in 1897, thanks principally to the Academy of Music but supported by the Corporation, was a broader church. Inspired by the Welsh Eisteddfod, the intent was to promote amateur musical performance and to sponsor distinctly 'Irish' composition. It remained a wholly Dublin-based organisation but had almost immediate nationwide appeal.[31]

In 1897 plans for an Irish literary theatre were first sketched out in Co. Galway by Lady Augusta Gregory, Edward Martyn and W. B. Yeats. It was an unlikely project involving a peripatetic group of writers of great ability but diverse vision, their patrons ranging from aristocratic cronies to Fenian veterans. But when *The Countess Cathleen*, their first production, opened in the Antient Concert Rooms in 1899 using amateur actors, the audience seems to have been puzzled rather than enthralled. It was roundly denounced by senior Catholic clergy for its celebration of an aristocratic woman selling her soul to feed the poor. Even when the theatre company dropped anchor at the Mechanics Institute in 1904 and a London patron paid for the building to be kitted out as the Abbey Theatre, it remained the smallest and most exclusive of the city's four licensed venues – a scarcity of cheap tickets saw to that. What, of course, made it so different was its experimental nature, its commitment to exclusively Irish drama shaped (initially anyway) by the mythological past, and its record of endless controversies, both public and internal. Inconsistent and ambiguous, Yeats was a superb publicist and his strong London connections ensured that Dublin's new theatre attracted distant attention almost from the beginning. He delighted in rubbishing the commercial stage-Irish drama offered in the larger theatres, in so doing belittling their cultural impact. However, by championing a playwright of J. M. Synge's quality and depth, the early Abbey earned the enormous attention bestowed upon it by posterity. Yeats and the Abbey team may have misjudged the wildly disapproving reaction in the pits during the first week of Synge's *Playboy of the Western World* in January 1907 and have caricatured their critics as merely boorish, but they did stand by their man.[32]

Edward Martyn was also involved (together with the artist Sarah Purser) in setting up An Túr Gloine, a cooperative workshop established off Pembroke Street in 1902, to develop stained glass-making in Ireland at a time when the strong demand for such glass from the churches was entirely met by British and German imports. As it turned out, the workshop was highly successful, involving gifted and mainly female alumni of the Metropolitan Art School, trained there by Alfred Child. His most distinguished student was Harry Clarke, son of a Yorkshire immigrant who had built up a church-decorating business and had branched into stained glass. Clarke's prodigious talents, both as a book illustrator and an artist in glass, threatened to draw him permanently to London, but he returned to the family business in North Frederick Street in 1914 and became part of the small Dublin coterie working in glass. Clarke led this group to international fame and a flow of commissions, both to his studios and An Túr, in the next generation. But with his technical virtuosity in glass and his 'characteristic delight in a medieval juxtaposition of the macabre and the sublime', the bizarre and the sexually ambiguous, he stood apart.[33]

Those who championed new kinds of theatre and of applied art worked in the shadow of what became a much larger cultural movement, the Gaelic League. This was established without fanfare in Dublin in 1893 to encourage the mass revival of spoken Irish. An unusual coalition of enthusiasts had for some time championed the preservation of the spoken language and in 1878, thanks to the almost single-handed enthusiasm of a National Bank clerk, David Comyn, the language had become an optional element in the curriculum in both national and intermediate schools. But the spark that led to the more ambitious initiative of 1893 was a stirring public lecture in Leinster Hall the previous autumn by Douglas Hyde, president of the newly formed Irish National Literary Society, 'the most important utterance of its kind since '48', reported Yeats. Hyde, an aspiring academic with finely tuned interests in the Irish language and its endangered oral riches, had spoken out with unusual clarity against 'men who read English books, and know nothing about Gaelic literature, nevertheless protesting as a matter of sentiment that they hate the country which at every hand's turn they rush to imitate', and he singled out the 'penny dreadfuls, shilling shockers, and still more, the garbage of vulgar English weeklies' which were making Ireland 'a nation of imitators, the Japanese of Western Europe'. In the depressing aftermath of the Parnellite split, the timing was favourable for a cultural new departure, an explicitly non-political, non-denominational movement committed to reviving the indigenous language, thereby restoring public access to the culture embedded within it and recreating an authentic sense of nationhood.

There had been earlier attempts to promote the old language, and the new League had a faltering start. A divide emerged between those who adopted Hyde's exclusively Gaelic vision of the future and those inspired by Yeats who sought to marry all the cultural ingredients from the Irish past, Protestant and pagan, into some kind of 'Celtic' renaissance. But in the early days this mattered little as the League began its gradual ascent to become the largest cultural organisation in the country's history, achieving a membership of around 16,000 in 1901 in 258 branches, and perhaps 40,000 by 1908 in 671 branches. There was some overlap between the Gaelic League and the Feis, but the revivalism of the League was at odds with the cosmopolitan tastes of the professional musicians involved in the latter. Some months after the first Feis in 1897, the League held the first Oireachtas na Gaeilge, filling the Rotunda with dancing competitions, singing and recitation. This annual festival rotated thereafter between venues around the country and dozens of county and local festivals were organised under the watchful eye of the Dublin board, the Coiste Gnotha. Travelling teachers were despatched to prospective branches, the most fertile ground being urban communities in English-speaking Ireland. Through its educational publications and its newspapers, notably *An Claidheamh Soluis*, nearly all of them Dublin-produced, the League projected a sense of purpose and excitement and made learning the language much easier. The census results did appear to indicate some success: the percentage in the city declaring bilingual

33. The shop and offices of 'Connradh na Gaedhilge' (sic), in Upper Sackville (O'Connell) Street in 1901. The Gaelic League was established in 1893 in a small room in Lower Sackville Street, but by 1901 it had come a long way, helped now by the success of their weekly paper An Claidheamh Soluis *and its enthusiastic young secretary of publications, Patrick Pearse.*

proficiency rose from less than 1 per cent in 1891 to 3.7 per cent twenty years later.[34]

The League's founders were a diverse group – priests and printers, student teachers, journalists and minor civil servants, clerks in the railways and the banks. Few of them were Dublin-born, but the original city branch remained much the largest with around 600 members in 1900. Timothy MacMahon's work on the League has shown that the Dublin membership was always socially mixed, albeit with the majority holding lower-middle- or skilled working-class occupations. Those born outside Dublin were over-represented in the city branch, and although it was strongly male at first, by the pre-war peak in 1907 about a third of its membership was female. From having one single large club, the League sprouted over fifty branches across the city and suburbs by 1903, many of them grafted onto trade societies and working men's clubs. The League's annual 'Language Procession' to the Mansion House became one of the great civic events, attracting up to 40,000 in 1903. Numbers, however, can be deceptive; there was a constant turnover of paid-up members, with only a minority taking language classes at any one time, suggesting that involvement in the League may have been a rite of passage for many, a liberating social environment where class, gender and generation could mix for a while in respectable late-night camaraderie. Hyde was a Roscommon rector's son, and there was a scattering of other Protestant activists in the movement. They achieved a modest victory in St Kevin's Church when the service on St Patrick's Day 1905 was conducted entirely in Irish. But in general there was growing hostility towards the revival of Irish in the city's Protestant-managed national schools after Irish was formally included as an optional subject. Protestant alienation grew in the following years as the championing of 'Irish-Ireland' became ever more shrill and as language revival seemed in danger of becoming an integral part of an ethno-religious nationalism that labelled Protestants as irredeemable 'west Britons'.[35]

One element in the success of the Gaelic League was the relative autonomy accorded to its local branches. Eoin MacNeill, a young civil servant who acted as League secretary in the early years, was passionately committed to the idea of a democratic, rural movement, supported by young, nationalistic Catholic clergy; the national centre would merely provide the printed resources, the organisational direction and the initial teachers but no more. One Dublin branch, the Keating, set up in 1901, exploited this autonomy to the full and became a stronghold for Cork- and Kerry-born revivalists, 'an elite within an elite'. It established the first Irish-language teacher-training college (in west Cork) and published its own magazine, *Banba*. It also sponsored its own Gaelic sports team and, unlike the League at large, developed strong links with 'advanced' republican politics.[36]

The custodian of advanced republicanism was still the oath-bound Irish Republican Brotherhood. After the 1870s its supporters found a succession of new issues to animate the cause, beginning with the short-lived Land League, but it was through sport that they sought a more durable 'front' organisation, both as a source of money and of recruits. City Fenians with their country colleagues were among those involved in the launch of the Gaelic Athletics Association (GAA) in 1884 and, although the Association was initially headquartered in Tipperary, Dublin was highly receptive. Indeed, its architect and first president was Michael Cusack, a gifted and somewhat eccentric Dublin teacher, then operating a successful 'grind-school' for candidates seeking entry into the police and the civil service. He was typical of many contemporaries, Irish and British, in his enthusiasm for competitive sports in general and for cricket, handball and rugby in particular (the latter blossoming with the growth of competition after the establishment of the Irish Football Union in 1874). Cusack was both a rugby coach and a vigorous forward, but in 1882 he switched his energies into a campaign for the revival of hurling, a sport known to him from his childhood in north Clare but unknown to late nineteenth-century Dublin. Out of his own grind-school (and with youths from a dozen counties) he launched a hurling club, the Metropolitan, in 1883 and was soon training and competing in the Phoenix Park. He used his skills as a publicist writing in *United Ireland* to generate public interest in hurling competition. Stung by the social exclusivism in some of Dublin's rugby, athletics and tennis clubs and by their mainly Protestant character, he began the crusade for a wholly self-regulated Irish sporting body that would be an agent of national regeneration, both physical and moral. He was one of the first to see the potential for modernising and regulating the diversity of traditional rural sports, some of them almost lost to memory, and in so doing to make participation exclusive to club members, whether it be athletics, hurling or a version of football. Early hurling clubs in the city drew heavily on new migrants, especially from north Munster, and the army of young sales assistants attached to the department stores proved willing recruits. By contrast, 'Gaelic' football appealed more to indigenous talent in the city and in north Co. Dublin, with 'Sons of the Sea' based in Ringsend earning famous early victories.[37]

Cusack was a divisive figure, but he was not responsible for the vicious infighting and sea-sawing fortunes of the early GAA. These arose from the IRB takeover of the central executive in 1886 and the resistance to this, both clerical and lay. Dublin was somewhat sheltered from the worst of the splits and the infighting, but by the mid-1890s it seemed that Cusack's bold initiative, in Dublin and elsewhere, was withering away. There had been 114 clubs active in the city and county in 1888 (perhaps a quarter of the national total), but that number had shrunk by about two-thirds in 1896. Meanwhile the first Dublin club committed to Association Football, Bohemians, was set up in 1891, but the 'Scottish game' only took off a decade later as Dublin clubs notched repeated successes in the Irish

Cup. However, from 1896 the GAA was in expansionary mode again, now with less overtly political aims. Dublin became the venue for All-Ireland championship games and from 1901 was the national administrative centre (such as it was). Almost a dozen city grounds were then used by GAA clubs, but Maurice Butterly's City and Suburban Racecourse (which had obliterated a swathe of market gardens beyond the North Circular Road) was from 1896 regularly used for GAA matches. This was a good location to control the flow of spectators, and income from ticketed entry was critical for the GAA which, unlike other sporting organisations, lacked wealthy patrons. Soaring attendance levels led to the outright purchase of the former racecourse in 1913, following a Louth/Kerry All-Ireland football final replay that had attracted a dangerously large turnout of 35,000 spectators. Thereupon 'Croke Park' became nationalist Ireland's sporting mecca. The GAA had already engineered a remarkably enduring marriage between localism and central authority, thanks to its elaborate participatory constitution that entrusted just enough power to Dublin to control and manage the rules of play and the development of club and county competition, but not too much. For unlike older cultural movements, the GAA was in Dublin but not of it. Munster and south Leinster, the heartlands of hurling, called the tune.[38]

The pre-war years were the heroic age for both the GAA and the Gaelic League. The two organisations reinforced one other, with heavy cross-membership and the common aims of cultural self-help and national regeneration. They were both shown public respect by the city government, with mayoral attendance at major championships, and the partial adoption c.1905 of bilingualism on the city's letterheads and on new street wall-plaques. And in their period of most rapid growth, from 1900 to 1906, a new kind of holistic separatism heavily infiltrated both organisations. Here the role of one Dubliner, a printer by training and a journalist by inspiration, was singularly important: Arthur Griffith. Hardly out of his apprenticeship, Griffith became involved with William Rooney, another Christian Brothers-educated north-sider, in promoting small literary debating clubs and ephemeral patriotic journals. But Griffith emigrated to South Africa in 1897, where he gained experience of newspaper editing. Then, within two years and at Rooney's encouragement, he came home to edit a new weekly for him, the *United Irishman*, its title echoing John Mitchel's call to arms in 1848. Although it was never to achieve huge circulation in what was a crowded market, the paper became the launch-pad for Griffith's distinctive

brand of radicalism. In the opinion of one young Paris-based reader, James
Joyce, 'it was the only paper in Dublin worth reading'.[39]

❧

Nationalist politics in 1898 was all about commemoration, specifically
about who owned the legacy of 1798 and 1848. On New Year's Eve a
vast torch-lit procession of wagons and bands skirted around the sites of
patriot memory, playing the 'Marseillaise' in Green Street where Newgate prison had once stood, pausing at the stroke of midnight outside St
Michan's church before crossing the river to St Catherine's, all the while
'Who fears to speak of '98' and other Young Ireland ballads were echoing
in the streets. But behind the pageantry was an ongoing turf-war involving
the two IPP factions and rival IRB-inspired groups. IRB men had initiated
plans for the commemoration and organised the New Year proceedings.
But the papers were full of the sordid skirmishing and rival committees of
commemoration before agreement was reached the following spring for a
day-long event on 15 August. An even larger peregrination of the city then
took place involving seventy bands, nearly eighty trade societies, dozens of
delegations from the provinces (notably Ulster), and at least one Kilkenny
hurling team. They proceeded to St Stephen's Green for the laying of the
foundation stone for a Wolfe Tone monument, carved out of Cave Hill in
Belfast. The Grand Marshall was Fred Allan, the Methodist manager of
the chief Parnellite newspaper, but he was also the secretary of the IRB's
Supreme Council; the master of ceremonies was John O'Leary, the veteran Fenian. The IRB may have had some 5,000 members nationally, but
police estimates put the numbers active in Dublin at no more than fifty
and that they presented little security threat. Yet the successful mobilisation of 'hundreds of thousands' on the streets of the city to celebrate the
rebel heroes of a century previous allowed the *Freeman's Journal* the next
day to observe (a little disingenuously), 'who yesterday in Dublin could
speak of "the failure" of the men of '98? Their spirit lives, and their principles live too'. As T. J. O'Keefe has observed, 'republicanism ... at a safe
historical distance seemed to enjoy an unprecedented respectability'. But
the momentary appearance of nationalist unity fractured immediately.
In the short run, the big men in the Irish Party won out, paving the way
for its reunification in 1900. Funds for the planned monument to Tone
evaporated, and John Redmond, the Irish Party leader, championed the

idea of a great Parnell monument in Sackville Street instead: this was completed in 1911 and, in front of a sea of cheering spectators, his unveiling
of the Chief's statue, framed by an oversized 'dull granite pylon', was for
Redmond 'the proudest action of my life'. But for the rising generation of
political activists in Dublin, swept up by the Gaelic League and the GAA,
there was something quite unappealing about Redmond's London-centred world of parliamentary politics, and it was the circle around Griffith
and Rooney who filled the gap, both with their frenetic journalism and
their many political interventions.[40]

Griffith remained as full-time editor of the *United Irishman* for seven
years, then (after a libel action) of the rebranded *Sinn Féin* for another
seven. At the same time he was always busy germinating literary and political initiatives, initially with Rooney until the latter's premature death in
1901. The first big opportunity came in the lead-up to the Anglo-Boer war.
Griffith used their paper during 1899 to provide an endless flow of publicity in support of the Boer cause and to generate opposition to army recruitment. Public meetings and protests during that autumn climaxed with
plans for a rally beside the Custom House in December (to protest at the
visit of Joseph Chamberlain, the Colonial Secretary, who was in town to
receive an honorary degree from Trinity College). The organisers ignored
a ban, and the chaotic consequences were running skirmishes between the
hundreds of Dublin Metropolitan Police (including the mounted reserve)
and some of their more intrepid supporters. (There were far more colourful figures present at these gatherings than Griffith, notably Maud Gonne:
to the public she was the luminous exemplar of Fenianism as fashion, but
for Griffith she was a providential ally.) Griffith was the choreographer,
both of the war protests and of the next round in 1900 against the visit
of a now very elderly Queen Victoria. Despite its intermittent suppression, the paper continued its treasonable words through the Boer War
and during the royal visit. Griffith's own political philosophy of 'inclusive
separatism' and anti-imperialism was radical but pragmatically non-vio-
lent, uncompromising but transparent, and was a challenge both to the
London-centred world of the IPP and constitutional politics, and to the
moribund world of insurrectionary separatism. He was sympathetic to the
Irish-Ireland cultural movements, but distinct from them; his mission was
to convince all Irish public representatives to disengage totally from the
institutions of the Union and by means of constructive abstention and,
if necessary, civil disobedience, to create a shadow state at home, based

on the principles of self-help. For Griffith, the sight of the Boer republics resisting the might of an armed empire was, while it lasted, utterly seductive. His forte remained campaigning journalism and when against his wishes diverse supporters came together in 1907 to form a new political party they adopted his title, Sinn Féin. The party's success in the Dublin municipal elections promised much, then ebbed away. But Griffith kept writing.[41]

Griffith's view of the world was a Dublin one. The other mould-breaking journalist of the era, D. P. Moran, was a late arrival in Dublin – from Waterford, via London. His weekly, *The Leader*, appearing first in 1900, was far more widely read than Griffith's periodicals, but this was because of the racy style and transgressive message. Running for more than two decades, Moran's journal championed a larger revival – moral, educational and commercial – one framed by Catholic institutions and owned by Catholic Ireland. Moran rejected the relevance of the patriot tradition and the inclusiveness of Dublin radicalism; no political movement led by Protestants could restore Irish fortunes, and the militarism of the Fenians was not the answer. He was contemptuous of the Yeatsian project ('Mr. Yeats does not understand us, and he has yet to write even one line that will strike a chord in the Irish heart. He dreams dreams. They may be very beautiful and "Celtic", but they are not ours'), and was dismissive of those tainted by Trinity College ('the price of Trinity is exile from the Gael'), developing these ideas at greater length in *The philosophy of Irish Ireland* (1905). Beneath his rough-house style, there was a serious argument, however: Catholics were still under-achieving in city and country. He caused quite a stir by highlighting Protestant dominance of the management grades in both the railway companies and the banks. But when a new Catholic Association was established in 1902 to lobby for competitive entry, to be backed by the threat of boycott of firms that refused to address their religious composition, Archbishop Walsh came out publicly against such incendiary talk. But Moran's economic version of revivalism, mixing respect for the cloth with visceral criticism of the status quo, helped widen clerical support for the new nationalism in all its forms.[42]

House and home

For most Dubliners who took an interest in public affairs, 'big politics'

dominated the headlines in the early years of the new century: the ageing Irish Parliamentary Party were all too comfortable in Westminster,
progressive conservatism was pushing for a final settlement of tenant land
purchase, and a selective 'greening' of the Dublin Castle bureaucracy was
taking place. Then came the Liberal victory in 1906, the final achievement
of Irish university reform in 1908, the 'People's budget' of 1909, and the
clipping of the powers of the House of Lords in 1911, meaning that it was
now a near certainty that a Home Rule Act would reach the statute book
and that the cut and thrust of national politics would revert to Dublin.
The city's newspapers and magazines thrived in this fevered environment,
a capital in waiting. The most striking journalistic innovation was the re-
launch of a halfpenny daily, the *Irish Independent* in 1905, funded by the
ample resources of William Martin Murphy. Applying lessons learnt by
Northcliffe with the English *Daily Mail*, Murphy employed a gifted team
of journalists and sub-editors to produce a punchy paper that put all the
other non-Unionist papers in the shade. Within a decade, the *Independent* with its sharpened news values had secured a national circulation of
around 120,000. It was unusual in being quite antagonistic towards the
IPP, a reflection of its owner's growing doubts that Home Rule would give
closure to Irish nationalism. But its editor T. R. Harrington (yet another
west Cork migrant) prided himself on being in tune with his readers'
changing tastes and views, and giving them what they wanted.[43]

'Small politics' also blossomed, however, thanks to the dramatic widening of the franchise for local elections. This, the result of Balfour's 1898
democratisation of Irish local government, brought tenement Dublin to
the ballot box by giving the vote to all male working-class householders
and lodgers, and to all female heads of household. Some 49,000 citizens
were eligible to vote in the first elections under the new arrangements in
January 1899, and Ciaran Wallace has estimated that where seats were contested, a remarkable 82 per cent exercised that right in wintry conditions
(a turnout surely never repeated). In the surviving townships, the opening
of the franchise had striking if somewhat less dramatic effects. They were
now rebranded as urban district councils and their first elections attracted
a high turnout of around 65 per cent. Each year thereafter a proportion
of council seats fell vacant, giving rise to constant but low-level electioneering until 1915. The party implications were at first sight not very dramatic: Parnellites vanquished anti-Parnellites in 1899, then after 1900 the
reunited Irish Party completely dominated representation in City Hall for

the next two decades, with the retail trade, especially publicans, still pre-eminent. Conservative/Unionists held a handful of seats, and other parties flourished briefly: organised craft labour translated its voting strength to win ten out of the sixty city seats in 1899, drawing on significant Protestant working-class votes, but it could not repeat that result again for two decades. It was overtaken by Griffith's party, Sinn Féin, in 1907, but this makeshift party peaked early in the Corporation and then faded as the IPP's fortunes were restored with the accelerating likelihood of Home Rule.[44]

In the 1900s Dublin Corporation was subject more than ever to government rules and Treasury controls, yet with its increased statutory powers it had an unprecedented impact on everyday life. Its ancient roles – monitoring public markets, maintaining street surfaces, overseeing new buildings, providing fresh water and street lighting, disposing of urban waste – had, as we have seen, been augmented in the Victorian period with many new powers: to inspect the quality of working-class accommodation, to clear condemned housing (for others to develop), to provide an integrated fire service, to maintain and improve public parks, to impose safety standards on food offered for sale (with some of these responsibilities being taken much more seriously than others). The lasting symbol of all this was the new Fruit and Vegetable Market, opened (after forty years of talk) in 1892 in the old markets area north of Pill Lane, a huge project involving major street clearance and costing some £84,000. Its highly decorative brick exteriors were a city showpiece (the Fish Market of 1897 was much less extravagant). But from the 1890s the Corporation took on responsibilities of a new order of complexity, what with the construction and subsequent management of several large working-class housing schemes, the generation of electricity both for civic needs (street lighting) and for general consumption, the development of cultural and educational services (public libraries and technical training courses), and after 1909 the administration of social welfare (the old-age pension). Such advances were, of course, more than matched by what was happening in Edwardian Belfast, and to a greater or lesser extent in every UK city. Peer pressure as well as UK-wide statutory changes helped drive this remarkable process of local government growth, a process that was only possible because of the somewhat stronger state of the city's finances from the 1890s (increased borrowing powers gained in 1891 were critical here).

The biggest infrastructural project of the era was the main drainage

scheme, long delayed for financial reasons until the mid-1890s. The demand
for this kind of grand solution to the disposal of the city's detritus was not
as acute as it had been at mid-century. Cholera was now a memory and the
great fear that infected air emanating from the rat-infested cesspools and
adulterated subsoils of the city was the principal vector of disease was now
discredited. But the environmental degradation of the river and the coastline kept the issue alive, and some diseases associated with bad sanitation
still persisted, not least typhoid. Drawing on old plans from Parke Neville's
time, the Corporation gave the go-ahead in 1896 for the construction of
two interceptor sewers, over seven miles in length in all, to run in parallel
on either side of the Liffey and designed to capture the fifty-four sewage
outfalls that then entered the river under the quays. Starting at Islandbridge, the works moved eastwards for several years; the interceptors were
eventually joined under Burgh Quay, from where a great tunnel was excavated down to Ringsend. There a massive pumping station was built to raise
the effluent and feed it to a series of treatment tanks at the Pigeon House,
which had a capacity to handle 117 million gallons. The residual sludge was
taken aboard a slurry ship at that point for dumping off Howth Head. The
project contractors were local but, predictably, much of the arduous work
was done by rural migrants. The scheme was completed in 1906 at a cost of
just over £500,000 and was celebrated as an elegant engineering solution,
generating much talk of a cleaner city and a less malodorous river.[45]

New utilities and expanded services (or their failure) invigorated
local politics precisely at the time when local democracy had become a
reality. With the antagonism between the city, where the Irish Parliamentary Party (or rather its surrogate, the United Irish League) controlled
the wards, and the wealthiest of the suburban councils (Rathmines and
Pembroke), where Conservative/Unionist interests remained dominant,
there was an ever-present climate of mutual criticism and controversy
about administrative inadequacies, cronyism or downright corruption
in their respective spheres of control. Drainage and municipal electricity
were obvious success stories for the city, and the four municipal technical schools established by the Corporation were immediately popular,
but the snail-like development of public libraries was less impressive: the
first two were opened in 1884, and although the overall number of books
borrowed trebled between 1890 and 1912, the public library service was
starved of funds. When a fine Carnegie-financed central library building
was completed in Great Brunswick Street in 1909, there was a delay of

four years before it was fully open to the public. But all the hostile talk of corruption overstated the reality, certainly by older (and later) standards, and it is easy to underestimate the level of administrative efficiency within all these local government bodies. Comparing the 'litter, discomfort and dirt' of Dublin in 1859 with the state of things in 1909, one old hand, the builder James Beckett, gave a very positive verdict: it was, he said, now 'well paved, well lighted, and fairly cleanable', a city of abundant water with a showpiece drainage system.[46]

After the city's abject failure in 1882 to win government support for boundary extension, the issue lay dormant until 1898. The case for continuing the autonomy of the suburban townships at a time of government growth was becoming weaker, and the Irish government seemed increasingly sympathetic to the Corporation's desire to engross the whole of greater Dublin. As the 1901 census revealed, no less than 31.8 per cent of the population of 383,178 encompassing the extended urban area was now resident outside the municipal boundaries in one of the nine suburban townships. But once again there was successful rearguard action by Rathmines and Pembroke (with a combined population of 58,401 in 1901). They played the political card in Westminster and managed to freeze the southern boundary of the city for another generation. By that point, every township, even Rathmines, had a Catholic majority, yet Conservative/Unionist councillors controlled both Rathmines and Pembroke, and no party dominated in Kingstown. The city did, however, win on two fronts in 1900: the southern urban district councils (as they were now styled) were now required to contribute to the city's overheads by means of a local tax harmonisation scheme, and its case for boundary extension to the west and north of the city was accepted by government. Kilmainham and Drumcondra Urban District Councils agreed terms with the city, and Unionist Clontarf was also drawn in (on the grounds that it could not possibly afford to invest in an independent drainage scheme). In the wake of these changes, the independent southern urban district councils remained the most dynamic in terms of population growth, with a 9.6 per cent rise in the decade 1901–11 compared with a mere 3.8 per cent rise within the enlarged city boundary. Thus even with the move towards local tax equalisation, the lure of suburban life remained.[47]

It was now conventional to contrast a stagnant Dublin at the end of Victoria's reign with the booming city of Belfast and to suggest that older comparisons of Dublin with London (with more than six million inhabitants by 1901) were now sadly irrelevant. Belfast, with a tenth of Dublin's population a hundred years earlier, had indeed caught up (or more than caught up, depending how the calculation is done) by 1891. With high levels of regular employment, heavy industrialisation, a skilled working class housed in vast swathes of purpose-built back-to-backs and a pro-business municipal government, Belfast seemed to be all the things that Dublin was not. The sectarian tensions that accompanied Belfast's tempestuous growth, the religious barriers that restricted its labour market and the huge occupational health problems of its mill proletariat were of course glossed over by those who used Belfast's ascendancy and Dublin's pathology to make the case against Home Rule, whether in 1886 or 1911. And insofar as there were distinctive social problems in Dublin, Unionists chose to blame the long years of nationalist municipal misgovernment.[48]

The focus of debate was initially on Dublin's death rate. Despite the heroic estimates of Sir William Wilde in former times, an accurate determination of civic death rates only became possible after 1879. Statistical evidence demonstrating that Dublin was a 'sick city' was already being debated before this, with the typhoid fever epidemic of that year causing something of a panic (it was the last occasion when distress in the countryside brought a wave of sickly beggars into the city). But long after such emergencies, Dublin's place in the international health rankings remained a matter of intense interest: in a league table of mortality in thirty world cities published in 1906, Dublin came out worst in western Europe with twice the death rate of London. However, between 1880 and 1914 there was real long-run improvement, albeit sluggish and uneven, with the positive trend stalling for some years in the late 1890s. The crude death rate, hovering around 30 per 1,000 in the early 1880s, had fallen by nearly a third by 1914. Such is the aggregate picture for the city and suburbs, but life expectancy remained very heavily correlated with neighbourhood and class. Indeed, the mortality gap actually widened between the top tier in the city – the families of professionals and those of independent means – and the bottom tier, the unskilled and the institutionalised (who formed two-fifths of the population). Cormac Ó Gráda has estimated that life expectancy of the former group improved very considerably between the 1880s and 1900s, from 53.4 to 60.3 years, while for the latter it was almost unchanged, moving from 31.8 years to 32.25 years. And his study of Pembroke township households in 1911 reveals the contrast operating spatially: 20.9 per cent of the children of working-class Ringsend had died

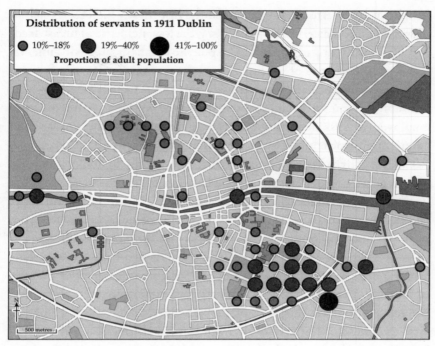

Map 5: Domestic servants in Dublin 1911. The survival of the 1901 and 1911 census-enumerator forms permits a dramatically sharper analysis of the social structure of the city than is possible for any other period. The 1911 data show a bunching of resident servants, principally female, in the high-status south-eastern districts of the city. But the number of such servants even there began to fall sharply from the 1920s.

before the age of five as opposed to 14.3 per cent in next-door leafy Sandymount. A more startling contrast was suggested by the Registrar General Thomas Grimshaw back in 1889: his data from the mid-1880s implied that the survival rates of the under-fives in the top social tier in Dublin was more than six *times* greater than for the children of the unskilled, and 'this ... is really something shocking in a civilised community'.[49]

The pernicious effects of city life on the health of young children, particularly those in congested lodgings or in institutional care, was common knowledge. However, in the late nineteenth century there had been a marked improvement in child survival rates across all UK cities, first affecting those over one year, later the very young. These improvements in early childhood came late to Dublin, but come they did, the mortality of 1–5 year olds falling most noticeably between the early 1880s and early 1890s, that of infants between the late 1890s and late 1900s. What lay behind such patterns? Some explained the historically high rates of child mortality on bad diet, family alcoholism, the low incidence of breast-feeding, or simply bad parenting; others put the emphasis on environmental issues, the prevalence of tenements and the consequential overcrowding and poor sanitation; yet others stressed the simple facts of poverty – that in Dublin an unusually large proportion of the working population were employed in unskilled, casual and low-paid jobs. Broadly similar (and conflicting) explanations were given as to why adult mortality remained persistently high. Daly has suggested that it is only by looking beyond 1914 that we can get close to an explanation for the overall trend: the city's crude death rate continued to fall sharply in the 1920s and 1930s (from 19.9 in 1913 to 14.4 per 1,000 in 1940); infant mortality fell from 147.2 per 1,000 in 1905–14 to 94.9 in 1930–39. Yet inner-city overcrowding was still pervasive in the 1930s, and medical support for low-income families had not significantly improved. What had changed was the cost of food (with free milk schemes and cheaper meat), the level of rent, and the range of welfare supports for the old, the sick and the unemployed with the spread of National Insurance – modest changes, but perhaps sufficient to have had real impact on the health of the bottom quartile of city households for whom the food budget would usually consume more than half the week's income. But of course it is possible that a stronger factor was the decline in the virulence of certain familiar diseases – smallpox, measles and enteric infections. Certainly there is evidence of this in the case of pulmonary tuberculosis, the hugely feared and slow-burning killer of young adults, particularly poorer males. The scourge of TB only peaked in the first decade of the twentieth century when mortality in Dublin was worse than in other Irish cities, but by the mid-1930s TB as a cause of death had fallen by almost two-thirds. How far it was public information campaigns and the hesitant introduction of sanatoria (the publicly funded Crooksling in 1911 and Peamount in 1912) that had helped to turn the tide remains unclear, but they did make some difference.[50]

At first sight, if the most rapid improvements in mortality did not occur until after 1920, then the social impact of all the public-health interventions championed by Chief Medical Officer Sir Charles Cameron and his small team over nearly fifty years must have been relatively modest. Were the clearing of the fever nests, the introduction of regular street-cleaning and a refuse-collection service, the near universal provision of flushing toilets and the clearing of the backyard ash-pits, all missing the main problem

of urban poverty? Cameron was the first to admit that the structural problems in the inner city, the low and uncertain income of unskilled households and the large pool of casual employment, limited the impact of his
Corporation team. An inveterate optimist, he was in the great Victorian
tradition of urban reformers, but he may have been a little too inclined to
assume that good regulations meant good practice, and to have tolerated,
particularly in his later years, the supineness of Corporation officials in the
face of special interests, be it the butchers with their dangerously under-
regulated abattoirs, the dairymen with their little regard for the purity of
the milk they supplied, or the many tenement owners who ignored health
regulations. Cameron openly admitted at the 1913 Housing Inquiry the
inability of his officers to enforce minimum standards of hygiene in up to
half the tenement houses in the city, given the weak sanctions available.[51]

Augustine Birrell, Chief Secretary from 1907 to 1916, had established
the Housing Inquiry in the wake of a particularly gruesome incident,
the collapse of two tenement houses in Church Street in which seven
people had been killed. It was undertaken by officers of the Local Government Board, a state agency based in the Custom House that in 1898 had
been given greatly enhanced powers over all local authorities. Relations
between it and Dublin Corporation were at best testy. The inquisition
was held in public in City Hall with the hearings lasting for several weeks;
the evidence of the seventy-six witnesses provided many headlines for the
newspapers. The tenement system was in the spotlight as never before.
Nearly everyone accepted the link between bad housing and ill-health as
axiomatic, but older witnesses tended to emphasise how much things had
improved, even as they conceded that there was still a major housing problem in Dublin. And indeed they had a point: the proportion of Dubliners
living in one-roomed dwellings was highest back in 1851 at 49 per cent,
and the total tenement population had peaked in 1871 at 29,952 families.
The 1911 census returned 20,564 such families in the city proper, 32.5 per
cent of the total city population, living in 5,322 one-room tenements; as a
proportion of the greater Dublin population they were somewhat smaller.
Yet despite these improvements, the deprivation of the under-class was
revealed in 1913 as never before, but with a new focus on the north side,
and in particular the transformation of the core streets of the Gardiner
estate into an almost unrelieved forest of tenements in the fairly recent
past. John Cooke, speaking for the NSPCC, presented a series of remarkable photographs of tenement life and was one of the few to articulate

the great fear in the tenement communities that housing 'reform' would render them homeless. But he added that

> in no city in these islands with which I am acquainted have the [tenement] children such a freedom, I might say such possession of the streets, as Dublin. Many thousands [of] little ones throng the thoroughfares, under no control, running moral and physical risks; ill-clad, ill-fed, ill-taught, undisciplined, how can they become useful citizens?

Then, 'straight from the streets the children are put to bed with dirty feet, hands and faces', and in the single family room, there were no dogs or cats, no caged birds, no flowers in the window, almost no printed material. Others contrasted the tall brick façades of Gardiner Street and Mountjoy Square, and behind them 'mostly ... single room tenements with open hall doors, the fanlights broken'.[52]

Even in 1913 the task of rehousing this teeming world of 20,000 families seemed beyond the capacity of either the private sector or the municipal authority. Some defended the numerous owners of tenement property (once, it seems, a profitable and streamlined business but no longer so, what with onerous city regulations and public hostility). There was the extraordinary case of the great Ballsbridge developer Joseph Meade, Lord Mayor in 1891–2, who followed up his time in office by acquiring nine houses on the north side of Henrietta Street, stripping them and reconstituting them as solid tenements; he had the resources to do a competent job and his motives were not, it seems, entirely mercenary. But it was as a slum landlord, not as one of Ballsbridge's biggest builder-developers, that he is remembered.

The long-serving Town Clerk was not alone in believing that it should not be the Corporation's job to solve the housing problem: 'if they are going to build houses for the people, I don't see why they should not provide them with umbrellas and top hats'. But other colleagues, following the recently completed suburban scheme in Inchicore, championed plans for public housing on the city's edge, specifically at Marino and at Cabra on the north side, where site costs would be much lower and cottages with gardens could be the norm. Most witnesses in 1913 recognised that inner-city initiatives had given a poor public return and that some, specifically the two five-storey blocks built in Foley Street (west of Amiens Street) were a social

disaster. These had been completed in 1905 and were among the largest
pre-war rehousing projects. It was a brave choice as Foley (formerly Montgomery) Street had remained the epicentre of prostitution in the city since
the 1880s – after the DMP had cleared the brothels from west of Grafton
Street; 460 apartments (mainly single-room units) were built there by the
Corporation, but there was little demand for them until the asking rents
were slashed. Many of the new tenants were the madams who continued
with their open brothels, and a substantial proportion of the city's prostitutes, for the most part country girls, stayed on in the area. (Some argued
that, large as it was, the Foley Street development failed because it was not
big enough.) In the final analysis, the inquiry looked for greater public
investment in housing, but it was highly critical of the Corporation and its
employees, not least the veteran Charles Cameron, for sloppy enforcement
of the regulations. The Chief Medical Officer was a convenient scapegoat.
However, within several months, he had published a measured and highly
effective apologia, and the Corporation also refused to accept any blame.
Cameron remained in office until his eighty-ninth year.[53]

The boldest voices at the inquiry had advocated full-blooded state
action – to remedy Dublin's discontents rather than rural Ireland's, as had
been the recent pattern. The most dramatic intervention came from Patrick Geddes, whose grand vision for a phoenix-like rebirth of Dublin had
a 'startling' impact: he called for city-wide planning to integrate housing
policy into wider metropolitan development. The father of the town-planning movement in Britain, he was encouraged to take a particular interest in Dublin several years earlier by his fellow Scot, Lady Aberdeen, wife
of the long-stay Liberal Lord Lieutenant (who held office from 1906 to
1915). Her sustained advocacy of craft industries and public-health reform,
in particular her championing of women's health issues, broke the social
taboos as to the proper role of a viceroy's consort, but she had real impact
in the causes she took up – the provision of pasteurised milk for infants
and the prevention and treatment of TB in adults. The interest in town
planning would, of course, have spread to Dublin without the Aberdeens –
the new Central Highways Committee of the Corporation had developed
a master plan for street-widening in the city core, but it was entirely to
suit business and changing traffic needs. But it is unlikely that the remarkable ratcheting up of public interest in urban planning between 1910 and
1914 would have occurred without the Scottish input. Geddes' words in
1913 had unrivalled authority: he advocated the adoption of democratic

planning through civic education and public consultation, and found
fault with recent Corporation initiatives that had been developed in isolation and had slavishly copied London's mistakes rather than continental
successes. He maintained that the Corporation's twelve completed housing schemes 'would have been more economical and more effective in the
past' had their interventions been made 'with more regard and less injury
to the fine town plan inherited from the eighteenth century, and ... with
more relation to docks, railways and manufactories in the nineteenth'.
Others echoed Geddes' call to utilise the past strengths of the city, draw
up a full city plan and establish a Dublin regional housing authority. A
follow-up to this was the Civic Exhibition in summer 1914, parts of which
were directly organised by Geddes. It was housed in the old Linen Hall
and on ten acres of Constitution Hill, an exhibition aiming for once not
to be an entertaining spectacle or a promotion of the exotic, but to challenge its 80,000 visitors to reflect and imagine their city's future through
the use of maps, plans and models relating to planning and public health
in Dublin, Cork and many other UK cities.[54]

Geddes was not a member of a rather different organisation active
since 1908 – the Georgian Society – the primary object of which was to
document eighteenth-century Dublin domestic architecture. Nearly all
of its members (about 300) were Protestant and many ex-landed families
supported the initiative. Iveagh and Pembroke were among the aristocratic
vice-presidents. Although prompted, it seems, by the early campaigns to
conserve the architecture of eighteenth-century Bath, it was primarily a
revealing act of retrospection, not a plea for conservation or social intervention. Four of the six lavish volumes published by the society between
1909 and 1915 dealt exclusively with Dublin, and they included a substantial photographic record of the more important townhouses in the once
upper-class residential districts, as well as making pioneering use of the
Public Record Office. The Society's president was J. P. Mahaffy, the best
known of Trinity College's great classical scholars, whose love of ancient
Greece was fully matched by his contempt for the Gaelic revival. The idea
of a heroic 'Georgian Dublin' past was thus born, attached, however, to
some problematic baggage.[55]

9

ERUPTION: 1913–1919

Larkin's war

As the Dublin Housing Inquiry conducted its long inquisition in City Hall, an extraordinary confrontation was coming to a climax on the streets outside. Initially it was a labour dispute centred on Murphy's Tramway Company, but it had escalated quite spectacularly. Remembered as the '1913 Lockout', it was one of the defining events in the city's history, later explored in fiction and film and ever resonant in the city's political culture, despite an even greater crisis visited on the city three years later. The five-month conflict is often portrayed as a simple class war between the men of capital and the teeming masses in the tenements, a view that overstates the link between housing and industrial relations and obscures the contingent elements of the melodrama, for it was the particular chemistry of the main protagonists and the misjudgements of third parties that actually made it such a bitter affair. But were there underlying factors that may have heightened the likelihood of such a conflagration?

The material display of wealth in 1913 was perhaps more conspicuous than in Victorian times. Although social segregation between city and suburbs, between the worlds of Summerhill and Shrewsbury Road, was now more complete than ever, the actual visibility of the rich in their new motor-cars (about a thousand were registered in Dublin by 1914) and their Bernardo furs was painfully obvious, and much of this wealth was Catholic wealth. Thus recourse to the language of class, rather than of race or religion, had new meaning and it was explosively effective. Yet Dublin's poor were almost certainly not getting poorer. Trends in wages since the 1880s were broadly benign: both skilled and unskilled wages in nominal and real terms had risen faster than the UK average. Differentials between craft and general earnings in the construction trades (which are the best documented) had narrowed over the three decades. Working hours in many sectors had improved – building sites now opened at 8 a.m., where 6 a.m. in summer had been the old convention, and in the wake of a four-month builders' strike in 1896 the working week had been cut from fifty-seven to fifty-four hours. National insurance against unemployment and medical accident was now becoming the standard for craft workers, and the coming of the old-age pension was a universal boon. Yet in the years immediately before 1913 unemployment had been growing again (despite the opening of the first labour exchanges), and there was a lull in big public-works projects. The working week for unskilled men still averaged around seventy hours.[1]

Compared with London or Liverpool, the recent challenge from organised labour in Dublin had been quite fragmented. Up to 1911 the established craft societies had stayed on top, very slow to evolve beyond their traditional roles of policing the terms of apprenticeship and the protection of wage differentials. The Dublin Trades Council had a long but uneventful past, its first tangible initiative in modern times being to host an Irish Trades Union Congress in 1894, but the Council remained completely dominated by the small craft bodies. Its evergreen secretary, the printer and journalist J. P. Nannetti, was in the first batch of Labour men to get into City Hall in 1898 and went on to win and hold the College Green seat in Westminster from 1900 until his death in 1915. Despite a long association with the GAA, he was no radical, and his cosy relationship with the Irish Parliamentary Party (IPP) helped him secure the mayoralty in 1906.

The process of absorption of local trade societies into cross-channel amalgamated unions had proceeded fitfully for decades, with relatively little consequence for the world outside. But the ripple effect from 'new unionism' was another matter, and the example of the London dock strike of 1889 and its demonstration of the success of an unskilled labour alliance employing occasionally militant methods caused an immediate frisson in Dublin. It was, after all, a former Dublin dockworker and Fenian,

Jim Connell, who composed 'The Red Flag' during the London strike, and May Day was first celebrated as a labour holiday in Dublin the following year. But the momentum soon lapsed. Over 1,000 labourers in the coalyards were organised by the London-based National Union of Dock Labourers (NUDL) in 1900 to strike for improved wages and conditions, but the coal importers stood firm, hired replacement non-union labour ('scabs') and secured the prosecution of twenty-four dockers. The union was nearly wiped out. General workers on the railways fared better and employers responded selectively to the petitions for modest improvement. Migrant 'agitators' had far more ambitious ideas, seeking ways to harness the huge but atomised army of carters, dockers and manual labourers in the city. James Connolly was by far the most important such figure, yet few would have believed that the minuscule Irish Republican Socialist Party, which he founded in 1896, his *Worker's Republic* paper started in 1898, or his anti-war protests the year following were more than the obscure actions of an autodidactic crank from the Edinburgh slums. He left the city in 1903 for seven years to go to the US, having been let down by his friends and demonised by the press as an atheist agitator. But Connolly had a formidable political mind, his application of Marxist ideas to contemporary Ireland revealing both originality and rare analytical depth. By the time he returned to Dublin in 1910, an agitator with a very different skill-set was in the ascendant, the Liverpool-born James Larkin, a man of rare energy and tactical guile and a public speaker whose magnetism was reminiscent of John Mitchel.

But Larkin was no team player.[2] His initial employment in Belfast and Dublin was to rebuild the NUDL in 1907, and within a year the coal-men were organised again. An attempt by the coal importers and the shipping companies to assert their right to employ non-union men caused a ten-day shut-down in July 1908 which ended with compromise, brokered by Dublin Castle. Four months later, the NUDL brought out some 3,000 carters across the city over a mixture of grievances, and political (and church) arbitration prevented the arrival of a huge force of Liverpool scabs. But the strikers won very little else. Larkin's extravagant militancy and independent initiatives brought about his dismissal from the union, whereupon he established the Irish Transport and General Workers Union (ITGWU) in 1909, scooping up NUDL members and recruiting general workers in the transport industries en masse under the symbol of the Red Hand. The nirvana proclaimed was an eight-hour working day, pensions for all, work schemes for the unemployed, industrial arbitration courts and selective nationalisation. Larkin proceeded in the belief that the city's unskilled labour force, numbering now over 20,000, would, if properly led, engage in coordinated industrial action for the greater good by means of 'sympathetic strikes'; in other words, once organised, they would act in solidarity, believing in the ideology of working-class unity. There had of course been instances of labour solidarity in the city back to 1780, but on such occasions the crafts had always dominated. What was new was Larkin's attempt to embed a sense of common working-class identity in all those who had never 'served their time', whether the semi-skilled in steady employment on the trams, the newsboys on the streets, or the casual workers hired and fired by the week along the docks and in the markets.[3]

The immediate aim of the ITGWU was to transform the terms and conditions of its burgeoning membership, in Dublin and the major Irish cities, but it moved slowly. Larkin was implicated in a financial scandal in 1910 over union funds (in Cork), but a short prison sentence helped to give him welcome notoriety. Shortly after his release, and working with a group of like-minded syndicalists, he won control of the Dublin Trades Council. In May 1911 he launched a penny weekly, the *Irish Worker*. Its savage cartoons, unfettered abuse and veiled threats against leading businessmen proved immensely popular. Soon it achieved spectacular sales of between 15,000 and 20,000, mainly in Dublin, with its blend of messianic socialism, name-calling and romantic Irish fiction. It had first appeared just ahead of the great wave of transport strikes in Britain, during which time the ITGWU organised rolling work stoppages by dockers and carters in support. But a sympathetic strike on the GSWR in mid-September 1911 was rather different: authorised by the long-established Amalgamated Society of Railway Servants (ASRS), which gave backing to its members' refusal to handle any 'tainted' goods coming from a timber firm in dispute with the ITGWU, the strike snowballed, leading within days to the closure of almost all mainline rail services. The railway companies responded in unison, dismissed everyone on strike, recruited men from England and sought military assistance from the Royal Engineers. This kept a skeleton service operating. After a fortnight, the ASRS, starved of financial support from England, caved in. Most staff were re-hired on their promise never again to take sympathetic strike action. It was a learning experience for all involved.[4]

In 1912 Larkin purchased the long-abandoned Northumberland

Hotel beside the Custom House as premises for the ITGWU. This was immediately renamed 'Liberty Hall', its ample rooms, cellars and kitchens allowing for group activities of all kinds. Located beside the wide spaces of Beresford Crescent, which for decades had been used as a marshalling point for demonstrations and public funerals, it was well chosen. By January 1913 Larkin had recruited over 24,000 members to the union, the great majority of whom were semi-skilled or unskilled, and were Dublin-based. For Larkin, the greater end was economic revolution, the sympathetic strike being developed as a political weapon to cripple Dublin's capitalist class. This meant attacking the Svengalian William Martin Murphy, with his multiple directorships, his control of the Chamber of Commerce and ownership of the tramways, the leading department store and the bestselling morning paper. It was quite a challenge, because Murphy was celebrated as one of the great employers in the city, a nationalist and the principal undertaker of the huge 1907 Irish International Exhibition in Ballsbridge (on the site of the future Herbert Park) which in six months had attracted 2.7 million visitors. And had he not copper-fastened his credentials as a good nationalist by refusing on that occasion to accept a knighthood from the king?[5]

Murphy anticipated the threat sooner than most. Operating his businesses on fairly low margins, he believed that any significant increase in labour costs would be gravely damaging, and that Larkinism was at least as sinister and as dangerous in fact as its rhetoric on class sounded. Yet throughout his long career he had cultivated the loyalty of his workforce, or rather of the skilled trades and their families, and believed that this would protect his interests. General operatives on the tramways had, none the less, been trying for more than two decades to negotiate terms and conditions and had failed to win a nine-hour day. In the wake of the 1911 rail strike, however, Murphy raised wages and shortened hours. But now he could see no possibility of compromise with an organisation that regarded industrial relations as low-intensity class warfare and seemed to be prompting labour militancy far outside its own membership. Some, like the shipping companies, disagreed with Murphy's bleak analysis; after a series of strikes they negotiated a deal with the ITGWU in the spring of 1913, Larkin disavowing the use of the sympathetic strike in return for union recognition and wage concessions. But when Larkin began a recruitment drive within the Dublin United Tramways Company (DUTC) some months later, Murphy warned his men that involvement

34. *The most famous of Ernest Kavanagh's many cartoons, this appeared in James Larkin's paper three days after William Martin Murphy had persuaded some 400 city employers not to retain any worker still a member of the Transport Union, and two days after the death of John Byrne, a labourer who had been assaulted by the police. Murphy's residence in Rathmines provided the ideal backdrop to depict him as the vulture poised to destroy the working man.*

in Larkin's union would bring instant dismissal. Sackings actually began elsewhere in his empire, in the *Independent* despatch office, but within two days 200 tramway workers were let go for refusing to handle *Independent* publications. Thus began a tit for tat, bringing the vast DUTC system almost to a standstill and it soon affected the main coalyards, the builders' suppliers, the building trade and much else. Most of the smaller general unions were swept up in the whirlwind, their men for the most part walking out in solidarity. Sabotage and petty violence worsened by the day, with stone-throwing, the sabotage of tramlines, attacks on 'scabs' and suspected strike-breakers, all of which involved the DMP from the beginning. But the police were ill-prepared for the challenge and displayed poor discipline when trying to cope with the vast and angry crowds around Liberty Hall. On the first Saturday night the police batoned to death two married labourers on Eden Quay and pursued their tormentors into the red-light world of Foley Street – where resentments over a recent clamp-down on prostitution had made them many enemies, male and female; the police seem to have run amok in the neighbourhood. The following day, a Sunday, police attempted to arrest Larkin in Sackville Street after his theatrical appearance at a window of the Imperial Hotel (owned by Murphy), and in so doing generated the largest street riot for a generation. Caught on camera, the events of 'Bloody Sunday', 31 August 1913, helped to damn the heavy-handedness of the authorities. Over 400 civilians from all parts of the city were injured in the baton charges and the panic that followed, during which shops were looted and trams wrecked. But all of the forty rioters arrested that day were drawn from Foley Street and the other rookeries east of Marlborough Street.[6]

Murphy was now the dominant voice in the Chamber of Commerce and in its Employers Executive Committee. He convinced most of the affiliated firms, about 400 employers, that the moment had come to break Larkinism and that all their employees who had been unwise enough to join the ITGWU must resign immediately and sign a declaration never to join such an organisation in the future. Some employers, notably Guinness's and the railway companies, more or less kept their distance, but most firms followed Murphy, expecting an early triumph over 'the labour dictator', although many watered down the precise undertakings demanded of their own employees. It was a high-risk strategy: liberal public opinion, particularly in Britain, was shocked at the apparent high-handedness both of employers and police. The 9,000 men 'locked out' of their jobs by mid-September, the 20,000 by October, garnered wide public sympathy, most importantly among Labour supporters in Britain. By then the first of many consignments of food had arrived in the port – packages of bread and tea, jam and biscuits, sugar and cheese, vegetables and potatoes, together with coal and cash. This remarkable largesse, overseen by the British TUC and channelled through the Dublin Trades Council, continued at full throttle until January and was wound down slowly thereafter. Worth by the end close to £94,000, TUC support allowed the battle to run for months and helps explain why, despite the huge surge of unemployment, the death rate rose only slightly at this time. The ITGWU's own funds might have covered strike pay for a month; the Lockout lasted for more than four.[7]

In the early weeks there were violent flashpoints around the city and

suburbs, usually involving strike-breaking by 'free workers' or employers –
in the Liberties, in the south docklands, and in the streets around Jacob's
(which were one of the largest employers fully backing Murphy). Some
1,000 Royal Irish Constabulary (RIC) men were drafted in to support the
DMP in the early weeks, and the army was brought in to provide regular
protection from late September. Military convoys protecting vulnerable
deliveries became a common sight on the streets for the next three months.
Critics of the employers, whether liberal or socialist, faulted the courts,
the police and the government for buttressing Murphy's campaign, and
many ridiculed the local IPP MPs for saying nothing and doing nothing.
Attempts by various parties to arbitrate in the dispute all foundered. The
apparent inflexibility of the employers lost them middle-ground support
both in Dublin and London, but this failed to weaken Murphy's steely
determination. By contrast, critics of the strikers continued to demonise
Larkin and exaggerated the collapse of law and order on and off the streets.
The violence was real and very occasionally fatal, but it was targeted on
scabs and other strike-breakers. Larkin jousted with the courts, and he and
his associates were repeatedly in and out of prison during the saga, but
given the increasingly militant language, the talk of arms, and the actual
establishment of a militia in November (the Irish Citizens Army), it was a
reflection of weakness at the political centre that the ITGWU continued
to operate so openly. (The Liberal government's dependence on Labour
support in Britain was a major factor here.) When not in prison, Larkin
spent much of the crisis in England and Scotland drumming up union
support. He was deputised on the ground by James Connolly, who had
returned from the US in 1910 to work full-time for the union in Dublin
and Belfast. The veteran socialist now had a much more developed belief
in syndicalism as a form of industrial warfare and a better grasp of tactics:
in early November he organised continuous mass pickets at the entrance
to disputed firms. This could not be sustained, however, perhaps because
Connolly was a less inspirational leader than Larkin.[8]

It is hard to gauge the level of wider public support for the warring
parties: apart from the *Irish Worker*, there was very little consistent support
for Larkin in the Dublin press, nationalist or Unionist. An unrestrained
war of words continued between the *Independent* and *Worker,* Larkin
trying to position his struggle within the city's Parnellite and Fenian traditions, Murphy's writers depicting Larkin as a foolish megalomaniac.
However, criticism of the employers' tough line appeared from time to

time even in *The Irish Times,* most memorably in stinging comments by artist, mystic and journalist George Russell (AE), who likened the coming fate of the employers of Dublin to the recent demise of the landed gentry:

> Despotisms endure [only] while they are benevolent ... You do seem to read history so as to learn its lessons ... It remained for the twen-tieth century and the capital city of Ireland to see an oligarchy of four hundred masters deciding openly upon starving one hundred thousand people, and refusing to consider any solution except that fixed by their pride ... You may succeed in your policy and endure your own damnation by your victory. The men whose manhood you have broken will loathe you, and will always be brooding and scheming to strike a fresh blow. The children will be taught to curse you. The infant being moulded in the womb will have breathed into its starved body the vitality of hate. It is not they – it is you who are blind Samsons pulling down the pillars of the social order.[9]

The dislocating effects on trade and employment touched most sectors of the city and the public demand for compromise was a constant refrain. Local fund-raising for families in distress organised by the Lord Mayor was very poorly supported, but the St Vincent de Paul's Society discreetly raised far more. In the course of 1913, the numbers in its night shelter and food kitchens doubled, and their direct aid to households also grew. Even at the end of the Lockout, public support for the cause must have remained quite strong: despite an abusive torrent of clerical and IPP warnings about socialism and its hidden supporters, Labour candidates endorsed by the Trades Council polled strongly in the local elections of January 1914, securing 42 per cent of the vote. Yet they won almost no seats.[10]

Commercial activity in the city was not as badly hit as the headlines might suggest. The trams ran a full service after the early weeks of the Lockout and the coal firms and the wholesale carters turned to mechanical alternatives and began to invest in lorries. Even the near total closure of the port from mid-November had less impact in the lead-up to Christmas than Liberty Hall expected. Probably the building industry was the most severely affected. Tactical errors by Larkin are usually seen as critical in bringing it all to an end in the New Year – his failure to win British TUC support for sympathetic strikes, and the split between him and the Catholic church over a scheme to send the children of affected workers to supportive (but non-Catholic) English homes, which left Larkin open to charges that he was uncaring in matters of religion. But the decisive factors were simply the wind-down of British financial support and the exhaustion of the union's own limited strike funds, forcing most of those locked out to seek re-employment on whatever terms, a majority of them in January 1914, the Jacob's women not until March. A minority, notably labourers in the building trade, had to make the pledge disavowing the ITGWU, but about a quarter of those locked out failed to be re-employed at all.[11]

Larkin's great moment had passed, and later in 1914 he moved off to the US, leaving the radical ground to James Connolly. But Connolly, even in the midst of the Lockout, was shifting his political focus from social militancy to a republican strategy – though that took some time to mature.[12]

Cosmopolis

Dublin in the aftermath of the Lockout reverted to its generally peaceful ways. Despite all the lurid publicity, it was largely a safe environment with less petty crime and far less public drunkenness than a generation earlier. Powerful electric light now bathed the main streets throughout the night, although much to the disgust of clerical reformers prostitution still flourished brazenly. The city was a strange mixture of the provincial and the cosmopolitan. The Irish Executive itself was less than ever Dublin-centred: Augustine Birrell, long-serving Chief Secretary, was rarely seen in the city and disliked being there. And despite the apparent proximity of Home Rule, the Irish Party and its appendages had in recent years decentralised political activity down to the local constituency level. From a distance, Dublin's political controversies seemed very local, whether it was housing reform, municipal taxes or union recognition. The great battles over Home Rule and the possible exclusion of parts of Ulster were now being played out in London, with almost none of the key actors based in Dublin. Irish Unionism was now Ulster Unionism, albeit led by the one-time Dublin barrister Edward Carson; the alarming threats of physical resistance to government plans that emanated from Ulster were attracting hardly any public support in Dublin, although some of the city's Orangemen made discreet preparations to support the Ulster Volunteer Force (UVF). There was, it is true, one last great rally by southern Unionists in

November 1913 which filled the Theatre Royal to hear Andrew Bonar Law, the Tory leader, give a passionate promise to protect the interests of Ulster. This was certainly not what many from south and west wished to hear, and he was spat at before the evening was over. *The Irish Times*, mouthpiece of mainstream southern Unionism, remained resolutely opposed to any partitionist solution to the Home Rule impasse.[13]

The cultural politics of theatre and literary revival, for all the heat they generated, were largely specific to the city. Even when something of potentially wider significance emerged, the proposal to create a purpose-built gallery of modern art that would accommodate the superb Impressionist collection brought together by Lady Gregory's nephew, Hugh Lane, the long-running debate degenerated in 1913 into a local spat over money and the Corporation's penury, not about the status of art in the modern world. Yeats's ringing contempt for those who had halted the scheme, whether by tepid support (Lord Ardilaun) or penny-pinching objections (Murphy), was singularly merited. The city's cultural marginality was more evident than ever in the book trade, where despite the liveliness of the newspaper press and presence of innovative 'craft' publishers (notably Elizabeth Yeats's Dun Emer Press), the focus was entirely inwards. The great 1907 International Exhibition, for all its spectacle and chutzpah, its crafts and curiosities, provided little evidence of industrial vitality. The great department stores, with their warehouses full of imported goods, dominated the 'Palace of Industries'. And in the more rarefied world of science and scholarship there was a palpable sense of the city's reduced international status: in 1908 the British Association for the Advancement of Science made its fourth visit to Dublin in seven decades, a highly prestigious moment when the city was on show to over 2,000 guests. But in contrast to earlier visits, this time there was no local scientific celebrity and very little in the way of local scientific discovery to report on, except for James Joly's work on radioactivity. Admittedly, the vast College of Science in Merrion Street, halfway to completion, looked very impressive, but this was a state initiative aimed at extending technical education that was strangely disconnected from indigenous scholarship.[14]

The city seemed to be controlled by an older generation, whether in business or the churches, Trinity College or City Hall, as suspicious of the avant-garde as of socialism, a collective negativity appearing to make Dublin, in young Joyce's famous words, 'the centre of paralysis'. There were, it is true, a few Medici figures, men of great wealth prepared to patronise

young talent: Murphy's fellow tramway and railway director Laurence
'Larky' Waldron was such a case. A highly successful stockbroker, briefly
an independent nationalist MP, a trustee of the National Library and governor of the National Gallery, Waldron held Sunday court in his Killiney
mansion, deliberately mixing the yacht-club set with the young artists. He
gave graphic and stained-glass commissions to the young Harry Clarke in
1913 and filled his house with exquisite reproduction Chippendale furniture, carved by James Hicks, the most accomplished city cabinet-maker.
But he was an eccentric exception.[15]

One of the many aims of Joyce's *Dubliners*, published (after much
difficulty in London) in June 1914, was to hold up a looking-glass to the
claustrophobic social world that he had left behind and reveal the hum-
bug of Catholic bourgeois respectability. But even Joyce could imagine
Dublin sometimes wearing 'the mask of a capital' as in the story 'After the
race', when it played host to exotic racing-cars and luxury yachts. For it still
could dazzle. The luxurious Shelbourne, rebuilt in the 1860s and raised to
six storeys, could reasonably claim to be a premier European hotel, now
tightly managed and attracting a record 49,671 guests in 1907, reflecting
the pull of the International Exhibition. Wealthy American visitors were
beginning to stay during the summer season (although on census night
in April 1911 most of the forty-eight guests were British, and the kitchen
staff German, Italian and Swiss). But every August, Horse Show time,
the old hotel was repossessed by its original patrons, the country gentry.
Among the surviving gentlemen's clubs, the Kildare Street Club remained
the most cosmopolitan as well as the most exclusive, the unique meeting
point for peers and wealthy ex-landlords, senior civil servants of a Tory
disposition, judges, military officers and a large clutch of Unionist bankers and brewers, railway directors and stockbrokers. Its membership had
remained at around 700 since the great rebuilding of the premises in the
1860s, but its composition had changed. Clergy had now gone and its
military and imperial character was much more pronounced: nearly 35 per
cent of the club were serving or retired members of regular Crown forces.
Reciprocal links with the Sports Club in Monaco and the Hunting Club
in Paris looked good but meant little, whereas relations with the Royal St
George Yacht Club and the Turf Club were what really mattered to many
members. All such clubs were exclusive male spaces, unlike the hotels and
the newly fashionable tea-rooms. In 1900 the popular Burlington Hotel in
Andrew Street was taken over by a former chef of the viceregal household,

35. *Pim Brothers' department store in Gt George's Street had been the city's largest store when it opened in 1857 and was now second only to Arnotts. Among the Quaker families prominent in Dublin business, the Pims had the most diverse range of industrial investments, keeping them all as privately owned family enterprises.*

Michel Jammet. With his brother, he set up the first haute cuisine restaurant in Dublin, and it soon became a city institution patronised by a mixed but well-heeled clientele. But the spot that best captured the era was Bewley's Oriental Café, which opened in Westmoreland Street in 1896 following the success of a smaller café in South Great George's Street. The Bewleys were neither the oldest nor the richest Quaker clan in town, but they had been shippers of China tea since the 1830s and had revived sugar-refining more recently. The cafés were distinctive for their exotic ambience (selling Chinese decorative goods), high-quality patisserie (produced by continental bakers), and the vigorous promotion of coffee. Westmoreland Street was never quite the same.[16]

American-style retailing appeared in 1914 with the opening of the first Woolworth store, taking over three shops at the top of Grafton Street and offering in its expansive interior vast counter displays of confectionery and hardware at discount prices, with the added novelty of a self-service cafeteria. British multiple stores had been locating in Dublin since the 1880s – one of the earliest was Tyler's, the Leicester boot manufacturers, which opened first in Earl Street and then opened in eight locations in the city. International branded foods and chocolates (led by Heinz, Cadbury and Nestlé) first appeared at the turn of the century and were soon household names. But the biggest grocery brands were local. Both Leverett & Frye and Findlaters operated ten city and suburban shops: Findlaters, 'the largest distributors of food products in Ireland', ran an efficient home-delivery service to distribute their brands of tea and coffee, whiskey and wine, cakes and sweets, oils, spices, syrups and much else, building on their much older practice of distinctive labels on the wines, ales and spirits which they had handled for eighty years.[17]

To those who could afford the tempting delights of such 'capital shops', there was now a superabundance of choice and a sense of the world opened up as never before to the discriminating consumer. With the tram or better still with a motor-car, suburban women had unprecedented access to the several hundred high-class retail establishments clustering around Grafton Street and George's Street, Henry Street and Capel Street, and the much smaller numbers on the main streets of Rathmines, Blackrock and Kingstown. But products exclusive to such shops gradually percolated down to less favoured outlets as products were recycled or prices fell – whether the used evening wear despatched to the clothes market in Francis Street or the proliferation of cut flowers, moving from specialist florists to the ubiquitous street sellers. The 'safety' bicycle, a hobby-product for upper-middle-class recreation in the 1880s, fell in price and by 1914 was beginning to be used for regular commuting by most young men.[18]

Cinema had also now arrived, one of the many by-products of a ubiquitous electricity supply. The earliest demonstration of the 'startling' medium had been in Dan Lowery's Music Hall in 1896, and in the next decade the Rotunda and the Queen's Theatre were adapted from time to time for short films. Joyce is usually credited as the first to see the commercial potential in Dublin of cheap picture-houses offering a constantly changing programme with live musical accompaniment. Certainly he came back to Dublin in 1909 with this in mind; with the financial backing of several Italian partners, he opened the Cinematograph Volta in Mary Street, showing mainly continental films with the titling in Italian. Joyce did not remain long enough to judge what he had started, but the partnership soon sold out to a British consortium, which had already opened the much grander Picture House on Sackville Street in 1910 and the Grafton Picture House in 1911. This was the start of a short boom in cinema development: by 1915 there were twenty-six small picture-houses operating in the city, an unusually strong uptake of the new technology and enough indeed to frighten the city's moral guardians, particularly when many of them were owned by 'aliens and Jews'. One such was the former green-grocer Maurice Elliman, whose third and most striking venue, the Theatre de Luxe in Camden Street, was opened in 1913. Like others built on prime retail streets, it was pitched towards a middle-class clientele. But many of the converted billiard-halls and warehouses showing movies attracted the boisterous custom of young working-class adults and teenagers.[19]

Why were many of these early cinemas Jewish-owned? Dublin's Jewish community until the late nineteenth century had been a tiny and fairly well-integrated part of the 'English' Sephardic diaspora. Their leading spokesman for many years, Lewis Harris, was elected to the Corporation in 1874 as a reform-minded independent (he died very shortly afterwards). Then, in the late 1870s, Ashkenazi Jews from Tsarist Lithuania, the 'Litvaks', began to arrive, soon becoming the largest new ethnic ingredient in the city since the Huguenot migration two centuries earlier. The Jewish population climbed to nearly 3,000 by 1911, and even though this was less than 1 per cent of the city's population, their impact was quite disproportionate. This was partly because of the marked propensity of the Litvaks to cluster together in the south-west of the city, settling on both sides of the South Circular Road along new artisanal streets that soon came to be known as Little Jerusalem, and partly because of their success as 'shilling-a-week' men, peddling clothes, light household goods and trinkets on tick, and lending money to poorer householders in town and country-side. As Ó Gráda has shown, the community enjoyed remarkable upward social mobility over two generations, reflected in their determined move southwards beyond the canal after the war. And even though their wider contribution to public life in the city was only evident in later times, their distinctive foods and manner of living did not go unnoticed. Indeed, the cinema managers among them were picked out for unsavoury criticism during the Lockout. Their success in the various commercial niches they occupied puzzled contemporaries, but others quickly copied them.[20]

Small numbers of Jewish students had for generations attended Trinity College, as had larger numbers of middle-class Catholics. But the old university remained an unambiguous stronghold of Unionism in a strongly nationalist city, its great self-confidence of early Victorian times long gone. Shocked by church disestablishment, its income hit by land reform and threatened by the Liberal appeasement of Irish nationalism,

Trinity had recast itself as a secular institution in 1873, paving the way for a very gradual transfer of control from clerical fellows to lay academics. This did not prevent the first of many condemnations of the institution by the Catholic hierarchy in 1875, or of ominous signs of stagnation. By the turn of the century, student numbers were only half those of the 1820s, and in some professional fields more than half of its graduates were emigrating. There was, it is true, major building development to the east of the College Park, reflecting a scientific turn and the welcome injection of Guinness money.

The fall in student numbers had also hit the old Queen's Colleges in Cork and Galway. By contrast, a number of unincorporated colleges (particularly in the medical field) were thriving in the capital, and some of the older secondary schools had developed third-level courses, preparing their students for examination by the vestigial Royal University. Castleknock and Blackrock Colleges had followed this path, and the Dominicans had established a small women's college, St Mary's, in 1893, but the trail-blazer was the old Newman/Woodlock institution in St Stephen's Green, known since 1882 as University College Dublin (UCD). It was fortunate to have had as its longest serving president a remarkably able Jesuit, Father William Delany, and UCD, like its sister institution, the Catholic Medical School in Cecilia Street, began a long period of expansion in the 1880s. By 1900 the combined student population of UCD and Cecilia Street was about half that of Trinity's, but they were still housed in unpretentious buildings and had to make do with limited resources. This 'scandal' of Catholic institutional poverty, side by side with Trinity's evident wealth, exercised both Delany and Archbishop Walsh for more than two decades, and the 'university question' remained after Irish land reform the one great issue that successive Liberal governments could not resolve to the satisfaction of the Irish Catholic hierarchy – not least because of Trinity's residual political leverage which was repeatedly deployed to defend its autonomy. The debate over university reform became public and ugly in its final stages, inflamed by several celebrated street scuffles involving students from UCD and TCD from the time of the Boer War, but also by the withering judgements on the respective academic standing of the two institutions made by academic elders who should have known better.[21]

Resolution came in 1908, with UCD becoming the strongest partner in a federation of the three colleges that constituted the new National University of Ireland (NUI); Trinity (and with it the University of Dublin) remained unaffected. The new NUI college, secular in fact but Catholic in ethos, moved into the Earlsfort Terrace buildings first used for the 1865 Exhibition, and in later years functioning as the examination halls of the Royal University. Grand building plans were drawn up and soon scaled down, but Rudolf Butler's monumental stone pavilion along the Terrace (completed in 1914) echoed Gandon's Custom House. The new dispensation transformed UCD's scale and its academic diversity, but early hopes of major state investment ran far ahead of what the Treasury was prepared to commit. Nevertheless, UCD's exuberant student culture, evident since the 1890s, reasserted itself in the reformed institution. And there was a remarkable array of scholarly talent in the new professorial team after 1909, from well-travelled physicists to outstanding Celticists, including veterans of the city's recent culture wars – Douglas Hyde, Eoin MacNeill, Thomas MacDonagh and Tom Kettle (the rising star in the IPP) being the best known. There was a palpable sense that they were preparing the elite that would soon take control of Home-Rule Ireland. There was still a pervasive Jesuit feel to the new college, but at its inception there had been a dramatic if temporary loss of clerical (specifically episcopal) authority: Delany was quite opposed to linking the new institution with the cultural revival, but the Gaelic League ran a very effective national campaign and managed to pressurise the NUI Senate in 1910 into making proficiency in the Irish language an essential requirement for admission to any of the NUI colleges.[22]

The older, more intimate UCD had left its mark on the pre-1908 graduates and echoes of this can be found in Joyce. One of his closest student associates, Francis Skeffington (who as 'McCann' appears in Joyce's posthumous novel *Stephen Hero* (1944)) made a singular mark on the pre-war city. Shortly after graduation, Skeffington was briefly UCD registrar before resigning over Delany's reluctance to admit women in 1904. Thereafter, he and his wife Hanna Sheehy became the most tireless and outspoken campaigners on 'the woman question', being heavily critical of the Irish Party's lack of support for the advancement of women. Their radicalism embraced many other causes, as they firmly rejected both the 'aristocratic' Castle and local clerical tyranny, and they discounted the cultural revival (whether Gaelic or Yeatsian) as a diversion from real social issues. However, the Sheehy-Skeffingtons only broke with the IPP in 1912 when they established the *Irish Citizen*, one of the many minor weeklies now flooding the news-stands. Their paper was unique in Dublin in its uncompromising advocacy of gender equality, its principal readership being drawn from the

1,000-odd members of the Irish Women's Franchise League which Hanna had co-founded in 1908. Shortly after its launch she partook in the first acts of civil disobedience by the IWFL (the stoning of Dublin Castle offices), which led to her temporary imprisonment and celebrity. Support for the cause was narrow, even though there had been public debate on the subject for at least thirty years. Most of the growing number of female teachers and nurses in the city were members of the Catholic religious orders and thus were outside the public sphere. But there were a few powerful voices, such as the veteran campaigner for access to higher education, Mary Hayden, now on the staff and governing body of UCD, and Sarah Harrison, now on the city council. But for all the relative marginality of the Sheehy-Skeffingtons, they stood out as the most active and fearless members of the intelligentsia, giving full-blooded support to Larkin in 1913, thereby earning Murphy's ridicule and Connolly's respect.[23]

The return of European war

In August 1907 the city's first triumphal arch was unveiled at the north-east corner of St Stephen's Green as a monument to the 250 members of the Royal Dublin Fusiliers who had perished in the Boer War. The garrison depot of Fusiliers, the principal east Leinster infantry regiment since the army reforms of 1881, was at Naas, Co. Kildare, but the rank and file were overwhelmingly city men, many of them poor. Indeed, at the time of the unveiling much was made of the distress of some hundreds of unemployed veterans in the city. The decision to locate the Fusiliers Arch opposite the top of Grafton Street was made by the Board of Works, who also supplied the architect. That it was the site chosen by the Corporation nine years earlier for a monument to Wolfe Tone was hardly coincidental, but the arch would have been controversial wherever it was erected. To the advanced nationalists, such an elaborate celebration of imperial arms was quite repugnant, but that was probably a minority view in 1907.[24]

Over the next six years the place of arms and armies changed profoundly in the minds of citizens. When the military were ordered onto the streets in 1913 in support of the unarmed city police during the Lockout, nothing like this had been seen since the Invincibles in 1882, and then only briefly. But by that point an unofficial militarisation of a kind not seen since the 1780s had spread through Unionist Ulster in opposition to

Home Rule – in the form of the Ulster Volunteer Force (UVF), a movement given muscle by the covert importation of 25,000 German rifles in April 1914 and their successful distribution. Months earlier, at a somewhat fractious meeting in the Rotunda in November 1913, a rival amateur militia, the Irish Volunteers (IV), was formally established, with the somewhat ambiguous mission of protecting the prospects for the successful passage of a Home Rule bill. Eoin MacNeill was the public face of the initiative, but the idea had been developed by a knot of IRB men, principally a young Belfast Quaker, Bulmer Hobson. With relatively lax rules over gun ownership prior to the crisis and little restraint on quasi-military association, both organisations had mushroomed, adopting the trappings and discipline of the British infantry and tutored by many ex-servicemen. Their very high visibility contributed to the gathering assumption that Home Rule was not going to be achieved without some kind of civil conflict. Also in the mix by spring 1914 were the rumours of a possible mutiny by officers in the Curragh if they were ordered to move against the UVF.

Recruitment into the Irish Volunteers had been a strongly urban phenomenon to begin with, attracting many army reservists, but its ranks were filled with the 'respectable' working class. By the summer of 1914, it was almost nationwide. A women's division, Cumann na mBan, was created in Dublin, its mission far too modestly conceived for the suffragists. Volunteering was a practical response to the growing realisation that the Liberal government would truncate Home Rule for peace's sake and offer some form of Irish partition to the Ulster Unionists. John Redmond and the IPP were fighting a difficult game inside and outside Westminster, one of Redmond's tactics being to take control of the executive of the Irish Volunteers in June 1914. But unknown to Redmond a group of Volunteer supporters (mainly London-based) were organising a modest gun-run, and some 900 German Mausers reached Howth late in July. The Dublin Volunteers, who were organised to collect and distribute these weapons in a very public show of strength, were intercepted by the DMP and Scottish troops on the Howth Road. The police failed to capture many weapons, and some hours later the soldiers from the same regiment were stoned by crowds on Bachelors Walk. In the return fire they killed four civilians. Six days later a further 600 rifles were covertly landed in north Co. Wicklow.[25]

If events far away had not interrupted the local course of events, some messy resolution of the crisis would probably have been found without Dublin being directly affected, although a bloodbath in Ulster would certainly have created novel sectarian tensions in the capital. But the First World War came in the early days of August, and there was an almost immediate reduction in the political temperature as the final iteration of Home Rule was left to be determined after the end of the war. Redmond's ambiguous declaration of support on the eve of hostilities and his appeal at Woodenbridge seven weeks later to Volunteers to enlist in Crown forces helped generate a wave of anti-German sentiment, nothing perhaps to compare with such feelings in Britain but strong enough for army recruitment in the city to reach unprecedented levels for a few months. In the first five months of the war, 7,283 men were recruited in the Dublin district (out of 21,187 recruited there by the end of 1916). Fraternal organisations and sports clubs channelled the enthusiasm of would-be recruits, and large employers, even Dublin Corporation, gave promises of job security or better to the thousands of well-employed young men willing to sign up. More traditional forms of recruitment were used to drum up support in the inner city, tapping at first the large pool of reservists. The old Liberties district seems to have been the most important source of recruits in greater Dublin, followed by the north inner city, and one of the companies in the Dublin Fusiliers was largely composed of dockers, Larkin's veterans. A very high proportion of the Fusiliers who boarded the troop ships were unmarried, and two-thirds were under twenty-five. The other side of this sentiment was a surge in war-related voluntary activity, unprecedented in its scale and intensity, mostly involving women, with the leadership generally Protestant. The ever-busy Lady Aberdeen moved quickly to have the State Rooms in Dublin Castle transformed into a Red Cross hospital, and dozens of other initiatives were launched in the early months of the war. Elsie Henry, wife of a College of Science professor, directed a scheme that had particular impact at the Front – the collection and preparation of sphagnum moss from around the country to be used to dress battlefield wounds in place of cotton-wool. As Clara Cullen has revealed, vast quantities found their way from the College of Science to field-hospitals in Flanders over the next few years.[26]

Henry noted in her diary in mid-August 1914 how the troop ships in Dublin port 'blow awful sirens every evening at 5 and 8; they sometimes sound like wailing banshees, and sometimes they roar and bellow like some devouring beast of the Apocalypse'. Such language hints at the fears running below the surface as to what modern industrial warfare might mean, but few Dubliners can have expected that artillery would be used within their own city. Redmond's fateful decision to support the war effort attracted overwhelmingly positive support in the Dublin media, but within days it split the Volunteer movement and MacNeill led the abstainers. Backed by the support organisations attached to the Irish Party, over 90 per cent of the 190,000 Volunteers stayed with Redmond's renamed 'National Volunteers', but in Dublin the result was rather different: nearly 30 per cent sided with MacNeill, even more in the inner city, less in the suburbs, least in Rathmines. The stock of weaponry, such as it was, remained disproportionately with the anti-war grouping.[27]

Support for the war among IPP-supporting nationalists receded very gradually. The particularly heavy losses suffered by the Dublin Fusiliers in Gallipoli were shocking enough, but the paltry recognition of their part in the campaign in official commentary was galling, as was the long delay in revealing just how badly the Allied forces had been worsted by the Turks. Redmond's National Volunteers, denied the kind of status that the UVF were being accorded, lost ground. They possessed large premises and an arms store in Rutland Square, but by 1916 there was a palpable sense of an organisation withering. It was a different story with MacNeill's Irish Volunteers, operating from – of all places – Kildare Street. One reason was the curious make-up of the organisation: on the surface it existed to check-mate the UVF and secure the full measure of Home Rule after the war, but since the split its growth had been covertly promoted by the Irish Republican Brotherhood. In other words, the secret republican organisation that had smouldered under the surface for a generation saw the war as a phoenix-like opportunity. Eleven days before Redmond's Woodenbridge speech, an IRB group, chaired by veteran Fenian Thomas Clarke, met in the Gaelic League headquarters and decided to organise an insurrection with German support and to plan for it in the tightest secrecy so that even friends active in the Volunteers would be unaware of what was contemplated.[28]

1916

The republican conspiracy, spanning twenty-one months and culminating in the events of Easter Week 1916, has enjoyed an extraordinary afterlife in history, memoir and literature. Yet elements of the story remain puzzling. How did a small group of easily identifiable advanced nationalists, well known to the police and to journalists, manage to develop plans for an

insurrection that took nearly everyone, apart from the participants, by surprise, given all the resources of the state and the technologies available to
it? From the initial contact made between trusted American confidantes
and the German embassy, the steady infiltration of men sworn to the IRB's
code of secrecy into command and control positions inside the Irish Volunteers and the Gaelic League, and the use of the Sinn Féin organisation as
a mask behind which to recruit, how come almost none of this was known
to the world outside or was apprehended by Dublin Castle? There is no
single answer. The insurrectionists were perhaps a bit lucky, and Clarke's
prison-hardened self-discipline and the utter loyalty of his deputy Seán
MacDiarmada were critical ingredients in taking it as far as it got. Successfully excluding both MacNeill (opposed to secret societies) and several
senior IRB men from the secrets of the so-called Military Council until
the final days suggested a fine degree of ruthless duplicity. Then there is the
tantalising issue of Larkin's successor: what was a socialist internationalist
doing in planning a national uprising together with petit bourgeois plotters who lacked any popular mandate? Connolly had, it seems, begun his
republican journey during the Lockout, a journey hastened by the prospect
of Irish partition and then by the international collapse of working-class
solidarity in August 1914. But it is hard to fathom the intellectual basis
for his conversion to the idea that national liberation was a prerequisite to
social revolution and that the Citizen Army should be the catalyst in seizing that liberation. However, the fact that Connolly and the IRB insurrectionists brokered an agreement in January 1916 to work together and that
they managed to entirely abide by that agreement suggests that participation in a nationalist revolt had become a cause sufficient to risk his life – as
long as there was a strong dose of democratic socialism in its title deeds.[29]

Food and fuel prices began to climb from the first weeks of European hostilities, and although inflation did not have acute welfare effects
until 1917, it contributed to the rapid decline of public enthusiasm for the
war during 1915. Muffled reports of the horrors of Flanders and Suvla Bay
and the sight of hospital ships on the quays discharging the war-wounded
for care in local institutions contributed too. Pacifism made little showing locally, apart from the Labour leader Thomas Johnson and the irre-
pressible Sheehy-Skeffingtons, but the looming danger that conscription
might be introduced became the issue that mobilised popular opposition
long before it was actually threatened. The funeral of O'Donovan Rossa
in Glasnevin in August 1915 was a telling moment when the last of the

*36. James and Margaret Pearse and family in the 1880s. James Pearse was a
gifted monumental sculptor in the inner city; he died in 1900 and the business
was gone by 1910. Their children, Patrick (who is standing) and Margaret,
Willie and Mary, went on to achieve national fame, thanks to Patrick's
extraordinary career, first as publicist for the Gaelic League, then as innovating
educationist, finally as the public face of revolutionary nationalism.*

original Fenians managed in death to establish the radical credentials of a
recent IRB recruit, Patrick Pearse. The event was tightly managed by the
Irish Volunteers, shots were fired beside the grave and, even though all
wings of nationalism were in attendance, it was the intoxicating oratory
from the Rathfarnham schoolteacher that everyone remembered:

> Life springs from death, and from the graves of patriot men and women
> spring live nations. The defenders of this Realm have worked well in
> secret and in the open. They think that they have pacified Ireland.
> They think that they have purchased half of us, and intimidated the
> other half. They think that they have foreseen everything. They think
> that they have provided against everything; but the fools, the fools,

the fools! They have left us our Fenian dead, and, while Ireland holds these graves, Ireland unfree shall never be at peace.

Pearse, poet, mystic and educational reformer, had grown up in Brunswick Street around his father's stonemasonry business. A product of the old UCD and called to the bar in 1901, he was one of the best-known Gaelic revivalists in the city, a passionate and imaginative editor of *An Claidheamh Soluis*. Since 1908 he had thrown his energies into St Enda's, an experimental private school, where he had sought to marry new educational psychology with the cultural revival, but the bilingual school (and a short-lived girls school) proved to be a heavy financial drain. Yet Pearse found time to be drawn into politics. A radical Home Ruler who came to despair of Home Rule, he was only admitted to the IRB late in 1913, but by the spring of 1915 he was in the inner sanctum, the director of military organisation for an imminent Dublin rising. It was a curious choice: he was a superb speaker and had great organisational energy, but he lacked knowledge of or any previous interest in military matters. Yet it was his arrival which consummated the marriage between revivalism and republicanism, his burning sense of a heroic past and the nobility of sacrifice that bewitched the faint-hearted. Joseph Plunkett, grandson of one of Rathmines' major house-builders, was an even stranger choice for the Military Council: young, wealthy and with literary, theatrical and scientific interests, he was shy and plagued by ill-health. It is all the more remarkable that he appears to have drafted the original plan for the Dublin insurrection with its emphasis on capturing and controlling strategic neighbourhoods and on garrisoning specific large buildings. It envisaged city Volunteers being organised into four battalions. Not everyone in the planning group was committed to such an emphasis on Dublin or to a big-bang strategy, but it seems to have been the majority view, always favoured by Pearse and (for very different reasons) by Connolly, who had made a point of studying street-fighting in Paris and more recently in Moscow. It was, of course, still assumed that in the regions where the Volunteers were strongest, independent action to pin down Crown forces would be taken.[30]

The plan for a republican insurrection quietly matured within the carapace of Volunteering. And the shrill rhetoric of Volunteers – nationalist, defensive and ambiguous – amplified the popularity of the militia and provided a purpose for the endless drills, weekend camps and formal reviews. These culminated in a huge but unauthorised review in College Green (beside King William's statue) on St Patrick's Day 1916, with Mac-Neill presiding. Despite menacing behaviour and the blocking of traffic, the police did not intervene. The next occasion for nationwide Volunteer reviews was scheduled for a month later on Easter Sunday. MacNeill was appalled to discover only days before the event that he had been duped, and that the planned countrywide reviews were in fact the cover for a rising. Then news came through that a large shipment of German arms had been intercepted in Kerry, so he publicly cancelled all Volunteer activity, only to find a day later that his colleagues had overriden his orders and decided to go ahead, albeit with an improvised plan concentrating very largely on Dublin.

A ragtag armed force of some 1,200, many of them perplexed at the sequence of commands and countermands, assembled on Easter Monday morning at Liberty Hall and Earlsfort Terrace, in a small park in Fairview and in Emerald Square (off Cork Street), and a few outside the city at Pearse's school, four-fifths of them under orders as Volunteers, the remainder Citizen Army men and women. Their numbers were under half the total that would have mustered on the previous day had the review not been cancelled. If the 872 men and women later arrested and interned is a guide to the social composition of those who marched out, participants with semi- or un-skilled occupations were a minority (36 per cent), and far behind the old backbone of city Fenianism, the skilled workers, clerks and shop assistants (58 per cent). Professional and business families contributed a mere 2 per cent – and a great many of these were very young indeed.[31]

Relatively little blood was shed in the midday seizure of the GPO (by the Headquarters Battalion), or during the next few hours with the capture of the Four Courts and Church Street area by the First Battalion of the Volunteers, Jacob's factory by the Second Battalion (they had originally been assigned Amiens Street station on the far side of the city), Boland's flour mill, Grand Canal Dock and Westland Row station by the Third, and the South Dublin Workhouse complex and the Marrowbone distillery by the Fourth (who alone had to fight to defend their positions on the first day). The capture and fortification of St Stephen's Green was the responsibility of the Citizen Army. Much the largest concentration of Volunteers was in the cavernous GPO (it grew to hold 408 people, including those who cooked and carried). In the first minutes of the revolt, a band of thirty Citizen Army men made to enter Dublin Castle, which was almost completely unprotected. Their leader, an amateur actor who had just starred as Robert Emmet, was perhaps not the best choice for such a task. After shooting the sentry, they withdrew as the gates were forcibly closed and they took over City Hall instead. With an unarmed police and a denuded garrison, the Castle remained at the mercy of snipers until relief arrived two hours later. Apart from a Castle guard of six men and about two dozen in the Ship Street barracks nearby, there were no more than 400 soldiers in 'immediate readiness' across all the city's barracks. Not since 1659 had an armed plot come quite so close to occupying the ancient symbol of London's authority in Ireland.[32]

The executive head of the Irish government, Sir Matthew Nathan, Under Secretary since August 1914, remained at his desk for the duration of the crisis. Since coming to Ireland he had followed the ever-absent Birrell's policy of accommodating nationalist, specifically Redmondite, concerns, always aware of the danger of 'Sinn Féin' agitators undermining Redmond's authority during the long wartime delay in finalising Home Rule. Even though Nathan authorised the closure late in 1914 of several radical papers, notably Griffith's *Sinn Féin*, and the principal IRB paper, *Irish Freedom*, others filled their place (Griffith was particularly adept at this), and anti-war sentiment was still able to circulate. Nathan was privately aware of the hardening of the public mood against the war and of declining support for the Irish Party, the National Volunteers and other support organisations, but Birrell in London remained convinced that the 'Sinn Féin' threat was exaggerated. The quality of police and military intelligence available to the Castle was very poor, not least as to the state of things in the city itself, with only a single mid-level spy feeding information. Great importance was given at government level to Sir Roger Casement's activities in Germany in 1915, less to Plunkett's trip to Berlin at the same time. And the capture of Casement in Kerry in Holy Week 1916 was invested with huge significance, when in fact he was marginal to Irish plans. The loss of the arms that had come with him was far more important. But Casement's capture did reflect high-quality British naval intelligence (via wire taps), which had picked up news of the arms shipment and of a planned Dublin rising a month before the event. The failure to transmit this critical information in a timely way, and Nathan's failure to determine its authenticity (when it did eventually reach him), was more a spectacular systems failure than personal incompetence. But the dramatic events surrounding Casement's capture led to the decision to search Liberty Hall and to carry out a large-scale round-up of Volunteer and Sinn Féin leaders – but not yet, not on an Easter Monday Bank Holiday.[33]

Monday's rebellion lasted for a week. In the first two days the four Dublin battalions consolidated their hold on the six neighbourhoods they had taken. Outposts were created in the upstairs of private houses and good sight-lines picked from behind old parapets. Barricades marked the edge of liberated districts or were built (as around St Stephen's Green) to block traffic and give cover to street-level movement. The police were stood down, street lights went out, the trams were stopped. All waited. Most Volunteers had very little idea of how things might unfold, whether German help was imminent, whether the rest of the country had risen. The leadership knew better, but even among them justification and motivation varied. All, however, seem to have shared a profound sense that whatever the outcome of their actions they were changing the course of Irish history, reigniting the separatist cause, and destroying Home Rule and all the corrupting compromises it stood for. The proclamation of the Republic at the GPO portico, the flying of the green flag echoing 1798 and of the tricolour of 1848, presented the armed rejection of British authority as a centuries-long, seamless and noble endeavour, almost a sacred act of acknowledgement of those who had gone before.

Emmet's rebellion carried particular potency for the rebels – an exclusively Dublin event, at its centre a heroic martyr and the timeless force of the speech from the dock. Pearse, with his near-devotion of Emmet, fanned this sense of history. But the wording of the 1916 Proclamation, which it seems he and Connolly largely wrote, was carefully measured and its enlightenment sense of a Republic claiming 'the allegiance of every Irishman and Irishwoman', offering 'religious and civil liberty, equal rights and equal opportunities to all its citizens ... cherishing all the children of the nation equally' reflected 1913, not 1803. As Padraig Yeates has observed, 'it could not have been drafted, let alone adopted ... anywhere in Ireland but Dublin', what with the city's 'unique milieu of radical nationalists, syndicalists, suffragists and socialists', and certainly its well-honed language suggested a convincing degree of ideological unity among the seven signatories. Despite invoking the Deity, it was a secular document, yet there was no anti-clericalism in this revolution. Quite the contrary, regular religious observance mattered to many of the participants, and a number of clergy gave pastoral support amid the gun-smoke. When old Archbishop Walsh was invited by the government to denounce the rebels, he declined, merely encouraging his flock to stay indoors. Upper-class Protestants might have been heavily implicated in the Howth gun-running, but where were they now? Countess Markievicz, assisted by her medical comrade Kathleen Lynn, were exceptional by their presence. And with Hobson sidelined within the IRB (for opposing the insurrectionary project) and Casement a prisoner in the Tower of London, the seven Proc-lamation signatories were all Catholic. It is true that one of them had mar-ried an Anglican (James Connolly), one had an Anglican father (Thomas Clarke), one had a Presbyterian mother (Thomas MacDonagh), and that Patrick Pearse's father had been a freethinker. But they were all in good standing with their confessors now.[34]

The reality on the streets in those first days was less edifying. With no police to be seen, large-scale looting began, both inside and beyond the areas controlled by Volunteer snipers, with grocery shops and department stores being targeted by women and children: 'ordinary shutters were use-less against this throng'. Stories of grand pianos being carried along Sack-ville Street and of looters wading through a foot-deep flood of wine in a Henry Street cellar may exaggerate, but probably thousands of tenement dwellers benefited from the temporary collapse of social order. Some of the first great fires were started by the looters (visible even from the Cur-ragh) and, despite their strong disapproval, neither Connolly nor Pearse ordered any counter-measures to this 'French Revolution in miniature'. Vigilantes on Grafton Street prevented a similar story south of the river, but the military ignored much of the looting that did take place.[35]

Major-General William Lowe, a cavalry officer based in the Curragh with little knowledge of the country, directed the military response. This began in earnest on the Wednesday with the arrival in Kingstown of large numbers of infantry. Lowe's strategy was to reinforce the physical division between rebels north and south of the river, specifically strengthening the corridor of streets running from Kingsbridge station east to Trinity Col-lege, and to establish control over the full length of the North Circular Road. The Sherwood Foresters were the first to enter the city from Kings-town, receiving a predictably warm welcome as they passed through the townships. Lacking machine guns or artillery support, they marched into an ambush near the canal at Mount Street Bridge, an outpost of the Third Battalion. With orders from Lowe to clear enemy fire before proceeding, the Foresters suffered terrible losses (twenty-eight killed and some 200

*37. Sackville (O'Connell) Street in flames: one of the more apocalyptic
images of the Rising, this was apparently taken on the fifth night,
capturing the scene southwards from the Rotunda Rooms into the smoke
and fires that were principally caused by artillery bombardment. The
Republican leadership surrendered unconditionally on the sixth day.*

wounded) at the hands of seventeen Volunteers. It was a costly demonstration of the new world of urban warfare and in neither of the other main
fire-fights – around the South Dublin Union and beyond the Four Courts
along North King Street – was there any such mass killing by either army.[36]

The artillery assault on Beresford Place and Sackville Street was a different matter. Lowe summoned the *Helga*, a fishery protection yacht from
Kingstown, to exploit the river and the open lie of the land. Combining
with field guns placed in Tara Street, the vessel pounded Boland's, Liberty Hall and then the blocks around the GPO; two days of incendiary
shells directed into Lower Sackville Street led to huge fires, both there and
along Abbey Street, 'the most dreadful conflagration ever seen in Dublin'.
Clery's, the Royal Hibernian Academy, Eason's, the *Freeman's Journal* and
the Alliance Gas building were among the household names reduced to
rubble before the end of the week, so that 'one would not know the different streets were it not for Nelson's Pillar as a guide'. Every building along
the east side from Eden Quay to Cathedral Place was destroyed, including

Lower Abbey Street, and on the west side from Middle Abbey Street to Henry Street. By contrast, buildings on the south side of the Liffey (apart from Lower Mount Street) were little affected because of the more confined sites the rebels had chosen for garrisoning. The first estimate after it was all over was that 196 buildings in the inner city had been destroyed by the weekend, valued at £2.5 million, but how far artillery was responsible was never clear. The old Linen Hall was burnt down by Volunteers, apparently to prevent their enemies from seizing it.[37]

As the GPO became a pyre, the leaders retreated, but were pinned down one block to the west before an unconditional surrender was negotiated between Pearse and Lowe late on Saturday. Other battalions surrendered the following day with considerable reluctance. To their adversaries the Volunteers appeared well disciplined, even chivalrous, but woefully out-gunned, despite what had happened in Mount Street and around Cork Street. But given the resources they set out with, mistakes were made which, if avoided, could certainly have prolonged the revolt into weeks, albeit with a much greater cost of human life and city fabric. Plunkett's plans had assumed at least twice the manpower than they had, but even with diminished numbers it would still have been possible to occupy the Castle, take hostages and hold it for a token period. Its capture was part of the plan, but no one had grasped the fact that it was almost completely undefended. Then there was the College campus located in the middle of the rebellion; it would certainly have been risky for the Volunteers to have tried to seize major buildings there, as this would have been resisted by the TCD training corps with its light arms, and the leadership may have feared that heavy loss of life in such an exchange would give the rising a sectarian appearance. The tactics in St Stephen's Green, the excavation of a series of light trenches, some of which were overseen by the Shelbourne, were almost comically inappropriate. This was a Citizen Army zone, commanded not by Connolly but by his deputy Michael Mallin and the Countess Markievicz, whose eccentric behaviour hid their exceptionally poor tactics.

Deficient logistical planning was everywhere apparent; food and medical supplies in the larger garrisons were quite inadequate, and were it not for the forceful ingenuity of the Cumann na mBan Volunteers, things would have been much worse. Even stranger was the rebels' failure to break key communication lines; the seizure of the GPO knocked out the Telegraph Instrument Room, but the twenty telephonists working in the Crown Alley Exchange were left untouched. Thanks to considerable makeshift ingenuity, a telephone service was operated by the head of the Irish Post Office from the Royal Hibernian Hotel throughout the week. Military communications between Kilmainham (the military command) and London were never broken, although non-official communications (and the postal service) were suspended for the duration of the crisis. Rail communication other than in the approaches to Westland Row were hardly interrupted; the Second Battalion's plan to occupy Amiens Street station miscarried, as did the First Battalion's sally towards Broadstone; both stations and, more critically, Kingsbridge continued to operate unmolested as railheads for incoming troops as they were brought in from country garrisons. Efforts to blow up railway bridges in Fairview and Cabra came to nothing, and there was not even the hint of a sniper in Kingstown or on the North Wall to halt the wave of troop reinforcements.[38]

When it was almost over, a far more senior officer arrived from London, General Maxwell, to take all necessary measures to restore order. The city had been under martial law since Tuesday, 25 April, and the army command was now the sole authority, controlling some 20,000 soldiers in and around the city. There was some but not a great deal of abuse of that overwhelming power. In what was later deemed to be one such abuse of military law, an officer from Portobello barracks executed three civilians, including Francis Sheehy-Skeffington, for acting suspiciously on the street. The pacifist feminist had been trying to organise an anti-looting initiative. About 3,500 prisoners were taken up, of whom ninety were court-martialled at the beginning of May and fifteen executed, including all the leaders and commandants except for the American-born Eamon De Valera, who had commanded Boland's Mills. There were various estimates of the death toll: the most conservative suggested 300 deaths and 2,600 injuries. Crown forces had 103 fatalities, the Volunteers perhaps 60, and the rest were civilian casualties, a reflection of how great was the collateral cost in choosing to locate an insurrection in the centre of a crowded city.[39]

The greatest uncertainty surrounding these events is how the city at large reacted. Shock and anxiety at first – over family safety, food supply, the breakdown of public security – and there were no shortage of stories in the first few days of citizens reprimanding the rebels. Women, probably older than most of the rebels, were, it seems, the most visible critics. Some were the 'separation women' with sons or husbands at the Front, but the early contempt for the rebels was much broader than that. Then, after the surrender, as the newspapers began to appear again, virtually all the Dublin press, including Murphy's *Independent*, could not find words of condemnation strong enough to denounce the men who by their actions had destroyed Dublin. But for all that, many non-combatants – including vast numbers of working-class Dubliners who were the passive but undiscriminating supporters of most nationalist causes – are likely to have sympathised to some degree with the men inside the GPO, their numbers swollen by the 300 or so latecomers who joined the rebels during the week. General Lowe's Staff Captain noted that 'tremendous cheers greeted the rebels as they surrendered' in St Stephen's Green, and that at the surrender of the Marrowbone Lane distillery in the Liberties, while 'there seemed to be great relief ... that hostilities had ceased, it was perfectly plain that all the admiration was for those who surrendered'. But the manner of their surrender, the universal experience of rough martial law in the city and the excruciating elongation of the fifteen executions in Kilmainham jail, all combined to radicalise nationalist public opinion. Their opponents called it the Sinn Féin rebellion, and those who survived the firestorm were happy to brand themselves as Sinn Féin when, less than a year later, they began to come out of jail. Pearse and the IRB plotters may have made many tactical mistakes in preparing for the Rising, but their predictions as to its political impact after they were gone proved entirely correct, and in the years ahead it was their version of the Irish future that triumphed within nationalist Ireland. A day before he surrendered, Pearse reminded the GPO Volunteers of the historical significance of what they had accomplished. They might not have won in a narrow sense, but they had 'redeemed Dublin from many shames, and made her name splendid among the names of cities', a sentiment that neutral observers were surprised to detect among non-combatants – that the rebels had put up a good fight and had not been humiliated.[40]

Radical victories

The horrors of the Somme and more than two years of war lay between the Dublin Rebellion and the Allied victory in November 1918. During that time the city was itself at peace, but the aftershocks of Easter 1916 did not subside. Martial law was ended within a week, but the intense military surveillance of opposition political activity continued as it became evident that support for the 'Sinn Féin' prisoners was solidifying. At least one popular weekly, *The Catholic Bulletin*, edited by Gaelic League radical

J. J. O'Kelly, went out of its way to endorse the actions of the rebels and published a mass of detail about the participants and their families. Then in June 1917, when many leading Volunteers were released from detention, they received an exuberant, almost victorious welcome in the city. One of those released, Thomas Ashe, commandant of the lone County Dublin battalion in 1916, was re-arrested, went on hunger strike and died in Mountjoy prison three months later; the charismatic schoolteacher from Kerry had emerged as one of the new leaders of the revolutionary movement and his sudden death after being force-fed was a propaganda disaster for the government. Against the Under Secretary's wishes, his body lay in state in City Hall, where even the Archbishop paid his respects, and the funeral, with 35,000 in the procession 'principally of Dublin people', was 'larger and even more impressive than that of Parnell'. Less than a month later, the IRB-backed Volunteers in effect took over Griffith's Sinn Féin party, rewrote its constitution and geared it up for electoral contests against the IPP. William Cosgrave of James Street, one of the founder members of Griffith's original Sinn Féin, having served with unusual distinction on the Corporation since 1908, had already demonstrated that an Easter Week veteran could handsomely defeat an IPP candidate in a parliamentary contest (at Kilkenny), and that set the pattern.[41]

Nevertheless, military recruitment continued, albeit at reduced levels, with some 7,000 volunteering from Dublin in the last two years of the war, but in the same period over 8,000 migrated from the city to civilian employment in Britain. But the old cry against conscription continued until it was on the point of implementation in spring 1918; a national anti-conscription conference in the Mansion House, drawing in all nationalist political parties, won full endorsement from the Catholic bishops and was immediately followed by a general strike for one day. It was an unprecedented and untypical display of nationalist unity, choreographed in Dublin, and had almost immediate results in forcing a government climb-down, followed by the arrest of seventy-three Sinn Féin leaders for supposedly hatching a new German plot.[42]

The fevered state of politics was rather disconnected from life on the street. Wartime inflation certainly hit hard, particularly in the last two years of war, making some necessities (coal, milk, even potatoes) almost beyond the reach of poor households. But wartime rent control, introduced in 1915, and progressive state wage-arbitration muffled the impact of inflation for many of those in employment. The flow of benefits to the wives and children of men on active service had a perceptible effect on the living standards of many semi- and unskilled working-class households, and the growth of demand (from 1916) for female labour from the two munitions factories, one on the North Wall, the much larger one (the National Shell Company) at the west end of the city, was the employment equivalent of a new Jacob's factory. As Yeates has shown, workhouse numbers fell in the course of the war, reported cases of child neglect declined sharply, and the quarterly death rate for the city, which averaged 22.5 per 1,000 for the war as a whole, fell to 18.75 per 1,000 between summer 1917 and summer 1918. Male employment was certainly hit by the severe production controls placed on brewing and distilling (the payroll in 1917 was half that of 1914), but other sectors such as shipbuilding and ship repair recovered. Given the bottlenecks in Britain, skilled labour was more mobile than ever and that brought earnings close to, or sometimes even ahead of, inflation. In sectors where it did not, there were several short-lived industrial disputes, notably in the port in 1916 and 1917. But most important of all for urban welfare, the war brought unprecedentedly high prices at the farm-gate for more than four years, and this translated into a strengthened demand for city trades and services, and the cattle market handled record numbers of bullocks and sheep on their way to the English market. Only the building trades, which might have expected a huge boost from reconstruction business, were left waiting as compensation settlements were thrashed out and as prospects for a major initiative (whether state or municipal) to rebuild the city centre receded. Lesser public servants, notably the DMP and other white-collar workers, were left nursing grievances over pay and compensation as inflation eroded their living standards and as they observed the widows and families of 1916 Volunteers being handsomely looked after (thanks to the well-run Volunteer Dependants' Fund).[43]

In the final weeks of the war, the global conflict finally came over the horizon. Not far from Kish Bank, the *Leinster,* one of the CDSPC's fast mail-boats, was steaming for Holyhead on an October morning, carrying a full complement of soldiers returning to the Front, as well as military nurses and civilians, when it was sunk by two U-boat torpedoes. The threat to cross-channel traffic had been there through the war, there had been near-misses before, but the loss of over 500 people on a merchant vessel within sight of land compounded the shock. The fact that only about a fifth of the casualties were civilian was rather downplayed. Within ten days U-boats were recalled from offensive duties in foreign waters, and within a month came the armistice. As in 1814, the city's mixed loyalties were never more apparent – students from Trinity College and the College of Surgeons celebrating exuberantly in the streets, while UCD students tore down the Union Jack from the National University headquarters. There were serious street fights into the night on both sides of the river.[44]

But serious minds were focused once again on electoral politics and the long-sought general election a month after the armistice. It was the first time women over thirty had the parliamentary vote. The odds on a complete rout of the Irish Party/United Irish League candidates, both in the city and across nationalist Ireland, were now shortening by the week. The Sinn Féin party, a far more formidable organisation with at least twenty-three clubs in the city, had matured and learnt from running the anti-conscription campaign; it was focused on getting its leaders out of jail and on launching the bid for international recognition of the Republic at the upcoming peace conference. And it now enjoyed the support of the main nationalist daily, Murphy's *Independent*. In the seven new city con-stituencies, Sinn Féin swept the board, winning 66.7 per cent of the votes cast, and also took three of the four county and suburban seats with 47.6 per cent of the vote. IPP candidates in city and county held almost a quar-ter of the vote but won no seats, while Unionists with half that vote won seats in Trinity College and in Rathmines, where a liberal Unionist busi-nessman and advocate of women's rights, Sir Maurice Dockrell, topped the poll. The Sinn Féin victory, nine MPs in greater Dublin (and seventy-three overall, thirty-six of them in prison), was an electoral revolution far surpassing the earthquake of 1885, and among the victors was the veteran Countess Markievicz in the Liberties constituency of St Patrick's.[45]

A month later, on 21 January 1919, the thirty-two Sinn Féin MPs then at liberty were accommodated by the non-party nationalist Lord Mayor, Laurence O'Neill, in the Round Room of the Mansion House. The meet-ing was conducted entirely in Irish and was witnessed by an estimated hun-dred journalists. With one or two exceptions, they were 'all young men, there being no grey hairs among them and very few wrinkled brows'. The assembly ratified the Proclamation of the Republic and declared itself to be the Parliament of the Irish Republic, Dáil Éireann. Apart from adopt-ing a provisional constitution, it passed a short 'democratic programme'. This was by any measure a radical manifesto, not perhaps Bolshevik, but in its earliest drafts too close to Marx for some of those pulling the strings. It built on the socialist aspirations contained in the 1916 Proclamation but went further, as when it declared the subordination of all private property 'to the public right and welfare', gave the commitment that 'no child shall suffer hunger or cold from lack of food, clothing and shelter', and declared that all were entitled to 'their proper education and training as citizens of a free and Gaelic Ireland'. Larkin's former deputies in the Transport Union, together with Thomas Johnson, the long-time president of the Irish TUC, wrote the document, and it reflected the leverage they had acquired by agreeing to stand back in the recent election and leave the electoral field to Sinn Féin. It was a unique moment of influence for working-class Dublin, and it soon passed.[46]

10

A CAPITAL ONCE AGAIN: 1920–1940

Tricolour time

At lunchtime on 25 May 1921 Gandon's Custom House was seized by over 100 Volunteers. They had orders to destroy the building. Within hours, all but the riverfront façade was a burnt-out shell. The rationale given at the time was simple: it was 'one of the seats of an alien tyranny', housing nine departments of government (principally the Local Government Board), and thus it was a necessary act of war undertaken by the 'Irish Army', acting under the authority of Dáil Éireann in their campaign to establish the Republic. John Dillon, leader of the now defunct Irish Parliamentary Party, watched it burn from O'Connell Bridge and noticed

> the crowds of silent people, afraid to express any opinion, and the appalling sight of the most beautiful [building] of Ireland ... deliberately destroyed by the youth of Ireland as the latest and greatest expression of idealism and patriotism.

It was a well-planned operation, involving all five Dublin battalions of the Volunteer army (by now generally referred to as the Irish Republican Army or IRA), and it was by far the most spectacular incident in the city during the two-year guerrilla war, as indeed was precisely the intention. Éamon de Valera as President of Sinn Féin believed that such an act would strengthen the leadership's hand prior to negotiating any truce with Crown forces and the Irish Executive. Seven weeks later, a truce was agreed, which bought peace and space for politics to resume. But the sack of the Custom House came at a heavy price: eight deaths, over 110 men arrested, and a landmark sacrificed.[1]

By that stage the city had been profoundly affected by two years of political violence, during which time the physical impact was much less than the psychological. Back in January 1919, after the first meeting of the Dáil, the Sinn Féin leadership had established a shadow government and a series of ministries, and politics in the broadest sense had come alive again. City Hall was the base for the shadow ministry of Local Government. But there was a gradual shift from this strategy of passive resistance and 'moral force' to one of guerrilla war and terrorist tactics. A majority of the Dublin-based Volunteer executive was against an offensive posture for many months, but when it came the violence in Dublin was sporadic, targeted and for most people invisible. Nevertheless, between 1918 and mid-1921 over 300 died in Dublin city and county from political violence, half of them civilians (14.4 per cent of the estimated national death toll). For much of this time there was a night-time curfew (of varying length), frequent disruptions of transport services and the virtual collapse of civilian policing in the face of Republican attack. These attacks had been directed at the detective wing of the DMP: eleven city policemen died in the first year of the conflict. But by mid-1920 Dublin Castle regarded the city police as politically compromised and its old intelligence-gathering capacity quite degraded. To fill the gap, large numbers of Auxiliaries (a new division of the RIC made up of young demobbed army officers and mainly English) were garrisoned in the Castle and they became the 'rapid response' force on Dublin's streets. Another new element of the RIC were the notorious 'Black and Tans' reservists; large numbers were based in the Phoenix Park, but they were used sparingly in the city. Thus, unlike the situation in 1916, Dublin became a uniquely militarised zone: in addition to the swollen and armed RIC, twelve infantry battalions ringed the city by late 1920, while rival intelligence-gathering agencies, military and police, struggled to penetrate the Republican movement. Surprisingly, until late November 1920 many officers lived away from barracks in commodious hotels and private accommodation. And civilian life did go on: the markets, even the Stock Exchange, functioned without a break. Theatre and more informal night-life continued, curfews permitting. Newspapers, despite censorship and

9. Built *c.* 1721 close to the Tenter Fields on the edge of the Liberties, the tall houses constituting Sweeney's Lane off Mill Street were ideal for family weaving enterprises. But, two centuries later, they were among the worst slum buildings in the city when photographed for the 1913 Housing Inquiry.

10. *Rubbish pickers*: one of sixty-six ink-and-wash sketches made by the young Hugh Douglas Hamilton in 1760 that together provide a unique naturalistic panorama of life on Dublin's streets and across the city's informal sector, which was then employing thousands. Here the scavenging women appear well-equipped and purposeful recyclers, and there is no hint of Hogarthian squalor or demeaning work.

11. Thomas Hickey, *Charles Lucas*, 1759. Still an 'enemy of his country' and in exile in London when drawn by Hickey, Lucas was soon to return to Dublin, a civic hero and mascot of the parliamentary 'patriots'.

Gandon : "'Pon my word, taking it all in all, that young man didn't do so badly by my Custom's House."

16. 'Pon my word, taking it all in all, that young man didn't do so badly by my Custom House': whether or not Gandon would have appreciated the aesthetic principles of twentieth-century architecture, the *Dublin Opinion* cartoonist W. H. Conn caught the generally positive contemporary reaction in 1953 to Michael Scott's Busáras building and to its location beside the reconstructed Custom House.

intimidation, continued to appear, although police action closed the *Freeman's Journal* for six weeks late in 1920, and during that time there was an IRA attack on the *Independent* premises which knocked it out for a short period as well. But there were always newspapers available; even the Dáil government's covert *Irish Bulletin,* produced mainly for the international press corps, continued to appear for sixteen months.[2]

Local government in the townships was little affected by the crisis. It was very different at City Hall, which was in the eye of the storm. First, soaring inflation and falling revenues brought about an acute financial crisis for the municipality in 1919. Then in January 1920 came the long-delayed nationwide local elections: Sinn Féin won a firm majority on the Council for the first time, and this led to a formal switch of allegiance by the Corporation to Dáil Éireann four months afterwards (such a switch happened much later in the townships). With such an act of defiance, the city's access to central government funds and credit was effectively cut off. As Sinn Féin had been declared illegal in November 1919 (together with all other nationalist organisations), the attendance of many councillors at public meetings was necessarily erratic. Pet Sinn Féin projects such as an extensive renaming of city streets were not carried through (except for Great Brunswick Street, where the choice of 'Pearse Street' seems to have been immediately accepted). The formal struggle between city and government culminated in December 1920: the military authorities took possession of City Hall and arrested several councillors in full public view. Thereupon the administrative staff and remaining council members retreated in some disarray to the Mansion House. But for a series of backroom understandings with the Bank of Ireland, the Corporation's ability to perform normal services during the revolutionary period would have collapsed.[3]

The cultural bodies close to republican politics – the Gaelic League and the Gaelic Athletics Association – were subject to constant harassment, but events at a Gaelic football game in Croke Park (between Dublin and Tipperary) on 21 November 1920 were of a different order. At breakfast-time that morning nineteen men, supposedly all army intelligence officers, were taken by surprise in city hotels or lodgings and shot at close quarters, some in front of their families. Fifteen of them died. This carnage caused official disarray and led, among other hurried responses, to a plan to detain the GAA teams and spectators after their Croke Park match in a search for arms, but those assigned to the task (Black and Tans, some Auxiliaries and regular infantrymen) were not trained for such a delicate mission. The arrival of the military almost immediately became a bloodbath after a fusillade was discharged into the 5,000-odd spectators and players, resulting in fourteen deaths. As David Leeson has shown, Croke Park was not a revenge attack as such, but rather a toxic mixture of panic and incompetence on the part of the Black and Tans, followed by a propaganda war (in Ireland and internationally) that the government comprehensively lost. Later that same night, two top Volunteers (Dick McKee, founder and commandant of the Dublin Brigade, and his deputy), who were detained for interrogation in Dublin Castle, were shot dead, allegedly while trying to escape. There were other incidents on and off the streets, and altogether thirty-six lives were lost as a result of the day's violence. 'Bloody Sunday', with all its barbaric twists, traumatised the city for weeks. A crackdown by the security forces was conducted through the following winter with an average of about eighteen police raids per day in Dublin. By the following May, 3,594 Dubliners had been interned as a result. With so many arrested, the Dublin Brigade of the IRA was under intense pressure in these months. In response, it widened its range of permitted targets.[4]

The Bloody Sunday assassination of off-duty army men revealed a central feature of the Republican campaign: the priority given to the slow accumulation of counter-intelligence about police and army activities, and then the ruthless use of that information. Here the crucial figure was Michael Collins. A west Cork man, like so many nationalist leaders of the previous generation, he combined a sharp strategic intelligence with charm and fearlessness. He had championed an aggressive policy against the weak links of Crown authority where others had had their reservations, and he devised ways of asserting a degree of centralised control over local military groups by monopolising the supply of operational intelligence and controlling its dissemination. He also sought (with less success) to act as a conduit in the supply of arms. His strongest city ally was Dick McKee. They assembled a group of full-time gunmen (the 'squad') in mid-1919, who in the early months were principally young Volunteers from Munster, and it was this group who carried out most of the attacks on DMP detectives in the first year of the war. But the aura that grew up around Collins as 'the Dublin pimpernel' masked the bluntness of his assassination tactics: the DMP detectives whom he hunted were not the threat they were made out to be and, as Jane Leonard has shown, of the fifteen executed on Bloody Sunday probably fewer than half were actually army intelligence officers. Several of the victims were entirely innocent.[5]

In the tradition of the Invincibles, Collins also supported attempts to assassinate the Lord Lieutenant, Viscount French, and at the end of 1919 he nearly succeeded. In Dublin since 1918, French had reinvigorated the viceregal office, but as an opinionated wartime general proud of his Irish roots he was dangerously out of touch and his conservative instincts only prolonged the crisis. He survived unscathed, but his close friend Frank Brooke, a Fermanagh Tory, chairman of the Dublin and South-Eastern Railway and a prominent figure in Dublin business, was less lucky. He was one of the few Unionist figures in the city to be assassinated during the war, shot as he sat in his Westland Row office.[6]

How then did the wider nationalist citizenry react to 'The Troubles' on their doorstep? There were moments of general popular arousal, as in April 1920 when seventy republican prisoners went on hunger strike in Mountjoy jail, seeking political status. Public sympathy welled up, the memory of Thomas Ashe was invoked, and huge numbers gathered outside the prison gates, apparently spontaneously, to recite the rosary. RAF planes were used to fly low over the crowds and drop warning notices. A one-day general strike was called and was so well supported that in less than a week the striking prisoners were all released. The fate of the small number of Volunteers sentenced to death also stirred intense emotion, most famously in the case of the young UCD medical student Kevin Barry, who was captured in action. He was the first to be executed since 1916, and his youth and demeanour fired public sympathy in the hours before his death and pushed most of his fellow students 'in the direction of the republican idea'. Another indicator of the state of public opinion was the prolonged transport dispute that began on the North Wall, and soon affected all the railway companies, over the handling of 'munitions' (meaning any military supplies for the army or police). Dockers began the campaign in May 1920, but railwaymen made it a far bigger affair when many of them embargoed trains carrying armed military personnel. Such actions meant suspension, but the men affected received financial support from their unions, despite the mounting strain this imposed. The sea became critical once again for the distribution of military supplies from Dublin to the provinces. However, in November the threat by government to force the railway companies into closure if they failed to provide a full service frightened the unions into a total climb-down. Some claimed that the railwaymen had been intimidated by the IRA into taking these actions, but there is no evidence that this was a factor.[7]

Two other straws in the wind, a year apart, give hints of changing public attitudes: the long-delayed municipal elections, which took place in January 1920, and the funeral of Archbishop Walsh in April 1921. Fourteen months after the fateful 1918 parliamentary election and a month before the city curfew was imposed, political violence in the city was still quite modest, yet a vote for Sinn Féin even in the local elections was now more explicitly an endorsement for militant republicanism than had been the case for those who voted in 1918. Given the ambiguous stance of many Labour and independent nationalist candidates, a direct comparison of the two elections is tantalising, but as Yeates has shown, first preference votes for Sinn Féin in the city (at 45 per cent) were only two-thirds of the party's 'plumper' vote in 1918 (and nationally the party's decline was even sharper); however, if the 'Republican Labour' vote is added to that for Sinn Féin, it suggests that more than half of the city's voters in 1920 backed republican candidates. Even in the townships Sinn Féin ended up with 36 per cent of the seats, their (admittedly lower) 1918 vote remaining firmer than in the city. Unionists still controlled Rathmines and Pembroke (very narrowly), but Sinn Féin took control in Kingstown. In that council one of their first actions was to restore the town's original name, albeit using the correct but unfamiliar Irish spelling, Dún Laoghaire. But the most eloquent evidence of Sinn Féin's ascendancy came in the spring of 1921 when old Archbishop Walsh died suddenly. With his patrician manner and careful ambiguities, he had managed to steer a narrow course since 1916 between explicit support for Sinn Féin and formal respect for lawful authority. In 1919 he endorsed the Dáil government's first efforts at fund-raising in America, but this gesture was not publicised at home where his equivocation helped to protect his popularity. But when the episcopal hearse emerged from the Pro-Cathedral there was no doubt: it was covered by a tricolour. This, it seems, was his parting wish. Yet at the same moment the Union flag was flying at half-mast in the Castle and at the Viceregal Lodge, if only as a matter of courtesy.[8]

The economic backdrop to this slow-burning revolution is often overlooked. The year 1919 saw economic recovery. Wartime price levels held up for a while and the leverage of organised labour remained strong. Despite a very noticeable growth in unemployment caused by demobilisation, sectors badly affected by the war – the drinks industries and the building trades – picked up, although international shortages of coal and other raw materials may have held back production. Nominal hourly wages in the Dublin building trades were close to treble their 1913 levels by the end of 1920, somewhat ahead of cost of living increases. But the short boom was ending in the second quarter of 1920 when the Dublin stock market began to edge back. The growing disruption to inland trade caused by the munitions dispute came precisely at the time when agricultural prices were softening, and a sharp fall in rural disposable income was everywhere evident by the spring of 1921, with agricultural prices continuing to fall for another year. Just how far economic recession fed the revolution is a moot point, but it can be no coincidence that the renewal of large-scale labour disputes in the city which aimed to hold onto wartime gains (notably the nine-month bricklayers' strike that began in October 1920) and the surge in registered unemployment paralleled the most active period of the city IRA. But Bloody Sunday also helped.[9]

Civil war

A truce in July 1921 led, after five anxious months, to the Anglo-Irish Treaty and the Treaty to the great divide within Sinn Féin in 1922 between those for whom the sovereign Republic was everything that they had fought for, and those who were prepared to accept an Irish Free State and dominion status within a partitioned Ireland. London was the venue for treaty negotiations, Dublin the stage for deciding its fate. At the end of 1921 the tortuous Treaty debates were conducted in Earlsfort Terrace in what was an entirely Sinn Féin assembly (its members having been elected unopposed in May 1921 to sit in what was officially the parliament of Southern Ireland as constituted under the Government of Ireland Act of 1920). The Treaty debates of the Second Dáil brutally exposed the tensions within the revolutionary movement, but with support in favour of the Treaty coming both from the old moral-force Sinn Féin of Arthur Griffith and those loyal to the military hero Michael Collins, the smart money was on acceptance of the grand compromise. Collins controlled the IRB, and although always playing something of a double game, he was now the towering symbol of the Treaty-as-victory. Within Dublin, the press, the Catholic Church, the battered business world and, almost certainly, the vast majority of the population shared an overwhelming longing for peace, a start to reconstruction and the restoration of Dublin as a capital once again. Yet among the city's republican intelligentsia, not least the women activists within Sinn Féin and the widows of 1916, there was a visceral distaste for the compromises inherent in the Treaty and a determination to remain utterly loyal to those who had given their lives to the cause. The strongest appetite for a return to war was among the IRA veterans in the south and the west, where the quiet months of the Truce had been used to train and re-arm. In such quarters there was an easily tapped antipathy to Dublin control and Dublin compromise, and their willingness to fight on for the Republic was helped by the decision of de Valera, despite being president of Dáil Éireann, to withdraw from the Dáil shortly after a slim majority had voted to ratify the Treaty.[10]

The formal handover of executive authority to the Provisional Government of the Irish Free State took place inside the Castle on 16 January 1922 when Viscount FitzAlan, the last viceroy and first Catholic to hold the office since 1690, did the honours with a minimum of fuss. Castle officials like Mark Sturgis even allowed themselves to feel some real sense of achievement at the outcome. The administrative handover took many months, with less than a thousand of the 21,000 public servants based in the twenty-six counties resigning. As the regime changed, the 300-odd civilian prisoners in Mountjoy jail gained no remission and were guarded by the same warders in the same uniforms – only long-serving political prisoners were released. The military pull-out of Crown forces was a particularly delicate affair: under the terms of the Treaty this could only be completed when the Free State had come into existence in December 1922 and after its constitution had been ratified by Westminster. The handover of barracks elsewhere around the country took place quite rapidly at first (and indeed, in February 1922 there was an almost constant tramp of soldiers through the city to the North Wall). But between April and December there was a very obvious massing of the remaining Crown forces in the Dublin area, especially to the west and north of the city where, by November, some 6,600 mainly infantry troops remained on duty. The final departure took place in mid-December, one of the more ironic moments coming when the Legion of Ex-Servicemen (later the British Legion) paraded en masse outside the ruins of Liberty Hall to salute the departing regiments, protected discreetly by the DMP and the Free State Army.[11]

Meanwhile the IRA sundered irrevocably on the fateful question: whether a republican army could give allegiance to a non-republican civil authority. The Sinn Féin organisation also split: a national conference in February 1922 voted to reject the Treaty. And despite fervent attempts to accommodate the many IRA commanders who felt that they were the unique custodians of the revolution without thereby diminishing the authority of a Dáil-based government, no common ground was agreed. A rump Army Convention met in Dublin on 26 March and delegates representing three-fifths of the IRA denounced the Treaty and in effect disowned the Dáil.[12]

Beggar's Bush barracks in the heart of Ballsbridge had been the first Dublin garrison to be handed over by Crown authorities. In a race against time it became headquarters for a vast makeshift fighting force, the national army of the Free State. The first recruits were drawn from IRA companies loyal to Collins, but they included large numbers of ex-servicemen as well as raw recruits. The new soldiers were first seen in public when they took over protection of the Bank of Ireland Guard Room a month later. But they would probably have been overwhelmed if the anti-Treaty IRA had united and moved against them. Instead, during April the Republicans seized a number of public buildings in the city and fortified them in an open challenge to the Provisional Government. There was a stand-off for almost two months, towards the end of which the 'pact' general election was held; Sinn Féin supporters faced a strange dilemma with pro- and anti-Treatyists standing in many of the now multi-seat constituencies. In Dublin city and county, only in the central constituency of 'Mid Dublin' was the anti-Treaty Sinn Féin vote stronger than the pro-Treaty one, but both sides were outpolled there by independent nationalists. Dublin for the most part stood by the Treaty, but the threat of imminent civil war was growing.[13]

Less than a week after the election, the British government instructed Crown forces to return to action and capture the Four Courts, a decision precipitated by the assassination of Field Marshal Sir Henry Wilson, one of Ulster's war heroes. It was thanks to the last-minute wisdom of General Nevil Macready, Commander-in-Chief in Ireland since 1920, that such an inflammatory intervention was put on hold. Instead, helped by the short-term loan of heavy artillery from the British command, the Free State Army attacked their erstwhile colleagues on 28 June. The Republicans were in a sense restaging 1916, holding out within another architectural symbol of the old regime, but they failed to evince much public sympathy in the city (despite the fact that anti-Treaty candidates had garnered about a fifth of first-preference votes in the city a week earlier). They seem to have underestimated the ruthless determination of the young government. It took two days of bombardment to force the Four Courts garrison into submission, and minutes later the heavily mined building was racked by explosions. A second Gandon landmark was partially destroyed, the Public Record Office beside it entirely so. The fighting ranged across the north inner city, destroying public buildings (notably the recently vacated Dublin headquarters of the Orange Order in Rutland Square), but once again Sackville Street bore the brunt of arson and artillery, with several department stores and institutions at the north end of the boulevard that had escaped in 1916 now being worst affected. Large-scale fighting in the city was over within ten days, but the Civil War continued in parts of Munster and the west for nearly a year. There the commercial disruption was very severe, whereas in the Dublin region the war was limited to a series of aftershocks, mainly arson attacks, which although sensational at the time did not change public opinion. The Phoenix Park races were held in July, and in August the Liffey Swim and Dublin Horse Show went ahead without incident. But the loss during the latter month of both Griffith (who died of natural causes in his Dublin bed) and of Collins (shot in west Cork) rocked the Provisional Government, but William Cosgrave, a veteran of Dublin Corporation's Finance Committee and more recently Dáil Minister of Local Government, emerged to become a remarkably effective President of the Executive Council, a position he held for a decade. The deaths in August steeled the new government into taking fierce retribution against their opponents, most notoriously when they authorised the summary execution of four leading Republican detainees held in Mountjoy jail (following the assassination of a Dáil member, Seán Hales, on Ormond Quay). Even state prisoners in 1798 had enjoyed a greater degree of due process than that. So when it came, it was a fratricidal, not an exhilarating, peace.[14]

But there were the literary legacies. In 1925 the Abbey Theatre, immersed in financial trouble, had against the odds secured government funding and official status as the National Theatre. Later that year it mounted a play that was intended to subvert the passions of civil war: *Juno and the Paycock* was the second in Seán O'Casey's Dublin trilogy, which, with its local authenticity and pungent Dublin humour, was an immediate success. O'Casey was a product of dockland working-class Protestantism and he had been a young activist in Connolly's Citizen Army in 1913, a radical socialist but not a revolutionary nationalist. Then in 1926 came

The plough and the stars, his even more bitter verdict on the events of 1916, staged in the Abbey despite official misgivings. The character of Rosie Redmond, the anti-heroic prostitute, was too much for some and ignited another bout of theatre disturbances (on the fourth night), but more broadly the uproar suggested that 'the gap between revolutionary heroics and the reality of violence ... [was] one which the stiffening orthodoxies of post-independence Dublin could not negotiate'. *Juno* was transformed into an early 'talkie' by Alfred Hitchcock in 1930, thereby giving O'Casey's resolutely unheroic reading of the Irish revolution an international audience. But his unromantic reading of 1916 was entirely lost when in 1936 John Ford and his Hollywood backers turned the *The plough and the stars* into an unproblematic affirmation of the Easter Rising.[15]

Rebuilding

The cost of reinstating property damaged prior to the Truce was shared by the two governments, but Cosgrave's fledgling government had to carry the whole financial costs of the Civil War and the huge levels of damage to property that occurred largely outside the capital. This meant that most of the brave ideas for state-sponsored national economic regeneration were put on the shelf for another day. The overriding imperative was securing the peace and balancing the books, and the regeneration of Dublin became a lesser priority. But as the smoke cleared, how did the Dublin business community react to this new order? The upper layers of business – the boardrooms of the banks, the stockbroking firms, the chartered accountants, the big exporting firms, the major building contractors – were still disproportionately Protestant, and the Chamber of Commerce more or less reflected this, even though it was now quite mixed in its religious make-up. During 1920, the Chamber had repeatedly denounced the prevailing 'state of terror', but had made strenuous efforts to modify the Government of Ireland bill, calling for a constitutional settlement far more radical than southern Unionists would recently have conceded: 'complete self-government ... subject only to the restrictions ... that Ireland should remain within the empire', and that Ulster be not coerced. In purely business terms, the prospect of partition was a very negative one, implying that the residual financial and legal services that Dublin still provided northern clients (despite the commercial ascendancy of Belfast) would be lost and the many north/south business partnerships might be sundered. In advocating a 'dominions' solution the Chamber was echoing the established editorial line of the *Irish Independent* and the political views of the late William Martin Murphy; then, during the Treaty negotiations, the Chamber lobbied successfully *against* British moves that would have made the continuation of free trade between the two jurisdictions binding.

So when the political settlement finally emerged in December 1921, it was ardently supported by liberal business interests, Protestant and Catholic, and accepted with some trepidation by more conservative Protestants, once it became evident that private property rights were unaffected, that there would be no restrictions on the movement of capital, and that the Free State would remain within the sterling area (the Irish bank rate was nevertheless pegged at a steady one cent above London to discourage capital outflows). The elder statesman of city Unionism, Andrew Jameson, managing director of the Bow Street distillery and a former Governor of the Bank of Ireland, had been one of those attempting to protect southern Unionism at the time of the Treaty, but the only constitutional concession that his group secured was the inclusion of an upper house in the Free State legislature, a senate that was supposed to provide the 'minority' with constitutional protection. It certainly gave its more articulate members, notably W. B. Yeats, a public platform, but Jameson's political leverage in the post-Treaty years was largely informal and covert, influencing the economic but not the social policies of the new administration. Some old businesses quietly folded like Hutton and Sons of Summerhill, coachmakers and Irish agents for Daimler and other expensive marques. Their market, it seems, had been eclipsed.[16]

Dublin-based banks remained highly profitable throughout the crisis, their stock-market valuations rising from the time of the Truce almost without interruption until the later 1920s. They had immediate back-door access to their new political masters, in particular the Bank of Ireland with the Irish Department of Finance. But in an untypically assertive move, the Chamber went political in 1923 and endorsed a panel of business candidates to run for the Dáil. Those chosen were for the most part Protestant, and two were successful, one of them John Good, the city's principal manufacturer of bricks, head of a large building firm that had constructed the aerodrome at Collinstown and chairman of Pembroke Council for many years. He became a Teachta Dála (TD), i.e. a parliamentary representative, for the eight-seater Co. Dublin constituency, and he held his seat through four subsequent general elections. As he said in 1933, 'he stood for the Treaty, both in the letter and the spirit'. The principal spat between old city business and the first Free State government came in 1924 over the future of the railway companies. Weighed down by huge reconstruction costs and wartime wage levels, the companies were unable to extract the anticipated levels of compensation from the state to get their balance sheets back in order. The solution, a state-imposed amalgamation of the principal railway companies, was bitterly opposed by all the vested interests, but to no avail. The government created the Great Southern Railways (with only the cross-border Great Northern Railway (Ireland) (GNRI) remaining independent), and in so doing Cosgrave ridiculed his business critics as 'peculiar specimens ... in antique furniture', 'so-called businessmen' who were the principal source of disorder in the state 'during these last few years'.[17]

This strange outburst from a socially conservative premier against the city's business lobby was soon forgotten. Its tone reflected the extreme political and financial pressures felt by the new Cumann na nGaedheal administration and Cosgrave's belief that the upsurge in labour disputes and unemployment over the previous two years had come about because of the self-serving behaviour of employers. In fact, what had happened was the delayed arrival in Dublin of the post-war industrial struggle already seen across Britain, in which organised labour attempted to protect wartime gains in money wages and working hours into an era of recession and falling prices. But the highly disturbed political climate in Ireland between 1920 and 1922 had weakened the resolve of many employers to push for local wage reductions until times were quieter and a more effective government was there to back them up. The Tramway Company led the way with wage reductions early in 1922. And 1923 seems to have been the year when more of the wartime gains were generally whittled back, despite a series of lengthy strikes. Nevertheless, real income and working conditions for those in employment, not least in the building industry, remained significantly higher in 1924 than in 1914, and probably higher than in most Scottish and English cities. A belief that the high cost of skilled labour was holding back Dublin's economic recovery became commonplace.[18]

The necessity for the total reform of city government became another prominent issue, reflecting the escalating burden of local taxation. On this there was an unlikely alliance between the Chamber of Commerce and the Free State government: using emergency powers created in 1923, the

Minister of Local Government ordered a public inquiry in March 1924 into the recent conduct of the Corporation and its financial management. The ensuing report was never published; instead, two months later the Minister suspended the Corporation and vested its powers in three commissioners. There were protests in the Dáil and the press at this action – in the words of the outgoing Lord Mayor, 'a gross insult to the citizens of Dublin' – which would indeed have been unimaginable under the old regime. The official reason given was that the Corporation had not been cooperating in government initiatives (refusing to consider lowering the wages of its general staff, tolerating nepotistic or corrupt practices and failing to cooperate in the planned merger of the DMP with the new national police force, An Garda Síochána, among other things). Cosgrave was acutely aware of the issues and supported the suppression of eighteen other local authorities at this time. But what probably sealed Dublin Corporation's fate were signs that it had become a platform for republican Sinn Féin, during and after the Civil War, at a time when the government was determined to use any legitimate excuse to come down hard on its opponents (it had survived a Free State army mutiny only weeks before). City Hall, for so long the shadow national parliament, was now silenced by a national government.[19]

The three commissioners ran the city for six years; the leading figure was Seamus Murphy who had worked directly under Cosgrave in various capacities since 1919. He saw the creative possibilities of the Commission: direct rule provided a unique opportunity for the restructuring of local government without short-term local political considerations dominating the debate. Rates were substantially reduced over the six years, water supply to the north side greatly improved, the number of Corporation tenants more than doubled and social services, specifically child welfare services, greatly expanded. Elaborate 'civic weeks' were organised in 1927 and 1929 involving military tattoos, historical pageants and firework displays, and there was a strikingly non-partisan effort to stimulate public interest in the city's culture and commerce. Strategic planning, forgotten since 1916, came back into vogue, and there was a new determination to complete the reconstruction of the city centre.[20]

But uppermost was the old question of the city boundaries. The Corporation had tried to seize the initiative in 1923 by drafting a private bill to bring the whole metropolitan region from Howth to Bray within its grasp. The Department of Local Government responded, its inspector recommending to government a more modest expansion, merely taking in Rathmines and Pembroke councils. This report led the Cabinet to widen the debate and set up a Greater Dublin Commission of Inquiry in July 1924, its membership a strange assortment of business, labour and academic figures. Its recommendations two years later were that Dún Laoghaire and parts adjacent should be absorbed into Greater Dublin; that budget policy and executive power be entrusted to a city manager answerable to the Minister for Local Government; that existing civic titles and offices be abolished, and that councillors' powers be severely circumscribed (but allowing them a veto on the budget). As Daly has observed, the report 'combined a disregard for the existing institutions with a distrust of local democracy' and it sank almost without trace in the Department, which was happy to continue direct rule by ministerial commission.

Then, at the end of 1929, the Local Government (Dublin) Act appeared: Rathmines and Pembroke after forty years of resistance were finally going to be absorbed, but not Dún Laoghaire; there would be special representation for business on a shrunken city council of twenty-five, and individual city managers for Dublin and Dún Laoghaire (Town Clerk Gerald Sherlock was named as the first post-holder for the city). But there was no element of strategic urban planning in the legislation: that, deputies were told, would follow. Under pressure, the government increased representation on the proposed city council to thirty-five and gave councillors somewhat greater discretionary power over the manager. The total area of the city, with green-field additions both to the north and the south-west, was doubled by the act. But the administrative changes were hardly revolutionary: Sherlock interpreted his new powers quite conservatively, handing back decision-making where possible to the Council and its committees, and in so doing he stood in contrast to his assertive opposite number in Cork where similar legislation had actually preceded the Dublin act. But the controversial business franchise, one of the few ideas to come out of the 1926 Commission, was abolished by the next government in 1935.[21]

In one of its final acts before dissolution in 1924, the old Corporation had officially renamed Sackville Street as O'Connell Street (*The Irish Times* among others refused to adopt this change for many years). The street itself had slowly come back to life from the revolutionary ashes: Clery's and Eason's had already been handsomely rebuilt before 1922, but much of the northern half was still a wasteland as business owners waited for building costs to fall (which they did not). Commercial rebuilding got going there in the mid-1920s despite ongoing haggling over compensation, building specifications, and whether or not new secondary streets were to be created. In the event, the only major improvement was a new street (Cathal Brugha Street) connecting up with Gloucester Street (now Seán MacDermott Street), which involved relocating the site of St Thomas's church (which had been destroyed in 1922). There was no attempt to reproduce eighteenth-century façades or nineteenth-century insertions in O'Connell Street, and stone rather than brick predominated in the new buildings. But Horace O'Rourke, City Architect from 1922 to 1944, used the innovative building legislation passed eight months after the Easter Rising to enforce fairly uniform cornice heights, fenestration lines and building materials. But with no state support, the new buildings were in general a sober and unexciting assemblage, the only architectural landmarks being the Gresham Hotel and the striking Venetian-style Savoy Cinema costing 'almost £200,000' by the time it opened in 1929. However, the GPO reappeared phoenix-like in the same year, its façade fully restored.[22]

There was a strange backdrop to the redevelopment of O'Connell Street: three visionary reports appeared, arguing for a drastic reorganisation of traffic and public buildings in the city, two of them making the case for a central traffic hub much further to the west. The genesis of these publications was the pre-war flurry of interest in town planning and the involvement of the leading British figures in the field, Patrick Geddes and Raymond Unwin, in trying to persuade the Corporation to take a unified approach to public housing development. They had made a strong case for abandoning further construction of inner-city working-class housing and instead creating low-density suburban communities. One of their recommendations had been that plans for municipal housing at Ormond Market should be halted, and that instead it be made the focal point for a set of north–south boulevards, a critical element of which would be a new Catholic cathedral. Out of their tantalising report came the idea for an international competition in 1914 to produce a city development plan. War and revolution intervened, but the winning submission (by the Liverpool-based Patrick Abercrombie) was eventually published in 1922: *Dublin of the future: The new town plan*, sponsored by the Civic Institute of Ireland, a local advocacy group with strong professional membership but no official standing, and it was dedicated somewhat wistfully to the long-departed Lord Lieutenant, the earl of Aberdeen, and Lady Aberdeen. Abercrombie characterised the Dublin of 1914 as at a similar stage to Paris on the eve of Haussmann's transformations. He imagined intervention on a similar scale and for a similar purpose (albeit with the provision of 'hygienic housing', a dimension missing in Haussmann and now a priority). Abercrombie's plan set out an extraordinary vision for an alternative Dublin and it received very favourable international notices, after publication.

In it he elaborated on the Geddes/Unwin idea of integrating the movement of all traffic at a central node far upstream from O'Connell Bridge. He suggested the creation of two piazzas facing one another across the river, one east of the Four Courts, the other below Christ Church, onto which no fewer than fourteen streets would converge, many of them newly cut. Under the northern piazza a central railway station would be built, the crossing point for two tunnels carrying all mainline trains. Pill Lane, of ancient notoriety, would become the centre of the city. Among the principal roads proposed was one continuing Abbey Street westwards to the northern piazza and from there an entirely new tree-lined 'Phoenix Park Mall' which would pass the Royal Barracks (transformed into an art gallery) on its way to the park entrance, the Wellington Monument closing the western vista. One of the more imaginative secondary routes would have exploited the palatial width of old Dominick Street as it ran from Broadstone station down to the Ha'penny Bridge before transecting Dame Street and terminating at a secondary hub west of St Stephen's Green. The plan advocated a wholesale clearance of the tenements and rehousing of the estimated 64,000 inhabitants to new suburbs integrated within the city plan: Crumlin to the south-west, Cabra to the north-west, and Drumcondra in the north, all linked to the central piazzas by dedicated avenues and connecting trams. Abercrombie suggested large-scale reclamation east of Irishtown and Clontarf on which public parks, private housing and a 'power citadel' for electricity generation would be built. The Catholic cathedral was now to be located on the old Linen Hall site, closing the vista up Capel Street. Even though it would have taken a military dictatorship and Guinness millions to realise this plan, its sheer audacity registered in the minds of architects and city officials for a generation, and it brought back into public discourse the legacy of the Wide Streets Commissioners. But the scale of these proposals was far beyond what John Beresford had ever imagined.[23]

At almost the same time, the Greater Dublin Reconstruction Movement published an alternative master plan, making the case for a 'new and spacious boulevard' running from Kilmainham Hospital, recast as site of the National Parliament, eastwards through the old city to College Green and ending up at a new town hall on the site of the GPO. That at least chimed with the WSC street plan, and it attracted press support. But in the *Dublin Civic Survey* (1925), also published by the Civic Institute, Abercrombie's radical plan was again to the fore. Here the lead author was O'Rourke, the City Architect, and much of it was a collation of new data on traffic, health, education, housing, employment and the physical state of the city. The *Survey* operated on the premise that Dublin as a capital reborn merited heavy investment by the new state and that its core should be thoroughly replanned to reflect a break with the past and to take account of the rise of motor traffic, not least of motor buses. New locations were suggested for the National Parliament (the Royal Hospital), a central railway station (Temple Bar), a municipal gallery (the rebuilt Four Courts), with the courts themselves moving to Dublin Castle. A strong case was made for a proliferation of parks within the city and gardens in the suburbs. But to achieve all this, 'drastic statutory powers' would be required. 'Demolition, demolition and more demolition is the only remedy for a building or a city falling into decay,' announced the City Architect. The ghost of Haussmann lingered on.

But there was no Louis Napoleon in the wings, no champion for such a grandiose metropolitan project, either within the Cumann na nGaedheal government or its successor, even though such a great public-works programme in Dublin would have dramatically addressed the city's pervasive unemployment. Insofar as Cosgrave's government had any views on the physical development of Dublin, it was not to reposition the city centre westwards but to concentrate the organs of government and Parliament in one area as cheaply as possible: the Castle was therefore left to the judges (until the Four Courts were rebuilt), together with the Revenue Commissioners and the police, and part of the new College of Science complex in salubrious Merrion Street was adapted to house the principal ministries of government. Cosgrave resisted plans to make the Chief Secretary's Lodge in the Park his official residence (it became home instead for American ambassadors to Ireland), although the first two Governor Generals were housed in the quiet vastness of the Viceregal Lodge nearby. As for a Parliament house, the RDS lecture theatre in Leinster House had been used by the third Dáil since September 1922, and the room was just about large enough. Other possibilities (College Green, Dublin Castle and particularly Kilmainham) all had enthusiastic advocates, but each was ruled out, principally on cost grounds, and the decision in 1924 to remain in Leinster House was taken almost by default. The Royal Dublin Society was well compensated, and thereafter it concentrated all its activities on the showground site in Ballsbridge. The first new building designed for a state ministry was not commissioned until 1939 (for the Department of Industry and Commerce) and it too was located in Kildare Street, now fully the Irish Whitehall. The fond hopes of Abercrombie and the Civic Institute that the centre of the city might be drawn back westwards and the site of the medieval town re-established as the urban core were stillborn. Yet their ideas were respected and Abercrombie remained involved at a distance as benign godfather of Dublin planning until the 1940s.[24]

Some public figures in the new state wanted to turn their back on Dublin altogether: 'really a foreign town', argued one government supporter from Mayo, 'the seat of the government ... should be far removed from the atmosphere of Dublin ... and from its foreign mode and method of thought'. But the absence of any 'vanity' state spending on Dublin projects prevented anti-metropolitan sentiment gaining ground. However, there was one local call on government that could not be disregarded: the Dublin 'housing question'. In the early months of the Free State, Cosgrave said on the record that 'no populace [thus] housed as so many of the people of Dublin are can be good citizens, or loyal and devoted subjects of the state, no matter what the state may be', and his instincts were to rebuild in the inner city. That did not happen. But helped by somewhat more ample government grants and loans, impressive public investment in Dublin housing during the 1920s did occur – there were 5,043 dwellings built between 1923 and 1931. However, nearly all the action was on the edge of the city and most of the new housing was designed, not for the most needy, but for the skilled working classes. Marino (once the lower reaches of the Charlemont demesne) had been identified as a prospective 'garden suburb' before 1914, and the realisation of this project overlooking Dublin Bay was hailed as one of the real achievements of the new order. The Corporation laid out a landscaped master plan for Marino and the adjoining Croydon Park, and four building firms (one of them German) constructed nearly 1,300 houses (with three to five rooms) by 1928. By this time the Corporation was laying out a grand boulevard on its northern rim to connect Clontarf, Drumcondra and Glasnevin, thereby creating a new north-east boundary for the city – 'Griffith Avenue' – and within less than a decade an even more northerly connector road, Collins Avenue, was begun. Indeed, 72 per cent of the 4,248 suburban houses developed by the Corporation between 1923 and 1931 were located north of the Liffey. It was entirely logical that City Hall's search for virgin land and optimum development sites should have focused on the outer north side because it had inherited a considerable land-bank there, and in addition green-field land prices were probably much lower there than anywhere on the south side.[25]

As Ruth McManus has documented, these houses were intended not for long-term renting but for 'tenant purchase', to be financed through a variety of schemes, some with very long repayment schedules. As in other Irish cities, ownership of the family home was emerging as an achievable aspiration, first in middle-class Dublin before the war, now more broadly in the 1920s. The statutory retention of rent control (introduced nationally to control wartime inflation in 1915) greatly reduced the attractions of speculative ownership of house property and encouraged private-sector builders in the 1920s and 1930s to target prospective owner-occupiers rather than *rentier* investors. Thanks to the availability of state subsidies for small-home purchasers and of rates remission on new houses, the financial barriers to private ownership were now becoming much lower, helped also by the emergence of house-building cooperatives (public utility societies) at this time.[26]

The spread of owner occupancy among the skilled working class was welcomed by church and state. But the congestion in the inner city was actually worsening. Imaginative plans to recycle some of the recently abandoned army barracks had modest results, Richmond/Keogh Barracks being the only instance of such a conversion into public housing (with the officers' mess reinvented as a children's milk depot). But there was little enthusiasm in the 1920s to turn any abandoned site within the city into tenement blocks. The onset of the Great Depression, mild as it initially was in Dublin, coincided with a switch in public priorities and a partial return to inner-city building. This policy change was prompted by the evident failure of garden suburbs to relieve the poverty of the inner city and by a fear that the Corporation was swamping private and cooperative developers in areas they were prepared to build. When new evidence was produced showing that the number of houses unfit for human habitation had actually risen by 15 per cent since 1914, there was a public outcry.

The shift in emphasis was well underway before Cosgrave's government was defeated at the polls in 1932, although de Valera's incoming Fianna Fáil administration has often been credited with the renewed drive to solve the housing crisis. The 1931 Housing Act (modelled on similar British legislation of 1930) doubled the grants available where families were being rehoused out of the slums and facilitated much speedier acquisition and clearance of tenement property. The new government sponsored stronger incentives, with the state undertaking to carry two-thirds of the interest charges on loans raised for slum clearance. In the following seven years the Corporation commissioned over 1,600 inner-city apartments, some with strikingly modernist exteriors but nearly all with fewer and smaller rooms than the suburban standard, and mass concrete became the principal building material. But small-house building by the Corporation continued in the suburbs where over 5,000 houses were added between 1932 and 1939, many of them on the north side.

By far the largest project, however, was in the south-west, on the open ground of Crumlin, a district favoured twenty years earlier by Abercrombie, lying over the canal, beyond the trams, airy and well watered. Much of the land was acquired by compulsory purchase order, and in five years over 3,200 two-storey houses were built to rehouse families from the inner city, many of the units being semi-detached or terraced, but most with only three rooms and a small garden. It was certainly the largest building project of the 1930s, and such was its scale that government officials in the Department of Local Government were directly involved – and they were later blamed for abandoning the high standards of the 1920s and bringing about a 'ruthless reduction of the specifications'. Demand for Crumlin houses (as for Cabra houses in the north-west) was nevertheless huge, and the initial rush of applications far exceeded what was on offer. Successful applicants were generally married couples with young families deemed able to afford the (subsidised) rent but not secure enough to commit to a purchase agreement. The houses themselves lacked the finish or diversity of the 1920s estates, and from the start there was a demographic uniformity about Crumlin (a pattern replicated in the other mass housing schemes over the next generation) that placed huge demands on schooling and on the very limited recreational facilities. A Garda station was constructed ahead of the first secondary schools, 'to control', it was claimed in 1945, 'the unruly crowds of workless adolescents'. For the transplanted children Crumlin may have given a greater sense of freedom, but for adults the weakening of communal and family networks, the end of informal visits to neighbours, and the loss of ready access to street markets, familiar shops and small pubs came at a price, and the high bus fares back to the city was a constant complaint, even though the distance from the city centre was less than two miles.[27]

Despite government rhetoric, state support for housing was not exclusively directed at slum clearance, and subsidies for private housing (and rural labourers' cottages) soaked up funds that could have supported a more muscular urban agenda. In the period of maximum house-building between 1932 and 1939, nearly 48 per cent of new housing units in the metropolitan area were built by private or cooperative developers, which tells its own story. The contrast between predominantly middle-class suburbs, with a growing preponderance of home-owners, and working-class suburbs where most households were now local authority tenants, was becoming starker. It is true that on the north side there were many gradations from the pockets of low-density garden suburbs in Glasnevin and Clontarf (which witnessed substantial private building in the inter-war years) to the new three-roomed Corporation houses in Cabra, and that there was often quite a heterogeneous social mix on some of the new estates, but on the south side local differences were sharper: the new town of Crumlin stood in stark contrast to the brick terraces of Harold's Cross, Terenure and Rathgar not far to the east. On the southern skirts of the city, on the edges of the Pembroke estate, house-building of an entirely different calibre was underway: the Mount Merrion 'garden estate', two houses to the acre, began in the mid-1920s and continued slowly, the chief builder-developer being John Kenny who had previously built the first phase of Marino on the far side of the city for the Corporation.[28]

Despite the scale of new public building, the ambitious targets of 1932 were not met. Labour shortages and a six-month strike in 1937 (which ended in union victory) were blamed, but the Corporation's exhausted credit was also a factor. Its borrowings in 1934 had stood at a little over £6 million, by 1939 they were just under £11 million (four-fifths of which related to housing programmes), and at that point, as Mary Daly has revealed, it was encountering serious difficulties with the banks and in floating further loans on the local capital market. Meanwhile the inner-city tenements festered. The Corporation launched yet another public inquiry in 1939, perhaps to increase the political pressure on government for greater direct financial support for slum clearance. The inquiry

38. Crumlin from the air, 1939. *Despite delays in the provision of primary schools and shops and the problems with water supply and public transport, the new south-western township was already developing a character of its own. And its proximity to the inner city, from where many of the Corporation tenants had come, softened the impact of the large-scale transplantation.*

reviewed the abundant evidence from 1913 and examined the recent building boom. Why had such energetic public building failed to diminish the problem? Some blamed the misallocation of scarce public funds towards grant-aiding private housing, others the recurring choice of creditworthy tenants over the most needy. City Hall's refusal to consider income-related differential rents (which worked well in Cork city) was certainly one bad decision for which it was responsible.[29]

Were changes in the city's demography also to blame? The slums may often have seemed like a stagnant pond, impossible to drain, but there was always a very considerable turnover of population. In some cases it was a final retreat for those unable (whether because of illness, death or unemployment) to make a go of it in the newer housing estates, in others their first step to better things, like the rookeries of old. There was indeed a remarkable and unexpected rise in the population of the city between

1926 and 1936. The population of greater Dublin rose from 505,654 to 586,925 – an increase of some 1.5 per cent p.a., which was a growth rate probably not seen since the early eighteenth century. Was this brought about by immigration from a depressed countryside and the downturn of agricultural employment in the 1930s, or was it because of the new curbs on transatlantic migration? Both these factors played a part, but Stanley Lyon estimated in 1943 that nearly 60 per cent of the population rise could be accounted for by natural increase within the Dublin registration district, and that making up much the largest segment of the 1930s migrants were young women in the sixteen to twenty-four age cohort. This implies that the spurt after 1932 in clerical and industrial jobs for young women may have been a major factor, but it is unlikely that such migrants settled in the slums. What the demographic data does suggest is a strong correlation between husband's occupation and the reported number of pregnancies of married women; in Lyon's survey in 1943 of Dublin maternity hospitals, around 50 per cent of births were to women whose husbands were semi-skilled or unskilled, but around 65 per cent of the births by women in their fourth or higher pregnancy were drawn from these social groups. If such patterns of high marital fertility continued into the post-war era of falling infant mortality rates, then indeed it offered the prospect of a teeming children's world in the working-class neighbourhoods. And so it turned out to be.[30]

Lemass and Dublin

The year 1932 was a memorable one in two respects. In June, the 1,500th anniversary of St Patrick's arrival in Ireland was celebrated with the visit of a papal legate and the holding of a Eucharistic Congress, a week-long event which put the international exhibitions of former times quite in the shade. It was choreographed by the church authorities, but city and state gave enthusiastic support, and the great set-pieces, the theatrical arrival of the legate to the city, the High Mass in the Phoenix Park, the closing ceremonies at O'Connell Bridge, attracted unprecedented numbers of international visitors and a vast Irish pilgrimage to the city in 127 special trains. The stage management of the event was innovative (there were 400 loudspeakers distributed across the city to broadcast the ceremonial events) and there was a general sense of exhilaration, of a city at last comfortable with itself. Some Protestant businesses were publicly supportive of the event, but most of non-Catholic Dublin seems have been quietly bemused.[31]

What added piquancy to the event was the very recent change of government and the coming to power of a coalition led by Fianna Fáil, the party formed by de Valera in 1926 when he broke with anti-Treaty Sinn Féin on the question of whether to enter the Free State Dáil and take an oath of allegiance offensive to republicans. Electoral support for Cosgrave's government had been falling in the city; it was hit by ministerial resignations, was slow to read growing social discontent and it lacked grassroots organisation. In contrast, Fianna Fáil built up an electoral organisation, which was backed (from late 1931) by an excellent daily newspaper, the *Irish Press*. The party's impact in the capital was at first less than in the south and west, and it picked up only five seats in the revived municipal elections in 1930, even though the rump Sinn Féin party had by then completely withdrawn from electoral contests. The principal organisers of Fianna Fáil nationally were both Dubliners: Gerald Boland and Seán Lemass. Boland came from a family with impeccable Fenian, Invincible and GAA credentials, was part of the republican garrison in Jacob's factory in 1916 and lost his more famous brother Harry in the Civil War; he won a rural seat (Roscommon) in 1923 and held it until 1961. Lemass's paternal grandfather had been a Parnellite city councillor, his father a prosperous hatter based at the south end of Capel Street, and the family also had strong Fenian and Parnellite associations. As a teenager he had been in the GPO in 1916 with his elder brother Noel, and was in the Four Courts when it was attacked by Free State forces. But the unexplained discovery of Noel's body in the Dublin mountains some months after the end of the Civil War (presumed to be an act of political revenge) propelled the young Lemass into the public eye and his tactical sharpness and organisational energy first became evident in 1924 when (at the second attempt) he headed the poll in a Dáil by-election for Dublin South City. That was in the name of 'abstentionist' Sinn Féin, but in 1927 he held the seat for Fianna Fáil and continued to represent an inner Dublin constituency for another thirty-nine years. Critical to his success and to the wider ascendancy of Fianna Fáil in Dublin was the winning and holding of broad working-class support. The official Labour party, which had maintained an awkward neutrality between the big parties in the 1920s, returned only a handful of TDs in 1932 and chose to back a minority Fianna Fáil administration – given the latter's commitment to industrial protection, unemployment relief, enhanced social welfare and a vigorous house-building programme.[32]

Thus began Fianna Fáil's remarkably long electoral dominance in the city – less evident in the middle-class suburbs – which helped keep the party in power for the next sixteen years, and indeed as the dominant political force in the country until the twenty-first century. From a Dublin perspective, one can see Fianna Fáil's victory in 1932 as the moment of triumph for that old craft and petit bourgeois Fenianism, pervasive but heretofore disempowered, over the city's dominant social groups. Its victory in Dublin may have involved a lot of rough talk about freemasons as the puppet-masters of Cosgrave's government, and also an element of ruthless electoral malpractice (in the form of well-organised impersonation), but that does not detract from the party's achievement in reinventing popular republicanism. For Lemass, the local face of the new party, the aim was very specifically the conquest of unemployment and industrial development, leaving it to others to worry about the small matter of cultural revival. Like many in the party, Lemass had made strongly anti-clerical noises in the past, but de Valera ensured that the new government for all its radical republican trappings would not take on the Catholic Church. Thus the scrupulously correct government welcome for the Eucharistic churchmen, which helped make the Congress a short moment of national healing.[33]

The local impact of Fianna Fáil's radicalism was mixed. The pace of housing construction certainly accelerated after 1932, but this was not peculiar to Dublin. The government's close attention to labour relations culminated in the introduction of union-friendly employment legislation in 1936, and urban wages seem to have held up in real terms throughout the decade, both for skilled and unskilled grades, especially in the building trades. This, however, did not prevent a disastrous six-month builders' strike in 1937, which was only ended by Lemass's intervention but led to little benefit for the strikers; other sectors, even the poorly organised charwomen and housemaids working in the banks and the department stores, reacted to the rising cost of living and pressed for a wage increase that year.[34]

The decision by the new government to introduce full-blooded protecting tariffs in 1932 caused alarm in the city, given its still dominant position as the country's commercial hub, yet it is hard to determine just how serious the disruption to wholesale business actually was. With the prospect of tit-for-tat tariffs from Britain, there were suspicions that the big export-dependent firms would scale back their Irish operations, and in the case of Guinness rumours circulated about a total withdrawal of the firm from Ireland. These rumours had currency since the company's acquisition of a large site in Manchester back in 1913, a move prompted in part by the political uncertainties surrounding Home Rule, but there had been no follow-up. But Guinness sales, while still vast, were slipping throughout the 1920s and market share was being lost in the critical English market. That concern was compounded in 1932 by a British threat, not directly prompted by Irish protectionism, that UK import duties might be imposed on the Dublin-brewed product if the firm did not move some of its production across the channel. This had the desired effect and prompted the Guinness board in the greatest of secrecy to search out a site in London for a stand-alone brewery to service the south of England. In 1934, only days before the plan became public knowledge, Lemass was informed, but he could then do very little about it. Brewing began at Park Royal in north-west London in 1936. However, Dublin remained the principal brewery. The export trade held up, and Guinness's cosseted workforce (still close to 2,400 in the early 1930s) were not adversely affected, although there was almost no fresh recruitment. And it is possible that the unspoken threat of further disinvestment from Ireland may actually have helped maintain good relations between the Fianna Fáil government and the city's largest industry. In the case of Jacob's, they had actually opened an English factory in 1913 (at Aintree), with political uncertainty in Ireland at least a subsidiary factor, and the firm decided to expand capacity there early in 1932. But production in Bishop Street remained strong through the 1930s and employment remained at around 2,500. Indeed, the high Irish tariffs on confectionery encouraged the biscuit giant to diversify in that direction. It had to contend with Quaker competition from Fry-Cadburys, which set up an Irish subsidiary company in 1933 and opened a large chocolate factory in the North Strand, and from Urney Chocolates, which started production in Tallaght.[35]

The selective introduction of tariffs by the first Free State government had already had an impact on the city, generating new light industry. Import duties on tobacco in 1923 had prompted the Imperial Tobacco Company to begin manufacturing cigarettes for the Free State market, first with a small factory in the Liberties in 1923, then with their Player's division opening a large plant in Glasnevin *c.*1925 and the Wills division establishing an art deco presence on the South Circular Road ten years

*39. Jacob's biscuit factory remained one of the largest sources of employment
in the inter-war period, despite having been in the eye of the storm during
both the 1913 Lockout and the Easter Rising. Its vast payroll of young
female employees was drawn from the Liberties and the inner south-western
suburbs, and they enjoyed the company's advanced social and medical services
and a factory swimming pool. But employment ceased on marriage.*

later. Meanwhile, Gallaher's of Belfast 'tariff-jumped' in 1931, building the
landmark 'Virginia House' on East Wall Road. In the case of whiskey,
it was the reverse story: duties on the Irish product entering the British
market (and prohibition in the United States) devastated the city's old
distilleries: the Scottish-owned Phoenix Park distillery closed in 1921, and
the Dublin Distillers Company, a partnership created in 1890, linking
two distilleries in the old city with the Jones Road firm in Drumcondra,
went out of business in 1926, leaving behind only two producers of Dublin
whiskey – Powers of John's Lane and John Jameson's off Smithfield – both
with falling order books.[36]

The onset of the Great Depression and the general race to protectionism opened up the prospect of far greater tariff manipulation. Under

Lemass's direction, the Department of Industry and Commerce was transformed into an industrial development agency with a panoply of novel legal and executive weapons at its disposal, the aim being the rapid creation of a self-sufficient economy and the exclusion of foreign capital from involvement in that process. It is no surprise that over the next few years manufacturing employment within the state jumped for the first time in a century. But the drive to attract industrial investment was rushed and often poorly executed; this was perhaps inevitable given the backdrop of a disastrous trade war between Dublin and London (over the issue of land annuities), which hit rural incomes severely and was not finally resolved until 1938. One of the principal elements of the new policy was the decentralisation of industrial development, but that was a failure: roughly two-thirds of the net increase in Free State manufacturing employment between 1926 and 1936 occurred in Dublin city and county (some 13,000 additional jobs), and throughout the 1930s and 1940s more than half of the Free State's industrial output was generated within Dublin city and county (albeit a somewhat declining share). Thus Lemassian industrialisation in its pre-war form favoured the capital, not the rural heartlands of Fianna Fáil support (and Cabinet colleagues, notably Gerry Boland, were particularly critical of this).

Much of the new industry was small, the skills involved fairly quickly learnt. In a survey carried out in 1948 of the 516 firms in the 'protected industries' across Dublin city and county, there was an average of only thirty-five employees per firm (very close to the national pattern) and headline-grabbing developments like the new Irish Glass Bottle factory at Charlotte Quay (completed in 1936 and employing around 400) were exceptional. More than a third of the new industrial jobs were in the 'ready-made' clothing trade: in Dublin city and county, both the number of firms and total employment more than doubled between 1931 and 1936. This was overwhelmingly female work, and at least a quarter of these operatives in 1936 were under eighteen. By contrast, in the metal trades, new employment was principally created for men and, helped by the revival of construction, employment numbers more than doubled. Some of the new entrepreneurs were immigrants, like Hyman Jacobovitch, and despite higher site costs in the capital it was accepted that incomers would have a natural preference for a Dublin location with its larger pool of skills, transport links, doorstep market and easy access to the bureaucrats in Industry and Commerce. Most of these new enterprises were labour-intensive and required electricity, not water-power, as an energy source, so factory location was widely dispersed around the city, although there was some clustering in the north-west and south-west suburbs, close to new housing developments.[37]

Fianna Fáil's industrial drive had collateral benefits for Dublin too. The sleepy Irish stock exchange saw an unprecedented number of company flotations in the years after 1932, many of them hybrid Irish/British enterprises designed to conform to the new investment controls. Some corporate lawyers like Arthur Cox specialised in precisely this field, and professional fortunes were made by those in the know and willing to facilitate government policy. Despite intense misgivings, the banks cooperated in the provision of trade credit and the only sector of financial services subject to direct interference by government was the insurance industry, very much dominated until then by UK-based companies. They were not challenged, but out of the small Irish-owned and financially distressed companies a new conglomerate, Irish Life, was created in 1939 with the state holding a majority share.[38]

The relatively subdued reactions of the business community to the highly interventionist policies of Fianna Fáil are at first sight surprising. One reason may have been the pervasive sense of economic crisis internationally and an acceptance that strange times demanded strange measures. But was there in addition a sense among Protestant business families of official coolness, even of exclusion. Fianna Fáil had certainly fanned fears of a malignant freemasonry at work, and such smears were easily extended to include all Protestant business. Both Lemass and Boland were for a time members of the Knights of St Columbanus, a fraternal lay organisation and originally Belfast-based, that put down roots in Dublin in the early 1920s. Its mission (a bit like the Afrikaner *Broederbond*) was discreetly to promote the advancement of Catholics in business and in other areas of civil society where they were under-represented. It is doubtful whether this influenced public policy (de Valera was quite opposed to secret societies), but with both the Freemasons and the Knights strengthening their respective organisations within the business world, this weakened the capacity of neutral organisations such as the Chamber of Commerce to speak with a strong voice. That said, Lemass was no bigot and was very loyal to those who worked with him and suspicious of those who did not, whatever their party or prayerbook. It is striking that some of the Protestant firms in the building trade like Crampton's and Brooks Thomas, the builders' providers, were among the great beneficiaries of the construction boom in the 1930s. Bewley's cafés also had a good decade, despite carrying heavy debts incurred with the extravagant fitting-out costs of the new premises in Grafton Street, complete with its stained-glass windows by Harry Clarke. Opened in 1927, the café soon attracted a huge and loyal custom.[39]

One new enterprise that owed nothing to protection and was dependent on the external markets was the Irish Hospitals' Sweepstake, a rare example of an Irish business providing a service legal in Ireland (from 1930) but illegal in Britain, a lottery tied to the outcome of classic race meetings that was conducted with theatrical impunity from Dublin. The promoters of the 'Sweep' sold it as an idea to fund the city's voluntary hospitals, which by 1930 were in varying degrees of financial trouble. Despite church disapproval, the scheme proved to be an extraordinary success, managed by Richard Duggan, a well-established Dublin bookmaker who had run earlier sweepstakes from the Continent; Joseph McGrath, former Volunteer and ex-government minister; and a logistical genius, Captain Spencer Freeman. Its success rested on several factors – tapping into the Irish diaspora in Britain and America, using old IRA networks to sell coupons and transfer the cash, and a superb knack for generating public excitement and media attention, notably when the lucky coupon-holders were to be assigned their horses for an upcoming classic. The operation was characterised by shrewd financial management and it made the three trustees immensely wealthy men at a time when new money was rare. Their takeover of the Irish Glass Bottle Company in 1932 and their involvement with a light-bulb factory (Solus) and a city laundry were only the most public demonstrations of their financial muscle. Meanwhile the city's first new hospital building in a generation was largely financed from the proceeds – the National Maternity Hospital in Holles Street. The hospital, half a century old and with a strongly Catholic ethos, had previously been tucked into several eighteenth-century houses. These were swept away and the site expanded to include Antrim House in Merrion Square. Only some chimneypieces and stucco was salvaged in the enthusiasm to build the new all-electric hospital.[40]

Setting the boundaries

Dublin Opinion first appeared in March 1922. It was certainly not the first satirical magazine in the modern city, but it was something special: whimsical, emollient, prescient and often very funny at a time of civil war, it was selling 40,000 copies a month by 1926 and for the next forty years it had no rival. Its first editor, Arthur Booth, was a Tramways clerk, its most prolific cartoonist, Charles Kelly, a civil servant, as was Tom Collins, the principal contributor. Remarkably, they avoided libel actions and were very rarely attacked by irate politicians. Their gently sardonic political cartoons have withstood endless reproduction ever since. *The Irish Statesman* (1923–30) had a more serious purpose; edited by Yeats's old friend AE – artist, poet and non-aligned public intellectual – the weekly was humane and internationalist, and became the main forum for politicians, writers and artists, some attracted to it by AE's advocacy of an Ireland based on cultural pluralism, others happily ignoring his defence of Anglo-Irish tradition. (Only in his visceral reaction to Cubism, when Mainie Jellett's work first appeared in Dublin, was AE uncharacteristically intolerant.) Another great survivor, *The Dublin Magazine* (1923–58), had a similar Protestant/Jewish south-side ambience, the sole editor Seamus O'Sullivan providing a well-tended platform for nearly all the poets and writers of the next generation. But it became cautiously introverted and avoided politics.[41]

Censorship was nevertheless in the air. After clerical lobbying, the Free State government introduced film censorship in 1923. In the same year, the first local review of Joyce's *Ulysses*, due to be published in *The Dublin Magazine*, was blocked by O'Sullivan's printer. The author of the review, Con Leventhal, established his own (single-issue) journal, *Klaxon,* to get it into print. Leventhal was also involved in *To-morrow* (1924), another culturally subversive magazine that was printed in Manchester after the Talbot Press baulked at publishing an anonymous essay (by Yeats) ridiculing contemporary bishops, such censorship by printers presumably reflecting an anxiety about losing church business. The many tracts of the Catholic Truth Society (established in 1899) and the *Catholic Bulletin* (1911–39) had long been targeting 'evil literature' and happily extended the attack to modernism and to any hint of covert Protestant influence. But it was joint pressure from churchmen, Catholic and Protestant, that led an initially reluctant government to establish the state censorship of books and magazines in 1929. The legislation was badly drafted and proved a blunt weapon, but Eason's, the principal importer of UK magazines, was quietly cooperative. Censorship infuriated the literary community, not surprisingly given that most of the books banned in the 1930s were literary rather than pornographic, but they got no support from the political opposition. Yeats's protests were loudest, just as they had been in 1925 when legislation to outlaw divorce was being considered. That measure was rightly seen as proof of the Catholic bishops' direct influence on Cosgrave's administration and it stirred Yeats to deliver his famous apologia in the Senate for the Irish Protestant tradition and for his caste ('no petty people') who, he asserted, were now under terminal threat.[42]

But the campaign against 'evil literature' was rather different from the divorce issue and it drew broader support, with even *The Irish Times* supporting the Jesuit Richard Devane (who ran a Dublin working-class retreat house) when he argued that

> the national morals are looser today [1925] than they were 20 years ago. The restraints of family life have been relaxed here, as everywhere; and in Ireland that laxity has been aggravated by the effects of our recent years of social and political disorder. The Churches have lost much of their influence over the young. The craze for amusement has induced late hours and extravagance, and the young generation is ready to take many risks. Symptoms of this moral decadence are the increase of the drinking habit among girls and ... 'all night dances'...

Devane was perhaps the most persistent of many lobbyists, pleading for controls on the foreign press and restrictions on public dance-halls, convinced that this would protect children at risk. Similarly, the long-serving Film Censor claimed he was primarily concerned to protect vulnerable youth, keeping in mind 'the memory of a crowd of children from the neighbouring slums attending the Picture House in Pearse Street' when he restricted the circulation of 'underworld films'. But within the debate on 'evil literature' was the sub-theme of birth control and its presumed links with promiscuity. There was strong pressure from the hierarchy in 1929 for a ban on the importation and sale of contraceptive devices. Literature advocating birth control was censored, but the government quietly resisted imposing an actual ban on the importation of such devices. Fianna Fáil, however, introduced the ban in 1935.

Was this perception of a great change in sexual behaviour real or imaginary? Alarming reports as to the prevalence of sexually transmitted disease were discussed at Cabinet in 1926, and indeed the numbers attending city hospitals in connection with venereal conditions rose sharply in the course of the decade. In the summer of 1925 extraordinary events took place in the Foley Street neighbourhood in the form of the 'cleansing' of Monto. This was a highly organised police crackdown on brothel-keepers that was coordinated with a vigorous 're-education' programme of the young prostitutes undertaken by lay Catholic vigilantes, who were drawn from the recently formed Legion of Mary. Such close cooperation between the Free State police in Dublin (led by a vigorous young Commissioner William Murphy) and the Legion enthusiasts would have been unthinkable before 1922, but the campaign to close Monto seems to have had only limited effects on the city's sex trade. It merely became less brazen. Admittedly, the numbers arrested for prostitution-related offences did fall away in the 1930s and, as Maria Luddy has shown, the old Magdalene asylums, which in Victorian times had sought to rescue 'fallen women' from a life of vice, had by now turned to catering primarily for ordinary unmarried mothers whose families wanted them conveniently tucked away, either for short-term confinement or for much longer detention, usually in one of the Magdalene-operated laundries.

In 1931–2 a government inquiry, the Carrigan Commission, was set up to consider raising the age of consent. The Garda Commissioner Eoin O'Duffy supplied a raft of statistics on sexual crime that suggested historically high levels of prosecutions in the 1920s, particularly for crimes involving minors. Dublin, however, was only part of a wider national trend. But such was the sensitivity surrounding the subject that the Carrigan report was never published, much to the consternation of social reformers in the city concerned about teenage prostitution and the lack of protection for young rape victims. Admission of the prevalence of such sexual practices threatened to undermine the dominant pulpit narrative of chaste Irish womanhood being threatened only by external decadence. But some perspective on the issue is provided by Stanley Lyon's surveys of the city birth rate in 1941 and 1942: Dublin's level of illegitimacy (almost certainly under-recorded) at 3.9 per cent was still very low by UK urban standards and only slightly higher than the Irish mean (around 3.5 per cent). Fifty-eight per cent of 'ex-nuptial' mothers were under twenty-five, compared to married mothers where only 16 per cent were as young. But among all married women the proportion of first births resulting from premarital conception was relatively high at 18 per cent, as was the proportion of first births within the first year of marriage (57 per cent); only 15 per cent of first births occurred after more than two years of marriage. In all, Lyon's wartime snapshot of the city echoed rural patterns of deferred marriage and the almost complete absence of fertility control within marriage, but there was also a strong hint here that conception preceded – and perhaps initiated – a great many city weddings that were staged in time to avert the desperate stigma attached to unmarried motherhood. During the war there was talk once again of a new wave of prostitution in the city, but the wilder fears of the moral police were as usual somewhat over-coloured.[43]

The campaign to outlaw evil literature was primarily concerned with sexual mores, but it became confused with revivalist demands for 'cultural protectionism' and for curbs on all Anglo-American media. The case for cultural protection was easily made: even with the launch of Fianna Fáil's *Irish Press* in 1931, the London dailies were probably selling more copies in Ireland than were the Dublin dailies, and the London Sundays (even after the banning of the *News of the World* in 1930) far outstripped Abbey Street's *Sunday Independent*. A tax was placed on all imported magazines in 1932 and on daily newspapers in 1933, and this reduced the sales of the English dailies by at least a third and boosted the three Dublin titles. However, the relentless spread of Anglo-American popular culture was not greatly affected. English women's magazines and teenage comics still dominated the news-stands. And cinema, despite censorship, was more popular than ever: in 1934–5 there was an average daily attendance of over 30,000 at the city's thirty-four cinemas, led by the new Savoy. It had recently become part of the entertainment portfolio controlled by the remarkable Elliman family; they had added the iconic Metropole cinema and ballroom in 1921 on the far side of Sackville Street to their pre-war picture-houses, and by 1939 they owned eight cinemas. They were now the dominant force in live entertainment, having taken over the Queen's (in 1934), the Gaiety (in 1936), and the vastness of the Theatre Royal (in 1939), following the British conglomerate ABC ceding majority control to the Ellimans' company (but maintaining a close relationship). One of the most prominent Jewish families in the city, the Ellimans knew precisely what their audiences wanted without stirring up trouble with churchmen or the censors. With an audience capacity of over 3,000, the rebuilt Theatre Royal was the focus of novelty. The policy there of cheap tickets and a regular turnover of international variety acts followed in the footsteps of New York's 'Radio City' and was in its own way as successful. When the singing cowboy Gene Autry riding Champion the Wonder Horse came up the steps of the Theatre Royal on 3 September 1939 to launch his latest singing Western, he drew a crowd of many thousands. But a new war and the curbs on international travel halted all that.

Cinema and dance-halls kept the city going: the small dance venues, operating under tight licensing controls from 1936, were relatively cheap ventures for their promoters, their live band music largely American-inspired. In 1937 there were fifty-four dance-halls licensed in the city, another thirty-nine in Co. Dublin. Thanks to the cinemas and these dance-halls, the young of the new suburbs flocked back into town. As one working-class woman remembered, in her day 'we had all our fun with neighbourhood groups. But now the boys and the girls, too, after they are sixteen are off all over the city to dances here and dances there and to movies and that sort of thing.'[44]

Then there was radio, which from the start was in government control: 2RN/Dublin began broadcasting on a minuscule budget in 1926, moving into the GPO in 1928. However, its signal only slowly reached beyond the Dublin and Cork city regions until the powerful Athlone transmitter came on air in 1933. Wireless sets thereafter became something of a social necessity; in 1939 around 40 per cent of Free State licence-holders lived within the Dublin region, which would suggest that nearly every second metropolitan household had access to a radio. But the growing popularity of Radio Éireann outside Dublin not only helped to foster a new sense of national identity, but also gave the service an opportunity to project the respectable values of bourgeois Dublin into the parlours and kitchens of rural Ireland.[45]

Terence Brown, surveying the intellectual history of the 1930s, has concluded that 'once more Dublin was a place to leave'. The sense of excitement and revolutionary tension of earlier decades had, it seems, been lost. Not, of course, that there were not moments of frisson, as in August 1933 when a new organisation, the National Guard, composed mainly of Free State army veterans who were bitter opponents of the Fianna Fáil government and their continuing links with the IRA, planned to march in a show of strength from Merrion Square to Glasnevin, parading in their blue shirts and fascist-style formations. Their leader, Eoin O'Duffy, had been Police Commissioner until his acrimonious dismissal by de Valera.

After months of minor scuffles between the Blueshirts and IRA supporters, the government, fearing not unreasonably the political intentions of
the marchers, banned the organisation and saturated the city streets with
police. O'Duffy blinked first, the army and police remained loyal to the
new administration, and there was no further challenge to government
authority.[46]

So was Dublin becoming boringly peaceful? Brown's contention is
that heterodoxy was marginalised and that the creatively inclined tended
now to scatter. Apart from the threat of censorship, the straitened budgets
of the national cultural institutions and the very modest support of the
arts by either public or private patrons were hardly encouraging. Harry
Clarke died prematurely in 1931 (although his stained-glass workshop
long outlived him) and his larger-than-life patron Larky Waldron had
died in 1923, his library and art collection dispersed. The National Library,
once the hub of the pre-revolutionary intelligentsia, was a quieter and a
poorer place, and the National Museum's staff numbers had begun a long
decline. The career of the Clongownian Thomas Bodkin is suggestive: he
was Hugh Lane's nephew, like him an art collector and critic, and at thirty
was on the board of the National Gallery, becoming its part-time director
in 1927. Yet he left Ireland in 1935 to take up a chair of fine art in Birmingham, but not before he vented his frustrations at the neglect of the Gallery
and Museum by native governments. (Later, after the war, he made the
case for a powerful sub-ministry of arts that would oversee all the publicly
funded cultural institutions, but the Arts Council that emerged in 1951
was a more modest undertaking.) The great days of the Abbey had also
passed, and although the Gate Theatre, a new venture opening in 1928,
managed to put down roots by offering contemporary and mainstream
European drama to more adventurous Dublin audiences, it was a modest operation, albeit highly successful on its own terms. In its early days,
the Gate did attract some exceptional talents, notably Denis Johnston,
a young Presbyterian barrister educated at Cambridge and Harvard of
strong communist sympathies. His first experimental script, focusing on
the resurrection of Robert Emmet in twentieth-century Dublin, had been
passed over by the Abbey, but was mounted by the Gate company in 1929
as *The Old Lady Says No!*. Its expressionism apparently bewildered audiences almost as much as its transgressive attack on Emmet as a deluded
fool offended them. It was startlingly different from the mainstream stage.
Johnston developed his short Dublin career with two further plays and

40. Hilda Roberts, Grafton Street. In the early years of the Irish Free State, old business names and old-style customers still dominated the city's premier retail street, the shoppers as always self-consciously well-dressed.

with film direction, but by 1936 he was in London and working for the BBC (where he rose almost to the top).[47]

Thus to Dubliners with education, creativity and ambition, the lure of London and Paris was perhaps never stronger, and this restlessness may have been coupled with a sense that the Irish public service, the police, even Dublin Corporation were now being colonised by folk from the provinces. Since 1924, public-service appointments from clerical grades upwards were in the hands of a very competent national commission, but this new meritocratic system did not allay suspicions that political and family influences from the world outside Dublin were working against the city in general, and against the English-educated in particular, when they competed against the product of the Christian Brothers schools. But the world of the arts was certainly not dead. The old RDS School of Art, which had been taken over by the Department of Science and Art in 1854 and then by the Irish Department of Education – now known to all as the Metropolitan School of Art – was rebranded as the National College of Art in 1936. Nestling in the shadows of Leinster House, it remained starved of funds but brought together a gifted team of teachers. In the wider arts world much rested on the shoulders of Dermod O'Brien, William Smith O'Brien's grandson, a fine if conservative artist in his own right: he was founder of the Arts Club in 1907 (which remained an ever-lively bolt-hole for painters and theatre folk), and he was a key figure in getting the Royal Hibernian Academy back on its feet after its destruction in 1916 and in rediscovering its educational mission. But it was his senior, Sarah Purser, practitioner and patron of the arts into her eighties and the grande dame of Mespil Row, who persuaded Cosgrave to endow the city with the state-owned Charlemont House as Dublin's gallery of modern art (it opened in 1933). She and Thomas Bodkin were centrally involved in the long battle to get the Hugh Lane collection out of legal limbo and back to Dublin (although it took until 1959 to negotiate a compromise agreement with the British National Gallery).[48]

Ex-Unionist Dubliners certainly felt marginalised by the 1930s. It was a quiet process, occasionally punctuated by dramatic incidents such as the destruction of royal statues in public places (that of William blown up by the IRA on Armistice Day 1928, George II in the Green being dealt with similarly in 1937), but more telling was the decline of the Free State Senate with its strong Protestant representation and de Valera's easy abolition of it in 1936. Granted, the first President elected under the new constitution of 1937 was Douglas Hyde, the Anglican founder of the Gaelic League and non-partisan to the last. But outside everyday professional life, the religious minorities retreated into their own associational culture based around parish, church, synagogue, school, sports and charity, and denominational barriers strengthened in the 1930s. Overt campaigns to boycott 'loyalist' businesses (notably by Sinn Féin in 1928) were unusual, but there was a touchy sense of vulnerability occasionally revealed in the pages of *The Irish Times*, though mostly it was nothing worse than irritation at the imposition of compulsory Irish in the elementary curriculum. Readers were, however, very well served by 'the old lady of Westmoreland Street', which had only two editors between 1907 and 1954, both of them pragmatic and insightful commentators on a world that they did not entirely like and both wholly committed to their paper. But other institutions linked to the old regime actually benefited in this climate: the RDS, once comfortably resettled in Ballsbridge, enjoyed a huge surge in membership in the 1920s and attendance at its lectures and recitals soared. And love of the horse, as always, transcended politics.[49]

The conduct of Armistice Day reflected the changing environment. Long after General Macready's troops had departed in 1922, many tens of thousands of veterans and their families gathered each 11th of November. For several years, College Green was the ceremonial focus, then St Stephen's Green, and finally the Wellington Monument in the Phoenix Park. But these public displays in military formation and the extravagant use of the Union Jack were somewhat provocative and played into the hands of republicans. After the establishment of the British Legion and the promotion of poppy sales, both Fianna Fáil and the Sinn Féin rump organised rival protests at such displays, some innocently promoting the Easter lily, others deploying petty violence and arson against the British Legion halls and the shops selling poppies. In 1933, citing fears of public disorder, de Valera's government forbade the Legion from publicly displaying the Union Jack, although still allowing the veterans their parade, but numbers at the formal events were already falling and the religious ceremonies now moved indoors to the Anglican cathedrals and parish churches. When the superb Lutyens-designed National War Memorial in Islandbridge was finally completed in 1939 (thanks largely to the efforts of Andrew Jameson and some earlier support from President Cosgrave), there was no ceremony whatsoever.[50]

College Green was always a lively place around Armistice Day and had been since 1919 when students from Trinity and UCD first traded political insults and proclaimed rival loyalties during the two minutes' silence. It still drew crowds in the early 1930s, with IRA supporters on occasion adding spice. Both universities had grown since the war, UCD's numbers rising from 1,017 in 1916–17 to 1,520 by 1929–30, and the college greatly increased its physical size after being allocated most of the College of Science in Merrion Street and the Albert Agricultural College (including its large farmlands) beyond Glasnevin. UCD graduates were strongly represented in the first Free State Cabinet, and filled many of the new appointments to the bench and to the upper grades of the reformed civil service. But after 1932, relations between Earlsfort Terrace and de Valera's government were far less intimate – too many professors were linked to Cosgrave's party and there was only a single UCD graduate in de Valera's first Cabinet. But if UCD was no longer centre-stage, Trinity seemed entirely out in the cold, a relic of the old regime decaying behind its high railings. Prospects of a large capital injection agreed with London in 1920 to meet post-war debts and to upgrade college facilities were compromised by the change of regime (it was, it seems, one of many financial details overlooked in the Treaty negotiations), and the Free State government had far more pressing calls on scarce resources than helping the old college compete with Oxbridge. But some of the wider changes helped Trinity, for with the introduction of Irish as a compulsory matriculation subject in all NUI colleges in 1913, Cork and Galway lost prospective business, and by the 1920s around half of the student body in TCD was non-Anglican for the first time in its history. Female students also reached critical mass, making up about a quarter of the total student body by then. Overall, Trinity's numbers rose sharply after the Great War and were on a par with UCD's total by 1930, its intake over 80 per cent Irish-born and more evenly spread across the island than in UCD's case.

The university's cultural isolation can indeed be exaggerated – de Valera was happy to chair a student debate in 1934 ('a tense occasion' when he told a packed audience that 'we want Trinity men not to have their hearts and their minds centred upon another country') and in 1937 he opened the new library attached to the college's war memorial. Indeed, its flag-waving loyalist students were not entirely representative. In a less than scientific poll of TCD student attitudes in 1938, more than half with political views declared themselves to be 'vaguely pink' or supporters of Fianna Fáil, Labour or Republican parties; 'nearly everyone' read *The Irish Times*, many the *New Statesmen* and the *Irish Press* ('for sport'). As to why they were there, 'nearly half ... came to be prepared for some definite profession', hardly surprising when over two-fifths of students came from professional families. That at least had not changed.[51]

11

THE MODERN
TURN: 1940–1972

Plato's cave?

Iveagh House, last of the city's private palaces, was bequeathed to the
nation by Rupert Guinness, the 2nd earl of Iveagh, in 1939. A three-day
sale of the contents in September was greeted as the end of an era, as Louis
Seize furniture slipped away at bargain prices. The government allocated
the house to the Department of External Affairs (then under de Valera's
direct charge), and its continental interiors admirably accommodated the
evolving departmental culture. But in 1939 External Affairs was focused
on keeping the world out rather than entering into dangerous alliances.
Neutrality as a policy won almost complete backing in the Dáil, but
within the city there were large numbers who felt otherwise. Thousands
of young men were reported as leaving on the mail-boats in the first days of
the Second World War, most of them reservists at that point. And neither
then nor later were those who wished to enlist in British forces prevented
from taking the train to Belfast (although the civilian exodus to British
factories and construction projects was to prove more important). There
were also about 500 German nationals in the city in 1939, some of them
Jewish refugees, but quite a few committed supporters of National Socialism. The most notorious was Adolf Mahr, distinguished archaeologist
and from 1934 director of the National Museum, who still found time
to run the local *Auslandsorganisation* of party members abroad and to

compose monthly reports on Irish politics. He was on holiday in Germany in September 1939 and spent the war there, overseeing radio broadcasts to Ireland. The only indigenous fascist movement, Ailtirí na hAiséirghe ('Architects of the resurrection'), evolved from a radical branch of the Gaelic League in 1940 to become an independent movement in 1942, led by a disaffected accountant, Gearóid Ó Cuinneagáin. It had more than a little resemblance to the Hitler Youth and achieved a public profile greater than its numbers justified.[1]

The citizens of most northern European cities were soon exposed to the horrors of total war and indiscriminate aerial attack. Dublin got off very lightly, even compared with other cities around the Irish Sea. De Valera's policy of formal neutrality from 1939 and the successful military survival of Britain during 1940–41 allowed Dublin to continue in a state of austere isolation. In the early years of the war the city had almost no protection against aerial attack, and the Irish Army's capacity to resist a ground invasion – whether German, British or American – was very modest. Contingency planning for the civil response to attack was remarkably slow to develop. The city did experience aerial attack on three nights in 1941, coinciding with the later stages of the German bombardment of British cities – in January and May, when bombs landed on Terenure and along the South and North Circular Roads. The May bombing was much the worst, coming six weeks after Belfast's blitz which killed over 900 people and brought some 3,000 refugees to Dublin; Dermot Moran, a student in Drumcondra, described for his parents in Kerry the moments leading up to the first Dublin bomb that May night:

> Long beams of light shot out in a vain endeavour to locate those who dared to infringe on our jealously-guarded neutrality. The anti-aircraft went into action from Collinstown. Coastal defences were in action. And all the while that demonic purring sound from overhead threatened our fair capital. More anti-aircraft guns went into action and then! the sinister whine of a falling bomb. I scarcely knew what to expect but waited ...

The last of four bombs landed in the North Strand district and caused twenty-eight fatalities, multiple injuries and damage to some 300 houses (it was apparently the result of pilot disorientation, induced by British radio jamming). Dublin was spared further physical destruction, but the cumulative effects of six years of the 'Emergency' were considerably greater than the collateral effects of the First World War. Shortages of fuel, food, essential raw materials and newsprint were much more onerous, and post-war dislocation continued for more than two years afterwards.[2]

In the first months of the war, Lemass's pet project began to take shape: the massive ministerial office block in Kildare Street to house the Department of Industry and Commerce. It had been agreed in principle in 1934, but to his frustration construction was delayed until 1939 and it was not completed until 1942. Its stern appearance was relieved by a prominent set of murals, interweaving mythology and industrialisation, most clearly in the plaque where Lugh, the god of light, is depicted releasing an aircraft into the sky. Gabriel Hayes, a mother of two young children, chiselled the limestone murals *in situ* (see Pl. 15). Her figures symbolising Ireland on the move were male, while an androgynous Éire formed the keystone over the main entrance. The female workforce, critical to the recent growth in industrial activity, was represented by a spinner and a youthful cigarette sorter. But the prospect of a mother working outside the home was contrary to the whole drift of government thinking in the pre-war years. Opportunities for women to stay at work had been seriously impaired by legislation in 1936 that overturned statutory advances in 1919 and required all women to resign from the public service on marriage with no hope of re-employment, even on widowhood, and excluded all women from certain categories of work. The Irish Women Workers Union and left-wing republicans were almost alone in their protests.[3]

Lemass left Industry and Commerce while his colossus was taking shape, for in the first days of the war, he was moved to the new Department of Supplies. Emergency legislation gave him sweeping powers there to control wages and prices, supervise imports, ration consumer goods and intervene in the management of public companies, even to prescribe profits. He held the post for the duration of the war and in 1942 took over the new Kildare Street office with his 600 staff. Lemass had a well-developed sense that the state should drive the economy if and when private business was unable to do so, or it was unwilling to serve what government deemed to be the national interest. He could point to the success of national parastatal organisations like the Electricity Supply Board (ESB), formed in 1927 to take over municipal power production and operate a national grid when Shannon hydroelectricity became available, and Aer Lingus, formed in 1936. They were proof that government involvement and 'semi-state' enterprise had none of the damaging effects that Dublin businessmen had warned about, and he had few scruples in extending the economic role of the state over the next six years.

Managing the economy was a daunting enough task, on the one hand maintaining an outward show of fastidious diplomatic neutrality, on the other trying to secure critical supplies from one of the belligerents without making concessions in return. The abundant supplies of porter, butter and lean cattle were the only strong cards with which the Irish government could negotiate. The real test came in 1941 as the British government imposed a covert economic squeeze to break de Valera's commitment to neutrality, cutting back on the supply of wheat, steel, coal and industrial raw materials at a time when there was almost no Irish-registered merchant shipping and no oil-refining capacity. Around New Year 1941 Dublin's petrol pumps ran dry, the quality of coal plummeted, bread prices rose and tea became scarce. The introduction of extreme fuel rationing cleared the streets of cars, and buses which had become ubiquitous during the 1930s gave way once again to the trams; suburban train services were reduced and became far less punctual, and inter-city travel more uncertain. 'Leather was such poor quality that people nailed metal tips or hob nails to the soles of their shoes, to save the leather. The sound of a crowd of people walking down O'Connell Street was a unique experience ...', recalled Rory Doyle, an apprentice printer. Bread rationing was not introduced until 1942, but by that time a wages standstill (introduced in the wake of a bruising two-month strike at Dublin Corporation in early 1940) and growing unemployment, not least in the new industrial firms dependent on spare parts from outside, was beginning to hit working-class health. The impact was particularly felt in new working-class suburban communities, where both rents and food prices were higher than in the inner city. Although the most acute disruption had passed by the end of 1942, the material effects of the crisis on weaker households intensified. Typhus reappeared after fifty years in 1943, TB was on the increase, rickets and scurvy became commonplace, and infant mortality fell back to the level of the early 1920s (gastroenteritis being the principal immediate cause).[4]

Building activity was drastically scaled back after 1940, fuel shortages pushing up the price of cement and bricks, and credit becoming scarce. In the case of the Corporation's Rialto project (the future Fatima Mansions), where fifteen blocks were planned, the site itself was prepared and the foundations poured in 1940–41, only to be left for post-war completion when building materials became affordable once again. For the rest of the war the Corporation reverted to a policy of reconditioning ancient housing stock, especially in the Gardiner Street and Summerhill area, giving tenement properties an extended lease of life. By 1942 very large numbers of building workers and men in allied crafts had crossed to Britain, some to take up well-paid employment in public works or in the war industries, others to enlist, so that by 1943 male unemployment in the city was only two-thirds of the 1939 level. But it was predominantly male work that was available in Britain: recorded female unemployment in Dublin doubled in the same period. For the Great Southern Railways (GSR), the first year of the war saw large numbers of railwaymen signing up for the Irish defence forces, whereas 1943 was the peak year for their exodus (in not quite such large numbers) to join Crown forces in Northern Ireland or Britain.[5]

The most decisive policy move by Lemass was in relation to this sector of the economy. In 1942 emergency powers were used to impose on the GSR a general manager with dictatorial powers – Percy Reynolds, a 1916 veteran who had very successfully developed private bus transport in the 1930s. He took over the company from its mainly Protestant directors, the 'old money', who were blamed for all the operating problems evident in the early stages of the war. Owning a large lorry fleet and an even larger fleet of provincial buses, the GSR had adapted to the decline of railway business, but not well enough. Reynolds was a strong and competent manager in Kingsbridge, and on his watch the railways and the canals coped in very difficult circumstances, not least in keeping Dublin's fuel famine at bay. Peter Rigney has documented the remarkable process, beginning in 1942, whereby hundreds of thousands of tons of turf were transported to Dublin from midland and western bogs each summer on specially adapted trains, much of it kept in open storage in the Phoenix Park. The precious stocks of coal were reserved for the railways themselves and for the Pigeon House power station (with the use of town gas strictly rationed). Plans for a mass evacuation of the city also centred on the railways: there were contingency arrangements in place by 1942 to move 145,000 people from the city at three days' notice, and 190 railway carriages were kept permanently in reserve to respond quickly to any aerial attack.[6]

'This city is dying. The frightful censorship and narrowness is sapping the life out of everything', reported Betty Chancellor, one of the Gate's leading actresses, to her future husband Denis Johnston in 1942, 'there is nobody to fight a battle because the place is full of drunken Blitz Gaels and Queens ...' Paranoid, anaesthetised, raffish, cosmopolitan – just some of the puzzlingly contradictory images conjured by those who wrote about wartime Dublin then and thereafter. Unprecedented travel restrictions certainly frustrated those with the means to travel abroad, and this contributed no doubt to what Elizabeth Bowen characterised as the city's 'claustrophobia and restlessness', but both she and Chancellor (one moment suggesting intellectual rigor mortis, and the next a decadent expatriate scene) are confusing witnesses. That there was intrusive political censorship throughout the war is not in dispute – it directly affected commercial cinema, newsprint and private postal correspondence – but what Clair Wills has shown is how much this was softened, at least for bourgeois Dublin, by the variety and vitality of theatre, the revival of orchestral concerts, the uncensored screenings in the Irish Film Society (with some 900 Dublin members by 1943), and the modernist Living Art group who mounted their first annual exhibition in 1943 in protest at what they saw as the stuffy old guard who controlled the Royal Hibernian Academy. Meanwhile, the Ellimans kept the huge Theatre Royal busy by nurturing indigenous comic talent and variety.

As for radio, although Radio Éireann was still under-resourced and its news service starchily controlled, with two orchestras and a repertory company it was now a major cultural institution in the city. Dubliners with access to wireless also had the BBC, to which they listened a great deal, both for its news and its wartime entertainment, and from time to time they tuned in to German radio and the strange English-language offerings of Francis Stuart and other Dubliners in exile. A sense of unreality and isolation was probably greatest in the first years of the war, when startling events were unfolding beyond the horizon, but this had eased substantially by 1944. Resident British pacifists and artists, American GIs on weekend trips from across the border, and the flotsam and jetsam of Dublin's small diplomatic corps mingled at the Red Bank, Jammets, the Unicorn and the well-regarded pubs. It helped make parts of the city feel like the Casablanca of the North. But there were many who bitterly resented their loss of freedom.[7]

The Bell is the most famous cultural legacy of the war, a monthly review launched in 1940; its financial backer was Peadar O'Donnell, the great left-wing republican from Donegal, its editor Seán O'Faolain, a Cork republican intellectual. With a circulation of never more than 3,000, it managed throughout the Emergency to stand back from immediate events and provide an unvarnished cultural, social and political commentary on contemporary Ireland and beyond, publishing poetry and fiction as well. Its editor railed against the folly of censorship, but the magazine's strength was its calm detachment from clerical or political agendas, combined with a knack for exposing unnoticed aspects of a changing society. And although Protestant writers contributed, this was truly a post-colonial enterprise, written from the inside against 'Little Irelandism', and designed not for an intimate Dublin readership but for liberal minds in provincial Ireland. While it helped to construct the idea of Dublin's cultural introversion during the war, the magazine's very vitality helped disprove the thesis.[8]

O'Donnell had been a leading figure in the IRA in the 1930s, a movement that had regrouped despite the ascendancy of Fianna Fáil. But his version of republican socialism lost out to a narrower, purely militant group, headed from 1938 by Seán Russell, a 1916 veteran from Buckingham Street, whose single-minded pursuit of military struggle was uncomplicated by radical politics. His subsequent attempts to secure German military support were entirely logical and predictable. Between his travels to the US, Germany and Russia, Russell was rarely on home ground, but it was with his inspiration that a fifty-strong IRA unit attacked the Magazine Fort in the Phoenix Park in December 1939 and stole over a million rounds of ammunition. The old days of intimacy between Fianna Fáil and the IRA were long gone by then, but the raid gave the government the resolve to intern IRA activists for the duration of the Emergency, some in the city, most in the Curragh Camp, and to tighten further its special powers. The 800-odd internees were indeed isolated, but out of this harsh regime literary talents of the next generation were shaped, most notably the unruly lad from Crumlin, Brendan Behan, one of the least adroit physical-force republicans in the IRA's history but one of working-class Dublin's most authentic voices: 'In public ... Rabelaisian, jocose, knowledgeable. In private ... difficulties and bewilderment[,] about which he was in fact much funnier.'[9]

Breakthrough

Alderman Tom Kelly, a product of the Townsend Street tenements and a close ally of Arthur Griffith from 1905, rarely spoke in the Dáil after he returned to politics in 1932 as a Fianna Fáil TD. But in 1941, the year before his death, he let fly at the misrepresentations of Dublin in the Dáil ('possibly the reason for that is that there are very few Dublin men here'); he rejected the picture of its terrible home-grown poverty and argued that it was too big because of immigration, and that with young people pouring in from the countryside, housing them was the problem – perhaps government should follow America's example and directly manage (and fund) the capital city. Others at the time wanted action on the radical recommendations of Local Government (Dublin) Tribunal of Inquiry (1935–8), which had made the case for a metropolitan Dublin council incorporating the whole of the city and county of Dublin, 'a financial and planning authority to work out its own salvation instead of being controlled by the Local Government Department'. Its recommendations were left on the shelf, opposed on financial grounds from within the Corporation and on political grounds by the Department of Local Government, although two lesser reforms followed: the Howth peninsula was brought into the city in 1940, and the remit of the City Manager was expanded, requiring him to act at the same time as the Manager for Co. Dublin. And in 1941 the city's 'Sketch Development Plan' was finally published.

This short document of sixty-two pages, written in 1939, was the culmination of three decades of debate. It was written at the behest of the Corporation, using its powers under the 1934 Town and Regional Planning Act to commission 'consultants' to produce a regional development plan. Its lead author was once again Patrick Abercrombie, who used the opportunity to revisit ideas dating back to 1914 and to refine them in the light of the rise of the motor-car, the likely impact of air travel and the declining importance of fixed-rail transport. The Plan argued once again that greater middle-class residence within the city should be encouraged and that new working-class housing should be in the suburbs; the central traffic hub should be moved westwards and a new 'central internal ring system' be created; the quays should be regenerated (with a Catholic cathedral now earmarked for Ormond Quay), and additional road bridges built. The need for urban parks and playgrounds was more precisely calibrated, and the case also made for a massive extension of the outer ring roads (specifically Griffith and Collins Avenues); planning controls should ensure that new building be in harmony with the old and should respect the 'magnificent brick houses built with a quiet Georgian dignity' (although the Plan also recommended the demolition of the west side of

Parliament Street to make way for a new headquarters for the Corporation). Unlike earlier blueprints, the 1941 Plan had official status. When it
was published, in 1943, the City Manager P. J. Hernon chose not to exaggerate its originality (strongly acknowledging the importance of the Wide
Streets Commissioners) or its potential to transform the city at a time of
wartime stringency, but it was a landmark.

The Town Planning Committee immediately watered down Abercrombie's bolder ideas, and the Corporation as a whole declined to use
the 1934 Act to assume wider regional responsibility for planning, ostensibly on grounds of cost. It failed even to produce a metropolitan plan
until 1957 and did so then only under legal duress. The 1934 Planning Act
placed no obligation on local authorities to develop a competence in planning, and the delay in developing regional planning functions was common to all Irish cities and reflected deeper issues. Politicians of the two
leading parties and civil servants in Local Government were very suspicious of the whole concept of planning at both urban and regional levels,
whether because of the hidden costs of compensation that might follow a
rigorous system of land zoning, or because of the loss of political control
that commitment to a potentially binding strategic plan implied. Thomas
Johnson, the Labour party leader, was an exception, Lemass showed some
interest in green belts in 1930, as did the young Erskine Childers in the
1940s (all Dublin-based politicians), but that was very rare. Most of those
who passionately campaigned for the passage of town and regional planning legislation and, after the passing of the 1934 and 1939 Acts, for their
implementation, were professional (and often Protestant) Dubliners,
over-influenced, some said, by British best practice, and that reduced the
impact of their advocacy. They may have received fulsome support in *The
Irish Times*, but there were no votes in planning.[10]

None of the principal recommendations of either the Tribunal or of
the 1939 Plan was implemented in the short term. There was no obligation
on local government bodies to become planning authorities until the 1963
Planning Act. It was, indeed, not until the 1980s that local government
reform was back on the agenda and the early 1990s before a new structure
for local government was finally agreed, dividing the Dublin county area
into four units (Dublin City, Fingal, South County and Dún Laoghaire/
Rathdown), and they in turn were to be coordinated by a Dublin Regional
Authority (but that was no more than 'a paper structure that you can just
fold away in the morning'). Yet the 1939 Plan did have a long afterlife in

one respect: it set out the case for a 'green belt', an 'agricultural reservation', that would commence four miles from the city centre and be four to six miles in width, within which there should be very tight controls on development, but allowing satellite towns within the belt to expand (from Malahide in the north-east to Tallaght in the south-west). The Plan argued for national controls to enforce a future ceiling on greater Dublin's population at 765,300, plus 61,500 in the satellites. And even though the Corporation chose to restrict their planning role to the county borough of the city, Dublin planners accepted the logic of a green belt and indeed the term was regularly used in post-war debate. In 1950 Michael O'Brien, the City Planning Officer, claimed that since the Plan 'we have tightened the urban fence and have formed the view that the maximum population to which [metropolitan] Dublin should reach would be 620,000', a figure below Abercrombie's projected ceiling. Post-war arterial roads, notably the southern ring road along the Grand Canal, were credited to the Plan, but the case for satellite towns was rejected until the 1960s. On the north side of the city, there was the special issue of the airport. As traffic built up, a decision was taken *c.*1947 to restrict any development within a 2.5-mile radius of the runways (later reduced), and this threw into relief the huge compensation issues that came with rigorous land zoning. Abercrombie's general projections continued to influence investment decisions on water and sewerage until at least the 1960s (and the fact that O'Brien as lone Planning Officer remained in post from 1936 into the 1970s may have helped that continuity). So, by default, Abercrombie's was the master plan for the next two decades, influencing the official Dublin 'planning scheme' agreed in January 1957, which was principally concerned with road improvement, and acting as a point of departure for Myles Wright, Colin Buchanan and the next generation of planning consultants who pondered the Dublin region's future in the 1960s.[11]

In the summer of 1939, the Gate Theatre, unusually for it, staged a realist drama set in contemporary Dublin, *Marrowbone Lane*. The author, Robert Collis, was no O'Casey, but his play about the overwhelming poverty of tenement Dublin and the failure of the authorities to resolve it was designed to be controversial and it ran for four weeks. It was, he said, inspired by Steinbeck and *The grapes of wrath*. Three years later, another Collis play was staged in the Gaiety, *The barrel organ*, which focused on TB. Collis was a paediatrician and, unusually in the city's intimate medical world, he had had extensive professional experience in London and

Baltimore. On returning to Dublin, he lost no chance to publicise the link between bad housing and children's health, and he was one of the founding members of an advocacy group, the Citizens Housing Council. He had two remarkable allies, former republican activists and lifelong medical pioneers: Kathleen Lynn, who had established St Ultan's, a specialist mother's and children's hospital, in the wake of the influenza epidemic in 1919, and Dorothy Stopford-Price, whose introduction of BCG inoculation at St Ultan's in 1937 was truly revolutionary (the hospital was chosen to lead a national campaign to eliminate juvenile TB under her direction in 1949). There was, of course, a very old tradition of medics campaigning for public-health reforms, but what made Collis and Lynn different was the combination of advanced medical knowledge, good political connections across the denominational divide and a flair for publicity. Through the war years Collis campaigned for the medical needs of the city's poorest children, but the introduction in 1943 of a universal children's allowance for families with more than two children probably had far wider impact than such latterday philanthropy. The restless Collis meanwhile enrolled with the Red Cross and was among the first doctors to help at the liberation of Belsen.[12]

The Corporation's 1939 Housing Report appeared in 1943, adopting (without acknowledgement) many of the policies advocated by Collis's Housing Council. Another medic, T. W. T. Dillon, reflecting on the report, scolded 'the wider public' for remaining in denial about the stinking, rat-infested conditions still tolerated by 23,000 city families, their men being 'the last to be employed, the first to be discharged ... their young sons and daughters leave school at 14 in a state of incredible ignorance. They have no chance of employment in a steady trade; dressed in rags, inarticulate, dirty and often dishonest, they drift into the street corner gangs which are the despair of social workers and the concern of the police.' Like Collis's plays, this Hobbesian portrait (appearing in the Jesuits' quarterly *Studies* in 1945) was designed to shock. Dillon held both the state and the municipality to account for badly designed policies and a lack of political will.[13] This has to be set against the bigger housing picture. Housing density across the city was extraordinarily uneven. Horner's mapping of the city in 1936 reveals a spectrum from Mountjoy ward in the north-east of over 450 people per hectare to that in the Rathmines and Ballsbridge districts of around 70 people per hectare; high density (more than 200 per hectare) was still strongly correlated with the inner city. That would change from the 1950s. One pointer to overall improvements in housing after 1936 comes in the shift in the persons-per-room ratio. Here we can see a long-term fall in average numbers per room: in 1936, in the urbanised county borough area (excluding Dún Laoghaire), the figure was 1.26 per room, falling to 1.14 by 1946; in the next fifteen years there was a much larger rate of decline to 0.93 in 1961, at which point the figure stabilised for many years. This trend was helped by a much slower rate of population growth between 1946 and 1961 in greater Dublin; the county borough, Dún Laoghaire and Co. Dublin together reached 718,332 by the latter date, still a considerable distance below Abercrombie's suggested maximum in the 1939 Plan. But also critically important was improvement at last in eradicating the tenements – not complete by 1961, but a transformation nonetheless.[14]

The year 1948 marked the step change, both in public housing and in the expansion of private-sector building. Scarcity of skilled labour, scarcity of building materials, appalling weather (notably the awful winter of 1946–7) and tight credit had delayed any post-war bounce, but the political mood in Dublin was for an end to austerity and a break with the familiar wartime faces. New parties contested the 1948 general election, with Clann na Poblachta capturing all the attention in the Dublin media. This was a left-wing republican party that combined a modernising agenda for social reform with a scathing rebuttal of Fianna Fáil's record in government. It campaigned for massive public spending, particularly in health, to create in effect an Irish welfare state. Clann polled well in the city, taking around a fifth of the vote and winning six seats (out of a national tally of ten), but not as well as many expected. Nevertheless it became a junior partner in the first Inter-Party government (1948–51), and one of its Dublin TDs, a young doctor with no political experience, was appointed Minister in the recently established Department of Health. This was the mercurial Noël Browne; in his time in office he greatly accelerated the TB eradication programme by introducing free hospital treatment for TB sufferers and by modernising and expanding the dedicated TB sanatoria, getting a huge 250-bed facility for child victims off the ground in west Dublin (at Ballyowen). The incidence of TB had been gradually falling for decades and many hands were involved in this, but Browne was credited, then and thereafter, as the white knight who conquered the scourge. He also proceeded with plans for free state healthcare for mothers and children, but this proved a radical step too far. The ensuing storm of protest from professional medical interests and, more damagingly, from the Catholic Hierarchy, led to his resignation in April 1951 and to the collapse of the coalition government shortly afterwards (although a diluted version of the Mother and Child scheme was quietly introduced by the next Fianna Fáil administration). Ironically the political firestorm came towards the end of a period of dramatically improved infant mortality after the war. A cluster of factors helped achieve this – improved post-war maternal nutrition and with it a rise in working-class breast-feeding, but the provision of a municipal infant health unit and of local public-health nurses also seems to have been of critical importance.[15]

At the formation of the Inter-Party administration in 1948, the Labour party had taken on the vital Ministry of Local Government, and the short-lived minister there, T. J. Murphy (another west Corkman) took up the cause of eradicating Dublin's slums with Brownite passion. Dublin was the centrepiece of his national ten-year housing programme that embraced both local-authority building and an incentivised private sector. The Corporation agreed to a target of building 3,000 houses p.a. (about double the rate achieved in 1932–9). In the first year they met that target, and between 1950 and 1952, despite some excruciating difficulties in securing funding, they managed to borrow £15 million to continue the housing programme. But the 1950s turned out to be a decade of false dawns, of economic expansion halted on at least two occasions by fiscal austerity and tight credit (in 1952 and 1956), of vacillating policies on the part of short-lived ministers, of labour scarcities in some years (because of heavy migration to Britain), and of labour disputes and unemployment protests in others. It was also a decade of endless headaches for the Corporation in its efforts to secure the capital loans necessary to sustain the building programme as first promised by government in 1948. However, a great deal was achieved in the first half of the 1950s, and the massive extensions to Crumlin and Cabra and the beginnings of entirely new working-class suburbs – notably Walkinstown in the south-west, Ballyfermot beyond Kilmainham to the west, Finglas to the north-west and Whitehall, Artane and Coolock/Raheny to the north-east – changed the shape of the city. The Corporation was involved in nearly fifty housing schemes in the course of the decade, some of them directly managed, most using private contractors, old and new. At least five building firms were involved in the creation of Ballyfermot alone. In appearance the new estates did not differ greatly from pre-war projects, but the introduction of the concrete block, pre-stressed concrete sections and aluminium window-frames helped speed up the building process. But, as McManus has shown, despite such standardisation, a large and paternalistic firm of builders like Crampton's still maintained a tight apprenticeship structure and a powerful battalion of craftsmen.[16]

Without an agreed city plan or a metropolitan planning authority, yet with politicians permanently hungry for new building, there was a danger of serious infrastructural bottlenecks. This repeatedly occurred in relation to school provision, recreational space, water supply, sewage disposal and road construction. Crumlin, the first of the massive suburbs, experienced pre-war deficits in all of these services; most alarming was the repeated experience of taps running dry. Indeed, water threatened to put an absolute brake on the city's growth when in 1935, for the first time, supplies from Vartry reservoir could not keep up with demand. Additional extraction from the old Rathmines reservoir at Bohernabreena and from the Grand Canal gave limited relief. But a solution for the future came in 1936 when the Corporation persuaded the ESB to enter a joint agreement to dam the headwaters of the Liffey above Poulaphouca, creating both further hydroelectric capacity and an abundant supply of Wicklow water for the western suburbs. The scheme was completed in 1944 and this immediately increased city water supply by a quarter. But post-war expansion on the north side created new concerns about water supply, with various stopgap measures taken until the mid-1960s, when another big agreement with the ESB gave access to the newly created Leixlip reservoir, thereby meeting demand from the burgeoning suburbs of Finglas and Ballymun. A related issue, which also threatened north-side development, was sewage disposal. After years of debate, the Department of Local Government agreed in principle during Murphy's time in office to the construction of a mains interceptor running across the northern suburbs to the sea. The scale of the project grew before work commenced in 1952. An immediate consequence was the extension of the city boundary to take in Baldoyle, Coolock and Finglas (the City wanted more but the County Council refused). The 'North Dublin Drainage Scheme' was directly managed by the Corporation and was for its time a massive project. The trunk sewer ran from Blanchardstown and Cabra across to the coast at St Anne's, then along the Bay to Sutton and Howth, and, with the help of four pumping stations, to a discharge point out at sea beyond the nose of Howth; linked to it were a number of feeder lines. The final cost was around £2 million, and at its peak the project employed 115 men, overseen by fewer than a dozen overworked city engineers. Parke Neville would have been impressed. But massive as it was, its designers underestimated the growth that lay ahead.[17]

Living with prosperity

After the short boom in the later 1940s, the general picture of the next decade is of a stuttering economy and a haemorrhaging countryside. Perhaps the picture is overdrawn, but there was certainly a downbeat character to the city in the 1950s. The literary and cultural world was small, male and, more than ever, centred on a few pubs and clubs (and pubs were still overwhelmingly male spaces). Patrick Kavanagh, the poor cobbler's son from Co. Monaghan who had first tramped to Dublin in his boots in 1931 to meet 'the poets' and bring home some books, best captured the incestuous mood of that world twenty years later, managing to be both the cantankerous countryman and the lyrically perceptive poet, subverting the official culture of the city and the self-serving patrons of the arts. Brian O'Nolan/Flann O'Brien, another Ulster migrant to the city a few years younger than Kavanagh, had on the surface a far more successful career in the civil service, ending up as head of the town-planning section in Local Government. Writing behind several masks in Irish and English, he found that his experimental writing was only appreciated after 'Myles na gCopaleen' became the premier columnist in *The Irish Times* (it started in Irish, but ran mainly in English from 1941 until his death in 1966). Post-modern before the term had been dreamt up, O'Brien's work drew on his extraordinary polymathic curiosity, his literary breadth and verbal playfulness, and through his columns and later writing he created a virtual world of surreal characters. Like Kavanagh, he was utterly subversive of the formal culture – despite being an insider in every respect and enjoying the quiet support of Lemass's old party rival, Seán MacEntee.[18]

If the 1950s were years of disappointment for most Dubliners, the 1960s were a time when their city changed more than anyone expected. A few statistics capture the story. Between 1951 and 1961, greater Dublin grew very slowly, the core county-borough area not at all (losing 2.2 per cent of its population between 1951 and 1956, and stagnating in the second half of the decade). The only areas of pronounced growth were in the

41. The poet Patrick Kavanagh directing operations outside Davy Byrne's pub in Duke Street on 'Bloomsday', 16 June 1954, watched by author Anthony Cronin. The convivial staging of the fiftieth anniversary of Bloomsday involved a convoy of horse-drawn cabs, beginning with the re-enactment of breakfast at the Martello tower in Sandycove. The event was a stab at the still prevailing disapproval of Joyce's work.

southern suburbs outside the boundary, ranging from Terenure across to Stillorgan, where owner-occupancy was the norm in the patchwork of new privately developed housing schemes. But population growth in the next inter-censal period soared: between 1961 and 1971 greater Dublin grew at about 1.7 per cent p.a., considerably faster than in the 1930s, the previous peak. One factor underpinning this growth was the stable low level of infant mortality in the 1960s, bringing Dublin close to national averages. The city's growth was still very uneven, inner city wards losing population, the suburbs old and new now driving the trend: in 1936 the wards within the canals had contained 54.5 per cent of the county-borough population, whereas by 1971 they accounted for only 18.9 per cent. There was an absolute fall in population in all these wards, with the Rotunda, Wood Quay and South Docks wards seeing the greatest residential collapse.[19]

Meanwhile, registered private cars in the city, reaching 25,000 in 1950, had doubled by 1960, then grew at a faster rate of 9 per cent p.a. for

a decade. The car by 1970 had changed the character of middle-class living, extending the suburbs and loosening the former influence of public
transport on residential patterns. The great age of the bicycle as a principal means of short-distance commuting had passed with the availability of cheap petrol and the opening up of a vast market in second-hand
cars. The urbanised area was itself expanding at an unprecedented rate.
Lower house densities and more land set aside for amenities meant not
just a lower-pressure city but the continued gobbling up of agricultural
land. Horner has estimated that between 1940 and 1971 800 acres a year
moved from rural to built-up uses and that by the early 1970s the city
was sprawling across 100 square miles, ten times its spatial dimensions in
1841. Controls over this process were weak and a high visual price was
now being paid for the woefully slow introduction of planning controls.
Back in 1925, one of the officers of the old Local Government Board had
warned about Dublin's 'centrifugal tendency ... Every motor car or 'bus
is a stimulus thereto, and the progress towards the mountains and the sea
should be thought out and orderly, rather than haphazard as heretofore'.
The planning enthusiasts of the 1920s believed that there was still time to
put in place land-use regulations that would contain the city and protect
the villages and the rural environment within its reach. Forty years later
it was evident that the opportunity to regulate such growth, if it ever had
existed, had now passed.[20]

Most saw the economic improvement, clearly visible by the early
1960s, in political terms, the result of Lemass finally taking over the leadership of Fianna Fáil from de Valera in 1959 and directing a radical shift
in economic policy away from pre-war protectionism and austerity. Now
the new orthodoxies were economic planning, foreign direct investment,
tariff reduction and export promotion, raising the prospects of an end to
emigration and high unemployment. Lemass was perhaps lucky: many of
these policy changes were already underway before 1959 and, more importantly, the international environment for the pursuit of such strategies
was particularly favourable. By the time of President Kennedy's triumphal
visit in June 1963 there was something more to celebrate than the coming home of a youthful émigré prodigy – although Kennedy's rhetoric in
Leinster House, televised live, had a striking impact on the public mood.
But whatever the fundamental causes of the new economic climate and
of the rise in incomes, Dublin in the 1960s benefited in a myriad of ways
from the wider Irish recovery. Lemass's government made great efforts to

secure trade-union support for economic planning, and the very generous national three-year wage agreement of 1964 was a landmark development. Real wages kept ahead of inflation and the gap between the average industrial wage and top professional incomes was beginning to narrow. Consumer credit and hire-purchase for cars and televisions drew in the working classes. But more fundamentally, these years can be seen as a bridge into the late twentieth century, the age when high mass consumption, cosmopolitan tastes, gender equity and increasingly secular values began to be embraced by most Dubliners.[21]

But such a transition was profoundly disturbing to the guardians of traditional belief. In the first two decades of independence, the Catholic Church in Dublin had been led by Edward Byrne: a personally courageous figure, he was neither as assertive nor as politically astute as Walsh, his predecessor, nor the Holy Ghost headmaster of Blackrock College, John Charles McQuaid, who succeeded him in 1940 (and who was helped along the way by well-timed diplomatic support from his friend de Valera). McQuaid was in post for thirty-two years, longer than Cullen a century before, but, like him, was a shy man of exceptional energy, administrative flair and a steely determination to copper-fasten the church's dominant position in the city. His family background was strongly medical and he had considerable interest in the arts. Despite the hundreds of building projects with which he was associated, his artistic side rarely showed, but he did display an unprecedented interest in public health, particularly that of the poorer sections of the urban working class. Early in 1941, with supplies of bread and fuel shrinking, he brought together some forty Catholic charitable agencies and oversaw the establishment of twenty-seven food centres in the city, which in the first year provided over two million meals. The focus was particularly on helping pregnant women and children through the Emergency. That set the tone for thirty years of personal involvement in numerous public-health initiatives, most notably the 324-bed children's hospital that was opened in Crumlin in 1956 on land donated by the archdiocese, and the religiously run Mount Carmel hospital in Dartry, which became the maternity hospital of choice for many south-side families. The sub-text to much of this energy was the purposeful exclusion of secular or cross-denominational agencies, whether it was the St John's Ambulance Brigade as an alternative agency running wartime food depots, or the threat of an amalgamated St Ultan's and the Children's Hospital in Harcourt Street, over which he would have little leverage.[22]

But, as Deirdre MacMahon has shown, Archbishop McQuaid for all his compassion was profoundly out of sympathy with the social trends evident around him and his illiberal attitudes came to seem decidedly out of place. His intervention in plans for the 1958 Dublin Theatre Festival (in what would have been its second year), with objections to a proposed stage version of *Ulysses* and to parts of a new O'Casey play, led to its entire cancellation, which may have seemed a successful outcome in Archbishop's House, but it outraged many more than just the fans of Joyce and O'Casey. It was indeed unusual in being a very public display of the power of the crozier which was usually exercised covertly, and the customary invisibility of his methods was one reason why they were normally so effective. His abiding concern was about protecting the faith and morals of his flock, not from proselytising Protestants – that issue was history – but from atheistic communism, decadent cross-channel media in all its forms and alcohol and drug abuse, all a reflection of his primary focus on working-class issues. He was central to the huge controversy over the state's Mother and Child scheme in 1951, having opposed earlier versions of the proposal in 1947, not just on the grounds that such a scheme might provide cover for the introduction of family planning services, but from a profound dislike of the state's creeping intrusion into family life. And throughout his time in office he displayed a stiff disregard for Protestant institutions of every type, clamping down on inter-denominational groups, and from 1944 zealously enforcing a ban on Catholic attendance at Trinity College (other than by special dispensation).[23]

His greatest impact on the life of the city and the diocese was in overseeing a relentless process of parish creation. McQuaid's record of twenty-three new city parishes was without precedent and the attendant church-building programme, funded by traditional forms of local fundraising and, from the mid-1960s, by professional fund-raisers, put considerable strain on diocesan finances. Not surprisingly, he declined to follow up his predecessor's enthusiasm for erecting a new Catholic cathedral in Merrion Square – or in any other location. The expansion of Catholic secondary schools during the McQuaid years was also impressive: in the diocese as a whole the number of such schools doubled between 1946 and 1966, with a further acceleration in the late 1960s at the moment when the state introduced its free-fees initiative for participating schools (the city's technical/vocational schools, which lay more directly within public control, were also expanding rapidly, but not as rapidly as the church-controlled sector). And while McQuaid did not share his friend de Valera's enthusiasm for language revival, on his watch four Catholic schools offering secondary education wholly in the Irish language became highly influential – Scoil Chaitríona (established in 1928) and Coláiste Mhuire (in 1931) on the north side, Coláiste Eoin (in 1968) and Coláiste Íosagáin (in 1971) in south Dublin, two girls' and two boys' schools, and all but the first with a strong Christian Brothers ethos. Between them they protected and strengthened revivalist networks across the public service, not least from provincial competition.

The newspapers of the 1940s and 1950s record an endless succession of episcopal blessings at school openings and hospital extensions. All of this church-orchestrated expenditure came at a time when the secular authorities, until the 1960s at least, were financially unable, or at least unwilling, to invest in the social infrastructure being demanded by an urban society where the comparisons with post-war British advances were constantly being made and which revealed a widening deficit. It is hard to imagine what the social consequences of a less engaged Catholic Church might have been. Never had Clonliffe seminary been so busy, nor had so many nuns and priests been visible on the streets of the city, most of them involved in pastoral, educational or medical provision in the widening suburbs. The total number of religious at the time of McQuaid's retirement in 1972 was close to the high-tide mark: there were 567 secular clergy and no fewer than 297 religious communities of clergy, nuns and brothers active within his diocese. One harbinger of the future was already evident by 1970: a change in the Church's involvement with wayward children. Since Cullen's era, vast numbers of unfortunate children had been sent by the courts into Catholic institutions, whether because of 'inadequate parental care, destitution, neglect, truancy, ... the commission of minor offences', or simply because of family poverty. At the beginning of McQuaid's episcopacy, the reformatories were full to overflowing: Artane on the Malahide Road, by far the largest in the country, had a resident population of 820 boys in 1940, all kept busy on the farm and in the workshops. But Artane was far too big and was woefully managed; the Christian Brothers in charge were badly trained, under-staffed and too often openly abusive of the children in their care; a few were sexual predators. Rumours that all was not well first circulated in the early 1960s, and McQuaid was in private highly critical of the institution. Numbers fell steeply during the decade until 1969, when the Brothers took the decision

42. Completed in 1941, the Corpus Christi Church catered for a new north-side parish carved out of Drumcondra. A striking granite basilica peppered with art deco references, it was designed by Robinson, Keefe and Devane, and was perhaps the most architecturally distinguished and self-confident of the many city churches opened during Archbishop McQuaid's long episcopacy.

to close the reformatory. It was perhaps a measure of a wealthier society and a more humane one that such places of detention were falling out of favour, and that the alternatives of adoption and fosterage were becoming much more common. There was also the hint of a more critical public attitude to previously inviolate church institutions. However, it was not until many years later that the gross deficiencies of institutions such as Artane would be fully revealed.[24]

Making and breaking

'Modernism' may have been McQuaid's enemy, but it was slow to show itself in his city. The artistic hothouse of the war years and the promise of creative experiment that came with it dissipated fairly quickly as the lure of larger European cities was reasserted. Domestic patrons of the arts, private or public, were limited and the trend was towards standardisation, not experimentation. The pre-eminent architectural practice after the war was Robinson, Keefe and Devane, and the senior partner, John Robinson, had been official architect to the Eucharistic Congress in 1932 and the designer of the Hospital Sweepstake headquarters in Ballsbridge (1938). He had scooped up a series of plum church commissions from Archbishop Byrne, most of them neo-Romanesque in style but some with contemporary nuances (such as Corpus Christi church in Drumcondra, completed in 1941). His firm championed art deco, most strikingly in the Gas Company's showrooms in D'Olier Street (1928) and the College of Catering in Cathal Brugha Street (1939), and Robinson himself had no love for the classical idiom of the older city. When making the case for Merrion Square as the site for the Catholic cathedral in 1942, he remarked of the surrounding terraces, 'their day is done – the Georgian era is over, and there is little sense in seeking to perpetuate it ... nothing is left for them but demolition ...'.[25]

Where Robinson reflected the eclectic and generally conservative tastes of his clients, the leading Dublin architect of the next generation was a total contrast. Michael Scott was a larger-than-life figure, a professional actor (briefly), artist, architect and cultural patron for nearly half a century. Trained as an architect but a natural actor, his first commission was in 1930 to design a permanent home for the Gate Theatre within the Rotunda's old Assembly Rooms. Later in the decade he was involved in fitting out several cinemas and the new Theatre Royal. But Gropius and Le Corbusier now became his inspiration, and friendship with Lemass helped secure him the commission to design the Irish Pavilion for the 1939 New York World's Fair, which was a great critical success. However, his masterpiece was the national bus station, commissioned in 1946 in the expansive early days of Córas Iompair Éireann (CIE), the state-owned national transport authority and successor to the GSR. The station was to be placed on a sensitive site in Beresford Place. Its bold internationalist style, innovative use of materials and huge cost caused professional and public controversy. As with his chassis-building plant designed for CIE in Inchicore, the bus station at Busárus became something of a white elephant, most of its vast office space being reassigned to government use. But when fully and meticulously completed in 1953 the building, thanks to its striking modernist appearance and location, was accepted as a symbol of a new Dublin. His firm's later public projects, even the reconstruction of the Abbey Theatre completed in 1966, did not have quite the same impact. Seán Rothery has characterised Scott as 'more of an impresario than an architect', since 'it wasn't so much what he did himself as the fact that he assembled a group of very talented people around him, stimulating a lot of creative thinking, which made things happen', and so it seems to have been with Busárus, where at least six young assistants (led by Wilfred Cantwell and Kevin Fox) actually did all the creative design work. But the era of the solo architect who could place his stamp on the city had passed. In a personal capacity, Scott was a highly influential champion of artistic innovation, thanks to his 'high regard for power', his magnetism and his artistic open-mindedness. Amongst much else he was the driving force behind Rosc, a formidable exhibition of contemporary international art that was first held at the RDS in 1967, but unlike Robinson he was also converted to the cause of protecting the architectural heritage of eighteenth-century Dublin.[26]

However, in an echo of times past, it was left to a young English architect to secure one of the most difficult architectural commissions in post-war Dublin, and on the strength of that to establish an international reputation. The project was a new main library for Trinity College. De Valera had in an unlikely way become supportive of the university's needs after the war and had agreed the first tranche of state funds in 1947 (a move cancelled the next year by the Inter-Party government and restored on de Valera's return to office in 1951), and he took a particular interest in the library where storage space was running out. From this came plans for a joint venture with the National Library. Objections from Archbishop McQuaid put paid to that. The university then went fund-raising for a decade on both sides of the Atlantic (bringing the Book of Kells on circuit), but securing pound-for-pound matching of funding from government was critical. An ambitious design brief was published in 1960 for a structure that would be sympathetic in height and line to its neighbours, two buildings of exceptionally strong architectural character (Burgh's Library and Woodward and Deane's Museum). Two hundred and eighteen entries were received in the architectural competition, and twenty-eight-year-old Vienna-born, English-trained Paul Koralek won the day and remained architect of the project. His Library (opened, appropriately, by de Valera in 1967) was an object lesson in the imaginative use of concrete and curved glass, its Le Corbusier influences evident in the detailing of the concrete and the boldness of the interior plan, its integration with the older architectural styles nearby a rare success.[27]

Almost no other contemporary building involved international competition on this scale, and most of Dublin's new public buildings were locally designed and built by local firms. One practice that left a real mark on the changing skyline was that of Desmond FitzGerald, designer of the first terminal at Dublin Airport (1940); he was more mathematician than artist, and was well attuned to cost and the particular needs of clients. On that basis he won commissions for two types of building that were new to post-war Dublin: commercial office blocks and private apartments. In the case of the latter, St Ann's, located close to Donnybrook bridge, was probably the first set of luxury apartments to be built in the city and it formed a discreet addition to the Pembroke landscape. But FitzGerald's office-buildings, notably the twelve-storey O'Connell Bridge House (1965) and D'Olier House (1970), were visually obtrusive in the centre of Dublin and completely out of sympathy with the older streetscape into which they were inserted.[28]

FitzGerald was also professor of architecture in UCD through the 1950s and 1960s. His sudden resignation from that position in 1969 was one of the more tangible results of the 'Gentle Revolution', a wave of student protests in 1968–9 in the overcrowded spaces of Earlsfort Terrace, which had spilled out onto the streets. A few of the student leaders were anarchists, some young socialists, and most were willing observers. Many of the issues were practical or professional, but the rhetoric of some of the student leaders mixed Berkeley with the Sorbonne. But, as Donal McCartney has observed, what was most remarkable was the contrast between the 1930s and the 1960s in student sentiment: pre-war student activists had been right-wing champions of the explicit Catholicisation of the campus and critical of their more secular professors (even though a number of academics were centrally involved in the Censorship Board and in the Catholic press). From 1960, student societies began to make anti-clerical gestures, and a more liberal secular atmosphere developed by the mid-1960s, even though clerical students, nuns and monks still made up an eighth of the student body. The domineering college president, Michael Tierney (in office from 1947 to 1964) was a major factor in this. A combative personality, he stamped on dissent and was committed to undoing 1908 and to transforming UCD into an independent Catholic university. In this he had the close support of Archbishop McQuaid. Not for nothing did student activists attack the college leadership as being 'in the grip of hoary, toothless senility'.[29]

Tierney did not get his Catholic university, but he did manage to move UCD from its cramped city-centre quarters two miles southwards. In 1933 the college had acquired Belfield, a small suburban property off the Bray road, for playing fields and, being unable to secure affordable space to expand on the old site, Tierney masterminded the purchasing of a collection of prime houses and villa properties around Belfield, starting in 1949, a portfolio which eventually amounted to some 300 acres. The planned exodus from the inner city became a great public and political controversy through the 1950s, but Tierney's terrier-like determination won out and the die was cast in 1960, when the decision was formally endorsed at government level. State funding for the new university campus came slowly, with the faculty of Science, the first to be completed, in 1964 and the Arts faculty not until 1970. The move came just ahead of a huge expansion in student numbers, and the south-side campus has remained a site of almost continuous construction activity ever since.[30]

The creation of Belfield was a key element in the cultural geography of the city that followed the introduction of postcodes in 1961. To its west lay Dublin 6 and the salubrious districts formerly ruled from Rathmines town hall, home of the 'Rathgar accent', if comics in the Theatre Royal were to be believed. It was an area that had seen a huge expansion in private mid-market housing since the 1940s. To the east and north of Belfield lay Dublin 4, which included nearly all of the old Pembroke township, Ballsbridge, Sandymount, Donnybrook and Mount Merrion. 'D4' came to be imagined across Ireland as the heartland of old and new money, of high fashion and subversive liberal values. Many ingredients were present in the concoction. The mecca of rugby at Lansdowne Road was a landmark in the district, not far from the American-owned Intercontinental Hotel with its 315 bedrooms (opened in 1963) and the startling circular honeycomb that became the new American Embassy in 1964. They soon attracted a cluster of mid-size office buildings, housing banks and insurance companies. Across the Dodder was the Royal Dublin Society complex and the Hospital Sweepstake; beyond that a large number of high-status secondary schools (some of which had only just moved out from the city), a few Protestant, most of them Catholic. But the cultural epicentre of Dublin 4 in the 1960s was Montrose, the site chosen for the state television service (and on which Ronnie Tallon, of the Scott Tallon and Walker partnership, built a chaste modernist block, the first of several commissions from the broadcaster). Telifís Éireann began broadcasting at the end of 1961 and managed to keep its distance from church and state in the early formative years. It also succeeded in breaking the complete dominance of the British television channels which had built up during the 1950s. Their signals were picked up via the tens of thousands of aerials that now brushed the Dublin skyline. But Telifís Éireann, despite the fact that more than half of its airtime in the early years was used to recycle imported content, was an agent of cultural revolution, far more than its radio parent, and was the purveyor of a sometimes cosy, sometimes edgy, modernity to provincial Ireland, most famously so with its Saturday-night chat show. Even the most deprived inner-city home soon had a TV.[31]

It was that inner city which caused great grief for RTE (as the state broadcaster had become in 1966). A soap opera set in 'Tolka Row' ran for several years, offering a fairly safe evocation of working-class lives, but then a documentary team produced a startling exposé in 1969, claiming that police were turning a blind eye to a new vice, illegal moneylending, and that at least 500 such moneylenders were using strong-arm tactics on their terrorised debtors. It was certainly not a new phenomenon; in the Emergency there had been dark talk about illicit moneylending in the city. But so graphic was this documentary that it caused a political storm and an official tribunal of inquiry (which somewhat unfairly focused on faulty journalistic practices rather than on the underlying social issues). *A week in the life of Martin Cluxton*, a RTE drama documentary aired in 1971, had even greater impact; in a minimalist manner it told a similar story of inner-city deprivation and of Borstal, of the stigmatising of certain streets and estates by potential employers, and of the social distance between the inner north-side of Dublin 1 and the sunny south side: 'babies don't get bit by rats in Foxrock'.[32]

By 1971 the old tenements had nearly all gone. Their elimination had been hastened by events in June 1963. Two women were killed in a house collapse in Bolton Street at the beginning of the month and ten days later, after some of the heaviest rainfall in decades, another tenement house collapsed on two young girls in Fenian Street, killing them both. 'Clear the slums' declared some of the banners in the subsequent protest marches, and the Corporation moved quickly to declare hundreds of dwellings 'dangerous', placing some 900 families and 326 individuals in need of immediate rehousing. It became a government issue, and indeed Lemass kept the pressure on his less than committed Minister of Local Government, Neil Blaney. As an emergency measure the state became directly involved in house construction, widening the remit of the National Building Agency, and this body took charge of addressing the Dublin crisis. The principal outcome was Ballymun, designed as a new suburb on the northern fringes of the city on old Albert College lands (specifically purchased from UCD for the purpose). The winning design was a mix of four-, eight- and fifteen-storey apartment blocks, thirty-six in all, plus 400 houses. By 1970 some 3,265 units had been created. French-inspired in their mode of construction, the towers grabbed the headlines; they were unlike anything in the city and a complete contrast to the cottage-and-garden philosophy of a previous generation. The seven fifteen-storey blocks, when completed in 1967, were seen as marking the final triumph over the tenements, each tower named after a 1916 signatory. Amply built and centrally heated, they promised a new life. Yet when they were handed over to Dublin Corporation in 1969 the problems were already beginning: the landscaping was poor, the lifts were unreliable, the heating broke down and, critically, there were too few commercial or educational facilities in place. A much-heralded town centre did not begin until the 1970s, by which stage there was a heavy turnover of tenancies (worse than the Crumlin story of three decades before): a landscape without trees, gardens or adequate recreational space. The NBA, somewhat chastened, went on to commission standardised housing on a smaller scale in other fringe suburbs in Tallaght, Coolock and Kilbarrack.[33]

However, in a detailed analysis of the 1971 census, Joseph Brady has revealed that the primary area of social disadvantage remained the inner city (especially in the docklands wards), a zone of high unemployment, petty crime, low car ownership, two-room dwellings and often elderly householders, albeit living in twentieth-century public housing rather than tenements. Dockers' numbers were falling from the 1940s (when there had been about 3,000 casual hands), and by the mid-1970s there was only a sixth of that number of jobs, though now well regulated. Industrial employment across the whole inner city was falling steeply from the early 1960s as manufacturers large and small capitalised on rising site values to cut and relocate in the western suburbs, often beyond convenient commuting distance for the lower-paid inner-city workers. In the suburbs they could draw on labour from newer local-authority estates, which in population terms were double the size of the inner city by 1971, their families bigger, the mean age younger and the levels of deprivation somewhat less.

Brady's classification system also picked out the 'old middle-class

43. *The radical high-rise approach to public housing had come about as a national solution to a specifically Dublin problem. In the pristine early days of Ballymun, its seven towers were filled with young couples and young children, and play space was at a premium.*

suburbs' and the 'new owner-occupied suburbs' as distinct city zones by 1971, at that point holding between them two-fifths of the population, with 'flatland' one of the growing intermediate zones. But what the published census data did not reveal was the depth of these social divisions and the uncertain level of social mobility between them. Alexander Humphreys, an American sociologist who did extensive fieldwork in the city between 1949 and 1951, cautiously suggested that there was increasing upward social mobility among artisanal families, but in Roy Geary's national study of the mid-1960s, the low mobility of native Dubliners relative to incoming migrants from rural Ireland was a striking finding, which reflected very sharp differences in schooling within the city across social groups. Bertram Hutchinson came to similar conclusions in 1969: that provincial, especially urban, migrants to Dublin were 'of higher social status than the Dublin-born themselves', a reflection that less well-off country migrants now made for England and there there were educational bottlenecks in the city. The extraordinary successes of the leading inner-city Christian Brothers schools – Synge Street on the south side and O'Connell Schools on the north – producing actors and entertainers, high-flyers in business and the public service, does not disguise the fact that higher education for those from a semi-skilled or unskilled background within the city remained utterly alien. As late as 1950, about 55 per cent of those leaving primary school in the city did not proceed to any secondary education: for the girls in skilled working-class families, the pressure was to leave and enter factory work; for the boys, to start an apprenticeship. As one informant told Humphreys c.1951, most artisanal families, if they had to choose between giving a girl or a boy secondary education, would choose the girl, 'because it would give her a better chance for a good marriage ... and that is much more necessary for her than for a boy. A boy will get along if he has a good trade and the ability ...'. He found that, in general, the elder children in a family were more likely to leave school and be put to work. Among labouring families, Humphreys found that if any child stayed in education beyond national school it would be a boy, but for no more than a year or two at vocational school. In predictable contrast, he found that all the teenage children of 'white-collar' families were sent to secondary school. After 1950, Dublin's school participation rates improved somewhat, helped by the expansion of vocational and secondary places and by the free-fees initiative in 1967, but in the inner city the proportion leaving school at fourteen was still 41.5 percent in 1971, and 43.5 per cent of the city's adult population still had had no secondary education, rising to nearly three-quarters in the inner city. Thus raising the minimum school-leaving age to fifteen in 1973 actually made a difference.[34]

The area of the city undergoing the most startling change of appearance in the 1960s was the old business district from Dame Street southwards to the Canal and eastwards around St Stephen's Green towards Ballsbridge. The era of the office block came suddenly to a city ill-prepared, and the results by international standards were little short of disastrous for the central city streetscapes. It attracted some very negative reactions in the international press. The largest single block was built on the site of the Ellimans' Theatre Royal, the vast art deco building acquired by the Rank Organisation after the war. They chose to demolish the twenty-five-year-old building and develop the site: the result, Hawkins House, cost about £750,000 to build, was twelve storeys high and had 126,000 square feet to rent at a guinea a foot; it was, in the words of the conservation campaigner Frank McDonald, 'easily the most monstrous pile of architectural rubbish ever built in Dublin'. Indeed, so intrusive was it on the skyline that the Corporation planning department later moved to impose severe height controls on all new building. But just at that time (1965) the Transport Union were completing their modernist offering on the most sensitive of riverside sites beside Butt Bridge: the soaring sixteen-storey Liberty Hall, designed by a structural engineer.[35]

There were some 200 office blocks built around the city between 1960 and 1985. Many were built on sites that had taken years to assemble, a process which added to the dilapidated appearance of many prime streets in the intervening period. The office-building boom was triggered by several factors: the example of post-war English cities where a similar kind of intensive city-centre development had become commonplace, especially in London, and where financial and technical expertise in property development had been built up in the process; then there was the new legal onus on the employers of clerical and administrative staff in the city to observe the 1958 Office Premises Act, which placed many existing offices in older houses outside the law. And there was also the more aggressive policy taken by Dublin Corporation towards supposedly dangerous buildings in the wake of the Fenian Street incident. Finally, there was the quite voracious demand for office space from banks, insurance companies and, equally, from the government, the public service and the semi-state sector (note that clerical workers rose from being 9.9 per cent of the city's workforce in 1946 to 17.6 per cent in 1971). Lemass and his circle were firmly of the view that vigorous urban redevelopment was good for employment, good for Ireland's image, and maybe even a timely reward for their own supporters. Despite the passage of time, the complicity of government ministers and party supporters in the property development bonanza of the 1960s remains unclear. It was a small world, it was a new game, the regulatory culture was weak, and rules were certainly bent. Behind the anodyne corporate names were a relatively small number of very active players and new dynasties of wealth emerged, most of them with links to the Fianna Fáil party. The early property buccaneers were a cultural mix, ranging from John Byrne, a north Kerryman who made a fortune in London dance-halls before arriving in Dublin, to Mont Kavanagh, a former tank commander in the war. By 1970, developers were the butt of media and public hostility, but the concrete kept flowing.[36]

The largest of several big building firms was Crampton's, themselves based in Ballsbridge. By the mid-sixties the old Protestant firm were employing around 700, more than half of them skilled tradesmen, some in the joinery shop, most at one of about two dozen projects that they were handling at any one time. Ruth McManus has documented the human side of this story, and it is remarkable just how well adapted they became to the fast-moving upbeat Fianna Fáil-dominated business world and how many of the prestige projects came their way. Collen's, another old Protestant building firm, seems to have adapted equally well, regularly employing up to 150 men on major projects. As John Walsh has shown, they played a critical role in the modernisation of the port, or rather the redesign of its newly reclaimed outer sections, to accommodate 'ro-ro' ferries. The earliest such facilities in the 1950s were blacked by the stevedores for some years, but Collen's designed more advanced facilities that were completed just ahead of the launch of the B & I car-ferry service in 1968. Shortly afterwards, Collen's built two vast container terminals on some thirty-six acres of reclaimed land. The character of the whole port was transformed within a decade. Overall ship tonnage rose from 2.7 million in 1938 to 5.9 million by 1972, but ship numbers grew more slowly: it was a case of larger vessels sourcing coal and other basic commodities much further afield than Cumbria.[37]

A radical change in the occupational make-up of the city was well established by the 1960s. For working-class men, casual work in all its forms was greatly diminished, and for women domestic service, especially full-time live-in employment, had shrunk dramatically since the 1930s. The Cattle Market, which as late as 1957 was handling nearly a quarter of a million fat stock during the season, went into a steep decline in the 1960s, with changes in cattle wholesaling (the spread of the out-of-town marts) and in the nature of the Anglo-Irish cattle trade (the rise in the export of stores), and in 1973 the market fell silent and was demolished. Light industry in the city, which had flourished in the protectionist 1930s, did not benefit from government policy in the 1960s and was marking time. The Anglo-Irish Free Trade Agreement of 1965 (despite a five-year grace period for Irish manufacturers) threatened many of the processing firms working for the home market, and the chocolate makers and the car-assembly firms knew that their days were numbered. Even one of the most successful post-war industries, Glen Abbey, had only a short future in 1970: it was the creation of the Barnes brothers, who had begun a small clothes manufacturing business in Clanbrassil Street in 1939 and after the war had moved their business out to Tallaght (before it was a suburb), concentrating on the manufacture of men's knitwear. Glen Abbey worked in alliance with Dunnes Stores, the first nationwide supermarket chain, and became a textbook success in the 1960s, widening its product range and developing overseas markets to become a publicly quoted company with a suburban workforce of 1,100 by the end of the decade. The industrial flight to the suburbs had also created factory clusters in Finglas and along the Long Mile Road in the south-west of the city, their workers usually young and disproportionately female. Soft-drinks and confectionery manufacturers all moved out, Cadbury from East Wall to Coolock, Jacob's abandoning their historic Bishop Street factory for a more flexible site in Tallaght in 1975, where Collen's created what became the largest industrial estate in the country and attracted international blue-chip companies (IBM, Wellcome, General Motors) to locate on their water-abundant estate. Powers and Jameson's, in a new embrace with Cork Distillers, abandoned manufacturing in the capital altogether in the early 1970s. Of the old firms, only Guinness remained unmoved. And one comparatively new firm, Jefferson Smurfit, cardboard box and packaging manufacturers, retained their base beside the lower Dodder as they concentrated on corrugated paper and exploited the opportunities of free trade. It was the classic case of a protection-era micro-factory seizing the opportunities of the 1960s, both at home and in the UK. A public company in 1964, it grew in an extraordinary fashion over the next generation to become a vast multinational conglomerate, a global business that far outgrew the Irish market but retained its base in Dublin 6.[38]

In 1969 the Irish Women's Liberation Movement and the Irish Family Planning Association were founded in Dublin. They had their champions in the media and indeed many actually worked in the media (notably *The Irish Times*). The pre-war controls on contraception and evil literature had been openly questioned in middle-class Dublin for some years, and while literary censorship controls were greatly relaxed in 1967, the ban on literature explaining family planning was not lifted for another dozen years. But Catholic doctors were in limited circumstances prescribing the pill. However, the papal encyclical *Humanae vitae* in 1968 and its unalloyed ban caused heart-searching, encouraging reformers to take direct action against the restrictions on contraception. A 'Fertility Guidance Clinic' was discreetly established in Merrion Square in 1969 by a group of seven medical practitioners, who offered women free contraceptive advice and assistance, and thus avoided legal prosecution. But the most celebrated moment came in 1971 when a group of forty-seven women returned on the train from Belfast with supposedly vast supplies of condoms to tease the customs officials at Amiens Street station into confrontation. Before the end of the decade, one Dublin magazine was proclaiming that a revolution in sexual habits was underway in the city, with opinion-poll evidence that 57 per cent of Dublin women in the eighteen to thirty-four age cohort now believed that sex outside marriage was permissible in certain circumstances, and with even more believing that it was far more common than five years previously. Sexual liberation of a different kind – the legalisation of homosexuality – was still far off, but at least the issue had tentatively entered the public domain in the 1960s, facilitated by the openness to British media. But whatever the law, there had been an openly gay coterie of artists during the war and the veteran couple Micheál Mac Liammóir and Hilton Edwards who had run the Gate Theatre for three decades were untouchable, the coming of Irish television only adding to Mac Liammóir's iconic status. Legal protection, however, was not achieved until 1993, and it took an epic sixteen-year legal battle (in Dublin and in Strasbourg) to achieve that landmark.[39]

Archbishop McQuaid stood down in 1972 and was dead in little more than a year. By then, the palace in Drumcondra was a quieter place, for the last Dublin prince of the church had become a permanent figure of controversy in the media, feared and disliked for his exalted view of episcopal authority; he in turn found the new world of television and public image intensely distasteful. And the generation of Dubliners who had been educated in the many schools he had helped to create displayed no particular loyalty towards him. But McQuaid and the political old guard had a final chance to put their stamp on the city's history with the fiftieth anniversary of the Easter Rebellion in 1966. Neither McQuaid nor Lemass, with an impeccable revolutionary record, chose to exploit the event. The low-intensity IRA 'border campaign' early in Lemass's premiership was perhaps a warning, and the destruction of Nelson's Pillar in February 1966, carried out by an IRA cell, discouraged grandstanding. The lively street protests of the openly Marxist Connolly Youth Movement (aligned with the Moscow-loyal Irish Workers' Party) was also a portent of changed times. Lemass's emollient message of outward-looking modernity did not go unchallenged in republican or socialist circles, but the Easter 1966 celebration brought together some 600 veterans, a huge military display and a crowd of 200,000, and it turned out to be a supremely calm affair. When the rebuilt Abbey Theatre, now firmly attached to the state, was reopened on the old site two months later, even the theatre riots of half a century earlier were harmlessly caricatured on stage in front of President de Valera. Plans were made for a Garden of Remembrance in Parnell Square, but initially this was a private initiative, only subsequently adopted by government. When it came to be officially opened and blessed, McQuaid saw to it that the event was an exclusively Catholic affair. One of the big commemorative events earlier that year had been the unveiling in College Green of Edward Delaney's striking copper-cast statue of Thomas Davis, Young Irelander and Protestant. The following year, his mildly subversive statue of Wolfe Tone, United Irishman and Protestant, was finally unveiled at the north-east corner of St Stephen's Green.[40]

Lemass retired late in 1966, dying five years later. During the years when he held the reins – whether at the Leopardstown races or the Dublin Horse Show, in Roland's restaurant in the Russell or the Shelbourne Bar – there had been an uninhibited display of new wealth in his city. Historians still debate whether this was what the pipe-smoking teetotaller from Capel Street with a fondness for the horses had really wanted.

12

MILLENNIUM CITY: 1972–2000

Measuring Dublin

'A thousand years old and a million strong': the civic commemorations in 1988 celebrating the first Viking settlement on the Liffey were based on a harmless but significant misreading of the historical evidence. Claims for the city's population size were closer to the mark: in Greater Dublin, i.e. the area constituting the city and the county, numbers had risen from 852,219 in 1971 to 1,024,429 in 1991, and 1,122,821 in 2002. Myles Wright's regional plan for Dublin in 1967 envisaged something even larger, a city-region that would include north Wicklow, south Meath and north Kildare. As part of this process, Wright recommended the creation of a series of protective green wedges (rather like Abercrombie's green belt), to lie between four proposed satellite towns, Tallaght, Clondalkin, Lucan and Blanchardstown; each of these towns he proposed should be allowed to grow to a maximum of 60,000–100,000 inhabitants. Wright predicted that the overall population of his region (city, county and commuter belt) would be 1.2 million by 1985. He was close: it reached nearly 1.3 million. The million mark had actually been crossed by 1971, but growth in the city and county of Dublin was actually slowing: between 1981 and 1996 the population grew by a mere 5.5 per cent. One element of this was the crude birth rate, which in Dublin as elsewhere in the Republic fell for the first time quite dramatically during the 1980s. However, in the wider region now being designated as the Greater Dublin Area (GDA), i.e. the four counties of Dublin, Meath, Kildare and Wicklow, population over the same fifteen years grew by 9.0 per cent. But even that was modest by Dublin's standards in the 1960s.

With a million Dubliners, the city could claim to be a European megalopolis, even if its demographic size relative to the Irish Republic as a whole was no longer growing, as had been the case for much of the twentieth century. In 1936, Dublin city and county had held nearly a fifth of the state's population (19.7 per cent) and that share rose through the era of rural emigration and provincial stagnation to 25.5 per cent in 1961, then through the booming sixties to 28.6 in 1971. But this was the ceiling; in 2002 Dublin city and county held virtually the same share. By comparison, the four-county GDA share rose from 26.1 per cent in 1936 to 35.7 in 1971 and continued to rise sharply into the 1980s. However, it too had nearly stabilised by the end of the century (it held 39.2 per cent of the Republic's population by 2002).[1]

Whatever the reasons for this stabilisation, it reflected a policy success, for decentralisation remained a standard goal of all political parties. But what went unrecognised in this was the longer established decentralisation of benefit – specifically, the net transfer of tax income paid by Dubliners to other regions within the state, narrowing the income differential between the metropolitan area and all other regions, which apart from the social equity argument may have had some effects on migration. The provincial drift to Dublin – such a powerful factor through most of its history – became far less important in the late twentieth century. More than a quarter of the city and county's inhabitants had been born in one of the thirty-one other counties in 1971 (26.3 per cent), but by 2002 the figure had fallen to 16.8 per cent, and if the transient and now much swollen third-level student population could be subtracted at the latter point, the proportion would be even lower. But the proportion born *outside* Ireland was rising: 6.6 per cent in 1971, 10.6 per cent in 2002. And while transient students may also have affected this trend, there was by the final years of the century the first wave of an international migration on a scale not seen since the late seventeenth-century Huguenot inflow: Asian students, African refugees and the first of many EU workers coming to Dublin, taking advantage of the opening of the European labour market after 1992. Most of these were young adults, some planning to move on, most to stay. Rainbow Dublin had finally arrived.[2]

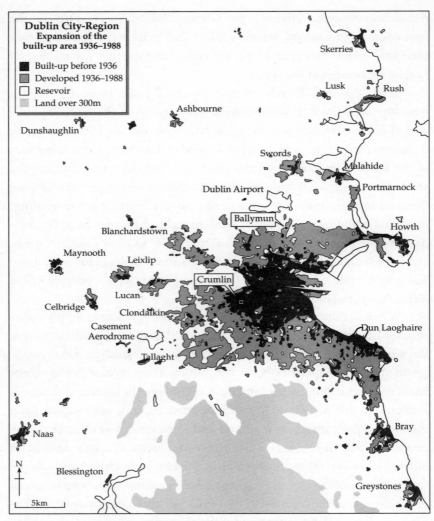

Map 6: The growth of Greater Dublin 1936–1988.

But if the overall advance of population was sedate, the growth of
Dublin's urban site was anything but. Arnold Horner has suggested a
jump in the land surface being urbanised each year between 1973 and 1988,
with the browning of some 1,100 acres p.a., far above the annual average
between 1936 and 1972. At the same time the inner city continued to lose
population, a trend not reversed until the 1990s when tax-driven urban
renewal schemes and the sprouting of city-centre apartment blocks dramatically altered the pattern. In retrospect, it can be seen that the toxic
combination of a weak and ill-regulated physical planning system, and a

legal system based on the 1937 constitution that gave an exceptional level of protection to private property rights, was little short of disastrous in terms of the optimum management of the city rim in an era of rapidly changing land values.

During this time, an era of prolonged if uneven inflation when over-all living standards were rising as never before, the gap widened between those who benefited – the four-fifths of Dubliners who were the owner-occupiers or were tenants of privately rented accommodation – and those who did not – the one-fifth of families who inhabited Corporation or local authority housing. More than in the past, there was a strong cor-relation between housing status and income. Unemployment levels, which rose during the 1970s with the decline of manual jobs and worsened in the 1980s, remained stubbornly high well until the mid-1990s, when over 18 per cent of the insured labour force was on the live register. One report, using early 1990s data, estimated that 67 per cent of local authority house-holds in the city fell below the poverty line, admittedly using very differ-ent poverty criteria from those being applied half a century previously. But it was still a sign of the abiding inequality of city life that the odds on local authority renters being defined as 'poor' were thirty-five times greater than for house-owners or mortgage-holders. It was really only in the final three years of the century with the onset of the huge construction boom that unemployment levels in the central black-spot wards shrank noticeably – for a while.[3]

Another dimension of inner-city problems was traffic congestion. A Dublin Transportation Study in 1971 marked the birth of new think-ing: it proposed an outer orbital ring-road for the city to end congestion and transform access to both port and airport. It envisaged that this route would necessitate heavy tunnelling under Dublin Bay. This was highly controversial. Much of the early opposition focused on the tunnel and its likely disastrous impact on the south-side coastal environment. That element of the plan was eventually abandoned, but the first part of what became a great C-shaped motorway, the fondly named 'Western Parkway', was built to the west of the city in 1986–90, with the sections stretching north-eastwards and south-eastwards being constructed over the follow-ing fifteen years. This, the M50, had the predictable effect, long before the first cars raced along it, of drastically reconfiguring property values, com-muting patterns and the basic economic geography of the city. One of the great beneficiaries of the M50 was the new town of Tallaght, one of the future satellites picked out by Myles Wright in 1967. Its early growth in the 1970s and 1980s was chaotic, but by the time it became the headquarters of the new South Dublin County Council in 1994 it had developed a diversity of retail, commercial and educational facilities and a third-level institute, and then in 1998 it became home for a giant hospital campus incorporating the Meath, the Adelaide and the Harcourt Street Children's Hospitals.[4]

The hospital complex came after three decades of amalgamation and resettlement of the city's other old voluntary hospitals – St Vincent's, Jervis Street, Sir Patrick Dun's all reappearing or being rebranded in modern suburban guises. Apart from hospitals, other service institutions also fled to the suburbs – the amalgamated banks (with Allied Irish Banks (AIB) settling on Royal Dublin Society land in Ballsbridge, the Mint to Sandyford), insurance companies, and the old Protestant schools (notably Wesley, High School and St Andrews) all travelling southwards in the 1970s. Only Trinity College stood firm in the centre, despite entering a period of massive growth in student numbers. But perhaps the single event that had most impact on Greater Dublin in these decades was the decision by the computer-chip giant Intel in 1989 to site its European manufacturing plant at Leixlip. It opened there in 1993 and soon had a workforce larger than that of Guinness at its peak – around 4,500. Its presence had a huge multiplier effect on west Dublin and north Kildare; the state's Industrial Development Authority (IDA) had already attracted a number of major computer-related firms to the Dublin region (as well as to Cork, Shannon and Galway), but its success in luring and holding Intel was the catalyst for drawing in a whole cluster of global hardware (and later software) corporations to the region. It is a measure of greater Dublin's attraction that such a development could occur despite the chaotic planning in the region and the pervasive traffic congestion, the high cost of living and defective communications. An IDA bias against Dublin in the 1960s and early 1970s was reversed in 1978, although a rhetorical commitment to industrial decentralisation persisted long afterwards. And by 1993 many of the infrastructural deficits across greater Dublin were at last being addressed with the help of EU Structural Funds.[5]

Resurrecting Dublin

With a spread-eagled urban region and a de-industrialising core, was the city as a social entity dying by the end of the twentieth century? Or if not dying, was there a slow termination of the historical bonds and sense of communal identity shared by the million residents of the Dublin region? Or, as Arthur Gibney, then one of the city's leading architects, posed the question in 1988, was the city 'over-run by the inhabitants of its hinterland' and by their provincial values, with a civil service, a police force and a party system 'conspicuously non-urban in birth and cultural background', sharing a common desire for better roads to the exclusion of civic values? He suggested that as a result of the mass suburbanisation of the indigenous Dubliners, 'the myth and memory of city life has nearly disappeared'. Quite apart from the impact of intrusive road schemes cutting through neighbourhoods, some of the cultural elements that had for generations shaped perceptions of community were becoming dramatically weaker. Even half a century earlier, the American sociologist Alexander Humphreys had noted that neighbourly solidarity was disappearing, not least in the new housing estates, and that extended family networks were shrinking. But far more tangible by the late twentieth century was the decline in religious practice and of respect for the cloth in Catholic Dublin. When Pope John Paul II arrived in the city at the beginning of his 1979 trip to Ireland, an observer of the million-strong crowd at the Wellington Monument in the Phoenix Park would have assumed that the state of the Catholic Church had never been stronger. But seminary numbers were falling and much worse was to come. In the following decades, the standing of the Church in Dublin was weakened by conservative leadership, then by a torrent of court revelations about clerical sexual abuse, followed by growing evidence of institutional cruelty in the reform schools and the Magdalene homes run by Catholic religious orders, stretching back many decades. There was a bitter public controversy in 1993 when part of High Park convent in Drumcondra (the old reformatory) was sold to a developer and 133 bodies of former inmates – 'fallen women' – were exhumed from the graveyard; there was embarrassing confusion as to the number and identities of the women interred, most or all of whom had toiled for years in the convent's commercial laundry. A taboo was lifted by such incidents, and much that had been privately suspected became the stuff of constant public debate. The corrosive effects of all this had still quite a distance to go in 2000, but falling mass attendance was making many of McQuaid's great churches obsolescent before their time.[6]

Less dramatic was the decline in the power of organised labour in the city. Through the Lemass era, links between the state and the big trade unions had greatly strengthened and membership continued to rise until c.1980. And while the role of these unions as 'social partners' in public policy-making became even stronger towards the end of the century, overall membership fell sharply. Many of the international 'sunrise' industries and the big multiple stores outlawed union membership and, more generally, the discipline of the trade and the family traditions of craft association were progressively weakened by the decline of manufacturing and the rise of office and professional employment. The one great bastion of union control remained the public services, the importance of which within the city economy grew relentlessly.[7]

In a more generic way, civic identity and loyalty to one's place were being weakened by commercial and technological change. Familiar names were falling by the way in Henry Street and Grafton Street, with the inward march of the British multiples in fashion and recreational products, operating on tighter margins and often lower labour costs: BHS, Marks & Spencer, Laura Ashley. The old department stores increasingly became the preserve of international concessionaires (although their survival was helped by the fact that both Switzer's and Clery's were for the first time run by women for many years). Many smaller specialist shops succumbed in the inflationary 1970s and depressed 1980s, and were not replaced. The same applied to eating out too, with the demise of Jammet's restaurant and its specialist staff of nearly seventy in 1967, and the opening nearby of the first McDonald's outlet in 1974. Haute cuisine, which had flourished briefly in post-war Dublin, was gone by the mid-1970s; the Russell Hotel, the other early Egon Ronay mecca, was demolished in 1974. Nouvelle cuisine emerged but in smaller, more discreet places, most of them in the southern suburbs. Commercial night-life did remain in the inner city, but where in the 1960s it had been all about glittering ballrooms (notably the Four Provinces, the National and the gleaming Olympic), disco ended all that; by the 1980s things became far more fragmented, although Leeson Street with its seventeen Georgian basement clubs was 'the strip' that catered for a diversity of late-night appetites. However, it was a suburban working-class barn of a ballroom, the Stardust in Artane, that caught world headlines in February 1981: it could draw up to 3,000 patrons, but there were some 800 present on the night of the infamous fire, when forty-eight were killed and 128 seriously injured.[8]

The growth of air travel also had profound cultural effects. Aer Lingus, firmly anchored in Dublin, remained a state-owned agency committed to building up tourism; thus the growth of Dublin as a tourist destination from the 1950s was closely connected to the airline's promotions and its close collaboration with hoteliers. North American carriers had been first to seize on the idea of promoting Dublin (and by extension Ireland) as a destination in the early 1950s, but Aer Lingus operating a North American service from 1960 became the principal agent of growth thereafter. The rise of the sun holiday and of package tourism out of Ireland came a little later, and when cheap air travel came to Dublin in the early 1990s – initiated by the commercial carrier Ryanair – families in every social class could afford the faraway break. One consequence was the huge growth of business at Dublin airport (with a 9.7 per cent passenger growth p.a. through the 1990s). Another more modest effect was the decline of local family recreation, whether to Bray, to Merrion Strand or to Dollymount, which up to the 1960s had attracted huge numbers out of the city in warm weather – and the abandonment of open-air baths and other Victorian relics.

The revolutionary cheapening of distance in every sense has been universal since the 1970s, its implications not fully recognised even by 2000. But Dubliners (and Irish people generally) who up until the 1980s had to cope with a particularly under-resourced state telephone service adopted mobile telephony in its earliest manifestations with particular relish. In a low-density city with overloaded city traffic, the fall in communication costs, local and distant, helped reduce a comparative economic disadvantage, even if there were hidden social costs. In the light of these, can one really talk about Dublin as a social organism by the turn of the millennium, what with its emptying churches, its forgotten trade halls, its homogenised high streets and suburban malls, its sanitised beer-halls and international coffee docks? There are, however, some compelling reasons for a positive view.

The political fact that the Irish state and Irish governments enjoyed greatly enhanced prestige and international profile from the 1970s brought lustre, profit and pride to its capital city. Admittedly, the spill-over of the Northern Ireland crisis split the Fianna Fáil government in 1970 and exposed a level of complicity in the arming of the Provisional IRA in the

North which threatened to compromise political stability in the Republic. More immediately shocking was a series of car-bombing incidents in
the city centre in 1973 and 1974, the last of which, on 17 May 1974, killed
twenty-six people in three separate car-bombs in Talbot Street, Parnell
Street and Nassau Street. The bombings took place during the Loyalist
Workers' Strike and the cars involved had been stolen that morning in
Belfast, but the motive behind the attacks was unclear. The huge death toll
stunned the city for weeks; implausible suspicions as to British state col-
lusion later became rather less implausible and have never been resolved.
The collateral effects of the Northern Troubles were indeed felt in Dublin
in many ways during the 1970s, not least in a huge growth in indictable
crime, falling detection rates and the proliferation of illegal firearms.[9]

But it was also the decade when Europe came to Dublin. The Irish
government assumed the presidency of the EEC for the first time in 1975
and with considerable fanfare hosted an EEC Council meeting in Dublin
Castle, two years after Irish and British entry into the Community. Despite
opposition from the Left, entry into the EEC had evoked far stronger
public support in Dublin than in London, coming as it did against the
backdrop of the Northern Troubles and in the wake of the first oil crisis.
The meeting was seen as something of a triumph for Irish diplomacy. The
return of the European Council every few years thereafter prompted the
Office of Public Works into repeated refurbishments of Dublin Castle
and then, prior to the 1990 summit, of other government buildings, which
were greatly extended and modernised, with UCD finally abandoning the
old College of Science building in Merrion Street. Charles Haughey, the
Taoiseach of the time, thereby secured his own Elysée Palace at a discount.

The 1980s were a decade of short-lived governments and parliamentary instability, but one unlikely dividend for Dublin was 'the Gregory
deal'. Haughey, the wealthy (or so it seemed), republican (or at least populist) Fianna Fáil politician who dominated the decade, needed one vote
in the Dáil to return to government in February 1982. The most divisive
figure of his generation and less than scrupulous in his methods to win
and hold power, he always had the capacity to surprise. He secured support from an unlikely source, Tony Gregory: the product of a north-side
tenement, Gregory had won a scholarship to O'Connell Schools and then
one to UCD, and had become a gifted teacher and a republican activist in
the 1960s (when he was heavily involved in the Dublin Housing Action
Committee (DHAC)). He was by no means the first to push for special

treatment for the inner city, but was exceptional both in his dogged advocacy and his life story. Very few had made it from the tenements to the higher grades of public service employment. In 1982, Gregory won a Dáil seat as a left-wing independent and entered Leinster House, a lone figure in casual dress. Within weeks he agreed to give Haughey the vital one vote in return for a long list of commitments – including government funding for some 2,000 houses in the inner city, the development of the now derelict Custom House Docks, a twenty-seven-acre site that the state was to acquire, and the creation of 3,746 jobs. It was an extraordinary compact that would have cost tens of millions. The Port and Docks Board, who for more than a decade had sought to become a development agency itself, felt cheated. However, the Haughey government collapsed at the end of that year and with it the Gregory programme. But the injection of Exchequer funds into the Corporation's housing budget during 1982 could not be recalled, and in the years following 'the deal', fine low-density public housing was erected in some of the most run-down neighbourhoods, notably on Summerhill and in the City Quay parish. And the problems of inner Dublin were brought to national attention.

The 1986 Urban Renewal Act, the product of Garret FitzGerald's coalition government, stirred further controversy: it introduced a suite of tax incentives and capital allowances designed to promote commercial development in parts of the docklands, in the north-east inner city and along the full length of the quays, and (a Gregory legacy) it established an autonomous agency, the Custom House Docks Development Authority, totally independent of the Corporation. Haughey adopted and expanded this policy after his return to power in 1987, with Gregory now a passive backbench observer. But more than the media or the professional planners, he had made a compelling case for inner-city regeneration and he kept the focus on the catastrophic eclipse of manual employment and the continuing low levels of educational participation. Heroin addiction had spread alarmingly among unemployed young adult males in the inner north side in 1979, and in its wake the levels of crime in the city centre soared and the city's prison population doubled in a decade (leading to the multiple occupancy of Mountjoy jail's old single cells). More sophisticated drug gangs emerged who were directly profiting from the opiate epidemic. This gave an added urgency to the case for central government intervention in inner-city matters. However, the focus of successive governments in the 1980s was on political subversives, not illicit drug wholesalers, and as a result heroin consumption became embedded in many working-class neighbourhoods.[10]

But if there was no grand programme of regeneration, there was a cluster of major city-centre projects that operated to mitigate the centrifugal tendencies of the age: in two of these the inspiration was entirely commercial, in two others public agencies took the lead. The commercial projects were predictable: two large retail centres that were inserted fairly brutally into prime shopping districts (the Ilac Centre off Henry Street in 1981, and the Stephen's Green Shopping Centre at the top of Grafton Street in 1988). The culmination of two decades of site purchases, corporate deals, legal disputes, spectacular bankruptcies and public controversy, these were ugly developments, but proved highly profitable. The Ilac project was all that was left of a naively ambitious Corporation plan of 1964 to develop on its own bat the whole precinct between Capel Street and O'Connell Street using powers of compulsory purchase. Both of the 1980s' centres were large (Stephen's Green had 100 units to offer) and each provided the novelty of covered car parks. Between them they helped maintain discretionary retail spending within the central district. The city faced competition from some twenty-eight suburban malls by then, most copying the innovative Stillorgan Shopping Centre that had opened on the Bray Road in 1966.

Later in the 1980s, two public initiatives were hatched that changed the inner city: the International Financial Services Centre (IFSC) on the Custom House Docks site, and the Temple Bar project on the south side of the Liffey, west of O'Connell Bridge. Both were run by statutory agencies completely outside the control of the Corporation, both were developed in the public gaze, and neither escaped controversy, not least because of their links with Charles Haughey. Even before returning to power in 1987, he was captivated by the idea of a special economic zone on the dockland site that had featured so largely in the Gregory deal five years previously, an enclave that would be the location for international banks and finance houses, offering them a discount on corporation tax liabilities for a set period. The IFSC was quickly established on the twenty-seven-acre site beside the river. It proved a well-timed move and drew in big names from the City of London during the 1990s, firms that were willing to locate back-office functions in this Irish equivalent of Canary Wharf. The initial development agency built apartments and a hotel, principally for the young professionals working in the new zone. And so successful was it that a remodelled agency, the Dublin Docklands Development Authority, emerged in 1997 with a wider brief. The lower port district, east of the IFSC, was utterly transformed over the next decade, a ramshackle dockland landscape replaced by a string of substantial office developments. It was financed in a series of private-public partnerships, with spillover effects further north with the private development of the Eastpoint Business Park on fifty acres of newly reclaimed land. The whole process went almost unnoticed by the city at large until public transport arrived. The two-centuries-old business district around Dame Street and College Green lost status quite suddenly as corporate law firms, stockbrokers and international banks were drawn eastwards to the IFSC district. Perhaps more than any other city development towards the end of the twentieth century, this great rebuilding of the docklands, north and later south of the river, 'a mini-Singapore ... now seeping out of the edges of old Dublin', symbolised the unquenchable optimism of builders and bankers. It was soon to prove spectacularly misjudged.[11]

Temple Bar was different. The late seventeenth-century network of streets lying between Dame Street and the Liffey were somewhat down at heel when they were chosen by CIE as an optimum site for a city bus terminal in 1976, and the company proceeded to acquire large numbers of shops and houses as they came on the market. Short-term shop tenants came to dominate the area, giving it the bohemian atmosphere of London's Portobello Road or New York's Greenwich Village, but there were few residents. Then, in 1986, a coalition of conservationists and local traders lobbied first the Corporation, then the government to save the area and grant special tax status for its development. Haughey was persuaded, CIE had to back off, and the idea expanded: Temple Bar would become a 'left bank' cultural hub, to be funded by European structural funds now becoming available for innovative urban regeneration projects. Temple Bar Properties (TBP), a non-profit agency, was established in 1991 to realise the plan, and over the following eight years some IR£22 million from Europe plus IR£15 million in national exchequer funding were spent on cultural and infrastructural investments within the twenty-eight-acre site. TBP also borrowed heavily to fund retail and residential development in the area, and over IR£100 million of commercial investment followed. A consortium of fourteen young UCD-trained architects (Group 91) won the initial competition to design the new cultural spaces and pedestrian streets, and with great flair they created a quite distinct neighbourhood in

*44. The International Financial Services Centre: the foundation stone for one of
the earliest blocks was laid by An Taoiseach Charles Haughey in September 1988,
bringing together the developers, financiers and senior civil servants who, for a
variety of motives, had championed this huge riverside regeneration scheme, a
scheme that over twenty years utterly transformed the inner port, shifted the central
business district downstream, and gave direct employment to some 25,000 people.*

the old city waterfront, complete with ten cultural centres and three open
spaces. Their plans were heavily influenced by then fashionable European
critics of architectural modernism, who rejected brutal functionalism
and rigid urban zoning and emphasised instead a respect for the inherited urban fabric and for the primacy of the pedestrian in street design.
Commercially, the new Temple Bar was a runaway success, new fortunes
were made, high-end apartments commanded top prices and the residential population grew ten-fold in the course of the 1990s. Its pubs and restaurants earned harmless notoriety in international media. But by 2000
it was plain for all to see that there was a huge gap between the cultural
theories adumbrated by Group 91 and the realities of 'nighttown' by the
Liffey. The 'youth recreational consumer demand', innocently envisaged in
the original application for European funding in 1990, had pretty successfully overwhelmed the lofty precepts of the 'New Urbanism'.[12]

But there were also suburban development hotspots. Wholesale
commercial activity increasingly concentrated on what had started out

45. The old suburban railway lines from Howth to the city and south-eastwards to Bray were electrified in 1981–4. The Dublin Area Rapid Transit (DART) was later extended northwards to Malahide and southwards to Greystones. Despite initial scepticism, traffic volumes soon exceeded projections. The DART helped define the middle-class world of the south-eastern suburbs, and a DART accent was deemed to be the patois of the youthful masses who packed the trains.

as industrial estates when first developed in the 1950s, notably in Finglas and along the Long Mile Road on the south-western approaches. Then, on the north side, the airport, which remained in state ownership, became a major centre of secondary employment, although if the imaginative plans from the 1950s to make Dublin into a major European airline hub had come off, the potential spin-offs would have been much greater. The former Albert College beside Ballymun was another catalyst: the eighty-five-acre site that was sold by UCD when its Agriculture faculty retreated south across the river became the campus for a new technical institute in 1979. This evolved to become Dublin City University in 1989, developing a strong business, science and technology mix that went some way towards addressing the low uptake of third-level education in the north of the city, its success as a garden-centred campus shaped by its inspirational designer Deirdre O'Connor. On the south side, the massive development of Belfield proceeded inexorably, but as it took place within an old zone of high amenity the impact in the immediate area was simply to inflate house prices. Further south, the Sandyford Industrial Park near Foxrock and the Leopardstown Racecourse was an unusual choice for commercial development in the 1960s, but lying within the Dún Laoghaire-Rathdown Council boundary and close to the future M50, it eventually (after thirty years) turned out to be highly profitable, and predictably it helped displace high-street retailers in the southern suburbs.[13]

Imagining Dublin

But what of more intangible things? What part did they play in reshaping the idea of Dublin? The big spectator sports had since their nineteenth-century inception divided rather than united Dubliners. Rugby was nurtured in higher status secondary schools, Catholic and Protestant, and the city's rival rugby clubs drew on this pool and thrived on ancient local rivalries. The code remained rooted in the south-side middle-class world, and even the winter internationals in Lansdowne Road had only sectional appeal until the commercialisation of the sport in the 1990s. Throughout the twentieth century, soccer had a stronger, albeit passive, following in the city itself; there were eight professional clubs linked to the Football Association of Ireland (FAI) when it was established after partition in 1921. Dublin clubs were linked to large employers (Guinness, Jacob's) or drew their support from particular districts (Shelbourne from around Ringsend; Shamrock Rovers, more broadly, the suburban south side; St Patrick's from Inchicore and Kilmainham; Home Farm from Drumcondra and Whitehall; and Bohemians drawing wide north-side support). But general interest in soccer was heightened when television brought English first-division games into every home, and in the eighties and nineties there were moments of universal soccer fever when the national Irish team performed Goliath-slaying feats in Lansdowne Road under the eye of Jack Charlton (even though few of the heroes were home-grown). There was even occasional talk of an English premier club being relocated to Dublin (famously so in the late 1990s when the FAI chose to block a move by a Dublin consortia to bring Wimbledon FC to the city).[14]

In the case of the GAA, with its strong club and county structure, there was always the potential for a strong Dublin team to excite city and county. But until the 1950s Dublin teams were dominated by provincial players, and not necessarily the best, so that there was little silverware for Dublin in either club or county championships, whether in hurling, football or camogie (the variant of hurling played by women, governed by slightly different rules). Dublin's modest status changed in the 1950s, and the ascendancy of St Vincent's club is usually given the credit. Established in the new garden suburb of Marino in 1931, the club was unusual in deliberately keeping country talent out. With strong Christian Brothers coaching and the abundant open spaces of Marino on which to practise, St Vincent's provided most of the players for the Dublin senior football team that achieved national dominance in the late 1950s, thereby generating for the first time (or so it was claimed) a degree of 'emotional tribalism' in the city and introducing 'the spirit of Knocknagow'. Seventy-three thousand spectators saw Dublin beat Derry in the All-Ireland final in Croke Park in 1958, and some 25,000 stood outside listening on loudspeakers. The country practices of bonfires and after-match parades were adopted, but they were concentrated on Marino and Donnycarney. Nevertheless the GAA's popularity was permanently strengthened across the city, as was evident by the wide range of clubs involved in the next run of national victories in the 1970s, when Dublin's double-blue colours flew in the heartlands of soccer. But Croke Park, despite modernisation in the 1930s and 1950s, was unable to cope with the autumn crowds that the championships were attracting (over 90,000 squeezed into one All-Ireland final in 1961). The stadium was entirely rebuilt between 1993 and 2005 at a cost of 260 million euros, 58 per cent of which was raised by the Association's national fund-raising, most of the rest from the state lottery. By 2000 it was by far the most prominent landmark on the north side of the city and is remarkable in being not just one of the largest sports stadia in Europe but much the largest created by an amateur sporting organisation. On completion, it chose to open its doors to the 'foreign' sports that it had been established to resist, but that was a sign of strength, not of weakness.[15]

Dublin supporters developed a particular mythology about Hill 16, the open north terrace of Croke Park, supposedly built from the rubble of O'Connell Street. The anthem of choice was 'Sweet Molly Malone', the fictive lady of the streets. The construction of such personae and, by extension, the attribution of distinct cultural habits to its citizenry (be it 'the cits' or 'the Dubs') was a very old game, whether in the press, on the stage, or in the efforts of anonymous ballad-mongers. But since the 1920s there had been a number of prominent Dublin performers who drew heavily on the city for their art and achieved celebrity far beyond their city in so doing. In internationalising elements of Dublin's cultural past, they helped not only to raise the global profile of the city, but intangibly altered the ways that Dubliners thought about themselves. The Abbey Theatre interpreters of O'Casey are an early example, some of whom took their skills as far as Hollywood. In the comic tradition, Jimmy O'Dea looms large: born in Bridgefoot Street, he had a professional career that ran from 1918 to 1964; he dominated the Gaiety pantomime for at least two decades and toured extensively in Ireland and Britain. His stage personae included the all-knowing street trader 'Biddy Mulligan, pride of the Coombe', and she travelled well. Like a few of his Abbey contemporaries, O'Dea made a successful transition to the screen, but never permanently left Dublin. His junior foil, Maureen Potter, moved comfortably between stage and television, and over a sixty-year career on the pantomime stage she cultivated her own cast of precisely etched 'Dubs', pompous males and coarse-cut females, gently exposing the class divisions of the city.[16]

In the 1960s a cluster of musical groups emerged out of Dublin that drew a rather different kind of spotlight on the city: The Dubliners formed as a folk ballad group with a Joycewards nod in 1962, and The Chieftains in 1963 as a five-piece band adapting traditional instruments and melodies. Both began with small live sessions in the city and (in the case of the Chieftains) local recording contracts, and each achieved enduring celebrity far beyond Ireland. Their popularity internationalised interest in the Irish ballad tradition and in Irish traditional music, and made the music pub a major ingredient in Dublin (and Irish) tourism, with hundreds of imitators of the original venue, O'Donoghue's of Merrion Row. Then came Dublin rock: Thin Lizzy (1969–85), a mercurial band led by the mesmeric Phil Lynott, the voice of a generation (for whom a statue was erected off Grafton Street, almost two decades after his death), and the Boomtown Rats (1975–86), Dublin's first punk band, who were full of anger and contempt for the hypocrisies around them, their concerts resonating around city campuses before they moved to London. A year after the Rats, U2 was formed – a motley group from a Protestant-run north-side comprehensive school, and their first recordings were also local. U2's subsequent rise to global celebrity was hard won, but their local apotheosis was assured when 50,000 fans packed Croke Park (of all places) in the summer of 1985. They wore their Dublin origins lightly but retained a discreet presence in the city, acting as patrons of newer talent, hoteliers and putative property developers. In the background, supporting the music industry (for such it had become), stood the old reliable fortnightly *Hot Press*, started in 1977; its mixture of left-leaning commentary, edgy investigative journalism and musical news projected a lively sense of an ever-changing Dublin music scene. Then, in 1992, out of the RTE stable came the most explicit commercialisation of the traditional musical practice in modern form: *Riverdance*, first produced as an intermezzo act during RTE's hosting of the Eurovision Song Contest. Such was its enduring global success that the format became a distinct category of live dance performance.

The venue for *Riverdance* was an old railway warehouse in the lower docks, the Point Depot, opened by Harry Crosbie, a local haulier, as a venue for large-scale musical performance in 1988 (holding 8,500). It had about seven times the capacity of the National Concert Hall (opened in 1981 in the former UCD Great Hall in Earlsfort Terrace). As in the Theatre Royal half a century before, many of the Point's acts were short-stay international visitors. Dublin in the 1980s, unlike other centres of popular music and youth culture in the English-speaking world, did not have local ethnic diversity to enrich its own popular music. It drew on an indigenous musical tradition certainly, and with unexpectedly exciting results from time to time. But Phil Lynott, the boy from Crumlin, was unusual in having that added extra – Caribbean ancestry on his father's side – and he revelled in his exotic image. When his bittersweet lyric 'Old Town' was released in 1982, a video was produced: the camera followed him as he gyrated through the crowds in Grafton Street and as he stood alone in a small ferry boat off the South Wall. It is one of the most atmospheric evocations of Dublin youth culture in its prime, hinting at the vulnerability both of the city and of the artist. Weeks later, the last cross-river ferry closed. Less than four years after that, Lynott was dead from a drugs overdose.[17]

Lynott had moved far from the ordinary world of working-class estates. But *fin de siècle* writers drew inspiration from it. Dermot Bolger's epic story *The journey home* (1990) was shaped by the marginalised youth of Finglas and was a savage indictment of the morally empty, drug-infested and corrupt city, from which the only redemption is a retreat to an older rural world. Roddy Doyle also exposed the north-side working class in a series of

46. Two Dublins: Phil Lynott scrutinised by a passing priest in St Stephen's Green, 1977. The scene was captured by the photographer who was working with Lynott's band, Thin Lizzy, in the production of their album covers.

raw but highly engaging novels; he began with a privately published work, *The Commitments* (1987), and won the Booker Prize with *Paddy Clarke ha ha ha* in 1993. Helped by critically acclaimed adaptations of his work for television and film (starting with *The Commitments*, which was shot in Ballymun), Doyle's Barrytown became the real Dublin for a new audience. His narratives turn on family, generational and gender conflicts, fought out against a backdrop of economic marginality and the near-total absence of religious belief or political ideology. All is rescued by the subversive humour, the self-knowledge and complete absence of pretence in a culturally impoverished and at times violent world. And because Doyle's Barrytown lacked cultural reference points beyond those of imported mass culture, its wider appeal rested on the fact that it could be Clichy-sous-Bois or any dystopic working-class suburb at the end of the line in any metropolis.[18]

Doyle then turned from that world to history and to 1916, with *A star called Henry* (1999). Fiction inspired by the revolutionary period in Dublin has not worn well, with the exception of Liam O'Flaherty's *The informer* (1925), and any temptation to capture the city's past on an epic scale had to operate under the enormous shadow cast by *Ulysses*. But one literary project did manage it: James Plunkett's *Strumpet city* (1969) may not have been in critical terms a literary masterpiece, but it was an epic, and in its impact on readers, and later on viewers, it has had no rival in evoking the Dublin of 1913. As a young union official, Plunkett had worked with James Larkin in old age, and later used his skills as a television producer to construct a vast tableau of the Lockout year. *Strumpet city* was a global bestseller (with sales of over a quarter of a million), thanks to its accessibility, humour and very graphic presentation of class divisions in the city. As a latterday Dickensian epic, it came across as a moral tale of the times and became the prism through which most Dubliners viewed the events of 1913. RTE's lavish dramatisation in 1980 (which was sold on to more than thirty countries) only served to reinforce its status. Yet by far the bestselling Dubliner of the twentieth century was Maeve Binchy – like Doyle a former teacher, but there the similarities end. A gifted journalist before her literary career, she was the beneficiary of the development of the global market for blockbuster fiction in paperback format. Her imagined world, first revealed in *Circle of friends* (1990), was an extension of bourgeois south Dublin, a world of social rather than material insecurity, where religion, guilt and traditional social restraints complicated the lives of her softly tortured characters.[19]

One of the local bestsellers of the 1990s evoked a different world: *Seventy years young: Memories of Elizabeth, Countess of Fingal*, a spirited account of upper-class life at the beginning of the century. Unnoticed when first published in London in 1937, it had far broader appeal in a very changed Dublin. For the social and associational divisions based on religion had almost disappeared by the 1990s. The principal institutions once associated with Protestant Dublin – Trinity College, *The Irish Times*, the Royal Dublin Society, the Royal Dublin Golf Club, the Bank of Ireland – were without exception emancipated from their denominational past, and even if certain symbols and cultural practices echoed that past, these were more likely to be treasured than resented by the inheritors. The case of *The Irish Times* is instructive. From the 1920s it characterised itself as the paper of business, but its loyal readership was heavily Protestant until the 1960s. Then, through a combination of strong editorial leadership by Douglas Gageby (who saw himself as a Protestant republican in the tradition of Wolfe Tone) and the growing demand for a liberal secular morning paper, its circulation consistently grew while that of other dailies fell. By the late 1990s it was selling more than 100,000 copies per day. It had become the paper of choice for middle-class Dublin – both women and men – and for all those who wished to keep up with middle-class Dublin. Its dominance was confirmed when the *Irish Press,* a paper of very high journalistic quality, folded in 1994. One of the ironies in the rise of *The Irish Times* was that when its financial survival had been in severe doubt in the inflationary 1970s, it was quietly bailed out by that other venerable institution, the Bank of Ireland, for reasons that do not seem to have been strictly commercial. Some of the paper's strongest voices, then and later, were schooled in the unique hothouse that was *Magill,* a monthly political magazine that ran from 1977 to the 1990s, its best scoops and sharpest commentary coming amidst the giddy politics of the 1980s. The guiding editorial hand was Vincent Browne, whose campaigning journalism stalked the line between brilliance and obsession and, like a latterday Watty Cox, he exposed the vanities and hinted at the corruption of those in power, and his journalists were more in touch with the unfolding crisis in the North than most of the Dublin media.[20]

Knowing Dublin

> The Dubliner, like his ancient city, is vanishing, all in the name of
> bureaucratic planning ... The complacency of these men in their ivory
> towers to move us around like chess men has gone too far ... We are
> talking while this insane planning, that makes provision for the motor
> car and the speculator, leaves out the most important thing, the heart
> of any great city, its people ...

So wrote Larry Dillon, a lifelong resident of the Liberties, in 1973. He was a pioneer of a new phenomenon, the community activist working outside local party political structures and critical of the policies being pursued by central and local government that were (he believed) corroding working-class communities. Dillon hit out at the grandiose road-widening schemes, the zoning regulations that facilitated property speculation and short-term dereliction, and the housing policies that had driven people to the suburbs. In Dillon's time there was a stop-start campaign for urban regeneration (thus pre-dating the Gregory deal), and the Liberties were one area to benefit from the construction of some small-scale public housing. The immediate background to this activism lay in disparate protest movements of the 1960s, specifically the politically orchestrated agitation over housing policy and the non-political protests at the destruction of houses of historic interest. The left-leaning Sinn Féin movement had seized on housing shortages to win support in the city, and the DHAC emerged as a far-left alliance advocating direct action against 'speculators' and encouraging those on the Corporation waiting lists to squat in vacant houses. On at least one occasion in 1969, it published the specific addresses of places in which to squat, 'some of the empty, surplus property owned by the foreign bums and parasites who have come to tear our city to shreds in order to build gaudy office blocks and expensive hotels'.[21]

This tradition of civic protest had begun in 1961, after the ESB announced that they were going to demolish a terrace of sixteen houses on Lower Fitzwilliam Street in order to create an integrated head-office for the organisation; the ESB as a national success story stood in high public regard. The boldness of the plan (apparently decades in the making) appealed to some: the houses in question formed a standard classical terrace dating from the 1790s and although in fairly good condition they were unsuitable for modern offices. Against them was the resurrected Irish Georgian Society, a group with little in common with the pre-1914 body beyond the name. It was led by members of the Guinness clan and their social circle. They had one very strong argument: the houses in question formed part of a unique vista of Georgian brick stretching southwards for more than half a mile towards the mountains, a perspective that would be utterly compromised by any modern infill. Artists and actors of all political colours spoke at a packed Mansion House rally organised by the Georgian Society; the earl of Pembroke, the ground landlord, sent his support. But the Society failed to secure political or professional support and the media were divided. The ESB ran an architectural competition for the project, which was won by Sam Stephenson and Arthur Gibney, then fledgling local architects, and Stephenson made clear his views on the 'shoddiness' of the threatened houses and the ridiculous 'antics' of the preservationists. But the Corporation, advised by Dáithí Hanly, the courageous City Architect, refused to support the plans for demolition, only to be overruled by the Minister for Local Government. And so the demolition went ahead in 1965. This was by no means the first demolition of sound eighteenth-century property for a large integrated development – after all, had not the old regime done precisely the same thing when demolishing thirteen houses in Upper Merrion Street for the College of Science at the beginning of the century?[22]

If Fitzwilliam Street was fought out in the newspapers and in Dublin Corporation, the next battle was on the ground. Here the proposal was to demolish a series of fine houses in St Stephen's Green, mainly from the 1760s, lying on the east side and running into Hume Street, in preparation for an office development (by no means the first such case in the neighbourhood). They were among a relatively small group of buildings listed in the Draft City Development Plan of 1967. When one of the houses, which was in state ownership (45 St Stephen's Green), was on the point of being demolished, a group of architectural students from nearby UCD, copying the DHAC's tactics, occupied it and remained there for six months through the winter and spring of 1969–70. They achieved international publicity and, unlike the Fitzwilliam Street case, they earned strong public and political support. Midway through the affair, the then Minister for Local Government Kevin Boland made his celebrated attack on the protesters, calling them 'aesthetic hijackers', 'pampered students', backed by 'a consortium of belted earls and their ladies and left-wing intellectuals'. All knew the Georgians that Boland was talking about. His argument was that the compensation the state would have to pay if planning permission were reversed would directly hit the budget for public housing. In June, there was a botched attempt by the property company involved to take forcible possession of the house; the roof was taken off, but then the occupiers retook the building. Some days later, government mediation led to a compromise of sorts: the buildings would all be demolished, but the revised planning permission would 'maintain as far as possible the existing quality and character of the streetscape', meaning facsimile façades on the street, a pastiche compromise that pleased hardly anyone but ended the affair. The decision had the unfortunate effect of encouraging similar very undistinguished faux-brick office development in the 1970s, and influencing the fad for 'Georgian' styling in new suburban housing.[23]

At this point the Corporation was once again in suspense, having refused to fix a rate to fund the new regional health authority, and between 1969 and 1973 a single commissioner ran the city with the manager's team. This weakened still further the planning review process. The Dublin Civic Group (formed in 1966) and the quirky trade monthly *Build* were the only consistent voices of dissent trying to restrain the juggernaut of office development. One of the Hume Street veterans, Deirdre Kelly, established the Living City Group in 1970 and became the most fearless community activist in the next decade – on the streets, in the courts and with her polemical *Hands off Dublin* (1975). But resident associations in many of the areas threatened by large-scale development and/or major road schemes were established, as indeed were tenant associations in areas of public housing. Political parties became involved, but usually discreetly, in such activity. Thanks to this civic activism, planning law and Corporation procedures became much more widely understood, and some resident associations used the law to good effect. The Upper Leeson Street association, observing the obliteration of the great Victorian houses in nearby Burlington Road, successfully resisted the wholesale transformation of their neighbourhood into another series of office blocks.[24]

The next battle, and much the greatest conservation issue of late twentieth-century Dublin, was Wood Quay. This concerned not Georgian but medieval and Viking Dublin. The background was the long ambition of the Corporation to bring its various administrative divisions, spread over a dozen or more locations, and most of its 6,500 staff, together on an integrated campus. The 1939 plan had pointed to Parliament Street as an appropriate site and from 1956 the Corporation began acquiring land immediately to the west of it. Twelve years later, it was ready to run an intimate competition with local developers, which Sam Stephenson won. The delay had been so long and so much had been invested in gathering the site that the Corporation management was now determined to keep going, knowing that it was developing a sensitive site that was visible right along the upper quays. But little if any official thought was given to the possibility that under the foundations of the buildings to be demolished, none of which can have been more than 300 years old, there might be much earlier archaeological riches. Yet up the hill beside High Street, archaeological investigations during road-widening in the 1960s (carried out with a marked lack of support from higher officialdom) had already revealed an unlikely treasure trove of eleventh- and twelfth-century house foundations and superb evidence of the material culture of the walled city just before the Normans. As it turned out, the alluvial clays of Wood Quay cloaked an even richer and older time capsule.

Between legal challenges and government involvement, redesigns and budgetary constraints, the project was repeatedly delayed. The exposure of a very early section of the city wall in 1973 only added to doubts about the choice of site. A pressure group, the Friends of Medieval Dublin, led by UCD historian Father F. X. Martin, secured a court order declaring the site a National Monument in 1978. In the following years, public protests over Corporation plans polarised opinion in the city and street marches were held, attracting on one occasion some 20,000 people and demonstrating a remarkably wide coalition of interests ready to denounce the Corporation's plans. The focus of the agitation was on the threatened hidden history of the site rather than on the aesthetics of Stephenson's proposed buildings – four massive bunkers squatting above the river (which seemed uncompromisingly out of character with their surroundings). The Corporation finally secured legal possession, with a three-month reprieve before bulldozers cleared the site in 1980. A vast amount of archaeological evidence was collected – and that was very much thanks to the delays won by the protesters – but it was a fraction of what had lain undisturbed up to that point. Two of Stephenson's ten-storey 'brutalist slabs' were swiftly built, but the plans for the other two were abandoned, and Scott Tallon Walker Architects brought the sorry saga to a conclusion with a more emollient riverfront building in 1994.[25]

Wood Quay was a defeat for archaeological conservation, but it helped transform official and political attitudes towards the city's heritage. It influenced the outcome of the local elections in 1979, when five of the forty-five elected were 'community' candidates and several were Wood Quay veterans. Amidst an increasingly supportive media, the environment correspondent of *The Irish Times,* Frank McDonald, was the white knight, and his 339-page exposé of thirty years of property development (*The destruction of Dublin,* 1985), became a bestseller. By the time municipal bureaucracy had completed their move into the Civic Offices in 1995, there had been a generational change within city government, a shift from those whose primary concern was traffic management, road-widening, car parks, main drainage and housing provision to the softer issues of inner-city regeneration and heritage management. Where once there had been accountants, road engineers and surveyors, the influence of architects, town planners and environmental engineers now belatedly came to the fore. Sentiment within the elected council came out much more strongly in favour of conservation, and there was a direct link between the embarrassment of Wood Quay and the decision to celebrate the supposed millennium of the city in 1988. For all the fireworks and fizz, this really did mark a political turning point, a move away from the cold war between city managers and conservation watchdogs, and official recognition of the cultural and commercial value of the city's early history.[26]

The politicians – some of them – also discovered heritage and environment. Charles Haughey in his later years was a case in point, saving Temple Bar from CIE (1987), establishing the National Heritage Council (1988) and supporting costly restoration programmes at the Custom House and in Dublin Castle. This official revaluation of the city's past led to Dublin's choice as European City of Culture in 1991 (it was after all European money that was the critical new ingredient in many of these top-down initiatives). During that year, the Dublin Writers Museum was opened in Parnell Square, the first City Archaeologist was appointed, the old Royal Hospital in Kilmainham was transformed, phoenix-like, to become the Irish Museum for Modern Art, and the Temple Bar Properties Company began its rescue and transformation of the waterside. The following year the Dublin Civic Trust was established, the most focused of a series of heritage groups concerned with the built environment. None of these initiatives had been championed by the municipal authority; the majority were government decisions and several were opportunistic responses to the availability of European funding. But the profound change in municipal thinking was reflected in the difficult decision as to how to renovate City Hall, once the Civic Offices had become the administrative centre of Dublin. The City Council (as it had now become) chose to sweep away nearly all the municipal modifications made since the city had taken over the building in 1851 and to restore it to its pristine neoclassical form when it had been the Royal Exchange. The superb quality of Thomas Cooley's great Rotunda was fully revealed in 2000 for the first time in 150 years.

However, as official Dublin rediscovered its history, the inherited weaknesses of local government, particularly in the suburban parts of Co. Dublin, were being publicly exposed in a series of sinister corruption tribunals, giving a sense of just how high the cost of weak regulation since the 1950s was turning out to be. Such post-mortems were possible in the very different environment of the 1990s: the winding down of three decades of civil conflict in Northern Ireland; the recovery of the economy; the end of emigration; a female president (and veteran of the Hume Street protests) in the Park. The legacy of misplaced shopping centres (notoriously, the siting of the Liffey Valley Centre out on the edge of the community it was suppose to serve) and of inappropriate road schemes remained, most visibly in the partially built Inner Tangent Road scheme now evident in the grossly over-widened Parnell Street. But the run-down shops and houses on that misshapen boulevard were the germination bed for ethnic traders, and there began the city's Chinatown, soon joined by a cascade of new traders from Korea and Nigeria springing up at the turn of the century.[27]

When it came to the city's celebration of the real millennium, two rather perverse ideas took hold. One was to lay an illuminated electric clock in the Liffey near O'Connell Bridge that would count down the seconds to the new age, the other a replacement monument for the long gone Nelson's Pillar. The river clock was a fiasco; it repeatedly stopped and had to be removed long before the actual millennium. Nelson's successor was the Monument of Light, a soaring 121-metre stainless steel spire, designed to be visible at night even from the outer suburbs. When it was finally completed (in 2003), it was claimed to be the world's tallest sculpture. Certainly its scale served to diminish the verticality of O'Connell Street. But it carried no cultural reference to place or city and unlike the Pillar it could not be climbed; it defied graffiti artists; visitors could gather beside it, but it could only be admired from a distance. To some, it suggested a city without a past.[28]

By contrast, one of the most memorable incidents of the 1988 millennium had been the arrival of a cast bronze statue near the bottom of Grafton Street, unveiled by the Jewish Lord Mayor, Ben Briscoe. There had been no public competition or discussion. Yet no public statue in the city has been so popular, not at least since William of Orange's early days in College Green. An oyster-seller by day, the lady of the night, Molly Malone, was given a well-nourished and buxom appearance by her sculptress, Jeanne Rynhart. But why Molly Malone? Long before the 1980s, the ballad had become a favourite among Dublin supporters in every code of sport; it was sung by the Wood Quay protesters as they marched through the city and was the official anthem of the City Millennium: a good melody, an authentic embodiment of Dublin resilience, a hint of transgressive ambiguity? Despite Corporation assertions that she was a real figure of the late seventeenth century, the conventional view has been that she was a music-hall invention of the late nineteenth. The ballad is first recorded in an American printing and apparently written by a Scot. Was she then yet another construct of Irish America who was quietly shipped 'home'? The ballad on which her fame rests may indeed be late nineteenth century, but in fact 'sweet Molly Malone' is older. She appears in at least one late eighteenth-century collection of light verse and may have even earlier associations. Thus her past, like all good history, is a bit of a tease.[29]

NOTES

Abbreviations used in notes

Anal. Hib.	*Analecta Hibernica*
CARD	J. T. Gilbert, *Calendar of the ancient records of Dublin in the possession of the municipal corporation of that city*, 19 vols (Dublin, 1889–1944)
Cal. S.P. Ire.	*Calendar of State Papers Ireland*
Casey, *Dublin*	Christine Casey, *Dublin: The city within the Grand and Royal Canals and the Circular Road with the Phoenix Park* [The Buildings of Ireland] (London, 2005)
Clark and Gillespie, *Two capitals*	Peter Clark and Raymond Gillespie (eds), *Two capitals: London and Dublin 1500–1840* (Oxford, 2001)
DIB	*Dictionary of Irish Biography* (Cambridge, 2009; online edition, 2010–)
DHR	*Dublin Historical Record*
DKR	Dublin and Kingstown Railway
DSER	Dublin and South Eastern Railway
ECI	*Eighteenth-Century Ireland: Iris an dá chultúr*
FJ	*Freeman's Journal*
GSWR	Great Southern and Western Railway
Gilbert, *Dublin*	J. T. Gilbert, *A history of the city of Dublin*, 3 vols (1st edn, Dublin, 1854–9; 3rd edn, Dublin, 1978)
HC	House of Commons sessional papers
HMC	Historical Manuscripts Commission

Hall, *Bank of Ireland*	F. G. Hall, *The Bank of Ireland, 1782–1946* (Dublin, 1949)
Hib. Jnl.	*Hibernian Journal*
Hist. Jnl.	*Historical Journal*
Ir. Geog.	*Irish Geography*
JCHI	*Journals of the House of Commons of Ireland*
JRSAI	*Journal of the Royal Society of Antiquaries of Ireland*
JSSISI	*Journal of the Statistical and Social Inquiry Society of Ireland*
IESH	*Irish Economic and Social History*
IHS	*Irish Historical Studies*
McDowell and Webb, *Trinity College*	R. B. McDowell and D. A. Webb, *Trinity College Dublin 1592–1952: An academic history* (Cambridge, 1982)
MGWR	Midland Great Western Railway
NAI	National Archives of Ireland
NESC	National Economic and Social Council
ODNB	*Oxford Dictionary of National Biography* (Oxford, online edition, 2004–)
O'Dwyer, *Lost Dublin*	Frederick O'Dwyer, *Lost Dublin* (Dublin, 1981)
PRIA	*Proceedings of the Royal Irish Academy*
PRONI	Public Record Office of Northern Ireland
TCD	Trinity College Dublin
TNA	The National Archives [Kew]
TNAPSS	*Transactions of the National Association for the Promotion of Social Science*
Trans. RHS	*Transactions of the Royal Historical Society*
UCD	University College Dublin
Warburton and Whitelaw, *Dublin*	James Warburton, James Whitelaw & Robert Walsh, *History of the city of Dublin, from the earliest accounts to the present time ...* 2 vols (London, 1818)

Preface

1. James Stephens, 'Dublin', in *Manchester Guardian Commercial*, Ireland supplement, 26 July 1923, p. 42.
2. Quoted in Gerry Smyth, 'The right to the city: Re-presentations of Dublin in contemporary Irish fiction', in Liam Harte and Michael Parker (eds), *Contemporary Irish fiction; Themes, tropes, theories* (Basingstoke, 2000), p. 13.
3. Fergus Campbell, *The Irish establishment 1879–1914* (Oxford, 2009), p. 54; John Ardagh, *Ireland and the Irish* (London,1994), p. 23.

Prologue: Dublin Town and the First Thousand Years

1.   John W. de Courcy, 'A bridge in its time: The River Liffey crossing at Church
      Street in Dublin', in *PRIA*, XC, C (1990), pp. 245–6; John W. de Courcy, 'Bluffs,
      bays and pools in the medieval Liffey at Dublin, in *Ir. Geog.*, XXXIII, 2 (2000),
      pp. 117–33; Geraldine and Matthew Stout, 'Patterns in the past: County Dublin
      1000 BC–1000 AD', in F. H. A. Aalen and Kevin Whelan (eds), *Dublin city and
      county: From prehistory to present...* (Dublin, 1992), pp. 11–21; Howard Clarke,
      'The diocese of Dublin to 1152', in James Kelly and Dáire Keogh (eds), *History
      of the Catholic diocese of Dublin* (Dublin, 2000), pp. 21–3, 26–8; Emer Purcell,
      'Michan: Saint, cult and church', in John Bradley, A. J. Fletcher and Anngret
      Simms (eds), *Dublin in the medieval world: Studies in honour of Howard B.
      Clarke*, (Dublin, 2009), pp. 132–7. For an alternative reading of the evidence on
      the routeways to the east coast, suggesting that Tara not Dublin was the focus:
      see Stout and Stout, 'Patterns in the past', pp. 15–16. On the ford downstream at
      Temple Lane, see Linzi Simpson, 'Viking warrior burials in Dublin ...', in Seán
      Duffy (ed.), *Medieval Dublin VI* (Dublin, 2005), p. 58.
2.   Clarke, 'The diocese of Dublin', pp. 24–5; Linzi Simpson, 'Forty years a-digging: A
      preliminary synthesis of archaeological investigations in medieval Dublin', in Seán
      Duffy, *Medieval Dublin I* (Dublin, 2000), p. 18; Simpson, 'Fifty years a-digging ...',
      in Duffy, *Medieval Dublin XI* (Dublin, 2011), pp. 18–20, 27; H. B. Clarke, 'Dublin
      to 1610', in Clarke, *Dublin, Part I: To 1610* [Irish Historic Towns Atlas, no. 11]
      (Dublin, 2002), pp. 1–2.
3.   Simpson, 'Forty years a-digging', pp. 24–5; Simpson, 'Viking warrior burials in
      Dublin ...', pp. 18–19, 50–60; Andrew Halpin, 'Development phases in Hiberno-
      Norse Dublin: A tale of two cities', in Duffy, *Medieval Dublin VI*, pp. 101–104;
      John Bradley, 'Problems of Scandinavian settlement in the hinterland of Dublin',
      in Bradley et al., *Dublin in the medieval world*, pp. 48–58.
4.   Donnchadh Ó Corráin, 'Viking Ireland: Afterthoughts', in H. B. Clarke et al.
      (eds), *Ireland and Scandinavia in the early Viking age* (Dublin, 1998), pp. 421–52;
      Clarke, 'Diocese of Dublin', pp. 30–33; D. N. Dumville, 'Old Dubliners and new
      Dubliners in Ireland and Britain: A Viking-age story', in Duffy, *Medieval Dublin
      VI* (Dublin, 2005), pp. 82–92; Clare Downham, 'Viking identities in Ireland', in
      Duffy, *Medieval Dublin XI* (Dublin, 2011), pp. 192–5.
5.   Ó Corráin, 'Viking Ireland', pp. 427–9; Clarke, 'Diocese of Dublin', p. 33; P. F.
      Wallace, 'The archaeology of Ireland's Viking-age towns', in Dáibhí Ó Cróinín
      (ed.), *A new history of Ireland*, vol. I: *Prehistoric and early Ireland* (Oxford, 2005),
      pp. 815–18.
6.   Clarke, 'Dublin to 1610', pp. 4–6; Simpson. 'Forty years a-digging', pp. 30–34;
      Wallace, 'Viking-age towns', pp. 819–23; Halpin, 'Development phases in
      Hiberno-Norse Dublin', pp. 104–109.
7.   Ó Corráin, 'Bilingualism in Viking-age Dublin', in Bradley et al., *Dublin in the
      medieval world*, pp. 65–7; *DIB*, 'Amlaíb Cuarán', 'Máel-Sechnaill'.
8.   H. B. Clarke, 'Myth, magic and the middle ages: Dublin from its beginnings
      to 1577', in Clarke (ed.), *Irish cities* (Cork, 1995), p. 89; Seán Duffy, 'Ireland's

Hastings: The Anglo-Norman conquest of Dublin', in Christopher Harper-Bill (ed.), *Anglo-Norman Studies* XX (Woodbridge, 1998), pp. 82–5; Anngret Simms, 'Origins and early growth', in Joseph Brady and Anngret Simms (eds), *Dublin through space and time* (Dublin, 2001), pp. 15–30; J. F. Lydon, 'Dublin in transition: From Ostman town to English borough', in Duffy, *Medieval Dublin II*, p. 137; Clarke, 'Dublin to 1610', pp. 2–4; Seán Duffy, 'The royal dynasties of Dublin and the Isles in the eleventh century', in Duffy, *Medieval Dublin VII* (Dublin, 2006), pp. 51–65; Bradley, 'Scandinavian settlement', pp. 42–4, 48–50.

9. Wallace, 'Viking-age towns', pp. 823–31; Margaret Murphy and Michael Potterton, *The Dublin region in the middle ages* (Dublin, 2010), pp. 360–61, 366–7. For the full excavation report, see Wallace, *The Viking Age buildings of Dublin: Medieval Dublin excavations 1962–81*, 1 (Dublin, 1992).

10. Poul Holm, 'The slave trade of Dublin, IXth to XIIth centuries', in *Peritia*, V (1986 [1989]), pp. 317–45; Michael Kenny, 'The geographical distribution of Irish Viking-Age coin hoards', in *PRIA*, LXXXVII, C (1987), pp. 524–5; Kenny, 'Coins and coinage in pre-Norman Ireland', in Ó Cróinín, *New History of Ireland*, I, pp. 845–51; Wallace, 'Viking-age towns', pp. 833–9; John Bradley, 'The topographical development of Scandinavian Dublin', in Aalen and Whelan, *Dublin city and county*, pp. 42–54; Bradley, *Dublin in the year 1000* (Dublin, 2003), pp. 5–10; Myles and Michael Gibbons, 'The search for the ninth-century *longphort*', in Seán Duffy (ed.), *Medieval Dublin VIII* (2008), p. 16.

11. Clarke, 'Diocese of Dublin', pp. 37–44; Clarke, 'Dublin to 1610', pp. 5–4; Clarke, '*Angliores ipsis Anglis*: The place of medieval Dubliners in English history', in Clarke, Jacinta Prunty and Mark Hennessy (eds), *Surveying Ireland's past: Multidisciplinary essays in honour of Anngret Simms* (Dublin, 2004), pp. 42–7; Donnchadh Ó Corráin, 'Bilingualism in Viking-age Dublin', in Bradley et al., *Dublin in the medieval world*, pp. 64–72; Adrian Empey, 'Intramural churches and communities in medieval Dublin', in Bradley, op. cit., pp. 250–51; Raghnall Ó Floinn, 'The late medieval relics of Holy Trinity church, Dublin', in Bradley, op. cit., pp. 383–9; http://www.british–history.ac.uk/report.aspx?compid=19184 [accessed 3 June 2013].

12. Small sections of the Norse wall survive within the Undercroft at Dublin Castle, and (as a reconstructed section) on the ground floor of the Civic Offices above Wood Quay.

13. Holm, 'Slave trade of Dublin', pp. 331, 341–2; Seán Duffy, 'Irishmen and Islesmen in the kingdom of Dublin and Man 1052–1171', in *Ériu*, XLIII (1992), pp. 120–22.

14. Clarke, 'Diocese of Dublin', pp. 44–50; Clarke, 'Dublin to 1610', pp. 4–6; Ailbhe MacShamráin, 'The emergence of the metropolitan see: Dublin 1111–1216', in Kelly and Keogh, *Diocese of Dublin*, pp. 51–62; James Lydon, 'The defence of Dublin in the middle ages', in Seán Duffy (ed.), *Medieval Dublin, IV* (Dublin, 2003), p. 64; Purcell, 'Michan: Saint, cult and church', pp. 131–3.

15. Aubrey Gwynn, 'Medieval Bristol and Dublin', in *IHS*, V, 20 (1947), p. 277; Ben Hudson, 'The family of Harold Godwinson and the Irish Sea province', in *JRSAI* CIX (1979), pp. 94–100; Holm, 'Slave trade of Dublin', pp. 341–2; F. J. Byrne, 'The

trembling sod: Ireland in 1169', in Art Cosgrove (ed.), *A new history of Ireland*, vol. II: *Medieval Ireland 1169–1534* (Oxford, 1987), pp. 21–8; Byrne, 'Ireland and her neighbours, *c.*1014–1072', in Ó Cróinín, *New History of Ireland*, I, pp. 887–91; http://www.vikingeskibsmuseet.dk/index.php?id=1321&L=1 [accessed 31 May 2013].

16. MacShamráin, 'Emergence of the metropolitan see', pp. 56–60; Byrne, 'The trembling sod', pp. 22–8.

17. Byrne, 'Diarmait Mac Murchada and the coming of the Anglo-Normans', in Cosgrove, *New history*, pp. 43–66; F. X. Martin, 'Allies and an overlord', in Cosgrove, pp. 75–9, 81–90, 95; Duffy, 'Ireland's Hastings', pp. 76–85.

18. MacShamráin, 'Emergence of the metropolitan see', pp. 60–62.

19. Byrne, 'Allies and an overlord', pp. 86–90; Barra Ó Donnabháin and Benedikt Hallgrímsson, 'Dublin: The biological identity of the Hiberno-Norse town', in Duffy, *Medieval Dublin II* (Dublin, 2001), pp. 65–87; Lydon, 'Dublin in transition', pp. 128–41; Duffy, 'Town and crown: The kings of England and their city of Dublin', in Michael Prestwich, Richard Britnell and Robin Frame (eds), *Thirteenth-century England X* (Woodbridge, 2005), p. 97; Emmett O'Byrne, 'Cultures in contact in the Leinster and Dublin marches, 1170–1400', in Duffy, *Medieval Dublin V* (Dublin, 2004), pp. 114–17; R. A. McDonald, 'Man, Ireland and England', in Duffy, *Medieval Dublin VIII*, p.135; *DIB*, 'Lorcán Ua Tuathail', 'Diarmait Mac Murchada'; Bill and Linda Doran, 'St Mary's Cistercian abbey: A ghost in the alleyways', in Bradley et al., *Dublin in the medieval world*, p. 188; Murphy and Potterton, *Dublin region*, pp. 374–5.

20. Murphy and Potterton, *Dublin region*, pp. 74–5, 84–6. For a map of the territorial liberty of Dublin, see H. B. Clarke, *The four parts of the city: Highlife and low life in the suburbs of medieval Dublin* (Dublin, 2003), p. 7.

21. Gwynn, 'Medieval Bristol and Dublin', p. 279; R. D. Edwards, 'The beginning of municipal government in Dublin', in *DHR*, I, 1 (1938), pp. 1–10; Lydon, 'Dublin in transition', pp. 129–33, 140; Duffy, 'Town and crown', pp. 97–117; MacShamráin, 'The emergence of the metropolitan see', pp. 60–62; Clarke, *'Angliores ipsis Anglis'*, pp. 48–50.

22. Clarke, *The four parts of the city*, pp. 12–13; Clarke, *Dublin to 1610*, pp. 14, 19; Alan Fletcher, 'God's jesters and the festive culture of medieval Ireland', in Duffy, *Medieval Dublin V*, pp. 277–8; Emer Purcell, 'The city and the suburb: Medieval Dublin and Oxmanstown', in Duffy, *Medieval Dublin VI*, pp. 199, 204–5, 207–9, 213.

23. Lydon, 'Dublin in transition', p. 131; 'Defence of Dublin', p. 65; Claire Walsh, 'Archaeological excavations at the abbey of St Thomas the Martyr', in Duffy, *Medieval Dublin I*, pp. 185–201; Clarke, *The four parts of the city*, pp. 10, 12; O'Byrne, 'Cultures in contact', pp. 112–23; Purcell, 'The city and the suburb', pp. 191, 198; Simpson, 'Fifty years a-digging', pp. 61, 88–9; Murphy and Potterton, *Dublin region*, pp. 94–5, 102–3.

24. Margaret Murphy, 'Archbishops and anglicisation: Dublin 1181–1271', in Kelly and Keogh, *Diocese of Dublin*, pp. 80, 84–7; Clarke, *The four parts of the city*, p. 16;

Charles Lyons, 'Dublin's oldest roof? The choir of St Patrick's Cathedral', in Duffy, *Medieval Dublin VII*, pp. 208–9; Casey, *Dublin*, pp. 604–18; Howard Clarke, 'Cult, church and collegiate church before 1220', 'Cathedral, close and community, *c*.1220–*c*.1550' and 'External influences, *c*.1220–*c*.1550', in John Crawford and Raymond Gillespie (eds) *St Patrick's Cathedral: A history* (Dublin, 2009), pp. 40–42, 45–8, 58, 74–93; *DIB*, 'Alexander Bicknor'; Murphy and Potterton, *Dublin region*, p. 372. With such achievements and two cathedrals in his diocese, Henry had some grounds for his claim that as archbishop of Dublin he was *ipso facto* 'primate' of Ireland: *DIB*, 'Henry of London'.

25. Raymond Gillespie, 'The coming of reform 1500–58', in Kenneth Milne (ed.) *Christ Church Cathedral Dublin: A history* (Dublin, 2000), p. 158; Lydon, 'Dublin in transition', p. 136; Clarke, *Dublin to 1610*, p. 23, entries for 'Guild Hall' and 'Tholsel'; E. W. Eggerer, 'The Guild Merchant of Dublin', in Duffy, *Medieval Dublin VI*, pp. 145–51. For the list of some 8,000 names on the first guild roll: Philomena Connolly and Geoffrey Martin (eds), *The Dublin guild merchant roll, c.1190–1265* (Dublin, 1992).

26. Wendy Childs, 'Ireland's trade with England in the later middle ages', in *IESH*, IX (1982), pp. 10–15; Childs and Timothy O'Neill, 'Overseas trade', in Cosgrove, *New history*, pp. 511–15; Tim Coughlan, 'The Anglo-Norman houses of Dublin: Evidence from Back Lane', in Duffy, *Medieval Dublin I*, pp. 232–3; Lydon, 'Dublin in transition', pp. 134–6; Halpin, 'Development phases in Hiberno-Norse Dublin', pp. 109–13; Clarke, *The four parts of the city*, p. 6; Margaret Murphy and Michael Potterton, 'Investigating living standards in medieval Dublin and its region', in Duffy, *Medieval Dublin VI*, pp. 240–45; B. M. S. Campbell, 'Benchmarking medieval economic development: England, Wales, Scotland, and Ireland, *c*.1290', in *Economic History Review*, LXI (2008), pp. 917–19; Murphy and Potterton, *Dublin region*, pp. 313–14, 364–7, 390, 418–26, 451–6, 469–86, 495.

27. Colm Lennon, *The lords of Dublin in the age of Reformation* (Blackrock, Co. Dublin, 1989), p. 84; De Courcy, 'A bridge in its time', pp. 247–9; Simpson, 'Forty years a-digging', pp. 57, 59, 62; Jessica McMorrow, 'Women in medieval Dublin: An introduction', in Duffy, *Medieval Dublin II*, pp. 205–15; Clarke, 'Dublin to 1610', pp. 7–9; Clarke, '*Angliores ipsis Anglis*', pp. 48–52; Lydon, 'Defence of Dublin', pp. 67–8, 70; Murphy and Potterton, 'Living standards', p.249; Simpson, 'Fifty years a-digging', pp. 66–7, 100; Crawford and Gillespie, *St Patrick's Cathedral*, p. 84; Murphy and Potterton, *Dublin region*, p. 415.

28. J. F. Lydon, 'The impact of the Bruce invasion 1515–27', in Cosgrove, *New history*, pp. 288–92.

29. Bernadette Williams, 'The Dominican annals of Dublin', in Duffy, *Medieval Dublin II*, pp. 153–68; O'Byrne, 'Cultures in contact', pp. 131, 133; M. B. Callan, 'Dublin's first heretic?', in *Anal. Hib* , XLIV (2013), p. 7.

30. Gearóid Mac Niocaill, 'Socio-economic problems of the late medieval town', in David Harkness and Mary O'Dowd (eds), *The town in Ireland* (Belfast, 1981), pp. 18–19; Maria Kelly, *A history of the Black Death in Ireland* (Stroud, 2001), pp. 76–7; Clarke, *The four parts of the city*, p. 8; Campbell, 'Benchmarking

medieval economic development', pp. 911, 913–15, 930–32; *DIB*, 'John Clyn'. The Clyn chronicle only survived in early-modern copies, from one of which an edition was published in 1849: Richard Burke (ed.), *The annals of Ireland by Friar John Clyn ...* (Dublin, 1849), p. 35.

31.   Lennon, *Lords of Dublin*, p. 96; Kelly, *Black Death in Ireland*, pp. 36, 79, 95–7.

32.   De Courcy, 'A bridge in its time', pp. 249–50; Kevin Down, 'Colonial society and economy in the high middle ages', in Cosgrove, *New history*, pp. 449–50; W. J. Smyth, 'Sixteenth- and seventeenth-century County Dublin', in Aalen and Whelan, *Dublin city and county*, p. 146; Williams, 'Dominican annals', pp. 155–6; Lydon, 'Defence of Dublin', pp. 70–74; Clarke, *'Angliores ipsis Anglis'*, p. 49; Simpson, 'Fifty years a-digging', p. 104; Doran and Doran, 'St Mary's Cistercian abbey', pp. 189–91; Murphy and Potterton, *Dublin region*, pp. 107–9.

33.   Clarke, *Dublin, part I: To 1610*, p. 22; Alan Fletcher, 'The annals and chronicles of medieval Dublin', in Duffy, *Medieval Dublin XI*, pp. 206–7; Murphy and Potterton, *Dublin region*, pp. 184–91. Cf. S. G. Ellis, *Ireland in the age of the Tudors: English expansion and the end of Gaelic rule* (London, 1998), pp. 31–5.

34.   Mary Clark and Raymond Refaussé (eds), *Directory of historic Dublin guilds* (Dublin, 1993), pp. 44–5; Alan Fletcher, 'The civic pageantry of Corpus Christi in fifteenth- and sixteenth-century Dublin', in *IESH*, XXIII (1996), pp. 73–84; Fletcher, 'Annals and chronicles', pp. 210–11; Empey, 'Intramural churches', p. 269; Colm Lennon, 'Fraternity and community in early modern Dublin', in Robert Armstrong and Tadhg Ó hAnnracháin (eds), *Community in early modern Ireland* (Dublin, 2006), pp. 167–78; Raymond Gillespie, 'Dubliners view themselves: The Dublin city chronicles', in Duffy, *Medieval Dublin VIII*, pp. 217–18, 221, 225.

35.   Childs, 'Ireland's trade with England', pp. 23–4, 27, 29; Lennon, *Lords of Dublin*, pp. 98–9; Timothy O'Neill, *Merchants and mariners in medieval Ireland* (Blackrock, 1987), pp. 74–5; Childs and O'Neill, 'Overseas trade', pp. 516–23; Simpson, 'Forty years a-digging', p. 43; C. P. Lewis, *A history of the county of Chester*, V, part 1: *The city of Chester ...* (London, 2003), pp. 60–84; Eggerer, 'Guild Merchant', pp. 156–7; Purcell, 'The city and the suburb', pp. 201, 205; Abi Cryerhall, 'Excavations at Hammond Lane', in Duffy, *Medieval Dublin VII* (Dublin, 2006), pp. 37–40, 49; Simpson, 'Fifty years a-digging', pp. 99–100; Murphy and Potterton, *Dublin region*, pp. 101, 146–51, 163–4, 264, 269, 402.

36.   Lydon, 'Defence of Dublin', pp. 26–7; Murphy and Potterton, *Dublin region*, pp. 264–82.

37.   Gillespie, 'Dubliners view themselves', pp. 220–21, 224–6; Randolf Jones, '"Hys worthy seruice in that vpror": Sir John Whyte and the defence of Dublin during Silken Thomas' rebellion, 1534', in Duffy, *Medieval Dublin XI*, pp. 275–97; Colm Lennon, 'The print trade, 1550–1700', in Gillespie and Andrew Hadfield (eds), *The Oxford history of the Irish book*, III: *The Irish book in English 1550–1800* (Oxford, 2006), p. 62; *DIB*, 'Gerald FitzGerald', 'Thomas FitzGerald'; Murphy and Potterton, Dublin region, pp. 264–83.

38.   Sir Anthony St Leger to King Henry VIII, 26 June 1541, in James Gairdner and R. H. Brodie (eds), *Letters and papers, foreign and domestic, Henry VIII* (London,

1898), XVI, no. 927; Brendan Bradshaw, *The dissolution of the religious orders in Ireland under Henry VIII* (Cambridge, 1974), pp. 78–81, 98–100, 110–19, 191, 220–22; Lennon, *Lords of Dublin*, pp. 38, 73, 77; Doran and Doran, 'St Mary's Cistercian abbey', pp. 191–2; Gillespie, 'The coming of reform, 1500–58', pp. 162–71; Gillespie, 'Reform and decay, 1500–98', in Crawford and Gillespie, *St Patrick's Cathedral*, pp. 160–63; Brendan Scott, 'The religious houses of Tudor Dublin: Their communities and resistance to the Dissolution, 1537–41', in Duffy, *Medieval Dublin VII*, pp. 214–32; *DIB*, 'Sir William Brabazon'; Murphy and Potterton, *Dublin region*, pp. 109–10.

39. Lennon, *Lords of Dublin*, pp. 14, 20, 28, 73, 81, 140–41; Raymond Gillespie, 'Religion and urban society: The case of early modern Dublin', in Clark and Gillespie, *Two capitals*, p. 226; Gillespie, 'The coming of reform, 1500–58', pp. 166–72; Gillespie, 'Reform and decay, 1500–98', pp. 160–68; James Murray, 'The diocese of Dublin in the sixteenth century', in Kelly and Keogh, *Diocese of Dublin*, pp. 95–111; Murray, *Enforcing the English Reformation in Ireland: Clerical resistance and political conflict in the diocese of Dublin 1534–1590* (Cambridge, 2009), pp. 30–32, 45–7, 53–4, 71–2, 80–81, 319.

40. Lennon, *Lords of Dublin*, pp. 139–40; Lennon, 'The print trade, 1550–1700', and Thomas O'Connor, 'Religious change, 1550–1800', in Gillespie and Hadfield, *The Irish book in English, 1550–1800*, pp. 62–5, 174–5.

41. Lennon, *Lords of Dublin*, pp. 144, 162–3, 215; ibid., 'Fraternity and community', pp. 170–71, 176–7; Clark and Refaussé, *Dublin guilds*, p. 34.

42. D. M. Woodward, *The trade of Elizabethan Chester* (Hull, 1970), pp. 26–31, 132–3; Lennon, *Lords of Dublin*, pp. 34–5, 38–46, 49–50, 53–5, 64–75, 80–81, 92–3, 97–105, 113–14, 118–23, 150–51, 266.

43. Ibid., pp. 87–91, 127, 128–65, 151–8; Christopher Maginn, 'The Baltinglass rebellion, 1580: English dissent or a Gaelic uprising?', in *Historical Journal*, XLVII, (2004), p. 232; *DIB*, 'Adam Loftus', 'Nicholas Nugent'. A gruesome engraving of O'Hurley's execution was published in 1587 in Antwerp in a Catholic tract on anti-Catholic persecution: Alan Ford, 'Martyrdom, history and memory in early modern Ireland', in Ian MacBride (ed.), *History and memory in modern Ireland* (Cambridge, 2001), pp. 47–8.

44. Andrew Carpenter, 'Literature in print 1550–1800', in Gillespie and Hadfield, *The Irish book in print 1550–1800*, p. 303; *DIB*, 'Arthur Grey'; Thomas Herron, 'Edmund Spenser's "Cleopolis" and Dublin', in Bradley et al., *Dublin in the medieval world*, pp. 454–6.

45. Lennon, *Lords of Dublin*, pp. 129–30, 144–9; Lydon, 'Defence of Dublin', p. 78; Gillespie, 'The coming of reform 1500–58', and 'The shaping of reform 1558–1625', in Kenneth Milne (ed.), *Christ Church Cathedral Dublin: A history* (Dublin, 2000), pp. 151–94; *DIB*, 'Sir William Brabazon'. On the controversies over government policy between the 1540s and 1590s, see Nicholas Canny, 'Revising the revisionist ...', in *IHS*, XXX, 118 (1996), pp. 242–54; Ciaran Brady, *A viceroy's vindication: Sir Henry Sidney's memoir of his service in Ireland, 1556–1578* (Cork, 2000).

46. Gillespie, 'The shaping of reform 1558–1625', pp. 191–3; Roland Budd, *'The platform of an universitie': All Hallows' priory to Trinity College, Dublin* (Dublin, 2001), pp. 32–55; *DIB*, ' Luke Challoner', 'Adam Loftus'.

47. Lennon, *Lords of Dublin*, pp. 26, 78.

48. Ibid., pp. 95–6, 123–7, 166–70; Lennon, 'The great explosion in Dublin, 1597', in *DHR*, XLII, 1 (1988), pp. 7–20.

1 The Fashioning of a Capital: 1600–1647

1. Colm Lennon, *The Lords of Dublin in the Age of Reformation* (Blackrock, Co. Dublin, 1989), pp. 31, 96.

2. J. H. Andrews, 'The oldest map of Dublin', in *PRIA*, LXXXIII, C (1983), pp. 205–37.

3. Lennon, *Lords of Dublin*, pp. 28, 120.

4. Gilbert, *Dublin*, I, p. 57; Barnabe Rich, *A new description of Ireland: Wherein is described the disposition of the Irish whereunto they are inclined* (London, 1610), p. 74.

5. Barnabe Rych [Rich], *A Catholicke conference between Syr Tady Mac Mareall a popish priest of Waterforde, and Patricke Plaine a young student in Trinity Colledge by Dublin in Ireland. Wherein is delivered the certayne maner of execution that was used upon a popish Bishop, and a popish Priest, that for several matters of treason were executed at Dublin the first of February, now last past 1611* (London, 1612), pp. 5–6.

6. Lennon, *Lords of Dublin*, p. 168.

7. *ODNB*, 'Henry FitzSimon'. Also, cf. Lennon, *Lords of Dublin*, p. 127.

8. Alderman Patrick Browne, quoted in Lennon, *Lords of Dublin*, p. 181.

9. Rich, *New description of Ireland*, p. 60.

10. Lennon, *Lords of Dublin*, p. 145; *DIB*, 'Luke Rochford'.

11. G. A. Little, 'The Jesuit university of Dublin', in *DHR*, XIII (1952), p. 41.

12. Alan Ford, 'Who went to Trinity? The early students of Dublin University', in Helga Robinson-Hammerstein (ed.), *European universities in the age of Reformation and Counter Reformation* (Dublin, 1998), pp. 53–74; *DIB*, 'Sir William Temple', 'James Ussher'.

13. 'Opinion of Robert Cogan', quoted in Constantia Maxwell, *Irish history from contemporary sources (1509–1610)* (London, 1923), p. 373.

14. [Richard Hadsor], *Advertisements for Ireland*, edited by George O'Brien (Dublin, 1923) (I am following Victor Treadwell's attribution of this tract to Hadsor (*IHS*, XXX, 119 (1996–7), pp. 305–36)); Lennon, *Lords of Dublin*, pp. 108–9; *DIB*, 'Nicholas Weston'.

15. Michael Perceval-Maxwell, *The outbreak of the Irish rebellion of 1641* (Dublin, 1994), p. 35; Donald Woodward, 'Irish trade and customs statistics 1614–1641', in *IESH*, XXVI (1999), pp. 54–80. The value of Dublin's exports in 1626 was almost 28 per cent of the Irish total: Raymond Gillespie, 'Dublin 1600–1700', in Peter Clark and Bernard Lepetit (eds), *Capital cities and their hinterlands in early modern Europe* (Aldershot, 1996), p. 94.

16. N. P. Canny, *Making Ireland British 1580–1650* (Oxford, 2001), p. 368; Raymond Gillespie, 'Print culture 1550–1700', and Colm Lennon, 'The print trade, 1550–1700', in Raymond Gillespie and Andrew Hadfield (eds), *The Oxford history of the Irish book*, III: *The Irish book in English 1550–1800* (Oxford, 2006), pp. 22, 70–71.

17. This proportion relates to the near 3,000 individuals lending money on the Dublin staple between 1597 and 1678, excluding the years 1638–1664. In all, 82 per cent were from within Leinster, 5 per cent from Ulster, 4 per cent from England and Wales, 4 per cent from Munster, and 3 per cent from Connacht: Jane Ohlmeyer and Éamonn Ó Ciardha (eds), *The Irish statute staple books, 1596–1687* (Dublin, 1998), p. 16. See also Canny, *Making Ireland British*, pp. 364–9.

18. Patricia Stapleton, 'The merchant community of Dublin in the early seventeenth century: A social, economic and political study' (Ph.D. dissertation, University of Dublin, 2008), pp. 108, 159.

19. Rich, *New description of Ireland*, p. 73.

20. 'Travels of Sir William Brereton, 1635', in C. L. Falkiner, *Illustrations of Irish history and topography …* (London, 1904), p. 390; Raymond Gillespie, *The transformation of the Irish economy 1550–1700* (Dundalk, 1991), p. 21.

21. *The Lady's Magazine* [London], V (1774), p. 675.

22. *CARD*, II, pp. 106, 113; Fitzpatrick, 'The Municipal Corporation of Dublin 1603–40' (Ph.D. dissertation, University of Dublin, 1984), pp. 163, 215.

23. Canny, *Making Ireland British*, pp. 369–70; Rolf Loeber, 'English and Irish sources for the history of Dutch economic activity in Ireland, 1600–89', in *IESH*, VIII (1981), pp. 70–85.

24. *CARD*, III, pp. 298–9.

25. Rich, *New description of Ireland*, p. 61; M. V. Ronan (ed), 'Archbishop Bulkeley's visitation of Dublin, 1630', in *Archivium Hibernicum*, VIII (1941), pp. 57–62.

26. *ODNB*, 'Wentworth, Thomas, first earl of Strafford'.

27. Quoted in Falkiner, *Illustrations of Irish history*, p. 23.

28. Wentworth, Dublin Castle, to Archbishop Laud, 27 September 1637; Howell, Dublin, to Sir Edward Savage, Dublin, 3 May 1639: in M. L. Kekewich (ed.), *Princes and peoples: France and the British Isles 1620–1714* (Manchester, 1994), pp. 23, 25–7.

29. 'Brereton's travels', in Falkiner, *Illustrations of Irish history*, p. 385; Raymond Gillespie, 'Dublin 1600–1700', pp. 86–7.

30. There were 226 freemen enrolled in 1638 alone, more than three times the annual average in the previous fifteen years: Stapleton, 'Merchant community of Dublin', p. 77.

31. Sir John Temple, *The history of the general rebellion in Ireland …* (7th edn, Cork, 1766), pp. 92–3. Cf. Andrew Hadfield, 'Historical writing, 1550–1700', in Gillespie and Hadfield, *The Irish book in English 1550–1800*, pp. 261–2.

32. Philip Bysse, Dublin, to 'dear brother', 16 February 1641[or 1642] (TCD MS 840, f. 100v.); Raymond Gillespie, 'War and the Irish town: The early modern experience', in Pádraig Lenihan (ed.), *Conquest and resistance: War in*

seventeenth-century Ireland (Leiden, 2001), pp. 308–10; Joseph Cope, *England and the 1641 Irish rebellion* (Woodbridge, 2009), pp. 45–9.

33. For the full database of the 1641 depositions, see http://1641.tcd.ie/index.php.

34. Gillespie, 'War and the Irish town', p. 300; Maighréad Ní Mhurchadha, *Fingal 1603–60: Contending neighbours in north Dublin* (Dublin, 2005), pp. 265–9; Kenneth Nicholls, 'The other massacre: English killings of Irish, 1641–3', in David Edwards, Pádraig Lenihan and Clodagh Tait (eds), *Age of atrocity: Violence and political conflict in early modern Ireland* (Dublin, 2007), pp. 184–8.

35. J. Skout [*recte* Scout], *Exceeding certain and true newes from Munster ...* ([London?], 2 January 1643), p. 5; Aidan Clarke, *The Old English in Ireland 1625– 42* (London, 1966), pp. 190–92, 199–202.

36. *CARD*, III, pp. xxvii, 393–4; Rolf Loeber and Geoffrey Parker, 'The military revolution', in Jane Ohlmeyer (ed.), *Ireland from independence to occupation 1641– 1660* (Cambridge, 1995), pp. 78–9; Gillespie, 'War and the Irish town', pp. 298, 300, 314. The dating and topography of these defences remain somewhat unclear, but a small section in Ardee Street in the Meath Liberties was recently exposed (vid. www.excavations.ie/Pages/Details.php?Year=&County=Dublin&id=11434 [accessed 2 April 2009]).

37. Pádraig Lenihan, *Consolidating conquest: Ireland 1603–1727* (Harlow, 2008), p. 119.

2 Court City: 1647–1690

1.   Raymond Gillespie, 'The Irish economy at war', in Jane Ohlmeyer (ed.), *Ireland from independence to occupation 1641–1660* (Cambridge, 1995), p. 177.

2.   Notably the great survivor Daniel Hutchinson: T. C. Barnard, *Cromwellian Ireland: English government and reform in Ireland 1649–1660* (Cambridge, 1972), pp. 81, 83–4. On the military burden on the city: Raymond Gillespie, 'War and the Irish town: The early modern experience', in Pádraig Lenihan (ed.), *Conquest and resistance: War in seventeenth-century Ireland* (Leiden, 2001), pp. 302–5.

3.   *CARD*, III, p. 451; R. J. Devenish and C. H. McLaughlin, *Historical and genealogical records of the Devenish families of England and Ireland* (Chicago, 1948), pp. 271–3. I am grateful to Colm Lennon for the latter reference.

4.   Maighréad Ní Mhurchadha, *Fingal 1603–60: Contending neighbours in north Dublin* (Dublin, 2005), p. 229.

5.   V. F. Snow and A. S. Young, *The private journals of the Long Parliament, 2 June to 17 September 1642* (New Haven, 1992), p. 134; *CARD*, III, p. xxxi. This would suggest a civilian population of somewhat over 20,000 and a total population of about 25,000.

6.   Gillespie, 'Irish economy', pp. 163–4.

7.   Edmund Borlase, *The history of the execrable Irish rebellion ...* (London, 1680), p. 213; *Lieut. General Jones's letter to the Council of State, of a great victory ...* (London, 1649), p. 3. Cf. [R. C], *The present condition of Dublin in Ireland ...* (London, 1649), p. 2; Micheál Ó Siochrú, *God's executioner: Oliver Cromwell*

and the conquest of Ireland (London, 2009), pp. 70–73. Whether many of those expelled were readmitted after the battle is unclear.

8. *Jones's letter*, p. 4.
9. *CARD*, IV, p. 501; R. T. Dunlop, *Ireland under the Commonwealth* (Manchester, 1913), p. 504; Gillespie, 'Irish economy', pp. 177–8; ibid., *The transformation of the Irish economy 1550–1700* (Dundalk, 1991), pp. 15–16.
10. *CARD*, IV, pp. 3–4.
11. *CARD*, III, p. 488; Barnard, *Cromwellian Ireland*, pp. 81–7; Rolf Loeber, 'English and Irish sources for the history of Dutch economic activity in Ireland, 1600–89', in *IESH*, VIII (1981), pp. 70–85.
12. *CARD*, IV, pp. 4, 108, 114–15.
13. *CARD*, III, p. 470; IV, pp. 3–4.
14. Gillespie, 'War and the Irish town', pp. 312–13; Phil Kilroy, 'Radical religion in Ireland 1641–1660', in Ohlmeyer, *Ireland*, pp. 207–9.
15. Dunlop, *Ireland under the Commonwealth*, pp. 436, 477.
16. *CARD*, IV, pp. 118, 558–9.
17. *CARD*, IV, pp. vi, 38; Dunlop, *Ireland under the Commonwealth*, pp. 434n, 505, 562.
18. Dunlop, op. cit., pp. 482, 486, 531; L. J. Arnold, *The Restoration land settlement in County Dublin, 1660–1688* (Blackrock, Co. Dublin, 1993), p. 144. For evidence of considerable settlement disturbance in the neighbourhood of the city, see W. J. Smyth, *Map-making, landscapes and memory: A geography of colonial and early modern Ireland, c. 1530–1750* (Cork, 2006), pp. 271–2.
19. Dunlop, *Ireland under the Commonwealth*, pp. 462, 492, 598.
20. Séamus Pender, *A census of Ireland circa 1659* (new edn, Dublin, 2005), pp. 363–80.
21. *CARD*, IV, p. 172; Aidan Clarke, *Prelude to restoration in Ireland: The end of the Commonwealth 1659–1660* (Cambridge, 1999), pp. 108–30, 156–60, 167–8.
22. Ibid., p. 249.
23. Quoted in ibid., p. 298.
24. T. C. Barnard, 'Conclusion', in Ohlmeyer, *Ireland*, p. 228.
25. Barnard, *Cromwellian Ireland*, pp. 83–4; Clarke, *Prelude*, pp. 196, 200–201.
26. *ODNB*, 'James Butler, first duke of Ormond'. On the pageantry surrounding Ormond's welcome: Robin Usher, *Protestant Dublin 1660–1760: Architecture and iconography* (Basingstoke, 2012), pp. 18–19.
27. Raymond Gillespie, 'Rev. Dr John Yarner's notebook: Religion in Restoration Dublin', in *Archivium Hibernicum*, LII (1998), pp. 30–41; *De Búrca Rare Books*, catalogue no. 95 (Dublin, 2010), pp. 9–12; Usher, *Protestant Dublin*, p. 70.
28. Arnold, *Restoration land settlement*, p. 146; *CARD*, IV, p. 259.
29. Arnold, *Restoration land settlement*, pp. 141–2. These calculations are based on Arnold (appendix, pp. 156, 160). No account is taken of unidentified land in either calculation here or (in 1670) of the Duke of York's grants or the expanded acreage of churchland.
30. Quoted in Arnold, op. cit., p. 80. See also pp. 48, 82–3.

31. Christopher Morash, *A history of Irish theatre 1601–2000* (Cambridge, 2002), pp. 12–19, 21–9. The first public dramatic production may in fact have been staged at the great banquet which the the earl of Orrery put on for Ormond in the 'great hall' of Thomas Court in the Meath Liberties, when one of Orrery's own compositions was performed: D. Deighnan, 'The Ormond–Orrery conflict 1640–1680 ...' (Ph.D. dissertation, Brown University, 1982), p. 668.

32. Albert Jouvin (de Rochefort), *Le voyageur d'Europe ...* (Paris, 1672), III, pp. 477–8.

33. Brian Gurrin, 'The hearth tax roll for Dublin City, 1663', in *Analecta Hibernica*, XXXVIII (2004), pp. 51–133; *DIB*, 'Marcus Trevor', 'Wentworth Dillon'. For use of the term 'over the water' for the city's north side, see Rowena Dudley, 'The Cheney letters 1682–85', in *IESH*, XXIII (1996), p. 103.

34. *Cal. S.P. Ire., 1663–5*, 17 June 1665, p. 591; John Dunton, *The Dublin scuffle*, ed. Andrew Carpenter (Dublin, 2000), pp. 209, 388; Usher, *Protestant Dublin*, pp. 174–5.

35. Arnold, *Restoration land settlement*, pp. 117–19; C. L. Falkiner, *Illustrations of Irish history and topography* (London, 1904), pp. 41–73; Usher, *Protestant Dublin*, pp. 25–6.

36. *CARD*, IV, pp. 256, 313, 401–402; V, p. 138; R. L. Greaves, *Dublin's Merchant-Quaker: Anthony Sharp and the community of Friends 1643–1707* (Stanford, 1998), p. 91; Rowena Dudley, 'St. Stephen's Green: The early years 1664–1730', in *DHR*, LIII, 2 (2000), pp. 157–79; T. C. Barnard, '"Grand metropolis" or "The anus of the world": The cultural life of eighteenth-century Dublin', in Clark and Gillespie, *Two capitals*, pp. 205–9; Desmond MacCabe, *St Stephen's Green* (Dublin, 2009), pp. 34–8, 54, 57, 60–67, 70, 93; Usher, *Protestant Dublin*, p. 174. MacCabe has suggested that the first reference to the Green being called a 'square' was in 1697 (op. cit., p. 44n).

37. *CARD*, IV, pp. 197–8; *Cal. S.P. Ire, 1669–70*, pp. 248–9.

38. Nuala Burke, 'An early modern suburb: The estate of Francis Aungier, earl of Longford', in *Ir. Geog.*, VI, 4 (1972), pp. 365–85; Usher, *Protestant Dublin*, pp. 175–7.

39. *Cal. S.P. Ire., 1663–5*, 17 June 1665, p. 591; Colm Lennon, *Dublin 1610–1756*, [Irish Historic Towns Atlas, no.19] (Dublin, 2008), p. 36 and facsimile of de Gomme's map.

40. *CARD*, IV, pp. 549–50; V, pp. 573–6. Yarranton's remarkable plan is reproduced in *CARD*, V, frontispiece.

41. For the 'Amory' lease: *CARD*, V, pp. 58–9.

42. *ODNB*, 'Sir William Ellis'; Usher, *Protestant Dublin*, pp. 80–81.

43. *CARD*, IV, p. 309.

44. *CARD*, IV, pp. 549–50.

45. Usher, *Protestant Dublin*, pp. 46–8.

46. TCD Hutchinson MSS 8556–8; *CARD*, V, pp. 303–4, 328, 331–5, 346, 383–4, 603–10; Sir Frederick Falkiner, *The foundation of the Hospital and Free School of King Charles II, Oxmantown, Dublin ...* (Dublin, 1906), pp. 90–98; Casey, *Buildings of Dublin*, p. 88.

47. Hutchinson MSS 8556–8; Usher, *Protestant Dublin*, pp. 185–8.

48. Jacqueline Hill, *From patriots to unionists: Dublin civic politics and Irish Protestant patriotism 1660–1840* (Oxford, 1997), pp. 48–55; Gillespie, 'Religion and urban society: The case of early modern Dublin', in Clark and Gillespie, *Two capitals*, pp. 234–5.

49. R. L. Greaves, *God's other children: Protestant nonconformists and the emergence of denominational churches in Ireland, 1660–1700* (Stanford, 1997), pp. 276–9, 285–99, 309–314; Greaves, *Merchant-Quaker*, pp. 13–14, 69–71, 147–54; Dudley, 'Cheney letters', pp. 99–100; Emer Purcell, 'The city and the suburb: Medieval Dublin and Oxmanstown', in Duffy, *Medieval Dublin VI*, p. 214; Simpson, 'Fifty years a-digging ...', in Duffy, *Medieval Dublin XI* (Dublin, 2011), pp. 84–5; Margaret Murphy and Michael Potterton, *The Dublin region in the middle ages* (Dublin, 2010), pp. 440–41. On the religious composition of the Meath Liberties, see Dunton's comments in 1698: Edward McLysaght, *Irish life in the seventeenth century* (Shannon, 1969), p. 385.

50. Smyth, *Map-making*, pp. 270–71.

51. C. H. Hull (ed.), *The economic writings of Sir William Petty* (Cambridge, 1899), II, pp. 496–8; R. A. Butlin, 'The population of Dublin in the late seventeenth century', in *Ir. Geog.*, V, 2 (1965), pp. 51–8.

52. Taking 'Birne' and 'Brin' together, they constituted 11 per cent of the 'principal Irish names' in the city, more than twice as many as the next most numerous surname, Doyle: Pender, *A census of Ireland*, p. 373. For the 1683–4 bills of mortality: *CARD*, V, pp. 610–12.

53. Hull, *Petty's writings*, II, p. 498; Colm Lennon, 'The print trade, 1550–1700', in Gillespie and Andrew Hadfield (eds), *The Oxford history of the Irish book*, III: *The Irish book in English 1550–1800* (Oxford, 2006), p. 73.

54. There were 66 full brothers in the Weavers Guild in 1675 and 121 in 1683, and 98 quarter-brothers in 1678 and 78 in 1684: Greaves, *Merchant-Quaker*, p. 76. Cf. Mary Clark and Raymond Refaussé (eds), *Directory of historic Dublin guilds* (Dublin, 1993). On the wider issue of Catholics and the Corporation: *CARD*, IV, pp. 399, 425, 527–8; V, pp. 130–31, 402–6; Hill, *Patriots to unionists*, pp. 32–5.

55. McLysaght, *Irish life*, p. 228; Mary Clark, 'Dublin city pipe water accounts, 1680', and 'Dublin city piper water accounts 1704/5', in *Irish Genealogist*, VII, 2 (1987), pp. 201–4; IX, 1 (1994), pp. 76–88.

56. *CARD*, V, p. 46; McLysaght, *Irish life*, p. 381; Usher, *Protestant Dublin*, pp. 40–44.

57. *CARD,* V, pp. 79, 106; Falkiner, *Hospital and Free School*, pp. 65–5; Lesley Whiteside, *A history of the King's Hospital* (Palmerstown, 1975); Edward McParland, *Public architecture in Ireland, 1680–1760* (London, 2001), p. 168.

58. *CARD*, V, pp. 202, 566–73.

59. *CARD*, V, pp. 10–11; Usher, *Protestant Dublin*, pp. 27–30. According to Dunton writing in 1699, 1,200 inmates were accommodated there after the battle of Aughrim, quadruple its normal intake: McParland, *Public architecture*, p. 66. For a magisterial essay on the Hospital: ibid., chapter 3.

60. McParland, *Public architecture*, p. 91.

61. *London Gazette*, 14 April 1684; Falkiner, *Illustrations*, pp. 34–5; McParland, *Public architecture*, pp. 91–2; Usher, *Protestant Dublin*, pp. 21–5, 31–2.

62. HMC, *Ormond MSS*, new ser., VIII, p. 343.

63. Greaves, *Merchant-Quaker*, p. 48.

64. See the anonymous journal of a Dublin Protestant recording the five years of Jacobite control in *Ormond MSS*, VIII, pp. 343–88. *Lillibulero*, the ever-popular Williamite ballad had complex origins: adopting a 1640s melody, it achieved celebrity after Lord Thomas Wharton championed it as an attack on Tyrconnel.

65. 'Dr King's observations on the state of Dublin after the battle of the Boyne', n.d, [c. Sept. 1690] (TCD MS 1738–1820/2310).

66. *London Gazette*, 9 July 1689.

67. 'Dr King's observations'; *Ormond MSS*, VIII, p. 385.

68. *Ireland's lamentation: Being a short, but perfect, full and true account of the situation, nature, constitution and product of Ireland* ... (London, 1689), pp. 26–8.

69. Raymond Gillespie, 'The Irish Protestants and James II', in *IHS*, XXVIII (1992), pp. 124–33.

70. H. J. Lawlor (ed.), 'The diary of William King D. D... .', in *JRSAI*, 5th ser., XIII (1903), p. 280. For Thomas Denton's observation on Ram's house, *c.*1687: Lennon, *Dublin 1610–1756*, p.37.

71. R. H. Murray (ed.), *Journal of John Stevens, containing a brief account of the war in Ireland, 1689–1691* (Oxford, 1912), pp. 93–4. Cf. J. G. Simms, *Jacobite Ireland 1685–91* (London, 1969), pp. 132–3.

72. Lawlor, 'Diary of William King', p. 144. King recorded a variety of rumours in his 1689 prison diary suggesting that the city would be burnt down. Cf. *A true and perfect journal of the affairs in Ireland since his majesty's arrival in this kingdom* (London, 1690), pp. 2–3, 8–10; *Ormond MSS*, VIII, p. 271; Simms, *Jacobite Ireland*, p. 145.

73. *A true account of seizing and securing the castle and city of Dublin for their majesties' service* ([London], 1690); *True and perfect journal*, pp. 8–12; *Ormond MSS*, VIII, 388. For Catholic confirmation of 'pillaging and plundering', see Valentine Rivers' report: Rev. N. Donnelly, *History of Dublin parishes*, II (Dublin, n.d. [c.1910]), pp. 215–16; Greaves, *Merchant-Quaker*, p. 62.

3 Injured Lady: 1690–1750

1. K. T. Hoppen, *The common scientist in the seventeenth century: A study of the Dublin Philosophical Society 1683–1708* (London, 1970), pp. 64, 78–9, 132–4.

2. 'Irish Catholics licensed to bear arms (1704)', in *Archivium Hibernicum*, IV (1915), pp. 59–65.

3. John Dunton, *The Dublin scuffle*, ed. Andrew Carpenter (Dublin, 2000), p. 177.

4. *CARD*, V, p. 509; VI, pp. 6–7, 184, 199, 224; Valentine Rivers, Lisbon, to Rev. R. Eustace, [1692], in Rev. N. Donnelly, *History of Dublin parishes*, II (Dublin, n.d. [c.1910]), p. 216; Jacqueline Hill, *From patriots to unionists: Dublin civic politics and Irish Protestant patriotism 1660–1840* (Oxford, 1997), pp. 67–8.

5. H. J. Lawlor (ed.), 'The diary of William King D.D... .', in *JRSAI*, 5th ser., XIII (1903), p. 272.

6. *CARD*, VI, pp. 137, 155–6, 162–3, 214–15.

7. Robert Munter, *The history of the Irish newspaper, 1685–1760* (Cambridge, 1967), pp. 27–8; Mary Pollard, *Dictionary of members of the Dublin book trade 1550–1800* (London, 2000), pp. 395–6.

8. Robin Usher, *Protestant Dublin 1660–1760: Architecture and iconography* (Basingstoke, 2012), pp. 101–9.

9. *DIB*, 'Sir Toby Butler', 'Sir Michael Creagh'. On the impact of the penal laws on the legal profession: Patrick Fagan, *Catholics in a Protestant country: The papist constituency in eighteenth-century Dublin* (Dublin, 1998), pp. 107–9, 115–17. Between 1704 and 1729, about 350 Catholics with Dublin addresses were registered on the convert rolls: Eileen O'Byrne (ed.) *The convert rolls* (Dublin, 1981).

10. Patrick Fagan, *The second city: Portrait of Dublin 1700–1760* (Dublin, 1986), p. 111.

11. Gilbert, *Dublin*, I, pp. 372–3; Thomas O'Connor, 'Religious change, 1550–1800', in Raymond Gillespie and Andrew Hadfield (eds), *The Oxford history of the Irish book*, III: *The Irish book in English 1550–1800* (Oxford, 2006), p. 186; *DIB*, 'Sir Thomas Hackett'.

12. Raymond Gillespie, 'Religion and urban society: The case of early modern Dublin', in Clark and Gillespie, *Two capitals*, pp. 231–4; T. C. Barnard, *Irish Protestant ascents and descents 1641–1770* (Dublin, 2004), chapter 5; William Gibson, 'The persecution of Thomas Emlyn 1703–5', in *Journal of Church and State*, XLVIII, 3 (2006), pp. 530–31.

13. G. A. Forrest, 'Religious controversy within the French Protestant communtiy in Dublin, 1692–1716', in Kevin Herlihy (ed.) *The Irish dissenting tradition* (Blackrock, 1995), p. 99; Raymond Hylton, *Ireland's Huguenots and their refuge 1662–1745* (Brighton, 2005), pp. 35, 112, 116.

14. Earl of Arran, Dublin, to the duke of Ormond, 2 May 1682 (*Ormond MSS*, VI, p. 359). The apprentices were presumably not in the main Catholic.

15. Based on Hylton's occupational data for the years 1692–1745, it would appear that a third of his database were merchants or in allied wholesale pursuits, and another 40 per cent were divided almost equally between luxury crafts, textile manufactures, clothing and apparel, and the medical or legal professions: Hylton, *Ireland's Huguenots*, p. 133. See also Jessica Cunningham, 'Dublin's Huguenot goldsmiths 1690–1750', in *Irish Architectural & Decorative Studies*, XII (2009), p. 162.

16. Edward McParland, *Public architecture in Ireland, 1680–1760* (London, 2001), pp. 163, 165–6; Muriel MacCarthy, 'Elie Bouhéreau, first keeper of Marsh's Library', in *DHR*, LVI, 2 (2003), pp. 132–45; Toby Barnard, 'Libraries and collectors, 1700–1800', Gillespie and Hadfield, *The Irish book in English 1550–1800*, pp. 120–22; *DIB*, 'Elie Bouhéreau'.

17. Mairéad Dunlevy, *Pomp and poverty: A history of silk in Ireland* (London, 2011), pp. 58–60.

18.   T. C. Barnard, *Making the grand figure: Lives and possessions in Ireland, 1641–1770*
      (London, 2004), p. 288; Colm Lennon, 'The medieval town in the early modern
      city', in John Bradley, A. J. Fletcher and Anngret Simms (eds), *Dublin in the
      medieval world: Studies in honour of Howard B. Clarke*, (Dublin, 2009), p. 444;
      Alan Smyth, David Dickson and Rolf Loeber (eds), 'Journal of a tour to Dublin
      and the counties of Dublin and Meath in 1699', in *Anal. Hib.*, XLIII (2012),
      pp. 47–67.

19.   Donald Woodward, 'The Anglo-Irish livestock trade in the seventeenth century',
      in *IHS*, XVIII, 72 (1973), pp. 508–13.

20.   Patrick Kelly, 'The Irish woollen export prohibition act of 1699: Kearney
      re-visited', in *IESH*, VII (1980), pp. 22–44; Kelly, 'William Molyneux and the
      spirit of liberty in eighteenth-century Ireland', in *ECI*, III (1988), pp. 133–48; James
      Kelly, 'Political publishing 1700–1800', in Gillespie and Hadfield, *The Irish book in
      English 1550–1800*, pp. 213, 216–18.

21.   *CARD*, VI, p. 179.

22.   Patrick Fitzgerald, 'Poverty and vagrancy in early modern Ireland' (Ph.D.
      dissertation, Queen's University Belfast, 1994), pp. 43–5, 47, 50, 108–9, 122, 126–7,
      129–35, 142.

23.   St John's Vestry minutes, 25 May 1680, quoted in Rowena Dudley, 'The Dublin
      parishes and the poor 1660–1740', in *Archivium Hibernicum*, LIII (1999), p. 89;
      Fitzgerald, 'Poverty and vagrancy', pp. 272, 341; R. L. Greaves, *Dublin's Merchant-
      Quaker: Anthony Sharp and the community of Friends 1643–1707* (Stanford, 1998),
      p. 58.

24.   *CARD*, V, p. 457; VI, p. 218; Greaves, *Merchant-Quaker*, p. 59.

25.   John Vernon, *Remarks on a paper, entitled, An abstract of the state of the work-house,
      for maintaining of the poor of the city of Dublin ...* (Dublin, 1716), pp. iii, 11–12.

26.   Ibid., pp. 34, 35, 36–7; *CARD*, VI, pp. 90–91, 219; T. K. Moylan, 'Vagabonds and
      sturdy beggars', in *DHR*, I, 2 (June 1938), pp. 42–3; David Dickson, 'In search of
      the old Irish poor law', in Rosalind Mitchison and Peter Roebuck (eds), *Economy
      and society in Scotland and Ireland 1500–1939* (Edinburgh, 1988), pp. 150–51;
      Fitzgerald, 'Poverty and vagrancy', pp. 241–3.

27.   Vernon, *Remarks*, p.11; Fitzgerald, 'Poverty and vagrancy', pp. 233–5, 284–5;
      Dudley, 'Dublin parishes', p. 82.

28.   James Kelly, 'Harvests and hardship: Famine and scarcity in Ireland in the late
      1720s', in *Studia Hibernica*, XXVI (1992), pp. 81, 92, 94–5.

29.   Joseph Robins, *The lost children: A study of charity children in Ireland 1700–1900*
      (Dublin, 1980), pp. 10–17.

30.   Dickson, 'Old Irish poor law', p. 151; Fitzgerald, 'Poverty and vagrancy', pp. 274–5,
      354–7, 388–9, 396; Dudley, 'Dublin parishes', p. 89.

31.   Laurence M. Geary, *Medicine and charity in Ireland 1718–1851* (Cork, 2004),
      pp. 13–19.

32.   McParland, *Public architecture*, pp. 76–8.

33.   Ibid., pp. 123–5; Mairéad Dunlevy, *Dublin Barracks: A brief history* (Dublin,
      2002), pp. 17–19; Usher, *Protestant Dublin*, pp. 130–38.

34. P. M. Kerrigan, *Castles and fortifications in Ireland 1485–1945* (Cork, 1995), pp. 135–6; Dunlevy, *Dublin Barracks*, pp. 25–9; John A. McCullen, *An illustrated history of the Phoenix Park: Landscape and management to 1880* (Dublin, 2009), p. 37. On Stoneybatter: Archbishop King to Viscount Palmerston, 8 October 1725, quoted in McParland, *Public architecture*, p. 44; Barnard, *Making the grand figure*, pp. 361–5.

35. Ibid., pp. 117, 119; Patrick Walsh, *The making of the Irish Protestant ascendancy: The life of William Conolly 1662–1729* (Woodbridge, 2010), pp. 130–35.

36. These data are taken from a 1732 return: TNA, CUST/20/100. Cf. Walsh, *Conolly*, pp. 134, 137, 142. The curate at Irishtown was on the Revenue payroll; another thirty-eight were employed in the collection of excise duties in the Dublin city district.

37. Jacqueline Hill, 'Dublin Corporation, Protestant dissent and politics 1660–1800', in Kevin Herlihy (ed.), *The politics of Irish dissent 1650–1800* (Dublin, 1997), pp. 30–32; *DIB*, 'Benjamin Burton'.

38. *A directory of Dublin for the year 1738* (Dublin, 2000); L. M. Cullen, *Princes and pirates: The Dublin Chamber of Commerce, 1783–1983* (Dublin 1983), pp. 25–8; Cullen, 'The Dublin merchant community in the eighteenth century', in Paul Butel and L. M. Cullen, *Cities and merchants: French and Irish perspectives on urban development 1500–1900* (Dublin, 1986), pp. 196–7.

39. *Cal. S.P. Ire. 1669/70*, p.683; David Dickson, 'The place of Dublin in the eighteenth-century Irish economy', in T. M. Devine and David Dickson (eds), *Ireland and Scotland 1600–1850* (Edinburgh, 1983), p. 190n.

40. *A letter from a shop-keeper in Dublin to His Grace the Duke of Bedford ... on public credit* (Dublin, 1760), pp. 7–10; *DIB*, 'Benjamin Burton'. For Damer's supposedly fabulous wealth at the time of his death in 1720, see Fagan, *Second city*, pp. 251–2.

41. Steven ffeary-Smyrl, '"Theatres of worship": Dissenting meeting houses in Dublin, 1650–1750', in Kevin Herlihy (ed.), *The Irish dissenting tradition 1650–1750* (Dublin, 1995), pp. 49–53; Jean Agnew, *Belfast merchant families in the seventeenth century* (Dublin, 1996), pp. 174–5, 184–5; Usher, *Protestant Dublin*, pp. 92–4.

42. Cullen, 'Dublin merchant community', pp. 199–200.

43. [Charles Abbot], 'A tour through Ireland N[orth] Wales, 1792' (TNA, PRO 30/9/23), f. 121; Ada K. Longfield, 'History of the Irish linen and cotton printing industry in the 18th Century', in *JRSAI*, 7th series, VII, 1 (1937), pp. 33–4; Dickson, 'The place of Dublin', pp. 182–4. One estimate suggested that by 1760, £400,000 'in specie' was annually taken north from Dublin, 'mostly from the banks', to finance the linen trade: *A letter on public credit*, p. 10.

44. Usher, *Protestant Dublin*, pp. 50–60, 76–80.

45. McParland, *Public architecture*, pp. 44–9; Usher, *Protestant Dublin*, pp. 81–2.

46. Munter, *The history of the Irish newspaper*, pp. 50–51; *DIB*, 'Edward Lloyd'.

47. David Hayton, 'The crisis in Ireland and the end of Queen Anne's ministry', in *IHS*, XXII, 87 (1981), p. 198.

48. Hill, *Patriots to unionists*, pp. 72–8.

49. Usher, *Protestant Dublin*, pp. 111–17.

582 Notes to pp. 132–43

50. For Conolly's business career: Walsh, *Conolly, passim*.

51. McParland, *Public architecture*, p. 191. Cf. Usher, *Protestant Dublin*, pp. 32–3, 138–41.

52. McParland, *Public architecture*, chapter 7.

53. Irvin Ehrenpreis, *Swift: The man, his works, and the age*, III: *Dean Swift* (London, 1983), pp. 157–9; James Kelly, 'Jonathan Swift and the Irish economy in the 1720s', in *Eighteenth-Century Ireland*, VI (1991), pp. 7–36; ibid., 'Harvest and hardship', pp. 65–105.

54. Munter, *The history of the Irish newspaper*, pp. 145–9; Brendan Twomey, *Smithfield and the parish of St. Paul 1698–1750* (Dublin, 2005), p. 45; Andrew Carpenter, 'Literature in print 1550–1800', in Gillespie and Hadfield, *The Irish book in print 1550–1800*, pp. 314–15.

55. Samuel Madden, *Reflections and resolutions proper for the gentlemen of Ireland, as to their conduct for the service of their country, as landlords, as masters ...* (Dublin, 1723), p. 32; Munter, *The history of the Irish newspaper*, pp. 153, 164–5; Kelly, 'Harvests and hardship', pp. 96–7; Patrick Kelly, 'The politics of political economy in mid-eighteenth-century Ireland', in S. J. Connolly (ed.), *Political ideas in eighteenth-century Ireland* (Dublin, 2000), pp. 105–29.

56. H. F. Berry, *A history of the Royal Dublin Society* (London, 1915), pp. 3–33; Munter, *The history of the Irish newspaper*, pp. 53, 152–3, 166.

57. J. L. McCracken, 'The social structure and social life, 1714–60', in T. W. Moody and W. E. Vaughan (eds), *A new history of Ireland*, IV: *Eighteenth-century Ireland 1691–1800* (Oxford, 1986), pp. 46–9; L. M. Cullen, 'Economic development 1750–1800' in Moody and Vaughan, op cit., p. 184; David Broderick, *The first toll-roads: Ireland's turnpike roads 1729–1858* (Cork, 2002), chapter 2.

58. For a statement of the case for canals: Madden, *Reflections*, pp. 190, 193.

59. McParland, *Public architecture*, pp. 147–57.

60. Munter, *The history of the Irish newspaper*, pp. 160–62; McDowell and Webb, *Trinity College*, p. 500; *DIB*, 'Francis Hutcheson'; Usher, *Protestant Dublin*, pp. 83–90. In fairness, Swift was a champion of female education: Norma Clarke, *Queen of the wits: A life of Laetitia Pilkington* (London, 2008), p. 47.

61. Hylton, *Ireland's Huguenots*, pp. 120–22.

62. *Reasons humbly offered against passing an act for the better preventing mischiefs that might happen by fire* (Dublin, 1713); Dickson, 'Large-scale developers and the growth of eighteenth-century Irish cities', in Butel and Cullen, *Cities and merchants*, pp. 115–16; Casey, *Dublin*, pp. 36–7, 193–200; A. P. W. Malcomson, *Nathaniel Clements: Government and the governing elite in Ireland, 1725–75* (Dublin, 2005), pp. 201–4; Usher, *Protestant Dublin*, pp. 189–93. Sash windows had, however, been introduced to Dublin by 1700, but were still uncommon in the 1720s: Barnard, *Making the grand figure*, p. 288.

63. During the controversy over the revaluation of the Irish currency in 1737, Swift reportedly warned Boulter in public that, 'if it had not been for him he would have been torn to pieces by the mob, and if he held up his finger he could make them do it that instant' (George Sackville to the Duke of Dorset, 6 October 1737, in

Sotheby's Catalogue of English Literature, 10 July 2012, Lot 13, Dorset papers [now in TCD Manuscripts Department]).

64. J. A. Oughton, autobiography memoir (National Army Museum [London], MS 8808–36–1), ff. 66–7; David Dickson, *Arctic Ireland: The extraordinary story of the great frost and forgotten famine of 1740–41* (Belfast, 1997), *passim*; R. S. Harrison, *Dr John Rutty (1698–1775) of Dublin: A Quaker polymath in the Enlightenment* (Dublin, 2011), pp. 52–5.

65. In the 1729 famine, some 3,635 people received funds from the city-wide parish collections which totalled over £900, almost half of whom were resident in the two south-west parishes of St Catherine's and St Nicholas without: Kelly, 'Harvest and hardship', pp. 90–91.

66. F. E. Dixon, 'Weather in old Dublin', in *DHR*, XIII, 3/4 (1953), p. 96; Michael Drake, 'The Irish demographic crisis of 1740–41', in T. W. Moody (ed.), *Historical Studies*, VI (London, 1968), pp. 101–24; Dickson, *Arctic Ireland*, *passim*.

67. Nuala Burke, 'A hidden church? The structure of Catholic Dublin in the mid-eighteenth century', in *Archivium Hibernicum*, XXXII (1974), pp. 81–2.

68. Patrick Fagan, 'The Dublin Catholic mob (1700–50)', in *Eighteenth-Century Ireland*, IV (1989), p. 134.

69. Herbert Davis and Louis Landa (eds), *Jonathan Swift: Irish tracts, 1720–1723, and sermons* (Oxford, 1968), p. 19; Munter, *The history of the Irish newspaper*, p. 142; Fagan, *Second city*, pp. 102–7; Fagan, 'Dublin Catholic mob', pp. 134–9; James Kelly, *The Liberty and Ormond boys: Factional riot in eighteenth-century Dublin* (Dublin, 2005), pp. 21–4.

70. I have followed Fagan's reading of the somewhat problematical 1731 evidence: Fagan, *Second city*, pp. 114–20.

71. Burke, 'Hidden church', pp. 88–9; Fagan, *Second city*, pp. 120–22, 127–32.

72. Alan Harrison, *The dean's friend: Anthony Raymond 1675–1726, Jonathan Swift and the Irish language* (Blackrock, Co. Dublin, 1999), chapter 2 and appendix 1.

73. Ibid., p. 50; Fagan, *Second city*, pp. 204–9.

74. Barnard, *Irish Protestant ascents and descents*, pp. 189–96.

75. Quoted in Fagan, *Second city*, pp. 203–4. Mary Lawrence of Merchants Quay, printer of at least the second edition of *Almanack an Gaoidheilg ar son uliana [bliana] an tighearna Criosda 1724* (Dublin, 1724), produced mainly educational material; her late husband had had strong Tory associations.

76. *DIB*, 'Aodh Buí MacCruitín'.

77. One tantalising estimate of city literacy levels comes from the 1690s: 70 per cent of the craftsmen signing bail bonds in the Tholsel court in 1693–4 could sign their names, compared to 20 per cent of the 'yeomen', i.e. (presumably) countrymen: Gillespie, 'Catholic religious cultures 1614–97', in James Kelly and Dáire Keogh (eds), *History of the Catholic diocese of Dublin* (Dublin, 2000), pp. 132–3; another document in 1730 suggests that 80 per cent of broad-cloth weavers could sign their name: Barnard, 'Print culture, 1700–1800', in Gillespie and Hadfield, *Irish book in English 1550–1800*, p. 43.

78.	Patrick Corish, *The Catholic community in the seventeenth and eighteenth centuries* (Dublin, 1981), p. 85.

79.	Munter, *The history of the Irish newspaper*, pp. 148–50; James Kelly, 'Political publishing, 1700–1800', in Gillespie and Hadfield, *Irish book in English 1550–1800*, pp. 223–4; *DIB*, 'John Harding'.

80.	Munter, *The history of the Irish newspaper*, pp. 102–4.

81.	Ibid., pp. 19, 40–49.

82.	Ibid., pp. 38, 55–66, 76–86, 95–100; T. C. Barnard, 'Print culture, 1700–1800', and Kelly, 'Political publishing, 1700–1800', in Gillespie and Hadfield, *Irish book in English 1550–1800*, pp. 51–3, 218–19.

83.	*Dickson's Dublin Intelligence*, 25 February 1728–9, quoted in Munter, *The history of the Irish newspaper*, p. 35; ibid., pp. 153–4; T. C. Barnard, '"Grand metropolis" or "The anus of the world": The cultural life of eighteenth-century Dublin', in Clark and Gillespie, *Two capitals*, p. 187.

84.	Mary Pollard, *Dublin trade in books 1550–1800* (Oxford, 1989), pp. 119, 197.

85.	Andrew Carpenter, *Verse in English from eighteenth-century Ireland* (Cork, 1998), pp. 24, 26–7, 278–95.

86.	A. C. Elias Jr., *Memoirs of Laetitia Pilkington* (Athens and London, 1997); Carpenter, *Verse in English*, pp. 31–3; Clarke, *Queen of the wits, passim*.

4 'This Now Great Metropolis': 1750–1780

1.	For comparative European city populations: Jan de Vries, *European urbanization 1500–1800* (London, 1984), appendix 1. Note that de Vries's estimate for Dublin in 1750 (90,000) is a serious underestimate. For the working estimate of 125,000 for Dublin: David Dickson, 'The place of Dublin in the eighteenth-century Irish economy', in T. M. Devine and David Dickson (eds), *Ireland and Scotland 1600–1850* (Edinburgh, 1983), p. 179; Patrick Fagan, *Catholics in a Protestant country: The Papist constituency in eighteenth-century Dublin* (Dublin, 1998), pp. 29, 33, 44. The Dublin figure is capable of further refinement.

2.	Cited in Peter Clark and Bernard Lepetit (eds), *Capital cities and their hinterlands in early modern Europe* (Aldershot, 1996), p. 4.

3.	T. C. Barnard, *Making the grand figure: Lives and possessions in Ireland, 1641–1770* (London, 2004), p. 306. For the search in Dublin for a bride for Pole Cosby in 1725: ibid., p. 296. For echoes of Dublin in eighteenth-century Naples: Brigitte Marin, 'Naples: Capital of the enlightenment', in Clark and Lepetit (eds), *Capital cities*, p. 163.

4.	Clark and Lepetit (eds), *Capital cities*, p. 4.

5.	McDowell and Webb, *Trinity College*, pp. 49–53; Tighernan Mooney and Fiona White, 'The gentry's winter season', in David Dickson (ed.), *The gorgeous mask: Dublin 1700–1850* (Dublin, 1987), pp. 2–4; T. C. Barnard, '"Grand metropolis" or "The anus of the world": The cultural life of eighteenth-century Dublin', in Clark and Gillespie, *Two capitals*, pp. 194–5; Barnard, *Making the grand figure*, pp. 288–91, 297–301; Alison Fitzgerald, 'The business of being a goldsmith in eighteenth-century Dublin', in Gillian O'Brien and Finola O'Kane (eds), *Georgian Dublin* (Dublin, 2008), p. 134.

6. F. G. James, *Lords of the ascendancy: The Irish House of Lords and its members 1600–1800* (Dublin, 1990), pp. 158–9; A. P. W. Malcomson, *The pursuit of the heiress: Aristocratic marriage in Ireland 1740–1840*, 2nd edn (Belfast, 2006), pp. 40–41. Another indicator of the overlap between ennobled families and wealthy commoners' families is suggested by the register of private sedan-chair owners in the 1780s; only two-fifths of those owning this highly visible status symbol were drawn from the former group: *A correct copy of the registry of private licensed sedan chairs, in the city of Dublin, as they appear on the Collector's Books, 25th March, 1786* (Dublin, 1786).

7. [Thomas Campbell], *A philosophical survey of the south of Ireland, in a series of letters to John Watkinson, M.D.*, 2nd edn (Dublin, 1778), pp. 31, 46; Barnard, 'Grand metropolis', pp. 191–2, 201–3; ibid., *Making the grand figure*, pp. 292–5, 361–6, 369. As for the physical appearance of these spaces, Barnard has unearthed details of one tavern, 'The Blackamoor's Head', off Church Street, which in 1730 had a well-lit parlour and a second 'long' room, a kitchen, 'some drinking boxes', and some discreet private rooms at the back of the premises, and it would have probably been respectable enough to receive the custom of gentlemen: Barnard, *Making the grand figure*, pp. 292, 353–4.

8. John Dunton, *The Dublin scuffle*, ed. Andrew Carpenter (Dublin, 2000), p. 182; *A letter of advice to a young poet* [Dublin, 1721], in *Jonathan Swift's Irish tracts 1720–1723*, ed. Herbert David (Oxford, 1968), p. 323; Gilbert, *Dublin*, II, p. 70; W. S. Clark, *The early Irish stage: The beginnings to 1720* (Oxford, 1955), *passim*; Christopher Morash, *A history of Irish theatre 1601–2000* (Cambridge, 2002), chapter 2.

9. Clark, *Early Irish stage*, p. 117; John Greene, 'The repertory of Dublin theatres, 1720–45', in *ECI*, II (1987), pp. 133–48.

10. Brian Boydell, *A Dublin musical calendar 1700–1760* (Blackrock, Co. Dublin, 1988), pp. 21–2; Morash, *History of Irish theatre*, pp. 42–9.

11. Chris Mounsey, 'Thomas Sheridan and the second Smock Alley Theatre riot, 1754', in *New Hibernia Review*, IV, 3 (2000), pp. 65–77; Morash, *History of Irish theatre*, pp. 58–66. Sheridan returned to Dublin in 1758 for a further season.

12. Boydell, *Dublin musical calendar*, pp. 48–9.

13. Ibid.; Barnard, *Making the grand figure*, pp. 358–9; Thomas O'Connor, 'Religious change, 1550–1800', in Raymond Gillespie and Andrew Hadfield (eds), *The Oxford history of the Irish book*, III: *The Irish book in English 1550–1800* (Oxford, 2006), p. 184.

14. Gilbert, *Dublin*, I, pp. 67–77; Andrew Carpenter, *Verse in English from eighteenth-century Ireland* (Cork, 1998), pp. 278–80.

15. Boydell, 'Music 1700–1850', in T. W. Moody and W. E. Vaughan (eds), *A new history of Ireland*, IV: *Eighteenth-century Ireland 1691–1800* (Oxford, 1986), pp. 570–81; Barnard, 'Grand metropolis', pp. 196–9.

16. Gary Boyd, *Dublin 1745–1922: Hospitals, spectacle and vice* (Dublin, 2006), pp. 202–3.

17. Cormac Ó Gráda, 'Dublin's demography in the early nineteenth century: Evidence from the Rotunda', in *Population Studies*, CL (1991), p. 46; Boyd, *Dublin 1745–1922*, pp. 81–2.

18. Campbell, *Philosophical survey*, p. 25; I. C. Ross (ed.), *Public virtue, public love: The early years of the Dublin Lying-in Hospital* (Dublin, 1986), pp. 20, 22–4; Edward McParland, *Public architecture in Ireland, 1680–1760* (London, 2001), pp. 84–6; Edel Sheridan-Quantz, 'The multi-centred metropolis: The social topography of eighteenth-century Dublin', in Clark and Gillespie, *Two capitals*, p. 270.

19. On Henry's private art collection: The Knight of Glin and James Peill, *Irish furniture* (New Haven and London, 2007), pp. 88–9.

20. Ross, *Public virtue*, p. 79; McParland, *Public architecture*, pp. 87–8.

21. Brian Boydell, 'Music', in Ross, *Public virtue*, p. 108.

22. Ross, *Public virtue*, pp. 47–50, 77–93; Brian Boydell, *Rotunda music in eighteenth-century Dublin* (Dublin, 1992).

23. Beatrice Bayley Butler, 'Lady Arabella Denny, 1707–1792', in *DHR*, IX, 1 (1946), pp. 1–20; Joseph Robins, *The lost children: A study of charity children in Ireland 1700–1900* (Dublin, 1980), pp. 23–7; Sarah Lloyd, '"Pleasure's golden bait": Prostitution, poverty and the Magdalen Hospital in eighteenth-century London', in *History Workshop Journal*, XLI (1996), pp. 55–6, 65–6; Rosemary Raughter, 'A natural tenderness: The ideal and the reality of eighteenth-century female philanthropy', in Maryann Valiulis and Mary O'Dowd (eds), *Women and Irish history* (Dublin, 1997), pp. 71–88; Barnard, *Making the grand figure*, pp. 294–5, 353–4; *DIB*, 'Arabella Denny', 'Teresa Mulally'.

24. McParland, *Public architecture*, p. 207.

25. [M. B.], *A letter to T— P—, esq; concerning a new bridge* ([Dublin], 1751), p. 7, quoted in Edward McParland, 'Strategy in the planning of Dublin 1750–1800', in Paul Butel and L. M. Cullen (eds), *Cities and merchants: French and Irish perspectives on urban development 1500–1800* (Dublin, 1988), pp. 98–9. Cf. James Rooney, Dublin, to [Sir Nicholas Bayly], 3 Nov., 4 Dec. 1753, Annesley MSS (PRONI, D619/21/B/111, 112); Eoin Magennis, *The Irish political system 1740–1765* (Dublin, 2000), p. 69. For opposition in the Liberties in 1761: W. C. Stubbs, 'Weavers' Guild', in *JRSAI*, XLIX (1919), p. 76.

26. *Georgian Society records*, III, pp. 74–98; Eamon Walsh, 'Sackille Mall: The first one hundred years', in Dickson (ed.), *The gorgeous mask*, pp. 34–7; Robin Usher, *Protestant Dublin 1660–1760: Architecture and iconography* (Basingstoke, 2012), pp. 194–6.

27. Barnard, *Making the grand figure*, pp. 299–300; A. P. W. Malcomson, *Nathaniel Clements: Government and the governing elite in Ireland 1725–75* (Dublin, 2005), pp. 202, 380; *DIB*, 'Nathaniel Clements'; John A. McCullen, *An illustrated history of the Phoenix Park: Landscape and management to 1880* (Dublin, 2009), pp. 50–52; Usher, *Protestant Dublin*, pp. 119–21, 134–6. Several of those who had worked on the Lying-in Hospital and its chapel, including Cramillion, also worked

on his Phoenix Park villa (the future Viceregal Lodge): Casey, *Dublin*, pp. 292–3, 300–301.

28. Alistair Rowan, 'The Irishness of Irish architecture', in *Architectural History*, XL (1997), p. 16; Casey, *Dublin*, pp. 497–8; Susan Roundtree. 'Brick in the eighteenth-century Dublin house', in Christine Casey, *The eighteenth-century Dublin town house: Form, function and finance* (Dublin, 2010), p. 78; Tony Hand, 'Supplying stone for the Dublin house', in Casey, op. cit., pp. 87–8; Loreto Calderón and Konrad Dechant, 'New light on Hugh Montgomerie ...', in Casey op. cit., pp. 187–94; Usher, *Protestant Dublin*, p. 176.

29. [Charles Abbot], 'A tour through Ireland N[orth] Wales, 1792' (TNA, PRO 30/9/23), f. 38; Casey, *Dublin*, pp. 498–501; Finola O'Kane, 'The Fitzwilliam family's development of Merrion Square', in Casey, *Eighteenth-century Dublin town house*, pp. 102–6. The first duke left debts of £148,000 in 1773; his heir was said to have enjoyed an income of only £7,000 a year: *DIB*, 'James Fitzgerald'. I am very grateful to Dr C. J. Woods for allowing me to make use of his transcription of Abbot's 'Tour' prior to publication.

30. Sheridan-Quantz, 'Multi-centred metropolis', p. 274.

31. Dickson, 'Large-scale developers and the growth of eighteenth-century Irish cities', in Butel and Cullen, *Cities and merchants*, pp. 120–21; Casey, *Dublin*, pp. 577–9; O'Kane, 'Fitzwilliam family's development', pp. 98–109; Conor Lucey, 'Classicism or commerce? The town house interior as commodity', in Casey, *Eighteenth-century Dublin town house*, pp. 236–7, plates 7, 10–13 in ibid.

32. J. H. Andrews, 'Introduction', in Paul Ferguson (ed.), *The A to Z of Georgian Dublin: John Rocque's maps of the city in 1756 and the county in 1760* (Dublin, 1998); John Montague, 'John Rocque and the *Exact survey of Dublin*', in Montague and Colm Lennon (eds), *John Rocque's Dublin: A guide to the Georgian city* (Dublin, 2010), pp. xi–xvi.

33. Campbell, *Philosophical survey*, p. 2. For Mrs Delany's evocative description of the prospect looking south from Glasnevin in 1744: Mary Delany to Ann Dewes, 19 July 1744, in *Letters from Georgian Ireland: The correspondence of Mary Delany 1731–68*, ed. Angelique Day (Belfast, 1991), pp. 181–2.

34. [Charles Abbot], 'A tour through Ireland N[orth] Wales, 1792' (TNA, PRO 30/9/23), f. 124; *The villa: or Glasnevin, a poem ...* (Dublin, 1754), pp. 5, 12; Finola O'Kane, '"The appearance of a continued city": Dublin's Georgian suburbia', in O'Brien and O'Kane, *Georgian Dublin*, pp. 120–26. Blackrock's popularity was helped even in the 1760s by a capacious inn, 'The sign of a ship', equipped with a 'spacious ballroom ... where an excellent band of music, a man cook and a good larder were to be found ...': F. E. Ball, *A history of the county Dublin*, 6 vols (Dublin, 1902), I, p. 23.

35. H. A. Gilligan, *A history of Dublin port* (Dublin, 1988), pp. 21–41.

36. The hall had been planned from the early 1730s and opened in 1745, its architect, Joseph Jarratt, being responsible among much else for the La Touche Bank building in Castle Street in the 1750s: Nicholas Sheaff, 'Jarratt and rococo', in *Irish Arts Review*, I, 3 (1984), pp. 50–51.

37. For the most insightful account of the Lucas affair: Jacqueline Hill, *From patriots to unionists: Dublin civic politics and Irish Protestant patriotism 1660–1840* (Oxford, 1997), pp. 83–111.

38. Robert Munter, *The history of the Irish newspaper, 1685–1760* (Cambridge, 1967), pp. 180–88; James Kelly, 'Political publishing 1700–1800', in Gillespie and Hadfield, *The Irish book in English 1550–1800*, pp. 225–6.

39. *A Dialogue between a Protestant and a Papist, concerning some late strange reports about an union, and the seditious consequences of them* ([Dublin], [c.1759]), p. 7.

40. James Kelly, *The Liberty and Ormond Boys: Factional riot in eighteenth-century Dublin* (Dublin, 2005), pp. 21, 30–31, 38–9. On rivalries between Oxmantown and Thomas Street at civic musters at the beginning of the seventeenth century: Emer Purcell, 'The city and the suburb: Medieval Dublin and Oxmanstown', in Duffy, *Medieval Dublin VI*, pp. 221–2.

41. Ab[raham] W[ilkinson], *The clothier's letter to the inhabitants off the Liberties* (Dublin, 1759), pp. 9–11; 'A Freeman', *A short but true history of the rise, progress and happy repression of several late insurrections ...* (Dublin, 1760), pp. 16–17, cited in Sean Murphy, 'The Dublin anti-union riot of 3 December 1759', in Gerard O'Brien (ed.), *Parliament, politics and people: Essays in eighteenth-century Irish history* (Blackrock, Co. Dublin, 1989), p. 5; Seamus Cummins, 'Extra-parliamentary agitation in Dublin in the 1760s', in R. V. Comerford (ed.), *Religion, conflict and coexistence in Ireland ...* (Dublin, 1990), pp. 121–5; Eoin Magennis, *The Irish political system 1740–1765* (Dublin, 2000), pp. 136–40; Vincent Morley, *Irish opinion and the American Revolution 1760–1783* (Cambridge, 2002), pp. 11–12; Kelly, *Liberty and Ormond Boys*, p. 39.

42. Quoted in Gilbert, *Dublin*, I, p. 292, and dated 1766. Cf. Kelly, 'Political publishing, 1700–1800', pp. 228–9.

43. *Dublin Magazine*, [I] (1762), p. 1; Máire Kennedy, 'Reading print, 1700–1800', in Gillespie and Hadfield, *The Irish book in English 1550–1800*, p. 154.

44. *DIB*, 'Peter Wilson'.

45. *Dublin directory, 1760;* Walter Harris, *The history and antiquities of the city of Dublin ...* (Dublin, 1766), 'Preface'; McParland, *Public architecture*, p. 84; Bernadette Cunningham, 'Historical writing, 1660–1750', in Gillespie and Hadfield, *The Irish book in English 1550–1800*, pp. 279–81; *DIB*, 'Edward Worth'; R. S. Harrison, *Dr John Rutty (1698–1775) of Dublin: A Quaker polymath in the Enlightenment* (Dublin, 2011), pp. xxi, 11, 19–20, 79, 85–7, 113–14, 120, 159–60, 187–9, 194–5, 204n, 216–17, 222, 232–4. For the estimate of the printing workforce: Colm Lennon, 'The print trade, 1550–1700', in Gillespie and Andrew Hadfield (eds), *The Oxford history of the Irish book*, III: *The Irish book in English 1550–1800* (Oxford, 2006), pp. 82–4; and for the estimate of the total number of Dublin imprints for the century: Kennedy, 'Reading print, 1700–1800', and James Kelly, 'Political publishing, 1700–1800', in Gillespie and Hadfield (eds), *The Irish book in English 1550–1800*, pp. 151, 219–21.

46. The Knight of Glin and James Peill, *Irish furniture* (New Haven and London, 2007), pp. 70–79.

47. L. M. Cullen, *Anglo-Irish trade 1660–1800* (Manchester, 1968), pp. 114, 159.

48. [Wilkinson], *The clothier's letter*, pp. 4–5; Dickson, 'The place of Dublin', pp. 186–8; L. M. Cullen, 'Eighteenth-century flour milling in Ireland', in Andy Bielenberg (ed.), *Irish flour milling: A history 600–2000* (Dublin, 2003), pp. 44–55.

49. James Rooney, Dublin, to Sir Nicholas Bayley, 8 March 1755 (Anglesey MSS: PRONI, D619/21/B/125).

50. Malcolm Dillon, *The history and development of banking in Ireland* (London, 1889), pp. 21–4; Cullen, *Anglo-Irish trade*, pp. 15, 163–5, 197, 199; Marie-Louise Legg, 'Money and reputations: The effects of the banking crises of 1755 and 1760', in *ECI*, XI (1996), pp. 74–87; Magennis, *Irish political system*, pp. 135–6; Malcomson, *Clements*, pp. 352–86.

51. *A letter from a shop-keeper in Dublin to His Grace the Duke of Bedford ... on public credit* (Dublin, 1760), pp. 11–12.

52. L. M. Cullen, *Princes and pirates: The Dublin Chamber of Commerce 1783–1983* (Dublin, 1983), pp. 34–5.

53. Ibid., pp. 35–7.

54. George Semple, *A treatise on building in water* (Dublin, 1776); *DIB*, 'George Semple'; Usher, *Protestant Dublin*, p. 116.

55. Gilbert, *Dublin*, II, p. 36. Cf. Toby Barnard, *A new anatomy of Ireland: The Irish Protestants* (London, 2003), p. 123.

56. McParland, 'Strategy in the planning', pp. 100–101; Mary Pollard, *Dictionary of members of the Dublin book trade 1550–1800* (London, 2000), 'Crampton, Philip'.

57. Edward McParland, 'The Wide Streets Commissioners', in *Quarterly Bulletin of the Irish Georgian Society*, XV, 1 (1972), pp. 1–32; Cullen, *Princes and pirates*, pp. 34–44; Casey, *Dublin*, pp. 351–7; Usher, *Protestant Dublin*, pp. 144–6.

58. Edward McParland, 'James Gandon and the Royal Exchange competition, 1768–69', in *JRSAI*, CII, 1 (1972), pp. 58–72; Edward McParland, *James Gandon: Vitruvius Hibernicus* (London, 1985), p. 38; Casey, *Dublin*, pp. 361–4; Usher, *Protestant Dublin*, pp. 161–3.

59. Jonathan Swift, *Directions to servants and miscellaneous pieces, 1733–1742*, ed. Herbert Davis (Oxford, 1973), pp. xxvi–vii, 89–92, 167–71; Sarah Foster, 'An honourable station in respect of commerce as well as constitutional liberty', in O'Brien and O'Kane, *Georgian Dublin*, p. 32. The 1734 riot was apparently directed against French cottons and woollens: Martyn J. Powell, *The politics of consumption in eighteenth-century Ireland* (Basingstoke, 2005), p. 174; Usher, *Protestant Dublin*, p. 170.

60. Charles Hendrick account book 1733–64 (NLI, uncat. MS); *Wilson's Dublin directory for the year 1763* (Dublin, 1763); *Wilson's Dublin directory for the year 1774* (Dublin, 1774); Hall, *Bank of Ireland*, p. 13; L. M. Cullen, *Economy, trade and Irish merchants at home and abroad* (Dublin, 2012), pp. 215, 224–5; *DIB*, 'Sir Nicholas Lawless'.

61. In *Wilson's Dublin directory 1768*, ninety-two merchants and traders were listed for Dame Street who were involved in some thirty-eight different trades. Cf. Sheridan-Quantz, 'Multi-centred metropolis', pp. 280–84; Barnard, *Making the*

grand figure, p. 287; Fitzgerald, 'The business of being a goldsmith', in O'Brien and O'Kane, *Georgian Dublin*, pp. 130–31.

62. Benjamin Houghton, *A faithful narrative of the conduct of Benjamin Houghton ... on the late risings and tumults ...* (Dublin, 1764), pp. 23–5; *Journal of the House of Commons of Ireland*, VII, pp. 190, 235, append. ccxlviii–ccli; Mairéad Dunlevy, *Pomp and poverty: A history of silk in Ireland* (London, 2011), pp. 75, 78. Houghton implicated four men – William Keating, James Corrogan, Patrick Muldoon and John Jackson – 'apprentices to journeymen weavers' as 'the principal actors' in the events of 8 August (*Faithful narrative*, p. 23), three of whom had Catholic-sounding names. Ten of the eleven masters whose stock was destroyed because of their links with Cottingham and King had Protestant-sounding names: *JHCI*, VII, append. ccxlix.

63. Fitzgerald, 'The business of being a goldsmith', in O'Brien and O'Kane, *Georgian Dublin*, p. 127. See also Fitzgerald, 'The production of silver in late Georgian Dublin', in *Irish Architectural and Decorative Studies*, IV (2001), pp. 24–6.

64. Mairéad Reynolds, 'Wedgwood in Dublin, 1772–1777', in *Irish Arts Review*, I, 2 (1984), pp. 36–8; Danny Parkinson, 'The Delamain family in Ireland', in *DHR*, XL, 2 (1996), p. 157; Barnard, *Making the grand figure*, pp. 127–8.

65. Alison Fitzgerald, 'Cosmopolitan commerce: The Dublin goldsmith Richard Calderwood', in *Apollo* (Sept. 2005), pp. 46–52; Review [of Glin and Peill, *Irish furniture* (London, 2007)], in *Apollo* (Sept. 2007), p. 118.

66. The fluctuations in raw and thrown silk imported into Dublin in this period were quite pronounced, but it was not until the 1770s that there is evidence of a long-term contraction in silk manufacturing: TNA, CUST/15.

67. Sarah Foster, 'Going shopping in eighteenth-century Dublin', in *things*, 4 (1996), pp. 48–50.

68. John Turpin, 'The School of Ornament of the Dublin Society in the eighteenth century', in *JRSAI*, CXVI (1986), p. 44. See also Turpin, 'The School of Figure Drawing of the Dublin Society in the eighteenth century', in *DHR*, XL, 1 (Dec. 1986), pp. 2–14; XL, 2 (1987), pp. 42–6; Gitta Willemson, *The Dublin Society Drawing Schools: Students and award winners 1746–1876* (Dublin, 2000); Anne Crookshank and the Knight of Glin, *Ireland's painters 1600–1940* (New Haven, 2002), pp. 83–92; Dunlevy, *Pomp and poverty*, pp. 67–70.

69. William Laffan (ed.), *The cries of Dublin &c: Drawn from the life by Hugh Douglas Hamilton, 1760* (Dublin, 2003).

70. Glin and Peill, *Irish furniture*, pp. 79–83; Joseph McDonnell, 'Stuccowork and English rococo carving in Russborough', in *Irish Architectural and Decorative Studies*, XIV (2011), pp. 111–12.

71. Richard Twiss, *A tour in Ireland in 1775* (London, 1776), p. 24; Joseph McDonnell, 'Joseph Henry of Straffan', in Michael MacCarthy (ed.), *Lord Charlemont and his circle* (Dublin, 2001), pp. 77–80; *DIB*, 'Joseph Leeson'. The value of Henry's lost cargo in 1745 was reportedly £60,000, no doubt a massive exaggeration: McDonnell, 'Stuccowork and English rococo carving', p. 112.

72. McParland, *Gandon*, pp. 34–5, 89; Cynthia O'Connor, *The pleasing hours: The grand tour of James Caulfeild (1728–99), traveller, connoisseur and patron of the arts* (Cork, 1999), part 3; Christine Casey, 'Newly discovered building accounts for Charlemont House and the Casino at Marino', in *Apollo* (June, 1999), pp. 45–7; Jane Meredith, 'Letters between friends: Lord Charlemont's library and other matters', in *Irish Architectural and Decorative Studies,* IV (2001), pp. 53–75; John Redmill, 'The buildings of William Chambers in Dublin', and Helen Byrne, 'Simon Vierpyl, (*c.*1725–1810), sculptor and stonemason', in MacCarthy, *Charlemont and his circle*, pp. 159–61, 186–9; Casey, *Dublin*, pp. 149–52; Usher, *Protestant Dublin*, p. 198.

73. McParland, *Gandon*, pp. 6, 38, 67,186; Casey, 'Building accounts', pp. 45–7; Redmill, 'Buildings of William Chambers', pp. 154–9; Byrne, 'Simon Vierpyl', pp. 182–6; and Teresa Watts, 'Lord Charlemont and vases', in MacCarthy, *Charlemont and his circle*, pp. 130–35.

74. Barnard, 'Grand metropolis', pp. 195–6, 199–201; Deana Rankin, 'Historical writing, 1750–1800', in Gillespie and Hadfield, *The Irish book in English 1550–1800*, p. 299.

75. James Kelly, 'Napper Tandy, radical and republican', in James Kelly and Uáitéar Mac Gearailt (eds), *Dublin and Dubliners* (Dublin, 1990), pp. 1–24; James Kelly, *Sir Edward Newenham MP, 1734–1814: Defender of the Protestant constitution* (Dublin, 2004); Padhraig Higgins, *A nation of politicians: Gender, patriotism, and political culture in late eighteenth-century Ireland*, (Madison, 2010), p. 224. For the statue: idem., pp. 74, 129n.

76. *FJ*, 26–28 February, 7–9 March 1771; Hill, *Patriots to unionists*, pp. 127–8; Vincent Morley, *Irish opinion and the American Revolution 1760–1783* (Cambridge, 2002), pp. 70–71.

77. Ibid., pp. 73–4.

78. Martyn J. Powell, 'The Society of Free Citizens and other popular political clubs, 1749–80', in James Kelly and M. J. Powell (eds), *Clubs and societies in eighteenth-century Ireland* (Dublin, 2010), pp. 245–55.

79. *Hib. Jnl.*, 19 July 1775, quoted in R. B. McDowell, *Ireland in the age of imperialism and revolution 1760–1801* (Oxford, 1979), p. 243. See also Hill, *Patriots to unionists*, pp. 142–4; Kelly, *Sir Edward Newenham*, pp. 100–103, 117–19; Morley, *Irish opinion*, pp. 76–7, 125–6.

80. Hill, *Patriots to unionists*, pp. 143, 147.

81. Ibid., pp. 125–6, 145; Higgins, *Nation of politicians*, p. 12.

82. Morley, *Irish opinion*, pp. 91–4, 128–9, 142–4; Kelly, *Liberty and Ormond boys*, pp. 33, 48.

83. Hugh Fenning, 'The archbishops of Dublin 1693–1786', in James Kelly and Dáire Keogh (eds), *History of the Catholic diocese of Dublin* (Dublin, 2000), pp. 206–14. Remarkably, a large scrapbook of Irish-language poetry and prose, a grammar-book, and a collection of Irish prayers survive, all transcribed by Carpenter as a teenager *c.*1745 while he attended Ó Neachtain's school: Brian Mac Giolla

Phádraig, 'Dr. John Carpenter: Archbishop of Dublin, 1760–1786', in *DHR*, XXX, 1 (1976), pp. 8–9.

84. Thomas Bartlett, *The fall and rise of the Irish nation: The Catholic question 1690–1830* (Dublin, 1992), pp. 50–55, 60–65, 75–81; Patrick Fagan, *Catholics in a protestant country: The papist constituency in eighteenth-century Dublin* (Dublin, 1998), pp. 97–8; Morley, *Irish opinion*, pp. 9–10.

85. *FJ*, 10 November 1779; Maureen Wall, 'The Catholic merchants, manufacturers and traders of Dublin 1778–1782', in *Reportorium Novum*, I, 2 (1959–60), pp. 298–323.

86. Bartlett, *Fall and rise of the Irish nation*, pp. 86–90.

87. Hall, *Bank of Ireland*, pp. 13–14; Morley, *Irish opinion*, pp. 192–8.

88. Hill, *Patriots to unionists*, pp. 146–8; Kelly, *Sir Edward Newenham*, p. 149; Stephen O'Connor, 'The Volunteers of Dublin 1778–84', in O'Brien and O'Kane, *Georgian Dublin*, pp. 68–77. Evidence on the total number of Dublin corps in existence between 1778 and 1780 is imprecise; the estimates here are drawn from data in Padhráig Ó Snodaigh, *The Irish volunteers, 1715–93* (Blackrock, Co. Dublin, 1995).

89. Edward Newenham to E. N. Newenham, 29 October 1779, quoted in Kelly, *Sir Edward Newenham*, p. 151; *Londonderry Journal*, 12 November 1779, quoted in Morley, *Irish opinion*, p. 226.

90. One petition in early 1779 spoke of 19,000 weavers in the Liberties on the verge of starvation, indicative more of the total size of textile families than of the actual state of distress: Bartlett, *Fall and rise of the Irish nation*, p. 93.

91. Danny Mansergh, *Grattan's failure: Parliamentary opposition and the people in Ireland 1779–1800* (Dublin, 2005), pp. 36–7, 40–44; James Kelly, 'Elite political clubs', in Kelly and Powell, *Clubs and societies*, pp. 268–74.

92. Hill, *Patriots to unionists*, pp. 146–7; Morley, *Irish opinion*, pp. 204–8; Powell, *Politics of consumption*, pp. 184–5; Higgins, *Nation of politicians*, pp. 83, 88, 94–6, 99, 110–14, 121–6.

93. James Kelly, '"The glorious and immortal memory": Commemoration and Protestant identity in Ireland 1660–1800', in *PRIA*, XCIV, C, 4 (1994), pp. 38–9; James Kelly, 'Francis Wheatley: His Irish paintings, 1779–1783', in A. M. Dalsimer (ed.), *Visualizing Ireland: National identity and the pictorial tradition* (London, 1993), pp. 145–63.

94. Hill, *Patriots to unionists*, pp. 148–9; Morley, *Irish opinion*, p. 228; Mansergh, *Grattan's failure*, pp. 31–6; Kelly, *Sir Edward Newenham*, pp. 148–9, 152–5; Higgins, *Nation of politicians*, pp. 70–72. For a Tandy-led demonstration outside Parliament in March 1778 (over a controversial paving bill): Mansergh, *Grattan's failure*, p. 38.

95. Morley, *Irish opinion*, pp. 232–3; Higgins, *Nation of politicians*, pp. 72–81. Higgins points out that some Volunteer corps were disinclined to celebrate: ibid., pp. 77–8.

5 Patriot Town: 1780–1798

1. Padhraig Higgins, *A nation of politicians: Gender, patriotism, and political culture in late eighteenth-century Ireland* (Madison, 2010), pp. 51–5, 232.

2. *Hib. Jnl.*, 21 August 1778, quoted in Higgins, op. cit., p. 42.

3. Robert Munter, *The history of the Irish newspaper, 1685–1760* (Cambridge, 1967), pp. 100–104, 175, 181–6, 189–91.

4. Ibid., pp. 87–8; James O'Toole, *Newsplan: Report of the Newsplan project in Ireland*, rev. edn (Dublin, 1998), pp. 291–5; Higgins, *Nation of politicians*, pp. 31–2; Colm Lennon, 'The print trade, 1700–1800', in Hadfield and Gillespie, *Irish book in English, 1550–1800*, pp. 77–8.

5. [Thomas Campbell], *A philosophical survey of the south of Ireland, in a series of letters to John Watkinson, M.D.*, 2nd edn (Dublin, 1778), p. 26; Brian Inglis, *The freedom of the press in Ireland 1784–1841* (London, 1954), p. 37; Vincent Morley, *Irish opinion and the American Revolution 1760–1783* (Cambridge, 2002), pp. 145–7; *DIB*, 'Frederick Jebb'; Higgins, *Nation of politicians*, pp. 40–41, 45–7.

6. Mathew Carey, *The urgent necessity of an immediate repeal of the whole penal code candidly considered* (Dublin, 1781), cited in Padhraig Higgins, 'Catholic identity, and the penal laws' (paper presented to the McNeil Center for Early American Studies symposium, 'Ireland, America, and the Worlds of Mathew Carey', October 2011); E. C. Carter II, 'Mathew Carey in Ireland, 1760–1784', in *Catholic Historical Review*, LI, 4 (1966), pp. 503–527; *DIB*, 'Mathew Carey'.

7. John FitzGibbon, Dublin, to William Eden, 18 November 1787, in D. A. Fleming and A. P. W. Malcomson (eds), *"A volley of execrations": The letters and papers of John FitzGibbon, earl of Clare 1772–1802* (Dublin, 2005), pp. 61–2; Inglis, *Freedom of the press*, pp. 21–48; Thomas Wall, *At the sign of Doctor Hay's Head* (Dublin, 1958), pp. 2–40; Higgins, *Nation of politicians*, pp. 46–7, 226–30; A. P. W. Malcomson, *John Foster (1740–1828): The politics of improvement and prosperity* (Dublin, 2011), pp. 65–9.

8. Carey, *Urgent necessity*, pp. 59, 64.

9. James Kelly, *Sir Edward Newenham MP, 1734–1814: Defender of the Protestant constitution* (Dublin, 2004), pp. 163–4; James Kelly, 'A "genuine" whig and patriot: Lord Charlemont's political career', in Michael MacCarthy (ed.), *Lord Charlemont and his circle* (Dublin, 2001), pp. 19–21; Danny Mansergh, *Grattan's failure: Parliamentary opposition and the people in Ireland 1779–1800* (Dublin, 2005), pp. 55–6.

10. *ODNB*, 'Henry Grattan'. On the threats by some Volunteers of direct action in the city if the constitutional demands were not conceded by 27 May 1782: Mansergh, *Grattan's failure*, p. 73.

11. Jacqueline Hill, *From patriots to unionists: Dublin civic politics and Irish Protestant patriotism 1660–1840* (Oxford, 1997), pp. 164–5. On the Irish Brigade (under the command of Lord Delvin in 1784): [Patrick Duigenan?], *The alarm: Or, an address to the nobility, gentry, and clergy, of the Church of Ireland, as by law established* (Dublin, 1783), p. 33; James Kelly, 'A secret return of the Volunteers in Ireland in 1784', in *IHS*, XXVI, 103 (1989), p. 284; Kelly, *Newenham*, pp. 157, 215–18.

12. Higgins, *Nation of politicians*, p. 213. For an intriguing description of the Volunteer convention in the Rotunda: Kelly, *Newenham*, pp. 202–6.

13. Kelly, 'Secret return', pp. 272–3, 284; Kelly, *Newenham*, pp. 223–5; Hill, *Patriots to unionists*, pp. 171–82; Higgins, *Nation of politicians*, pp. 214–15, 220–21; Jim Smyth, *The men of no property: Irish radicals and popular politics in the late eighteenth century* (Basingstoke, 1992), p.138.

14. James Kelly, 'Scarcity and poor relief in eighteenth-century Ireland: The subsistence crisis of 1782–4', in *IHS*, XXVIII, 109 (1992), pp. 40–62.

15. Ibid., p. 47; James Kelly, 'The resumption of emigration from Ireland after the American War of Independence: 1783–1787', in *Studia Hibernica*, XXIV (1988), pp. 76–7. In 1800 Jacob Geoghegan, a Francis Street silk manufacturer, put the numbers employed 'in the silk manufacture in all its branches in Dublin' at between 5,000 and 6,000, which would suggest some recovery in the intervening period: *Union with Ireland: Evidence taken before the committee of the Irish House of Commons on the subject of legislative union* (H.C., 1833 [517]), p. 4.

16. Hill, *Patriots to unionists*, p. 178; Higgins, *Nation of politicians*, pp. 229–31; Brian Henry, *Dublin hanged: Crime, law enforcement and punishment in late eighteenth-century Dublin* (Blackrock, Co. Dublin, 1994), pp. 66–7.

17. Smyth, *Men of no property*, pp. 136–7; Hill, *Patriots to unionists*, pp. 173–5; Kelly, *Newenham*, pp. 220–23; Martyn J. Powell, *The politics of consumption in eighteenth-century Ireland* (Basingstoke, 2005), p.179; Higgins, *Nation of politicians*, pp. 225–33.

18. Hill, *Patriots to unionists*, pp. 178–82; Kelly, 'Lord Charlemont's political career', pp. 26–8; Kelly, *Newenham*, pp. 213–15, 218–24; Higgins, *Nation of politicians*, pp. 215–17, 220–23.

19. Mansergh, *Grattan's failure*, pp. 99–100. For recognition by Eden of this group as early as the autumn of 1781, although their influence was limited in the following two short viceroyalties until Rutland's arrival early in 1784: A. P. W. Malcomson, *John Foster: The politics of the Anglo-Irish ascendancy* (Oxford, 1978), p. 43.

20. William Stevens, *Hints to the people, especially to the inhabitants of Dublin* (Dublin, 1799), pp. 9, 11; Malcomson, *John Foster*, pp. 387–95.

21. *DIB*, 'Walter Wade'; Malcomson, *John Foster (1740–1828): The politics of improvement*, pp. 348–9.

22. Warburton and Whitelaw, *Dublin*, II, pp. 973–5; David Dickson, 'Aspects of the rise and decline of the Irish cotton industry', in L. M. Cullen and T. C. Smout (eds), *Comparative aspects of Scottish and Irish economic and social history 1600–1900* (Edinburgh, [1977]), pp. 101–3; James Kelly, 'Prosperous and Irish industrialization in the late eighteenth century', in *Journal of the County Kildare Archaeological Society*, XVI (1985–6), pp. 441–67; Henry, *Dublin hanged*, pp. 66–7.

23. [Sir Thomas Bond], *National advantages to be derived from adopting the following plans ...* (Dublin, 1799), p. 15; David Dickson, 'The place of Dublin in the eighteenth-century Irish economy', in T. M. Devine and David Dickson (eds), *Ireland and Scotland 1600–1850* (Edinburgh, 1983), p. 183.

24. Hall, *Bank of Ireland*, pp. 30–35, 50–60, 508–12; David Dickson and Richard English, 'The La Touche dynasty', in David Dickson (ed.), *The gorgeous mask: Dublin 1700–1850* (Dublin, 1987), pp. 22–3; *DIB*, 'William Eden', 'David La Touche III'; W. A. Thomas, *The stock exchanges of Ireland* (Liverpool, 1986), pp. 2–7, 136; Malcomson, *John Foster (1740–1828):Politics of improvement*, p. 60; L. M. Cullen, *Economy, trade and Irish merchants at home and abroad* (Dublin, 2012), pp. 224–8.

25. L. M. Cullen, *Princes and pirates: The Dublin Chamber of Commerce, 1783–1983* (Dublin 1983), pp. 43–53; Cullen, *Economy, trade and Irish merchants*, p. 224; Malcomson, *John Foster (1740–1828):Politics of improvement*, pp. 37–8.

26. Stanley H. Palmer, *Police and protest in England and Ireland 1780–1850* (Cambridge, 1988), p. 119; Ann C. Kavanaugh, *John FitzGibbon, Earl of Clare: A study in personality and politics* (Dublin, 1997), pp. 198–201; *DIB*, 'John Fitzgibbon (1748–1802)'; The Knight of Glin and James Peill, *Irish furniture* (New Haven and London, 2007), p.179.

27. *Animadversions on the street robberies in Dublin …* (Dublin, 1765), pp. 6–13.

28. Ibid., p. 19.

29. Maurice O'Connell, 'Class conflict in a pre-industrial society: Dublin in 1780', in *Irish Ecclesiastical Record*, CIII (1965), pp. 93–106; Smyth, *Men of no property*, p.134; Hill, *Patriots to unionists*, p. 202. The grouping of parishes into divisions was first attempted in the 1774 Paving Board legislation, which divided the city into five divisions.

30. J. D. Herbert, *Irish varieties for the last fifty years …* 1st ser. (London, 1836), pp. 77–82; Henry, *Dublin hanged*, pp. 62–5, 119–28; Denver O'Mahony, 'Sir Lucius O'Mahony, 3rd baronet 1731–95' (unpublished M.Litt. dissertation, University of Dublin, 2001), pp. 242–9; Mary Lyons (ed.), *The memoirs of Mrs Leeson, madam 1727–97* (Dublin, 1995), pp. 69–71; *DIB*, 'Richard Crosbie'. It seems that Crosbie's 1785 flight may have been trumped by a M. Rousseau at Navan some months previously.

31. Palmer, *Police and protest*, p. 123; Henry, *Dublin hanged*, pp. 99–100.

32. Bernadette Doorley, 'Newgate prison', in Dickson, *Gorgeous mask*, pp. 124–30; Henry, *Dublin hanged*, pp. 16–17, 19, 35–6, 100; Desmond MacCabe, *St. Stephen's Green* (Dublin, 2009), pp. 122–3.

33. Palmer, *Police and protest*, pp. 117–21, 128–9; Hill, *Patriots to unionists*, pp. 183–5; Kavanaugh, *John FitzGibbon*, pp. 97–9; Henry, *Dublin hanged*, p. 100; Neal Garnham, 'Police and public order in eighteenth-century Dublin', in Clark and Gillespie, *Two capitals*, pp. 82–7.

34. 'Abbot's tour, 1792', ff. 25–6; Brian Henry, 'Crime, law enforcement and punishment in Dublin 1780–95' (Ph.D. dissertation, University of Dublin, 1992), pp. 56, 108; Henry, *Dublin hanged*, pp. 34, 67, 77, 91, 95, 98, 164–5. Cf. Herbert, *Irish varieties*, pp. 81–2; Palmer, *Police and protest*, pp. 122–4.

35. Ibid., pp. 123–8.

36. Ibid., p. 133; Hill, *Patriots to unionists*, pp. 246–7.

37. Smyth, *Men of no property*, p. 145; Henry, *Dublin hanged*, p. 76; Kavanaugh, *FitzGibbon*, pp. 160–97, 248–9; Malcomson, 'Introduction', in Fleming and Malcomson, '*A volley of execrations*', pp. xv–xlviii: James Kelly (ed.), *Proceedings of the Irish House of Lords* (Dublin, 2008), I, pp. xxxiv–v.

38. Murray Fraser, 'Public building and colonial policy in Dublin, 1760–1800', in *Architectural History*, XXVIII (1985), pp. 112–3; *ODNB*, 'John Beresford'.

39. John Coleman, 'Luke Gardiner (1745–98): An Irish dilettante', in *Irish Arts Review*, XV (1999), pp. 164–7.

40. The haven-master estimated in 1774 that the existing Custom House Quay could accommodate a maximum of thirty-two vessels of 100 tons if roped together in four tiers, whereas berthage for sixty-five vessels was now needed: *Considerations on the removal of the Custom-House humbly submitted to the public* (Dublin, 1781), pp. 7–10. See also ibid., pp. 15–16, 37–9.

41. Ibid., appendix, pp. 4–6, 8–15. Interestingly, Luke Gardiner was noted as being only 'neutral' in the Commons debate on the Customs House move: James Kelly (ed.), 'Review of the House of Commons, 1774', in *ECI*, XIX (2004), p. 175.

42. 'Abbot's tour, 1792', f. 28; Edward McParland, *James Gandon: Vitruvius Hibernicus* (London, 1985), pp. 41–3; Fraser, 'Public building', pp. 108–11; McParland, 'Strategy in the planning of Dublin 1750–1800', in Paul Butel and L. M. Cullen, *Cities and merchants: French and Irish perspectives on urban development 1500–1900* (Dublin, 1986), pp. 97–104; E. M. Johnston-Liik, *History of the Irish parliament, 1692–1800* (Belfast, 2002), III, p. 66; A. P. W. Malcomson, *Archbishop Charles Agar: Churchmanship and politics in Ireland 1760–1810* (Dublin, 2002), pp. 143–8, 156, 158–60. Malcomson has noted the political support for the Ellis/Agar position given by Speaker Sexton Pery, even though he was a Sackville Street resident: ibid., pp. 147–8.

43. Thomas J. Mulvany (ed.) *The life of James Gandon . . . from materials collected . . . by his son, James Gandon* (Dublin, 1846), pp. 44–5, 55–64; Fraser, 'Public building', pp. 109–110; McParland, *Gandon*, pp. 40–41.

44. Ibid., pp. 47–9, 71; Fraser, 'Public building', p. 112. Coping with massive dampness and flooding was a continuing problem in the building: McParland, *Gandon*, p. 59. The warehouses and docks added in the following decade cost in the order of £100,000.

45. T. M. Truxes, *Irish-American trade 1660–1783* (Cambridge, 1988), pp. 74–6; Fraser, 'Public building', p. 107; Karen Cheer, 'Irish maritime trade in the eighteenth century: A study in patterns of trade, market structures, and merchant communities' (unpublished MA thesis, Victoria University of Wellington, NZ, 2008), pp. 12–15, 34–6, 42–5, 60–61. [http://researcharchive.vuw.ac.nz/bitstream/handle/10063/895/thesis.pdf?sequence=1, accessed 7 February 2013].

46. McParland, *Gandon*, pp. 33, 48, 51, 55–7, 58, 66, 68–70.

47. Malcomson, *John Foster*, p. 359. For a retrospective view that it was always Tories like Beresford, not Whigs, who had championed metropolitan improvement: 'Viator', *Letters to the right honorable Robert Peel . . . relating to the improvement of*

'*the district of the metropolis' and principally the earl of Meath's Liberties* ... (Dublin, 1816), p. 27.

48. John Beresford, Greenwood, to James Gandon, September 1781, in Mulvany, *Gandon*, p. 57; Nuala Burke, 'Dublin 1600–1800: A study in urban morphogenesis' (unpublished Ph.D. dissertation, University of Dublin, 1972), pp. 396–7, 403; Fraser, 'Public building', p. 112; McParland, *Gandon*, pp. 70–71; Andrew Kincaid, *Postcolonial Dublin: Imperial legacies and the built environment* (Minneapolis, 2006), pp. 2–4.

49. McParland, *Gandon*, pp. 72–4, 97; H. A. Gilligan, *A history of Dublin port* (Dublin, 1988), pp. 51–6. The most strident criticism of the new public buildings, and of Gandon in particular, was made in Anon. [Thomas Malton?], *Letters addressed to Parliament, and to the public in general; on various improvements of the metropolis* (Dublin, 1787).

50. McParland, *Gandon*, pp. 74–6.

51. Warburton and Whitelaw, *Dublin*, II, p. 1082; McParland, *Gandon*, pp. 75–6, 87; Fraser, 'Public building', pp. 114, 117.

52. Ibid., pp. 113–14, 119–20. Fraser has noted that Rutland spoke approvingly in 1784 of the rationale behind the great plans as 'calculated not more for ornament and splendour than for health, convenience and security': ibid., p. 114.

53. McParland, *Gandon*, p. 94; Fraser, 'Public building', pp. 106, 114–15. Between 1782 and 1792 the Commission received £50,000 from state grants and £ 76,500 from the coal tax; in addition £100,000 was borrowed in two tranches, in 1784 and 1790: ibid., p. 115.

54. Edward McParland, 'The Wide Streets Commissioners', in *Quarterly Bulletin of the Irish Georgian Society*, XV, 1 (1972), pp. 1–32; Fraser, 'Public building', p. 115.

55. McParland, 'Wide Streets Commissioners', p. 21; McParland, *Gandon*, p. 76; Fraser, 'Public building', p. 118.

56. Seamus Grimes, *Ireland in 1804* (Dublin, 1980), pp. 21–2; McParland, *Gandon*, pp. 95–6, 149–64.

57. Fraser, 'Public building', p. 115; C. E. F. Trench, 'William Burton Conyngham (1733–1796)', in *JRSAI*, CXV (1985), p. 54; Johnston-Liik, *History of Irish parliament*, III, p. 327. On the sickly reputation of the Viceregal Lodge in the 1780s and 1790s: Caroline Gallagher, 'State and domestic arrangements in the household of the Lord Lieutenant of Ireland, 1794–95', in *Archivium Hibernicum*, LXII (2009), p. 242.

58. David Broderick, *The first toll-roads: Ireland's turnpike roads 1729–1858* (Cork, 2002), pp. 94–7. Luke Gardiner stirred up a storm in 1786 when he proposed that all approach roads to the city should become toll-bearing: Diarmuid Ó Gráda, 'The rocky road to Dublin: Transport modes and urban growth', in *Studia Hibernica*, XXII/XXIII (1982–3), p. 8.

59. In the objections to the original 1763 bill, Viscount Fitzwilliam prevented the Circular Road from coming any further east than Leeson Street into what later became Fitzwilliam Square, and later acts specified that no tolls were to be levied on sections running through the Fitzwilliam estate; Henry Monck, with

development plans in the north-west side of town, also opposed the original route as it went through his property in Stoneybatter, on the grounds that the new road would be lined with cabins, making it 'a filthy suburb' rather than 'an agreeable country road': *JHCI*, VI (1760–65), p. 279. Speaker Ponsonby's strong support for the bill secured its passage. In the amending Acts of 15 & 16 Geo. III, *c.* 28, and 17 & 18 Geo. III, *c.*10, the line of the North Circular Road was pushed further north, and the north and south roads were divided into separate financial entities; the latter act also authorised a new downstream ferry where the ends of the road faced each other across the Liffey.

60.   Philip Luckombe, *A tour through Ireland: Wherein the present state of that kingdom is considered* (London, 1780), p. 38; Ó Gráda, 'The rocky road to Dublin', pp. 134–8; Fraser, 'Public building', p. 117; Broderick, *Toll-roads*, pp. 94–8; Casey, *Dublin*, p. 205.

61.   Ibid., pp. 200–204.

62.   John Montague and Colm Lennon (eds), *John Rocque's Dublin: A guide to the Georgian city* (Dublin, 2010), pp. 70–71.

63.   *CARD*, XI, pp. 171, 265–8, 321–3; V. T. H. and D. R. Delany, *The canals of the south of Ireland* (Newton Abbot, 1966), pp. 32–47; Hill, *Patriots to unionists*, p. 161.

64.   Some 102 tons of dung was supplied from Dublin to Kerdiffstown demesne beside the canal near Sallins in 1786 at 2s.6d per ton: Dublin City Library and Archives, Edward Hendrick's account-book, 1783–9.

65.   William Chapman, *Observations on the advantages of bringing the Grand Canal round by the circular road into the River Liffey ...* (Dublin, 1785), pp. 4–5; *Names of the proprietors of Grand Canal stock, and the amount, as it stood in the company's ledger on the 1st day of June, 1800* (Dublin, n.d. [*c.*1800]); Delany and Delany, *Canals of the south of Ireland*, pp. 37, 49–51.

66.   'Abbot's tour, 1792', f. 37; W. A. Thomas, *The stock exchanges of Ireland* (Liverpool, 1986), pp. 136–7.

67.   Ibid., pp. 80–87; Thomas Bartlett (ed.), *Revolutionary Dublin 1795–1801: The letters of Francis Higgins to Dublin Castle* (Dublin, 2004), pp. 254–5.

68.   Mansergh, *Grattan's failure*, pp. 111–13.

69.   Hill, *Patriots to unionists*, pp. 186–90; Mansergh, *Grattan's failure*, pp. 111–12.

70.   W. G. Strickland, 'The state coach of the Lord Mayor of the city of Dublin and the state coach of the earl of Clare, Lord Chancellor of Ireland', in *JRSAI*, LI (1921), pp. 52–61. Significantly, the figure of Liberty on the roof of the mayoral coach rested on three elements: Magna Carta, the charters of Dublin, and the Reform Act of 1760.

71.   Herbert, *Irish varieties*, 1st series, pp. 71–6; Andrew Carpenter, *Verse in English from eighteenth-century Ireland* (Cork, 1998), pp. 103–7; Hill, *Patriots to unionists*, pp. 194–5.

72.   Sir John Carr, *The stranger in Ireland: Or a tour in the southern and western parts of that country in the year 1805* (Philadelphia, 1806), p. 77; 'P. M. and F. O'K.', 'The Assembly House, South William Street', in *DHR*, I (1938), pp. 28–32; Bartlett, *Revolutionary Dublin*, p. 79; Usher, *Protestant Dublin*, pp. 153–8.

73. Henry, *Dublin hanged*, pp. 164–6.

74. Hugh Gough, 'Book imports from continental Europe in late eighteenth-century Ireland: Luke White and the *Société Typographique de Neuchâtel*', in *Long Room*, XXXVIII (1993), pp. 35–48; Máire Kennedy, 'Readership in French: The Irish experience', and Kennedy and Geraldine Sheridan, 'The trade in French books', in Graham Gargett and Geraldine Sheridan (eds), *Ireland and the French Enlightenment, 1700–1800* (Basingstoke, 1999), pp. 3–20, 173–96; Kennedy, 'Foreign language books, 1700–1800', in Raymond Gillespie and Andrew Hadfield (eds), *The Oxford history of the Irish book*, III: *The Irish book in English 1550–1800* (Oxford, 2006), pp. 368–82.

75. J. H. Stewart, 'The fall of the Bastille on the Dublin stage', in *JRSAI*, 5th series, LXXXIV, 1 (1954), p. 83; Stewart, 'The French Revolution on the Dublin stage', in *JRSAI*, 5th series, XCI, 2 (1961), p. 192.

76. Smyth, *Men of no property*, pp. 91–3; David Dickson, 'Paine and Ireland', in Dickson, Dáire Keogh and Kevin Whelan (eds), *The United Irishmen: Republicanism, radicalism and rebellion* (Dublin, 1993), pp. 137–41; Hill, *Patriots to unionists*, p. 227; Mansergh, *Grattan's failure*, pp. 116–25; Ultán Gillen, 'Opposition political clubs and societies 1790–98', in James Kelly and M. J. Powell (eds), *Clubs and societies in eighteenth-century Ireland* (Dublin, 2010), pp. 302–3.

77. Earl of Charlemont to Charles Haliday, 15 December 1791, quoted in Kelly, 'A "genuine" Whig and patriot', pp. 31–2. Cf. Mansergh, *Grattan's failure*, p. 131.

78. The best edition of the Drennan correspondence is Jean Agnew (ed.), *The Drennan–McTier letters*, 3 vols (Dublin, 1998–9). Cf. *DIB*, 'William Drennan'.

79. Thomas Bartlett, *The fall and rise of the Irish nation: The Catholic question 1690–1830* (Dublin, 1992), p. 124; Hill, *Patriots to unionists*, p. 239; C. J. Woods, 'The personnel of the Catholic Convention, 1792–3', in *Archivium Hibernicum*, LVII (2003), pp. 26–76. On Byrne as the largest importer at Dublin port in 1785: Cheer, 'Irish maritime trade', p. 94.

80. Quoted in Bartlett, *Fall and rise of the Irish nation,* p. 130. The meeting took place in November.

81. *Declaration of the Catholic Society of Dublin* (Dublin, 1791), p. v; Hill, *Patriots to unionists*, pp. 195–6, 230.

82. Smyth, *Men of no property*, p. 60; Bartlett, *Fall and rise of the Irish nation,* pp. 139–41.

83. *Walker's Hibernian Magazine*, January–June 1792, p. 458.

84. Bartlett, *Fall and rise of the Irish nation*, chapters 8 and 9; Hill, *Patriots to unionists*, pp. 213–37.

85. Drennan to Sam McTier, 1 November 1792 (Agnew, *Drennan–McTier letters*, I, p. 422); *Proceedings at the Catholic meeting of Dublin, duly convened on Wednesday, October 31, 1792 ...* (Dublin, 1792), p. 18; R. D. Edwards, 'Minute book of the Catholic Committee, 1773–92', in *Archivium Hibernicum*, IX, (1942), pp. 2–172; Hill, *Patriots to unionists*, pp. 229–31.

86. Ibid., pp. 224–5.

87. The best overview of this period remains Nancy Curtin, *The United Irishmen: Popular politics in Ulster and Dublin 1791–8* (Oxford, 1994), chapters 1 and 2.

88. John Binns, silk mercer and canal promoter, was absent but remained a supporter of Catholic relief within the Corporation: *DIB*, 'John Binns'. On William Paulet Carey's critical views on the elitism of society's leadership: Smyth, *Men of no property*, pp. 140–41; Michael Durey, 'The Dublin Society of United Irishmen and the politics of the Carey–Drennan dispute, 1792–94', in *Hist. Jnl.*, XXXVII, 1 (1994), pp. 91–108.

89. The key sources remain R. B. McDowell, 'The proceedings of the Dublin Society of United Irishmen', in *Anal. Hib.*, XVII (1949), pp. 3–143, and his 1940 study of the Society's personnel, reprinted with amendments in McDowell, *Historical essays 1938–2001* (Dublin, 2003), pp. 223–54. See also Mary Pollard, *Dictionary of members of the Dublin book trade 1550–1800* (London, 2000), pp. 73–5, 99–101; *DIB*, 'John Ashenhurst', 'Patrick Byrne', 'John Chambers'; Cheer, 'Irish maritime trade', pp. 94–5. For Bond's reported wealth: Bartlett, *Revolutionary Dublin*, p. 98n; C. J. Woods, 'Samuel Turner's information on the United Irishmen 1797–8', in *Anal. Hib.*, XLII (2011), p. 203. Tandy's eldest son James with about forty other 'respectable persons' opposed universal suffrage and withdrew from the Society on its adoption: McDowell, *Historical essays*, p. 251. On Catholic land speculation: Stevens, *Hints*, p. 25.

90. Smyth, *Men of no property*, pp. 97–8; Durey, 'Dublin Society', pp. 91, 104–8; Curtin, *United Irishmen*, pp. 52–5, 95; Mansergh, *Grattan's failure*, pp. 158–9, 163–4.

91. Mansergh, *Grattan's failure*, pp. 132–3; *DIB*, 'Napper Tandy'.

92. *DIB*, 'Lord Edward FitzGerald'.

93. Curtin, *United Irishmen*, pp. 147–8; *DIB*, 'John Burk'.

94. Drennan to Martha McTier, – May, 2 May, 8 May 1793 (Agnew, *Drennan–McTier letters*, I, pp. 531, 533–4, 541–2); McParland, *Gandon*, p. 97; Bartlett, *Revolutionary Dublin*, p. 114; Smyth, *Men of no property*, p. 144. See Tone's broadside on the social impact of the war: 'A Liberty weaver', *To the manufacturers of Dublin ... March 1793* (n.p., 1793), in T. W. Moody, R. B. McDowell and C. J. Woods (eds), *The writings of Theobald Wolfe Tone, 1763–98*, I (Oxford, 1998), pp. 419–21.

95. Mel Doyle, 'The Dublin guilds and journeymen's clubs', in *Saothar*, III (1977), pp. 8–10; C. R. Dobson, *Masters and journeymen: A prehistory of industrial relations 1717–1800* (London, 1980), *passim*; J. W. Boyle, *The Irish labor movement in the nineteenth century* (Washington, 1988), pp. 13, 15–16; Smyth, *Men of no property*, pp. 142–6; Henry, *Dublin hanged*, pp. 65, 75–6; Lennon, 'The print trade, 1700–1800', p. 80.

96. Smyth, *Men of no property*, pp. 144–6; Bartlett, *Revolutionary Dublin*, pp. 79, 88. On recollections of the Light Horsemen as enforcers: *Fourth report of the commissioners of inquiry into the collection and management of revenue arising in Ireland* (H.C. 1822 [634]), p. 291.

97. Smyth, *Men of no property*, pp. 112–14, 120, 146–52; Tommy Graham, 'The transformation of the Dublin Society of United Irishmen ... 1791–96', in Thomas

Bartlett et al., *1798: A bicentenary perspective* (Dublin, 2003), pp. 139–41; Mansergh, *Grattan's failure*, p. 154.

98. *Irish Magazine*, VIII (1815), p. 420; Warburton and Whitelaw, *Dublin*, II, pp. 1135–7; Bartlett, *Revolutionary Dublin*, p.100n.; Smyth, *Men of no property*, pp. 147–8, 153–4; Michael Durey, *Transatlantic radicals and the early American republic* (Lawrence, KS, 1997), pp. 104–5, 115. For a literary evocation of the Struggler's Inn 'in Wine Tavern-street': Lady Morgan, *The O'Briens and the O'Flahertys: A national tale* (London, 1827), pp. 242–6, 279. This profile of Pill Lane trade is based on an analysis of *Wilson's Dublin directory*, 1792; about a third of the ninety-odd businesses listed were related to textiles or clothing. At least two of the silk men there got great business in supplying United Irish demand in the North with green ribbons: Bartlett, *Revolutionary Dublin* , p. 145.

99. Bartlett, *Revolutionary Dublin*, pp. 88, 159n; Smyth, *Men of no property*, pp. 139, 146–7, 150–52; Kevin Whelan, *The tree of liberty: Radicalism, Catholicism and the construction of Irish identity 1760–1830* (Cork, 1996), p. 77; Hill, *Patriots to unionists*, pp. 241–2, 247; Graham, 'Transformation of the Dublin Society', pp. 141–5; Gillen, 'Opposition political clubs', pp. 291–2, 297, 307.

100. Hill, *Patriots to unionists*, pp. 231–3.

101. Ibid., p. 243.

102. Mansergh, *Grattan's failure*, pp. 169–70.

103. Deirdre Lindsay, 'The Fitzwilliam episode revisited', in Dickson, Keogh and Whelan, *United Irishmen*, pp. 197–208; Mansergh, *Grattan's failure*, pp. 178–84.

104. Fraser, 'Public building', 118; Malcomson, *John Foster (1740–1828): The politics of improvement*, p.110; Kelly, *Proceedings of the Irish House of Lords*, II, pp. 450, 463–4, 482–3, 512, 515–20, 528–9, 574; III, pp. 52–5. Two decades later J. C. Beresford was criticised for the slow completion of Lower Abbey Street, which left the old inhabitants in their houses surrounded by debris and without compensation until at least 1815: *Irish Magazine*, IX (Nov. 1815), p. 498. The overall development costs incurred by the Wide Streets Commission in the Lower Sackville/Abbey Street development were enormous and absorbed over two-fifths of their total expenditure between *c.*1780 and *c.*1815: Warburton and Whitelaw, *Dublin*, II, p. 1082.

105. *Orations delivered at a ... meeting of the Roman Catholics of the city of Dublin, held at Francis-Street Chapel ... on the grand question of Catholic emancipation* (Cork, 1795) p. 25; Mansergh, *Grattan's failure*, pp. 194–5.

106. Bartlett, *Revolutionary Dublin*, pp. 77–8; Smyth, *Men of no property*, pp. 149–50; Hill, *Patriots to unionists*, p. 245.

107. Ibid., pp. 246–7.

108. Sir Richard Musgrave, *Memoirs of the different rebellions in Ireland ...*, 4th edn (Fort Wayne, 1995), pp. 197–8, 268–9; Bartlett, *Revolutionary Dublin*, pp. 112–13, 115; Mansergh, *Grattan's failure*, pp. 207–8; *DIB*, 'Henry Sirr'. On the efforts by less radical Catholic leaders to form a yeomanry corps in 1797 and its rejection by government: Bartlett, *Revolutionary Dublin*, pp. 124–6.

109. *A list of the counties of Ireland, and the respective Yeomanry corps in each county, according to their precedence, established by lot on the 1st June, 1798, Dublin Castle* (Dublin, 1798); Alexander Stewart, *The Irish Merlin, or Gentleman's almanack: for the year of our lord, 1798* (Dublin, 1798), pp. 90, 95; Hill, *Patriots to unionists*, pp. 254–5; Allan Blackstock, *An ascendancy army: The Irish yeomanry 1796–1834* (Dublin, 1998), pp. 18, 131; Blackstock, 'The Irish yeomanry and the 1798 rebellion', in Bartlett et al., *1798*, p. 343.

110. Mansergh, *Grattan's failure*, p. 210.

111. Dáire Keogh, *'The French disease': The Catholic Church and radicalism in Ireland 1790–1800* (Dublin, 1993), pp. 43–5, 77–88.

112. Ibid., pp. 129–31.

113. Bartlett, *Revolutionary Dublin*, pp. 152–3, 158, 169, 192, 203.

114. Drennan, Dublin, to McTier, – March 98 (Agnew, *Drennan–McTier letters*, II, p. 374); Inglis, *Freedom of the press*, pp. 98–104; Pollard, *Dictionary*, pp. 552–3; Thomas Graham, 'Dublin in 1798', in Dáire Keogh and Nicholas Furlong (eds), *The mighty wave: The 1798 rebellion in Wexford* (Blackrock, Co. Dublin, 1996), pp. 66–7; Woods, 'Samuel Turner's information', 190–93.

115. James Wilson, 'Orangeism in 1798', in Bartlett et al., *1798*, pp. 359–62.

116. Dickson, 'Taxation and disaffection in late eighteenth-century Ireland', in Samuel Clark and J. S. Donnelly (eds), *Irish peasants: Violence and political unrest 1780–1914* (Madison, 1983), pp. 48–51, 57–8; Thomas, *The stock exchanges of Ireland*, pp. 7–11; Gillian O'Brien, 'Camden and the move towards union 1795–1798', in Dáire Keogh and Kevin Whelan (eds), *Acts of union: The causes, contexts and consequences of the act of Union* (Dublin, 2001), pp. 118–19; Bartlett, *Revolutionary Dublin*, p. 254; Malcomson, *John Foster (1740–1828): Politics of improvement*, pp. 115–19.

117. *Irish Magazine*, VII (1814), p. 482; Ruán O'Donnell, *Robert Emmet and the rebellion of 1798* (Dublin, 2003), pp. 45, 56; Bartlett, *Revolutionary Dublin*, pp. 92, 179, 191, 263, 309. 'Maiden ray' was another name for skate fish.

118. McDowell and Webb, *Trinity College*, pp. 76–8; O'Donnell, *Emmet and 1798*, pp. 62–8, 222n.

119. Bartlett, *Revolutionary Dublin*, p. 243.

120. O'Donnell, *Emmet and 1798*, pp. 52, 58, 68. Evidence on the whereabouts of United Irish cells was acquired by the Castle when the Bridgefoot Street timber-yard of Edward Rattigan was ransacked by yeomanry and his papers seized: see ibid., p. 74. For the panic at Francis Street Chapel in late June 1798 after a rumour circulated that the yeomanry were going to burn the church down: Bartlett, *Revolutionary Dublin*, pp. 257–8.

121. Durey, *Transatlantic radicals*, pp. 128–9; O'Donnell, *Emmet and 1798*, pp. 55–8. Richard McCormick who, with MacNeven, had been a long-serving Catholic leader, had already fled to France in February 1798; Keogh managed to keep his head below the parapet.

122. Thomas Graham, '"An union of power?": The United Irish organisation', in Dickson, Keogh and Whelan, *United Irishmen*, pp. 250–5; Graham, 'Dublin in

1798', in ibid., pp. 67–71; Curtin, *United Irishmen*, p. 258; O'Donnell, *Emmet and 1798*, p.73; Bartlett, *Revolutionary Dublin*, p. 90n.

123. Musgrave, *Rebellions in Ireland*, p. 192. Musgrave's account of the rising in Dublin, for all its special pleading, remains a key source: ibid., pp. 191–202. Cf. O'Donnell, *Emmet and 1798*, chaps. 2 and 3.

124. Rev. William Bennett, quoted in Graham, 'An union of power', p. 253. Cf. Musgrave, *Rebellions in Ireland*, p. 192.

125. Ibid., pp. 190–2; Graham, 'Dublin in 1798', p. 77; O'Donnell, *Emmet and 1798*, pp. 78–9.

126. Quoted in O'Donnell, *Emmet and 1798*, p. 86.

127. Bartlett, *Revolutionary Dublin*, p. 246. Cf. ibid., pp. 249–51.

128. Musgrave, *Rebellions in Ireland*, pp. 269, 275; O'Donnell, *Emmet and 1798*, pp. 88–9, 94–100, 103–6, 115, 138–9, 234–6n; Bartlett, *Revolutionary Dublin*, 247, 253–4, 257, 259–63.

129. Thomas Pakenham, *The year of liberty: The story of the great Irish Rebellion of 1798* (London, 1969), p. 287; Bartlett, *Revolutionary Dublin*, p. 264n and appendix; O'Donnell, *Emmet and 1798*, pp. 137–8.

130. There were rumours of a city rising to occur three days before the French were defeated at Ballinamuck; yeomanry flooded the city streets but there was no substance to the rumour: O'Donnell, *Emmet and 1798*, pp. 113–17.

131. Musgrave, *Rebellions in Ireland*, pp. 201–202; John Gamble, *Society and manners in early nineteenth-century Ireland*, ed. Breandán MacSuibhne (Dublin, 2011), p. 58; Pakenham, *Year of liberty*, p. 124; O'Donnell, *Emmet and 1798*, pp. 83–4, 228n–229n; Bartlett, *Revolutionary Dublin*, p. 247n.

6 Apocalypse Deferred: 1798–1830

1. *Proposals for publishing by subscription, a print of the portico of the Parliament House, Dublin; from a view taken by Mr. James Malton* ([London, n.d.]); Maurice Craig (ed.), *James Malton's Dublin views* (Dublin, 1981), pp. x–xii; Anne Crookshank and the Knight of Glin, *The watercolours of Ireland* (London, 1994), pp. 97–8; Claire Connolly, 'The Irish novel and the moment of union', in Michael Brown, Patrick M. Geoghegan and James Kelly (eds), *The Irish act of union, 1800: Bicentennial essays* (Dublin, 2003), pp. 171–2. Malton's relationship with Gandon remains elusive: *DIB*, 'James Malton'.

2. Patrick M. Geoghegan, 'The Catholics and the Union', in *Trans. RHS*, 6th series, X (2000), p. 247.

3. Richard Jebb, *A reply to a pamphlet entitled, argument for and against an union …* (London, 1799), p. 46.

4. *Orations delivered at a … meeting of the Roman Catholics of the city of Dublin, held at Francis-Street Chapel … on the grand question of Catholic emancipation* (Cork, 1795) p. 13; *Evidence taken before the committee of the Irish house of commons on the subject of the legislative union* (HC, 1833 [517]); G. C. Bolton, *The passing of the Irish act of union: A study in parliamentary politics* (Oxford, 1966), p. 130.

5.   Daniel Mansergh, 'The union and the importance of public opinion', in Dáire
     Keogh and Kevin Whelan (eds), *Acts of union: The causes, contexts and consequences
     of the act of union* (Dublin, 2001) p. 129; Patrick M. Geoghegan, *The passing of the
     Irish act of union: A study in high politics 1798–1801* (Dublin, 1999), p. 249.

6.   James Quinn, 'Dublin Castle and the act of union', in Brown et al., *Irish act of
     union*, pp. 97–9. Leading Catholic laymen like MacDonnell were tempted for a
     time to support the Whig opposition: Marquis of Buckingham to Lord Grenville,
     26 January 1799, in HMC, *Dropmore MSS*, IV, p. 455.

7.   *The Times*, 17, 26 January 1799; Thomas Bartlett (ed.), *Revolutionary Dublin
     1795–1801: The letters of Francis Higgins to Dublin Castle* (Dublin, 2004), p. 323;
     Mansergh, 'Union and public opinion', pp. 129–30, 136–7; Jacqueline Hill, *From
     patriots to unionists: Dublin civic politics and Irish Protestant patriotism 1660–1840*
     (Oxford, 1997), pp. 259–62; James Kelly, 'The failure of opposition', in Brown et
     al., *Irish act of union*, pp. 112, 123–4.

8.   This estimate includes Dublin editions of works published elsewhere, but excludes
     speeches etc.: W. J. McCormack, *The pamphlet debate on the union between Great
     Britain and Ireland 1797–1800* (Blackrock, Co. Dublin, 1996), *passim*.

9.   Bishop Percy [of Dromore] to Mrs Percy, 21 January 1799, quoted in Bolton, *Act
     of union*, p. 126. See also ibid., pp. 130–31; *Proceedings and debates of the parliament
     of Pimlico, in the last session of the eighteenth century* (Tripilo [i.e. Dublin],
     1799–1800); [Sir Thomas Bond], *National advantages to be derived from adopting
     the following plans ...* (Dublin, 1799), p. 23; William Stanley, *Commentaries on
     Ireland* (Dublin, 1833), pp. 73–5; David Dickson, *Old world colony: Cork and south
     Munster 1630–1830* (Cork, 2005), pp. 475–6; John Gamble, *Society and manners
     in early nineteenth-century Ireland*, ed. Breandán MacSuibhne (Dublin, 2011),
     p. 55. The 'Dalkeyan empire' was an ironic reference to Dalkey, the small village of
     fishermen and quarrymen close to Bullock harbour.

10. Kelly, 'Failure of opposition', pp. 271, 283.

11. Bolton, *Passing of the Irish act of union*, pp. 194–6; S. J. Connolly, 'Aftermath and
     adjustment', in W. E. Vaughan (ed.), *A new history of Ireland*, V: *Ireland under the
     union: I – 1801–70* (Oxford, 1989), pp. 1–2, 4; Allan Blackstock, 'The union and
     the military, 1801–c.1820', in *Trans. RHS*, 6th series, X (2000), pp. 333–9; A. P. W.
     Malcomson, *John Foster (1740–1828): The politics of improvement and prosperity*
     (Dublin, 2011), p. 151.

12. *DIB*, 'William MacNeven', 'John Sweetman', 'Richard McCormick', 'Charles Ryan',
     'John Keogh', 'Thomas Braughall'. Keogh was, however, suspected of involvement
     in the 1803 rebellion, but nothing incriminating was found in his house: P. M.
     Geoghegan, *Robert Emmet: A life* (Dublin, 2002), p. 151.

13. *Wilson's Dublin directory*, 1806, p. 163; Geoghegan, *Emmet*, pp. 154–83. On
     the prudential refusal of the Carpenters' Society to join the conspiracy: Ruán
     O'Donnell, *Robert Emmet and the rising of 1803* (Dublin, 2003), p. 37.

14. O'Donnell, *Emmet and 1803*, pp. 28–9, 54–5, 60–61; Thomas Bartlett, '"The cause
     of treason seems to have gone out of fashion in Ireland": Dublin Castle and Robert

Emmet', in Anne Dolan, P. M. Geoghegan and Darryl Jones (eds), *Reinterpreting Emmet: Essays on the life and legacy of Robert Emmet* (Dublin, 2007), pp. 16–22.

15. Bartlett, *Revolutionary Dublin*, pp. 289–90, 309, 311; Geoghegan, *Emmet*, p. 122; O'Donnell, *Emmet and 1803*, pp. 108–9.

16. Geoghegan, *Emmet*, pp. 124–7, 134–5, 171–2, 214–44; O'Donnell, *Emmet and 1803*, pp. 15, 18, 50; *DIB*, 'John Allen', 'Philip Long', 'William Dowdall'.

17. Geoghegan, *Emmet*, pp. 127–8, 172; *DIB*, 'Jemmy Hope'.

18. Geoghegan, *Emmet*, pp. 165–82; O'Donnell, *Emmet and 1803*, pp. 50–109.

19. Geoghegan, *Emmet*, pp. 155–64, 211–12, 244–54; O'Donnell, *Emmet and 1803*, pp. 40–41.

20. Geoghegan, *Emmet*, pp. 135, 164–5.

21. 'Return of prisoners, August 1803': TNA, HO/100/118; Seamus Grimes, *Ireland in 1804* (Dublin, 1980), p. 20.

22. Peter Pearson, *Dun Laoghaire – Kingstown* (Dublin, 1981), p. 17; P. M. Kerrigan, *Castles and fortifications in Ireland 1485–1945* (Cork, 1995), pp. 167–78.

23. Rev. James Whitelaw, *An essay on the population of Dublin* (Dublin, 1805), pp. 15–23; *Wilson's Dublin directory 1806*, p. 163; *Second report from the select committee on the local taxation of the city of Dublin: Minutes of evidence* (HC 1823 [549]), pp. 222–9; R. B. McDowell, *The Irish administration 1801–1914* (London, 1964), pp. 57–8; Stanley H. Palmer, *Police and protest in England and Ireland 1780–1850* (Cambridge, 1988), pp. 150–54.

24. Palmerston to Elizabeth Temple, 12 September 1808, in K. Bourne (ed.), *The letters of the third viscount Palmerston to Laurence and Elizabeth Sulivan, 1804–1863* (Camden Society, 4th series, XXIII [1979], p. 104; Palmer, *Police and protest*, pp. 150–59; Gamble, *Society and manners*, pp. 50–51. Cf. J. C. Curwen, *Observations on the state of Ireland principally directed to its agriculture and rural population* (London, 1818), II, p. 126. On the rise in city crime during the post-war recession: Warburton and Whitelaw, *Dublin*, II, pp. 1035–7.

25. Thomas Bartlett, *The fall and rise of the Irish nation: The Catholic question 1690–1830* (Dublin, 1992), p. 319; *DIB*, 'Walter Cox'; Elizabeth Tilley, 'Periodicals', in J. H. Murphy, *The Irish book in English 1800–1891* (Oxford, 2011), pp. 145–9. On Beresford: *Irish Magazine*, VII (1814), pp. 482–4.

26. *Irish Magazine*, VII (1814), p. 490. Cf. ibid., VIII (1815), p. 148.

27. *Irish Magazine*, VIII (1815), p. 465.

28. Palmerston to Temple, 12 September 1808; Gamble, *Society and manners*, p. 22; David Dickson, 'Death of a capital? Dublin and the consequences of union', in Clark and Gillespie, *Two capitals*, pp. 115–17; Gillian O'Brien, '"What can possess you to go to Ireland?": Visitors' perceptions of Dublin 1800–30', in Gillian O'Brien and Finola O'Kane (eds), *Georgian Dublin* (Dublin, 2008), pp. 21–9.

29. *The Patriot*, 23 April 1814; Charles Maturin, *Women: Or pour et contre* (Edinburgh, 1818), II, pp. 167–8; P. F. Garnett, 'The Wellington Testimonial', in *DHR*, XIII, 2 (1952), pp. 48–61; *DIB*, 'Charles Maturin'; Desmond MacCabe, *St Stephen's Green* (Dublin, 2009), pp. 233–42; Sharon Murphy, 'Maria Edgeworth's representations of Georgian Dublin', and Julie Anne Stevens, 'Views of Georgian

Dublin: Perspectives of the city', in O'Brien and O'Kane (eds), *Georgian Dublin*, pp. 147–50, 157–61; John A. McCullen, *An illustrated history of the Phoenix Park: Landscape and management to 1880* (Dublin, 2009), pp. 158–66. The huge delay in completing the Wellington Testimonial was partly because of Wellington's own objections (in 1829) to its becoming a monument to his support of emancipation; the final round of work was only done after his death.

30. William Stevens, *Hints to the people, especially to the inhabitants of Dublin* (Dublin, 1799), pp. 18–19.

31. *Treble almanack for 1798* (Dublin, 1798), part I; Mary Bryan, 'Fitzwilliam Square Dublin' (M.A. dissertation, UCD, 1995), p. 22. Those returning their town residence as Parliament, 'quarters' or 'Royal Navy' are assumed not to have had Dublin houses at that point.

32. Edward McParland, 'Francis Johnston, architect, 1760–1829', in *Quarterly Bulletin of the Irish Georgian Society*, XII (1969), pp. 96–131; *DIB*, 'Francis Johnston'.

33. Edward McParland, 'The Wide Streets Commissioners', in *Quarterly Bulletin of the Irish Georgian Society*, XV, 1 (1972), pp. 23–6; Murray Fraser, 'Public building and colonial policy in Dublin, 1760–1800', in *Architectural History*, XXVIII (1985), pp. 118–19. In the years 1812–15, 56 per cent of the Commissioners' revenues (exclusive of rental income) came from the Treasury grant, the remainder from local coal, card and Dublin club taxes; in 1823–5 the Treasury contribution had fallen to 38.6 per cent of a budget that had only fallen by about 10.7 per cent: *Wide Streets (Dublin): Accounts and papers* (H.C. papers, 1828 [81]), p. 12.

34. Warburton and Whitelaw, *Dublin*, II, pp. 1080–82; *Wide Streets (Dublin): Accounts and papers*, p. 12; Stefanie Jones, 'Dublin reformed: The transformation of the municipal government of a Victorian city 1840–1860' (Ph.D. dissertation, University of Dublin, 2001), pp. 89–92. Quayside improvements were preceded by the reconstruction of the quay walls along the whole length of the river within the city and were funded by the 'Anna Livia tax' (43 Geo.III, *c.*127). For a review of the Wide Streets works in the west of the city and how they might be improved, see 'Viator', *Letters to the right honorable Robert Peel ... relating to the improvement of the 'the district of the metropolis' and principally the earl of Meath's Liberties ...* (Dublin, 1816), *passim*.

35. Whitelaw, *Population of Dublin*, p. 26. Sir John Newport, speaking in the House of Commons on 4 May 1824, put the building costs of St George's church at £50,000, but on 3 April 1827 said that it was 'already upwards of £40,000'; the far higher figure of £90,000 was conventionally quoted: *The Times*, 5 May 1824, 4 April 1827.

36. McParland, 'Wide Streets Commissioners', p. 23, plate 20; 'Dictionary of Irish architects' [http://www.dia.ie/architects]; Merlo Kelly, 'Gardiner's Royal Circus', in *UCD Yearbook 2012*, pp. 127–9. [http://issuu.com/ucdschoolofarchitecture/docs/ucd_architecture_yearbook_2012]. On the remarkable decline of the Gardiner family after 1800: A. P. W. Malcomson, *The pursuit of the heiress: Aristocratic marriage in Ireland 1740–1840*, 2nd edn (Belfast, 2006), pp. 178–85.

37. Bryan, 'Fitzwilliam Square Dublin', pp. 21–6, 28, and appendix.

38.   Whitelaw, *Population of Dublin*, pp. 14–15; Sir John Carr, *The stranger in
       Ireland: Or a tour in the southern and western parts of that country in the year 1805*
       (Philadelphia, 1806), p. 32; Re. James Hall, *Tour through Ireland* ... (London,
       1813), I, pp. 39–40; Charles, Lord Colchester (ed.), *The diary and correspondence of
       Charles Abbot* (London, 1861), I, p. 293; Dickson, 'Death of a capital?', pp. 117–19;
       MacCabe, *St Stephen's Green*, pp. 217–18.

39.   *Treble almanac for 1798*; Eamon Walsh, 'Sackille Mall: The first one hundred years',
       in Dickson (ed.), *The gorgeous mask*, pp. 42–3; Dickson, 'Death of a capital?',
       p. 124; MacCabe, *St. Stephen's Green*, p. 351. Cf. Michael Maley's 1823 estimate of
       the upper-class exodus since the Union: *Second report on local taxation of Dublin*,
       p. 140.

40.   'Viator', *Letters to Peel*, pp. 19–20; The Knight of Glin, 'Introduction', in
       Luttrellstown Castle, Clonsilla ... [Christie's sale catalogue, 26–28 September 1983]
       (Dublin, 1982), [p. ix]; Kevin Bright, *The Royal Dublin Society 1815–1845* (Dublin,
       2004), pp. 35–6. For the purchase of Powerscourt House for the Stamp Office in
       1807: A. P. W. Malcomson, *John Foster (1740–1828): The politics of improvement
       and prosperity* (Dublin, 2011), pp. 358–9.

41.   'Abbot's tour, 1792', f. 20; Gilbert, *Dublin*, II, pp. 305–7; III, pp. 39–40, 289;
       McParland, 'Johnston', pp. 119, 124; McParland, 'Wide Streets Commissioners',
       pp. 13–14; R. B. McDowell, *Land and learning: Two Irish clubs* (Dublin, 1993),
       pp. 14–18, 44–6; M. J. Powell, 'Convivial clubs in the public sphere 1750–1800', in
       James Kelly and M. J. Powell (eds), *Clubs and societies in eighteenth-century Ireland*
       (Dublin, 2010), pp. 359, 362, 365, 371–2; Kelly, 'The Bar Club 1787–93', in Kelly
       and Powell (eds), *Clubs and societies*, p. 377. However, Daly's numbers were falling
       after 1815 to judge from the club tax receipts: *Dublin taxes: Returns to ... the House
       of Commons* (HC, 1821 [420]), p. 9; *Second report on local taxation of Dublin*,
       p. 255.

42.   Evidence of Alderman Jacob West, in *Third report of the commissioners of inquiry
       into the collection and management of the revenue of Ireland* (HC, 1822 [606]),
       pp. 20–21.

43.   Warburton and Whitelaw, *Dublin*, II, p. 975; *Fourth report of the commissioners
       of inquiry into the collection and management of revenue arising in Ireland* (HC,
       1822 [634]), pp. 224–5, 260, 266, 273–81; *Report of the select committee on artisans
       and machinery* (HC, 1824 [51]), p. 466; *Report from the select committee on
       manufactures, commerce, and shipping* (HC, 1833 [690]), pp. 408–9; Richard
       Harrison, 'Dublin Quakers in business, 1800–1850' (M.Litt. dissertation,
       University of Dublin, 1987), p. 180. In 1821 Jacob Geoghegan of Francis Street,
       who was then one of the largest dealers in the silk trade, employed fifty looms,
       but this was perhaps only 3 per cent of the total number of surviving looms; his
       weavers owned their loom-frames but the firm owned the valuable tackling and
       harness: *Fourth report into revenue*, pp. 279, 281.

44.   Warburton and Whitelaw, *Dublin*, II, p. 975; *Evidence taken before the committee of
       the Irish house of commons on the subject of the legislative union*, p. 13; *Fourth report
       into revenue*, pp. 234–41; Harrison, 'Dublin Quakers', p. 168; *DIB*, 'Joshua Pim'.

Finglas Mill was burnt down in 1828: Samuel Lewis, *A topographical dictionary of Ireland* (London, 1837), I, p. 629.

45. Warburton and Whitelaw, *Dublin*, II, pp. 983–4; *Fourth report into revenue*, pp. 170–86; *Select Committee on artisans and machinery*, pp. 282–7; *First report of evidence from the select committee on the state of the Poor in Ireland: Minutes of evidence* (HC, 1830 [589]), p. 277; Lena Boylan, 'The mills of Kildrought', in *Journal of the Co. Kildare Archaeological Society*, XV (1974–5), pp. 364–8. The Kilmainham mills were eventually acquired by Edward Cecil Guinness in 1881 to create female employment for the families of Guinness operatives, but it was closed down in 1887 after the public flotation of the brewery: S. R. Dennison and Oliver MacDonagh, *Guinness 1886–1939: From incorporation to the Second World War* (Cork, 1998), p. 121.

46. Hall, *Tour through Ireland*, pp. 484–5; *Fourth report into revenue*, pp. 323–6; Mary Pollard, *Dictionary of members of the Dublin book trade 1550–1800* (London, 2000), pp. 379–84, 648–9; Lewis, *Topographical dictionary*, I, pp. 134, 321; II, p. 542; Patrick Lynch and John Vaizey, *Guinness's brewery in the Irish economy 1759–1876* (Cambridge, 1960), pp. 120–22; Akihiro Takei, 'The first Irish linen mills, 1800–1824', in *IESH*, XXI (1994), pp. 30–31; L. M. Cullen, 'Eighteenth-century flour milling in Ireland', in Andy Bielenberg (ed.), *Irish flour milling: A history 600–2000* (Dublin, 2003), pp. 54–5, 58; *DIB*, 'Sir Edward McDonnel'; Malcomson, *John Foster (1740–1828): Politics of improvement*, pp. 84, 86, 243. For an interpretative map of the water-powered industries along the Dodder and its tributaries in 1837: T. W. Freeman, *Pre-famine Ireland* (Manchester, 1957), p. 166.

47. *Fourth report into revenue*, p. 342; *Second report of the commissioners appointed to consider and recommend a general system of railways for Ireland* (Dublin, 1838), appendix B, p. 113; *Copy of the evidence taken before the commissioners of inquiry in 1833–4 pertaining to the corporation of Dublin ...* (House of Lords sessional papers, 1840 [120]), pp. 122–3; Lynch and Vaizey, *Guinness's brewery*, pp. 119, 123–4, 154n; E. B. Maguire, *Irish whiskey: A history of distilling in Ireland* (Dublin, 1973), pp. 168–9, 248–50; Colin Rynne, *Industrial Ireland 1750–1930: An archaeology* (Cork, 2006), p. 245.

48. *Fourth report into revenue*, pp. 285–8, 304–7, 314–16; *Report on artisans and machinery*, pp. 294–5; Jim Cooke, *Charles Dickens's Ireland: An anthology* (Dublin, 1999), pp. 144–9; *DIB*, 'Henry Jackson'.

49. R. C. Cole, *Irish booksellers and English writers 1740–1800* (London, 1986), pp. 150–72, 182–90; Kenneth Ferguson, 'A list of master printers, and George Barnes's observations of employment in the Dublin printing trade, 1803', in *Long Room*, XLVII (2002), pp. 28–32; Christopher Morash, *A history of the media in Ireland* (Cambridge, 2010), pp. 60–62; Niall Ó Ciosáin, *Print and popular culture in Ireland 1750–1850* (Dublin, 2010), pp. 64–6; Charles Benson, 'The Dublin book trade', in J. H. Murphy (ed.), *The Irish book trade in English 1800–1891* (Oxford, 2011), pp. 27–46; *DIB*, 'James Whitelaw'.

50. *Fourth report into revenue*, pp. 325–6; *Evidence taken before the committee of the Irish house of commons on the subject of the legislative union*, pp. 4–5; Nini Rodgers,

Ireland, slavery and anti–slavery 1612–1865 (Basingstoke, 2007), pp. 139–40; L. M. Cullen, *Economy, trade and Irish merchants at home and abroad* (Dublin, 2012), pp. 107, 116.

51.   Jedidiah Morse, *The American universal geography ...* (Boston, n.d. [*c.*1796]), p. 176; Warburton and Whitelaw, *Dublin*, II, p. 977; Evidence of Jonathan Sisson, in *Report of the select committee on the silk trade* (HC 1831–2 [678]), pp. 836–40, 930; David Dickson, 'Aspects of the rise and decline of the Irish cotton industry', in L. M. Cullen and T. C. Smout (eds), *Comparative aspects of Scottish and Irish economic and social history 1600–1900* (Edinburgh, [1977]), pp. 110–11; Mary Campion, 'An old Dublin industry: Poplin', in *DHR*, XIX, 1 (1963), pp. 2–15; David O'Toole, 'The employment crisis of 1826', in David Dickson (ed.), *The gorgeous mask: Dublin 1700–1850* (Dublin, 1987), pp. 157–71; Hill, *Patriots to unionists*, pp. 286–7.

52.   *Fourth report into revenue*, p. 332; Stanley, *Commentaries*, pp. 72–3, 160.

53.   *Account of the House of Industry ...* (HC 1828 [176]); Jacinta Prunty, *Dublin slums 1800–1925: A study in urban geography* (Dublin, 1999), pp. 203–5. The institutions were the Hardwicke Fever Hospital (1803), the Bedford Asylum for Children (1806), the Richmond Surgical Hospital (1811), the Richmond Asylum (1811–15) and the Whitworth Chronic Hospital (1818).

54.   J. A. Paris, *The life of Sir Humphrey Davy* (London, 1831), I, pp. 340–46; *Report of the select committee on the Royal Dublin Society* (HC, 1836 [445]), pp. 2–3, 20, 217, 238; Bright, *Royal Dublin Society*, pp. 15, 28, 32, 34–40, 53–6, 59, 63–5, 245.

55.   *1833–4 evidence pertaining to the corporation of Dublin*, pp. 601–4; H. A. Gilligan, *A history of Dublin port* (Dublin, 1988), pp. 90–92, 109–10.

56.   NAI, CSO/RP/1819/312; CSO/RP/1822/93; CSO/RP/1822/2719; 'Viator', *Letters to Peel*, p. 28; Pearson, *Dun Laoghaire – Kingstown*, pp.18–28; Gilligan, *Port of Dublin*, pp. 119–20; Rob Goodbody, *The Metals: From Dalkey to Dun Laoghaire* (Dún Laoghaire, 2010), pp. 28–45, 52–5.

57.   *Twenty-second report of the commissioners of inquiry into the collection and management of the revenue arising in Ireland and Great Britain: Post-Office revenue* (HC 1830 [647]), p. 44; *Second report on railways for Ireland*, p. 72; John Kennedy, *The history of steam navigation* (Liverpool, 1903), p. 26; R. C. Jarvis, 'Parkgate packet', in *Notes and Queries*, CXCI (1946), pp. 40–41; Philip Bagwell, 'The Post Office steam packets 1821–36 and the development of shipping on the Irish Sea', in *Maritime History*, I (1971), pp. 4–9; Paul Johnson, *The birth of the modern: World society 1815–1830* (New York, 1991), pp. 179–83; G. W. Place, *The rise and fall of Parkgate, passenger port for Ireland 1686–1815* (Manchester, 1994), pp. 128–42; E. J. Guildi, 'The road to rule: The expansion of the British road network, 1726–1848', (Harvard Ph.D, dissertation, 2008), pp. 155–6.

58.   *Pigot & Co.'s Provincial Directory of Ireland 1824*, p. 117; *Partnerships (Ireland): Return from the Registry of Deeds* (HC, 1863 [379]), p. 2; Bagwell, 'Post Office steam packets', pp. 9–14; W. A. Thomas, *The stock exchanges of Ireland* (Liverpool, 1986), pp. 138–41; Place, *Parkgate*, pp. 103–11; Freda Harcourt, 'Charles Wye Williams and Irish steam shipping 1820–50', in *Journal of Transport History*, XIII,

2 (1992), pp. 145–6, 160n. In 1819, John Foster recalled that the 1781 Act had initially been turned down in Whitehall as being foreign to British commercial practice, and that indeed the draft Irish legislation had been 'taken from a French law-book': Hansard, *Commons debates*, 1819, XL, c.126 (5 May 1819).

59. *First report of evidence from the select committee on the state of the poor in Ireland: Minutes of evidence* (HC, 1830 [589], pp. 100, 261; Harrison, 'Dublin Quakers', pp. 179–85; *DIB*, 'Charles Williams'.

60. *First report on state of the poor*, p. 277; *Twenty-second report of the commissioners of inquiry into the collection and management of the revenue arising in Ireland and Great Britain: Post Office revenue* (HC, 1830 [647]), pp. 44, 715–21; *Fourth report of the commissioners appointed to inquire into the management of the Post Office Department* (HC 1836 [49–51]), appendix H, p. 242; Kennedy, *Steam navigation*, pp.180–83; Gilligan, *Port of Dublin*, pp. 105–7; Harcourt, 'Charles Wye Williams', pp. 142–62. Williams' father Thomas was Bank of Ireland Secretary for over forty years. On the difficulties that the City of Dublin encountered in the 1830s trying to increase the capital it could raise and its attempts to secure limited liability: Thomas, *Stock exchanges*, pp. 142–3.

61. Curwen, *Observations on the state of Ireland*, pp. 104–5; William Martin, *A commercial guide through Dublin for 1825 ...* (Dublin, 1825), pp. 23–4; *Nineteenth report of the commissioners of inquiry into the collection and management of revenue arising in Ireland and Great Britain* (HC, 1829 [353]), p. 352; *Dublin almanac and general register of Ireland ... for 1836* (Dublin, 1836), appendix; McDowell, *The Irish administration*, pp. 83–6; Mairéad Reynolds, *A history of the Irish Post Office* (Dublin, 1983), pp. 44–7; Harcourt, 'Charles Wye Williams', pp. 147, 160n; Ruth Delany and Ian Bath, *Ireland's Royal Canal* (Dublin, 2010), pp. 321, 325–6; O'Brien, 'Visitors' perceptions of Dublin', p. 26. In fact it was not until the 1830s that Sackville Street became the passenger terminus for the great mail-coaches (in place of Capel and Bolton Streets), a status it had to share with Dawson Street where most of the southern and western coach services terminated.

62. Patrick Henchy, 'Nelson's Pillar', in *DHR*, X, 2 (1948), pp. 53–63; Hill, *Patriots to unionists*, pp. 276–7; *DIB*, 'Valentine O'Connor'.

63. *The new picture of Dublin* (Dublin, 1828), pp. 335–8; Lewis, *Topographical dictionary*, I, pp. 557–8; *Georgian society records*, III, p. 98; V. J. McNally, *Reform, revolution and reaction: Archbishop John Thomas Troy and the Catholic church in Ireland 1787–1817* (Lanham, MD, 1995), pp. 26–8; Dáire Keogh, '"The pattern of the Flock": John Thomas Troy, 1786–1823', and Michael McCarthy, 'Dublin's Greek Pro-Cathedral', in James Kelly and Dáire Keogh (eds), *History of the Catholic diocese of Dublin* (Dublin, 2000), pp. 226–6, 231–5, 237–46; Casey, *Dublin*, pp. 53–5, 126–30, 473. The suggestion that before 1803 Troy tried to buy the site in the widened Lower Sackville Street on which the GPO was subsequently erected, but then abandoned the idea of building on such a strategic location lest it stir up hostility to emancipation, is only apocryphal: Dermod McCarthy, *Saint Mary's Pro-Cathedral* (Dublin, 1988), pp. 7–8.

64. Keogh, 'Troy', pp. 233–5; Emmet Larkin, *The pastoral role of the Roman Catholic Church in pre-famine Ireland 1750–1850* ((Dublin, 2006), pp. 159–62.

65. Myles Dungan, *Conspiracy: Irish political trials* (Dublin, 2009), pp. 53–84.

66. Brian MacDermot (ed.), *The Catholic question in Ireland and England 1798–1822: The papers of Denys Scully* (Dublin, 1988), p. xii; Oliver MacDonagh, *The hereditary bondsman: Daniel O'Connell 1775–1829* (London, 1988), pp. 88–9, 97–125, 133–44; Bartlett, *Fall and rise of the Irish nation*, pp. 295, 298–300; Hill, *Patriots to unionists*, p. 317; MacDonagh, *Hereditary bondsman*, pp. 133–44; Fergus O'Ferrall, *Catholic emancipation: Daniel O'Connell and the birth of Irish democracy 1820–30* (Dublin, 1985), p. 4.

67. *Pigot's directory 1824*, pp.120–21; Deirdre Lindsay, 'The Sick and Indigent Roomkeepers Society', in Dickson, *Gorgeous mask,* pp. 147–8; *Battersby's registry for the Catholic world ... 1853* (Dublin, 1853), pp. 269–70. The Dublin General Dispensary in Temple Bar, established in 1782 'for administering medical and surgical relief to the sick and diseased poor' was in practice also a mixed body from an early stage.

68. Hill, *Patriots to unionists*, pp. 306–7, 317–18, 341.

69. *Report on local taxation (1823)*, pp. 212–17; *Minutes of evidence taken before the select committee of the House of Lords appointed to inquire into the state of Ireland* (HC, 1825 [181]), p. 144.

70. Joep Leerssen, *Remembrance and imagination: Patterns in the historical and literary representation of Ireland in the nineteenth century* (Cork, 1996), pp. 77–9; Hill, *Patriots to unionists*, pp. 320–23. For William Turner de Lond's panorama of the king's entry into Sackville Street: Anne Crookshank and the Knight of Glin, *Irish painters 1600–1940* (London, 2002), p. 203.

71. O'Ferrall, *Catholic emancipation*, pp. 1–3, 13–15, 17, 30–32; Hill, *Patriots to unionists*, pp. 320–29; Morash, *Irish theatre*, pp. 94–102; *DIB*, 'Frederick Jones', 'Luke White'; Shunsuke Katsuta, 'Conciliation, anti-Orange politics and the sectarian scare: Dublin politics of the early 1820s', in *DHR*, LXIV, 2 (2011), pp. 142–59.

72. *The new picture of Dublin* (Dublin, 1821), p. 151; O'Ferrall, *Catholic emancipation*, pp. 67–9; MacDonagh, *Hereditary bondsman*, pp. 206–14, 220–23, 230–32; Bartlett, *Fall and rise of the Irish nation*, pp. 329–33.

73. Inglis, *Freedom of the press*, pp. 166–9, 184–9; O'Ferrall, *Catholic emancipation*, pp. 36–9; MacDonagh, *Hereditary bondsman*, pp. 208, 244–7, 249–56; Bartlett, *Fall and rise of the Irish nation*, p. 335; Hill, *Patriots to unionists*, pp. 341–2. The estimate of Dublin newspapers publishing at least once a week in 1824 is based on the listing in *Pigot's directory 1824*, p. 80, but excludes the *Irish Farmers' Journal* and adds the *Morning Register*.

74. *National Magazine*, II (1831), p. 452; Carmel Connell, *Glasnevin cemetery, Dublin, 1832–1900* (Dublin, 2004). pp. 7–15.

75. Maturin, *Women*, p. 102; F. E. Dukes, *Campanology in Ireland: A study of bells, bell-founding, inscriptions and bell-ringing* (Blackrock, Co. Dublin, 1994),

pp. 87–120. There were also bells in the GPO, the Royal Hospital and the
Foundling Hospital.

76. Hill, *Patriots to unionists*, pp. 333–5; Irene Whelan, *The Bible war in Ireland: The
'Second Reformation' and the polarization of Protestant–Catholic relations 1800–
1840* (Dublin, 2005), pp. 153–8; John Crawford, *The Church of Ireland in Victorian
Dublin* (Dublin, 2005), pp. 35–42, 56–7.

77. Dukes, *Campanology*, pp. 33–40, 102–3. Cf. Hugh O'Connor's evidence on
the socially poisonous atmosphere between the parties: *Report from the select
committee on the state of Ireland* (HC, 1825 [129]), p. 143.

78. John James McGregor, *New picture of Dublin* (Dublin, 1828), pp. 208–13; June
Eiffe, 'Lyons, Co. Kildare', in *Quarterly Bulletin of the Irish Georgian Society*,
XXVII (1984), pp. 1–37; Crookshank and Glin, *Ireland's painters*, pp. 179–80;
'Dictionary of Irish architects', http://www.dia.ie/architects. The Royal Irish
Institution offered lavish facilities to new artists but it had a decidedly *ancien
régime* flavour; the prime mover was none other than Town Major Henry Sirr, who
managed to persuade the duke of Leinster (Lord Edward's nephew) to be the first
patron.

79. McGregor, *New picture of Dublin* (1828), pp. 213–16; John Ryan, 'William Thomas
Mulvany', in *Studies*, XII, 47 (1923), pp. 378–9; D. F. Moore, 'The Royal Hibernian
Academy', in *DHR*, XXI, 1 (1966), pp. 30–34; *DIB*, 'William Ashford', 'Martin
Cregan', 'William Cuming', 'Francis Johnston', 'Thomas V. Mulvany'; Crookshank
and Glin, *Irish painters*, pp. 181–4. Fifteen of the thirty-one collectors listed in 1821
resided on the north side of the Liffey; only a quarter were aristocratic: McGregor,
New picture of Dublin, pp. 305–7. Johnston's collection housed in Eccles Street
must have been one of the largest: it took eighteen days to dispose of what
remained of his furniture, paintings and sculpture in 1835: Casey, *Dublin*, p. 285.

7 A Tale of Four Cities: 1830–1880

1. Queen Victoria, *Leaves from the journal of our life in the Highlands, from 1848 to
1861 ...* (New York, 1868), pp. 231–43; Jim Cooke, *Charles Dickens's Ireland: An
anthology* (Dublin, 1999), p. 4; John Mitchel, *The last invasion of Ireland (perhaps)*,
ed. Patrick Maume (Dublin, 2005), pp. 215–16; James Loughlin, 'Allegiance and
illusion: Queen Victoria's Irish visit of 1849', in *History*, LXXXVII, 288 (2002),
pp. 498–505. Cf. Thomas Carlyle's much more negative impressions of his visit
in July 1849: http://carlyleletters.dukejournals.org/cgi/content/long/24/1/
lt-18490704-TC-JAC-01: [accessed 30 October 2011].

2. Captain Thomas Larcom's vice-presidential address to the Society in June 1850,
Journal of the Dublin Statistical Society, II (1849–51); http://www.tara.tcd.ie.
elib.tcd.ie/ bitstream/2262/7782/1/jssisiVolII1_23.pdf: [accessed 27 Sept. 2010];
Thomas Jordan, 'The present state of the dwellings of the poor, chiefly in Dublin',
in *Journal of the Dublin Statistical Society*, II, 8 (1857), pp. 12–19; E. D. Mapother,
'The sanitary state of Dublin', in *JSSISI*, IV, 27 (1864), pp. 62–76; Stefanie Jones,
'Dublin reformed: The transformation of the municipal government of a Victorian

city 1840–1860' (Ph.D. dissertation, University of Dublin, 2001), pp. 236–9. One author whose social-realist fiction was largely set in Dublin is the under-rated May Laffan: H. K. Kahn, *Late nineteenth-century Ireland's political and religious controversies in the fiction of May Laffan Hartley* (Greensboro, NC, 2005).

3. The first of the thirty-three sheets constituting the five-foot (1/1056) town plan of the city was published in 1840 and the six-inch single-sheet map of the city was published in 1844: J. H. Andrews, *A paper landscape: The Ordnance Survey in nineteenth-century Ireland* (Oxford, 1975), pp. 229, 251, 275, 333, 335. The large-scale maps were put to immediate use in designing a new layout of municipal wards in 1850, scrapping those created at the time of municipal reform: *City of Dublin: Abstract of report … for dividing the city … into new wards* (HC, 1850 [559]).

4. R. B. McDowell, *The Irish administration 1801–1914* (London, 1964), pp. 282–3; Andrews, *Paper landscape*, pp. 140, 173, 186; Jacinta Prunty, *Dublin slums 1800–1925: A study in urban geography* (Dublin, 1999), pp. 20–25, 72; *DIB*, 'Sir Thomas Larcom'.

5. M. E. Daly, *Dublin: The deposed capital – A social and economic history, 1860–1914* (Cork, 1986), p. 3; Cormac Ó Gráda, *Black '47 and beyond: The Great Irish Famine in history, economy and memory* (Princeton, NJ, 1999), p. 173; David Dickson, 'Death of a capital? Dublin and the consequences of union', in Clark and Gillespie, *Two capitals*, pp. 118–19. Estimates for 1821–41 are based on the latter, and for those post-1841 on Daly. Cf. *Census of 1821*, pp. xxii–iii.

6. *Census of Ireland for … 1861, Part V: General report* (H.C. [1863 [3204-IV], pp. 18, 24; *Thom's official directory of the United Kingdom … 1896* (Dublin, 1896), p. 1279 [an annual publication since 1844, appearing first as *Thom's Irish almanac and official directory*, then from 1881 as *Thom's official directory …* , and cited thereafter as simply *Thom's directory*]; Daly, *Deposed capital*, pp. 3–4, 16; Dickson, 'The demographic implications of Dublin's growth 1650–1850', in Richard Lawton and Robert Lee (eds), *Urban population development in western Europe from the late-eighteenth to the early-twentieth centuries* (Liverpool, 1989), pp. 184–5.

7. *Census of Ireland for … 1851, Part VI* (HC 1856 [2134]), p. xlvii; Garret FitzGerald, 'The decline of the Irish language 1771–1871', in Mary Daly and David Dickson (eds), *The origins of popular literacy in Ireland: Language change and educational development 1700–1920* (Dublin, 1990), pp. 63–4, 70–72.

8. Sixty-two per cent of women in the 16–25 age cohort could read and write compared with only 48 per cent in the 36–45 cohort: *1841 census*, pp. 20–21.

9. *Second report of the commissioners of public instruction, Ireland* (HC, 1835 [46–7]), pp. 79b–123b; *Census of Ireland for the year 1851, part VI* (HC, 1856 [2134]), p. xlii. At that point enrolment numbers were rising most noticeably in schools in the west and north of the city, and were stationary or declining in most schools in the south-east, suggesting that the decline in child employment and improvements in Catholic provision may have been drivers of schooling in poorer parishes.

10. Catholic over-fives in the western wards ranged between 27.0 and 31.9 per cent illiterate, compared with a north-east average of 18.5 per cent and a south-east average somewhat higher at 21.3 per cent: *1861 census*, (HC, 1863 [3204-III]),

pp. 15–21. Cf. Mary Daly, 'Catholic Dublin: The public expression in the age of Paul Cullen', in Dáire Keogh and Albert McDonnell (eds), *Cardinal Paul Cullen and his world* (Dublin, 2011), p. 140.

11. The areas covered in 1834 and 1861 differ slightly, making precise comparisons problematic, but the results suggest that Protestant decline after 1834 was least in the north-western parishes and quite pronounced in the south-western parishes: *First report of the commissioners of public instruction, Ireland* (HC, 1835 [45]), pp. 89b–140b; *1861 census*. On the 1834 Commission: D. Miller, 'Mass attendance in Ireland in 1834', in S. J. Brown and D. W. Miller (eds), *Piety and power in Ireland 1760–1960: Essays in honour of Emmet Larkin* (Belfast and Notre Dame, 2000), pp. 159–61. On the pronounced decline in church attendance levels in Church of Ireland parishes in the south-west of the city during the century: John Crawford, *The Church of Ireland in Victorian Dublin* (Dublin, 2005), pp. 147–8. On Anglican-Presbyterian relations: ibid., pp. 68, 72. On funding the Abbey Presbyterian church: Alex Findlater, *Findlaters: The story of a Dublin merchant firm 1774–2001* (Dublin, 2001), pp. 38–40.

12. Daly, *Deposed capital*, pp. 18–19.

13. *Census of Ireland 1881, part I* (HC, 1881 [3042]), pp. 72–3; Dickson, 'Death of a capital?', p. 119; Tony Farmar, *Privileged lives: A social history of middle-class Ireland 1882–1989* (Dublin, 2010), p. 12. See Dickson, op. cit., for the parishes included in this computation and for fuller data. Note that the comparison is slightly compromised by changes in parish boundaries. Acres here refer to statute acres, not Irish acres.

14. *First report of the commissioners appointed to inquire into the municipal corporations in Ireland* (HC, 1835 [23–28]), pp. 115–6; Dickson, 'Death of a capital?', pp. 120–21.

15. On Wilde and 1841: T. G. Wilson, *Victorian doctor: Being the life of Sir William Wilde*, 2nd edn (Wakefield, 1972), pp. 130–32; Prunty, *Dublin slums*, pp. 40–48.

16. *Dublin almanac and general register of Ireland for … 1836* (Dublin, [1836]); Catherine de Courcy, *Dublin Zoo: An illustrated history* (Cork, 2009); Elizabeth Tilley, 'Periodicals', in J. H. Murphy, *The Irish book in English 1800–1891* (Oxford, 2011), p.148.

17. *Wilson's Dublin directory, 1788*; *Dublin almanac, 1836*; Wilson, *Victorian doctor*, pp. 230–32. Some of the RCSI licentiates were not practising surgeons, so this somewhat overstates their dominance.

18. *National Magazine*, II (1831), p. 453n; Dr [Dominic] Corrigan, *Ten days in Athens* (London, 1862), p. 194; Wilson, *Victorian doctor*, pp. 119–29, 140–42, 151–6, 205–12; L. M. Geary, *Medicine and charity in Ireland 1718–1851* (Dublin, 2004), pp. 13–39; *DIB*, 'Abraham Colles', 'Philip Crampton', 'Robert Graves', 'Robert William Smith'; *ODNB*, 'Richard Carmichael', 'Abraham Colles', 'Dominick Corrigan'. For the city's pre-famine voluntary hospitals: Geary, op. cit., pp. 18–19.

19. Warburton and Whitelaw, *Dublin*, II, pp. 708–16; *First report of the select committee on the state of disease and the condition of the labouring poor in Ireland* (HC 1819 [314]), pp. 78–9, 83; John James McGregor, *New picture of Dublin*

(Dublin, 1828), p. 291; *Dublin almanac, 1836*, p. 300; George Nicholls, *Poor laws, Ireland: Three reports* (London, 1838), pp. 89, 126; Joseph Robins, *The miasma: Epidemic and panic in nineteenth-century Ireland* (Dublin, 1995), pp. 48, 56–9; Audrey Woods, *Dublin outsiders: A history of the Mendicity Institution 1818–1998* (Dublin, 1998), chapters 2–6; Prunty, *Dublin slums*, pp. 25–36, 63–4, 206–9, 215, 218–27; Jones, 'Dublin reformed', pp. 221–3; Geary, *Medicine and charity*, pp. 83–5. The precursor of the Fever Hospital was the Sick Poor Institution opened as a charitable dispensary in Meath Street in 1793: Warburton and Whitelaw, *Dublin*, II, p. 708.

20. Nicholls, *Poor laws, Ireland*, pp. 88–90, 127, 143–5; Peter Froggatt, 'The response of the medical profession to the Great Famine', in E. M. Crawford (ed.), *Famine: The Irish experience 900–1900* (Edinburgh, 1989), pp. 140–48; Robins, *Miasma*, p. 123; Prunty, *Dublin slums*, pp. 211, 227–31; Ó Gráda, *Black '47*, p. 187. Thomas Willis, *The hidden Dublin: The social and sanitary condition of the working classes in the city of Dublin* [1845], ed. David Dickson (Dublin, 2002), pp. 36–7; Jones, 'Dublin reformed', pp. 206–8.

21. *Census of Ireland, 1851: Tables of death* (HC, 1856 [2087]); E. M. Crawford, 'William Wilde's Table of Irish famines', in Crawford, *Famine*, pp. 1–30; Froggatt, 'Medical profession', pp. 150–51; Robins, *Miasma*, pp. 69–72, 75, 132, 141; Ó Gráda, *Black '47*, p. 178. For Ellen Palmer's graphic diary of the cholera epidemic at Rush in 1849: Robins, op. cit., pp. 144–8.

22. John Gamble, *Society and manners in early nineteenth-century Ireland*, ed. Breandán MacSuibhne (Dublin, 2011), p. 28; *Dublin almanac, 1836*; Stephen Gwynn, *The famous cities of Ireland* (London, 1915), p. 260; David Dickson, 'The place of Dublin in the eighteenth-century Irish economy', in T. M. Devine and David Dickson (eds), *Ireland and Scotland 1600–1850* (Edinburgh, 1983), p. 85. By 1860 64 per cent of the Queen's Counsel with Dublin addresses were living on the Fitzwilliam/Pembroke estate: *Thom's directory, 1860*, p. 889.

23. Jacqueline Hill, 'The intelligentsia and Irish nationalism in the 1840s', in *Studia Hibernica*, XX (1980), pp. 96–8; R. F. Foster, 'Lord Randolph Churchill and the prelude to the Orange card', in F. S. L. Lyons and R. A. J. Hawkins (eds), *Ireland under the union – varieties of tension: Essays in honour of T. W. Moody* (Oxford, 1980), pp. 240–42; Daire Hogan, *The legal profession in Ireland 1789–1922* (Dublin, 1986), pp. 3–7, 11, 23–6, 32–4, 79–85, 95,113, 163–4; *DIB*, 'Tristram Kennedy'; Fergus Campbell, *The Irish establishment 1879–1914* (Oxford, 2009), pp. 80, 158–9, 166, 168.

24. *Dublin almanac, 1836*; *Select committee of the House of Commons to inquire into the … establishment of joint stock banks in England and Ireland* (HC, 1837 [531]), pp. 231–67; *F J*, 21, 24, 25 February 1853; Malcolm Dillon, *The history and development of banking in Ireland* (London, 1889), pp. 52–9; *Report from the select committee of the House of Lords … on the management of railroads …* (HC, 1847 [489]), pp. 43–4; K. A. Murray, *Ireland's first railway* (Dublin, 1981), pp. 30, 38–40, 218; G. L. Barrow, *The emergence of the Irish banking system, 1820–1845* (Dublin, 1975), pp. 73–4, 77–9, 89; W. A. Thomas, *The stock exchanges of Ireland*

(Liverpool, 1986), p. 141; *King's Inns admission papers*, p. 324; *DIB*, 'Peirce Mahony'. In later life Mahony moved from Merrion Square and Gresham Terrace to live at the Priory in Stillorgan, but he had a family house in Kildare Street, where he died.

25. Warburton and Whitelaw, *Dublin*, II, pp. 987–8; Hall, *Bank of Ireland*, pp. 455–71. By comparison, Home's establishment cost £16,000: *Commercial guide through Dublin* (Dublin, 1825), pp. 46, 59; Barrow, *Irish banking system*, pp. 3–6, 63; Thomas, *Stock exchanges*, pp. 89, 94. Northumberland Buildings near the Custom House, on the site of the future Liberty Hall, was like the Royal Arcade in a number of respects: built in the 1820s as a hotel, shops and coffee rooms, its success was limited: O'Dwyer, *Lost Dublin*, p. 65.

26. McGregor, *New picture of Dublin*, pp. 302–3; *Dublin almanac, 1836*; Thomas, *Stock exchanges*, pp. 78–82, 102–3, 106–8, 141; Richard Harrison, 'Dublin Quakers in business, 1800–1850' (M.Litt. dissertation, University of Dublin, 1987), pp. 257, 265–6, 282–4, 321. Home opened a hotel and 'mart' on Usher's Quay shortly after the fire.

27. Warburton and Whitelaw, *Dublin*, II, pp. 990–91; *1833–4 evidence pertaining to the Corporation of Dublin*, pp. 241, 610–11, 620; *Thom's directory, 1860*, pp. 1128, 1134, 1526–7; Harrison, 'Dublin Quakers', pp. 170–71, 207–8; L. M. Cullen, *Princes and pirates: The Dublin Chamber of Commerce, 1783–1983* (Dublin 1983), pp. 58–68, 74, 76; Tony Farmar, *Heitons – A managed transition: Heitons in the Irish coal, iron and building markets 1818–1996* (Dublin, 1996), pp. 22–3; Jacqueline Hill, *From patriots to unionists: Dublin civic politics and Irish Protestant patriotism 1660–1840* (Oxford, 1997), pp. 360–61.

28. Harrison, 'Dublin Quakers', pp. 210–16, 266, 270–73, 321–6; Murray, *Ireland's first railway*, pp. 13–15, 21–3; Peter Pearson, *Dun Laoghaire – Kingstown* (Dublin, 1981), pp. 46–8; Joseph Lee, 'Merchants and enterprise: The case of early Irish railways 1830–1855', in L. M. Cullen and Paul Butel (eds), *Négoce et industrie en France at en Irlande aux xviiie at xixe siècles* (Paris, 1980), p. 144; Fergus Mulligan, *William Dargan: An honourable life 1799–1867* (Dublin, 2013), pp. 30–51.

29. Joseph Lee, 'Railway labour in Ireland, 1833–56', in *Saothar*, V (1979), p. 14; Pearson, *Dun Laoghaire*, pp. 53–4, 57–8, 60–61; Séamas Ó Maitiú, *Dublin's suburban towns 1834–1930* (Dublin, 2003), pp. 24–5.

30. *Second report on railways for Ireland*, pp. 100, 103–4; *Thom's directory, 1847*, p. 181; Murray, *Ireland's first railway*, p. 31; Harrison, 'Dublin Quakers', p. 216; Lee, 'Merchants and enterprise', pp. 147–8; Thomas, *Stock exchanges*, pp. 109–10.

31. *Second report on railways for Ireland*, p. 44; Thomas, *Stock exchanges*, pp. 99–101.

32. On Vignoles' prescient plans to connect the DKR and the GSWR: *Second report on railways for Ireland*, Appendix A, pp. 32–4.

33. *Second report on railways for Ireland*, Appendix A, pp. 88–92; Appendix B, pp. 46–7; *Mail coach contract (Ireland)* (HC, 1843 [561]), pp. 7–8; *Thom's directory, 1847*; Lee, 'Merchants and enterprise', pp. 144, 146 147, 151, 154–5; Ruth Delany, *The Grand Canal of Ireland* (Dublin, 1995), pp. 164–8. Edward McDonnell, the paper-maker, became chairman in 1849. For the initial battle

over the northern railway route into Dublin: *Minutes of evidence taken before the committee on the Dublin and Drogheda Railway* (London, 1836).

34.　*The Irish tourist's handbook for visitors to Ireland* (London, 1852), pp. 27–8. Both Pim and his ally Perry used highly dubious means to defeat plans for a line from Portarlington through Athlone to Galway: Lee, 'Merchants and enterprise', pp. 153–4. The MGWR also took over freight operations on the Grand Canal Company between 1853 and 1860 but had a testy relationship with the canal company thereafter: Delany, *Grand Canal*, pp. 180–82. The north-side failure to secure funding for 'New Street' was, however, a complex story involving many others apart from the MGWR company: Jones, 'Dublin reformed', pp. 300–306.

35.　John D'Alton, *History of Drogheda, with its environs: And a memoir of the Dublin and Drogheda Railway* (Dublin, 1844), pp. xxv–vii; Jeanne Sheehy, 'Railway architecture: Its heyday', in *Journal of the Irish Railway Record Society*, XII, 68 (1975), pp. 134–5; Lee, 'Merchants and enterprise', pp. 143–5, 155; Thomas, *Stock exchanges*, p. 110. For the proposal to site the south-western terminus several hundred metres downstream beside Barrack Bridge on the site of what became part of the Guinness brewery: *Second report on railways for Ireland*, p. 37, Appendix A, p. 4; *ODNB*, 'Sancton Wood'. The later neglect of the original Kingstown line by the DSER ('the filthiest line in the whole empire') was reported even at Westminster: House of Commons debates, 16 May 1878 (*Hansard*, CCXL, c.16).

36.　*National Magazine*, I, 1 (July 1830), p. 30; *Thom's directory, 1860*; Charles Haliday, *A statistical inquiry into the sanitary condition of Kingstown*, ed. T. M. Madden (Dublin 1867); Daly, *Deposed capital*, pp. 174–6; Stella Archer and Peter Pearson, *The Royal St George Yacht Club: A history* (n.p., n.d. [1987]); pp. 1–22, 69–70, 83–7; Peter Pearson, *Between the mountains and the sea: Dun Laoghaire–Rathdown county* (Dublin, 1998), pp. 190–91; Campbell, *Irish establishment*, p. 34. For a list of the 502 members of the Royal St George in 1845: Archer and Pearson, op. cit., pp. 137–40.

37.　*Census of 1821*; *Thom's directory, 1860*; *1861 census*; Ó Maitiú, *Dublin's suburban towns*, pp. 25–7, 31–2.

38.　The general Towns Improvement Act of 1847 provided the template for the private Rathmines act: Ó Maitiú, *Dublin's suburban towns*, pp. 32–7; Daly, *Deposed capital*, p. 153.

39.　*FJ*, 20 August 1849, 28 September 1849, 22 September 1850, 21 April 1851, 10 February 1853; *Thom's directory, 1847*, p. 1388; *1861 census*; Susan Roundtree, 'Mount Pleasant Square', in Mary Clark and Alastair Smeaton (eds), *The Georgian squares of Dublin: An architectural history* (Dublin, 2006), pp. 123–53; Ó Maitiú, *Dublin's suburban towns*, pp. 28–38; Daly, *Deposed capital*, pp. 152–9 226–33. For Stokes' own apologia on his retirement: *Irish Times*, 7 December 1877.

40.　*Municipal boundaries commission (Ireland), I: Evidence, with appendices* (HC, 1880 [C.2725]), pp. 178, 184, 188; Daly, *Deposed capital*, pp. 159–62; Ó Maitiú, *Dublin's suburban towns*, pp. 38–9. The roads laid out at mid-century were Burlington and Raglan Roads, and after 1863, Clyde, Elgin, Ailesbury, Northumberland, Gilford, St Mary's and Simmonscourt Roads, Bushfield Terrace, Carlisle Avenue, Carlisle

Terrace and parts of Morehampton and Shelbourne Rds. I am very grateful to Dr
Susan Galavan for information on the Meade family.

41. *DIB*, 'William Dargan'; Mulligan, *Dargan*, pp. 157–62, 168–73.

42. A. C. Davies, 'Ireland's Crystal Palace, 1853', in J. M. Goldstrom and L. A. Clarkson
(eds), *Irish population, economy and society: Essays in honour of the late K. H.
Connell* (Oxford, 1981), pp. 249–70; Mulligan, *Dargan*, pp. 126–45.

43. Stephanie Rains, *Commodity culture and social class in Dublin 1850–1916* (Dublin,
2010), pp. 29–44; Mulligan, *Dargan*, pp. 145–50.

44. Nicholas Sheaff, *Iveagh House: An historical description* (Dublin, 1978); Rains,
Commodity culture, pp. 67–77; Casey, *Dublin*, pp. 497–8.

45. Casey, *Dublin*, pp. 602–23. Subsequent work on the cathedral after his death
brought the final expenditure to around £250,000: Andy Bielenberg, 'Late
Victorian elite formation and philanthropy: The making of Edward Guinness', in
Studia Hibernica, XXXII (2002/3), p. 136.

46. Roger Stalley, 'George Edmund Street and the restoration of Christ Church
Cathedral 1868–78', in Kenneth Milne (ed.), *Christ Church Cathedral Dublin*
(Dublin, 2000), pp. 353–72; Casey, *Dublin*, pp. 320–27; *DIB*, 'Henry Roe';
Michael O'Neill, 'Nineteenth-century architectural restoration', in John Crawford
and Raymond Gillespie (eds), *St. Patrick's Cathedral: A history* (Dublin, 2009),
pp. 340–45.

47. Gwynn, *Famous cities of Ireland*, p. 261; *DIB*, 'Lord John George de la Poer
Beresford', 'Thomas Davis'; Dickson, '1857 and 1908: Two moments in the
transformation of Irish universities', in David Dickson, Justyna Pyz and
Christopher Shepard (eds), *Irish classrooms and British empire: Imperial contexts in
the origins of modern education* (Dublin, 2012), pp. 184–7.

48. *FJ*, 24 January 1831, 2 February 1833, 17 Janunary 1838.

49. Hill, *Patriots to unionists*, pp. 362–76; Jones, 'Dublin reformed', pp. 8–17.

50. *First report of the commissioners appointed to inquire into the municipal corporations
in Ireland* (HC, 1835 [23–28]); *1833–4 evidence pertaining to the Corporation of
Dublin*, p. 393. Cf. Hill, *Patriots to unionists*, pp. 350–54, 364–71, 377–8.

51. K. H. Hoppen, *Elections, politics and society in Ireland 1832–1885* (Oxford, 1984),
p. 37; Hill, *Patriots to unionists*, pp. 379–80; Jones, 'Dublin reformed', pp. 31–3.

52. *Thom's directory, 1847*; Jacqueline Hill, 'The intelligentsia and Irish nationalism in
the 1840s', in *Studia Hibernica*, XX (1980), pp. 73–109; Hill, *Patriots to unionists*,
pp. 363–76, 380–81; Jones, 'Dublin reformed', pp. 11–20, 26–9.

53. 6 & 7 William IV, c.29; Hill, *Patriots to unionists*, pp. 379–80; Jones, 'Dublin
reformed', pp. 17–19, 35–6. The Paving Board had a long history of administrative
deficency, having had to be restructured in 1805–7 and 1826–7 and, although
relatively well managed after 1827, its budget soared to more than £39,000 p.a. by
the late 1840s, by which time there was mounting evidence of systemic failure:
ibid., pp. 94–111. For a satirical attack on the new Dublin police force: James
Henry, *An account of the proceedings of the government metropolitan police in the city
of Canton* (Dublin, 1840).

54. Hill, *Patriots to unionists*, pp. 381–2; Jones, 'Dublin reformed', pp. 33–4, 42–52, 121–70.

55. *Report from the select committee on local government and taxation of towns (Ireland)* (HC, 1876 [352]), pp. 69–70, 97, 162, 168; Ó Gráda, *Black '47*, p. 189; Prunty, *Dublin slums*, pp. 69–70; Jones, 'Dublin reformed', pp. 170–95, 249–62, 274–80, 291–2, 436; Lydia Carroll, *In the fever king's preserves: Sir Charles Cameron and the Dublin slums* (Dublin, 2011), p. 55. On Parke Neville: Jones, op.cit., pp. 280–85.

56. *Irish Times*, 15 September 1860, 21 February 1863; *Select committee on local government and taxation*, pp. 127, 156; [May Laffan], *Christy Carew* (London, 1880), I, p. 212; O'Dwyer, *Lost Dublin*, p. 139; Daly, 'Catholic Dublin', p. 133; Jones, 'Dublin reformed', pp. 288–90. The Assembly Rooms in William Street continued as the venue for the Lord Mayor's court and the basement was the headquarters (from the 1860s) for the new city Fire Brigade.

57. Jones, 'Dublin reformed', pp. 363–76. On the 1863 controversies for a connecting railway and a central station: Hugh Campbell, 'Railway plans and urban politics in nineteenth-century Dublin', in Ralf Roth and Marie-Noëlle Polino (eds), *The city and the railway in Europe* (Aldershot, 2003), pp. 183–6, 191–9.

58. *Irish Times*, 29 April 1861; Parke Neville, *Report to the right hon. the Lord Mayor, aldermen and councillors of the city of Dublin on the general state of the public works of the city under their control* (Dublin, 1869), pp. 79–81; ibid., *On the water supply of the city of Dublin* (London, 1874), pp. 29–34; *Select committee on local government and taxation*, pp. 97, 299; Daly, *Deposed capital*, pp. 248–50; Mary Daly, Mona Hearn and Peter Pearson, *Dublin's Victorian houses* (Dublin, 1998), pp. 83–5; Jones, 'Dublin reformed', pp. 380–430; Michael Corcoran, *Our good health: A history of Dublin's water and drainage* (Dublin, 2005), pp. 47–59; Carroll, *Fever king's preserves*, pp. 59–60. The architects of the 1851 accord within the Corporation – Codd and Guinness – were firmly supportive of Vartry; some opponents of the scheme, notably the earl of Meath, were handsomely bought off: Jones, 'Dublin reformed', pp. 393, 396–7, 426, 429. For Rathmines' independent water policy, first staking all on a Grand Canal supply until the 1880s, then building the Bohernabreena reservoir on the headwaters of the Dodder: Ó Maitiú, *Dublin's suburban towns*, pp. 86–97. The Corporation did reach an agreement some years later with the Grand Canal to supply water to the breweries and distilleries.

59. Daly, *Deposed capital*, pp. 117–51.

60. Neville, *Report ... on the general state of the public works of the city*, pp. 25, 50–56; Daly, *Deposed capital*, p.10; Liam Clare, 'The rise and demise of the Dublin cattle market 1863–1973', in D. A. Cronin, Jim Gilligan and Karina Holton (eds), *Irish fairs and markets: Studies in local history* (Dublin, 2001), pp. 181–9, 195.

61. *Irish Times*, 26 October 1863; *FJ*, 31 July 1871; *Municipal boundaries commission*, pp. 28, 196, 198; Daly, Hearn and Pearson, *Dublin's Victorian houses*, pp. 32–4; Ruth McManus, *Dublin 1910–1940: Shaping the city and suburbs* (Dublin, 2002), pp. 308–10; Casey, *Dublin*, pp. 659, 667; Rains, *Commodity culture*, pp. 51–3.

62. *Irish Times*, 26 October 1863; *FJ*, 26 August 1872, 22 February 1883; *Third report of H.M. commissioners for inquiring into the housing of the working classes, Ireland* (HC, 1884–85 [4547]), p. 97; F. J. Murphy, 'Dublin trams 1872–1959', in *DHR*, XXXIII, 1 (1979), pp. 2–5; *DIB*, 'James Lombard', 'William Martin Murphy'; Rains, *Commodity culture*, pp. 48–50, 57.

63. Ronald Nesbitt, *At Arnotts of Dublin* (Dublin, 1993), pp. 6–27; Rains, *Commodity culture*, pp. 2–3, 13–29, 43–4, 53–8.

64. Rains, *Commodity culture*, pp. 94–6, 133–5.

65. *Slater's national commercial directory of Ireland* (Manchester, 1846), pp. 181–2, 215–6; William Carleton, *The autobiography*, 2nd edn (Belfast, 1998), pp. 167–8. On the most famous and innovative of the early nineteenth-century academies: Christopher Stray, 'A pedagogic palace: The Feinaiglian Institution and its textbooks', in *Long Room*, XLVII (2002), pp. 14–25.

66. *Report of the commissioners appointed by … the Lord Lieutenant of Ireland to inquire into the endowments, funds, and actual condition of all schools endowed for the purpose of education in Ireland* (HC, 1881 [2831]), pp. 63, 101, 177–8; *Thom's directory, 1896*, p. 866; *Intermediate education (Ireland): Final report of the commissioners* (HC, 1899 [9511–3]), pp. 141–2, 187; Anon., *The school roll: From the beginning of the [Rathmines] School in 1858 till its close in 1899* (Dublin, 1932); A. V. O'Connor and S. M. Parkes, *Gladly learn and gladly teach: Alexandra College and School 1866–1966* (Dublin, n.d. [1984]), pp. 4–31; Richard Pine and Charles Acton, *To talent alone: The Royal Irish Academy of Music, 1848–1998* (Dublin, 1998), pp. 33–95; W. J. R. Wallace, *Faithful to our trust: A history of the Erasmus Smith Trust and the High School* (Blackrock, Co. Dublin, 2004), p. 121; Clara Cullen, 'The Museum of Irish Industry, Robert Kane and education for all in the Dublin of the 1850s and 1860s', in *History of Education*, XXXVIII, 1 (2009), pp. 99–113; David Fitzpatrick, *'Solitary and wild': Frederick McNeice and the salvation of Ireland* (Dublin, 2012), p. 64; Justyna Pyz, 'St. Columba's College: An Irish school in the age of empire', in Dickson, Pyz and Shepard, *Irish classrooms*, pp. 124–33; http://revpatrickcomerford.blogspot.ie/2010/04/home-communion-set-and-communion-of.html [accessed 30 Nov. 2012].

67. M. P. Magray, *The transforming power of the nuns: Women, religion and cultural change in Ireland 1750–1900* (New York, 1998), pp. 9–10, 80–81; M. M. Kealy, *Dominican education in Ireland, 1820–1930* (Dublin, 2007), pp. 46–7, 74, 78, 8–7; *DIB*, 'Daniel Murray'.

68. *Return to an order of … the House of Commons, dated 17 June 1864 for a copy 'of the special reports recently made to the Commissioners of National Education in Ireland on the convent schools in connection with the board'* (HC, 1864 [405]), pp. 64–5, 72–3, 77–8; Barry Coldrey, *Faith and fatherland: The Christian Brothers and the development of Irish nationalism 1838–1921* (Dublin, 1988), pp. 34–6; Magray, *Transformation of the nuns*, pp. 61–2, 82–3, 119–20; Angela Bourke et al. (eds), *The Field Day anthology of Irish writing* (Cork, 2002), V, pp. 658–9; *DIB*, 'Teresa Ball', 'Paul Cullen', 'May Laffan Hartley', 'Daniel Murray', 'Catherine McAuley'; Daly, 'Catholic Dublin', pp. 140–42.

69. *Thom's directory, 1860*, pp. 769, 1596–7; *FJ*, 7 March 1864; *Report of the commissioners appointed by ... the Lord Lieutenant of Ireland to inquire into the endowments, funds, and actual condition of all schools endowed for the purpose of education in Ireland* (HC, 1881 [2831]), pp. 125, 129; Coldrey, *Faith and fatherland*, pp. 19–22, 103–4; *DIB*, 'Philip Dowley', 'Jules Leman'.

70. Pauric Travers, '"Our Fenian dead": Glasnevin cemetery and the genesis of the republican funeral', in James Kelly and Uáitéar Mac Gearailt (eds), *Dublin and Dubliners* (Dublin, 1990), pp. 64–8; Clare Murphy, 'Varieties of crowd activity 1867–79', in Peter Jupp and Eoin Magennis, *Crowds in Ireland c.1720–1920* (Basingstoke, 2000), p. 182. The suburban Catholic churches of the 1830s were in St Peter's, Phibsboro; St John the Baptist's, Clontarf; St Mary's, Haddington Road; the first church in Rathmines; and St Brigid's, Cabinteely. The only church completions of the 1840s were those of St Audoen's; Blackrock; Dalkey; and the first church in Kingstown. The new churches of Cullen's era were: in the 1850s, St Catherine's, Meath Street; St James's; St Laurence O'Toole's, Seville Place; Mary Immaculate, Rathmines; Star of Sea, Sandymount; the University Church; Fairview; Ballybrack; and Chapelizod; the new churches in the 1860s were: City Quay; St Saviour's Dominick Street; Raheny; Sacred Heart, Donnybrook; Mount Argus, Harold's Cross, Rathgar; and Monkstown; those of the 1870s were: St Augustine and John's, Thomas Street; St Kevin's, SCR; Holy Family, Aughrim Street; St Mary and All Angels, Church Street; Holy Cross, Clonliffe; Rathfarnham; Inchicore; and Dundrum: Peter Costello, *Dublin churches* (Dublin, 1989). Cf. Emmet Larkin, *The pastoral role of the Roman Catholic Church in pre-famine Ireland 1750–1850* (Dublin, 2006), pp. 158, 162–3; Daly, 'Catholic Dublin', p. 136; Ciaran O'Carroll, 'The pastoral vision of Paul Cullen', in Keogh and McDonnell, *Cullen*, pp. 122–3; John Montague, 'Paul Cullen, J. J. McCarthy and Holy Cross Church, Clonliffe', in Keogh and McDonnell, *Cullen*, pp. 262, 270–73, 276; Fintan Cullen, 'Visualizing Ireland's first cardinal', in Keogh and McDonnell, op. cit., pp. 403–13; http://www.dia.ie/architects/view/851/BYRNE-PATRICK [accessed 11 December 2011].

71. Miller, 'Mass attendance in 1834', pp. 171–4; Daly, 'Catholic Dublin', pp. 135–6.

72. John Coolahan, *Irish education: Its history and structure* (Dublin, 1981), pp. 18–19, 24–8; O'Dwyer, *Lost Dublin*, p. 139; Donal McCartney, *UCD: A national idea – The history of University College, Dublin* (Dublin, 1999), pp. 1–17; *DIB*, 'John Henry Newman', 'Bartholomew Woodlock'; Eileen Kane, 'Paul Cullen and the visual arts', in Keogh and McDonnell, *Cullen*, pp. 111–14; Ian Ker, '"Not an equal, but ... one of his subjects": John Henry Newman's perception of the archbishop of Dublin', in Keogh and McDonnell, *Cullen*, pp. 277–88; Dickson, '1857 and 1908', pp. 190–93.

73. *DIB*, 'Bartholomew Woodlock'; Eileen Kane, 'Paul Cullen and the visual arts', in Keogh and McDonnell, *Cullen*, pp. 111–14; Joseph Doyle, 'Cardinal Cullen and the system of national education in Ireland', in Keogh and McDonnell, *Cullen*, p. 203; Montague, 'Cullen and Clonliffe', in ibid., pp. 261–76; Dickson, '1857 and 1908', pp. 190–93.

74. O'Carroll, 'Pastoral vision of Cullen', pp. 123–7; Daly, 'Catholic Dublin', p. 130.

75. *Thom's directory, 1860*; *Report from the Select Committee on Poor Relief (Ireland)* (HC, 1861 [408]), pp. 196–9; *Ninth report of the inspector appointed to visit the reformatory and industrial schools of Ireland* (HC, 1871 [461]), p. 30; J. V. O'Brien, *'Dear, dirty Dublin': A city in distress 1899–1916* (Berkeley, CA,1982), pp. 173–4; Joseph Robins, *The lost children: A study of charity children in Ireland 1700–1900* (Dublin, 1980), pp. 292–306; Virginia Crossman, 'Cullen, the relief of poverty and the development of social welfare', in Keogh and McDonnell, *Cullen*, pp. 158–64; Margaret Ó hÓgartaigh, 'Paul Cullen, the Mercy Missions and the Mater Hospital', in ibid., pp. 181–2, 186–8. Glencree Reformatory held up to 240 boys, the Catholic one for girls at High Park, 45, and the two Protestant ones 70 places between them: *Return showing the name and locality of every reformatory school in Ireland* (HC, 1861 [421]), p. 1. On the 'unruly girls' of the South Dublin workhouse in 1860–1: Anna Clark, 'Wild workhouse girls and the liberal imperial state in mid-nineteenth century Ireland', in *Journal of Social History*, XXXIX, 2 (2005), pp. 389–409.

76. *FJ*, 9, 11 November 1861; Travers, '"Our Fenian dead"', pp. 57–9.

77. *FJ*, 4 May 1848; Oliver MacDonagh, *The hereditary bondsman: Daniel O'Connell 1775–1829* (London, 1988), pp. 244–5;

78. *Northern Star and National Trades Journal*, 12 January 1848; *Belfast Newsletter*, 14 March 1848; *FJ*, 23, 24, 26 March; 6 April; 4, 16 May 1848; *DIB*, 'Patrick O'Higgins'.

79. Donal Kerr,*'A nation of beggars'?: Priests, people, and politics in Famine Ireland 1846–1852* (Oxford, 1994), pp. 127, 150–51, 160; Donal Kerr, 'Daniel Murray', in Kelly and Keogh, *Catholic diocese of Dublin*, pp. 258–9; Gary Owens, 'Popular mobilisation and the rising of 1848: The clubs of the Irish Confederation', in L. M. Geary (ed.), *Rebellion and remembrance in modern Ireland* (Dublin, 2001), pp. 51–63; Sean Ryder, 'Young Ireland and the 1798 rebellion', in Geary, op. cit., pp. 145–7; *DIB*, 'Charles Patrick Meehan'; Roisín Higgins, 'The *Nation* reading rooms', in Murphy, *Irish book in English*, pp. 264–7. The *OED* credits Frederick Jebb in 1779 as the first to use the term of 'passive resistance' in a political context (see chapter 5).

80. Joseph Denieffe, *A personal narrative of the Irish Revolutionary Brotherhood ... from 1855 to 1867 ...* (New York, 1906), p. 25; Charles Gavan Duffy, *Four years of Irish history, 1845–1849* (London, 1883), pp. 759–63; Robert Kee, *The green flag: A history of Irish nationalism* (London, 1972), pp. 261–9; R. V. Comerford, 'Anglo-French tension and the origins of Fenianism', in Lyons and Hawkins, *Ireland under the union*, pp. 152–5; *DIB*, 'Terence MacManus', 'Thomas Luby'; James Quinn, 'The IRB and Young Ireland: Varieties of tension', in Fearghal McGarry and James McConnel (eds), *The black hand of republicanism: Fenianism in modern Ireland* (Dublin, 2009), pp. 3–6; Marta Ramón, 'National brotherhoods and national leagues' in McGarry and McConnel, op. cit., pp. 23–5.

81. P. J. Stephenson, 'Hidden and vanishing Dublin: I', in *DHR*, I, 2 (1938), pp. 50–64; Shin-ichi Takagami, 'The Dublin Fenians 1858–79' (Ph.D. dissertation,

University of Dublin, 1990), pp. 18–37, 57–107; Ramón, 'National brotherhoods', pp. 22–3; *ODNB*, 'James Stephens'; *DIB*, 'Kevin Izod O'Doherty', 'Richard D'Alton Williams'.

82. *FJ*, 17 September 1865; Denieffe, *Personal narrative*, pp. 25–7; Takagami, 'Dublin Fenians', pp. 23–6; Quinn, 'IRB and Young Ireland', pp. 6–15; Matthew Kelly, 'The *Irish People* and the disciplining of dissent', in McGarry and McConnel, *Black hand of republicanism*, pp. 34–52.

83. Stephenson, 'Hidden and vanishing Dublin', p. 64; Takagami, 'The Fenian rising in Dublin, March 1867', in *IHS*, XXIX, 115 (1995), pp. 340–62; D. P. McCracken, *Inspector Mallon: Buying Irish patriotism for a five-pound note* (Dublin, 2009), pp. 24–31. The *Irishman* paper, controlled by Richard Pigott, became the dominant if more quirky mouthpiece for Fenianism in the late 1860s: *DIB*, 'Richard Pigott'.

84. *FJ*, 27 December 1870; Breandán Mac Giolla Choille, 'Dublin trades in procession 1864', in *Saothar*, I, 1 (1975), pp. 18–29; J. W. Boyle, *The Irish labor movement in the nineteenth century* (Washington, 1988), p. 83; Takagami, 'The Dublin Fenians after the Rising 1867–79', in Taro Matsuo (ed.), *Comparative aspects of Irish and Japanese economic and social history* (Tokyo, 1993), pp. 182–237.

85. Canon John O'Hanlon, *Report of the O'Connell Monument Committee* (Dublin, 1882), pp. xlvi–vii; Foster, 'Lord Randolph Churchill', pp. 246–7; H. F. Kearney, '1875: Faith or fatherland? The contested symbolism of Irish nationalism', in Brown and Miller, *Piety and power*, pp. 65–80; *DIB*, 'John O'Mahony'; Ramón, 'National brotherhoods', pp. 28, 31.

86. Fergus D'Arcy, 'Wages of labourers in the Dublin building industry, 1667–1918', in *Saothar*, XIV (1989), pp. 23–5, 28; ibid., 'Wages of skilled workers in the Dublin building industry, 1667–1918', in *Saothar*, XV (1990), pp. 28–32, 36; Andy Bielenberg, *Ireland and the industrial revolution: The impact of the industrial revolution on Irish industry 1801–1922* (London, 2009), pp. 158–63, 197.

87. J. W. Hammond, 'The founder of "Thom's Directory"', in *DHR*, VIII, 2 (1946), pp. 49–52, 55–6; Daly, *Deposed capital*, pp. 45–6; *DIB*, 'Alex Thom'; Charles Benson, 'Workers in printing and bookbinding', in Murphy, *Irish book in English*, pp. 89–97. Thom's obituarist claimed that he had 'spared no labour and grudged no expenditure' in publishing the *Directory*, and had 'never at all recouped the pecuniary outlay': *FJ*, 23 December 1879. It originally sold for half a guinea before being pitched at a standard price of one guinea.

88. Fergus D'Arcy and Ken Hannigan (eds), *Workers in union* (Dublin, 1988), pp. 62–5, 97–104; Boyle, *Irish labor movement*, pp. 54–49, 92–99; Emmet O'Connor, *A labour history of Ireland 1824–1960* (Dublin, 1992), pp. 30–32.

89. Anne Jellicoe, 'The condition of young women employed in manufactories in Dublin', in *Transactions of the National Association for the Promotion of Social Science, Dublin 1862* [*TNAPSS*] (London, 1863), pp. 640–45; *Census of Ireland, 1871*; Wilson, *Victorian doctor*, pp. 128–9; Daly, *Deposed capital*, pp. 40–42; Bielenberg, *Industrial revolution*, p. 113.

90. Daly, *Deposed capital*, pp. 36–7; Colin Rynne, *Industrial Ireland 1750–1930 : An archaeology* (Cork, 2006), pp. 278–9; Bielenberg, *Industrial revolution*, pp. 116–18. Pims of Greenmount and the two Jameson distilling firms built housing for their workers in the 1850s.

91. *Dublin almanac, 1836; Thom's directory, 1880* and *1896;* Arnold Wright, *Disturbed Dublin: The story of the great strike of 1913–14* (London, 1914), pp. 20–21; Patrick Lynch and John Vaizey, *Guinness's brewery in the Irish economy 1759–1876* (Cambridge, 1960), pp. 214–41; Daly, *Deposed capital*, pp. 23–31; Elizabeth Malcolm, 'The rise of the pub', in J. S. Donnelly and K. A. Miller (eds), *Irish popular culture 1650–1850* (Dublin, 1998), pp. 51–2, 68, 71; S. R. Dennison and Oliver MacDonagh, *Guinness 1886–1939: From incorporation to the Second World War* (Cork, 1998), pp. 6–8, 10, 94–6, 121–4, 130–31; Findlater, *Findlaters*, pp. 23–9, 32–6, 52–3, 75–87; Michael Purser, *Jellett, O'Brien, Purser and Stokes: Seven generations, four families* (Dublin, 2004), pp. 34–5; Rynne, *Industrial Ireland*, p. 247; Bielenberg, *Industrial Ireland*, pp. 79–87.

92. Jordan, 'Dwellings of the poor', p. 18; Mapother, 'Sanitary state of Dublin', p. 62; Nugent Robertson, 'The condition of the dwellings of the poor in Dublin', in *TNAPSS 1862*, p. 520; Daly, *Deposed capital*, pp. 21–2; Prunty, *Dublin slums*, p. 39; Anastasia Dukova, 'Crime and policing in Dublin, Brisbane and London *c*.1850–1900' (Ph.D. dissertation, University of Dublin, 2012), p. 82. There were actually fourteen traders present in Fordham's Alley: *1836 directory*.

93. *1836 directory*; Robertson, 'Dwellings of the poor', pp. 518–19; Willis, *Hidden Dublin*, pp. 10, 64–5, 72, 75, 77; Daly, *Deposed capital*, pp. 278–9; Jones, 'Dublin reformed', p. 299; Maria Luddy, *Prostitution and Irish society 1800–1940* (Cambridge, 2007), pp. 20–21, 41.

94. John O'Daly, *The poets and poetry of Munster ...* (Dublin, 1849), pp. xv–xvi; C. P. Meehan (ed.), *The poets and poetry of Munster*, 4th edn (Dublin, [1884]), pp. xx, xxiv–v, xxxi–lvi; Carleton, *Autobiography*, pp. 164–5.

95. Asenath Nicholson, *Annals of the famine in Ireland*, ed. Maureen Murphy (Dublin, 1998), pp. 12–13, 36–46, 50–57; Séamus Enright, 'Women and Catholic life in Dublin 1766–1852', in Kelly and Keogh, *Catholic diocese of Dublin*, pp. 281–4; F. O. C. Meenan, *St. Vincent's Hospital 1834–1994* (Dublin, 1995), pp. 10–31; Prunty, *Dublin slums*, pp. 241–7, 254–5; *DIB*, 'Mary Aikenhead', 'Margaret Aylward'.

96. *Census of Ireland, 1841*, p. lxxxii; ibid., Appendix [*Report upon the tables of death*], pp. lxxiii–lv; Willis, *Hidden Dublin*, pp. 22, 35, 49, 54, 69, 71, 92; Daly, *Deposed capital*, pp. 241–2; Prunty, *Dublin slums*, pp. 45–7, 109–12; J. G. Martin, 'The Society of St. Vincent de Paul as an emerging social phenomenon in mid-nineteenth century Ireland', (MA dissertation, National College of Ireland [NCEA], 1993), pp. 60–86, 147–8, 199; Jones, 'Dublin reformed', pp. 213–14; M. B. Ní Chearbhaill, 'The Society of St. Vincent de Paul in Dublin, 1926–1975' (MA dissertation, NUI Maynooth, 2008), pp. 7–14. Willis's son, a medical doctor, became first secretary of the St Vincent de Paul Society in Dublin.

97. Jordan, 'Dwellings of the poor', p. 17; Robertson, 'Dwellings of the poor', pp. 517, 519, 521, 595; Parke Neville, 'City of Dublin sewerage', in *TNAPSS 1862*, p. 527;

Prunty, *Dublin slums*, pp. 115–18; Woods, *Dublin outsiders*, pp. 132–44; Willis, *Hidden Dublin*, p.81; Jones, 'Dublin reformed', pp. 295–8, 338–41, 345–51; Carroll, *Fever king's preserves*, pp. 44–5, 70–5, 98–9.

98. *Irish Times*, 21 December 1880; *Appendix to the report of the departmental committee appointed by the Local Government Board of Ireland to inquire into the housing conditions of the working classes in the city of Dublin: Minutes of evidence with appendices* (HC, 1914 [7317]), pp. 16, 185; O'Brien, *'Dear, dirty Dublin'*, pp. 102–3; Daly, *Deposed capital*, pp. 241–3, 278–97; Prunty, *Dublin slums*, pp. 109–28; Jones, 'Dublin reformed', pp. 270–71; Colum O'Riordan, 'The Dublin Artisans' Dwellings Company', in *Irish Architectural & Decorative Studies*, VII (2004), pp. 160–3; Carroll, *Fever king's preserves*, pp. 73–4, 103–6. On the not entirely ineffective but unpaid parish officers of health, operating in most of the city from 1819: Jones, 'Dublin reformed', pp. 203–5.

8 Whose Dublin? 1880–1913

1. T. W. Moody and R. A. J. Hawkins with Margaret Moody (eds), *Florence Arnold-Forster's Irish journal* (Oxford, 1988), p. 307; Dana Arnold, 'Decimus Burton's work in the Phoenix Park 1832–49', in *Bulletin of the Irish Georgian Society*, XXXVII (1995), pp. 57–75; ibid., 'Trans-planting national cultures: The Phoenix Park, Dublin (1832–49), an urban heterotopia', in Dana Arnold, *Cultural identities and the aesthetics of Britishness* (London, 2004), pp. 78–84; Casey, *Dublin*, pp. 288–307; John A. McCullen, *An illustrated history of the Phoenix Park: Landscape and management to 1880* (Dublin, 2009), pp. 75–6, 111–43, 276–7.

2. [Percy Fitzgerald], 'Dublin society', in *Dublin University Magazine*, LXIII (1864), pp. 7–10; R. F. Foster, 'Lord Randolph Churchill and the prelude to the Orange card', in F. S. L. Lyons and R. A. J. Hawkins (eds), *Ireland under the union – varieties of tension: Essays in honour of T. W. Moody* (Oxford, 1980), pp. 238–40; Joseph Robins, *Champagne and silver buckles: The viceregal court at Dublin Castle 1700–1922* (Dublin, 2001), pp. 132–7; Patricia Pelly and Andrew Tod (eds), *Elizabeth Grant of Rothiemurchus: The Highland lady in Dublin 1851–56* (Dublin, 2005), pp. 268–70, 334; *ODNB*, 'James Hamilton, first duke of Abercorn'; *DIB*, 'George Howard, 7th earl of Carlisle'.

3. Fergus D'Arcy, 'Unemployment demonstrations in Dublin, 1879–1882', in *Saothar*, XVII (1992), pp. 15–23. For city antipathy to the land agitation insofar as it was hurting urban employment: M. E. Daly, *Dublin: The deposed capital – A social and economic history, 1860–1914* (Cork, 1986), pp. 59–60.

4. *FJ*, 15 March 1880; *Irish Times*, 20 March 1880; T. D. Sullivan, *Recollections of troubled times in Irish politics* (Dublin, 1905), pp. 138–44; A. J. Nowlan, 'Phoenix Park public meetings', in *DHR*, XIV, 4 (1958), pp. 102–13; D. P. McCracken, *Inspector Mallon: Buying Irish patriotism for a five-pound note* (Dublin, 2009), pp. 41–2; *DIB*, 'Thomas Brennan', 'Patrick Egan', 'Andrew Kettle'. On fond memories of the private garden attached to the Chief Secretary's Lodge in 1880: Moody and Hawkins (eds) *Arnold-Forster's Irish journal*, p. 48.

5. Myles Dungan, *Conspiracy: Irish political trials* (Dublin, 2008), pp. 176–81; McCracken, *Mallon*, pp. 57–9.

6. Myles Dungan, 'Enforcing silence: *United Ireland*, the Irish nationalist press and British governance, 1881–1891' (Ph.D. dissertation, University of Dublin, 2012), pp. 77–8; *DIB*, 'Timothy Harrington', 'Thomas Sexton'; 'A. M. Sullivan'. Brennan and Egan emigrated to the United States.

7. *Report from the select committee of the House of Lords appointed to enquire into the state of Ireland in respect of crime ...* (HC, 1839 [486]), pp. 1002–3; R. B. McDowell, *The Irish administration 1801–1914* (London, 1964), pp. 144–5; J. V. O'Brien, *'Dear, dirty Dublin': A city in distress 1899–1916* (Berkeley, CA,1982), pp. 179–88; Anastasia Dukova, 'Crime and policing in Dublin, Brisbane and London *c*.1850–1900' (Ph.D. dissertation, University of Dublin, 2012), pp. 71–2, 105, 113, 238–40; *DIB*, 'James Carey'; Dungan, *Conspiracy*, pp. 181–216; McCracken, *Mallon*, pp. 10–16, 65–157. Carey won over 51 per cent of the vote in the Trinity Ward election in a three-cornered contest: *Irish Times,* 27 November 1881.

8. *Irish Times*, 27 November 1883; Sullivan, *Recollections*, pp. 225–6; Daly, *Deposed capital*, pp. 214–15, Stephanie Rains, *Commodity culture and social class in Dublin 1850–1916* (Dublin, 2010), pp. 102–18. For Sullivan's stinging attack on the historic despoliation of the city by local Tories: *Irish Times*, 3 December 1883.

9. Brian Walker, *Parliamentary election results in Ireland, 1801–1922* (Dublin, 1978), pp. 372, 388, 394; W. L. Feingold, *The revolt of the tenantry: The transformation of local government in Ireland 1872–1886* (Boston, 1984), pp. 105, 113, 195, 200; H. A. Gilligan, *A history of Dublin port* (Dublin, 1988), pp. 98–9; W. N. Osborough, *Law and the emergence of modern Dublin: A litigation topography for a capital city* (Dublin, 1996), pp. 46–51.

10. *DIB*, 'William Walsh', 'Edward MacCabe'.

11. R. K. Irvine (ed.), *The commercial year book of the Dublin Chamber of Commerce* (Dublin, 1917), pp. 185–8; O'Brien, *'Dear, dirty Dublin'*, pp. 63–4; Thomas Morrissey, SJ, *William Martin Murphy* (Dundalk, 1997), pp. 4–17, 31; Andy Bielenberg, 'Entrepreneurship, power and public opinion in Ireland: The career of William Martin Murphy', in *IESH*, XXVII (2000), pp. 25–33; Rains, *Commodity culture*, pp. 93, 168–9.

12. *Irish Times*, 12, 27 October 1891; *FJ*, 12 October 1891; Walker, *Parliamentary election results*, pp. 344–9; C. J. Woods, 'The general election of 1892: The Catholic clergy and the defeat of the Parnellites', in Lyons and Hawkins, *Ireland under the union*, pp. 293, 208; Morrissey, *Murphy*, pp. 11–12, 18–30; David Fitzpatrick, *Harry Boland's Irish revolution* (Dublin, 2003), p. 25. For the remarkable butcher from Blackrock who defeated Murphy in the 1892 election: *DIB*, 'William Field'.

13. *FJ*, 25 April 1859; L. M. Cullen, *Eason & son: A history* (Dublin, 1989), pp. 43–7, 53–4, 56–7, 63–5, 76–7.

14. *FJ*, 8 April 1889; *Thom's directory, 1896*, pp. 991–2; A. J. Litton, 'The growth and development of the Irish telephone system', in *JSSISI*, XX, 5 (1962), pp. 81–5; S. R. Dennison and Oliver MacDonagh, *Guinness 1886–1939: From incorporation*

to the Second World War (Cork, 1998), p. 116n; Christopher Morash, *A history of the media in Ireland* (Cambridge, 2010), pp. 83–7; Desmond Norton, 'Stewart and Kincaid, Irish land agents in the 1840s', UCD Centre for Economic Research Working Papers 2002, WP/08, pp. 13–15; http://www.ucd.ie/economics/research/papers/2002/WP02.08.pdf: [accessed 12 Feb. 2011]; Rains, *Commodity culture*, pp. 144, 165n, 170.

15. Rolf and Magda Loeber, *A Guide to Irish fiction 1650–1900* (Dublin, 2006), pp. xci–xcii.

16. Cullen, *Eason & son*, pp. 80–82; Alex Findlater, *Findlaters: The story of a Dublin merchant firm 1774–2001* (Dublin, 2001), pp. 315–19; Loeber and Loeber, *Irish fiction*, pp. xci–xcix; Rains, *Commodity culture*, pp. 131–2; Elizabeth Tilley, 'Periodicals', in J. H. Murphy, *The Irish book in English 1800–1891* (Oxford, 2011), pp. 164–70; Loeber and Loeber, 'James Duffy and Catholic nationalism', and 'Popular reading practice', in Murphy op. cit., pp. 115–21, 223– 6, 231–2; John Strachan and Claire Nally, *Advertising, Literature and Print Culture in Ireland, 1891–1922* (Basingstoke, 2012), pp. 108–36.

17. *DIB*, 'David Plunket' (created Baron Rathmore), 'Edward Gibson' (created Baron Ashbourne).

18. *Irish Times*, 13 July 1881; Martin Maguire, 'The organisation and activism of Dublin's Protestant working class 1883–1935', in *IHS*, XXIX, 113 (1994), pp. 76–7; Martin Maguire, '"Our people": The Church of Ireland and the culture of community in Dublin since disestablishment', in Raymond Gillespie and W. A. Neely (eds), *The laity and the Church of Ireland 1000–2000: All sorts and conditions* (Dublin, 2002), pp. 283–4.

19. Daly, *Deposed capital*, pp. 230–33; Alvin Jackson, 'The failure of Unionism in Dublin, 1900', in *IHS*, XXVI, 104 (1989), pp. 377–95; Maguire, 'Dublin's Protestant working class', pp. 80–82.

20. Daly, *Deposed capital*, p. 33; Dennison and MacDonagh, *Guinness 1886–1939*, pp. 66–73, 116; Séamas Ó Maitiú, *W. & R. Jacob: Celebrating 150 years of Irish biscuit making* (Dublin, 2001), pp. 26–30; *DIB*, 'Sir Henry Cochrane'. On the rise of other commercial bakery firms in the city: Andy Bielenberg, *Ireland and the industrial revolution* ...(Basingstoke, 2009), p. 72.

21. Patrick Lynch and John Vaizey, *Guinness's brewery in the Irish economy 1759–1876* (Cambridge, 1960), pp. 186–97; J. U. Sharkey, *St. Anne's: The story of a Guinness estate* (Dublin, 2002), pp. 31–67; *ODNB*, 'Arthur Cecil Guinness'; *DIB*, 'Arthur Cecil Guinness'.

22. House of Commons debates, 13 July 1875 (*Hansard*, CCXV, cc1396–1404); *Irish Times*, 4 June 1880; W. P. Coyne, *Ireland, industrial and agricultural* (Dublin, 1902), pp. 179–80; H. F. Berry, *A history of the Royal Dublin Society* (London, 1915), pp. 290–91, 311–12; R. A. Jarrell, 'The Department of Science and Art and Control of Irish Science, 1853–1905', *IHS*, XXIII, 92 (1983), pp. 330–39; Elizabeth Crooke, *Politics, archaeology and the creation of a National Museum of Ireland* ... (Dublin, 2000), pp. 113–23; *DIB*, 'William Archer'; John Walsh, *Collen: 200 years of building and civil engineering in Ireland* (Dublin, 2010), pp. 10–12.

23. *1914 Dublin housing conditions report*, pp. 118–20, 182–5; Daly, *Deposed capital*, pp. 296–9, 306–8; F. H. A. Aalen, 'The working-class housing movement in Dublin, 1850–1920', in Michael Bannon (ed.) *The emergence of Irish planning 1880–1920* (Dublin, 1985), pp. 145–53; Findlater, *Findlaters*, pp. 58–60; Colum O'Riordan, 'The Dublin Artisans' Dwellings Company', in *Irish Architectural & Decorative Studies*, VII (2004), pp. 157–83. The company's only major interest beyond the canals was in Harold's Cross.

24. Lynch and Vaizey, *Guinness's brewery*, pp. 189–97; Rains, *Commodity culture*, p. 112.

25. *1914 Dublin housing conditions report*, pp. 15, 19–20, 37, 52, 195; O'Brien, *'Dear, dirty Dublin'*, pp. 26–7; Daly, *Deposed capital*, pp. 299–304; Aalen, 'Working-class housing', pp. 153–9; Dennison and MacDonagh, *Guinness 1886–1939*, pp. 16–23, 29, 35–6, 127–30; Jacinta Prunty, *Dublin slums 1800–1925: A study in urban geography* (Dublin, 1999), pp. 141–2; Andy Bielenberg, 'Late Victorian elite formation and philanthropy: The making of Edward Guinness', in *Studia Hibernica*, XXXII (2002/3), pp. 133–54; Emma Cullinan, 'Nellie's Iveagh flat ...', in *Irish Times*, 5 October 2006; *ODNB*, 'Edward Cecil Guinness'. Benjamin Lee Guinness had been considering a plan for clearing dilapidated property around the cathedral as far back in 1865: Aalen, 'Working-class housing', pp. 154–5.

26. *Thom's directory, 1896*, p. 1311; Padraig Yeates, *Lockout: Dublin 1913* (Dublin, 2000), pp. 260–64; John Crawford, *The Church of Ireland in Victorian Dublin* (Dublin, 2005), pp. 60–66; *DIB*, 'William Conyngham Plunket'; Fergus Campbell, *The Irish establishment 1879–1914* (Oxford, 2009), p. 279; David Fitzpatrick, *'Solitary and wild': Frederick McNeice and the salvation of Ireland* (Dublin, 2012), pp. 55, 58; Barry Crosbie, *Irish imperial networks: Migration, social communication and exchange in nineteenth-century India* (Cambridge, 2012), pp. 199–201, 213–15.

27. *Irish Times*, 7 December 1905; W. J. MacCormack, *Fool of the family: A life of J. M. Synge* (London, 2000), pp. 74–6, 176–7; W. A. Neely, 'The laity in a changing society 1830–1900', in Raymond Gillespie and W. A. Neely (eds), *The laity and the Church of Ireland 1000–2000: All sorts and conditions* (Dublin, 2002), p. 204; Maguire, '"Our people"', in Gillespie and Neely, op. cit., pp. 277, 280, 284; Crawford, *Church of Ireland*, pp. 41–6, 54–5, 67–85, 146–76; Campbell, *Irish establishment*, pp. 210, 236. Merrion Hall was in Lower Merrion Street. Several of the prominent Protestant lay organisations were interdenominational – notably the YMCA and the Dublin City Mission. According to a young cavalry office garrisoned in Dublin from 1912 to 1914, at that time there were 'no Nationalists among [the] Masons': ('Extracts from the letters of ... Captain Vane de Vallence': *Irish Times*, 4 May 1976).

28. Jackson, 'Failure of Unionism', pp. 377–95; Maguire, 'Dublin's Protestant working class', pp. 81–2; Maguire, '"Our people"', p. 278; Crawford, *Church of Ireland*, pp. 43, 75.

29. David Allsobrook, *Liszt: My travelling circus life* (London, 1991), pp. 126–58; Christopher Morash, *A history of Irish theatre 1601–2000* (Cambridge, 2002), pp. 76–93, 106; *DIB*, 'Dion Boucicault'.

30. *Irish Times*, 12 January 1877, 18 October 1884, 29 October 1886, 14 August 1889, 12 May 1892; [May Laffan], *Flitters, tatters and the counselor*, new edn (London, 1883), pp. 23–5, 44–7; Christopher Fitz-Simon, 'The Dublin theatre during the years leading up to the opening of the Abbey Theatre', in *DHR*, LIII, 1 (2000), pp. 19–32; Morash, *Irish theatre*, pp. 103–13; Robert O'Byrne, *Dublin's Gaiety Theatre: The grand old lady of South King Street* (Dublin, 2007), pp. 11–17. On Adam Findlater's involvement in the Star of Erin/Empire Palace: Findlater, *Findlaters*, pp. 232–49.

31. [Percy Fitzgerald], 'Dublin society', in *Dublin University Magazine*, LXIII (1864), pp. 10–11; O'Brien, *'Dear, dirty Dublin'*, pp. 47–9; Harry White, *The Keeper's recital: Music and cultural history in Ireland, 1770–1970* (Cork, 1997), pp. 98–117; Richard Pine and Charles Acton, *To talent alone: The Royal Irish Academy of Music, 1848–1998* (Dublin, 1998), pp. 96–8, 154, 160, 194–207, 213–19, 223–34, 237; *DIB*, 'Michele Esposito'.

32. Morash, *Irish theatre*, pp. 115–38; *DIB*, 'Frank Fay', 'William Fay', 'Annie Horniman', 'Edward Martyn', 'John Millington Synge'.

33. Nicola Gordon Bowe, *The life and work of Harry Clarke* (Dublin, 1994); *DIB*, 'Harry Clarke'.

34. John Hutchinson, *The dynamics of cultural nationalism: The Gaelic revival and the creation of the Irish nation state* (London, 1987), pp. 163–7; *DIB*, 'David Comyn'. Two of the League's most successful publications were Eugene O'Growney's *Simple lessons in Irish: Giving the pronunciation of each word* (Dublin, 1894) and Seán Ó Cuív's *Irish made easy: Being lessons, stories, songs etc. in simplified spelling* (Dublin, 1907).

35. Seán Ó Lúing, 'Douglas Hyde and the Gaelic League', in *Studies*, LXII, 246 (1973), pp. 123–38; Mark Storey, *Poetry and Ireland since 1800: A source book* (London, 1988), pp. 78–84; Janet Egleson Dunlevy and Gareth Dunlevy, *Douglas Hyde: A maker of modern Ireland* (Berkeley, 1991), pp. 182–6; T. G. McMahon, *Grand Opportunity: The Gaelic revival and Irish society, 1893–1910* (Syracuse, 2008), pp. 89–92, 98–9, 102–3, 107–11, 114–15, 156–161, 184; Seamus Ó Maitiú, 'A spent force: *An Claidheamh Soluis* and the Gaelic League in Dublin 1893–1913', in Francis Devine, Mary Clark and Máire Kennedy (eds), *A capital in conflict: Dublin city and the 1913 Lockout* (Dublin, 2013), pp. 281–309.

36. Hutchinson, *Dynamics of cultural nationalism*, pp. 120–27; *DIB*, 'John Joseph O'Kelly', 'Shan O'Keeffe'; Ó Maitiú, *'An Claidheamh Soluis'*, p. 305. On the ambience of a revivalist household: Desmond Ryan, *Remembering Sion: A chronicle of storm and quiet* (London, 1934), pp. 62–4.

37. R. V. Comerford, *Ireland* (London, 2003), pp. 217–24; Paul Rouse, 'Michael Cusack: Sportsman and journalist', in Mike Cronin, William Murphy and Paul Rouse (eds), *The Gaelic Athletics Association 1884–2009* (Dublin, 2009), pp. 47–60; Paul Rouse, 'Gunfire in Hayes's Hotel: The IRB and the founding of the GAA', in Fearghal McGarry and James McConnel (eds), *The black hand of republicanism: Fenianism in modern Ireland* (Dublin, 2009), pp. 72–85. The Irish Football Union became the Irish Rugby Football Union in 1879. Cusack published

and largely wrote the remarkable *Celtic Times,* but it ran for less than a year in
1887.

38. *Irish Times,* 27 February 1899, 28 March 1899; Hutchinson, *Dynamics of cultural
    nationalism,* pp. 155–8; Neal Garnham (ed.), *The origins and development of football
    in Ireland* (Belfast, 1999), p. 22; Fitzpatrick, *Harry Boland,* pp. 32–3; William
    Nolan (ed.), *The Gaelic Athletics Association in Dublin 1884–2000* (Dublin 2005),
    I, pp. 3–113; Rouse, 'Gunfire in Hayes's Hotel', pp. 82–4. Cusack was caricatured
    as the xenophobic 'Citizen' in the Cyclops episode of James Joyce's *Ulysses*: *DIB*,
    'Michael Cusack'.

39. Hutchinson, *Dynamics of cultural nationalism,* pp. 168–73; *DIB,* 'William
    Rooney'; Ciaran Wallace, 'Local politics and government in Dublin city
    and suburbs 1899–1914' (Ph.D., University of Dublin, 2010), pp. 279–81;
    Frank Callanan, 'Why Joyce, the "bohemian aesthete", was also a political
    controversialist', in *Irish Times,* 22 January 2011. Joyce, however, disliked Griffith's
    anti-Semitism, as is evident in his subsequent journalism: James Joyce, *Dubliners,*
    ed. Terence Brown (new edn, London, 1992), p. xxvii.

40. *Irish Times,* 1 January, 16 August 1898; *FJ,* 16 August 1898; T. J. O'Keefe, 'The
    1898 efforts to celebrate the United Irishmen: The '98 centennial', in *Eire-
    Ireland,* XXIII, 2 (1988), pp. 51–73; Senia Paseta, '1798 in 1898: The politics of
    commemoration', in *The Irish Review,* XXII (1998), pp. 46–53; Yvonne Whelan,
    'Monuments, power and contested space: The iconography of Sackville Street
    ... before Independence (1922)', in *Ir. Geog.,* XXXIV, 1 (2001), pp. 28–30; Owen
    McGee, 'Fred Allan (1861–1937): Republican, Methodist and Dubliner', in
    DHR, LVI, 2 (2003), pp. 210, 215–16; Casey, *Dublin,* p. 220; McCracken, *Mallon,*
    pp. 166–7, 177–83. The Tone monument was not completed until 1967 (then badly
    damaged when it was bombed by the UVF in 1971).

41. McCracken, *The Irish Pro-Boers 1877–1902* (Johannesburg, 1989), pp. 44–87; ibid.,
    Mallon, pp. 196–207; *DIB,* 'Arthur Griffith'.

42. *The Leader,* 22 December 1900; A. E. Clery, 'The Gaelic League 1893–1919',
    in *Studies,* VIII, 31 (1919), pp. 401–406; Hutchinson, *Dynamics of cultural
    nationalism,* pp. 173–8, 185; Patrick Maume, *The long gestation: Irish nationalist
    life 1891–1918* (Dublin, 1999), pp. 59–63; *DIB,* 'D. P. Moran'; Campbell, *Irish
    establishment,* pp. 189–90; Strachan and Nally, *Advertising, literature,* pp. 72–84.

43. Cullen, *Eason & son,* p. 355; Morrissey, *Murphy,* pp. 26–36; Bielenberg, 'William
    Martin Murphy', pp. 34–7; *DIB,* 'William Martin Murphy', 'Timothy R.
    Harrington'; Campbell, *Irish establishment,* p. 141; Patrick Maume, 'William
    Martin Murphy, the *Irish Independent* and middle-class politics, 1905–19',
    in Fintan Lane (ed.) *Politics, society and the middle class in modern Ireland*
    (Basingstoke, 2010), pp. 230–40; Morash, *History of the media,* pp. 122–3; Ciaran
    Wallace, 'Fighting for Unionist Home Rule: Competing identities in Dublin
    1880–1929', in *Journal of Urban History,* XXXVIII, 38, 5 (2012), pp. 932–49.

44. Wallace, 'Local politics and government', *passim.* For the electorate and voting
    levels, op. cit., pp. 104, 109, 127. Cf. O'Brien, *'Dear, dirty Dublin',* pp. 77–81.

45.   Daly, *Deposed capital*, pp. 251–5; Michael Corcoran, *Our good health: A history of Dublin's water and drainage* (Dublin, 2005), pp. 91–100; Cormac Ó Gráda, *Jewish Ireland in the age of Joyce: A socioeconomic history* (Princeton, 2006), pp. 40–41; *DIB*, 'Thomas Sexton'. Between 1892 and 1912 the city's debt rose from £1,258,013 to £2,625,695, slightly faster than the growth in annual revenue (from £270,588 to 499,792). The rateable valuation for the city over the period grew by 42.0 per cent (half of this coming from the north-side townships added in 1900). Less than one third of the 1912 municipal debt related to loans drawn down for housing developments: *1914 Dublin housing conditions report*, p. 160.

46.   James Beckett, 'The building trade in 1859 and 1909', in *The Irish Builder: Jubilee Number* (Dublin, 1909), p. 34; O'Brien, *'Dear, dirty Dublin'*, pp. 57–9, 74–5, 98.

47.   *Census of Ireland, 1901, 1911*; Wallace, 'Local politics and government', pp. 89–90.

48.   O'Brien, *'Dear, dirty Dublin'*, p. 130; Ó Gráda, *Jewish Ireland*, pp. 34–6, 38–9.

49.   T. W. Grimshaw, 'Child mortality in Dublin', in *JSSISI*, IX (1890), append. 12–13; *1914 Dublin housing conditions report*, p. 98; F. H. A. Aalen, 'Health and housing in Dublin, c.1850–1921', in F. H. A. Aalen and Kevin Whelan (eds), *Dublin city and county: From prehistory to present* (Dublin, 1992), pp. 284–6; Prunty, *Dublin slums*, pp. 153–7. Ó Gráda's data relate to the years 1883–7 and 1901–10: Ó Gráda, *Jewish Ireland*, pp. 35–7, 235n. The Pembroke study is a sample of 2,649 couples and relates to household responses relating to family deaths between 1901 and 1910, excluding therefore families that died out or departed during those years: Ó Gráda, 'Infant and child mortality in Dublin a century ago', in Marco Breschi and Lucia Pozzi (eds), *The determinants of infant and child mortality in past European populations* (Udine, Italy, 2004), pp. 89–104. Cf. Daly, *Deposed capital*, pp. 242–6, 270, 274.

50.   Grimshaw, 'Child mortality', pp. 3–19; *1914 Dublin housing conditions report*, p. 53; O'Brien, *'Dear, dirty Dublin'*, pp. 111–14; Daly, *Deposed capital*, pp. 268–70; Aalen, 'Health and housing in Dublin', pp. 284–6; Prunty, *Dublin slums*, pp. 153–5; Cormac Ó Gráda, *A new economic history of Ireland 1780–1939* (Oxford, 1994), pp. 436–41; ibid., *Jewish Ireland*, pp. 34–42, 167–8, 257n; Greta Jones, *'Captain of all these men of death': The history of tuberculosis in nineteenth- and twentieth-century Ireland* (Amsterdam, 2001), pp. 75–85, 151; Jones, 'The campaign against tuberculosis in Ireland 1899–1914', in Elizabeth Malcolm and Greta Jones (eds), *Medicine, disease and the state in Ireland 1650–1940* (Cork, 1999), pp. 177–84. On wages and food expenditure (in wartime Dublin): *The Carnegie United Kingdom trust: Report on the physical welfare of mothers and children: IV, Ireland*, ed. E. C. Bigger (Dublin, 1917), p. 32.

51.   *1914 Dublin housing conditions report*, pp. 43–4, 49–50; Sir Charles Cameron, *Reminiscences* (Dublin, 1913), pp. 164–7; O'Brien, *'Dear, dirty Dublin'*, pp. 122–4; Daly, *Deposed capital*, pp. 287–9; Carroll, *Fever king's preserves*, pp. 211–24; Aalen, 'Health and housing', pp. 292–4; Ó Gráda, *Jewish Ireland*, p. 41.

52.   *1914 Dublin housing conditions report*, pp. 101–104, 345; Aalen, 'Health and housing', pp. 280–83; Kate Cowan, '"The children have such freedom ...": The children of Dublin 1913', in Devine et al., *Capital in conflict*, pp. 129–44. On the

street children, cf. Joyce, *Dubliners* (1992), pp. xix, 66. For revealing tenement memories from this era gathered by the North Inner City Folklore Project: Terry Fagan et al. (eds.) *Monto: Madams, murder and black coddle* (Dublin, n.d. [*c.*2002]), pp. 54–8, 61–4.

53. *1914 Dublin housing conditions report*, pp. 8, 16, 29–30, 49, 54, 67, 125, 192, 200–201, 207, 209, 331; O'Brien, *'Dear, dirty Dublin'*, pp. 12–14, 61, 13, 143, 149–50, 155–6, 190–95; Aalen, 'Health and housing', pp. 280–83; Prunty, *Dublin slums*, pp. 19–70; Fagan et al., *Monto*, pp. 10–18, 39; Maria Luddy, *Prostitution and Irish society 1800–1940* (Cambridge, 2007), pp. 22–3, 26–30, 34–6, 44–5; Yeates, *Lockout*, pp. 53–4, 553; *DIB*, 'Joseph Michael Meade'; Carroll, *Fever king's preserves*, pp. 211–24. Sarah Harrison gave evidence that despite Foley Street being a 'bad neighbourhood', she saw that 'the rooms … [are] generally kept clean and tidy': *1914 Dublin housing conditions report*, p. 100. I am indebted to Dr Susan Galavan for information on the Meade family.

54. *The Times*, 16 July 1914; *1914 Dublin housing conditions report*, pp. 205–206, 208–11; O'Brien, *'Dear, dirty Dublin'*, pp. 69, 109; M. J. Bannon, 'The genesis of modern Irish planning', in Bannon, *A hundred years of Irish planning*, I: *The emergence of Irish planning, 1880–1921* (Dublin, 1985), pp. 191–241; M. E. Daly, *The buffer state: The historical roots of the Department of the Environment* (Dublin, 1997), pp. 202–3; Ruth McManus, *Dublin 1910–1940: Shaping the city and suburbs* (Dublin, 2002), pp. 49–50; Andrew Kincaid, *Postcolonial Dublin: Imperial legacies and the built environment* (Minneapolis, 2006), pp. 34–43; *DIB*, 'Ishbel Maria Gordon'; Christopher Harvie, *A floating commonwealth: Politics, culture and technology on Britain's Atlantic coast, 1860–1930* (Oxford, 2008), pp. 217–18.

55. *Georgian Society Records*, I, pp. v–xiii; IV, pp. xvii–xxiii.

9 Eruption: 1913–1919

1. J. V. O'Brien, *'Dear, dirty Dublin': A city in distress 1899–1916* (Berkeley, CA, 1982), pp. 64, 204–6, 213; Emmet O'Connor, *A labour history of Ireland* (Dublin, 1992), p. 54; Padraig Yeates, *Lockout: Dublin 1913* (Dublin, 2000), pp. 84, 493; Cormac Ó Gráda, *Jewish Ireland in the age of Joyce: A socioeconomic history* (Princeton, 2006), pp. 40–41. Cf. Liam Kennedy, 'The cost of living in Ireland', in David Dickson and Cormac Ó Gráda (eds), *Refiguring Ireland: Essays in honour of L. M. Cullen* (Dublin, 2003), p. 262.

2. O'Brien, *'Dear, dirty Dublin'*, p. 215; J. L. Hyland, *James Connolly* (Dundalk, 1997), *passim*; Tony Farmar, *Heitons – A managed transition: Heitons in the Irish coal, iron and building markets 1818–1996* (Dublin, 1996), p. 46; Yeates, *Lockout*, pp. 102–3; O'Connor, *Labour history*, pp. 47–61; *DIB*, 'James Connolly', 'J. B. Nannetti'.

3. The 1911 census returned 20,288 general labourers, factory labourers and coal-heavers: O'Brien, *'Dear, dirty Dublin'*, pp. 203, 216–19.

4. Farmar, *Heitons*, pp. 57–8. Yeates' *Lockout: Dublin 1913* remains the definitive work. Cf. Peter Rigney, 'Trade unionism on the Great Southern and Western Railway 1890–1911' (BA dissertation, Dept. of History, Trinity College Dublin,

1977); O'Brien, *'Dear, dirty Dublin'*, pp. 220–40; Thomas Morrissey, SJ, *William Martin Murphy* (Dundalk, 1997), pp. 41–59; Patrick Maume, *The long gestation: Irish nationalist life 1891–1918* (Dublin, 1999), pp. 236–7; John Newsinger, 'Jim Larkin and *The Irish Worker*', in Francis Devine, Mary Clark and Máire Kennedy (eds), *A capital in conflict: Dublin city and the 1913 Lockout* (Dublin, 2013), pp. 193–214; Leeann Lane, 'George Russell and James Stephens: Class and cultural discourse, Dublin 1913', in Devine et al., *A capital in conflict*, p. 341.

5. Ken Finlay, *The biggest show in town: Record of the International Exhibition, Dublin 1907* (Dublin, 2007); Stephanie Rains, *Commodity culture and social class in Dublin 1850–1916* (Dublin, 2010), pp. 185–97; Tony Farmar, *Privileged lives: A social history of middle-class Ireland 1882–1989* (Dublin, 2010), pp. 93–8.

6. Yeates, *Lockout*, pp. xiii–iv, 47–75, 145, 324; O'Connor, *Labour history*, pp. 61–5; Andy Bielenberg, 'Entrepreneurship, power and public opinion in Ireland: The career of William Martin Murphy', in *IESH*, XXVII (2000), pp. 31–2; *DIB*, 'James Larkin'. O'Brien suggests that there were twelve distinct riots around the city in the first weekend of the Lockout: O'Brien, *'Dear, dirty Dublin'*, p. 226.

7. Yeates, *Lockout*, pp. 54–6, 68, 72–3, 79, 156, 163, 199, 288, 322, 339, 583; Maume, *Long gestation*, pp. 235–40; Bielenberg, 'Murphy', pp. 31–3. Non-TUC donations amounted to more than £13,000: Yeates, *Lockout*, p. 323. For a tantalising survey and analysis of Dublin working-class diets *c.*1904: *Royal commission on the poor laws* (HC, 1910 [5070]), pp. 143–91.

8. O'Brien, *'Dear, dirty Dublin'*, pp. 230–31; Farmar, *Heitons*, p. 61; Yeates, *Lockout*, pp. 70–75, 165–7, 177.

9. *Irish Times*, 7 October 1913, quoted in Yeates, *Lockout*, pp. 217–19. Cf. ibid., p.346.

10. Peter Murray, 'Electoral politics and the Dublin working class before the First World War', in *Saothar*, VI (1980), pp. 8–25; O'Brien, *'Dear, dirty Dublin'*, pp. 92, 234, 236; Yeates, *Lockout*, pp. 333–4, 500–514; Patrick Maume, 'William Martin Murphy, the *Irish Independent* and middle-class politics, 1905–19', in Fintan Lane (ed.) *Politics, society and the middle class in modern Ireland* (Basingstoke, 2010), pp. 238–40; Kate Cowan, '"The children have such freedom ...": The children of Dublin 1913', in Devine et al., *Capital in conflict*, p.138.

11. O'Brien, *'Dear, dirty Dublin'*, pp. 236–7; Fergus D'Arcy, 'Larkin and the Dublin Lock-out', in Donal Nevin (ed.), *James Larkin: Lion of the fold* (Dublin, 1998), p. 45; Yeates, *Lockout*, pp. 496–7, 519–21, 524, 528, 568, 578; Andy Bielenberg, *Ireland and the industrial revolution: The impact of the industrial revolution on Irish industry 1801–1922* (London, 2009), p. 164.

12. Morrissey, *Murphy*, pp. 56–9; Yeates, *Lockout*, pp. 499–500; Maume, *Long gestation*, pp. 237–9. On the impact of the Lockout on the profits of Heitons, the dominant coal firm: Farmar, *Heitons*, pp. 62, 65.

13. W. B. Wells, *Irish indiscretions* (London, 1922), pp. 21–2; O'Brien, *'Dear, dirty Dublin'*, pp. 163, 188, 194–5, 423; Fergus Campbell, *The Irish establishment 1879–1914* (Oxford, 2009), pp. 155–79; R. B. McDowell, *Crisis and decline: The fate of the southern unionists* (Dublin, 1997), pp. 47–50; Martin Maguire, '"Our people": The Church of Ireland and the culture of community in Dublin since

disestablishment', in Raymond Gillespie and W. A. Neely (eds), *The laity and the Church of Ireland 1000–2000: All sorts and conditions* (Dublin, 2002), p. 290.

14.   O'Brien, *'Dear, dirty Dublin'*, pp. 53–6, 60; Yeates, *Lockout*, pp. 142–4; Lucy McDiarmid, *The Irish art of controversy* (Dublin, 2005), pp. 10–49; *DIB*, 'Elizabeth Yeats'; Rains, *Commodity culture*, pp. 188–90, 196; David Dickson, '1857 and 1908: Two moments in the transformation of Irish universities', in David Dickson, Justyna Pyz and Christopher Shepard (eds), *Irish classrooms and British empire: Imperial contexts in the origins of modern education* (Dublin, 2012), p.194; Ciaran Wallace, 'A bridge to the future: Hugh Lane's Municipal Gallery of Modern Art', in Devine et al., *Capital in conflict*, pp. 261–80.

15.   *Irish Times*, 29 December 1923; Nicola Gordon-Bowe, 'A regal blaze: Harry Clarke's depiction of Synge's *Queens*', in *Irish Arts Review*, (Summer 2006), pp. 196–205; *DIB*, 'Laurence Waldron'. On James Hicks: http://hicksfurniture. samcrichton.com/about.html [accessed 1 June 2013].

16.   Census of Ireland, 1911 (http://www.census.nationalarchives.ie/ pages/1911/ Dublin/ Trinity_Ward/ St__Stephen_s_Green__North/87552/); Stephen Gwynn, *The famous cities of Ireland* (London, 1915), pp. 262, 267; James Joyce, *Dubliners*, ed. Terence Brown (new edn, London, 1992), pp. 35–42; Joyce, *Dubliners*, ed. Jeri Johnson (Oxford, 2000), pp. ix–xvii; Tony Farmar, *The legendary lofty clattery café: Bewley's of Ireland* (Dublin, 1988), pp. 28–31; R. B. McDowell, *Land and learning: Two Irish clubs* (Dublin, 1993), pp. 76, 84–91; Walter Starkie, *Scholars and gypsies: An autobiography* (London, 1963), pp. 15–16; Michael O'Sullivan and Bernardine O'Neill, *The Shelbourne and its people* (Dublin, 1999), pp. 15–34, 38; Rains, *Commodity culture*, p. 130; Campbell, *Irish establishment*, p. 141. The Café de Paris in Lincoln Place, opened in 1860, was probably the first restaurant to offer French cuisine: Mairtín Mac Con Iomaire, 'The changing geography and fortunes of Dublin's *haute cuisine* restaurants, 1958–2008', in *Food, Culture and Society*, XIV, 4 (2011), p. 527. Cf. James Stephens, *The charwoman's daughter* (London, 1912), pp. 14–15.

17.   Barbara Walsh, *When the shopping was good: Woolworths and the Irish main street* (Dublin, 2011), pp. 6–10; Alex Findlater, *Findlaters: The story of a Dublin merchant firm 1774–2001* (Dublin, 2001), pp. 128–33, 320–25.

18.   Farmar, *Privileged lives*, pp. 21–2, 85–8.

19.   *Dublin commercial year book, 1917*, pp. 125–6; O'Brien, *'Dear, dirty Dublin'*, pp. 46–7; Peter Costello, *James Joyce : The years of growth 1882–1915* (Dublin, 1992), pp. 288–93; Findlater, *Findlaters*, pp. 234–5; *DIB*, 'Maurice Elliman'; Christopher Morash, *A history of the media in Ireland* (Cambridge, 2010), pp. 107–12; Kevin and Emer Rockett, *Film exhibition and distribution in Ireland, 1909–2010* (Dublin, 2011), pp. 15–47.

20.   Ó Gráda, *Jewish Ireland*, chapters 1, 3, 4, 5, 8 and 9; Rockett and Rockett, *Film exhibition*, pp. 26–7, 43. See also Joseph Edelstein's controversial novel, *The moneylender* (Dublin, 1908).

21.   McDowell and Webb, *Trinity College*, chapters 9, 10 and 12; Senia Paseta, *Before the revolution: Nationalism, social change and Ireland's Catholic elite 1879–1922*

(Cork, 1999), pp. 53–75; Sean Farragher, 'Eamon de Valera and Blackrock 1898–1921', in Gabriel Doherty and Dermot Keogh (eds), *De Valera's Irelands* (Cork, 2003), pp. 34–41; Dickson, '1857 and 1908', pp. 194–200.

22. John Hutchinson, *The dynamics of cultural nationalism: The Gaelic revival and the creation of the Irish nation state* (London, 1987), pp. 138–9, 166–7; Paseta, *Before the revolution*, pp. 62–75; Donal McCartney, *UCD: A national idea: the history of University College, Dublin* (Dublin, 1999), chapters 1–4; Casey, *Dublin*, p. 488.

23. Yeates, *Lockout*, pp. 221–6, 362–7; *DIB*, 'Sarah Harrison', 'Francis Sheehy-Skeffington', 'Hanna Sheehy-Skeffington'; Farmar, *Privileged lives*, pp. 44–5, 49–50, 63–4.

24. *Irish Times*, 5 June, 20 August 1907; Casey, *Dublin*, p. 533.

25. Charles Townshend, *Easter 1916: The Irish rebellion* (London, 2005), pp. 20–21, 39–47, 54–7.

26. Keith Jeffery, *Ireland and the Great War* (Cambridge, 2000), pp. 41–2; Séamas Ó Maitiú, *Dublin's suburban towns 1834–1930* (Dublin, 2003), pp. 194–5; Townshend, *Easter 1916*, pp. 60–61; Tom Burke, 'Whence came the Royal Dublin Fusiliers?', in *Ir. Sword*, XXIV (2004/5), pp. 452–6; Maume, 'William Martin Murphy', p. 240; Padraig Yeates, *A city in wartime: Dublin 1914–1918* (Dublin, 2011), pp. 32, 42, 47, 65; Clara Cullen, *The world upturning: Elsie Henry's Irish wartime diaries, 1913–1919* (Dublin, 2012), p. 4; http://www.ucd.ie/merrionstreet/1910_war.html [accessed 21 December 2012].

27. Yeates, *City in wartime*, p. 36; Cullen, *World upturning*, p. 54.

28. Jeffery, *Ireland and the Great War*, pp. 44–5; Townshend, *Easter rising*, pp. 76–8.

29. León Ó Broin, *Dublin Castle and the 1916 rising* (Dublin, 1966), p. 153; *DIB*, 'James Connolly'; Townshend, *Easter 1916*, pp. 90–116, 119; Fearghal McGarry, *The rising: Easter 1916* (Oxford, 2010), p. 105; Yeates, *City in wartime*, p. 89.

30. *Oration of P.H. Pearse over Rossa's grave* (n.d., n.p. [Dublin: Fergus O'Connor, 1915:]); Ó Broin, *Dublin Castle,* pp. 52, 165; Townshend, *Easter 1916*, pp. 12–13, 92–100, 113–16, 143–4; *DIB*, 'Patrick Pearse', 'Joseph Plunkett'; McGarry, *The rising*, pp. 92, 104–6, Yeates, *City in wartime*, p.74.

31. Ó Broin, *Dublin Castle*, pp. 70, 153–5; Jeffery, *Ireland and the Great War*, pp. 26–7; Peter Hart, *The IRA at war 1916–1923* (Oxford, 2003), pp. 124–5; Townshend, *Easter 1916*, pp. 116–21; Michael Purser, *Jellett, O'Brien, Purser and Stokes: Seven generations, four families* (Dublin, 2004), p. 161; McGarry, *The rising*, pp. 83, 124–7, 133.

32. Ó Broin, *Dublin Castle*, p. 97; Townshend, *Easter 1916*, pp. 100–101, 124–5, 131–8, 152–64, 181, 184; McGarry, *The rising*, p. 3.

33. Ó Broin, *Dublin Castle*, pp. 29, 34, 41–2, 53, 73, 78, 80, 86, 102–3, 144, 147–8, 166–7; Townshend, *Easter 1916*, pp. 80–81, 87–9, 103–8, 126–8, 144–5, 148–51; McGarry, *The rising*, pp. 94–5, 112, 115; Yeates, *City in wartime*, p. 89.

34. Liam de Paor, *On the Easter Proclamation and other declarations* (Dublin, 1997), pp. 41–5, 48–51, 72–6; Townshend, *Easter 1916*, pp. 53–6, 160–62, 165–6, 263; Brian Crowley, 'The strange thing I am', in *History Ireland*, XIV (http://www.

historyireland.com/volumes/volume14/issue2/news/?id=114021); McGarry, *The rising*, pp. 98, 135; Yeates, *City in wartime*, p. 93.

35. O'Brien, *'Dear dirty Dublin'*, p. 259; Keith Jeffery (ed.), *The Sinn Fein rebellion as they saw it* (Dublin, 1999), pp. 52–3; Findlater, *Findlaters*, pp. 270, 272; Townshend, *Easter 1916*, pp. 263–5; Clair Wills, *Dublin 1916: The siege of the GPO* (London, 2009), pp. 49–51; McGarry, *The rising*, pp. 144–6, 148.

36. Townshend, *Easter 1916*, pp.183–6, 203–5.

37. *Thom's directory, 1920*, p. 2300; L. M. Cullen, *Eason & son: A history* (Dublin, 1989), pp. 201–3; Frances Taylor and D. A. Levistone Cooney, 'Momentous days: Occasional diaries of Frances Taylor', in *DHR*, XLVII, 1 (1994), p. 81; Townshend, *Easter 1916*, pp. 191–2, 205; Joseph Brady, 'Reconstructing Dublin city centre in the late 1920s', in Clarke, Prunty and Hennessy, *Surveying Ireland's past*, pp. 640–41; Yeates, *City in wartime*, p. 110.

38. Ó Broin, *Dublin Castle*, pp. 98, 126; Jeffery, *The Sinn Fein rebellion*, p. 61; Townshend, *Easter 1916*, pp. 100–102, 110, 166–9, 175–9, 205, 210–13, 248–53, 256–7, 259–60; McGarry, *The rising*, p. 199. Telephone and telegraph links with Belfast were however cut in north Co. Dublin by Richard Mulcahy.

39. Townshend, *Easter 1916*, pp. 186–8, 192–5; McGarry, *The rising*, p. 188; Yeates, *City in wartime*, pp. 107–8.

40. Townshend, *Easter 1916*, pp. 244, 245, 267; Maume, 'William Martin Murphy', pp. 241–3; McGarry, *The rising*, pp. 127, 142–4, 203. For Capt. Harry de Courcy-Wheeler's remarkable account of the surrenders: Findlater, *Findlaters*, pp. 274–87.

41. *DIB*, 'John Joseph O'Kelly'; Yeates, *City in wartime*, pp. 207–11.

42. Ibid., pp. 148–9, 306.

43. Lionel Smith Gordon and Cruise O'Brien, *Starvation in Dublin* (Dublin, 1917), pp. 9, 13–18; Mervyn Miller, 'Raymond Unwin and the planning of Dublin', in Michael Bannon (ed.) *The emergence of Irish planning 1880–1920* (Dublin, 1985), pp. 182–96; Jeffery, *Ireland and the Great War*, pp. 30–32; Liam Clare, 'The rise and demise of the Dublin cattle market 1863–1973', in D. A. Cronin, Jim Gilligan and Karina Holton (eds), *Irish fairs and markets: Studies in local history* (Dublin, 2001), pp. 193–4; Yeates, *City in wartime*, pp. 134, 140–41, 143, 150–51, 172–3, 248–50, 260, 271, 277, 305, 307.

44. Jane Leonard, 'Survivors', in John Horne (ed.) *Our war: Ireland and the Great War* (Dublin, 2008), p. 214; Yeates, *City in wartime*, pp. 254–8; Roy Stokes, *Death in the Irish Sea: The sinking of the R.M.S. Leinster* (Cork 1998); http://www.rmsleinster.com/sinking/sinking.htm.

45. Brian Walker, *Parliamentary election results in Ireland, 1801–1922* (Dublin, 1978), pp. 388–9; Maume, 'William Martin Murphy', pp. 243–4.

46. *Irish Times*, 22 January 1919; Yeates, *City in wartime*, pp. 298–9; Padraig Yeates, *A city in turmoil: Dublin 1919–21* (Dublin, 2012), pp. 4–5.

10 A Capital Once Again: 1920–1940

1. *Irish Times*, 28 May 1921; Michael Hopkinson, *The last days of Dublin Castle: The diaries of Mark Sturgis* (Dublin, 1999), pp. 181–2; William Sheehan, *Fighting for Dublin: The British battle for Dublin 1919–1921* (Cork, 2007), pp. 53–4; Padraig Yeates, *A city in wartime: Dublin 1914–1918* (Dublin, 2011), p. 274.

2. W. B. Wells, *Irish indiscretions* (London, 1922), pp. 131–9; Peter Hart, *Mick: The real Michael Collins* (London, 2005), pp. 172–3, 211–19; Sheehan, *Fighting for Dublin*, p. 10; Patrick Maume, 'William Martin Murphy, the *Irish Independent* and middle-class politics, 1905–19', in Fintan Lane (ed.) *Politics, society and the middle class in modern Ireland* (Basingstoke, 2010), p. 244; Eunan O'Halpin, 'Counting terror: Bloody Sunday and *The dead of the Irish Revolution*', in David Fitzpatrick, *Terror in Ireland 1916–1923* (Dublin, 2012), p. 152.

3. Richard Abbott, *Police casualties in Ireland 1919–1922* (Dublin, 2000), pp. 40–72; Séamas Ó Maitiú, *Dublin's suburban towns 1834–1930* (Dublin, 2003), p. 202; Sheehan, *Fighting for Dublin*, pp. 11–12; Padraig Yeates, *A city in turmoil: Dublin 1919–21* (Dublin, 2012), pp. 78–82, 116, 142.

4. Donal McCartney, *UCD: A national idea – The history of University College, Dublin* (Dublin, 1999), pp. 107–8; David Leeson, 'Death in the Afternoon: The Croke Park massacre, 21 November 1920', in *Canadian Journal of History*, XXXVIII, 1 (2003), pp. 45–65; Hart, *Collins*, p. 272; Yeates, *City in turmoil*, pp. 163, 257, 203–4; O'Halpin, 'Counting terror', pp. 141–5, 155.

5. Anne Dolan, 'Killing and Bloody Sunday, November 1920', in *Historical Journal*, XL, 3 (2006), pp. 789–810; Jane Leonard, '"English dogs" or "poor devils"? The dead of Bloody Sunday morning', in Fitzpatrick, *Terror in Ireland*, pp. 102–40.

6. Hart, *Collins*, pp. 206, 220–23, 239–43; *DIB*, 'Richard McKee'; Yeates, *City in turmoil*, pp. 16, 164.

7. Charles Townshend, 'The Irish railway strike of 1920: Industrial action and civil resistance in the struggle for independence', in *IHS*, XXII, 83 (1979), pp. 265–82; Sean Lyons, 'A portrait of dislocation: The economy of Ireland 1920–1924' (BA dissertation, Dept. of History, Trinity College Dublin, 1989), pp. 28–9; McCartney, *UCD*, pp. 106–7; Sheehan, *Fighting for Dublin*, pp. 12–13, 18–19, 21–2; Yeates, *City in turmoil*, pp. 136–8, 185–7.

8. *Irish Times*, 15 April 1921; Ó Maitiú, *Dublin's suburban towns*, pp. 201–2; Yeates, *City in turmoil*, pp. 77–81, 248–51. Even in Rathmines, Sinn Féin attracted 39.5 per cent of first preferences: Ó Maitiú, op. cit., p. 199.

9. Lyons, 'Portrait of dislocation', pp. 14–19, figs 41–2; Ruth McManus, *Dublin 1910–1940: Shaping the city and suburbs* (Dublin, 2002), p.75.

10. Tom Garvin, *1922: The birth of Irish democracy* (Dublin, 1996), pp. 44–5, 88, 97–8; David Fitzpatrick, *The two Irelands 1912–39* (Oxford, 1998), pp. 109–11.

11. T. J. Barrington, 'Public administration 1927–36', in Francis MacManus (ed.), *The years of the great test* (Dublin 1962), p. 80; Hopkinson, *Last days of Dublin Castle*, p. 227; M. E. Daly, *The buffer state: The historical roots of the Department of the Environment* (Dublin, 1997), pp. 96–103; Anthony Kinsella, 'Goodbye Dublin: The British military evacuation', in *DHR*, LI, 1 (1998), pp. 10–22; Mary

Rogan, *Prison policy in Ireland: Politics, penal-welfarism and political imprisonment* (London, 2011), pp. 22–3.

12. M. G. Valiulis, *Portrait of a revolutionary: General Richard Mulcahy* (Dublin, 1992), pp. 122–7, 138; Fitzpatrick, *Two Irelands*, pp. 125–6.

13. On the military handover of Beggar's Bush: *Irish Times,* 2 February 1922. In the Mid-Dublin constituency the independent nationalists Laurence O'Neill (the Lord Mayor) and Alderman Alfie Byrne (the future Lord Mayor) attracted between them 59.6 per cent of the vote, whereas the one pro-Treaty Sinn Féin candidate took 14.7 per cent, and three anti-Treaty Sinn Féin took between them 19.6 per cent: Micheal Gallagher, 'The pact general election of 1922', in *IHS*, XXI, 84 (1981), p. 414; http://www.electionsireland.org/results/general/03dail.cfm [accessed 7 January 2013].

14. D. A. Levistone Cooney (ed.), 'Momentous Days: Occasional diaries of Frances Taylor', in *DHR*, XLVII, 1 (1994), pp. 81–6; Garvin, *1922*, pp. 49, 55, 60, 92–3, 98–102, 116, 130; Fitzpatrick, *Two Irelands,* pp. 127–9. On Griffith's last days: Oliver St John Gogarty, *As I was going down Sackville Street* (London, 1968), pp. 192–6. On a revealing running commentary on the atmosphere in Civil War Dublin by John Dillon and his daughter: Joachim Fischer and John Dillon (eds), *The correspondence of Myles Dillon, 1922–25* (Dublin, 1999).

15. Robert Welch (ed.) *The Oxford companion to Irish literature* (Oxford, 1996), p. 407; Maria Luddy, *Prostitution and Irish society 1800–1940* (Cambridge, 2007), pp. 226–7; Adrian Frazier, *Hollywood Irish: John Ford, Abbey actors and the Irish revival in Hollywood* (Dublin, 2011), pp. 59, 62, 80–98.

16. L. M. Cullen, *Princes and pirates: The Dublin Chamber of Commerce, 1783–1983* (Dublin 1983), pp. 92–101; R. B. McDowell, *Crisis and decline: The fate of the southern unionists* (Dublin, 1997), pp. 105–6, 117–18, 139–44, 148–62; *DIB*, 'Andrew Jameson'; John Walsh, *Collen: 200 years of building and civil engineering in Ireland* (Dublin, 2010), pp. 37–41.

17. *Irish Times*, 27 August 1923, 19 April 1924, 16 January 1933, 10 May 1941; T. K. Daniel, 'Griffith on his noble head: The determinants of Cumann na nGaedheal economic policy 1922–32', in *IESH*, III (1976), pp. 56–60; Lyons, 'Portrait of dislocation', p. 38, figs. 58–9; M. E. Daly, *Industrial development and Irish national identity 1922–1939* (Dublin, 1992), p. 139; Daly, *Buffer state*, p. 108; Bob Montgomery, 'Past Imperfect', in *Irish Times*, 8 December 2004; Garvin, *1922*, p. 164; Maume, 'William Martin Murphy', pp. 242–4; Yeates, *City in turmoil*, p. 164; Ruth McManus, *Dublin 1910–1940: Shaping the city and suburbs* (Dublin, 2002), p. 96. The Anglican John Good left £1,000 to St Vincent de Paul 'for the benefit of the scheme to enable poor Dublin children to visit the seaside during the summer months': *Irish Times*, 20 September 1941.

18. *Irish Times*, 8 February 1922, 2 April 1924, 23 October 1925; Lyons, 'Portrait of dislocation', pp. 26–7; McManus, *Dublin 1910–1940*, pp. 77–9, 102. Two other Protestants in the building trade, James Beckett of Foxrock and Henry Dockrell of Dún Laoghaire, were prominent supporters of Cosgrave, the former holding one of the Dublin South City seats from 1927 until his death in 1938, the latter one

of the Dublin County seats from 1932 to 1948. James Beckett was first cousin of Samuel Beckett's father: *DIB*, 'James Beckett', 'Sir Maurice Dockrell'.

19. *Irish Times,* 24 May, 6 June 1924; Cullen, *Princes and pirates,* pp. 100–101; Marie O'Neill, 'Dublin Corporation in the troubled times 1914–24', in *DHR,* XLVII, 1 (1994), pp. 68–70; Daly, *Buffer state,* pp. 119–23; Daly, 'Dublin the restored capital: Civic identity in an independent Ireland', in H. B. Clarke, Jacinta Prunty and Mark Hennessy (eds), *Surveying Ireland's past: Multidisciplinary essays in honour of Anngret Simms* (Dublin, 2004), p. 567; McManus, *Dublin 1910–1940,* pp. 81–2; *DIB,* 'Noel Lemass'.

20. Daly, 'Dublin the restored capital', pp. 571–3; Ruth McManus, *Crampton built* (Dublin, 2008), p. 74.

21. *Irish Times,* 11 April, 23 August 1930; Michael Bannon, 'Irish planning 1921–1945', in Bannon, *Planning: The Irish experience 1920–1988* (Dublin, 1989), pp. 38–40; Daly, *Buffer state,* pp. 122–30; Daly, 'Dublin the restored capital', pp. 568–74; Mark Callanan and J. F. Keogan, *Local government in Ireland: Inside out* (Dublin, 2003) pp. 125–6, 128–9; Ó Maitiú, *Dublin's suburban towns,* pp. 210–16.

22. *Irish Times,* 11 July 1929, 31 December 1929; Desmond Fisher, *Broadcasting in Ireland* (London, 1978), pp. 20–21; Mervyn Miller, 'Raymond Unwin and the planning of Dublin', in Michael Bannon (ed.) *The emergence of Irish planning 1880–1920* (Dublin, 1985), pp. 182–96; Bannon, 'Irish planning from 1921 to 1945', pp. 15–16, 19–20; Nial Osborough, *Law and the emergence of modern Dublin: A litigation topography for a capital city* (Dublin, 1996), p. 50; Daly, *Buffer state,* pp. 110–12; McManus, *Dublin 1910–1940,* pp. 49, 70–74, 169; McManus, *Crampton built,* pp. 52–3; Andrew Kincaid, *Postcolonial Dublin: Imperial legacies and the built environment* (Minneapolis, 2006), pp. 44–6; Casey, *Dublin,* pp. 214–19; Kevin and Emer Rockett, *Film exhibition and distribution in Ireland, 1909–2010* (Dublin, 2011), p. 74.

23. Patrick Abercrombie, *Dublin of the future: The new town plan* (Liverpool, n.d. [1922]), pp. 3–4, 9, 36, 51–8 (available at http://archive.org/stream/ cu31924024428629#page/no/mode/2up); McManus, *Dublin 1920–1940,* pp. 50–68; Kincaid, *Postcolonial Dublin,* pp. 13, 46–53, 99–101; *ODNB,* 'Patrick Abercrombie'; *DIB,* 'Patrick Abercrombie'.

24. Bannon, 'Irish planning 1921–1945', pp. 16–26; McManus, *Dublin 1910–1940,* pp. 67, 83–6; Kincaid, *Postcolonial Dublin,* pp. 102–4; Yvonne Whelan, 'Written in space and stone', in H. B. Clarke, Jacinta Prunty and Mark Hennessy (eds), *Surveying Ireland's past: Multidisciplinary essays in honour of Anngret Simms* (Dublin, 2004), pp. 587–94, 609; Daly, 'Dublin the restored capital', pp. 574– 6; *DIB,* 'H. T. O'Rourke'.

25. Bannon, 'Irish planning 1921–1945', pp. 33–4; McManus, *Dublin 1910–1940,* pp. 80, 93–4, 125–6, 140, 167, 182–96, 263, 363; McManus, *Crampton built,* pp. 64–7. The speaker was Joseph MacBride, TD for South Mayo: Whelan, 'Written in space and stone', p. 593.

26. Cullen, *Princes and pirates,* p. 104; Daly, *Buffer state,* pp. 206–10, 216–17, 360; McManus, *Dublin 1910–1940,* pp. 93–4, 119–20, 126, 140, 145–6, 151, 341–4.

27.   T. W. T. Dillon, 'Slum clearance: Past and future', in *Studies*, XXXIV, 133 (1945),
      p. 19; A. J. Humphreys, *New Dubliners: Urbanization and the Irish family*
      (London, 1966), pp. 186–7, 206–7; Cullen, *Princes and pirates*, p. 104; Daly, *Buffer
      state*, pp. 217–18, 238, 242–3; Billy French, 'Crumlin the way it was', in *DHR*, LIII,
      1 (2000), p. 15; McManus, *Dublin 1910–1940*, pp. 129, 133, 191, 137–9, 148, 178, 213–
      15, 218, 225–6; McManus, *Crampton built*, pp. 103–4, 109–17; Kincaid, *Postcolonial
      Dublin*, pp. 86–7. Brendan Behan's younger brother Brian was a famous case in
      point, going 'wild' in Crumlin before being sent aged twelve to Artane Industrial
      School for three years: *DIB*, 'Brian Behan'.

28.   Humphreys, *New Dubliners*, p. 183; Daly, *Buffer state*, pp. 220–21, 241; McManus,
      Dublin 1910–1940, pp. 379–81; McManus, *Crampton built*, pp. 109–10; Tony
      Farmar, *Privileged lives: A social history of middle-class Ireland 1882–1989* (Dublin,
      2010), pp. 151–2.

29.   'Artifex', in *Irish Times*, 23 April, 3 May 1938; Daly, *Buffer state*, pp. 238–48;
      McManus, *Dublin 1910–1940*, pp. 121, 225, 374.

30.   Stanley Lyon, 'Some observations on births in Dublin in the years 1941 and 1942',
      in *JSSISI*, XVII (1942–7), pp. 154–66: Humphreys, *New Dubliners*, p. 204.
      Population statistics for greater Dublin (Dublin city, Dún Laoghaire and Co.
      Dublin) are drawn from Andrew MacLaran, *Dublin: The shaping of a capital*
      (London, 1993), pp. 37, 164. For John Good's comments on the immigration of
      agricultural labourers into Dublin: *Irish Times*, 16 January 1933.

31.   Terence Brown, *Ireland: A social and cultural history, 1922–2004*, 4th edn
      (London, 2004), pp. 38–9; Farmar, *Privileged lives*, pp. 177–86.

32.   John Horgan, *Seán Lemass: The enigmatic patriot* (Dublin, 1997), pp. 4–5; Bryce
      Evans, *Seán Lemass: Democratic dictator* (Cork, 2011), pp. 46–7, 84. For one
      participant's memories of events around the birth of Fianna Fáil: C. S. Andrews,
      Man of no property, 2nd edn (Dublin, 2001), pp. 52–8.

33.   Tom Garvin, 'Change and the political system', in Frank Litton (ed.), *Unequal
      achievement: The Irish experience 1957–82* (Dublin, 1982), pp. 34–6; Andrews,
      Man of no property, pp. 245–7; Farmar, *Privileged lives*, pp. 154, 172–4; Evans,
      Lemass, pp. 55–6, 63–4, 78–80. At its first electoral outing early in 1927, Fianna
      Fáil attracted 25.2 per cent of votes cast in the two city constituencies but managed
      to increase its city share at every election up to 1938 (bar a single slight reverse
      in 1937); in 1938 it attracted a plurality of city votes (52.8 per cent). In the new
      'Townships' constituency (Pembroke and Rathmines) it was not far behind,
      attracting 47.7 per cent there in 1938, helped by the vote-catching ability of the
      Minister of Finance Seán MacEntee: http://electionsireland.org/results/index.
      cfm.

34.   Petition of housemaids to the Secretary, Bank of Ireland, 22 March 1937 (Bank of
      Ireland archives, Vault 5/13/3). I am grateful to Robert Dickson for this reference.

35.   Cullen, *Princes and pirates*, p. 105; S. R. Dennison and Oliver MacDonagh,
      Guinness 1886–1939: From incorporation to the Second World War (Cork, 1998),
      pp. 46–7, 162, 169, 213–16, 235–7, 248–58; Daly, *Industrial development* , pp. 100–
      101, 121; Emmet O'Connor, *A labour history of Ireland 1824–1960* (Dublin, 1992),

pp. 128–30; Séamas Ó Maitiú, *W. & R. Jacob: Celebrating 150 years of Irish biscuit making* (Dublin, 2001), pp. 34, 60, 77–9; Akihiro Takei, 'The political economy of the Irish flour-milling industry 1922–45', in Andy Bielenberg (ed.), *Irish flour milling: A history 600–2000* (Dublin, 2003), p. 141; Evans, *Lemass*, p. 95. The figure of 2,390 relates to 1930, compared to a figure of just over 2000 for 1908, but productivity was now affected by a shorter working week (44 compared to 48 hours) and the older average age of the workforce: Dennison and MacDonagh, *Guinness 1886–1939*, p. 237.

36. McManus, *Crampton built*, pp. 60–64. Employment in tobacco processing in Dublin city and county stood at 1,871 in 1931, and actually declined somewhat in the 1930s: *Irish industrial year book, 1939* (Dublin, 1939), p. 79.

37. *Irish industrial year book, 1939*, pp. 127–8, 179–81, 279, 302–3; *Commission on emigration and other population problems 1948–1954* (Dublin, n.d. [1954]), pp. 164–5; David Johnston, *The interwar economy in Ireland* (Dundalk, 1985), pp. 20–30; Daly, *Industrial development*, pp. 48–9, 56, 77, 107–9, 112, 115, 180; Horgan, *Lemass*, p. 75; *DIB*, 'Gerald Boland'; Evans, *Lemass*, pp. 85, 89–91; Cormac Ó Gráda, *A new economic history of Ireland 1780–1939* (Oxford, 1994), pp. 398–400; Diarmuid Ó Gráda's 'The rocky road to Dublin: Transport modes and urban growth', in *Studia Hibernica*, XXII/XXIII (1982–3), pp. 108–13; Joseph Brady, 'Reconstructing Dublin city centre in the late 1920s', in Clarke, Prunty and Hennessy, *Surveying Ireland's past*, pp. 660–61; McManus, *Crampton built*, pp. 86–94.

38. Farmar, *Privileged lives*, p. 136; Daly, *Industrial development*, pp. 136–42;

39. Cullen, *Princes and pirates*, pp. 105–7; Tony Farmar, *The legendary lofty clattery café: Bewley's of Ireland* (Dublin, 1988), pp. 31–9; Fitzpatrick, *Two Irelands*, p. 188; McManus, *Crampton built*, pp. 86–93, 103–4, 109–18, 124–9; Farmar, *Privileged lives*, p. 141; Evans, *Lemass*, pp. 99–100, 102, 112. On the apparent exclusion of a Protestant firm, the accountants Craig Gardners, from semi-state business in the 1930s: Tony Farmar, *A history of Craig Gardner & Co.: The first hundred years* (Dublin, 1988), pp. 133–4.

40. Ibid., pp. 145–52; McManus, *Crampton built*, pp. 100–3; Farmar, *Privileged lives*, pp. 159–67; *DIB*, 'Richard Duggan', 'Spencer Freeman', 'Joseph McGrath'.

41. Brown, *Ireland*, pp. 120–29, 167; L. M. Cullen, *Eason & son: A history* (Dublin, 1989), p. 188; Michael Purser, *Jellett, O'Brien, Purser and Stokes: Seven generations, four families* (Dublin, 2004), pp. 174–5; *DIB*, 'Arthur Booth', 'Thomas Collins', 'Charles Edward Kelly', 'Seamus O'Sullivan'.

42. Cullen, *Eason & son*, pp. 268–76, 281–2; McDowell, *Crisis and decline*, pp. 183–4; Fitzpatrick, *Two Irelands*, pp. 226–3; *DIB*, 'Abraham Jacob Leventhal'.

43. *Irish Times*, 7 November 1925; Lyon, 'Births in Dublin', pp. 152–3, 155–6, 158–9; Francis MacManus, *The Yeats we knew* (Cork, 1965), p. 32; Brown, *Ireland*, pp. 62, 68–78, 130–32, 149, 151; J. J. Lee, *Ireland, 1912–1985: Politics and society* (Cambridge, 1989), pp. 157–9; Ó Gráda, 'The rocky road to Dublin', pp. 202–3; Cormac Ó Gráda , 'Ireland 1907–1947', in Donal Nevin (ed.), *James Larkin: Lion of the fold* (Dublin, 1998), p. 14; Terry Fagan et al. (eds.) *Monto: Madams, murder*

and black coddle (Dublin, n.d. [*c.*2002]), pp. 91–100; Fitzpatrick, *Two Irelands*, pp. 227–9; Mark Finnane, 'The Carrigan Committee of 1930–31 and the "moral condition of the Saorstát"', in *IHS*, XXXII, 128 (2001), pp. 519–36; Diarmaid Ferriter, *The transformation of Ireland 1900–2000* (London, 2004), pp. 320–24; Peter Martin, 'Irish censorship in context', in *Studies*, XCV, 379 (2006), pp. 261–8; Clair Wills, *That neutral island: A cultural history of Ireland during the Second World War* (London, 2007), pp. 323–5; Luddy, *Prostitution and Irish society*, pp. 115–17, 120–22, 194–237, 243–4; *DIB*, 'Richard Devane', 'Frank Gallagher'; Christopher Morash, *A history of the media in Ireland* (Cambridge, 2010), pp. 138–43, 156–7. For trends in registered illegitimate births in Dublin city and county from 1923 to 1949: Lindsey Earner-Byrne, *Mother and child: Maternity and child welfare in Dublin, 1922–60* (Manchester, 2007), p. 175.

44. *Dáil debates*, 13 January 1938; Humphreys, *New Dubliners*, p. 185; Cullen, *Eason & son*, pp. 347–9, 354–8; Rockett and Rockett, *Film exhibition*, pp. 73–7, 412–13, 446; *DIB*, 'Maurice Elliman'; *Guardian*, 5 October 1998, 'Obituaries'.

45. Seán Lemass, in Seanad Éireann, 11 December 1946 (http://oireachtasdebates. oireachtas.ie/debates); Brown, *Ireland*, p. 153; Johnston, *Interwar economy*, p. 42; Richard Pine, *2RN and the origins of Irish radio* (Dublin, 2002), pp. 138–79; Farmar, *Privileged lives*, p. 137; Morash, *History of the media*, pp. 131–7.

46. David Thornley, 'The Blueshirts', in MacManus (ed.), *Years of the great test*, p. 47; Brown, *Ireland*, pp. 166–7.

47. *Irish Times*, 18, 22 November 1924; Desmond Ryan, *Remembering Sion: A chronicle of storm and quiet* (London, 1934), pp. 71–3; Brown, *Ireland*, pp. 124–5; Bruce Arnold, 'Politics and the arts in Ireland', in Litton, *Unequal achievement*, pp. 282–8; Rory Johnston (ed.), *Orders and desecrations: The life of the playwright Denis Johnston* (Dublin, 1992), pp. 50–69; *DIB*, 'Denis Johnston'.

48. P. M. Dickinson, *The Dublin of yesterday* (London, 1929), pp. 49–81; Terence de Vere White, 'Social life in Dublin 1927–37', in MacManus, *Years of the great test*, pp. 26–7; Brian Fallon, *An age of innocence: Irish culture 1930–1960* (Dublin, 1999), pp. 141–5; Purser, *Jellett, O'Brien, Purser and Stokes*, pp. 185–8; *DIB*, 'Thomas Bodkin', 'Dermod O'Brien', 'Sarah Purser'.

49. F. S. L. Lyons, 'The minority problem in the 26 Counties', in MacManus, *Years of the great test*, pp. 99–103; Brown, *Ireland*, p. 114; McDowell, *Crisis and decline*, pp. 175–6, 179–81, 188–90; McManus, *Crampton built*, p. 76.

50. *Irish Times*, 12 November 1925; McDowell, *Crisis and decline*, p. 170; Tom Burke, '"Poppy Day" in the Irish Free State', in *Studies*, XCII, 368 (2003), pp. 349–58. The last formal flying of the Union Jack within TCD was in 1935 on George V's Jubilee: McDowell and Webb, *Trinity College*, p. 434.

51. *Sydney Morning Herald*, 13 November 1933; Lyons, 'Minority problem in the 26 Counties', pp. 97–9; Brown, *Ireland*, pp. 115–16; Webb and McDowell, *Trinity College*, p. 507; McDowell, *Crisis and decline*, pp. 171–5, 204–11. About 100 students were interviewed in 1938 by postgraduates R. B. McDowell and Conor Cruise O'Brien, of whom 26 expressed no interest in politics, and of the remainder 11 were 'pink', 14 supported Fianna Fáil, 9 Labour, and 5 supported

the Republicans: R. B. McDowell, *Historical essays, 1938–2001* (Dublin, 2003), pp. 218–21.

11 The Modern Turn: 1940–1972

1. *Irish Times*, 30 September 1939; *DIB*, 'Gearóid Ó Cuinneagáin', 'Adolf Mahr'; Clair Wills, *That neutral island: A cultural history of Ireland during the Second World War* (London, 2007), pp. 51–3, 60–61, 110, 364, 367.

2. Dermot Moran, Drumcondra, to 'Dear Dad', 1–2 June 1941 (http://northstrandbombing.wordpress.com/2012/07/16/dermot-morans-letter/#more-4010); M. E. Daly, *The buffer state: The historical roots of the Department of the Environment* (Dublin, 1997), pp. 252–7; Wills, *Neutral island*, pp. 41, 89, 208–16, 231, 315.

3. [Angela Rolfe and Raymond Ryan], *The Department of Industry and Commerce, Kildare St. Dublin* (Dublin, 1992), pp. 21–35; David Fitzpatrick, *The two Irelands 1912–39* (Oxford, 1998), p. 234; Casey, *Dublin*, p. 476; Bryce Evans, *Seán Lemass: Democratic dictator* (Cork, 2011), pp. 83, 86, 96, 114–15, 116.

4. Daly, *Buffer state*, pp. 261–2; Enda Delaney, 'Irish migration to Britain, 1939–1945', in *IESH*, XXVIII (2001), p. 70; Roddy Doyle, *Rory & Ita* (London, 2002), pp. 123, 129–49; Lindsey Earner-Byrne, *Mother and child: Maternity and child welfare in Dublin, 1922–60* (Manchester, 2007), pp. 49, 96–102; Wills, *Neutral island*, p. 258; Peter Rigney, *Trains, coal and turf: Transport in Emergency Ireland* (Dublin, 2010), pp. 73–98, 136.

5. T. W. T. Dillon, 'Slum clearance: Past and future', in *Studies*, XXXIV, 133 (1945), pp. 14, 19; J. T. Carroll, *Ireland in the years* (Dublin, 1975), p. 91; Daly, *Buffer state*, pp. 273–7, 291; Wills, *Neutral island*, pp. 238–9; Ruth McManus, *Crampton built* (Dublin, 2008), pp. 137–8; Rigney, *Trains, coal and turf*, pp. 147–8; Evans, *Lemass*, pp. 105, 124–5, 135–6.

6. Daly, *Buffer state*, pp. 255, 263–70; Wills, *Neutral island*, p. 209; Rigney, *Trains, coal and turf*, pp. 44–56, 76–7, 103–17, 155–62.

7. Desmond Fisher, *Broadcasting in Ireland* (London, 1978), pp. 21–2; Terence Brown, *Ireland: A social and cultural history, 1922–2004*, 4th edn (London, 2004), p. 209; J. P. McGlone, *Ria Mooney: The life and times of the artistic director of the Abbey Theatre* (Jefferson, NC, 2002), p. 77; Benjamin Grob-Fitzgibbon, *The Irish experience during the Second World War* (Dublin, 2004), pp. 40–55; Wills, *Neutral island*, pp. 163, 188–95, 203, 264, 271, 276–7, 281–4, 302–5.

8. Brown, *Ireland*, pp. 202–4; Christopher Morash, *A history of the media in Ireland* (Cambridge, 2010), p. 145; Wills, *Neutral island*, pp. 291–302, 305.

9. *DIB*, 'Sean Russell'; Anthony Cronin, *Dead as doornails*, 2nd edn (Dublin, 1999), p. 15; Wills, *Neutral island*, pp. 93–4, 335.

10. Patrick Abercrombie, Sydney Kelly and Manning Robertson, *Dublin: Sketch development plan* (Dublin, 1943); *Dáil debates*, 19 March 1941; Frank MacDonald, *The destruction of Dublin* (Dublin, 1985), p. 11; Arnold Horner, 'The Dublin region, 1880–1982: An overview on its development and planning', in Michael

Bannon (ed.), *The emergence of Irish planning* (Dublin, 1985), pp. 49–60; Michael
Bannon, 'Irish planning from 1921 to 1945', in Bannon, *Planning: The Irish
experience* (Dublin, 1989), pp. 35, 39–40, 43–9, 59–60, 64–70; K. I. Nowlan, 'The
evolution of Irish planning 1934–1964', in Bannon, *Planning*, pp. 73–7; Daly,
Buffer state, pp. 285–6; *DIB*, 'Thomas Kelly'. The Tribunal had also advocated an
aggressive green-field acquisition policy by the Corporation, some of which should
be 'sterilised'.

11.   *Sketch Development Plan*; Michael O'Brien, 'The planning of Dublin', in *Journal
of the Town Planning Institute,* XXXVI (1949–50), pp. 208–10; *Irish Times,*
15 January 1957; T. J. Barrington, 'Whatever happened to *Irish* government?',
in Frank Litton (ed.), *Unequal achievement: The Irish experience 1957–82*
(Dublin, 1982), pp. 93–5; Horner, 'Dublin region 1880–1980', pp. 60–62; ibid.,
'Geographical aspects of recent local government reform in the Dublin area',
in *Ir. Geog.*, XXIX, 2 (1991), pp. 128–34; Nowlan, 'Evolution of Irish planning',
pp. 83–4; Bannon, 'Irish planning 1921–1945', pp. 9, 52–6, 55–6; Adam Marshall,
'EU structural funding in Ireland's capital city: Europeanization and regeneration
in Dublin 1989–2003', in *Ir. Geog.*, XL, 2 (2007), pp. 176–7. By 1950 Dublin
airport was already handling 212,000 passengers per annum: *Dáil debates*, 18 April
1950.

12.   Robert Collis, *Marrowbone Lane* (Monkstown, 1943); Margaret Ó hOgartaigh,
'St. Ultan's: A woman's hospital for infants', in *History Ireland*, (July 2005),
pp. 36–9; Earner-Byrne, *Mother and child*, pp. 108–11; *DIB*, 'Robert Collis',
'Kathleen Lynn', 'Dorothy Stopford-Price'. Collis's tenement drama can be
compared with that of another famous city doctor, Oliver St John Gogarty, whose
(anonymous) *Blight: The tragedy of Dublin* (Dublin, 1917), was performed in the
Abbey Theatre: Maria Luddy, *Prostitution and Irish society 1800–1940* (Cambridge,
2007), p. 189.

13.   Dillon, 'Slum Clearance', pp. 13–20; Arnold Horner, 'From city to city-region:
Dublin from the 1930s to the 1990s', in F. H. A. Aalen and Kevin Whelan (eds),
Dublin city and county: From prehistory to present (Dublin, 1992), pp. 331–2,
336; Ó Gráda, 'Ireland 1907–1947', in Donal Nevin (ed.), *James Larkin: Lion
of the fold* (Dublin, 1998), p. 15; *DIB*, '(William) Robert Fitzgerald Collis';
Wills, *Neutral island*, pp. 260–61. Confirming this picture of labouring parents'
increased anxieties about their children roaming far and wide some years later: A.
J. Humphreys, *New Dubliners: Urbanization and the Irish family* (London, 1966),
p. 203.

14.   *Census of Ireland 1961*, IV, table 3; *Census of Ireland 1971*, VI, table 4; Horner, 'City
to city-region', p. 335; Ó Gráda, 'Ireland 1907–1947', p. 13. At this point Dublin
no longer had the highest room density in the state (Limerick city was briefly the
worst).

15.   James Deeny, *To cure and to care: Memoirs of a chief medical officer* (Dun Laoghaire,
1989), pp. 99, 161–78; Catriona Clear, *Women of the house: Women's household
work in Ireland 1922–61* (Dublin, 2000), pp. 126–7; Earner-Byrne, *Mother and
child,* pp. 63–5, 99–101, 128–44, 155–63; McManus, *Crampton built*, pp. 218–19;

DIB, 'Noel Browne'. Infant mortality rates in Dublin City had improved in the 1920s, but then registered no real improvement until the dramatic falls in 1948–9: Earner-Byrne, *Mother and child,* pp. 48–9. At least a third of full-term deliveries were still in the home or in small nursing homes in the early 1940s, and the rising share of hospital deliveries after the war presumably boosted perinatal survival rates: Michael Solomons, *Pro Life ? The Irish question* (Dublin, 1992), p. 7.

16. Daly, *Buffer state*, pp. 336, 337, 343–4, 347–52, 365–9, 373; McManus, *Crampton built*, p. 183. On the experience of a young brickie employed by Cramptons at Ballyfermot: Billy French, *The journeyman: A builder's life* (Dublin, 2002), pp. 36–43.

17. *Dáil debates*, 22 February, 18 July 1951, 12 March 1952; O'Brien, 'Planning of Dublin', p. 209; Michael Corcoran, *Our good health: A history of Dublin's water and drainage* (Dublin, 2005), pp. 123–45. The completion of the Dodder Valley scheme in 1973, at a cost of £3 million, running for *c.*10 miles from Tallaght to Ringsend, had a similar effect two decades later, spurring on building activity in Tallaght, while the Greater Dublin Drainage Scheme, constructed in the mid-1970s, much of it along the Grand Canal, was crucial in allowing the satellite town development of Lucan, Clonadalkin and Blanchardstown: J. P. Haughton, 'The urban-rural fringe of Dublin', in N. Stephens and R. E. Glasscock (eds), *Irish geographical studies in E. Estyn Evans* (Belfast, 1970), p. 364.

18. Patrick Kavanagh, *The green fool* (London, 1971), pp. 298–305; Cronin, *Dead as doornails*, pp. 98–107, 113–23; Tony Farmar, *Privileged lives: A social history of middle-class Ireland 1882–1989* (Dublin, 2010), pp. 193–4, 250; Robert Welch (ed.), *The Oxford companion to Irish literature* (Oxford, 1996), pp. 401–2; Pat Walsh, *Patrick Kavanagh and* The Leader: *The poet, the politician and the libel trial* (Cork, 2010) pp. 64–7.

19. Farmar, *Privileged lives*, p. 223.

20. *Census of Ireland, 1936*, I, table 11; *Census of Ireland, 1956*, I, table 11; *Census of Ireland, 1961*, I, table 11; *Census of Ireland, 1966*, VI, table 9; *Census of Ireland, 1971*, VII, table 9; Haughton, 'Urban-rural fringe', p. 361; Horner, 'The Dublin region 1880–1982', pp. 25, 34; Bannon, 'Irish planning 1921–1945', pp. 33–5; Andrew MacLaran, *Dublin: The shaping of a capital* (London, 1993), p. 37.

21. Farmar, *Privileged lives*, pp. 197–9, 232–9.

22. Deirdre MacMahon, 'Archbishop John Charles McQuaid, archbishop of Dublin 1940–72', in James Kelly and Dáire Keogh (eds), *History of the Catholic diocese of Dublin* (Dublin, 2000), pp. 349–80; Earner-Byrne, *Mother and child*, pp. 16–17, 50, 91–6, 103–8; *ODNB*, 'Edward Byrne'; *DIB*, 'Edward Byrne'.

23. Donal McCartney, *UCD: A national idea – The history of University College, Dublin* (Dublin, 1999), pp. 202–3, 211; MacMahon, 'McQuaid', pp. 367–71.

24. James Lydon, 'The silent sister: Trinity College and Catholic Ireland', in C. H. Holland (ed.) *Trinity College Dublin and the idea of a university* (Dublin, 1992), pp. 43–51; MacMahon, 'MacQuaid', p. 380. On Artane Reformatory and its modern history: Justice Seán Ryan (ed.), *Commission to inquire into child abuse* [The Ryan report] (Dublin, 2009), I, pp. 106–284 (http://www.

childabusecommission.com/rpt/pdfs/CICA-VOL1–07.PDF [accessed 12 Nov. 2013]).

25. Patrick Abercrombie et al., 'The Dublin Town Plan (with comments)', in *Studies, XXXI,* 122 (1942), p. 165; Andrew Kincaid, *Postcolonial Dublin: Imperial legacies and the built environment* (Minneapolis, 2006), pp. 104–8; *DIB,* 'J. J. Robinson'.

26. Brian Fallon, *An age of innocence: Irish culture 1930–1960* (Dublin, 1999), p. 246; Evans, *Lemass,* pp. 106–7; *DIB,* 'Michael Scott'; http://archiseek.com/2009/michael-scott-1905-1989/ [accessed 12 April 2012].

27. J. V. Luce, *Trinity College Dublin: The first 400 years* (Dublin, 1992), pp. 162–7; Frank McDonald, 'ABK – bold, brutal and just turned 40', in *Irish Times,* 25 April 2002 (*Property Supplement*); McManus, *Crampton built,* pp. 256–7.

28. *DIB,* 'Desmond Fitzgerald'; Frank McDonald, *The destruction of Dublin* (Dublin, 1985), pp. 34–9.

29. McCartney, *UCD,* pp. 133–4, 146–9, 165–91, 212–15, 345–92.

30. Ibid., pp. 227–79, 389–92.

31. National Economic and Social Council Report 55: *Urbanization – Problems of growth and decay* (Dublin, 1981), p. 187; McDonald, *Destruction of Dublin,* pp. 47–61; Robert O'Byrne, 'The modern master' [Ronnie Tallon], in *Irish Times,* 27 January 2001, p. 9; McManus, *Crampton built,* pp. 262–71, 306–7; Morash, *History of the media,* pp. 166–82; Farmar, *Privileged lives,* pp. 231–2, 239, 306.

32. *Report of the commission on vocational organization* (Dublin, 1943), p. 267; Evans, *Lemass,* p. 241; http://wheresgrandad.com/2012/05/17/a-week-in-the-life-of-martin-cluxton/ [accessed 23 March 2012].

33. NESC 55: *Urbanization,* pp. 174–82; Haughton, 'Urban-rural fringe, p. 366; Daly, *Buffer state,* pp. 475–6; Sinead Power, 'The development of the Ballymun housing scheme, Dublin, 1965–1969', in *Ir. Geog.,* XXXIII (2000), pp. 199–212; Ruth McManus, *Dublin 1910–1940: Shaping the city and suburbs* (Dublin, 2002), p. 295.

34. Humphreys, *New Dubliners,* pp. 63, 125–30, 150, 153–4, 176–7, 196–201, 204–5, 208–9; Bertram Hutchinson, *Social status and inter-generational mobility in Dublin* (Dublin, 1969), pp. 7–9; *Census of Ireland, 1971,* 12, table 13a and 13b; NESC 55: *Urbanization,* pp. 184, 188; Farmar, *Privileged lives,* pp. 195–6.

35. *Irish Times,* 10 December 1964; McDonald, *Destruction of Dublin,* pp. 2–3, 32–4, 39–42; Frank McDonald and Kathy Sheridan, *The builders: How a small group of property developers fuelled the building boom and transformed Ireland,* 2nd edn (Dublin, 2009), pp. 29–31.

36. NESC 55: *Urbanization,* p. 192; McDonald, *Destruction of Dublin,* pp. 13–17, 23–8, 31–61.

37. H. A. Gilligan, *A history of Dublin port* (Dublin, 1988), pp. 184, 199–202, 261–2; John Walsh, *Collen: 200 years of building and civil engineering in Ireland* (Dublin, 2010), pp. 92, 103–4 111–22.

38. Humphreys, *New Dubliners,* pp. 213, 217; NESC 55: *Urbanization,* pp. 180, 196; James Wickham, 'Doing Dublin down', in *Irish Times,* 27 June 1979; S. A. Brophy, *The strategic management of Irish enterprise 1934–1984: Case studies from leading Irish companies* (Dublin, 1985), pp. 103–33, 140–65; Gilligan, *Port of Dublin,*

p. 197; Liam Clare, 'The rise and demise of the Dublin cattle market 1863–1973',
in D. A. Cronin, Jim Gilligan and Karina Holton (eds), *Irish fairs and markets:
Studies in local history* (Dublin, 2001), pp. 196–202; *DIB*, 'Colm Barnes', 'Jefferson
Smurfit'; Walsh, *Collen*, pp. 102–3, 106–9. The venerable British and Irish Steam
Packet Company was universally known in the twentieth century as 'the B & I
line'.

39. 'Adultery Irish style', in *Magill*, 1 April 1978; Solomons, *Pro Life ?*, pp. 17–19, 21,
27–9; Cronin, *Dead as doornails*, pp. 14–16; Linda Connolly, *The Irish women's
movement: From revolution to devolution* (Dublin, 2003), pp. 111–29; Diarmaid
Ferriter, *Occasions of sin: Sex and society in modern Ireland* (London, 2009),
pp. 405–17, 433–4, 487–506; Farmar, *Privileged lives*, pp. 220–21, 295–6, 303.
On the prevalence *c.*1951 of the rhythm method among white-collar families as a
means of family planning, and reportedly the complete absence of contraception:
Humphreys, *New Dubliners*, p. 211.

40. *Irish Times*, 19 July 1966, 2, 3 December 1968. Statues of James Larkin (in
O'Connell Street) and James Connolly (in Beresford Place) were erected in 1977
and 1996 respectively. On the city's first gay bar, The George, opened in 1985: *Irish
Times*, 16 April 2010, p. 19.

12 Millennium City: 1972–2000

1. http://www.cso.ie/en/media/csoie/census/documents/pser_map2.pdf; *Census of
Ireland, 1971*; *2002*; Arnold Horner, 'The Dublin region, 1880–1982: An overview
on its development and planning', in Michael Bannon (ed.), *The emergence of Irish
planning* (Dublin, 1985), pp. 62–6; Arnold Horner, 'From city to city-region:
Dublin from the 1930s to the 1990s', in F. H. A. Aalen and Kevin Whelan (eds),
Dublin city and county: From prehistory to present (Dublin, 1992), pp. 339–50.

2.. *Census of Ireland, 1971*, XI, pt. 2, table 2; *2002*, IV, table 33/4/33. On inter-
regional income transfer, see Garret FitzGerald's commentary in the *Irish Times*,
24 July 2010. The impact of immigration on Dublin shows up dramatically in a
comparison of the 2002 and 2006 censuses, with the sudden appearance in the
latter of many districts in the north inner city and the north-west suburbs with
more than a quarter of their population non-Irish born.

3. Brian Nolan et al., *Where are poor householders? The spatial distribution of poverty
and deprivation in Ireland* (Dublin, 1998), pp. 10–11, 20–21, 26–7, 45–7, 66–74.

4. Joseph Brady, 'Population change in Dublin', in *Ir. Geog.*, XXI (1988), p. 44;
Horner, 'City to city-region', pp. 344–50; Andrew MacLaran and Michael Punch,
'Tallaght: The planning and development of an Irish town', in *Journal of Irish
Urban Studies*, III, 1 (2004), pp. 17–40; Horner, 'Re-knotting Ireland in late Celtic
Tiger times', in *Ir. Geog.*, XLIII, 1 (2010), pp. 25–9.

5. *National Economic and Social Council Report 55: Urbanization – Problems of
growth and decay* (Dublin, 1981), p. 195; D. B. Rottman and P. J. O'Connell, 'The
changing social structure', in Frank Litton (ed.), *Unequal achievement: The Irish
experience 1957–82* (Dublin, 1982), pp. 80–81. On the state's failure to halt the

growth of the Dublin region: M. A. G. Ó Tuathaigh, 'The regional dimension', in Kieran Kennedy (ed.), *Ireland in transition: Economic and social change since 1960* (Cork, 1986), pp. 120–32.

6. A. J. Humphreys, *New Dubliners: Urbanization and the Irish family* (London, 1966), pp. 182–7; NESC 55: *Urbanization,* p. 197; *Irish Times,* 5 May 1988, 25 August, 8, 21 September 1993; Diarmaid Ferriter, *The transformation of Ireland 1900–2000* (London, 2004), pp. 572–3. For an astonishingly uncritical review of High Park's activities in the 1960s, when there were 150 women in the care of the nuns working in the laundry: *Irish Times,* 1 October 1968.

7. James Wickham, 'Doing Dublin down', in *Irish Times,* 27 June 1979.

8. Máirtín Mac Con Iomaire, 'The changing geography and fortunes of Dublin's *haute cuisine* restaurants, 1958–2008', in *Food, Culture & Society,* XIV, 4 (2011), pp. 525–45. The legendary Mary Guiney ran Clery's from 1967 until her death at 103 in 2004, and Margaret Hamilton Reid was chairman of the Switzer group from 1956 until its takeover in 1973: *Irish Times,* 1 May 2010. On the bitter and unresolved controversy over the Stardust disaster: http://www.rte.ie/news/2009/0123/stardustreport.pdf.

9. 'Review of the decade: A supplement', *Irish Times,* 28 December 1979, p. iii.

10. Geoffrey Dean et al., 'The opiate epidemic in Dublin 1979–83', in *Irish Medical Journal,* LXXVIII, 4 (1985), pp. 107–10; *Magill,* 1 March 1982, 1 November 1983, 1 March 1984, 1 August 1988; Niamh Moore, *Dublin docklands reinvented: The post-industrial regeneration of a European city quarter* (Dublin, 2008), pp. 71–100; *Irish Times,* 5 January 2009; Mary Rogan, *Prison policy in Ireland: Politics, penal-welfarism and political imprisonment* (London, 2011), pp. 156–9. The full details of 'the Gregory deal' were not published until many years later: http://www.maureenosullivan.ie/uploads/4/4/9/3/4493629/gregorydeal. pdf [accessed 30 December 2012]. A 1996 study estimated that there were by then 4,105 hard-drug addicts in the metropolitan area, 87 per cent of them unemployed, with over 6.2 per cent of the 15–30 age cohort in one north-central police district believed to be addicts: Eamonn Keogh, 'Illicit drug use and related criminal activity in the Dublin metropolitan area', pp. 7, 11: http://lenus.ie/hse/bitstream/10147/265274/1/ [accessed 31 March 2013].

11. Frank McDonald, *The destruction of Dublin* (Dublin, 1985), pp. 161–4, 267–75; A. J. Parker, 'Planned retail developments in Dublin', in *Ir. Geog.,* XIII (1980), pp. 83–8; *Irish Times,* 18 May 1987 and 31 October 2001 (*Commercial Property* supplement, p. 1); Colm Keena, *Haughey's millions: Charlie's money trail* (Dublin, 2001), pp. 195–214; Kevin Myers, 'An Irishman's diary', in *Irish Times,* 6 January 2006; Moore, *Dublin docklands,* pp. 112–35; Frank McDonald and Kathy Sheridan, *The builders: How a small group of property developers fuelled the building boom and transformed Ireland,* 2nd edn (Dublin, 2009), pp. 31–6, 165–6; Ruth McManus, *Crampton built* (Dublin, 2008), pp. 443–6.

12. Diane Payne and Peter Stafford, 'The politics of urban regeneration in Dublin', in J. R. Gupta (ed.), *Urban development debates in the new millennium* (New Delhi, 2005), pp. 98–110; Andrew Kincaid, *Postcolonial Dublin: Imperial legacies and*

the built environment (Minneapolis, 2006), pp. 189–200; Adam Marshall, 'EU structural funding in Ireland's capital city: Europeanization and regeneration in Dublin 1989–2003', in *Ir. Geog.*, XL, 2 (2007), pp. 170–77. For buyers queuing up to seven days to purchase lofty apartments in The Granary in Temple Bar: *Irish Times*, 23 February 1995 (*Property Supplement*, p. 1).

13. Shane O'Toole, 'Where the sun only rises', in *Sunday Tribune Magazine*, 24 October 1999.

14. For soccer fever: Roddy Doyle, *The van* (London, 1991), p. 508.

15. William Nolan (ed.), *The Gaelic Athletics Association in Dublin 1884–2000* (Dublin 2005), I, pp. 313–21, 376–7, 436–41, 467–89; http://comeheretome. com/2012/10/09/the-dublin-dons/ [accessed 21 Dec. 2012]; http://foot.ie/ threads/52439-Croke-park-funding [accessed 19 December 2012].

16. *DIB*, 'Jimmy O'Dea', 'Maureen Potter'.

17. *Magill*, 1 June 1985; *DIB*, 'Phil Lynott'; http://comeheretome.com/2011/01/23/1-classic-dublin-music-videos-phil-lynott-old-town-1982/ [accessed 21 December 2012]. On the National Concert Hall: McManus, *Crampton built*, pp. 391–4. On the prehistory of the Dublin singing pub: Elizabeth Malcolm, 'The rise of the pub', in J. S. Donnelly and K. A. Miller (eds), *Irish popular culture 1650–1850* (Dublin, 1998), p. 52.

18. Brian Donnelly, 'Roddy Doyle: From Barrytown to the GPO', in *Irish University Review*, XXX, 1 (2000), pp. 17–31; Fintan O'Toole, 'Greendale RIP ...', in *Irish Times*, 12 May 2007.

19. *DIB*, 'Maeve Binchy', 'James Plunkett'; John Cunningham, 'From *Disturbed Dublin* to *Strumpet City*: The 1913 "history wars", 1914–1980', in Francis Devine, Mary Clark and Máire Kennedy (eds), *A capital in conflict: Dublin city and the 1913 Lockout* (Dublin, 2013), pp. 367–72.

20. Bertram Hutchinson, *Social status and inter-generational mobility in Dublin* (Dublin, 1969), pp. 6–7; *Elizabeth, Countess of Fingal, Seventy years young: Memories ...* (Dublin, 1991); Andrew Whittaker, 'The Bank of Ireland and *The Irish Times*', in Whittaker (ed.), *Bright, brilliant days: Douglas Gageby and The* Irish Times (Dublin, 2006), pp. 171–7; Christopher Morash, *A history of the media in Ireland* (Cambridge, 2010), p. 190. For the history of the Royal Dublin at Dollymount: *Irish Times*, 4 October 1954. For *Magill's* cover stories through the 1980s: http://politico.ie/index.php?option=com_content&view=article&id=592 2&Itemid=471 [accessed 6 August 2013].

21. *Irish Times*, 4 December 1968; *Squatter*, June 1969 (http://cedarlounge.files. wordpress.com/2008/06/dhac-1969.pdf) [accessed 23 Dec. 2012]; L. P. Dillon, 'The Liberties of tomorrow', in Elgy Gillespie (ed.), *The Liberties of Dublin* (Dublin, 1973), p. 106; McDonald, *Destruction of Dublin*, p. 62; Andrew MacLaran, 'Industrial property development in Dublin 1960–82', in *Ir. Geog.*, XVIII (1985), pp. 44–9; Horner, 'City to city-region', pp. 349–50; Michael Punch, 'Inner-city transformation and renewal: The view from the grassroots', in P. J. Drudy and Andrew MacLaran, *Dublin: Economic and social trends, 3* (Dublin, 2001), pp. 40–42; McManus, *Crampton built*, pp. 385–8. On the proliferation of

hotels in the 1960s: McDonald, op. cit., pp. 69, 256. For the reflections in 1979 of a pioneering community activist in Ballyfermot: John Montgomery, 'Ballyfermot: A working class community', in Raynor Lysaght et al., *Dublin History Workshop* (Millennium Edition) (Dublin, 1988), pp. 10–12.

22. McDonald, *Destruction of Dublin*, pp. 18–29; McDonald and Sheridan, *The builders*, pp. 21–2; Casey, *Dublin*, p. 573; *DIB*, 'Dáithi Hanly'.

23. McDonald, *Destruction of Dublin*, pp. 78–99; McManus, *Crampton built*, pp. 316–17.

24. McDonald, *Destruction of Dublin*, pp. 68–9, 78–99, 110–11; *DIB*, 'Deirdre Kelly'.

25. Desmonde Roche, 'Local government', in Litton, *Unequal achievement*, pp. 145–6; John Ardagh, *Ireland and the Irish: Portrait of a changing society* (London, 1994), p. 126; Frank McDonald, 'New city manager', in *Irish Times*, 10 July 1996; *DIB*, 'F. X. Martin'.

26. Tony Farmar, *Privileged lives: A social history of middle-class Ireland 1882–1989* (Dublin, 2010), p. 304.

27. For overviews of the Flood Tribunal and the Quarryvale/Liffey Valley saga, see *Irish Times*, 10 May 2000, p. 10, and 20 May 2000, p. 8.

28. Yvonne Whelan, 'Written in space and stone: Aspects of the iconography of Dublin after independence', in Clarke, Prunty and Hennessy, *Surveying Ireland's past*, p. 607.

29. *Irish Times*, 12 September 1989; *Guardian*, 18 July 2010.

LIST OF
ILLUSTRATIONS

List of Maps

Colour Plates

Black and White Plates

BIBLIOGRAPHICAL
NOTE

General

Sir John Gilbert (1829–1898) is the founding figure in the modern study of Dublin's history, and his *History of Dublin*, 3 vols (Dublin, 1854–9), despite its many limitations, is still an authoritative work on the inner city. His *Calendar of the ancient records of Dublin*, 19 vols (Dublin, 1889–1944) remains the principal source for the study of municipal government over four centuries. However, his monumental endeavours were not followed up, with the only major additions in the next generation being F. E. Ball's *A history of the Co. Dublin*, 6 vols (Dublin, 1902–20), Weston St John Joyce's *The neighbourhood of Dublin* (Dublin, 1912), and the Georgian Society of Ireland's *Records of eighteenth-century domestic architecture and decoration in Dublin*, 5 vols (1909–13). Things began to change when the *Dublin Historical Record*, journal of the Old Dublin Society, was launched in 1938, and it has successfully blended scholarly and popular writing on all periods of the city's past in an eclectic mix, many of its articles illuminating the history of small places and obscure citizens.

More recent historical research on Dublin has concentrated on three distinct periods of the city's history: the Viking/Norse and early Norman centuries (900–1300); the 'long' eighteenth century; and the era of Yeats and Joyce, of the Easter Rising and the Irish Revolution (*c*.1890–1925). Archaeological discovery rather than historical documentation has shaped scholarly writing on the early medieval city, whereas a proliferation of sources – documentary, literary, architectural and pictorial – has allowed for a much more diverse treatment of eighteenth-century Dublin. But even for that period there is a pronounced imbalance between the voluminous writings on architecture, the arts, theatre and print culture, and the very modest literature on business and work, on class, gender, religion and the marginalised. Conversely, research on Dublin during the modern revolutionary era has focused on precisely these missing themes and on housing, public health, labour organisation and political dissent, as well as on the rich cultural history of those years.

There have been few modern attempts to capture all these strands in a single study or to survey the city's general history over the long run. Peter Somerville-Large's *Dublin: The fair city* (London, 1979) remains the best attempt; H. A. Gilligan's *History of the port of Dublin* (Dublin, 1988), Andrew MacLaran's *Dublin: The shaping of a capital* (London, 1993) and Siobhán Kilfeather's *Dublin: A cultural and literary history* (Dublin, 2005), although more selective in their concerns, also provide valuable overviews. There have been several excellent multi-authored volumes of essays that provide a composite picture of the city's evolution: Art Cosgrove (ed.), *Dublin through the ages* (Dublin, 1988); James Kelly and Uáitéar Mac Gearailt (eds), *Dublin and Dubliners: Essays in the history and literature of Dublin city* (Dublin, 1990); F. H. A. Aalen and Kevin Whelan (eds), *Dublin city and county: From prehistory to the present ...* (Dublin, 1992); Peter Clark and Raymond Gillespie (eds), *Two capitals: London and Dublin 1500–1840* (Oxford, 2001); and Joseph Brady and Anngret Simms (eds), *Dublin through space and time* (Dublin, 2001). And in the same category and broader in scope than their titles might suggest are Paul Butel and L. M. Cullen (eds), *Cities and merchants: French and Irish perspectives on urban development 1500–1900* (Dublin, 1986); James Kelly and Dáire Keogh (eds), *History of the Catholic diocese of Dublin* (Dublin, 2000); and Ruth McManus and Lisa-Marie Griffith (eds), *Leaders of the city: Dublin's first citizens, 1500–1950* (Dublin, 2013). H. B. Clarke (ed.), *Irish cities* (Cork, 1995) offers vignettes of Dublin measured against the history of seven other cities.

Three reference works have appeared in recent years that proved of critical importance in writing this book. First were the fascicles relating to Dublin that form part of the ongoing *Irish Historic Towns Atlas* (IHTA) project. Two have been published so far, *Dublin part I: To 1610*, edited by H. B. Clarke (Dublin, 2002), and *Dublin part II: 1610–1757*, edited by Colm Lennon (Dublin, 2008). These provide essential topographical data and contain reproductions of historical maps of the city that are of a very high quality. Second has been Christine Casey's *Dublin: The city within the Grand and Royal Canals and the Circular Road with the Phoenix Park* (London, 2005), a volume in Yale's Pevsner-inspired 'Buildings of Ireland' series. Thirdly has been the magnificent *Dictionary of Irish Biography*, edited by James McGuire in 9 vols (Cambridge, 2009), the online version of which (Cambridge, 2010–) has been used here.

Several thematic surveys spanning the centuries with a strong Dublin centre of interest have appeared in the fields of painting, printing, theatre and film. The writings of Anne Crookshank and the Knight of Glin, with *The watercolours of Ireland* (London, 1994), and *Ireland's painters 1600–1940* (New Haven, 2002), remain pre-eminent in their field. In printing, publishing and bookselling, the pioneer was Mary Pollard with her *Dublin's trade in books 1550–1800* (Oxford, 1989) and the *Dictionary of members of the Dublin book trade 1550–1800* (London, 2000). These have provided a firm foundation for many of the contributions to the 'Oxford History of the Irish Book' series: Raymond Gillespie and Andrew Hadfield (eds), *The Irish book in English 1550–1800* (Oxford, 2006); J. H. Murphy (ed.), *The Irish book in English 1800–1890* (Oxford, 2011); and Clare Hutton (ed.), *The Irish book in English 1891–2000* (Oxford, 2011). Meanwhile Rolf and Magda Loeber's *Guide to Irish fiction, 1650–1900* (Dublin, 2006) provides the first database of Irish imaginative literature. These have been joined by other magisterial surveys of

Irish cultural production where Dublin's role was central, notably Christopher Morash's *A history of Irish theatre 1601–2000* (Cambridge, 2002), and Kevin and Emer Rockett's *Magic lantern, panorama and moving picture shows in Ireland, 1786–1909*, and *Film exhibition and distribution in Ireland, 1909–2010* (Dublin, 2011).

On the evolution of Dublin's spaces and places, two definitive histories appeared together: Desmond MacCabe, *St Stephen's Green* (Dublin, 2009) and John McCullen, *An illustrated history of the Phoenix Park ...* (Dublin, 2009). But a much older grand survey remains unpublished (but heavily used): Nuala Burke's 'Dublin 1600–1800: A study in urban morphogenesis' (Ph.D. dissertation, University of Dublin, 1972). This has influenced all subsequent writing on the physical development of the streetscape, notably Niall McCullough's visually elegant *Dublin: An urban history/The plan of the city* (Dublin, 2007). But the precursor of all such work was Maurice J. Craig's *Dublin: A social and architectural history 1660–1860* (London, 1952). This was written a decade before the brutal redevelopment of the eighteenth-century city had begun, and is an evergreen text that has never gone out of print, a measure of the sharpness of its architectural judgements, its exhilarating style and its eye for telling detail.

Before 1600

Definitive reports on the great archaeological discoveries in the old city more than a generation ago have yet to be published. The most authoritative source remains Patrick Wallace, *The Viking Age buildings of Dublin*, 2 vols (Dublin, 1992). However, *Medieval Dublin,* edited by Seán Duffy, has appeared annually since 2000, and these volumes have allowed reports on recent archaeological investigations of the Norse and early Norman town to reach print quite promptly, and they have also provided an excellent forum for the presentation of historical research on the Dublin region up to and including the sixteenth century. Many of the contributors have also published in edited collections, notably in Howard Clarke (ed.), *Medieval Dublin: The living city* (Dublin, 1990), and *Medieval Dublin: The making of a metropolis* (Dublin, 1990); in Conleth Mannin (ed.), *Dublin and beyond the Pale: Studies in honour of Patrick Healy* (Bray, County Wicklow, 1998); and in John Bradley, A. J. Fletcher and Anngret Simms (eds), *Dublin in the medieval world: Studies in honour of Howard B. Clarke* (Dublin, 2009). The history of the city's two cathedrals from the time of their medieval foundation has also been the subject of multi-authored volumes – Kenneth Milne (ed.), *Christ Church Cathedral Dublin: A history* (Dublin, 2000) and John Crawford and Raymond Gillespie (eds), *St. Patrick's Cathedral: A history* (Dublin, 2009) – but that other great medieval institution, Dublin Castle, lacks an all-encompassing architectural or social history.

There have been relatively few monographs on the medieval city, but the magisterial survey by Margaret Murphy and Michael Potterton, *The Dublin region in the middle ages* (Dublin, 2010), includes much that is relevant to urban development, as does Áine Foley, *The royal manors of medieval Co. Dublin: Crown and community* (Dublin, 2013). Maria Kelly, *The great dying: The Black Death in Dublin* (Stroud, 2003), contextualises the city's greatest medieval crisis. Several short synoptic essays are particularly useful, notably Anngret Simms, 'Medieval Dublin: A topographical analysis', in *Irish Geography*, XII (1979), pp. 25–41; Poul Holm, 'The slave trade of Dublin, IXth to XIIth centuries', in *Peritia*, V (1986 [1989]), pp. 317–45; John Bradley, *Dublin in the year 1000* (Dublin, 2003); and H. B. Clarke, the outstanding historian of medieval Dublin whose work appears throughout the collections mentioned above but also includes 'The bloodied eagle: The Vikings and the development of Dublin', in *Irish Sword*, XVIII (1991), pp. 91–119; *The four parts of the city: Highlife and low life in the suburbs of medieval Dublin* (Dublin, 2003); and 'From Dyflinnarskiri to the Pale: Defining and defending a medieval city-state, 1000–1500', in Jennifer ní Ghrádaigh and Emmett O'Byrne (eds), *The March in the islands of the medieval west* (Leiden, 2012), pp. 35–52.

Our understanding of sixteenth-century Dublin has been transformed by Colm Lennon, beginning with his *Richard Stanihurst the Dubliner 1547–1618* (Dublin, 1981) and *The lords of Dublin in the age of Reformation* (Blackrock, Co. Dublin, 1989), and he has published prolifically ever since, his later work being reflected in his IHTA contributions and in 'Fraternity and community in early modern Dublin', in Robert Armstrong and Tadhg Ó hAnnracháin (eds), *Community in early modern Ireland* (Dublin, 2006), pp. 167–78. Among the burgeoning literature on the Irish Reformation and Counter-Reformation in Dublin, the contributions of Helga Robinson-Hammerstein on the origins of Trinity College – 'Royal policy and civic pride: Founding a university in Dublin', in David Scott (ed.), *Treasures of the mind ...* (London, 1991), pp. 1–15 – and of James Murray on the transformation of St Patrick's Cathedral – *Enforcing the English Reformation in Ireland: Clerical resistance and political conflict in the diocese of Dublin 1534–1590* (Cambridge, 2009) – are particularly suggestive.

Seventeenth-century Dublin

Raymond Gillespie has made a prodigious contribution to the city's history in the seventeenth century, both as an interpreter and editor. *Reading Ireland: Print, reading and social change in early modern Ireland* (Manchester, 2005) encapsulates much of this, but 'Dublin 1600–1700: A city and its hinterlands', in Peter Clark and Bernard Lepetit (eds), *Capital cities and their hinterlands in early modern Europe* (Aldershot, 1996), pp. 84–104, gives an excellent summary of his ideas on the city's wider social history. On economic change in the early seventeenth century, see also Patricia Stapleton, 'The merchant community of Dublin in the early seventeenth century: A social, economic and political study' (Ph.D. dissertation, University of Dublin, 2008), which complements Brendan Fitzpatrick, 'The Municipal Corporation of Dublin 1603–40' (Ph.D. dissertation, University of Dublin, 1984). On the social impact of war in the 1640s, Gillespie's essay, 'The Irish economy at war', in Jane Ohlmeyer (ed.), *Ireland from independence to occupation 1641–1660* (Cambridge, 1995), pp. 160–80, provides a good overview, and for the wider history of urban poverty in the seventeenth century, Patrick Fitzgerald's 'Poverty and vagrancy in early modern Ireland' (Ph.D. dissertation, Queen's University Belfast, 1994), opens up the field. On the city's growth, R. A. Butlin, 'The population of Dublin in the late seventeenth century', in *Ir. Geog.*, V, 2 (1965), pp. 51–66, remains valuable.

Dublin features centrally in T. C. Barnard's classic study, *Cromwellian Ireland: English government and reform in Ireland 1649–1660* (Cambridge, 1972), and L. J. Arnold's

The Restoration land settlement in County Dublin, 1660–1688 (Blackrock, Co. Dublin, 1993) explores some of the consequences. Maighréad Ní Mhurchadha's *Fingal 1603–60: Contending neighbours in north Dublin* (Dublin, 2005) traces the upheavals in the city's northern hinterland.

A number of writers since Maurice Craig have seen the Restoration era after 1660 as a point of departure for longer studies, including Rowena Dudley, 'St. Stephen's Green: The early years 1664–1730', in *DHR*, LIII, 2 (2000), pp. 157–79, and Robin Usher in his major survey, *Protestant Dublin 1660–1760: Architecture and iconography* (Basingstoke, 2012). Similarly Edward McParland, in his magisterial *Public architecture in Ireland, 1680–1760* (London, 2001), takes Ormond's later building projects as the beginning of a golden age of architectural achievement.

On economic change as it affected Dublin, L. M. Cullen's *Anglo-Irish trade 1660–1800* (Manchester, 1969) provides the foundations for all modern writing and is still the guidebook. On the growth of government in Restoration Dublin and the centralisation of finance, Sean Egan's 'Finance and the government of Ireland 1660–85' (Ph.D. dissertation, University of Dublin, 1983) is a key source. R. L. Greaves, *Dublin's Merchant-Quaker: Anthony Sharp and the community of Friends 1643–1707* (Stanford, 1998) is an important case-study of an innovative manufacturer. Nuala Burke has documented the beginnings of speculative housing development in 'An early modern suburb: The estate of Francis Aungier, earl of Longford', in *Ir. Geog.*, VI, 4 (1972), pp. 365–85. On the city's new intellectual life, K. T. Hoppen's *The common scientist in the seventeenth century: A study of the Dublin Philosophical Society 1683–1708* (London, 1970) remains the principal study. A wider context for this is provided in the earlier sections of R. B. McDowell and D. A. Webb's *Trinity College Dublin 1592–1952; An academic history* (Cambridge, 1982).

Eighteenth-century Dublin

Jacqueline Hill's *From patriots to unionists: Dublin civic politics and Irish Protestant patriotism 1660–1840* (Oxford, 1997) is the outstanding study of the political culture of the freemen of Dublin during the era of the Protestant monopoly of power, but it can be supplemented by James Kelly's many biographical studies of city-based politicians, notably that of *Sir Edward Newenham MP, 1734–1814: Defender of the Protestant constitution* (Dublin, 2004). Of the national political figures who left a profound mark on Dublin, several have been well served in modern biographies, notably Philip O'Regan's *Archbishop William King of Dublin (1650–1729) and the constitution in church and state* (Dublin, 2000); A. P. W. Malcomson's *Nathaniel Clements: Government and the governing elite in Ireland, 1725–75* (Dublin, 2005), his *Archbishop Charles Agar: Churchmanship and politics in eighteenth-century Ireland, 1760–1810* (Dublin, 2002), and his *John Foster (1740–1828): The politics of improvement and prosperity* (Dublin, 2011).

For those less privileged, Raymond Hylton's *Ireland's Huguenots and their refuge 1662–1745* (Brighton, 2005) illuminates a major story. On Presbyterian Dublin, Michael Brown's *Francis Hutcheson in Dublin, 1719–1730: The crucible of his thought* (Dublin, 2002) examines a formative moment. On the public life of Catholic Dubliners, Patrick Fagan's *The second city: Portrait of Dublin 1700–1760* (Dublin, 1986), 'The Dublin Catholic mob

(1700–50)', in *Eighteenth-Century Ireland*, IV (1989), pp. 133–42, and *Catholics in a Protestant country: The Papist constituency in eighteenth-century Dublin* (Dublin, 1998) have been pioneering works. But Nuala Burke's 'A hidden church? The structure of Catholic Dublin in the mid-eighteenth century', in *Archivium Hibernicum*, XXXII (1974), pp. 81–92, is still useful, and Cormac Begadon, 'The renewal of Catholic religious culture in eighteenth-century Dublin', in John Bergin et al. (eds), *New perspectives on the penal laws* (Dublin, 2011), pp. 227–47, opens a new debate.

Political life and the widening of print culture were intimately connected, as Robert Munter, *The history of the Irish newspapers, 1685–1760* (Cambridge, 1967), James W. Phillip, *Printing and bookselling in Dublin, 1670–1800: A bibliographical enquiry* (Dublin, 1998) and Brian Inglis, *The freedom of the press in Ireland 1784–1841* (London, 1954) eloquently demonstrate. Several other trades and crafts have been closely studied, notably the silk trade by Mairéad Dunlevy in *Pomp and poverty: A history of silk in Ireland* (London, 2011); the stuccodores by C. P. Curran in *Dublin decorative plasterwork of the seventeenth and eighteenth centuries* (London, 1967), and by Joseph McDonnell in *Irish decorative stuccowork and its European sources* (Dublin, 1991); the cabinet-makers by the Knight of Glin and James Peill, in *Irish furniture* (London, 2007); and the goldsmiths by Alison FitzGerald, in 'The business of being a goldsmith in eighteenth-century Dublin', which appears in a fine potpourri of new research edited by Gillian O'Brien and Finola O'Kane, *Georgian Dublin* (Dublin, 2008). And on the new materiality of the age, T. C. Barnard's *Making the grand figure: Lives and possessions in Ireland* (London, 2004) is a ground-breaking survey, the retail dimension of which is explored in Sarah Foster's '"Ornament and Splendour": Shops and shopping in Georgian Dublin', in *Irish Decorative and Architectural Studies*, XV (2013), pp. 12–33. Martyn J. Powell's *The politics of consumption in eighteenth-century Ireland* (Basingstoke, 2005) brings it all back to matters of power and conflict.

On the intersection of politics and business, L. M. Cullen's *Princes and pirates: The Dublin Chamber of Commerce, 1783–1983* (Dublin 1983) presented an entirely new reading as to why merchants cooperated, and his *Economy, trade and Irish merchants at home and abroad, 1600–1988* (Dublin, 2012) brings together a number of major papers on Dublin commercial history. Useful in establishing Dublin trade in the wider scheme of things is David Dickson's 'The place of Dublin in the eighteenth-century Irish economy', in T. M. Devine and David Dickson (eds), *Ireland and Scotland 1600–1850* (Edinburgh, 1983), pp. 177–92, and T. M. Truxes's *Irish-American trade 1660–1783* (Cambridge, 1988).

The social history of upper-class Dublin in this period has been well served, and major work includes A. P. W. Malcomson, *The pursuit of the heiress: Aristocratic marriage in Ireland 1740–1840*, 2nd edn (Belfast, 2006); Michael MacCarthy (ed.), *Lord Charlemont and his circle* (Dublin, 2001); I. C. Ross (ed.), *Public virtue, public love: The early years of the Dublin Lying-in Hospital* (Dublin, 1986); Brian Boydell, *A Dublin musical calendar 1700–1760* (Blackrock, Co. Dublin, 1988), and his *Rotunda music in eighteenth-century Dublin* (Dublin, 1992); James Kelly and M. J. Powell (eds), *Clubs and societies in eighteenth-century Ireland* (Dublin, 2010); and Christine Casey (ed.), *The eighteenth-century Dublin town house: Form, function and finance* (Dublin, 2010).

The contrasts in lifestyle are explored in David Dickson (ed.), *The gorgeous mask: Dublin 1700–1850* (Dublin, 1987) and, more specifically in Michael Drake's 'The Irish demographic crisis of 1740–41', in T. W. Moody (ed.), *Historical Studies*, VI (London, 1968), pp. 101–24. Other food crises that convulsed the city have been examined by James Kelly in 'Harvests and hardship: Famine and scarcity in Ireland in the late 1720s', in *Studia Hibernica*, XXVI (1991–2), pp. 65–105, and in 'Scarcity and poor relief in eighteenth-century Ireland: The subsistence crisis of 1782–4', in *IHS*, XXVIII, 109 (1992), pp. 40–62. The medical response to such social deprivation is explored in R. S. Harrison, *Dr John Rutty (1698–1775) of Dublin: A Quaker polymath in the Enlightenment* (Dublin, 2011). Rutty was fascinated by water and Patrick T. Ryan has reconstructed a detailed history of the city's supply in 'The water supply of early modern Dublin: Archaeology, history, cartography' (Ph.D. dissertation, University College Dublin, 2007).

On the architectural transformation of the eighteenth-century city, Edward McParland has been the exemplary guide, ranging from his essay on 'The Wide Streets Commissioners', in the *Quarterly Bulletin of the Irish Georgian Society*, XV, 1 (1972), pp. 1–32, to his superb *James Gandon: Vitruvius Hibernicus* (London, 1985). Others who have explored strategic urban development include Murray Fraser, 'Public building and colonial policy in Dublin, 1760–1800', in *Architectural History*, XXVIII (1985), pp. 102–23; Mary Clark and Alastair Smeaton (eds), *The Georgian squares of Dublin: An architectural history* (Dublin, 2006); Mairéad Dunlevy, *Dublin Barracks: A brief history* (Dublin, 2002); and Brendan Twomey, *Smithfield and the parish of St. Paul 1698–1750* (Dublin, 2005). The best introduction to developments by mid-century is John Montague and Colm Lennon (eds), *John Rocque's Dublin: A guide to the Georgian city* (Dublin, 2010).

Modern work on the politicisation of lower-class Dubliners is voluminous. A logical starting-point is James Kelly's *The Liberty and Ormond boys: Factional riot in eighteenth-century Dublin* (Dublin, 2005), and Sean Murphy's 'The Dublin anti-union riot of 3 December 1759', in Gerard O'Brien (ed.), *Parliament, politics and people: Essays in eighteenth-century Irish history* (Blackrock, Co. Dublin, 1989), pp. 49–68. Others who have reinterpreted the shifting dynamics of eighteenth-century popular politics include Vincent Morley in *Irish opinion and the American Revolution, 1760–1783* (Cambridge, 2002), and Padhraig Higgins in *A nation of politicians: Gender, patriotism, and political culture in late eighteenth-century Ireland* (Madison, 2010). Jim Smyth's *The men of no property: Irish radicals and popular politics in the late eighteenth century* (Basingstoke, 1992) and Nancy Curtin's *The United Irishmen: Popular politics in Ulster and Dublin 1791–8* (Oxford, 1994) traverse the major turning points of the 1780s and 1790s and document the new political landscape. This is examined with even closer precision in Thomas Bartlett (ed.), *Revolutionary Dublin 1795–1801: The letters of Francis Higgins to Dublin Castle* (Dublin, 2004). But Marianne Elliott's biography of the son of a city coach-maker, *Wolfe Tone: Prophet of Irish independence* (London, 1989) remains the most engrossing introduction to the world of Dublin radicalism. Also important for the 1790s are R. B. McDowell, *Historical essays 1938–2001* (Dublin, 2004); C. J. Woods, 'The personnel of the Catholic Convention, 1792–3', in *Archivium Hibernicum*, LVII (2003), pp. 26–76; Dáire Keogh, *'The French disease': The Catholic Church and radicalism in Ireland 1790–1800* (Dublin, 1993); and Tommy Graham's three essays, 'The transformation of the Dublin Society of United Irishmen ... 1791–96', in Thomas Bartlett et al., *1798: A bicentenary perspective* (Dublin, 2003), pp. 136–46; '"An union of power": The United Irish organization, 1795–1798', in

David Dickson, Dáire Keogh and Kevin Whelan (eds), *The United Irishmen: Republicanism, radicalism and rebellion* (Dublin, 1993), pp. 244–55; and 'The shift in United Irish leadership from Belfast to Dublin, 1796–1798', in Jim Smyth (ed.), *Revolution, counterrevolution and union: Ireland in the 1790s* (Cambridge, 2000), pp. 55–66.

On the responses of the state and the city to crime and subversion, Stanley H. Palmer, *Police and protest in England and Ireland 1780–1850* (Cambridge, 1988), Neal Garnham, *The courts, crime and the criminal law in Ireland, 1692–1760* (Blackrock, Co. Dublin, 1996), and Brian Henry, *Dublin hanged: Crime, law enforcement and punishment in Dublin, 1780–1795* (Dublin, 1993), debate the issues from somewhat different angles.

Nineteenth-century Dublin

There has been a flurry of work on Dublin and the parliamentary union of 1801 and on the insurrection of 1803, both well represented in Dáire Keogh and Kevin Whelan (eds), *Acts of union: The causes, contexts and consequences of the act of Union* (Dublin, 2001); Michael Brown, Patrick M. Geoghegan and James Kelly (eds), *The Irish act of union, 1800: Bicentennial essays* (Dublin, 2003); and Anne Dolan, Patrick M. Geoghegan and Darryl Jones (eds), *Reinterpreting Emmet: Essays on the life and legacy of Robert Emmet* (Dublin, 2007). But Ruán O'Donnell's *Robert Emmet and the rebellion of 1798* and *Robert Emmet and the rising of 1803* (Dublin, 2003) offer a close reading of the insurrection and its origins.

By contrast, the historical literature on Dublin in the following decades is limited, despite the huge expansion in the availability of primary sources, both quantitative and qualitative. Constantia Maxwell, *Dublin under the Georges 1714–1830* (Dublin, 1936), although very dated in its approach, gives a sense of the wealth of descriptive material commenting on city life. David Dickson's 'Death of a capital? Dublin and the consequences of Union' (in Gillespie and Clark, *Two capitals*, 2001, pp. 111–31) undermines some of the old assumptions as to the long-term impact of the Union; Alison FitzGerald, 'The production of silver in late Georgian Dublin', in *Irish Decorative and Architectural Studies*, IV (2001), pp. 9–47, comes to similar conclusions. The growth of Dublin's financial sector in the period can be explored in F. G. Hall, *The Bank of Ireland 1783–1947* (Dublin, 1949), and in F. G. Barrow, *The emergence of the Irish banking system, 1820–1845* (Dublin, 1975), but W. A. Thomas, *The stock exchanges of Ireland* (Liverpool, 1986) and Cormac Ó Gráda, *A new economic history of Ireland 1780–1939* (Oxford, 1994) provide more nuanced accounts. On the crucial part played then by Quakers in trade and manufacturing, Richard Harrison, 'Dublin Quakers in business, 1800–1850' (M.Litt. dissertation, University of Dublin, 1987) is a pioneering study.

On Dublin's role in the transport revolution, Ruth Delany's *Ireland's Royal Canal: 1789–1992* (Dublin, 1992) and *The Grand Canal of Ireland* (Dublin, 1995) are the standard works, and are complemented by Diarmuid Ó Gráda's 'The rocky road to Dublin: Transport modes and urban growth', in *Studia Hibernica*, XXII/XXIII (1982–3), pp. 128–48. Railway construction has been studied by K. A. Murray, *Ireland's first railway* (Dublin, 1981), and by Joseph Lee, notably in 'Merchants and enterprise: The case of early Irish railways 1830–1855', in L. M. Cullen and Paul Butel (eds), *Négoce et industrie en France at en Irlande aux xviiie at xixe siècles* (Paris, 1980), pp 143–58. The greatest Irish railway builder has his biographer at last with Fergus Mulligan's *William Dargan: An honourable life 1799–1867* (Dublin, 2013).

On the landed classes and the city in the nineteenth century, R. B. McDowell, *Land and learning: Two Irish clubs* (Dublin, 1993) is a suitable point of entry, and Joseph Robins, *Champagne and silver buckles: The viceregal court at Dublin Castle, 1700–1922* (Dublin, 2001) and James Meenan and Desmond Clarke (eds), *RDS: The Royal Dublin Society 1731–1981* (Dublin, 1981) offer complementary perspectives. On the professions, there is a worthy corpus of histories of the major medical and legal institutions and of individual pioneers, but little on the process of professionalisation or on the collective ascendancy of lawyers and medics in the city's political and social life. Daire Hogan's *The legal profession in Ireland 1789–1922* (Dublin, 1986) opens up bigger issues, as does Nial Osborough in *Law and the emergence of modern Dublin: A litigation topography for a capital city* (Dublin, 1996).

Much the same applies to the history of city education, but several of the institutional histories have broader application, notably A. V. O'Connor and S. M. Parkes, *Gladly learn and gladly teach: Alexandra College and School 1866–1966* (Dublin, n.d. [1984]); James H. Murphy, *Nos autem: Castleknock College and its contribution* (Dublin, n.d. [1996]), and Fergus D'Arcy, *Terenure College 1860–2010: A history* (Dublin, 2010), as do contributions in David Dickson, Justyna Pyz and Christopher Shepard (eds), *Irish classrooms and British empire ...* (Dublin, 2012). Niall Ó Ciosáin's *Print and popular culture in Ireland 1750–1850*, 2nd edn (Dublin, 2010) explores the new world of literacy, while L. M. Cullen's *Eason & son: A history* (Dublin, 1989) documents the evolution of the city's greatest newsagent. Charles Benson's 'The Dublin book trade 1800–50' (Ph.D. dissertation, University of Dublin, 2000) reveals a surprisingly adaptive printing industry.

There is much still to be written on Dublin and the Great Famine. On the demographic background, Cormac Ó Gráda's 'Dublin's demography in the early nineteenth century: Evidence from the Rotunda', in *Population Studies*, XLV (1991), pp. 43–54, and David Dickson's 'The demographic implications of Dublin's growth 1650–1850', in Richard Lawton and Robert Lee (eds), *Urban population development in western Europe from the late-eighteenth to the early-twentieth centuries* (Liverpool, 1989), pp. 178–89, are starting points. The most perceptive commentary on the crisis itself is by Ó Gráda in *Black '47 and beyond ...* (Princeton, 1999) and in his *Ireland's Great Famine: Interdisciplinary perspectives* (Dublin, 2006). Audrey Woods, *Dublin outsiders: A history of the Mendicity Institution 1818–1998* (Dublin, 1998), Thomas Willis, *The hidden Dublin: The social and sanitary condition of the working classes in the city of Dublin* [1845], ed. David Dickson (Dublin, 2002), and Laurence M. Geary, *Medicine and charity in Ireland 1718–1851* (Cork, 2004), explore social and medical conditions in the lead-up to the crisis, and the institutional response after it hit.

On the transformation of municipal governance after 1840, Stefanie Jones, 'Dublin reformed: The transformation of the municipal government of a Victorian city 1840–1860' (Ph.D. dissertation, University of Dublin, 2001) is the first full exploration of the subject, but Mary Daly's classic study, *Dublin: The deposed capital – A social and economic history, 1860–1914* (Cork, 1986), casts its net back to the 1840s. Daly's study traces the growth of local government through an era of enormous change, and plots it against a rigorous analysis of social and economic changes in city and suburbs. Jacinta Prunty, *Dublin slums 1800–1925: A study in urban geography* (Dublin, 1999), builds on this, investigating in great detail the politics of housing, health and social intervention across the nineteenth century. Lydia Carroll, *In the fever king's preserves: Sir Charles Cameron and the Dublin slums* (Dublin, 2011) is the first study of the long-lived champion of Dublin's public health. And Michael Corcoran, *Our good health: A history of Dublin's water and drainage* (Dublin, 2005) is particularly strong on this period.

On the revolution in the role and status of the Catholic Church in the city, Emmet Larkin's *The pastoral role of the Roman Catholic Church in pre-famine Ireland 1750–1850* (Dublin, 2006) is useful, but more definitive are the many contributions to Dáire Keogh and Albert McDonnell (eds), *Cardinal Paul Cullen and his world* (Dublin, 2011). M. P. Magray, *The transforming power of the nuns: Women, religion and cultural change in Ireland 1750–1900* (New York, 1998) goes some way in tracing the rise of the female religious orders, which is treated more concretely in F. O. C. Meenan, *St. Vincent's Hospital 1834–1994* (Dublin, 1995) and M. M. Kealy, *Dominican education in Ireland 1820–1930* (Dublin, 2007). Work on the social history of Dublin Protestantism in the nineteenth century is more modest, but the point of entry here is John Crawford, *The Church of Ireland in Victorian Dublin* (Dublin, 2005).

The growth of major cultural institutions in the city is set in a wider context by R. A. Jarrell in 'The Department of Science and Art and control of Irish science, 1853–1905', *IHS*, XXIII, 92 (1983), pp. 330–39. But two substantial works now dominate the field: Peter Somerville-Large's *1854–2004: The history of the National Gallery of Ireland* (Dublin, 2004) and Marie Bourke's *The story of Irish museums 1790–2000: Culture, identity and education* (Cork, 2011). On the wider physical changes in the city, Mary Daly, Mona Hearn and Peter Pearson's *Dublin's Victorian houses* (Dublin, 1998) and Michael Barry's *Victorian Dublin revealed ...* (Dublin, 2011) provide fine overviews in text and image. Of the many works on the new suburbs, Séamas Ó Maitiú, *Dublin's suburban towns 1834–1930* (Dublin, 2003) and Peter Pearson, *Between the mountains and the sea: Dun Laoghaire–Rathdown county* (Dublin, 1998), stand out. On commercial and industrial architecture, Colin Rynne, *Industrial Ireland 1750–1930: An archaeology* (Cork, 2006) and Michael O'Neill, *Bank architecture in Dublin: A history to c.1940* (Dublin, 2012) are pioneering surveys of the field.

On the later nineteenth-century economy, the two business histories of the Guinness brewery are pre-eminent: Patrick Lynch and John Vaizey, *Guinness's brewery in the Irish economy, 1759–1856* (Cambridge, 1960) and S. R. Dennison and Oliver MacDonagh, *Guinness 1886–1939: From incorporation to the Second World War* (Cork, 1998). Andy Bielenberg's 'Late Victorian elite formation and philanthropy: The making of Edward Guinness', in *Studia Hibernica*, XXXII (2002/3), pp. 133–54, documents the dispersal of some of that wealth. The wider retailing revolution is examined in Stephanie Rains, *Commodity culture and social class in Dublin 1850–1916* (Dublin, 2010), and fleshed out in lush detail in Alex Findlater, *Findlaters: The story of a Dublin merchant firm 1774–2001* (Dublin, 2001). A small number of other businesses have been examined, notably Ronald Nesbitt's *At Arnotts of Dublin* (Dublin, 1993); Tony Farmar's *Heitons – A managed transition: Heitons in the Irish coal, iron and building markets 1818–1996* (Dublin, 1996); and Séamas

Ó Maitiú's *W & R Jacob: Celebrating 150 years of Irish biscuit making* (Dublin, 2001). Also important is Andy Bielenberg's work: 'Entrepreneurship, power and public opinion in Ireland: The career of William Martin Murphy', in *IESH*, XXVII (2000), pp. 25–33; his edited volume, *Irish flour milling: A history 600–2000* (Dublin, 2003); and, on the drinks industries as well as on other industrial and construction sectors, his *Ireland and the industrial revolution: The impact of the industrial revolution on Irish industry 1801–1922* (London, 2009) is now the standard work. On those who inhabited the commanding heights, Fergus Campbell's *The Irish establishment 1879–1914* (Oxford, 2009) is a remarkable prosopographical study of business and other elites and challenges conventional assumptions about Protestant decline.

Emmet O'Connor's *A labour history of Ireland 1824–1960* (Dublin, 1992) is the best introduction to the growth of labour organisation in the city, but the trends in working-class standards of living remain opaque. Fergus D'Arcy's two papers, 'Wages of labourers in the Dublin building industry, 1667–1918' and 'Wages of skilled workers in the Dublin building industry, 1667–1918', in *Saothar: Journal of the Irish Labour History Society*, XIV (1989), pp. 17–32, and XV (1990), pp. 21–37, are the only sources for longitudinal data. John Lynch, *A tale of three cities: Comparative studies in working-class life* (Basingstoke, 1998), explores the contrasts in working-class experience in Dublin, Belfast and Bristol around the end of the nineteenth century.

Discussion of the city's distinctive place in nineteenth-century Irish politics is embedded in the general political histories. However, Jacqueline Hill's work on the 1840s highlights the capital's decisive role in the evolution of Irish nationalism, notably 'The intelligentsia and Irish nationalism in the 1840s', in *Studia Hibernica*, XX (1980), pp. 73–109; 'Religion, trade and politics in Dublin, 1798–1848', in Paul Butel and L. M. Cullen (eds), *Cities and merchants: French and Irish perspectives on urban development 1500–1900* (Dublin, 1986), pp. 247–59; and 'The 1847 general election in Dublin City', in Allan Blackstock and Eoin Magennis (eds), *Politics and political culture in Britain and Ireland, 1750–1850 ...* (Belfast, 2007), pp. 41–64. The character of Dublin radicialism in 1848–9 remains tantalising, but see John Hutchinson, *The dynamics of cultural nationalism: The Gaelic revival and the creation of the Irish nation state* (London, 1987); Gary Owens, 'Popular mobilisation and the rising of 1848: The clubs of the Irish Confederation', in L. M. Geary (ed.), *Rebellion and remembrance in modern Ireland* (Dublin, 2001), pp. 51–63; and James Quinn, *John Mitchel* (Dublin, 2008). Several of the contributors in Fearghal McGarry and James McConnel (eds), *The black hand of republicanism: Fenianism in modern Ireland* (Dublin, 2009) explore the links between Young Ireland and Dublin Fenianism, but the key study is Shin-ichi Takagami's 'The Dublin Fenians 1858–79' (Ph.D. dissertation, University of Dublin, 1990). The subsequent role of Dublin in the shaping of cultural nationalism is illuminated in T. G. McMahon, *Grand Opportunity: The Gaelic revival and Irish society, 1893–1910* (Syracuse, 2008), and in Patrick Maume, *The long gestation: Irish nationalist life 1891–1918* (Dublin, 1999).

Dublin policing developed a strongly political character, as D. P. McCracken's *Inspector Mallon: Buying Irish patriotism for a five-pound note* (Dublin, 2009) reveals. Jim Herlihy's *The Dublin Metropolitan Police ...* (Dublin, 2001) is the first general history of the force, and Anastasia Dukova has extended this in a transnational study, 'Crime and policing in Dublin, Brisbane and London *c*.1850–1900' (Ph.D. dissertation, University of Dublin, 2012). Prostitution is the only crime category to have been studied in depth, with Maria Luddy's *Prostitution and Irish society 1800–1940* (Cambridge, 2007), but the long battle to suppress the excesses of Donnybrook Fair is studied in Ó Maitiú's *The humours of Donnybrook ...* (Blackrock, Co. Dublin, 1995). Tim Carey's *Mountjoy: The story of a prison* (Cork, 2000) examines the principal penal institution of the era.

Sports history has been slow to develop, but Alan Bairner (ed.), *Sport and the Irish: Histories, identities, issues* (Dublin, 2005), and Mike Cronin, William Murphy and Paul Rouse (eds), *The Gaelic Athletics Association 1884–2009* (Dublin, 2009), open up the debate. Meanwhile William Nolan (ed.), *The Gaelic Athletics Association in Dublin 1884–2000* (Dublin 2005) is a remarkable encyclopaedia of club organisation, parish endeavour and individual prowess.

After 1900

J. V. O'Brien, *'Dear, dirty Dublin': A city in distress 1899–1916* (Berkeley, 1982) is still the best introduction to the early twentieth-century city, but Cormac Ó Gráda, *Jewish Ireland in the age of Joyce: A socioeconomic history* (Princeton, 2006) gives a far more nuanced sense of the hybridity of the city with its new Jewish community. On the intersection of local and national politics, Alvin Jackson, 'The failure of Unionism in Dublin, 1900', in *IHS*, XXVI, 104 (1989), pp. 377–95, provides an intriguing introduction, and Ciaran Wallace takes a wider perspective in 'Fighting for Unionist Home Rule: Competing identities in Dublin 1880–1929', in *Journal of Urban History*, XXXVIII, 5 (2012), pp. 932–49. The democratisation of local politics after 1898 is reconstructed in Wallace's 'Local politics and government in Dublin city and suburbs 1899–1914' (Ph.D. dissertation, University of Dublin, 2010). The politico-religious divisions in the capital are explored in Senia Paseta, *Before the revolution: Nationalism, social change and Ireland's Catholic elite 1879–1922* (Cork, 1999), and in contributions to Fintan Lane (ed.), *Politics, society and the middle class in modern Ireland* (Basingstoke, 2010). The physical expression of these tensions is explored in Yvonne Whelan, *Reinventing modern Dublin: Streetscape, iconography and the politics of identity* (Dublin, 2003). But Tony Farmar, *Privileged lives: A social history of middle-class Ireland 1882–1989* (Dublin, 2010) suggests that class rather than religion or politics may have been the great divider.

Study of the new Dublin media, their cultural and political impact, has proliferated. Kevin Rafter (ed.), *Irish journalism before independence: More a disease than a profession* (Manchester, 2011) brings much of this work together, but see also Mark O'Brien and Kevin Rafter (eds), *Independent newspapers: A history* (Dublin, 2012) and John Strachan and Claire Nally, *Advertising, literature and print culture in Ireland, 1891–1922* (Basingstoke, 2012). Recent work on the 1913 labour war and its background is brought together in Francis Devine, Mary Clark and Máire Kennedy (eds), *A capital in conflict: Dublin city and the 1913 Lockout* (Dublin, 2013), but Donal Nevin (ed.), *James Larkin: Lion of the fold* (Dublin, 1998) is still valuable, and Padraig Yeates provides the best single account in *Lockout: Dublin 1913* (Dublin, 2000). Similarly, Yeates, *A city in wartime: Dublin 1914–1918* (Dublin, 2011) provides a detailed narrative history of the city through war and rebellion. Keith Jeffery, *Ireland and the Great War* (Cambridge, 2000) gives an admirable overview, complemented by John Horne (ed.), *Our war: Ireland and the Great War* (Dublin, 2008). On Dublin and war recruitment, Tom Burke's 'Whence came the Royal Dublin Fusiliers?', in *Irish Sword*, XXIV (2004/5), pp. 452–6, is enlightening.

On the Easter rebellion itself, the literature is huge and growing. León Ó Broin, *Dublin Castle and the 1916 rising* (Dublin, 1966) and F. X. Martin, *Leaders and men of the Easter Rising* (London, 1967) remain the most useful of the many works produced at the time of the fiftieth anniversary, but now Charles Townshend, *Easter 1916: The Irish rebellion* (London, 2005); Keith Jeffery, *The GPO and the Easter Rising* (Dublin, 2006); Clair Wills, *Dublin 1916: The siege of the GPO* (London, 2009); and Fearghal McGarry, *The Rising: Easter 1916* (Oxford, 2010), are the best general studies of the rebellion. On Dublin and the War of Independence, Padraig Yeates again provides the best narrative synopsis, with *A city in turmoil: Dublin 1919–1921* (Dublin, 2012), but recent biographies of the revolutionary leadership based in Dublin provide a rich sense of the social world in which they operated, notably John Horgan's *Seán Lemass: The enigmatic patriot* (Dublin, 1997); Peter Hart's *Mick: The real Michael Collins* (London, 2006); and David Fitzpatrick's *Harry Boland's Irish revolution* (Cork, 2003). Marie O'Neill, 'Dublin Corporation in the troubled times 1914–24', in *DHR*, XLVII, 1 (1994), pp. 68–70, and Sheila Carden, *The alderman: Alderman Tom Kelly (1868–1942) and Dublin Corporation* (Dublin, 2007), are also valuable. Broader interpretative surveys help to position the role of Dublin in the War of Independence, notably Michael Laffan's *The resurrection of Ireland: The Sinn Fein party, 1916–1923* (Cambridge, 1999) and Charles Townshend, *The Republic: The fight for Irish independence 1918–23* (London, 2013).

On the long debate over the re-planning of central Dublin, the essays in Michael Bannon (ed.), *A hundred years of Irish planning*, I: *The emergence of Irish planning, 1880–1921* (Dublin, 1985) and *Planning: The Irish experience 1920–1988* (Dublin, 1989) are crucial. But Ruth McManus, *Dublin 1910–1940: Shaping the city and suburbs* (Dublin, 2002) is now the standard work on the physical development of the city in this period. Mary Daly's 'Dublin the restored capital: Civic identity in an independent Ireland', in H. B. Clarke, Jacinta Prunty and Mark Hennessy (eds), *Surveying Ireland's past: Multidisciplinary essays in honour of Anngret Simms* (Dublin, 2004), pp. 565–83, asks pertinent questions of a complex process, some of which are taken up in Andrew Kincaid's innovative study, *Postcolonial Dublin: Imperial legacies and the built environment* (Minneapolis, 2006). Sean Rothery, *Ireland and the new architecture, 1900–1940* (Dublin, 1991) establishes architectural trends and controversies, and Terence Brown et al. (eds), *Building for government: The architecture of state buildings ... 1900–2000* (Dublin, 1999) examines the public projects.

On the complex history of Dublin's municipal housing, two works provide fascinating evidence from different perspectives: Mary Daly's *The buffer state: The historical roots of the Department of the Environment* (Dublin, 1997) and Ruth McManus's *Crampton built* (Dublin, 2008), a history of one of the principal building firms involved. There are few business histories that focus specifically on the early or mid-twentieth century beyond those already mentioned, but see Daly's *Industrial development and Irish national identity 1922–1939* (Dublin, 1992); Maurice Manning, *Electricity supply in Ireland: The history of the E.S.B.* (Dublin, 1984); Peter Rigney's *Trains, coal and turf: Transport in Emergency Ireland* (Dublin, 2010); John Walsh's *Collen: 200 years of building and civil engineering in Ireland* (Dublin, 2010); and Barbara Walsh, *When the shopping was good: Woolworths and the Irish main street* (Dublin, 2011), examine the bigger picture. On the service sector, Tony Farmar, *A history of Craig Gardner & Co.: The first hundred years* (Dublin, 1988) is highly revealing on the rise of the accountancy profession.

The cultural climate in the post-independence era is magisterially surveyed in Terence Brown, *Ireland: A social and cultural history, 1922–2004*, 4th edn (London, 2004), and the particularities of Archbishop McQuaid's regime is (somewhat gratuitously) exposed in John Cooney, *John Charles McQuaid: Ruler of Catholic Ireland* (Dublin, 1999). Terry Fagan et al. (eds) *Monto: Madams, murder and black coddle* (Dublin, n.d. [c.2002]) provide a local study of the Catholic Church's moral crusade in action. The lively history of the 'Catholic' university is ably covered in Donal McCartney, *UCD: A national idea – The history of University College, Dublin* (Dublin, 1999). The fate of Protestant Dublin reverberates in R. B. McDowell's *Crisis and decline: The fate of the southern unionists* (Dublin, 1997), and is subject to finer analysis in Martin Maguire, 'The organisation and activism of Dublin's Protestant working class 1883–1935', in *IHS*, XXIX, 113 (1994), pp. 76–7, and in his '"Our people": The Church of Ireland and the culture of community in Dublin since disestablishment', in Raymond Gillespie and W. A. Neely (eds), *The laity and the Church of Ireland 1000–2000: All sorts and conditions* (Dublin, 2002), pp. 283–4.

On trends in urban living standards and public health, Catriona Clear, *Women of the house: Women's household work in Ireland 1922–61*, and Clare Wills, *That neutral island: A cultural history of Ireland during the Second World War* (London, 2007), cross new territory, but the many memoirs of tenement life and working-class childhoods provide a more graphic introduction to the human cost of bad housing. Here Kevin C. Kearns's work, notably his *Dublin tenement life: An oral history* (Dublin, 1994), is a rich source. Mary Daly, '"An attitude of sturdy independence": The state and the Dublin hospitals in the 1930s', in Elizabeth Malcolm and Greta Jones (eds), *Medicine, disease and the state in Ireland 1650–1940* (Cork, 1999), pp. 234–52, and Lindsey Earner-Byrne, *Mother and child: Maternity and child welfare in Dublin, 1922–60* (Manchester, 2007) provide the best introduction to the politics of health and the rise of family social services.

On the mid-century 'modern turn' in the city's development, there is abundant contemporary commentary but little retrospective analysis. Erika Hanna's *Modern Dublin: Urban change and the Irish past, 1957–1973* (Oxford, 2013) is a pioneering attempt to do just that, and John Bowman's *Window and mirror: RTÉ television 1961–2011* (Cork, 2011) plots the transformation of popular culture after 1960 – as moderated by 'Dublin 4'. Two essays by Arnold Horner give a geographer's spatial perspective: 'Changes in population and in the extent of the built-up area in the Dublin city-region, 1936–1988', in *Irish Geography*, XXIII (1990), pp. 50–55; and 'From city to city-region: Dublin from the 1930s to the 1990s', in F. H. A. Aalen and Kevin Whelan (eds), *Dublin city and county: From pre-history to the present ...* (Dublin, 1992), pp. 327–58. Andrew MacLaran's edited collection, *Dublin in crisis* (Dublin, 1991), provides a snapshot of the many prescriptions at what was then a tipping point in the city's development. On the impact of the office development, the classic if partisan account remains Frank McDonald, *The destruction of Dublin*

(Dublin, 1985), together with his follow-up, *The construction of Dublin* (Dublin, 2000). Diane Payne and Peter Stafford, 'The politics of urban regeneration in Dublin', in J. R. Gupta (ed.), *Urban development debates in the new millennium* (New Delhi, 2005), pp. 98–110, and Niamh Moore, *Dublin docklands reinvented: The post-industrial regeneration of a European city quarter* (Dublin, 2008), help take the story to the turn of the century and the eve of the 'bubble'.

Exploring the social background of the city's literary celebrities has generated a huge literature. Those most sensitive to that background include Roy Foster, in *W. B. Yeats: A life*, 2 vols (Oxford, 1998, 2003); Judith Hill, in *Lady Gregory: An Irish life* (Cork, 2011); W. J. McCormack, *Fool of the family: A life of J. M. Synge* (London, 2000); Terence Brown, in his 'Introduction' to James Joyce, *Dubliners* (London, 2000); Ian Gunn and Clive Hart, *James Joyce's Dublin ...* (London, 2004); Vivien Igoe, *James Joyce's Dublin houses ...* 2nd ed. (Dublin, 2007); Joep Leerssen, in *Remembrance and imagination ...* (Cork, 1996); David Krause, in *Sean O'Casey and his world* (London, 1976); Eoin O'Brien, in *The Beckett country: Samuel Beckett's Ireland* (Monkstown, Co. Dublin, 1986); and Anthony Cronin, *No laughing matter: The life and times of Flann O'Brien* (London, 1989). And in a different kind of exercise, Gerry Smyth, 'The right to the city: Re-presentations of Dublin in contemporary Irish fiction', in Liam Harte and Michael Parker (eds), *Contemporary Irish fiction: Themes, tropes, theories* (Basingstoke, 2000), pp. 13–34, discusses later twentieth-century writers who have sought in fiction to get the measure of modern Dublin and modern Dubliners.

INDEX